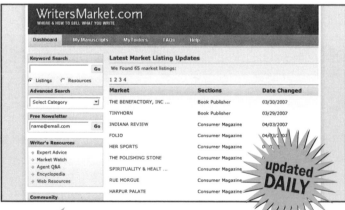

2009

GUIDE TO LITERARY AGENTS®

Chuck Sambuchino, Editor

WRITER'S DIGEST BOOKS
CINCINNATI, OH

Editorial Director, Writer's Digest Books: Jane Friedman
Managing Editor, Writer's Digest Market Books: Alice Pope

Guide to Literary Agents Web site: www.guidetoliteraryagents.com
Writer's Market Web site: www.writersmarket.com
Writer's Digest Web site: www.writersdigest.com
F + W Publications Bookstore: http://fwbookstore.com

Distributed in Canada by Fraser Direct
100 Armstrong Ave.
Georgetown, ON, Canada L7G 5S4
Tel: (905) 877-4411

Distributed in the U.K. and Europe by David & Charles
Brunel House, Newton Abbot, Devon, TQ12 4PU, England
Tel: (+44) 1626 323200, Fax: (+44) 1626 323319
E-mail: postmaster@davidandcharles.co.uk

Distributed in Australia by Capricorn Link
P.O. Box 704, Windsor, NSW 2756, Australia
Tel: (02) 4577-3555

Distributed in New Zealand by David Bateman Ltd.
P.O. Box 100-242, N.S.M.C., Auckland 1330, New Zealand
Tel: (09) 415-7664, Fax: (09) 415-8892

Distributed in South Africa by Real Books
P.O. Box 1040, Auckland Park 2006, Johannesburg, South Africa
Tel: (011) 837-0643, Fax: (011) 837-0645
E-mail: realbook@global.co.za

ISSN: 1078-6945
ISBN-13: 978-1-58297-548-1
ISBN-10: 1-58297-548-5

Cover design by Claudean Wheeler
Interior design by Clare Finney
Production coordinated by Greg Nock
Illustrations ©Dominique Bruneton/PaintoAlto

Attention Booksellers: This is an annual directory of F + W Publications. Return deadline for this edition is December 31, 2009.

Contents

SEALING THE DEAL

PERSPECTIVES

MARKETS

RESOURCES

INDEXES

From the Editor

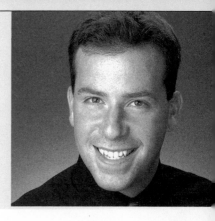

The publishing industry is constantly in motion. Genres and categories are hot one day, then nowhere to be seen the next. Editors change their preferences as quickly as they change jobs. Small, independent publishing houses get gobbled up while the big houses in New York create more imprints. But one thing that *hasn't* changed in recent years is the necessity of having a good literary agent to sell your work.

As agents continue to play a crucial role in getting writers' work noticed and bought, new agencies continue to appear—and that means more reps looking for new work!

So how do you contact these agents? Simply finding e-mails for agents is fairly easy. You can probably scour message boards on the Internet and find what you're looking for. But what's important—are the *details* of that agency. Do you know the preferred method of contact? Whether they consider submissions in your genre? The categories they're actively seeking right now? These little—and extremely valuable—details are in every listing of this book, and they are what sets *Guide to Literary Agents* apart from other agent databases, whether print or online.

Flipping through these pages, you'll notice that *GLA* no longer lists agents that solely represent scripts. That's because *Screenwriter's & Playwright's Market*, the ninth book in Writer's Digest Books market series, is set to debut in January 2009. *GLA* is now solely devoted to literary agents and writers' conferences.

Speaking of conferences, check out the event listings to find a gathering in your area. It's the largest number we've ever listed. Almost all conferences have agents in attendance who are there for one specific reason: To meet and sign writers like yourself. To find out how to make the most of a writers' conference, see the article on page 52. Other articles you should check out include agent Mollie Glick's no-nonsense approach to crafting a great book proposal (page 41) and agent Katharine Sands' breakdown on pet peeves and everything *not* to do when contacting reps and submitting work (page 71). Everything else you need to know about the road to publishing success is also spelled out in this book's instructional articles.

As always, stay in touch with me at **www.guidetoliteraryagents.com/blog.** Also, please continue to pass along success stories, improvement ideas and news from the ever-changing agent world. With all the new agents looking for clients, I thought last year was a good time to be a new writer—and it was. This year appears just as promising, so dust off that manuscript, and go find yourself an agent!

Chuck Sambuchino
literaryagent@fwpubs.com

How to Use
This Book

Searching for a literary agent can be overwhelming, whether you've just finished your first book or you have several publishing credits on your résumé. More than likely, you're eager to start pursuing agents and anxious to see your name on the spine of a book. But before you go directly to the listings of agencies in this book, take time to familiarize yourself with the way agents work and how you should approach them. By doing so, you will be more prepared for your search and ultimately save yourself effort and unnecessary grief.

Read the articles

This book begins with feature articles that explain how to prepare for representation, offer strategies for contacting agents, and provide perspectives on the author/agent relationship. The articles are organized into three sections appropriate for each stage of the search process: **Getting Started**, **Contacting Agents** and **Sealing the Deal**. You may want to start by reading through each article, and then refer back to relevant articles during each stage of your search.

Since there are many ways to make that initial contact with an agent, we've also provided a section called **Perspectives**. These personal accounts from agents and published authors offer information and inspiration for any writer hoping to find representation.

Decide what you're looking for

A literary agent will present your work directly to editors or producers. It's the agent's job to get her client's work published or sold and to negotiate a fair contract. In the **Literary Agents** section, we list each agent's contact information and explain what type of work the agency represents as well as how to submit your work for consideration.

For face-to-face contact, many writers prefer to meet agents at **Conferences**. By doing so, writers can assess an agent's personality, attend workshops and have the chance to get more feedback on their work than they get by mailing submissions and waiting for a response. The conferences section is divided into regions, and lists only those conferences agents and/or editors attend. In many cases, private consultations are available, and agents attend with the hope of finding new clients to represent.

Utilize the extras

Aside from the articles and listings, the book offers a section of **Resources**. If you come across a term with which you aren't familiar, check out the Resources section for a quick explanation. Also, note the gray tabs along the edge of each page. The tabs block off each section so they are easier to flip to as you conduct your search.

Frequently Asked Questions

1 **Why do you include agents who are not seeking new clients?** Some agents ask that their listings indicate they are currently closed to new clients. We include them so writers know the agents exist and know not to contact them at this time.

2 **Why do you exclude fee-charging agents?** We have received a number of complaints in the past regarding fees, and therefore have chosen to list only those agents who do not charge fees.

3 **Why are some agents not listed in *Guide to Literary Agents?*** Some agents may not have responded to our requests for information. We have taken others out of the book after receiving very serious complaints about them.

4 **Do I need more than one agent if I write in different genres?** It depends. If you have written in one genre and want to switch to a new style of writing, ask your agent if she is willing to represent you in your new endeavor. Most agents will continue to represent clients no matter what genre they choose to write. Occasionally, an agent may feel she has no knowledge of a certain genre and will recommend an appropriate agent to her client. Regardless, you should always talk to your agent about any potential career move.

5 **Why don't you list more foreign agents?** Most American agents have relationships with foreign co-agents in other countries. It is more common for an American agent to work with a co-agent to sell a client's book abroad than for a writer to work directly with a foreign agent. We do, however, list agents in the United Kingdom, Australia, Canada and other countries who sell to publishers both internationally and in the United States. If you decide to query a foreign agent, make sure they represent American writers (if you're American). Some may request to only receive submissions from Canadians, for example, or UK residents.

6 **Do agents ever contact a self-published writer?** If a self-published author attracts the attention of the media or if his book sells extremely well, an agent might approach the author in hopes of representing him.

7 **Why won't the agent I queried return my material?** An agent may not answer your query or return your manuscript for several reasons. Perhaps you did not include a self-addressed, stamped envelope (SASE). Many agents will discard a submission without a SASE. Or, the agent may have moved. To avoid using expired addresses, use the most current edition of *Guide to Literary Agents* or access the information online at www.WritersMarket.com. Another possibility is that the agent is swamped with submissions. Agents can be overwhelmed with queries, especially if the agent has recently spoken at a conference or has been featured in an article or book. Also, some agents specify in their listing that they never return materials of any kind.

Finally—and perhaps most importantly—are the **Indexes** in the back of the book. These can serve as an incredibly helpful way to start your search because they categorize the listings according to different criteria. For example, you can look for literary agents by name or according to their specialties (fiction/nonfiction genres). Similarly, you can search for script agents by name or according to format (e.g., plays/sitcoms). Plus, there is a General Index that lists every agent and conference in the book.

Listing Policy and Complaint Procedure

Listings in *Guide to Literary Agents* are compiled from detailed questionnaires, phone interviews and information provided by agents. The industry is volatile, and agencies change frequently. We rely on our readers for information on their dealings with agents and changes in policies or fees that differ from what has been reported to the editor of this book. Write to us (*Guide to Literary Agents*, 4700 E. Galbraith Road, Cincinnati, OH 45236) or e-mail us (literaryagent@fwpubs.com) if you have new information, questions or problems dealing with the agencies listed.

Listings are published free of charge and are not advertisements. Although the information is as accurate as possible, the listings are not endorsed or guaranteed by the editor or publisher of *Guide to Literary Agents*. If you feel you have not been treated fairly by an agent or representative listed in *Guide to Literary Agents*, we advise you to take the following steps:

- First try to contact the agency. Sometimes one phone call, letter or e-mail can clear up the matter. Politely relate your concern.

- Document all your correspondence with the agency. When you write to us with a complaint, provide the name of your manuscript, the date of your first contact with the agency and the nature of your subsequent correspondence.

We will keep your letter on file and attempt to contact the agency. The number, frequency and severity of complaints will be considered when deciding whether or not to delete an agency's listing from the next edition.

Guide to Literary Agents reserves the right to exclude any agency for any reason.

Do I Need an Agent?

Preparing for Representation

A writer's job is to write. A literary agent's job is to find publishers for her clients' books. Because publishing houses receive more and more unsolicited manuscripts each year, securing an agent is becoming increasingly necessary. Finding an eager and reputable agent can be a difficult task. Even the most patient writer can become frustrated or disillusioned. As a writer seeking agent representation, you should prepare yourself before starting your search. Learn when to approach agents, as well as what to expect from an author/agent relationship. Beyond selling manuscripts, an agent must keep track of the ever-changing industry, writers' royalty statements, fluctuating reading habits—and the list goes on.

So, once again, you face the question: Do I need an agent? The answer, much more often than not, is yes.

WHAT CAN AN AGENT DO FOR YOU?

For starters, today's competitive marketplace can be difficult to break into, especially for unpublished writers. Many larger publishing houses will only look at manuscripts from agents—and rightfully so, as they would be inundated with unsatisfactory writing if they did not. In fact, approximately 80 percent of books published by the major houses are acquired through agents.

But an agent's job isn't just getting your book through a publisher's door. The following describes the various jobs agents do for their clients, many of which would be difficult for a writer to do without outside help.

Agents know editors' tastes and needs

An agent possesses information on a complex web of publishing houses and a multitude of editors to ensure her clients' manuscripts are placed in the right hands. This knowledge is gathered through relationships she cultivates with acquisition editors—the people who decide which books to present to their publisher for possible publication. Through her industry connections, an agent becomes aware of the specializations of publishing houses and their imprints, knowing that one publisher only wants contemporary romances while another is interested solely in nonfiction books about the military. By networking with editors, an agent also learns more specialized information—which editor is looking for a crafty Agatha-Christie-style mystery for the fall catalog, for example.

Agents track changes in publishing

Being attentive to constant market changes and shifting trends is another major requirement of an agent. An agent understands what it may mean for clients when publisher A merges

To-Do List for Fiction Writers

1. **Finish your novel** or short story collection. An agent can do nothing for fiction without a finished product.

2. **Revise your novel.** Have other writers offer criticism to ensure your manuscript is as polished as possible.

3. **Proofread.** Don't ruin a potential relationship with an agent by submitting work that contains typos or poor grammar.

4. **Publish** short stories or novel excerpts in literary journals, proving to potential agents that editors see quality in your writing.

5. **Research** to find the agents of writers whose works you admire or are similar to yours.

6. **Use the indexes in the back of this book** to construct a list of agents who are open to new writers and looking for your type of fiction (e.g., literary, romance, mystery).

7. **Rank your list.** Use the listings in this book to determine the agents most suitable for you and your work and to eliminate inappropriate agencies.

8. **Write your synopsis.** Completing this step will help you write your query letter and be prepared for when agents contact you.

9. **Write your query letter.** As an agent's first impression of you, this brief letter should be polished and to the point.

10. **Read about the business** of agents so you are knowledgeable and prepared to act on any offer. Start by reading this book's articles section completely.

with publisher B and when an editor from house C moves to house D. Or what it means when readers—and therefore editors—are no longer interested in Westerns, but instead can't get their hands on enough suspense novels.

Agents get your manuscript read faster

Although it may seem like an extra step to send your manuscript to an agent instead of directly to a publishing house, the truth is an agent can prevent writers from wasting months sending manuscripts that end up in the wrong place or buried in someone's slush pile. Editors rely on agents to save them time as well. With little time to sift through the hundreds of unsolicited submissions arriving weekly in the mail, an editor is naturally going to prefer a work that has already been approved by a qualified reader (i.e., the agent) that knows the editor's preferences. For this reason, many of the larger publishers accept agented submissions only.

Agents understand contracts

When publishers write contracts, they are primarily interested in their own bottom line rather than the best interests of the author. Writers unfamiliar with contractual language may find

To-Do List for Nonfiction Writers

1 **Formulate a concrete idea** for your book. Sketch a brief outline making sure you have enough material for an entire book-length manuscript.

2 **Research** works on similar topics to understand the competition and determine how your book is unique.

3 **Write sample chapters.** This step should indicate how much time you will need to finish and if your writing needs editorial help.

4 **Publish** completed chapters in journals and/or magazines. This validates your work to agents and provides writing samples for later in the process.

5 **Polish your outline** so you can refer to it while drafting a query letter and you're prepared when agents contact you.

6 **Brainstorm** three to four subject categories that best describe your material.

7 **Use the indexes in this book** to find agents interested in at least two of your subject areas and who are looking for new clients.

8 **Rank your list.** Narrow your list further by reading the listings of agencies you found in the indexes, and organize the list according to your preferences. Research agent Web sites to be even more selective.

9 **Write your query.** Give an agent an excellent first impression by professionally and succinctly describing your premise and your experience.

10 **Read about the business** of agents so you're knowledgeable and prepared to act on any offer. Start by reading this book's articles section completely.

themselves bound to a publisher with whom they no longer want to work. Or, they may find themselves tied to a publisher who prevents them from getting royalties on their first book until subsequent books are written. Agents use their experiences and knowledge to negotiate a contract that benefits the writer while still respecting the publisher's needs. After all, more money for the author will almost always mean more money for the agent—another reason they're on your side.

Agents negotiate—and exploit—subsidiary rights

Beyond publication, a savvy agent keeps in mind other opportunities for your manuscript. If your agent believes your book will also be successful as an audio book, a Book-of-the-Month Club selection or even a blockbuster movie, she will take these options into consideration when shopping your manuscript. These additional opportunities for writers are called subsidiary rights. Part of an agent's job is to keep track of the strengths and weaknesses of different publishers' subsidiary rights offices to determine the deposition of these rights regarding your work. After the contract is negotiated, the agent will seek additional moneymaking opportunities for the rights she kept for her client.

Getting Started

Agents get escalators

An escalator is a bonus that an agent can negotiate as part of the book contract. It is commonly given when a book appears on a bestseller list or if a client appears on a popular television show. For example, a publisher might give a writer a $30,000 bonus if he is picked for a book club. Both the agent and the editor know such media attention will sell more books, and the agent negotiates an escalator to ensure the writer benefits from this increase in sales.

Agents track payments

Since an agent only receives payment when the publisher pays the writer, it's in the agent's best interest to make sure the writer is paid on schedule. Some publishing houses are notorious for late payments. Having an agent distances you from any conflict regarding payment and allows you to spend your time writing instead of making phone calls.

Agents are advocates

Besides standing up for your right to be paid on time, agents can ensure your book gets a better cover design, more attention from the publisher's marketing department or other benefits you may not know to ask for during the publishing process. An agent can also provide advice during each step of the process, as well as guidance about your long-term writing career.

ARE YOU READY FOR AN AGENT?

Now that you know what an agent is capable of, ask yourself if you and your work are at a stage where you need an agent. Look at the To-Do Lists for fiction and nonfiction writers on pages 6 and 7, and judge how prepared you are for contacting an agent. Have you spent enough time researching or polishing your manuscript? Does your nonfiction book proposal include everything it should? Is your novel completely finished and thoroughly revised? Sending an agent an incomplete project not only wastes your time, but also may turn off the agent in the process. Literary agents are not magicians, and they can't solve your personal problems. An agent will not be your banker, CPA, social secretary or therapist. Instead, agents will endeavor to sell your book because that's how they earn their living.

Moreover, your material may not be appropriate for an agent. Most agents do not represent poetry, magazine articles, short stories, or material suitable for academic or small presses; the agents' commission does not justify spending time submitting these types of works. Those agents who do take on such material generally represent authors on larger projects first, and then adopt the smaller items as a favor to the client.

If you strongly believe your work is ready to be placed with an agent, make sure you're personally ready to be represented. In other words, consider the direction in which your writing career is headed. Besides skillful writers, agencies want clients with the ability to produce more than one book. Most agents will say they represent careers, not books.

WHEN DON'T YOU NEED AN AGENT?

Although there are many reasons to work with an agent, an author can benefit from submitting his own work directly to a book publisher. For example, if your writing focuses on a very specific area, you may want to work with a small or specialized press. These houses are usually open to receiving material directly from writers. Small presses can often give more attention to a writer than a large house can, providing editorial help, marketing expertise and other advice directly to the writer.

Academic books or specialized nonfiction books (such as a book about the history of Rhode Island) are good bets if you're not with an agent. Beware, though, as you will now be responsible for negotiating all parts of your contract and payment. If you choose this path, it's wise to use a lawyer or entertainment attorney to review all contracts. If a lawyer special-izes in intellectual property, he can help a writer with contract negotiations. Instead of giving the lawyer a commission, the lawyer is paid for his time only.

And, of course, some people prefer working independently instead of relying on others to do their work. If you're one of these people, it's probably better to shop your own work instead of constantly butting heads with an agent. Let's say you manage to sign with one of the few literary agents who represent short story collections. If the collection gets shopped around to publishers for several months and no one bites, your agent may suggest retooling the work into a novel or novella(s). Agents suggest changes—some bigger than others—and not all writers think their work is malleable. It's all a matter of what you're writing and how you feel about it.

Agents Tell All

Expert Answers to Some Common (and Not So Common) Questions

T here are some questions writers ask time and time again. A handful of the most common ones are answered below by several professional literary agents as well as one script and literary manager.

What's a common mistake you see with query letters?

Length is an issue. Even though I accept online queries, I still want the query to come in somewhere close to one page. I think that writers often think that because it's online, I have no way of knowing that it's more than a page. Believe me, I do. Queries that are concise and compelling are the most intriguing.

—**Regina Brooks,** *founder, Serendipity Literary Agency*

When you're reading a partial for a YA novel, let's say . . . what things turn you off when reading a manuscript? What kills a writer's chances of getting signed with you?

There's no need to tell an agent or manager that your project is like no other they've ever seen. If it's good, the writing will stand on its own. If it's not solid writing, then there's probably a reason why we've never seen something like it published. Another thing that turns me away from a sample is sloppy proofreading.

—**Margery Walshaw,** *literary and script manager, Evatopia*

What are the most common things you see writers do wrong during an in-person pitch at a writers' conference?

Two things: One, some authors don't seem to understand their true "hook," or most interesting aspect of their work. One writer I met spoke about his young adult fantasy novel, but it wasn't until the end of his pitch that he mentioned how his book was inspired by Japanese folklore and myths. How cool! That is what I would have wanted to hear first. Until then, it sounded like just another young adult fantasy. Two: some authors over-praise their work. Some people told me how wonderful, great, amazing, funny, etc. their projects were. Coming from the author, such statements make me a bit skeptical. Of course the writer thinks his or her own work is amazing, but what is it about your work that makes it so fabulous? Why is it wonderful? I want more concrete information about an author's work so I can really think about where the book might fit in the market.

—**Taryn Fagerness,** *literary agent, Sandra Dijkstra Literary Agency*

If someone queries you with a novel, but has no fiction accomplishments or accolades, should they mention their nonfiction/poetry awards in the query? Will that help?

None of that really makes much of a difference, because it's all in the writing. If the novel's good, it doesn't matter whether the author's a dishwasher or a housewife. And plenty of fine nonfiction writers just can't produce fiction that works—I see it all the time. That said, if Michiko Kakutani sent me her novel, I might promote it to the top of my reading pile.

    —**Jim Donovan,** *founder, Jim Donovan Literary*

I've heard that nothing is taboo anymore in young adult books, and you can write about topics such as sex and drugs. Is this true?

I would say this: Nothing is taboo if it's done well. Each scene needs to matter in a novel. I've read a number of "edgy" young adult books where writers seem to add in scenes just for shock value and it doesn't work with the flow of the rest of the novel. "Taboo" subjects need to have a purpose in the progression of the novel—and of course, need to be well written!

    Taboo topics do, however, affect whether the school and library market will pick up the book—and this can have an effect on whether a publisher feels they can sell enough copies.

    —**Jessica Regel,** *literary agent, Jean V. Naggar Literary Agency*

Simply put, concerning middle grade and young adult—how are they different? Subject matter? Length?

As a disclaimer, there are exceptions to these rules, with the fantasy genre being a big one. But, typically, middle grade novels run between 20,000-40,000 words and feature protagonists aged 9-13. Young adult novels run between 40,000-65,000 words and feature protagonists aged 14+. The type of relationship at the core of a project can also tell you how to characterize it: MG often revolves around a protagonist's relationships with family and friends, while a story heavily driven by a romantic relationship is going to be YA.

    —**Michelle Andelman,** *literary agent, Andrea Brown Literary Agency*

A lot of people want to write a memoir, but few are good. What do you look for in a memoir?

Memoir is such a tricky genre. Everyone has a story (when I go to writing conferences, memoir writers are usually the overwhelming majority), and, unfortunately, you are right—few are good and many are overly sentimental. I look for two main things: a unique story and great writing. Memoirs should read like novels; they should have suspense, conflict, emotion, character development, dialogue and narrative arc. On top of all that, it's a tough question to ask about one's own story, but authors should ask it: Why will people be interested in me?

    —**Taryn Fagerness,** *literary agent, Sandra Dijkstra Literary Agency*

If you were teaching a course on writing nonfiction book proposals, but only had 60 seconds to talk, what would you say?

Three things. 1) Spill the beans. Don't try to tantalize and hold back the juice. 2) No BS! We learn to see right through BS, or we fail rapidly. 3) Get published small. Local papers, literary journals, Web sites, anything. The more credits you have, the better. And list them all (although not to the point of absurdity) in your query. Why does everyone want to pole-vault from being an unpublished author to having a big book contract? It makes no sense. You have to learn to drive before they'll let you pilot the Space Shuttle.

    —**Gary Heidt,** *literary agent, FinePrint Literary Management*

What can writers do to craft better book proposals?

Nonfiction proposals should be fairly easy to write. There's a lot of information available to writers on how to write "the greatest," "the most compelling," "the no-fail" nonfiction proposal, so I'm often surprised when authors fail to mention their reasons and credentials for writing the work. Like publishers, I often jump to the credentials section of the proposal before getting to the meat of the proposal. I need to know why an author is qualified to write what they're writing and how their work differs from what has already been published on the topic they've chosen.

> —**Janet Benrey,** *founder, Benrey Literary*

If an author envisions a five-book series for his story and even has three manuscripts completed, is it still best to query you regarding the first one only? Will the "series talk" come later?

We've been seeing a lot more of these types of "series" presentations lately—the feeling being that the author needs to present a future "franchise" for the agent and publisher to get them more interested in representation and publishing their work. This is not necessarily the case. In fact, it may send up a red flag about the author's expectations. I always try to downplay the series pitch (to publishers) unless there has already been a strong brand presence established in the marketplace. My advice to writers is to sell the first one; when it sells well, the editor and publisher will be very happy to listen to ideas for books two and three. Also, feedback can come from the publisher's sales and marketing teams, who will suggest (based on the success of book one) that the author write another book or make a series out of the original.

> —**John Willig,** *founder, Literary Services Inc.*

When an author sits down to pitch you, what is some advice you can give them?

One word: Relax. If you're relaxed, you can pitch your story a lot better than if you're in a panic, or scared of the big bad agent sitting in front of you. And I will want to know three things before getting into the story line: 1) Is it finished? 2) How many words? 3) What is the genre? Then give me about three sentences on the story. And, if you can, tell me what makes your book different from all the others out there of the same ilk—and don't tell me your voice because I know this—all voices are different. I want to know if you have a different hook.

> —**Cherry Weiner,** *founder, Cherry Weiner Literary Agency*

Can you help define the category "Christian Living" and give a few book examples?

The Christian Living category of books represents a huge umbrella that covers a multitude of topics. Christian Living works can include books on issues of importance to women, men and teenagers; Christian Living books can be about parenting, marriage, family life, divorce, breast cancer, healing, health, faith journeys, spiritual challenges, leadership and devotionals. [One] series that I've contracted is for three books with a theme of taking faith to the next level. These were written by a pastor of a large church and the audience will be members of churches across the country who are interested in working through a study program that deals with parenting and other topics.

> —**Janet Benrey,** *founder, Benrey Literary*

When you receive a nonfiction book proposal, how detailed should the author's promotional plan be?

As long as it needs to be and still be realistic. I see marketing plans all the time along the lines of "I'll be happy to be on Oprah," or other things that the author hopes will happen.

That's not realistic. I just want to hear what the author can really do that will help sell or promote the book, not pie-in-the-sky wishful thinking.

—**Jim Donovan,** *founder, Jim Donovan Literary*

Let's say an acquaintance calls you and says, "An agent wants to represent me, but she's new and has no sales. Is that OK?" How would you answer that?
An agent with little or no sales who has been an assistant at a leading agency will have just as much clout getting to an editor perhaps as an established agent, at least initially. One of the things I always advise writers to do is to ask an interested agent—that is, one who's made an offer of representation—"Why do you want to be my agent?" They will then hear a very clear thumbnail sketch of how that agent will sound agenting. Secondly, you're listening for strategy and prognosis: How will that agent work with you and what is their prognosis for your career?

—**Katharine Sands,** *literary agent, Sarah Jane Freymann Literary Agency*

Assessing Credibility

The Scoop on Researching Agents

Many people wouldn't buy a used car without at least checking the odometer, and savvy shoppers would consult the blue books, take a test drive and even ask for a mechanic's opinion. Much like the savvy car shopper, you want to obtain the best possible agent for your writing, so you should do some research on the business of agents before sending out query letters. Understanding how agents operate will help you find an agent appropriate for your work, as well as alert you about the types of agents to avoid.

Many writers take for granted that any agent who expresses interest in their work is trustworthy. They'll sign a contract before asking any questions and simply hope everything will turn out all right. We often receive complaints from writers regarding agents *after* they have lost money or have work bound by contract to an ineffective agent. If writers put the same amount of effort into researching agents as they did writing their manuscripts, they would save themselves unnecessary grief.

The best way to educate yourself is to read all you can about agents and other authors. Organizations such as the Association of Authors' Representatives (AAR; www.aar-online.org), the National Writers Union (NWU; www.nwu.org), American Society of Journalists and Authors (ASJA; www.asja.org) and Poets & Writers, Inc. (www.pw.org), all have informational material on finding and working with an agent.

Publishers Weekly (www.publishersweekly.com) covers publishing news affecting agents and others in the publishing industry. The Publishers Lunch newsletter (www.publishersmar ketplace.com) comes free via e-mail every workday and offers news on agents and editors, job postings, recent book sales and more.

Even the Internet has a wide range of sites where you can learn basic information about preparing for your initial contact, as well as specific details on individual agents. You can also find online forums and listservs, which keep authors connected and allow them to share experiences they've had with different editors and agents. Keep in mind, however, that not everything printed on the Web is solid fact; you may come across the site of a writer who is bitter because an agent rejected his manuscript. Your best bet is to use the Internet to supplement your other research.

Once you've established what your resources are, it's time to see which agents meet your criteria. Below are some of the key items to pay attention to when researching agents.

LEVEL OF EXPERIENCE

Through your research, you will discover the need to be wary of some agents. Anybody can go to the neighborhood copy center and order business cards that say "literary agent," but that title doesn't mean she can sell your book. She may lack the proper connections with others in the publishing industry, and an agent's reputation with editors can be a major strength or weakness.

Agents who have been in the business awhile have a large number of contacts and carry the most clout with editors. They know the ins and the outs of the industry and are often able to take more calculated risks. However, veteran agents can be too busy to take on new clients or might not have the time to help develop the author. Newer agents, on the other hand, may be hungrier, as well as more open to unpublished writers. They probably have a smaller client list and are able to invest the extra effort to make your book a success.

If it's a new agent without a track record, be aware that you're taking more of a risk signing with her than with a more established agent. However, even a new agent should not be new to publishing. Many agents were editors before they were agents, or they worked at an agency as an assistant. This experience is crucial for making contacts in the publishing industry and learning about rights and contracts. The majority of listings in this book explain how long the agent has been in business, as well as what she did before becoming an agent. You could also ask the agent to name a few editors off the top of her head who she thinks may be interested in your work and why they sprang to mind. Has she sold to them before? Do they publish books in your genre?

If an agent has no contacts in the business, she has no more clout than you do. Without publishing prowess, she's just an expensive mailing service. Anyone can make photocopies, slide them into an envelope and address them to "Editor." Unfortunately, without a contact name and a familiar return address on the envelope, or a phone call from a trusted colleague letting an editor know a wonderful submission is on its way, your work will land in the slush pile with all the other submissions that don't have representation. You can do your own mailings with higher priority than such an agent could.

PAST SALES

Agents should be willing to discuss their recent sales with you: how many, what type of books and to what publishers. Keep in mind, though, that some agents consider this information confidential. If an agent does give you a list of recent sales, you can call the publishers' contracts department to ensure the sale was actually made by that agent. While it's true that even top agents are not able to sell every book they represent, an inexperienced agent who proposes too many inappropriate submissions will quickly lose her standing with editors.

You can also find out details of recent sales on your own. Nearly all of the listings in this book offer the titles and authors of books with which the agent has worked. Some of them also note to which publishing house the book was sold. Again, you can call the publisher and affirm the sale. If you don't have the publisher's information, simply go to your local library or bookstore to see if they carry the book. Consider checking to see if it's available on Web sites like Amazon.com, too. You may want to be wary of the agent if her books are nowhere to be found or are only available through the publisher's Web site. Distribution is a crucial component to getting published, and you want to make sure the agent has worked with competent publishers.

TYPES OF FEES

Becoming knowledgeable about the different types of fees agents may charge is vital to conducting effective research. Most agents make their living from the commissions they receive after selling their clients' books, and these are the agents we've listed. Be sure to ask about any expenses you don't understand so you have a clear grasp of what you're paying for. Described below are some types of fees you may encounter in your research.

Office fees

Occasionally, an agent will charge for the cost of photocopies, postage and long-distance phone calls made on your behalf. This is acceptable, so long as she keeps an itemized account of the expenses and you've agreed on a ceiling cost. The agent should only ask for office expenses after agreeing to represent the writer. These expenses should be discussed up front, and the writer should receive a statement accounting for them. This money is sometimes returned to the author upon sale of the manuscript. Be wary if there is an up-front fee amounting to hundreds of dollars, which is excessive.

Reading fees

Agencies that charge reading fees often do so to cover the cost of additional readers or the time spent reading that could have been spent selling. Agents also claim that charging reading fees cuts down on the number of submissions they receive. This practice can save the agent time and may allow her to consider each manuscript more extensively. Whether such promises are kept depends upon the honesty of the agency. You may pay a fee and never receive a response from the agent, or you may pay someone who never submits your manuscript to publishers.

Officially, the Association of Authors' Representatives' (AAR) Canon of Ethics prohibits members from directly or indirectly charging a reading fee, and the Writers Guild of America (WGA) does not allow WGA signatory agencies to charge a reading fee to WGA members,

Warning Signs! Beware of . . .

Important

- Excessive typos or poor grammar in an agent's correspondence.

- A form letter accepting you as a client and praising generic things about your book that could apply to any book. A good agent doesn't take on a new client very often, so when she does, it's a special occasion that warrants a personal note or phone call.

- Unprofessional contracts that ask you for money up front, contain clauses you haven't discussed or are covered with amateur clip-art or silly borders.

- Rudeness when you inquire about any points you're unsure of. Don't employ any business partner who doesn't treat you with respect.

- Pressure, by way of threats, bullying or bribes. A good agent is not desperate to represent more clients. She invites worthy authors but leaves the final decision up to them.

- Promises of publication. No agent can guarantee you a sale. Not even the top agents sell everything they choose to represent. They can only send your work to the most appropriate places, have it read with priority and negotiate you a better contract if a sale does happen.

- A print-on-demand book contract or any contract offering you no advance. You can sell your own book to an e-publisher any time you wish without an agent's help. An agent should pursue traditional publishing routes with respectable advances.

as stated in the WGA's Artists' Manager Basic Agreement. A signatory may charge you a fee if you are not a member, but most signatory agencies do not charge a reading fee as an across-the-board policy.

Reading fees vary from $25 to $500 or more. The fee is usually nonrefundable, but sometimes agents agree to refund the money if they take on a writer as a client, or if they sell the writer's manuscript. Keep in mind, however, that payment of a reading fee does not ensure representation.

No literary agents who charge reading fees are listed in this book. It's too risky of an option for writers, plus nonfee-charging agents have a stronger incentive to sell your work. After all, they don't make a dime until they make a sale. If you find that a literary agent listed in this book charges a reading fee, please contact the editor at literaryagent@fwpubs.com.

Critique fees

Sometimes a manuscript will interest an agent, but the agent will point out areas requiring further development and offer to critique it for an additional fee. Like reading fees, payment of a critique fee does not ensure representation. When deciding if you will benefit from having someone critique your manuscript, keep in mind that the quality and quantity of comments varies from agent to agent. The critique's usefulness will depend on the agent's knowledge of the market. Also be aware that agents who spend a significant portion of their time commenting on manuscripts will have less time to actively market work they already represent.

In other cases, the agent may suggest an editor who understands your subject matter or genre and has some experience getting manuscripts into shape. Occasionally, if your story is exceptional or your ideas and credentials are marketable but your writing needs help, you will work with a ghostwriter or co-author who will share a percentage of your commission, or work with you at an agreed upon cost per hour.

An agent may refer you to editors she knows, or you may choose an editor in your area. Many editors do freelance work and would be happy to help you with your writing project. Of course, before entering into an agreement, make sure you know what you'll be getting for your money. Ask the editor for writing samples, references or critiques he's done in the past. Make sure you feel comfortable working with him before you give him your business.

An honest agent will not make any money for referring you to an editor. We strongly advise writers not to use critiquing services offered through an agency. Instead, try hiring a freelance editor or joining a writer's group until your work is ready to be submitted to agents who don't charge fees.

Revisions and Self-Editing

Get Your Work Ready for Submission

by James Scott Bell

ubmitting a novel without rewriting is like playing hockey naked. You're just not equipped to put your best, um, face on things. And sooner rather than later, a well-placed puck is going to hit you where it hurts most. That puck is editors' and agents' built-in prejudice against weak material. They are tuned to say *No*. That's why you rewrite. You want to take out all those *No* reasons.

Rewriting is one of the most important—if the not *the* most important—parts of writing. In that first draft you've completed is plenty of gold, but also plenty of waste that needs excising. So it's time to get to work.

THE TIME TO REVISE

So you have a completed manuscript. This is a crucial time. What you must avoid is any temptation to stop and do wholesale revisions *before you have read the entire manuscript once*.

Think of this process as Google Earth. You want to get a complete overview of your "earth." Your novel. Your story as a whole. You can spin the earth a little here and there to get a better view, but stay up top. You'll tag a few places to visit later, to zoom in on. That'll be the nuts and bolts of revision.

First, it's essential to give yourself a break from the first draft. At least two weeks. During this "cooling phase," try to forget about your book completely. Then try to read the manuscript through in a couple of sittings—three or four at the most. What you want to create is the feeling of being a fresh reader, getting into this book for the first time.

Don't stop to make changes at this point. You may jot a few things down, notes to yourself and the like, but keep going to get the overall impression of the book. Too many writers just sit down and read a manuscript page by page, making changes as they come up. Big or small, each item is dealt with the moment it's seen. Much better is to go from large to small. To start with the most crucial aspects and work your way down to the final step, which is *The Polish*.

MAKING BIG-PICTURE REVISIONS

When it comes to revision, I've found that most writers need a systematic approach. Think of this, then, as your ultimate revision checklist. Apply these questions to every manuscript you write.

JAMES SCOTT BELL is a novelist and writer. This article excerpted with permission from *Write Great Fiction: Revision and Self-Editing* (Writer's Digest Books).

Lead Character

- Is my Lead worth following for a whole novel? Why?
- How can I make my Lead "jump off the page" more?
- Do my characters sufficiently contrast? Are they interesting enough on their own?
- Will readers bond to my Lead because he:
    - . . . cares for someone other than himself?
    - . . . is funny, irreverent, or a rebel with a cause?
    - . . . is competent at something?
    - . . . is an underdog facing long odds without giving up?
    - . . . has a dream or desire readers can relate to?
    - . . . has undeserved misfortune, but doesn't whine about it?
    - . . . is in jeopardy or danger?

Opposition Character

- Is the opposition character just as fully realized as the Lead?
- Is his behavior justified (in his own mind)?
- Are you being "fair" with the opposition?
- Is he as strong or (preferably) stronger than the Lead, in terms of ability to win the fight?

Plot

- Is there any point where a reader might feel like putting the book down?
- Does the plot feel forced or unnatural?
- Is the story out of balance? Too much action? Too much reaction?

The Opening

- Do I open with some part of the story engine running? Or am I spending too much time warming up?
- How do my opening pages conform to Hitchcock's axiom ("A good story is life with the dull parts taken out")?
- What is the *story world* I'm trying to present? What mood descriptions bring that story world to life for the reader?
- What is the tone of my novel going to be? Are the descriptions consistent with that mood?
- What happens in Act I that's going to compel the reader to keep reading? What danger to the lead?
- Is there enough conflict in the setup to run through the whole book?

Middles

- Do I deepen character relationships?
- Why should the reader care what's happening?
- Have I justified the final battle or final choice that will wrap things up at the end?
- Is there a sense of death (physical, professional, or psychological) that overhangs?
- Is there a strong adhesive keeping the characters together (such as moral or professional duty, physical location, or other reasons characters can't just walk away)?

Endings

- Are there loose threads left dangling? (You must either resolve these in a way that doesn't distract from the main plotline, or go back and snip them out.)
- Do I give a feeling of resonance? (The best endings leave a sense of something beyond the confines of the book covers.)
- Will the readers *feel* the way I want them to feel?

Scenes

- Is there conflict or tension in every scene?
- Do I establish a viewpoint character?
- If the scene is action, is the objective clear?
- If the scene is reaction, is the emotion clear?

Exposition

- Do I have large chunks of information dumped in one spot?
- Is my exposition doing *double duty*? Cut out any exposition that doesn't also add to the mood or tone of your novel.

Voice, Style, & Point of View

- Are there sections where the style seems forced or stilted? (Try reading it out loud. Hearing it will often help identify places to be cut or modified.)
- Is the POV consistent in every scene?
- If writing in first person, can the character see and feel what it is I describe?
- If writing in third person, do I slip into the thoughts of other characters rather than sticking to the POV character in the scene? Do I describe something the character can't see or feel?

Setting & Description

- Have I brought the setting to life for the reader?
- Does the setting operate as a "character"?
- Are my descriptions of places and people too generic?
- Are my descriptions doing "double duty" by adding to the mood or tone?

Dialogue

- Can I put in non-sequiturs, or answer a question with a question, and so on?
- Can I change some attributions—*he said, she said*—to action beats?
- Does my dialogue have conflict or tension, even between allies?

Theme

- Do I know what my theme is?
- Has a different theme emerged in the writing? Am I fighting it?
- Have I woven in thematic elements naturally?
- Have I avoided "the lecture"?

THE POLISH

Now, before you send off the manuscript, give it one more going over. This won't take long in comparison, but it will add that extra sparkle that could make all the difference.

Chapter Openings

- Can you begin a little further in?
- Does the opening grab? Have a hint of conflict or action?
- Do most of your chapters begin the same way? Vary them.

Chapter Endings

- Do most of your chapters end the same way? Vary them.
- Can you end the chapter earlier? How does it feel? If it's better, use it.

Dialogue

- Is there plenty of "white space" in your dialogue exchanges?
- Can you cut any words to make the dialogue tighter?

Word Search

- Do a word search for those repeated words and phrases you tend to overuse, then modify them accordingly.
- Look for overuse of the words "very," "really," and "suddenly."
- Adverbs are usually not necessary, and the emotion you're trying to clarify can be better shown through action.

Big Moments

- Identify five big moments in your manuscript. After each moment, make a list of 10 ways you can heighten that moment, make it more intense, and give it more juice.

WHAT THE PROCESS LOOKS LIKE

Below are two versions of a section from my novel, *Sins of the Fathers*. The first is my original. The second shows a little of the thinking process that goes into self-editing.

Original Version

First came the children.

In Lindy's dream they were running and screaming, dozens of them, in some sunlit field. A billowing surge of terrified kids, boys and girls, some in baseball garb, others in variegated ragtag clothes that gave the impression of a Dickens novel run amok.

What was behind them, what was causing the terror, was something dark, unseen. In the hovering over visions that only dreams afford, Lindy sought desperately the source of the fear.

There was a black forest behind the field, like you'd see in fairy tales. Or nightmares.

She moved toward the forest, knowing who it was, who was in there, and she'd meet him coming out. It would be Darren DiCinni, and he would have a gun, and in the dream she kept low to avoid being shot herself.

Moving closer and closer now, the screams of the scattering children fading behind her. Without having to look behind she knew that a raft of cops was pulling up to the scene.

She wondered if she was going to warn DiCinni, or was she just going to look at him?

Would he say anything to her, or she to him?

The dark forest had the kind of trees that come alive at night, with gnarly arms and knotted trunks. It was the place where the bad things lived.

Lindy didn't want to go in, but she couldn't stop herself.

That's when the dark figure started to materialize, from deep within the forest, and he was running toward her.

Edited Version

First came the children.

In Lindy's dream they were running and screaming, dozens of them, in some sunlit field. A billowing surge of terrified kids, boys and girls, some in baseball garb, others in variegated ragtag clothes that gave the impression of a Dickens novel run amok.

Getting Started

~~What was behind them, what was causing the terror, was something dark, unseen.~~ [Weak sentence structure. Rethink. Check "dark." I use it a lot!] In the ~~hovering over visions~~ [Confusing.] that only dreams afford, Lindy sought desperately the source of the fear.

~~There was~~ [Sentences starting with "There" are generally weak. Rethink.] a black forest behind the field, ~~like you'd see~~ [Using "you" in this way can be effective in some places, but overuse is not good. Rethink.] in fairy tales. Or nightmares.

She moved toward the forest, ~~knowing who it was, who was in there,~~ [Awkward.] and she'd meet him coming out. ~~It would be Darren DiCinni, and he would have a gun, and in the dream she kept low to avoid being shot herself.~~ [See if I can strengthen this dramatic image.]

Moving closer and closer now, the screams of the scattering children fading behind her. Without having to look behind she knew that a raft of cops was pulling up to the scene.

~~*She wondered if she was going to warn DiCinni, or was she just going to look at him?*~~ [Tighten.]

Would he say anything to her, or she to him?

~~The dark forest had the kind of trees that come alive at night, with gnarly arms and knotted trunks. It was the place where the bad things lived.~~ [Rethink. There's "dark" again.]

Lindy didn't want to go in, but she couldn't stop herself.

~~That's when~~ [Unneeded verbiage.] the dark figure started to materialize, from deep within the forest, and ~~he~~ [How do we know it's *he*?] was running toward her.

LEARNING TO BE A REAL WRITER

Self-editing is the ability to *know* what makes fiction work. You learn to be your own guide so you may, as Renni Browne and Dave King put it in *Self-Editing for Fiction Writers*, "See your manuscript the way an editor might see it—to do for yourself what a publishing house editor once might have done."

By self-editing exercises and revising your work, you'll be operating on all cylinders. This is how you become a real writer. Cutting, shaping, adding, subtracting, working it, making it better, that's what real writing is all about. This is how unpublished writers become published.

Know Thy Genre

Realize Your Category,
but Beware Following Trends

by Michael J. Vaughn and Andrea Reeves

Agents appreciate it when writers can define the category of their work. A pitch that includes the sentence, "My novel is a police procedural," is much stronger than a sentence such as "My work is a romantic paranormal Western—but it's got some humor in it, too, and some detective elements, as well." The former is easy to place on bookstore shelves, and that's what agents want to do (because that's what editors want to do). But the latter? Not as much. That's why it's important to know your genre, and your subgenre.

If an agent says on her Web site that she's looking for "splatterpunk" and "cyberpunk," do you know for sure if your work qualifies? If you submit something and label it splatterpunk, but the agent quickly deduces that it's not even close, she may just stop reading after two pages—and your window with her has abruptly closed.

Whether you're writing horror or fantasy, there are many classifications as to how exactly your work fits into the market. Here are definitions for the little brothers of all the big categories.

ROMANCE

Romances, typically, are predictable—and that's no accident. People read romances for a reason: They enjoy the formula. It's the process leading to the resolution and the immersion of the reader into another life that's important. That formula in question, in its "pure" form, focuses on one relationship between a man and woman and ends happily ever after.

Romance subgenres

Chick-Lit: often humorous romantic adventures geared toward single working women in their twenties and thirties.

This genre gained steamed five years ago thanks to the success of books such as *Bridget Jones's Diary*. It focuses on careers, clothes and empowerment. The heroine doesn't always get the guy, but she does usually attain success somehow.

Christian: romances in which both hero and heroine are devout Christians, typically focused on a chaste courtship, and mentioning sex only after marriage.

Contemporary: a romance using modern characters and true-to-life settings.

MICHAEL J. VAUGHN is a fiction reviewer for *Publishers Weekly* and author of *Double Blind*, a novel. He defined all the subgenres listed in this article.

ANDREA REEVES is a freelancer and journalist based in Ohio.

Fantasy: A popular market, according to Farrell, that blends fantasy or paranormal with romance.

Erotica: also called "romantica," a romance in which the bedroom doors have been flung open and sexual scenes are described in candid language. These novels are ever popular, and more multi-racial and cultural heroines are taking the spotlight.

Glitz/Glamor: focused on the jet-set elite and celebrity-like characters.

Historical: a romance taking place in a recognizable historical period.

Multicultural: a romance centered on non-Caucasian characters, largely African-American or Hispanic.

Paranormal: involving some sort of supernatural element, ranging widely to include science fiction/fantasy aspects such as time travel, monsters or psychic abilities.

Romantic Comedy: a romance focused on humor, ranging from screwball antics to witty interplay.

Romantic Suspense: a novel in which an admirable heroine is pitted against some evil force (but in which the romantic aspect still maintains priority).

Sensual: based on the sensual tension between hero and heroine, including sizzling sex scenes.

Spicy: a romance in which married characters work to resolve their problems.

Sweet: a romance centered on a virgin heroine, with a storyline containing little or no sex.

Young Adult: written with the teenage audience in mind, with a suitably lower level of sexual content.

HORROR

"Horror, for me, is the compelling 'don't want to look/must look' sense of awe we feel under the breastbone," says Mort Castle, author of *Writing Horror* (Writer's Digest Books). Horror is that genre that seeks to give the reader goosebumps, lock the doors or leave the lights on at night, whether it be through the subgenres of vampires, ghosts, urban fantasy, the psychological or the apocalypse.

Horror subgenres

Child in Peril: involving the abduction and/or persecution of a child.

Comic Horror: horror stories that either spoof horror conventions or that mix the gore with dark humor.

Creepy Kids: horror tale in which children—often under the influence of dark forces—begin to turn against the adults.

Dark Fantasy: a horror story with supernatural and fantasy elements.

Dark Mystery/Noir: inspired by hardboiled detective tales, set in an urban underworld of crime and moral ambiguity.

Erotic Vampire: a horror tale making the newly trendy link between sexuality and vampires, but with more emphasis on graphic description and violence.

Fabulist: derived from "fable," an ancient tradition in which objects, animals or forces of nature are anthropomorphized in order to deliver a moral lesson.

Gothic: a traditional form depicting the encroachment of the Middle Ages upon the 18th century Enlightenment, filled with images of decay and ruin, and episodes of imprisonment and persecution.

Hauntings: a classic form centering on possession by ghosts, demons or poltergeists, particularly of some sort of structure.

Historical: horror tales set in a specific and recognizable period of history.

Magical Realism: a genre inspired by Latin-American authors, in which extraordinary forces or creatures pop into otherwise normal, real-life settings.

Psychological: a story based on the disturbed human psyche, often exploring insane, altered realities and featuring a human monster with horrific, but not supernatural, aspects.

Quiet Horror: subtly written horror that uses atmosphere and mood, rather than graphic description, to create fear and suspense.

Religious: horror that makes use of religious icons and mythology, especially the angels and demons derived from Dante's Inferno and Milton's Paradise Lost.

Science-Fiction Horror: SF with a darker, more violent twist, often revolving around alien invasions, mad scientists, or experiments gone wrong.

Splatter/Splatterpunk: an extreme style of horror that cuts right to the gore. This sub-genre, which first appeared in the '80s, lives up to its name—explicit, gruesome violence.

Supernatural Menace: a horror tale in which the rules of normal existence don't apply, often featuring ghosts, demons, vampires and werewolves.

Technology: stories featuring technology that has run amok, venturing increasingly into the expanding domain of computers, cyberspace, and genetic engineering.

Weird Tales: inspired by the magazine of the same name, a more traditional form featuring strange and uncanny events (Twilight Zone).

Young Adult: horror aimed at a teen market, often with heroes the same age, or slightly older than, the reader.

Zombie: tales featuring dead people who return to commit mayhem on the living.

THRILLER/SUSPENSE

A thriller is "any story that keeps you on the edge of your seat and, likely, up all night," says Robert S. Levinson, author of *Where the Lies Began* and *As a Dead Man*.

Thriller subgenres

Action: a story that often features a race against the clock, lots of violence, and an obvious antagonist.

Comic: a thriller played for laughs, whether through a spoof of the genre or wisecracking interplay between the protagonists.

Conspiracy: a thriller in which the hero battles a large, powerful group whose true extent only he recognizes.

Crime: a story focused on the commission of a crime, often from the point of view of the criminals.

Disaster: a story in which Mother Nature herself is the antagonist, in the form of a hurricane, earthquake or some other natural menace.

Eco-Thriller: a story in which the hero battles some ecological calamity—and often has to also fight the people responsible for creating that calamity.

Erotic: a thriller in which sex plays a major role.

Espionage: the classic international spy novel, which is enjoying a resurgence with one important change: where spies used to battle enemy spies, they now battle terrorists.

Forensic: a thriller featuring the work of forensic experts, whose involvement often puts their own lives at risk.

Historical: a thriller taking place in a specific and recognizable historic period.

Horror: a story—generally featuring some monstrous villain—in which fear and violence play a major part, complete with graphic descriptions.

Legal: a thriller in which a lawyer confronts enemies outside as well as inside the courtroom, generally putting his own life at risk.

Medical: a thriller featuring medical personnel, whether battling a legitimate medical threat such as a world-wide virus, or the illegal or immoral use of medical technology.

Military: a thriller featuring a military protagonist, often working behind enemy lines or as part of a specialized force.

Police Procedural: a crime thriller that follows the police as they work their way through a case.

Political Intrigue: a thriller in which the hero must ensure the stability of the government that employs him.

Psychological: a suspenseful thriller in which the conflict between the characters is mental and emotional rather than physical—until an often violent resolution.

Romantic: a thriller in which the protagonists are romantically involved.

Supernatural: a thriller in which the hero, the antagonist, or both have supernatural powers.

Technological: a thriller in which technology—usually run amok—is central to the plot.

SCIENCE FICTION/FANTASY

Science fiction was slowly created throughout the early- and mid-20th century. And when Neil Armstrong set foot on the moon in 1969, that event brought sci-fi into the mainstream. Over time, aliens have invaded the genre, robots have taken over, time travel has opened up new worlds, and technology has sometimes made the future bleak.

Women have also infiltrated science fiction, according to Richard Curtis, president of Richard Curtis Associates, Inc. "Women's influence in fantasy and science fiction has become prominent and the traditional men's domain has now been opened to more love interest and relationships than hardware, guns and space war," he says.

Sci-fi/Fantasy subgenres

Alternate History: speculative fiction that changes the accepted account of actual historical events, often featuring a profound "what if?" premise.

Arthurian Fantasy: reworkings of the legend of King Arthur and the Knights of the Round Table.

Bangsian Fantasy: stories speculating on the afterlives of famous people.

Biopunk: a blend of film noir, Japanese anime and post-modern elements used to describe an underground, nihilistic biotech society.

Children's Fantasy: a kinder, gentler style of fantasy aimed at very young readers.

Comic: fantasy or science fiction that spoofs the conventions of the genre, or the conventions of society.

Cyberpunk: stories featuring tough outsiders in a high-tech near future where computers have produced major changes in society. It typically has countercultural antiheroes who find themselves trapped in a dehumanized future.

Dark Fantasy: tales that focus on the nightmarish underbelly of magic, venturing into the violence of horror novels.

Dystopian: stories that portray a bleak future world. Stories where the apocalypse occurs, whether in the form of a nuclear bomb, asteroids, disease, or even a political regime, fit this genre.

Erotic: SF or fantasy tales that focus on sexuality.

Game-Related Fantasy: tales with plots and characters similar to high fantasy, but based on a specific role-playing game like Dungeons and Dragons.

Hard Science Fiction: tales in which real present-day science is logically extrapolated to the future.

Heroic Fantasy: stories of war and its heroes, the fantasy equivalent of military science fiction.

High/Epic Fantasy: tales with an emphasis on the fate of an entire race or nation, often featuring a young "nobody" hero battling an ultimate evil.

Historical: speculative fiction taking place in a recognizable historical period.

Mundane SF: a movement that spurns fanciful conceits like warp drives, wormholes and faster-than-light travel for stories based on scientific knowledge as it actually exists.

Military SF: war stories that extrapolate existing military technology and tactics into the future.

Mystery SF: a cross-genre blend that can be either an SF tale with a central mystery or a classic whodunit with SF elements.

Mythic Fiction: stories inspired, or modeled on, classic myths, legends and fairy tales.

New Age: a category of speculative fiction that deals with occult subjects such as astrology, psychic phenomena, spiritual healing, UFOs and mysticism.

Post-Apocalyptic: stories of life on Earth after an apocalypse, focusing on the struggle to survive.

Romance: speculative fiction in which romance plays a key part.

Religious: centering on theological ideas, and heroes who are ruled by their religious beliefs.

Science Fantasy: a blend in which fantasy is supported by scientific or pseudo-scientific explanations.

Social SF: tales that focus on how characters react to their environments—including social satire.

Soft SF: tales based on the more subjective, "softer" sciences: psychology, sociology, anthropology, etc.

Space Opera: a traditional good guys/bad guys faceoff with lots of action and larger-than-life characters.

Spy-Fi: tales of espionage with SF elements, especially the use of high-tech gadgetry.

Steampunk: a specific type of alternate history in which characters in Victorian England have access to 20th century technology.

Superheroes: stories featuring characters endowed with superhuman strengths or abilities.

Sword and Sorcery: a classic genre often set in the medieval period, and more concerned with immediate physical threats than high or heroic fantasy.

Thriller SF: an SF story that takes on the classic world-at-risk, cliffhanger elements of a thriller.

Time-Travel: stories based on the concept of moving forward or backward in time, often delving into the existence of parallel worlds.

Urban Fantasy: a fantasy tale in which magical powers and characters appear in an otherwise normal modern context, similar to Latin American magical realism.

Vampire: variations on the classic vampire legend, recently taking on many sexual and romantic variations.

Wuxia: fantasy tales set within the martial arts traditions and philosophies of China.

Young Adult: speculative fiction aimed at a teenage audience, often featuring a hero the same age or slightly older than the reader.

MYSTERY/CRIME

"The difference between thrillers and mysteries that there's a puzzle in the mystery. If you can disentangle it, it will lead you to the answer," says Jean V. Naggar, founder of her own agency in Manhattan.

Philip Marlowe coolly smokes a cigarette in a dark alley. Sherlock Holmes searches for the tiniest clue, his eye magnified by a magnifying glass. It's Gil Grissom uses the latest scientific methods to get to the bottom of the case. Theses characters are all synonymous to specific mystery genres.

True, they're all male, but diversity is on the rise in mystery, with more variety in gender, race, religion, sexuality and regional characteristics, bringing social issues into the mix, bringing attention to crimes against different groups. Even women writers of mystery have risen recently. Throughout the past 25 years, the number of professional women private eye characters in print jumped 1,000%—and that likely has to do with readership. "There are more female readers of traditional genres than there used to be," says Curtis. "But the writer who can still appeal to male readers is going to be warmly received."

Mystery/Crime subgenres

Amateur Detective: a mystery solved by an amateur, who generally has some profession or affiliation that provides ready access to information about the crime.

Child in Peril: a mystery involving the abduction or persecution of a child.

Classic Whodunit: a crime that is solved by a detective, from the detective's point of view, with all clues available to the reader.

Comic (Bumbling Detective): a mystery played for laughs, often featuring a detective who is grossly unskilled (but often solves the crime anyway, owing to tremendous good luck).

Cozy: a mystery that takes place in a small town—sometimes in a single home—where all the suspects are present and familiar with one another, except the detective, who is usually an eccentric outsider.

Courtroom Drama: a mystery that takes place through the justice system—often the efforts of a defense attorney to prove the innocence of his client by finding the real culprit.

Dark Thriller: a mystery that ventures into the fear factor and graphic violence of the horror genre.

Espionage: the international spy novel—here based less on action than on solving the "puzzle"—is today less focused on the traditional enemy spies than on terrorists.

Forensic: a mystery solved through the forensics lab, featuring much detail and scientific procedure.

Heists and Capers: an "antihero" genre which focuses on the planning and execution of a crime, told from the criminal's perspective.

Historical: a mystery that takes place in a specific, recognizable period of history, with much emphasis on the details of the setting.

Inverted: a story in which the reader knows "whodunit," but the suspense arises from watching the detective figure it out.

Locked Room: a mystery in which the crime is apparently committed under impossible circumstances (but eventually elicits a rational explanation).

Medical: generally involving a medical threat (e.g., a viral epidemic), or the illegitimate use of medical technology.

Police Procedural: a crime solved from the perspective of the police, following detailed, real-life procedures.

Private Detective: Focused on the independent snoop-for-hire, these have evolved from tough-guy "hard-boiled" detectives to the more professional operators of today.

Psychological Suspense: mysteries focused on the intricacies of the crime and what motivated the perpetrator to commit them.

Romantic: a mystery in which the crime-solvers fall in love.

Technothriller: a spinoff from the traditional thriller mystery, with an emphasis on high technology.

Thriller: a suspense mystery with a wider—often international—scope and more action.

Woman in Jeopardy: focuses on a woman put into peril by a crime, and her struggles to overcome or outwit the perpetrator.

Young Adult: a story aimed at a teenage audience, with a hero detective generally the same age or slightly older than the reader, pursuing criminals who are generally less violent—but often just as scary—as those in adult mysteries.

CONCERNING TRENDS

Although it's important to be knowledgeable in defining your subgenre, don't fall into the trap of trying to capitalize on category trends by quickly composing a technothriller, if that particular category is hot right now. As any agent will tell you, books take years to write and publish, and you'll be behind the curve. Steve Laube, president of the Steve Laube Agency said he spends time thwarting copycats. "I usually try to coach a writer against writing to the market. If they do, it's too late. The market has moved on," says Laube, an agent to Christian writers. "I'm tired of query letters that say, 'My book is the next *Left Behind* or *Purpose-Driven Life*.' Writers should spend their time and effort writing a fabulous book and letting it stand on its own merit."

Consider vampire fiction. Anyone following trends should know that vampire novels were hot a few years. Every editor wanted to get their hands on not just horror—but vampire horror: stories with those blood-sucking creatures of the night. But now, times have changed, according to Richard Curtis, president of Richard Curtis Associates, Inc. "I think vampires are coming to an end, and if it was up to me, I would drive a stake through their hearts and never read another vampire book again," he says.

But before you dismiss trends altogether, realize the crucial difference between following trends for copycat purposes and simply keeping an eye on them. Let's say you wrote three novels back in your younger years, and just recently, you've promised yourself to review all three manuscripts and do some hefty rewriting. If you get word that superhero young adult novels are in high demand right now, and one of your novels in the drawer is indeed a superhero young adult manuscript, then you should pull it out immediately and see if you can polish it in a reasonable amount of time for possible submission.

NOW BACK TO WRITING

While you're defining your story and reading other excellent fiction works in your category, don't forget to put the writing first. Putting your finger on the exact subgenre you're composing has its benefits, but if you try to follow all the parameters of one specific subject area, you may pin yourself into a corner. Not to mention, there is always the possibility of editors and agents simply disagree on what exactly constitutes "romantica."

When Faith Meets Prose

An Agent Talks Christian Writing

by Chip MacGregor

When Bethany House Publishers released Janette Oke's *Love Comes Softly* in 1979, a change swept through Christian publishing like fire across a prairie. Just like that, "inspirational fiction" was in demand. Years later, books such as Frank Peretti's *This Present Darkness*, followed by the Left Behind books, emerged as a genre-busting success stories in the publishing world. In less than 10 years, the market demand for inspirational fiction propelled even the most reluctant houses to make room on their lists for this hot new market segment. Christian fiction emerged as a significant part of the contemporary publishing scene—and has been the fastest growing area in all of publishing over the past four years. Because so much has changed—in fiction and nonfiction—it's important that you know how the markets are shifting and how your submissions are impacted by everything.

CHANGES IN FICTION

Today, nearly 30 years since Oke's groundbreaking release, much has changed. In the '80s, the majority of publishers who took up the fiction torch did so with a missionary zeal. Perceiving the new genre as another opportunity to spread the Gospel, some publishers required novelists to declare the tenets of faith in their work. Though a few may still provide specific guidelines for this approach, evangelism has become far less of an expected element when editors consider manuscripts.

Christian publishers are still evangelical, but readers have grown more skeptical and publishers have responded to this. Readers want clarity, but they also want room to reason for themselves. As a result, more Christian publishers are releasing generally redemptive novels with more subtle faith messages in place of the overt expository approach. In addition, more general market houses are willing to accept manuscripts that contain clearly Christian content—an area where many of them once feared to tread. The conversation has largely shifted from one of "message" to one of "craft." What every publisher wants is a well-written book that touches readers' emotions. Consequently, we are seeing an increase in novels written *by* Christians rather than novels written *for* Christians. While this may seem like a slight distinction, it has helped broaden the categories and the quantity of novels published.

From novels dealing with tough contemporary issues such as child abuse and AIDS, to humorous historicals and edgy mysteries, Christian fiction has broadened considerably and

CHIP MacGREGOR runs MacGregor Literary, an agency that works with Christian authors seeking publication in both CBA and ABA markets. You can read more of his thoughts on his Web site: www.ChipMacGregor.com.

now includes such categories as suspense, police procedurals, romance, relationships, science-fiction, fantasy, and chick-lit. The categories themselves have becoming more diverse and numerous as years go by.

So what's behind the shift? In one word: money. With the growth of religious fiction, there's a lot of money to be made. Publishing houses in the Christian Booksellers Association (CBA) have historically found revenue from fiction books to be relatively insignificant—until recently. Now there are Christian novels showing up on bestseller lists everywhere, so the market is presenting a huge opportunity.

CHANGES IN NONFICTION

If Christian fiction is the fastest growing segment of publishing, Christian nonfiction is by far the most dynamic. With one distinction remaining exclusive to Christian nonfiction titles (they are all based on the belief that only God can help readers make lasting change), all publishers seek to provide relevant and timely titles in response to current cultural trends. That goal is universal. In CBA, we're seeing more thoughtful books, more charismatic books, more books from people of color, more of a concern for social justice issues, more books from a postmodern perspective, more inclusive theology, and more multimedia books. Where once nearly all inspirational nonfiction titles were categorized as "Christian living," we're now seeing spiritual themes woven into cookbooks, travel books, relationship titles, and everything from business and finance to health and history. Humor, how-to, politics, marriage, parenting, singles, sports, and pop culture titles can all be found on CBA bestseller lists.

2007 offered the greatest number of Christian books ever published, and that has led to growth in publishing categories. Memoirs used to be dead, but we're currently experiencing a renaissance of spiritual memoir and creative nonfiction (true stories told using fiction techniques), with the purpose of delivering truth to readers. One thing remains the same with nonfiction: Tastes will change, generations will mature, and hot topics will die and be reborn.

THE RISE OF THE CHRISTIAN AGENT

Most publishing houses have policies requiring authors to send proposals through an agent—an ever-growing trend that has caused a huge growth among Christian literary agents. Professional writers need the expertise and counsel of experienced agents, regardless of whether they write for the CBA market or the American Booksellers Association (ABA).

"The only difference in submitting to a Christian agent is in the content of the material," says Steve Laube, an agent focused on Christian books who has his own agency. "Publishing is a business. The thought that Christian agents should be approached any differently is wrong. We expect the same level of professionalism in the proposals we review. There are still authors who try and navigate the labyrinth of publishing on their own, but it is becoming less and less advised."

Janet Grant, another CBA agent, agrees. "The only way for writers to protect their intellectual property and, more importantly, their writing ministry, is to trust an expert with the legal details of their contracts," she says.

Agenting is a relationship business. We do business with people we like and trust. So before setting out to find someone to sell your work, it's critical to find the *right* agent to represent you. This can seem daunting, but it really boils down to doing your research and being patient. Make a list of the things you need most in an agent. Find out who offers the services you want. Study agent Web sites. Check to see which agents are listed as faculty at local writing conferences.

As with any other business, the best way to build relationships is face to face, and conferences are your best bet for separating yourself and your work from the masses. These days, most agents are only able to give careful consideration and valuable feedback to writers they meet. There are exceptions, but we tend to take writers who invest in conferences far more seriously than those who merely slap a query in the mail and invest in a stamp. So show up—and be ready to ask questions: *Who do you represent? What houses have you done business with in the past year? How many deals have you done? What are your expectations of authors?* By asking some basic questions, you can quickly determine which agents might fit your particular style.

RESOURCES FOR CHRISTIAN WRITERS

There are writing conferences all over the country for Christian writers, usually featuring experienced authors and publishing professionals. A good conference is a great way to make introductions, ask questions, hear instructional presentations, and connect with others who are also trying to make it as writers.

Nationally, those that consistently deliver a high caliber of writers include the following:

- Mount Hermon in California (www.mounthermon.org)
- Write to Publish at Wheaton College (www.writetopublish.com)
- The Festival of Faith and Writing at Calvin College (www.calvin.edu/academic/engl/festival)
- The Annual Conference of the American Christian Fiction Writers (www.acfw.com)

There are good regional Christian conferences all over, and Jerry Jenkins' Christian Writers' Guild (www.christianwritersguild.com) also produces some excellent conferences.

The CBA (www.cbaonline.org) is the trade organization for retailers, and the most influential group in Christian publishing. The Evangelical Christian Publishers Association (ECPA; www.ecpa.org) is the trade organization for publishers. Both organizations put on national

Christian Fiction's New Directions

Below is a list of titles where fiction has blended with Christian/inspirational.

- Francine Rivers' *Redeeming Love*, a novel that retells the story of the prophet Hosea in a new way, making it largely the story of a farmer who falls in love with a prostitute.
- Bette Nordberg's *A Season of Grace*, which examined one Christian family's response to a member getting diagnosed with AIDS.
- Elizabeth Musser's *The Swan House*, exploring racial turmoil in '60s Atlanta.
- Lisa Samson's *Tiger Lillie*, which got Christian readers willing to explore questions about sexuality with a new honesty.
- Neta Jackson's influential Yada Yada series have followed a series of women as they've gone through life-changing events.
- Ann Tatlock's *All the Way Home* honestly explores discrimination in a Christian culture.
- Karen Kingsbury's *Between Sundays* caused readers to consider what would happen if our past mistakes were suddenly brought to light.

and regional gatherings for people in publishing to connect and do business. There are also hundreds of Christian ministries, magazines, e-zines, and newsletters that present writing opportunities to up-and-coming authors. And there are a wide variety of product-related Christian businesses that sometimes need writers—greeting cards, toys, games, art, jewelry, and the like. A great source for all things Christian is Sally Stuart's *Christian Writer's Market Guide*, published annually by Waterbrook.

GETTING STARTED

Christian publishing is still growing, and it's headed in all directions, so make sure you get involved if inspirational writing is up your alley. But remember: Though the Christian market is in some ways unique, it still exists in the realm of publishing—and that realm is a business. Make sure you work on your craft and learn about the business of publishing and proper submission protocol. If you've got passion and faith in your heart, and professionalism in your pen, then there's no better time to start writing Christian works than now.

Avenues to an Agent

Getting Your Foot in the Door

Once your work is prepared and you have a solid understanding of how literary agents operate, the time is right to contact an agent. Your initial contact determines the agent's first impression of you, so you want to be professional and brief.

Again, research plays an important role in getting an agent's attention. You want to show the agent you've done your homework. Read the listings in this book to learn agents' areas of interest, check out agents' Web sites to learn more details on how they do business, and find out the names of some of their clients. If there is an author whose book is similar to yours, call the author's publisher. Someone in the contracts department can tell you the name of the agent who sold the title, provided an agent was used. Contact that agent, and impress her with your knowledge of the agency.

Finding an agent can often be as difficult as finding a publisher. Nevertheless, there are four ways to maximize your chances of finding the right agent: submit a query letter or proposal; obtain a referral from someone who knows the agent; meet the agent in person at a writers' conference; or attract the agent's attention with your own published writing.

SUBMISSIONS

The most common way to contact an agent is through a query letter or a proposal package. Most agents will accept unsolicited queries. Some will also look at outlines and sample chapters. Almost none want unsolicited complete manuscripts. Check the ''How to Contact'' subhead in each listing to learn exactly how an agent prefers to be solicited.

Agents agree to be listed in directories such as *Guide to Literary Agents* to indicate what they want to see and how they wish to receive submissions from writers. As you start to query agents, make sure you follow their individual submission directions. This, too, shows an agent you've done your research.

Like publishers, agencies have specialties. Some are only interested in novel-length works. Others are open to a variety of subjects and may actually have member agents within the company who specialize in only a handful of the topics covered by the entire agency.

Before querying any agent, first consult the Agent Specialties Indexes in the back of this book for your manuscript's subject, and identify those agents who handle what you write. Then, read the agents' listings to see which are appropriate for you and your work.

REFERRALS

The best way to get your foot in an agent's door is through a referral from one of her clients, an editor or another agent she has worked with in the past. Since agents trust their clients, they'll usually read referred work before over-the-transom submissions. If you are friends

Communication Etiquette

Via Mail

- Address the agent formally and make sure her name is spelled correctly.
- Double-check the agency's address.
- Include a SASE.
- Use a clear font and standard paragraph formatting.
- A short handwritten thank-you note can be appropriate if the agent helped you at a conference or if she provided editorial feedback along with your rejection.
- Don't include any extraneous materials.
- Don't try to set yourself apart by using fancy stationery. Standard paper and envelopes are preferable.

Via E-mail

- Address the agent as you would in a paper letter—be formal.
- If it's not listed on the Web site, call the company to get the appropriate agent's e-mail address.
- Include a meaningful subject line.
- Keep your emotions in check: Resist the temptation to send an angry response after being rejected, or to send a long, mushy note after being accepted. Keep your e-mails businesslike.
- Don't type in all caps or all lower case. Use proper punctuation and pay attention to grammar and spelling.
- Don't overuse humor—it can be easily misinterpreted.
- Don't e-mail about trivial things.

On the Phone

- Be polite: Ask if she has time to talk, or set up a time to call in advance.
- Get over your "phone phobia." Practice your conversation beforehand if necessary.
- Resist the urge to follow up with an agent too quickly. Give her time to review your material.
- Never make your first contact over the phone unless the agent calls you first or requests you do so in her submission guidelines.
- Don't demand information from her immediately. Your phone call is interrupting her busy day and she should be given time to respond to your needs.
- Don't call to get information you could otherwise obtain from the Internet or other resources.
- Don't have your spouse, secretary, best friend or parent call for you.

In Person

- Be clear and concise.
- Shake the agent's hand and greet her with your name.
- Be yourself, but be professional.
- Maintain eye contact.
- Don't monopolize her time. Either ask a brief question or ask if you can contact her later (via phone/mail/e-mail) with a more in-depth question.
- Don't get too nervous—agents are human!

Contacting Agents

with anyone in the publishing business who has connections with agents, ask politely for a referral. However, don't be offended if another writer will not share the name of his agent.

CONFERENCES

Going to a conference is your best bet for meeting an agent in person. Many conferences invite agents to give a speech or simply be available for meetings with authors, and agents view conferences as a way to find writers. Often agents set aside time for one-on-one discussions with writers, and occasionally they may even look at material writers bring to the conference. These critiques may cost an extra fee, but if an agent is impressed with you and your work, she'll ask to see writing samples after the conference. When you send your query, be sure to mention the specific conference where you met and that she asked to see your work.

When you're face to face with an agent, it's an important time to be friendly, prepared and professional. Always wait for the agent to invite you to send work to them. Saying "I'll send it to your office tomorrow" before they've offered to read it comes off wrong. Don't bring sample chapters or a copy of your manuscript unless you've got a professional critique arranged beforehand. Agents will almost never take writers' work home (they don't have the suitcase space), and writers nervously asking agents to take a look at their work and provide some advice could be considered gauche.

Remember, at these conferences, agents' time is very valuable—as is yours. If you discover that agent who's high on your list recently stopped handling your genre, don't hunt her down and try to convince her to take it on again. Thank the agent for her time and move on to your next target.

If you plan to pitch agents, practice your speech—and make sure you have a pitch that clocks in at less than one minute. Also have versions of your pitch for 2-minute pitches and 3-minute pitches, depending on the conference. Keep your in-person pitch simple and exciting—letting the agent become interested and ask the follow-up questions.

Because this is an effective way to connect with agents, we've asked agents to indicate in their listings which conferences they regularly attend. We've also included a section of Conferences, starting on page 253, where you can find more information about a particular event.

PUBLISHING CREDITS

Some agents read magazines or journals to find writers to represent. If you have had an outstanding piece published in a periodical, an agent wanting to represent you may make contact. In such cases, make sure the agent has read your work. Some agents send form letters to writers, and such representatives often make their living entirely from charging reading fees and not from commissions on sales.

However, many reputable and respected agents do contact potential clients in this way. For them, you already possess attributes of a good client: You have publishing credits and an editor has validated your work. To receive a letter from a reputable agent who has read your material and wants to represent you is an honor.

Occasionally, writers who have self-published or who have had their work published electronically may attract an agent's attention, especially if the self-published book has sold well or received a lot of positive reviews.

Recently, writers have been posting their work on the Internet with the hope of attracting an agent's eye. With all the submissions most agents receive, they probably have little time to peruse writers' Web sites. Nevertheless, there are agents who do consider the Internet a resource for finding fresh voices.

Synopsis Writing

Summing Up Your Novel For an Agent

by Pam McCutcheon

I t's no secret: Most novelists hate writing synopses—but if you want to sell your work, a synopsis is a vital part of the sales package. Since many agents initially ask for just the first few chapters of your work, it's not enough to have scintillating prose with well-drawn characters and an intriguing idea; the editor must also be convinced you can sustain the story for the full length of the novel.

To do this, you need a well-written summary that explains your entire story from beginning to end. If you're unpublished, editors want to ensure your story ends appropriately; and if you *are* published, the synopsis may be all the editor sees. Once the editor falls in love with your story, she may use the synopsis to sell your story at the buying meeting, to write the back cover blurb, and/or to give the cover artist some idea of what your story is about. So you must make your synopsis shine as brightly as your manuscript.

Unfortunately, once you've written a 400-page book, it's tough to know how to condense it down to eight or 10 pages—or worse, one or two. Here are a few tips to help you figure out what to put in—and what to leave out.

Use the correct format. This is the same format you would use in writing your manuscript: one-inch margins, double-spacing, ragged right margin, white paper, etc. Write the synopsis in third person, present tense, no matter what your manuscript is written in. (To see a completed synopsis, look at the example on page 38.)

Watch your length. Most editors and agents have a distinct preference for what they want to see, and it often varies from one person to another in the same literary agency. The rule used to be to have approximately one page of synopsis for every 30-50 pages of text. That makes for a six- to 12-page synopsis when you're finished. Lately, though, agents are requesting shorter and shorter synopses—even as short as one or two pages. To be safe, draft up a ''long synopsis'' as well as a ''short synopsis.'' To discover an agent's specific preference, research their submission guidelines using this book, the Internet, or call and ask—then give them the length they ask for. If you're uncertain how many pages to send, err on the short side.

Know your target market. Make sure you know how your story fits within your targeted genre. There are certain expectations for each, and you need to ensure these are met in your synopsis or you run the risk of being rejected. For example, in a romance, you must show

An award-winning fiction author and popular writing instructor, **PAM McCUTCHEON** has published two how-to books for writers: *Writing the Fiction Synopsis: A Step by Step Approach* and *The Writer's Brainstorming Kit: Thinking in New Directions* (with Michael Waite). She lives in Colorado.

Formatting Your Synopsis

Use a header. Type your real last name and the title of the manuscript on the left. On the right, type "Synopsis" and the page number; this allows the editor to tell page 5 of the ms. from page 5 of the synopsis if it's dropped.

Type the title of your manuscript and "Synopsis." Use the same font as the rest of the synopsis

This is an example of how to show the setting, the protagonist's name and occupation, her internal goal and her internal conflict.

This shows the plot point that sends her in a new direction and a next external goal.

Additional internal and external conflict and another plot point.

Always capitalize the names of major characters when they are introduced.

Writer/Romancing the Stone   Synopsis-1

John Q. Writer
123 Main St.
Writertown, NY 10000
john@johnqwriter.com
(212) 555-1234

SYNOPSIS

ROMANCING THE STONE

by John Q. Writer

JOAN WILDER is a New York romance novelist who would like nothing better than to find her dream man, a man like the bold hero in her stories. But she's too timid to go after what she wants, unlike her sister Elaine who's lived the life of adventure Joan has only written about.

Joan's life is soon turned upside down when she receives a treasure map in the mail from Elaine's murdered husband—a map marking the location of a priceless treasure, El Corazon. Now, Elaine has been kidnapped and the only way Joan can ransom her is to take the map to Cartagena, Colombia.

Writer/Romancing the Stone   Synopsis-2

Though the thought of going to Colombia terrifies her, Joan is determined to save her sister. Unfortunately, when she gets there, she is tricked onto the wrong bus by COLONEL ZOLO, the butcher who killed Elaine's husband. When the bus has an accident with a Jeep, Colonel Zolo tries to kill Joan to steal the map but is foiled by the Jeep's owner, JACK COLTON.

Jack is disgusted. He lost $15,000 worth of birds in that Jeep, money that he planned to use to buy a boat and sail around the world. Now his ticket to success and the easy life is lost and he has to start all over again. The last thing he wants to hear is complaints from this strange woman.

the development of the relationship. For a mystery, you need to show the clues, red herrings, and suspects. For a fantasy, we need to know the rules of the world you have set up, and so on. I can hear some of you saying, "Duh!" but surprisingly, many writers leave out these elements. They get so caught up in the external plot that they forget to show these all-important genre expectations.

Make the characters interesting and sympathetic. Summing up the plot is crucial, but don't concentrate so much on the plot that the characters don't come alive. Show us the major characters' goals (what they want), motivations (why they want it) and conflicts (why they can't have it). Then at the end, show if they achieved their goals or not, and how they've grown as a result of the story. That will help your readers care about what happens to them. Try to briefly show us the characters' emotions on their journey.

Use transitions. Don't tell your story with a series of unconnected declarative sentences: "She yelled. He retaliated. They left." It makes for disjointed reading and interrupts the smooth flow of the story. Sometimes, writers who use transitions with ease and skill in their manuscripts somehow still fail to use them in their synopses. The objective is to make your synopsis flow as easily as your manuscript—to make the story so interesting that the reader will continue reading without a hitch from beginning to end.

So, connect those ideas from one sentence or one paragraph to the next to show how each plot point and character change are related to one another and affect what comes next. Even if you have to use such phrases as "Meanwhile, back at the ranch . . ." or "What Harold didn't realize was . . .", it's worth it to make your story read smoothly.

Keep your tone consistent. Don't use widely varying moods in the synopsis; it does nothing but confuse the reader. For example, don't start off describing a horrible, angst-filled character background, and then segue into a humorous romp. It leaves the agent baffled, wondering what kind of story it really is. Make sure your tone is consistent throughout the synopsis—and that it matches the tone of your novel.

Keep the authorial voice silent. Don't insert comments in the synopsis that address the agent directly to ensure she "gets it," such as "The conflict is . . ." or "At this point in the story . . ." Talking directly to the reader jerks her out of the flow of the story. Also avoid telling the agent the story is heartrending, humorous, exciting, etc. If you tell the agent how to feel, you run the risk of offending her. Quite literally, the agent will be the judge of whether your story makes her feel the way you intended.

Leave out irrelevant details. Don't get so caught up in the minutia of your intricate plot, fascinating research, historical period, or speculative world that the synopsis is stuffed with irrelevant details and characters. In the synopsis, we don't really need to know how a spinning wheel works or what a minor character looks like—unless it's necessary for understanding the plot or the major character(s). Save the details for the story itself—and include them there only if they're relevant.

Keep names to a minimum. Don't refer to all of your 20-plus characters by name. In a short synopsis, that's a lot of names to remember. Just mention the names of the key protagonist(s) and antagonist(s). Don't mention secondary characters by name unless they show up several times in the synopsis. Instead, refer to them by function or relationship: the cab driver, the housekeeper, Sarah's daughter, Joel's boss, etc. It will make it a lot easier for your readers to follow.

Use dialogue sparingly. The problem with including or using dialogue in the synopsis is that you are usually slowing down to telling the story word by precious word, which makes the pacing very erratic and takes up a lot of unnecessary space in the synopsis. Instead, summarize the gist of the conversation and move on.

Make the ending complete. Make sure you explain key character motivations (why they do the things they do) and tie up loose ends of plot and character development. Never commit the unpardonable sin of telling the agent she has to read the whole story to find out how it ends—unless you want an immediate rejection. Instead, at the end, show the resolution of the main characters' goals and conflicts, and the resolution of the plot. If you're unsure if anything is missing, give your synopsis to someone who knows nothing about your story and ask him to tell you if he has any unanswered questions after reading it.

Final advice. Remember that the synopsis is a summary of the story told in narrative form, as if you were relating it to a friend over a cup of coffee. Though some of the minor formatting details may vary from one person to person, if you just tell your story and follow the tips above, you should have a winning synopsis.

Book Proposals

Five Elements of a Nonfiction Proposal

by Mollie Glick

One of the most exciting parts about being an agent is the opportunity to introduce new ideas to the world. When an agent stumbles across a brilliant nonfiction proposal—the kind of proposal that sends a chill up her spine—she knows immediately that she's going to take it on. Such a connection often feels like magic, but the truth is, it's more like alchemy. Sure—in order to transform metal into gold, you need the philosopher's stone, and in order to write a brilliant book, you need a brilliant premise, but in both cases you also need to start out with the correct basic elements.

There are lots of ways to think about book proposals. Some agents, like Jean Naggar, president of The Jean V. Naggar Literary Agency, think of proposals as a blueprint for what the finished book is going to look like. Other agents, like Richard Morris of Janklow & Nesbit, think of it as an author's first chance to show off his/her unique narrative voice. In this tough market—a market in which editors are looking for reasons to reject projects rather than reasons to accept them—I think of proposals as an argument for why an editor can't afford *not* to take a book on. Any way you look at it, a book proposal is your first chance to prove that you've got all of the elements needed to spin your raw idea into a literary goldmine.

So what exactly are the essential elements that publishers and agents are looking for when they read your proposal? Five Things:

1. An original idea. What fresh, original and engaging idea will your book present?

2. But not *too* original. What published books share the same audience as your book? Why were those books successful, and why will your book appeal to the same readers?

3. A clear sense of what you want to achieve and how you're going to get there. What's the scope of your book? How are you going to set about gathering and presenting your information?

4. Why is this an important book? How is your book different (and better than) other similar books? Why is now the time to publish a book on your chosen subject?

5. Why are you the go-to-guy (or gal) to write a book on this subject? You may have heard the word "platform" floating around and wondered what it means. Put simply, there are two kinds of platforms, and ideally you want to demonstrate that you've got both. *First*: What makes you an expert and the clear choice to write the book you're proposing? *Second*: What media connections do you have that will help you reach your intended audience with your message?

MOLLIE GLICK is a literary agent with the Jean V. Naggar Literary Agency (www.jvnla.com) in New York City. She handles a variety of fiction, nonfiction and young adult work.

Now that you know the five crucial elements of a proposal, it's time to think about the shape your proposal is going to take. There are no hard and fast rules about what shape works, so long as it presents all of the raw materials listed above, but the following format will get you started if you're looking for a basic framework:

The first thing to include is an **Overview** or **Abstract** section. This is your chance to lay out the basic premise of your book in a clear, concise way. You'll want to include a few lines describing the idea behind your book, as well a bit of preliminary information about why the book is important, and why you're the one to write it. Try and keep this section short and sweet—ideally no longer than one page. You'll revisit many of the topics you touch on in this section later in more depth, so all you need to present here is the big picture.

If your **Overview** is on the long side, you might consider including information about the proposed length, structure and format of your book in a separate **Format** section. This is also a good opportunity to reveal how long it will take you to deliver the finished manuscript after you've signed a contract with a publisher.

Another place to expound on some of the information you glossed over in your Overview is the **About the Author** or **Author Bio** section. For example, if in the Overview, you said you were an Ivy-League-educated therapist who has made guest appearances on several national television shows, then here's where you'll explain that you graduated with a PhD from Harvard in 1991, and that the shows you've appeared on are "Oprah," "60 Minutes" and "Dateline." Try to make sure that you make a case in this section for both elements of your platform—your expert platform and your media platform. If you've published previous books, you'll list them here; and if you've published articles, you may want to mention them here, and then include them as **Clips** at the very end of the proposal.

But what if you're not a big name expert with national media exposure? In that case, use the About the Author section to talk about how/why you became interested in the topic of your book, and how you'll gain access to the information you need to include. If your platform is on the weaker side, you can also choose to present your bio later in the proposal, after you've already made a good case for the book.

The next section to include is a **Market** or **Audience** section. This is where you'll explain why there's a need for your book, and who is going to buy it. The more statistics and figures you can include here the better. Prove that different types of readers exist who will be interested in the book. If you want to write a book on architecture, for example, show circulation numbers for architecture-oriented magazines. Those who spend money on such magazines are the same readers who will spend money on your book.

And after you've argued that there are tons of readers out there, waiting to buy your book, you've also got the chance to explain how you plan to reach those readers in a **Publicity** or **Marketing Plan** section. The Publicity/Marketing section is a great place to talk about any particular promotional idea you've come up with, and/or media connections or networks you plan to use in promoting your book. That said, make sure that all the plans you include here are realistic, self-motivated and achievable—this is not the time to say that your book is a perfect fit for "Oprah" or that with the thousands of dollars of marketing money your publisher gives you, you plan to buy ad space in *The New York Times*.

Once you've explained who's going to buy your book, and how you're going to get the book into your audience's hands, it's time to face off against the competition. There are two ways you can approach your **Comparative Analysis** section. One route is to include successful books that would appeal to a similar audience, and make an argument that your book will be just as successful. Another approach is to talk about all of the books written on similar topics, and then explain why your book is different and better. Or you can include both of these elements. The one rookie mistake you *won't* want to make is playing down the competition and only including unsuccessful or small books on similar topics. If one or more pivotal books have been published in your field, and you fail to mention them, you'll look either uninformed or dishonest. The trick is to acknowledge all the competitors, then explain why your book is different and better. For example, maybe the definitive book on the subject is 10 years out of date, or your book includes more thorough research.

After the Comparative Analysis, include a thorough, well-organized **Chapter Outline**, explaining how many chapters you'll be writing, what topics you're covering, and how one topic will flow into the next. I like to have my authors write their Chapter Outlines in paragraph form, rather than in bullets, because it gives them another chance to demonstrate their writing style, but a bulleted chapter outline is also acceptable.

Finally, once you've provided your reader with a good overview of your plans, it's time to make good on the promises you've made, delivering one to three **Sample Chapters**. Take your time with these—they're the part of the proposal that most resembles a finished book, and although you'll ideally incorporate your unique narrative voice throughout the proposal, the sample chapters are your chance to really show it off.

As you've probably figured out by now, different parts of the proposal will be more or less important depending on the kind of book you're writing. If you're a public figure writing a tell-all, your bio, clips and sample chapter will be the most important parts. If you're a self-help writer, you'll need to prove your expert credentials, your target audience, and how you

Components and Elements They Include

This overview of proposal components relates to the five elements listed on page 41.

Overview/Abstract
A little bit of everything: your original idea, the scope of your book, why this is an important book, and why you're the person to write it (1, 3, 4, 5)

Format
Gives a sense of how you're going to deliver the material (3)

About the Author/Author Bio/Clips
Shows why you're the go-to-guy or gal to write this book (5)

Audience
Demonstrates the importance of your book (4)

Publicity/Marketing Plans
Shows how you plan to meet your goals and reach your intended audience (3)

Comparative Analysis
Shows how your book is similar to and differs from the competition (1, 2, 4)

Chapter Outline
Gives a better sense of your premise, and how you're going to pull all of your material together (1, 3)

Samples Chapters
Lets you explore aspects of your idea in greater depth, to demonstrate that you've got an engaging narrative voice (1, 3, 4, 5)

plan to reach that audience. And if you're a mother writing a personal story about raising an autistic child, you'll want to emphasize the size of your audience and the strength of your narrative voice. But regardless of which components of the proposal you choose to emphasize, what's most important is that your proposal incorporates each of the five elements necessary to spin your idea into gold.

The Next Steps

Further Reading and Research

Book proposals are complicated projects. Typically, they're not short—running anywhere from 12-30 pages. They require a ton of research and a lot of ideas on how you'll market the book and get readers into the bookstore (or on Amazon) to buy your product. To learn more about the proposal writing process—and see examples—here are two good books for further reading:

- *Bulletproof Book Proposals*, 2006, by Pam Brodowsky and Eric Niehaus (Writer's Digest Books); ISBN-13: 978-1582973678.

- *How to Write a Book Proposal*, 2004, by Michael Larsen (Writer's Digest Books); ISBN-13: 978-158297-2510.

The Query Letter

How to Hook an Agent

The query letter is the catalyst in the chemical reaction of publishing. Overall, writing a query letter is a fairly simple process that serves one purpose—getting an agent or editor to read your manuscript. A query letter is the tool that sells you and your book using brief, attention-getting words. Fiction and nonfiction query letters share the same basic elements, but there are differences you should consider for each category.

FICTION QUERIES

Here's a general rule of thumb when querying an agent for a fiction manuscript: Do not contact the agent regarding your novel until the entire manuscript is written and ready to be sent. A query letter for a work of fiction generally contains the following elements.

- **The hook.** This paragraph should be written to hook the agent and get her to request a few chapters or the whole manuscript. The hook is usually a special plot detail or a unique element that's going to grab the agent's attention.
- **About the book.** It is important to provide the agent with the technical statistics of your book: title, genre and word count. An easy way to estimate your manuscript's word count is to multiply the number of manuscript pages by 250 and then round that number to the nearest ten thousand. Simply starting your query with basic information is a safe route to go, especially if you don't have a referral.
- **The story.** This is the part of your letter where you provide a summary of your plot, introduce your main characters and hint at the main conflict that drives the story. Be careful not to go overboard here, either in content or in length. Only provide the agent with the basic elements she needs to make a decision about your manuscript. Cliffhangers are allowed. You want an agent to wonder what happens next.
- **The audience.** You must be able to tell the agent who the intended audience is for your novel. Many writers find it helpful to tell the agent the theme of their novel, which then signifies the intended audience and to whom the novel will appeal.
- **About you.** List any writing groups to which you belong, publishing credentials, awards won, etc. Remember, though, if you don't have any of the above, don't stress your inexperience or dwell on what you haven't accomplished.
- **The closing.** Make sure you end your query on a positive note. You should thank the agent for her time and offer to send more information (a synopsis, sample chapters or the complete manuscript), upon request. Be sure to also mention that you've enclosed a self-addressed, stamped envelope (SASE) for the agent's convenience.

NONFICTION QUERIES

Unlike fiction manuscripts, it is acceptable to query an agent about a nonfiction book before the manuscript is complete. The following seven elements should be included in a nonfiction query.

• **The hook.** The hook is usually a special detail or a unique element that's going to grab the agent's attention and pull her in. Oftentimes, nonfiction writers use statistics or survey results, especially if the results are astounding or unique, to reel in the agent.

• **The referral.** Why are you contacting this particular agent? A recommendation from an author she currently represents, an acknowledgment in a book they have represented, or because the agent has a strong track record of selling books on the subject about which you're writing? No matter the answer, knowing what type of work the agent represents shows her that you're a professional.

• **About the book.** It is important to provide the agent with the technical statistics of your book, including the title and sales handle—a short, one-line statement explaining the primary goal of your book. In his book *How to Write a Book Proposal* (Writer's Digest Books), agent Michael Larsen says that a book's handle "may be its thematic or stylistic resemblance to one or two successful books or authors." One example Larsen uses to further explain a sales handle is "*Fast Food Nation* meets fashion." Essentially, the handle helps the agent decide whether your book is a project she can sell.

• **Markets.** Tell the agent who will buy your book (i.e., the audience) and where people will buy it. Research potential markets according to various demographics (including age, gender, income, profession, etc.), and then use the information to find solid figures that verify your book's audience is significant enough to warrant publication. The more you know about the potential markets for your book (usually the top three or four markets), the more professional you appear to the agent. Use bullet points if necessary.

• **About you.** Tell the agent who you are and why you are the best person to write this book. In this paragraph, you should only provide qualifications that are relevant to your book, including career and academic background and publication credentials (as they relate to the subject of your book).

Mistakes to Avoid

- Don't use any cute attention-getting devices such as colored stationery or odd fonts.

- Don't send any unnecessary enclosures, such as a picture of you or your family pet.

- Don't waste time telling the agent you're writing to her in the hopes that she will represent your book. Get immediately to the heart of the matter—your book.

- Don't try to "sell" the agent by telling her how great your book is or comparing it to those written by best-selling authors.

- Don't mention that your family, friends or "readers" love it.

- Don't send sample chapters that are not consecutive chapters.

• **The closing.** Make sure you end your query on a positive note. Thank the agent for her time and tell her what items you have ready to submit (proposal, sample chapters, complete manuscript, etc.) upon request. Also mention that you've enclosed a self-addressed, stamped envelope (SASE) for the agent's convenience.

FORMATTING YOUR QUERY

There are no hard-and-fast rules when it comes to formatting your query letter, but there are some widely accepted guidelines like those listed below, adapted from *Formatting & Submitting Your Manuscript*, by Jack and Glenda Neff, and Don Prues (Writer's Digest Books).

- Use a standard font or typeface (avoid bold, script or italics, except for publication titles), such as 12-point Times New Roman.
- Your name, address and phone number (plus e-mail and fax, if possible) should appear in the top right corner or on your letterhead. If you would like, you can create your own letterhead so you appear professional. Simply type the same information mentioned above, center it at the top of the page and photocopy it on quality paper.
- Use a 1-inch margin on all sides.
- Address the query to a specific agent—preferably the one who handles the type of work you're writing.
- Keep it to one page.
- Include a SASE or postcard for reply, and state in the letter you have done so (preferably in your closing paragraph).
- Use block format (no indentations or extra space between paragraphs).
- Single-space the body of the letter and double-space between paragraphs.
- Thank the agent for considering your query letter.

Bad Fiction Query

The author's phone number and e-mail address are missing.

Vincent Barnes
1302 Amateur Road
Sheboygan, WI 53081

May 1, 2008

General Agents, Inc.
10 Anywhere Drive
Detroit, MI 48215

Always address your query to a specific agent.

Dear Sir/Madam,

Do not query an agent if your fiction manuscript is not finished and fully revised.

I'm about to finish my novel and wanted to give you a heads up because I know I'll need an agent to help sell it. Please take a look at the enclosed sample chapters and let me know if you think publishers will like my book.

Don't ask an agent for advice or criticism—that's not the agent's job nor the purpose of the query.

This is my first time writing a romance novel, but I've had a couple science articles published in online magazines. I worked in a hospital laboratory for 15 years and thought it would be fun to trade in all those cold hard facts for a good old-fashioned love story.

Never mention that this is the first book you've written—it singles you out as an amateur. While it's good to have publishing credits or professional expertise, they're only worth mentioning if they are relevant to the book being proposed.

My novel—titled *Many Miles of Love*—is about a shy midwestern girl named Lauren who falls in love with Ray, a boisterous salesman from Baltimore. The couple goes through many highs and lows together, including being separated from one another several times due to circumstances beyond their control. In the end, of course, they are able to come together and make a happy life for themselves.

The book will probably end up around 70,000 words and will be read mostly by women. I've already had a variety of family members look over the beginning chapters, and all of them are curious to know what happens next.

This is vague and has no "hook" to capture the agent's attention. What will make it different from other romance novels?

I put in an application with the U.S. Copyright Office last week. I've also been doing some research on how much authors get paid for novels these days. When you respond, please include any information on possible advances and royalties for my book.

Many thanks,

Vincent Barnes

You should describe your potential audience more specifically than just men or women. Also, mentioning that your family likes the book will get you nowhere. You would be better served to point out if it has been read/critiqued by a few local writing groups.

Don't mention copyright information or payment expectations. This is simply a query to assess an agent's interest in your novel.

Good Fiction Query

Brent Thompson
62 Fiction Drive
Naples, FL 34104
(630)555-6009
brent.thompson@email.com

February 27, 2008

Mr. Alexander Diaz
The Best Literary Agency
546 Representative Blvd.
New York, NY 10001

Dear Mr. Diaz,

I heard you speak at the Southwestern Florida Writer's Conference last month, where you mentioned an interest in seeing more young adult fiction submissions filled with both adventure and heart. I have just the story for you—a 60,000-word novel geared toward preteen and teenage boys titled *The Mysterious Map.*

The book opens in the North Carolina countryside, where 15-year-old Rowan Hampton has discovered a secret map. He's certain it will lead to treasure, but he and his best friend Karl soon realize the clues are of a more personal nature. As they move from town to town, Rowan begins to question details of his childhood that now seem unclear. What really happened to his younger sister? Can he trust everything his parents say? Who left him this map, and where will it lead?

I'm a native of the Carolinas, where I taught middle-school English for 35 years. While I was teaching, a few chapters of Rowan's journey were published in the *Lowland's Literary Journal.* After retiring last year, I dedicated myself to completing the novel.

My manuscript is ready to be sent at your request.

I look forward to hearing from you.

Sincerely,

Brent Thompson

Address your query to a specific agent.

Say why you have chosen to query this particular agent.

Always state your novel's genre, title and word count.

Briefly tell what the novel is about.

Provide relevant background information about yourself, including professional experience, publishing credentials, etc.

Bad Nonfiction Query

Contacting Agents

The author's address and phone number are missing—include all pertinent contact information.

Always address your query to the agent's full name, even if you've seen it shortened elsewhere. It's professional to make a formal first impression.

Questions can prove to be an interesting way to "hook" an agent, but don't be too vague. Ask a question nobody is asking—one that shows why your book is unique.

Only send these materials if requested in the agent's submission guidelines. Also, don't bother telling an agent what your friends think; show the agent why the book must be published and must be written by you.

Try to include a few main points that differentiate your book from others on the market. Also, make sure you are enough of an expert to provide this information to potentially thousands of readers.

Juanita Nielson
Kansas City, MO
badwriter@email.com

March 30, 2008

Charles Mortenson
Agent & Agent Representatives
39 W. Main St.
Boston, MA 02209

Dear Chuck,

Did you know there are actually six branches—or types—of yoga that people can practice? Did you know that chanting the word "Om" stems from the scientific theory that the universe is constantly in motion?

For more enlightening information on yoga, please look over my outline and sample chapters and let me know if you think this book will interest publishers. I have already shared my idea with a few friends and they all agree I would be great at writing this book.

I've been taking yoga classes on and off for several years now, and they have really helped me get through some tough times. I want to write a book about yoga so other people can see the benefits of it. I have never attempted to write a book before, but I've been taking some local college courses and even attended a writers' conference last year.

Yoga has been such a big trend lately that there are probably lots of interested readers out there. I know other books about yoga have already been published, but mine will be more personal and geared toward people who don't know much about the physical and spiritual practice.

I've been a stay-at-home mom for the past 8 years, and think this book can signify a new direction for my life. Hopefully with your help selling and an editor's help revising, this book can land on the bestseller list.

Thanks for your time,

Juanita Nielson

Don't pitch an idea based on a trend because trends eventually fade. Make sure you have a deep grasp on who your target readers will be, and make sure you will actually be able to reach them if they aren't already reading books on your topic.

Don't point out your (or the book's) shortcomings. If it needs editorial help, get some before you send it to an agent.

Good Nonfiction Query

Gayle Matthews
1999 Published Way
Durham, CA 95938
(773)555-6868
gmatthews@email.com

July 30, 2008

Lynn Kobayashi
Kobayashi & Brown, Inc.
55 Acceptance St. NW
Seattle, WA 98101

Always address a specific agent.

Dear Ms. Kobayashi,

The hook: Provide concrete information and indisputable reasoning for why your book fills a void in the market. Explain how your target audience fits into the proposal.

California, Washington and Oregon have long been the wine centers of the United States, but they are far from being the only places people can learn about and enjoy the vineyard culture. Nearly every state in the country—including Alaska—has a winery, and many of them are producing quality, affordable products. Recent research shows that wine is the favored alcoholic drink among Americans, and that almost all who drink it regularly are purchasing American wines. However, many do not have the time or money to travel all the way to the West Coast to do tours and tastings.

Explain a few details about the book, as well as why you are querying this particular agent.

Your Web site states you specialize in travel writing, so I'd like to propose a series of guidebooks that take people on tours of local vineyards. The books would be categorized by region (Northeast, Mid-Atlantic, Southeast, Midwestern, etc.) and would focus on the best wineries to visit in each neighboring state. Not only would each entry provide specific travel details, but information on the vineyard's history, specialties and overall atmosphere would also be included. There would also be a tremendous opportunity for beautiful photography and detailed maps.

If possible, talk about your book from a sales perspective.

Since no other travel books about wine have been broken down in this manner, there are multiple sales opportunities. Aside from national bookstores, the guidebooks could be marketed in vineyards, wine shops, tourism bureaus and local specialty stores in each region.

Provide professional background information relevant to the writing of this book.

I have been a professor of Viticulture and Enology for the past 12 years and help organize an annual conference with other wine professionals to discuss industry trends. I have a deep love for both wine and travel, and have already visited more than 100 wineries across the country. I also write a syndicated newspaper column about wine and have contributed to both consumer and trade magazines on the topics of travel and vineyards.

Show you've followed the agent's submission guidelines and make a polite offer.

Enclosed are a detailed outline, professional bio and three sample chapters. I would be glad to go over more specifics of my proposal at your convenience.

Sincerely,

Gayle Matthews

Wheeling and Dealing

Make the Most Out of a Writers' Conference

by Chuck Sambuchino

Writing is a solitary task. It means a lot of time sitting at the computer, researching facts online, checking your e-mail, and staring at that first chapter you've rewritten 18 times but still doesn't seem to work. If you want to be a writer, you're going to spend plenty of time alone, but at the same time, you need to understand the importance of networking and making friends who are fellow scribes. That's where writers' conferences come in.

Conferences are your rare and invaluable opportunities to simply get out there—to mingle, network, have fun, and meet new contacts that can help further your career. There are plenty of conferences all across the country and beyond. Now you just need to know how to maximize a conference's worth, and you'll be all set.

CONFERENCES: THE BASICS

Conferences are events where writers gather to meet one another and celebrate the craft and business of writing. Attendees listen to authors and publishing professionals who present on various topics of interest. Each day is filled with sessions regarding all aspects of writing, and attendees will likely have a choice of which sessions to attend. For example, you can attend the "Query Letter Writing" session versus other panels on "The Secrets of Mystery Writing" and "The Secrets of Successful Book Proposals" held at the same time. To find out what speakers and sessions will be included, check the event's official Web site or e-mail the coordinator.

Since they usually take place during a weekend, you may have to clear your Friday schedule to see all speakers. Also, conferences are not to be confused with *retreats*, which are longer outings that include a lot of writing assignments. Retreats typically have small attendance and cost more because of the personal attention.

Some conferences are longstanding, while others are brand new. Most are not out to make money—and few could, even if they wanted to. A regional writers group usually organizes them, and the organizers are likely all volunteers. For example, the Southeast Mystery Writers of America hosts Killer Nashville, while the Space Coast Writers' Guild organizes the Space Coast Writers' Conference in Cocoa Beach.

CHUCK SAMBUCHINO is the editor of *Guide to Literary Agents* as well as the editor of *Screenwriter's & Playwright's Market* and the assistant editor of *Writer's Market*. He presents at many writers' conferences. To learn more about him, visit his blog at www.guidetoliteraryagents.com/blog.

HOW DO YOU FIND CONFERENCES?

Conferences are all over the place. With approximately 200 per year in the U.S., you can find them in practically every state and area of the country—and then there are even more in Canada. Some areas are hotspots, such as New York, Texas and California, whereas other states may not have a lot of choices, but still have at least one annual event nearby.

To find a conference, you can use print directories, online directories or simply a search engine. This book—*Guide to Literary Agents*—lists a whole smorgasbord of conferences in its back section, while *GLA*'s sister publications, such as *Children's Writer's & Illustrator's Market*, will list conferences specific to the book's target readers. Also, conferences advertise in magazines (such as *Writer's Digest*) and are featured in writing-related newsletters, such as Absolute Write and Writer Gazette. Subscribe to free newsletters to get conference alerts along with plenty of other helpful info.

Helpful online directories exist—especially for genre fiction writers. Look online for the Web sites of the Romance Writers of America, the Mystery Writers of America, or the Society of Children's Book Writers and Illustrators, and you will find lists of upcoming conferences that are great value to scribes of those categories.

Another option is to simply use Google. The results are usually incomplete, but helpful enough. Try searching for "writers conference (month and year)" and see what comes up. You won't find a ton of gatherings that way, but searches will provide a few promising leads. Since conferences sometimes pop up out of nowhere without a whole lot of hubbub, this can be a good way to find newer events.

No matter where you find a conference listing, you will want to immediate check out the conference Web site, where updated lists of speakers, time, dates and registration forms can be found.

WHO WILL YOU MEET?

Perhaps the most valuable aspect of a conference is writers' ability to meet the power players and decision makers in the publishing world. In addition, they can make contacts and form partnerships with their fellow writers. Here are three different types of people you will meet.

Peers and writers

This is where the schmoozing comes in. Besides classes and presentations, there are usually dinners as well as meet-and-greet opportunities, not to mention simply banding together at night and hitting the hotel lobby or nearby bar to relax and talk. Perhaps you didn't even know the regional writers' group in charge existed, and may be able get involved with the organization.

Editors

As an editor myself, I spend a lot of time at conferences meeting with writers one-on-one and essentially answering any and all questions that they have for me. Editors specialize in presenting sessions and workshops, teaching everything from craft and characters to book proposal writing and the basics of agents.

Agents

Perhaps the biggest draw, agents attend conferences for a specific reason: to find potential clients. They are bombarded with pitches and request writing samples from those attendees who dazzle them with a good idea or pitch. Short of an excellent referral, conferences are the best way to snag an agent, so take advantage of meeting one. (I found my literary agent at a conference. Trust me: They work.)

Usually it works like this: You will schedule a short amount of time to pitch your idea to an agent. Your "elevator pitch" should be relatively short, and then there's some time for the agent to ask questions. If the agent is interested in seeing some of your work, she will pass you a business card and request a "partial" (a sample of the manuscript, such as the first 30 pages or the first three chapters). If the agent is not interested, she will say so. When an agent requests your manuscript, you can send it in and put "Requested Material" on the envelope (or in the e-mail) so it gets past the slush pile.

While there are designated times to pitch agents, it should be said that agents are usually ready for pitches at all times from all sides. However, beware crossing the line into "annoying." Don't pitch agents in the restroom. Don't interrupt them if they're having a conversation. If an agent is sitting down with fellow agents and trying, for a brief moment, not to talk business, don't hover around waiting for eye contact so you can step in and pitch.

The simple fact that you're *at* a conference shows that you're dedicated and professional. That in itself is enough to get agents' attention. Though writers still find in-person pitching quite nerve-wracking, the good news is that agents are not the mean stereotypes you may have in mind. They are almost all friendly booklovers like you.

HOW TO MAXIMIZE THE VALUE

If you want to make the most out of a conference, you have to stay busy and get involved. Go to presentations; hang out at late-night fiction readings; and make sure to stay for the whole shebang. Sign up for pitch slams and meet the power players in attendance. A little face time can pay off down the line. If you're involved with the sponsoring organization, offer to volunteer. If you pick up an agent from the airport, for example, that's plenty of one-on-one time in the car to slip in a pitch or two.

Make sure you schmooze. When you sit down at the dinner banquet, ask people what they're working on. Networking can be as simple as "I'll pass your name on to so-and-so, and I'd be appreciative if you could give me a referral to such-and-such." If you don't have business cards, make some basic ones just so others can know your contact info.

An unfortunate truth about conferences is that they can be a hit on the wallet. Some are affordable ($100-200) while others not so much ($700+). It all depends on how long the conference is, what is included, the price the conference paid to fly in speakers, etc. I've spoken at conferences where the crowd gathered at a Days Inn, and another where the event was hosted in a posh San Francisco hotel. Can you guess which event cost more? In addition to the basic conference cost, you have to budget money for "extras." Sometimes, the little things at a conference, such as 10-minute pitch sessions with agents or an editor's personal critique of your work, will mean an additional cost. If you want to truly make the most of a conference, you will need to indulge in some extras. When all is said and done, you may have to take a day off work and spend a chunk of money on costs and hotels. Think of it as an annual writing vacation for you and budget money early in the year. If you gain contacts that lead to writing assignments down the line, the conference will pay for itself before you know it!

KNOW WHICH ONE IS RIGHT FOR YOU

With so many to choose from, how can you know which one is the best investment? Obviously, proximity will play a factor, as we can't all afford a ticket to the Maui Writers' Conference. Look for events in your area and start from there. Some locations, such as Tennessee and Colorado, have a surprisingly large number of gatherings each year.

Ask yourself: "What do I want to get out of this?" Is it simply to recharge your batteries and get motivated? Because a general goal like that can be accomplished by most conferences. Do you have a polished and ready manuscript that needs an agent? Look for conferences with not only agents in attendance, but agents (or acquiring editors, as they function basically the same) in attendance that handle your specific area of work, be it science fiction, medical nonfiction, or whatever else.

Conferences usually have either a general focus on all subjects of writing, or a more narrow purpose. With some looking, you can find conferences devoted to screenwriting, playwriting, romance, mysteries, fantasy, science fiction, medical thrillers, and more.

GET OUT THERE!

Now that you know the ins and outs of a writers' conference, all that's left is for you to hunt down an event and sign up for 2008 or 2009. Going to a gathering and pitching agents may seem intimidating, especially if you're going alone, but the payoff is definitely worth it, and you're likely to make several friends who can ensure you don't go to a conference alone again. At the very least, you'll get some tips on how to start the befuddling first chapter that never seems to click.

Sign on the Dotted Line

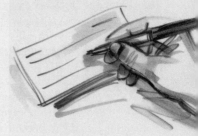

Research Your Options and Beware of Scams

Once you've received an offer of representation, you must determine if the agent is right for you. As flattering as any offer may be, you need to be confident that you are going to work well with the agent and that she is going to work hard to sell your manuscript.

EVALUATE THE OFFER

You need to know what to expect once you enter into a business relationship. You should know how much editorial input to expect from your agent, how often she gives updates about where your manuscript has been and who has seen it, and what subsidiary rights the agent represents.

More importantly, you should know when you will be paid. The publisher will send your advance and any subsequent royalty checks directly to the agent. After deducting her commission—usually 10 to 15 percent—your agent will send you the remaining balance. Most agents charge a higher commission of 20 to 25 percent when using a co-agent for foreign, dramatic or other specialized rights. As you enter into a relationship with an agent, have her explain her specific commission rates and payment policy.

Some agents offer written contracts and some do not. If your prospective agent does not, at least ask for a "memorandum of understanding" that details the basic relationship of expenses and commissions. If your agent does offer a contract, be sure to read it carefully, and keep a copy for yourself. Since contracts can be confusing, you may want to have a lawyer or knowledgeable writer friend check it out before signing anything.

The National Writers Union (NWU) has drafted a Preferred Literary Agent Agreement and a pamphlet, *Understand the Author-Agent Relationship*, which is available to members. The union suggests clauses that delineate such issues as:

- the scope of representation (One work? One work with the right of refusal on the next? All work completed in the coming year? All work completed until the agreement is terminated?)
- the extension of authority to the agent to negotiate on behalf of the author
- compensation for the agent and any co-agent, if used
- manner and time frame for forwarding monies received by the agent on behalf of the client
- termination clause, allowing client to give about 30 days to terminate the agreement
- the effect of termination on concluded agreements as well as ongoing negotiations
- arbitration in the event of a dispute between agent and client.

If you have any concerns about the agency's practices, ask the agent about them before you sign. Once an agent is interested in representing you, she should be willing to address any questions or concerns that you have. If the agent is rude or unresponsive, or tries to tell

What Should I Ask?

The following is a list of topics the Association of Authors' Representatives suggests authors discuss with literary agents who have offered to represent them. Please bear in mind that most agents are not going to be willing to spend time answering these questions unless they have already read your material and wish to represent you.

1. Are you a member of the Association of Authors' Representatives or do you adhere to their basic canon of ethics?

2. How long have you been in business as an agent?

3. Do you have specialists at your agency who handle movie and television rights? Foreign rights?

4. Do you have subagents or corresponding agents in Hollywood and overseas?

5. Who in your agency will actually be handling my work? Will the other staff members be familiar with my work and the status of my business at your agency?

6. Will you oversee or at least keep me apprised of the work that your agency is doing on my behalf?

7. Do you issue an agent/author agreement? May I review the language of the agency clause that appears in contracts you negotiate for your clients?

8. How do you keep your clients informed of your activities on their behalf?

9. Do you consult with your clients on any and all offers?

10. What are your commission rates? What are your procedures and time frames for processing and disbursing client funds? Do you keep different bank accounts separating author funds from agency revenue? What are your policies about charging clients for expenses incurred by your agency?

11. When you issue 1099 tax forms at the end of each year, do you also furnish clients—upon request—with a detailed account of their financial activity, such as gross income, commissions and other deductions and net income for the past year?

12. In the event of your death or disability, what provisions exist for my continued represenatation?

13. If we should part company, what is your policy about handling any unsold subsidiary rights to my work?

Reprinted with the permission of the Association of Authors' Representatives (www.aar-online.org).

Sealing the Deal

you that the information is confidential or classified, the agent is uncommunicative at best and, at worst, is already trying to hide something from you.

AVOID GETTING SCAMMED

The number of literary agents in the country, as well as the world, is increasing. This is because each year, aspiring authors compose an increasing number of manuscripts, while publishing houses continue to merge and become more selective as well as less open to working directly with writers. With literary agents providing the crucial link between writers and publishers, it's no wonder dozens of new agencies sprout up each year in the United States alone.

While more agencies may seem like a good thing, writers who seek to pair up with a successful agent must beware when navigating the murky waters of the Internet. Because agents are such a valuable part of the process, many unethical persons are floating around the online publishing world, ready to take advantage of uninformed writers who desperately want to see their work in print.

To protect yourself, you must familiarize yourself with common agent red flags and keep your radar up for any other warning signs. First of all, it can't be stressed enough that you should never pay agents any fees just so they consider your work. Only small fees (such as postage and copying) are acceptable—and those miniscule costs are administered *after* the agent has contacted you and signed you as a client.

A typical scam goes something like this: You send your work to an agency and they reply with what seems like a form letter or e-mail, telling you they love your story. At some point, they ask for money, saying it has to do with distribution, production, submissions, analysis or promotion. By that point, you're so happy with the prospect of finding an agent (you probably already told family and friends) that you nervously hand over the money. Game over. You've just been scammed. Your work may indeed end up in print, but you're likely getting very little if any money. To be a successful author, publishers must pay you to write; you must never pay them.

When a deal seems too good to be true, it likely is. If you want to learn more about a particular agent, look at her Web site. If she doesn't have a Web site (some small agents do not), look in this book to see if she has legitimate sales in the industry. Google her name: You'll likely find a dozen writers just like you discussing this agent on an Internet forum asking questions such as "Does anyone know anything about agent so-and-so?" These writer-oriented Web sites exist so writers like you can meet similar persons and discuss their good/bad experiences with publications, agents and publishing houses.

Protect yourself from scams by getting questions answered before you make any deals. When an abundance of research material is not available, you must be cautious. Ask around, ask questions and never pay upfront fees.

If you've been scammed

If you have trouble with your agent and you've already tried to resolve it to no avail, it may be time to call for help. Please alert the writing community to protect others. If you find agents online, in directories or in this book who aren't living up to their promises or are charging you money when they're listed as non-fee-charging agents, please let the Web master or editor of the publication know. Sometimes they can intervene for an author, and if no solution can be found, they can at the very least remove a listing from their directory so that no other authors will be scammed in the future. All efforts are made to keep scam artists out, but in a world where agencies are frequently bought and sold, a reputation can change overnight.

If you have complaints about any business, consider contacting The Federal Trade Commission, The Council of Better Business Bureaus or your state's attorney general. (For full details, see Reporting a Complaint below). Legal action may seem like a drastic step, but sometimes people do it. You can file a suit with the attorney general and try to find other writers who want to sue for fraud with you. The Science Fiction & Fantasy Writers of America's Web site offers sound advice on recourse you can take in these situations. For more details, visit www.sfwa.org/beware/.

If you live in the same state as your agent, it may be possible to settle the case in small claims court. This is a viable option for collecting smaller damages and a way to avoid lawyer fees. The jurisdiction of the small claims court includes cases in which the claim is $5,000 or less. (This varies from state to state, but should still cover the amount for which you're suing.) Keep in mind that suing takes a lot of effort and time. You'll have to research all the necessary legal steps. If you have lawyers in the family, that could be a huge benefit if they agree to help you organize the case, but legal assistance is not necessary.

Above all, if you've been scammed, don't waste time blaming yourself. It's not your fault if someone lies to you. Respect in the literary world is built on reputation, and word gets around about agents who scam, cheat, lie and steal. Editors ignore their submissions and writers avoid them. Without clients or buyers, a swindling agent will find her business collapsing.

Meanwhile, you'll keep writing and believing in yourself. One day, you'll see your work in print, and you'll tell everyone what a rough road it was to get there, but how you wouldn't trade it for anything in the world.

Reporting a Complaint

If you feel you've been cheated or misrepresented, or you're trying to prevent a scam, the following resources should be of help.

- The Federal Trade Commission, Bureau of Consumer Protection. While the FTC won't resolve individual consumer problems, it does depend on your complaints to help them investigate fraud, and your speaking up may even lead to law enforcement action. Visit www.ftc.gov.

- Volunteer Lawyers for the Arts is a group of volunteers from the legal profession who assist with questions of law pertaining to the arts. Visit www.vlany.org.

- The Council of Better Business Bureau is the organization to contact if you have a complaint or if you want to investigate a publisher, literary agent or other business related to writing and writers. Contact your local BBB or visit www.bbb.org.

- Your state's attorney general. Don't know your attorney general's name? Go to www.attorneygeneral.gov. This site provides a wealth of contact information, including a complete list of links to each state's attorney general Web site.

Sealing the Deal

SEALING THE DEAL

Improve Your Book Contract

Nine Negotiating Tips

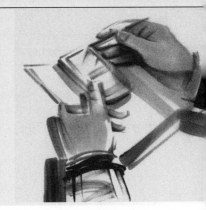

by The Authors Guild

E ven if you're working with an agent, it's crucial to understand the legal provisions associated with book contracts. After all, you're the one ultimately responsible for signing off on the terms set forth by the deal. Below are nine clauses found in typical book contracts. Reading the explanation of each clause, along with the negotiating tips, will help clarify what you are agreeing to as the book's author.

1. Grant of Rights

The Grant of Rights clause transfers ownership rights in, and therefore control over, certain parts of the work from the author to the publisher. Although it's necessary and appropriate to grant some exclusive rights (e.g., the right to print, publish and sell print-book editions), don't assign or transfer your copyright and use discretion when granting rights in languages other than English and territories other than the United States, its territories and Canada. Also, limit the publication formats granted to those that your publisher is capable of exploiting adequately.

- Never transfer or assign your copyright or "all rights" in the work to your publisher.
- Limit the languages, territories and formats in which your publisher is granted rights.

2. Subsidiary Rights

Subsidiary rights are uses that your publisher may make of your manuscript other than issuing its own hardcover or paperback print book editions. Print-related subsidiary rights include book club and paperback reprint editions, publication of selections, condensations or abridgments in anthologies and textbooks and first and second serial rights (i.e., publication in newspapers or magazines either before or after publication of the hardcover book). Subsidiary rights not related to print include motion picture, television, stage, audio, animation, merchandising and electronic rights.

Subsidiary rights may be directly exploited by your publisher or licensed to third parties. Your publisher will share licensing fees with you in proportion to the ratios set forth in your contract. You should receive at least 50 percent of the licensing proceeds.

- Consider reserving rights outside the traditional grant of primary print book publishing rights, especially if you have an agent.

- Beware of any overly inclusive language, such as "in any format now known or hereafter developed," used to describe the scope of the subsidiary rights granted.
- Make sure you are fairly compensated for any subsidiary rights granted. Reputable publishers will pay you at least 50 percent of the proceeds earned from licensing certain categories of rights, much higher for others.

3. Delivery and Acceptance

Most contracts stipulate that the publisher is only obligated to accept, pay for and publish a manuscript that is "satisfactory to the publisher in form and content." It may be difficult to negotiate a more favorable, objective provision, but you should try. Otherwise, the decision as to whether your manuscript is satisfactory, and therefore publishable, will be left to the subjective discretion of your publisher.

- If you cannot do better, indicate that an acceptable manuscript is one which your publisher deems editorially satisfactory.
- Obligate your publisher to assist you in editing a second corrected draft before ultimately rejecting your manuscript.
- Negotiate a nonrefundable advance or insert a clause that would allow you to repay the advance on a rejected book from re-sale proceeds paid by a second publisher.

4. Publication

Including a publication deadline in your contract will obligate your publisher to actually publish your book in a timely fashion. Be sure that the amount of time between the delivery of the manuscript and the publication of the book isn't longer than industry standard.

- Make sure you're entitled to terminate the contract, regain all rights granted and keep the advance if your publisher fails to publish on or before the deadline.
- Carefully limit the conditions under which your publisher is allowed to delay publication.

5. Copyright

Current copyright law doesn't require authors to formally register their copyright in order to secure copyright protection. Copyright automatically arises in written works created in or after 1978. However, registration with the Copyright Office is a prerequisite to infringement lawsuits and important benefits accrue when a work is registered within three months of initial publication.

- Require your publisher to register your book's copyright within three months of initial publication.
- As previously discussed in Grant of Rights, don't allow your publisher to register copyright in its own name.

6. Advance

An advance against royalties is money that your publisher will pay you prior to publication and subsequently deduct from your share of royalty earnings. Most publishers will pay, but might not initially offer, an advance based on a formula which projects the first year's income.

- Bargain for as large an advance as possible. A larger advance gives your publisher greater incentive to publicize and promote your work.
- Research past advances paid by your publisher in industry publications such as *Publishers Weekly*.

7. Royalties

You should earn royalties for sales of your book that are in line with industry standards. For example, many authors are paid 10 percent of the retail price of the book on the first 5,000 copies sold, 12.5 percent of the retail price on the next 5,000 copies sold, and 15 percent of the retail price on all copies sold thereafter.

- Base your royalties on the suggested retail list price of the book, not on net sales income earned by your publisher. Net-based royalties are lower than list-based royalties of the same percentage, and they allow your publisher room to offer special deals or write off bad debt without paying you money on the books sold.
- Limit your publisher's ability to sell copies of your book at deep discounts—quantity discount sales of more than 50 percent—or as remainders.
- Limit your publisher's ability to reduce the percentage of royalties paid for export, book club, mail order and other special sales.

8. Accounting and Payments

Your accounting clause should establish the frequency with which you should expect to receive statements accounting for your royalty earnings and subsidiary rights licensing proceeds. If you are owed money in any given accounting period, the statement should be accompanied by a check.

- Insist on at least a bi-annual accounting.
- Limit your publisher's ability to withhold a reserve against returns of your book from earnings that are otherwise owed to you.
- Include an audit clause in your contract which gives you or your representative the right to examine the sales records kept by the publisher in connection with your work.

9. Out of Print

Your publisher should only have the exclusive rights to your work while it is actively marketing and selling your book (i.e., while your book is "in print"). An out-of-print clause will allow you to terminate the contract and regain all rights granted to your publisher after the book stops earning money.

It is crucial to actually define the print status of your book in the contract. Stipulate that your work is in print only when copies are available for sale in the United States in an English language hardcover or paperback edition issued by the publisher and listed in its catalog. Otherwise, your book should be considered out of print and all rights should revert to you.

- Don't allow the existence of electronic and print-on-demand editions to render your book in print. Alternatively, establish a floor above which a certain amount of royalties must be earned or copies must be sold during each accounting period for your book to be considered in print. Once sales or earnings fall below this floor, your book should be deemed out of print and rights should revert to you.
- Stipulate that as soon as your book is out of print, all rights will automatically revert to you regardless of whether or not your book has earned out the advance.

Know Your Rights

Breaking Down Industry Lingo

Most writers who want to be published envision their book in storefronts and on their friends' coffee tables. They imagine book signings and maybe even an interview on "Oprah." Usually the dream ends there; after all, having a book published seems exciting enough. In actuality, a whole world of opportunities exists for published writers beyond seeing their books in print. These opportunities are called subsidiary rights.

Subsidiary rights, or subrights, are the additional ways that a book can be presented. Any time a book is made into a movie or excerpted in a magazine, a subsidiary right has been sold. If these additional rights to your book are properly exploited, you'll not only see your book in a variety of forms, but you'll also make a lot more money than is possible on book sales alone.

Unfortunately, the terminology of subsidiary rights can be confusing. Phrases such as secondary rights, traditional splits, or advance against royalty could perplex any writer. And the thought of negotiating the terms of these rights with a publisher can be daunting.

Although there are many advantages to working with agents, the ability to negotiate subrights is one of their best qualities. If the agent knows a house can make money with a right, she will grant that right to the publisher when the contract is negotiated. Otherwise, the agent will keep, or retain, certain rights for her clients, which she will try to exploit by selling them to her own connections.

If you want to work with an agent, there are two reasons why you should have a basic understanding of subrights. First, you'll want to be able to intelligently discuss these rights with your agent. (Although, you should feel comfortable asking your agent any question you have about subrights.) Second, different agents have more expertise in some subright areas than others. If you think your book would make a great movie, you should research the agents who have strong film connections. A knowledge of subrights can help you find the agent best suited to help you achieve your dreams.

An agent negotiates subrights with the publishing house at the same time a book is sold. In fact, the sale of certain subrights can even determine how much money the publisher offers for the book. But the author doesn't get paid immediately for these rights. Instead, the author is paid an advance against royalties. An advance is a loan to the author that is paid back when the book starts earning money. Once the advance is paid, the author starts earning royalties, which are a predetermined percentage of the book's profit.

The agent always keeps certain rights, the publisher always buys certain rights and the others are negotiated. When an agent keeps a right, she is then free to sell it at will. If the agent does sell it, the money she receives from the purchasing company goes immediately to the author, minus the agent's commission. Usually the companies who purchase rights pay royalties instead of a one-time payment.

If the publisher keeps the right, any money that is made from it goes toward paying off the advance. Because the publisher kept the right, they will keep part of the money it makes. For most rights, half the money goes to the publisher and half goes to the writer, although for some rights the percentages are different. This separation of payment is called a traditional split because it has become standard over the years. And, of course, the agent takes her commission from the author's half.

Most agents have dealt with certain publishers so many times that they have preset boiler-plate contracts. This means they've already agreed to the terms of certain rights, leaving only a few rights to negotiate. The following describes the main subrights and discusses what factors an agent takes into account when deciding whether or not to keep a right. As you read through this piece, carefully consider the many opportunities for your book, and encourage your agent and publisher to exploit these rights every chance they get.

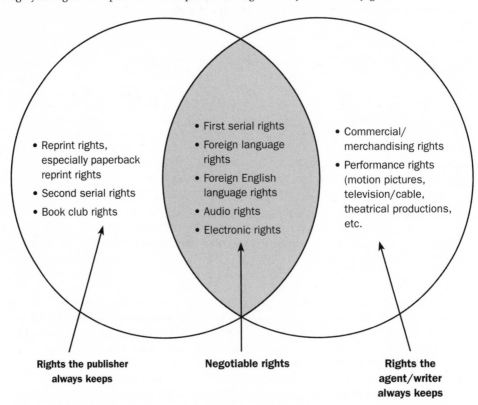

Rights the publisher always keeps

- Reprint rights, especially paperback reprint rights
- Second serial rights
- Book club rights

Negotiable rights

- First serial rights
- Foreign language rights
- Foreign English language rights
- Audio rights
- Electronic rights

Rights the agent/writer always keeps

- Commercial/ merchandising rights
- Performance rights (motion pictures, television/cable, theatrical productions, etc.

RIGHTS THE PUBLISHER ALWAYS KEEPS

The following subrights are always kept by the publisher and are often called nonnegotiable rights. Money earned from these rights is split between the publisher and the author, and the author's share goes toward paying back the advance. Selling these rights helps repay the advance faster, which hopefully means the writer will receive royalty checks sooner.

Reprint rights

In publishing, a reprint right refers to the paperback edition of the book. When a hardcover book is reprinted in paperback, the reprint right has been used. According to Donald Maass of the Donald Maass Literary Agency, "In deals with major trade publishers, it's a long-standing practice to grant them control of reprint rights. However, in some cases—a small-press deal, for instance—we withhold these rights." Traditionally, if a hardcover book sold really well, paperback houses bought the rights to reprint the book in a more affordable version. Any money earned from the paperback was then split 50/50 between the publisher and writer. Paperback houses often paid substantial amounts of money for these reprint rights.

But the recent consolidation of publishing houses has changed the value of reprint rights. "In the old days, most books were hardcover, and paperbacks were cheap versions of the book," explains Maass. "Today, so many paperback publishers have either merged with a hardcover publisher or begun their own hardcover publisher that the business of selling reprint rights has diminished." Now, many publishers make what is called a hard/soft deal, meaning the house will first print the book in hardcover and, if the book sells well, it will then reprint the book in paperback. This type of deal can still benefit writers because they no longer have to split the money earned from reprint with the publisher. Instead, they earn royalties from both the hardcover and paperback versions.

Book club rights

These days, it seems that a book club exists for every possible interest. There are the traditional book clubs, like Book-of-the-Month and its paperback counterpart, the Quality Paperback Book Club. But there are also mystery book clubs, New Age book clubs, book clubs for writers and artists and even online book clubs. Most book clubs are very selective, and you should be flattered if your book is chosen. Like reprint rights, any money made from book club rights is split 50/50 between the publisher and the writer. If an agent believes a book will appeal to a certain book club's audience, she will target the manuscript to publishers who have a good relationship with—or who own—that book club.

Serial rights

A serial is an excerpt of the book that appears in a magazine or in another book. To have your book serialized is wonderful because excerpts make additional money for you and provide great publicity for your book. There are actually two types of serial rights: first serial and second serial. First serial means the excerpt of the book is available before the book is printed. A second serial is an excerpt that appears after the book is in bookstores. First serial rights are actually negotiable; sometimes the right to use them is kept by the agent. Usually an agent's decision is based upon her knowledge of the publications available in the book's subject. If she doesn't know the various magazines, she will let the publisher have this right. Second serial rights, however, are almost always granted to the publisher.

Nonfiction books are more commonly excerpted than fiction. Nonfiction usually stands alone well, and magazines are eager to use these excerpts because they usually cost less than hiring a freelancer to write original material. While rare, serialized fiction still pops up every now and then. For example, a portion of Haruki Murakami's *Kafka on the Shore* (Knopf) appeared in *The Paris Review*.

NEGOTIABLE RIGHTS

The owner of these subrights is always determined when the book is sold. Often an agent and editor must compromise for these rights. In other words, an agent may agree to sell foreign rights if she can keep electronic rights. Or, an editor will offer more money if he can obtain the audio rights to a book.

Foreign language rights

If your book might appeal to audiences in countries where English isn't spoken, then you'll want an agent who has good connections with foreign co-agents. According to James Vines

Sealing the Deal

of The Vines Agency, Inc., foreign co-agents work on behalf of U.S. agencies and approach foreign publishers with manuscripts and proposals. They typically have appointments booked at big trade shows like Frankfurt Book Fair, London Book Fair and BookExpo America, where a lot of foreign deals happen. Usually an agent charges a 20 percent commission when a foreign co-agent is used, and the two split the earnings.

"All of my clients have benefited from the sale of foreign rights," continues Vines. For example, *Kokology* (Fireside 2003), by Tadahiko Nagao and Isamu Saito, started as a big phenomenon in Japan, selling more than four million copies." Vines sold the book to Simon & Schuster, and then worked with a co-agent to sell it all over the world.

When agents are considering how a book will do abroad, they must be aware of trends in other countries. "Most agents try to stay on top of the foreign markets as much as possible and listen to what foreign co-agents have to say," says Vines. He also points out that writers can benefit from different subrights over a period of time depending on how well a subright is selling.

Many publishing houses have foreign counterparts, and often an agent will grant the publisher these rights if she knows the book can be printed by one of these foreign houses. If the publisher has foreign language rights, the author receives an average of 75 percent of any money made when the book is sold to a foreign publisher.

British rights

Like foreign language rights, the owner of a book's British rights can sell the book to publishers in England. Australia was once included in these rights, but Australian publishers are becoming more independent. If an agent keeps these rights, she will use a co-agent in England and the two will likely split a 20 percent commission. If a publisher has these rights, the traditional split is 80/20, with the author receiving the larger share.

Electronic rights

Several years ago, Stephen King caused a big commotion in the publishing world first by using an electronic publisher for his book, *Riding the Bullet*, and then by self-publishing his serialized novel, *The Plant*. Many publishing professionals worried that King would start a trend drawing writers away from publishers, while others claimed only high-profile writers could ever compete successfully with the vast amount of information on the Web. Regardless, King's achievement showed that readers are paying attention to the Internet.

Basically, electronic rights refer to the hand-held electronic, Internet and print-on-demand versions of a book. This right is currently one of the hottest points of contention between agents and publishers because the potential for these rights is unknown—it is quite possible that electronic versions of a book will make a lot of money one day.

This area of publishing is changing so rapidly that both agents and editors struggle with how to handle electronic rights. Many publishers believe any version of a book is the same material as the printed book, and, therefore, they should own the rights. Agents worry, however, that if the publisher lets the book go out of print, the rights to the book will never be returned to the author.

Audio rights

Before people feared that the Internet would cause the end of traditional book publishing, people worried about audio versions of books. In actuality, audio books have complemented their printed counterparts and have proved to be a fantastic source of additional income for the person who owns the rights to produce the book in audio form—whether through cassette tape, compact disc or uploading onto an iPod.

Many publishers own audio imprints and even audio book clubs, and if they are successful with these ventures, an agent will likely grant the audio rights to the publisher. The traditional split is 50/50. Otherwise, the agent will try to save this right and sell it to a company that can turn it into a profit.

RIGHTS THE AGENT/WRITER ALWAYS KEEPS

When a book is sold, an agent always reserves two rights for her authors: performance and merchandising. Some books are naturally more conducive to being made into films or products, and when they do, there is usually a lot of money to be made. A smart agent can quickly identify when a book will be successful in these areas.

Performance rights

Many writers fantasize about seeing their book on the big screen. And a lot of times, agents share this dream—especially for best-selling titles. If your agent feels your book will work well as a movie, or even as a television show or video game, she will sell these rights to someone in the entertainment industry. This industry works fairly differently than the publishing industry. Usually a producer options the right to make your book into a movie. An option means the producer can only make the movie during a specific amount of time, such as one year. If the movie isn't made during that time period, the rights revert back to the writer. You can actually option these rights over and over—making money for every option—without the book ever being made into a movie.

As with foreign rights, agents usually work with another agent to sell performance rights. Usually these agents live in Los Angeles and have the connections to producers that agents outside California just don't have. Agents normally take a 20 percent commission from any money made from performance rights. That 20 percent will be split if two agents partnered to sell the rights.

Merchandising rights

Merchandising rights create products—calendars, cards, action figures, stickers, dolls—that are based on characters or other elements of your book. Few books transfer well into such products, but they can be successful when they do. If a producer options the performance rights to your book, the merchandising rights are usually included in the deal.

For example, agent Steven Malk of Writers House made wonderful use of these two rights for his client Elise Primavera and her book, *Auntie Claus* (Silver Whistle/Harcourt 1999). According to Malk, "When I first read the manuscript of *Auntie Claus* and saw a couple of Primavera's sample illustrations, I immediately knew the book had a lot of possibilities in the subrights realm. First of all, the character of *Auntie Claus* is extremely memorable and unique, and from a visual standpoint, she's stunning. Also, the basic concept of the book is completely fresh and original, which is very hard to accomplish with a Christmas book.

"The first thing I did was to approach Saks Fifth Avenue with the idea of featuring *Auntie Claus* in their Christmas windows. In addition to using the book as the theme for their window displays, they created some merchandise that was sold through Saks. It's a perfect project for them; the character of Auntie Claus is so sophisticated and refined, and it seemed ideal for their windows."

Like Malk did for Primavera, many agents successfully exploit subsidiary rights every day. If you want the most for your book, look for an agent who has the know-how and connections to achieve your publishing potential.

The Next Steps

So You Have an Agent—Now What?

by Chuck Sambuchino

I n this book, we've told you all about contacting and securing agents. Details on everything from writing to pitching to getting the most out of your subsidiary rights are included in these pages. But should your hard work and passion pay off in a signed deal with a big-shot agent, the journey isn't over. Now it's time to learn what lies in store after the papers are signed.

LET YOUR AGENT WORK

In the time leading up to signing a contract, you may have bantered around plenty with your agent—realizing you both love the New York Yankees and Kung Pao Chicken. But don't let this camaraderie allow you to forget that the relationship is a business one first and foremost. Does this mean you can't small talk occasionally and ask your agent how her children are doing? No. But don't call every day complaining about the traffic and your neighbor's habit of mowing his lawn before the sun comes up.

Your agent is going to read your work again (and again . . .) and likely suggest possible changes to the manuscript. "When you sign with an agent, you should go over next steps, and talk about what the agent expects from you," says Sorche Fairbank, principal of the Fairbank Literary Agency. "This can vary with each author-agent relationship, and on the type of book project. We (at the Fairbank agency) are fairly hands-on with shaping and polishing a proposal or manuscript, and there often is quite a bit of work to be done before we and the author feel it's ready to send out.

"If you have a nonfiction project, there is certain to be some final tweaking of the proposal and sample chapter(s)," Fairbank says. "If you have a novel, then I hope you would be . . . taking any agent advice on tightening and polishing it. Go through it one more time and weed out extraneous words, overused pet words and phrases, and stock descriptions."

KEEP WRITING

If you're not working with your agent on rewrites and revisions, it's your responsibility to continue creating. One challenge is over—another begins. As your agent is trying hard to sell your work and bring home a nice paycheck, you're expected to keep churning out material for her to sell. Keep her informed of what you're working on and when it'll be ready.

Stay passionate. Once you've convinced yourself that your first book was not a fluke,

---

CHUCK SAMBUCHINO is the editor of *Guide to Literary Agents* and an assistant editor of *Writer's Market*. He is a former staffer on *Writer's Digest*. To contact him or learn more, visit www.guidetoliteraryagents.com.

you've convinced yourself that you're a capable writer—and a capable writer needs to keep writing and always have material to sell. Always be considering new projects and working on new things, but give preference to the first work that got you a contract. Rewrites and revisions—wanted by agents and editors alike—will likely take months and become somewhat tedious, but all that frustration will melt away when you have that first hardcover book in your hands.

SELLING THE BOOK

When the book is as perfect as can be, it's time for your agent to start shopping it to her publishing contacts. During this process, she'll likely keep you abreast of all rejections. Don't take these to heart—instead, learn from each one, especially those with editors who have kindly given a specific reason as to why they don't want the book. "When the project is being shopped around, discuss rejections with your agent. There may be patterns that point to a fixable weak spot," Fairbank says.

Your book may be bought in a pre-empt. That's when a publishing house tries to beat other potential buyers to your work and offers a solid price in the hopes of securing your book early and avoiding a bidding war. An actual bidding war—or "auction"—happens when a work is so stunningly marvelous that every house in town wants it bad enough to compete against each other, offering different perks such as a large advance and guaranteed ad dollars. Traditionally, the best deal (read: most money and enthusiasm) wins and signs. After the auction was finished for Elizabeth Kostova's *The Historian*, her advance was a cool $2 million. (Note: First-time novelists will likely get an advance of $50,000 to $75,000, but hey, anything can happen!)

Your agent will submit the work to publishers (either exclusively or simultaneously, depending on her opinion) and hold a private auction if need be to secure the best deal possible. Fairbank says it's important for writers to relax during the auction process and not call every 30 minutes for an update. "In an auction, everything should go through the agent, but writers may be called upon to do a few things," she says. "I have had some cases where it made sense to bring the author around to meet with the various interested houses, usually to drive home the author's expertise and promotability. In every instance, it increased the size of the offers. There have also been times where a particular house asked for more specifics on something, and I needed my author ready to respond ASAP."

PROMOTE YOURSELF

Besides continuing to write and revise, the most important thing a writer needs to focus on is promotion. It's likely your work will not have the benefit of countless publicists setting up interviews for you. How you want to promote your work is up to you.

According to Regina Brooks, president of Serendipity Literary Agency, "It's always a great time to research who you might want on your team once the book is published (e.g., publicists, Web developers, graphic artists, etc.). Often times, authors wait until the last minute to start researching these options. The more lead time a publicist has to think about your project, the better. This is also an ideal time to attend conferences to network and workshops to tighten your writing skills."

GO WITH THE FLOW

An agent's job is to agent. That means knowing which people are buying what, and where they're headed if a move is in the works. Throughout the editing process, you'll work hand-in-hand with your agent and editor to revise and polish the manuscript. But let's say the editor makes the not-so-uncommon decision to switch jobs or switch houses. Ideally, an agent will shepherd you through the change.

Sealing the Deal

"It happens more often than we'd like," says Brooks. "When it does, you hope that someone in-house will be as excited about the project as the acquiring editor initially was, but there's no guarantee." Fairbank agrees: "The most important thing the author and agent can do in that case is take a deep breath, pick up the phone, and wholeheartedly welcome the new editor to the book team. Once they have their feet under them and have reviewed your work, ask them what they think, and listen to any questions or comments they may have."

In addition to switching editors at publishing houses, a writer must concern himself with the possibility of his agent hitting the lottery and quitting (or just quitting without hitting the lottery, which is more probable). To protect yourself, make sure that this scenario is clearly addressed in your contract with the agent. "It really depends on the initial written agreement between the agent and the author," says Brooks. "It's important that the agreement cover such situations in their termination language. This assures that all parties including the publishing company know how to proceed with royalty statements, notices, etc."

AND WHAT IF . . . ?

A difficult question that may come up is this: What should you do if you think your agent has given up on you, or isn't fulfilling her end of the bargain? (In other words, how do you get out? *Can* you get out?) First, consider that if an agent is trying and failing to sell your manuscript, then at least the *trying* part is there. It could just be an unfortunate instance where you and an agent both love a work but can't find anyone else who feels the same. This is no one's fault. As far as simply quitting an agent is concerned, you can't opt out of a contract until the contract says so.

A similar dilemma involves authors who have a satisfactory agent but want out in favor of one perceived to be better. If you already have an agent, but others are calling in hopes to work with you, the new agents likely don't know you already possess representation. Obviously, you need to tell them you are currently represented. That said, you most likely can't just switch agents because you're under contract. When the time comes when you can legally opt out of a contract (and you think your agent has had ample time to make a sale), consider your options then.

GET READY FOR YOUR RIDE

Hopefully, you'll never need to experience the difficulty and confusion of switching agents and/or editors. Hopefully, your work will smoothly find a house and then a large audience once it's published. Just remember that the smoother things go, the less excuses exist for you not to keep writing then promote the heck out of your work. Simply do what you do best (write) and continue to learn what you can about the publishing world. As Fairbank puts it so simply, "Be available, willing, and ready to help your agent."

Agents' Pet Peeves

Avoid These Peeves and Get Your Work Read

by Katharine Sands

To peeve or not to peeve . . . that is the question.

For the savvy wordsmith, this means heeding agent peeves, the universally cited blights any writer would do well to avoid. Some peeves are decades old, while the advent of technology has created new ones. For a new understanding of how to attract and how not to annoy, here are examples of *querial killers*: the mistakes writers make that we agents see and dislike on a daily basis. When you set out to woo, win and work with a literary agent, avoid these peeves to make sure your manuscript—whether fiction or nonfiction—gets read.

QUERY LETTER PET PEEVES

OK. First that granddaddy of gripes: How writers misaddress agents. For example, let's say you're writing a cold query letter to agent Ivana Schmooze. The correct salutation is: "Dear Ms. Schmooze"; it is not "Dear Ivana Schmooze," "Dear Ivana," "Dear Agent," "Dear Meredith Bernstein," or "Dear Sirs." An anonymous agent once addressed this peeve by saying: "No addressing me as Sir/Madam. To my mind, there are only several agents who can pull this one off, and it's usually after hours."

On to the Cadillac of classic peeves: submitting your work to dozens of agents at the same time. While this may seem like a surefire way to reach out to many potential agents and up your chances for success, it will end up working against you. Yes, getting an agent to represent you *is* a numbers game, but an e-mail blast to countless reps dings the place in the agent brain marked auto-reject and this is guaranteed to land your submission in the circular file (recycle bin). Why? This is the mark of the obvious amateur—a writer that doesn't respect basic submitting-to-an-agent etiquette. If you're thinking about e-blasting agents, remember that it may be a timesaver, but we ourselves save some time by deleting these submissions. When introducing your work (or yourself) to an agent, show you are ready for the literary marketplace by selecting your agent candidates with a serious and intelligent eye. Sending to multiple agents scattershot does not attract their attention. If your e-query doesn't end up in the trash, it's likely stuck in a spam filter. Make sure your submission does not become spam-a-lot.

TECHNOLOGY AND THE INTERNET

A query letter is designed to hook an agent; what it's not supposed to do is simply point them to Web sites. "My new peeve is a query made up of links," says Rita Rosenkranz, who has

KATHARINE SANDS is an agent with the Sarah Jane Freymann Literary Agency in New York City. She is the editor of *Making the Perfect Pitch: How to Catch a Literary Agent's Eye* (Watson-Guptill Publications, 2004).

an agency in New York. "I think a submission, especially via e-mail, should have at least a basic description about the work and the author, duplicating the content of a query letter sent through the mail. I feel the author is taking a self-defeating shortcut when the correspondence is made up only of links or attachments, requiring the agent to investigate these one by one."

Breakout success stories from the blogosphere where writers are blogging their way into agents' hearts is indeed happening, but blog-like submissions where the query is chatty and unfocused is a turn-off for agents. One has to kiss a lot of frogs to find a prince, and we have to riff a lot of blogs to find a print.

Even though it may seem like an agent needs only invest a few seconds to find a viable client, agents do not see a cyber scavenger hunt quite this way. To an agent, a writer stands out from the throng and shows preparedness by a crisp perfect pitch—one that gets the agent to say *yes*. A pitch is not the beginning of your book; it is the introduction to your potential as an author. The best pitches create a moment, pose a provocative question, or give a flavor for the project. Sarah Jane Freymann, an agent in Manhattan, shares: "If you are able to sum up your entire book with a title or one-line description, that's gold."

On that note, avoid the tendency to use lines that sound like they came right out of *The Player*, such as "It's *Sex and the City* meets *Silence of the Lambs*." Titles or ideas that are derivative do not fly; for example, we still see a spate of Dan Brown-inspired ones—*The Michelangelo Zone* or *The Cellini Code*. These are easy to decline.

CONCERNING REJECTIONS AND CRITICISM

Reactions to rejection spawn several agent peeves. Says agent Janet Reid of FinePrint Literary Management: "(Writers) just have to get over the idea that our response of 'It's not right for me' is some sort of comment on the value or quality of your work. It's not. It's only a comment about whether it resonates with me *and* whether I can sell it. I pass on really good stuff all the time."

Ah, but here is a new nettle: Writers posting comments on a Web site from a letter of rejection to create the impression of a blurb. This is false advertising since the agent is, in fact, declining to represent the work, not extolling it. This is fast becoming a big no-no; plus, publishing pros know these are probably from rejection letters, so it really doesn't serve a writer to claim a host of agents is championing their work, when they are merely being polite and encouraging.

At a conference, some writers react badly to being critiqued. If you are ready for an agent meeting, steady yourself for the hot seat. Your work will be deconstructed in a way unlike that of a supportive writing group, retreat, MFA program, or workshop. Best use of the time is to 1) understand where and why the agent suggests next steps about what to do, and 2) listen to feedback, whether or not it's agreeable. Agents do strive to be sensitive when rendering professional opinions about personal stories and we understand how emotional it can be to be reviewed, but our most helpful evaluation is an honest one.

AND THE REST

For more ways not to vex, consider this potpourri of peeves:

We see a lot of channeled and cosmic-inspired material. Hey, maybe your spirit guides did select the agency, but all forms of faith are a matter between you and your god, not you and your agent. (Besides, how do I know my spirit guides are simpatico with yours?) Connection with the divine is best left to the heavens and out of your pitch.

Red flags wave when a writer starts to huff and puff for any reason. Always behave professionally. Remember that how you interact is an important indicator of how you will work with your publisher. An agent is an author advocate, but functions a bit like an officer of the court. We do not swear oaths, but are instead bound to represent each side honestly.

You want your agent to act like a tigress on the prowl? Not likely in today's publishing climate. The martini-swilling dragon lady of your dreams who fights on your behalf for every deal point has been replaced by increasingly impersonal dealings with the corporate politics of a publishing imprint of a media behemoth. The new criteria: not how tough agents are, but how effective we can be as ambassadors for your writing.

Your attorney (a cousin in Florida who practices maritime law and has never seen a publishing contract) is unlikely to be a welcome part of the negotiation process. Agents not only have experience in negotiating contracts, but also a vested interest in your success and legal protections. It is not in your interest to obtain inaccurate legal advice, or to want the agent to address every issue that might arise for the Slovakian theme park rights from your 15th international bestseller (when you are really just starting out).

SO NOW YOU KNOW . . .

Whether meeting with you or reading your pitch letter, agents want to be engaged—to zero in on the zeitgeist, find hooks and sales engines, identify the intended audience, and be impressed by a writer's voice. We need to determine the answer to two pressing questions: *Why you? Why now?* The guiding principle is to remember that agents are looking first for a reason to keep reading, and then for a reason to represent you. Be certain you give us crystal clear answers—fast. We cherry-pick our clients, and want things to progress smoothly and happily. We want writers to get as close to their ultimate dreams and goals as possible, and a good way to start is to avoid agent pet peeves and make sure your next submission isn't sunk by a *querial killer.*

A Background Matters

Platform—and How to Get One

by Ally E. Peltier

In today's highly saturated book market, a strong publicity and marketing campaign requires that authors have a solid platform to get the kind of media attention necessary for sales—especially if you're writing nonfiction. But what is a platform, and how do you acquire one?

In the publishing industry, the term "platform" refers to everything about you that helps your publisher sell your book, such as credentials, useful connections and public presence. Next to writing ability, your platform is the most important selling point you have when approaching agents and publishers. Even a few key elements, referred to as "planks," can improve your chance of success.

CREATING A PRESENCE

A sturdy nonfiction platform is built on the following:

- Educational or professional experience
- Substantial personal experience
- Membership or officer standing in relevant organizations
- Print or Internet credits
- A mailing list obtained via a speaking schedule or Internet presence
- An established following, such as through newsletters or blog subscribers
- A reputation as an "expert" with local or international media.

A nonfiction author's background is critical for two reasons: History shows that potential readers will choose books by experts over non-experts; it's easier for marketing and publicity departments to get media attention for credentialed authors. Those credentials need not include an academic degree if your other planks are significant, but the right degree always helps. For example, if you're writing about heartburn, being a gastroenterologist or a nutritionist gives you a strong advantage. If you aren't a certified professional, getting one to write your introduction and endorse your book will help. Ultimately, your platform must illustrate that readers can and will trust you as an authority.

Marketing fiction, however, relies more on visibility than credentials. A well-constructed fiction platform includes connections to published writers; an established readership and mailing list via a newsletter, blog or other serial publications; prior publications; and any

ALLY E. PELTIER (www.ambitiousenterprises.com) is a writer, editor and publishing consultant, formerly of Simon & Schuster. Her work has appeared in a variety of places, including *Writers' Journal, Circle* magazine and J3tlag.com.

connections you have that might lead to a book review, serial sale, interview, book signing or other appearance.

For fiction, it matters less if you have a degree. However, having a degree in medieval history, for example, would be an advantage for the author of a novel set in the Middle Ages. A master's degree in creative writing always may also help you stand out. It means you may have connections via your academic program to other published authors who might provide endorsements. It also conveys a devotion to writing as a career, thus increasing the possibility that you'll produce more than just one novel (in other words, that you're a better long-term investment than a non-degree writer). And it gives you more opportunities to teach at universities and notable conferences, which increases your visibility and opens venues for sales.

BUILDING PLANKS

The more planks you have, the stronger your platform; a great platform takes a lot of guess-work out of an essentially risky process. Your platform lets publishers know that you under-stand book promotion, which is increasingly the author's responsibility. It tells them how marketable you are. It tells them where they can expect to gain some relatively effortless sales, or at least some valuable attention. And it gives them an indication of where the audience is—bigger audiences equal greater expected sales, which can get you a bigger ad-vance. If no one's heard of you, publishers may be more cautious—hence a smaller advance, if you get an offer at all.

The key to developing a great platform is to keep building using increasingly bigger planks. Put as much effort into your platform as you do your writing, and you'll have more than just a leg to stand on.

FOUR KEYS FOR BEGINNERS

Here are four exercises for writers to try on their way to building a platform and identifying the best avenues for you to reach potential book buyers.

1. Make a list of potential audiences for your topic. For example, if you're writing a book for new mothers, look for OB/GYN associations, groups devoted to parenting advice, resources for new grandparents, etc. If you're writing a novel about a new mother, do a similar search. This will generate a list with multiple purposes.

2. Build your network. First, get involved in key organizations: Become a member, obtain an official position, offer to write for their newsletter or Web site or volunteer to work at events. Second, spend time networking with people who share your subject of interest by attending meetings, joining message forums or chat groups or participating in conferences. These connections will serve as resources for further developing your platform. Don't over-look smaller local organizations, either, as face-to-face contacts are more likely to want to help you out when you call on them.

3. Beef up your résumé. Choose three topics relevant to your subject on which you could write or speak. Next, pitch your ideas to at least five venues from your potential audience list. Unless you already have great contacts, start small—using each achievement to build up to bigger venues. For example, query a small Web site or local publication first. Then pitch your second idea to a slightly larger publication, and so on. Or offer a free workshop to members of a local organization of which you are a member. Then see if you can interest an education center in paying you. The goal is to obtain contacts, credits and a mailing list complete with names, addresses and e-mail addresses. Publishers love authors with regular speaking engagements and publications because they know that these generate audiences predisposed to buying your book. Collecting e-mail addresses allows you to sign up target readers to get a free newsletter that you send out.

Perspectives

4. Build an audience for your work online. Myspace and Blogger have become hugely popular places to blog—Myspace even has a subscription feature. Blogs are also great for obtaining feedback and contacts. Yahoo Groups allows you to create and manage a distribution list for your e-publication for free. Create a Web presence and tell everyone you know: Add it to your business cards, your e-mail signature—everywhere you can think of. Get as many unique visits or subscriptions as possible so that you'll have hard stats proving that people want to read your work—even a small following can help get your material read and considered more seriously by potential publishers.

Having a platform is no longer a bonus for an author—it's a necessity, so don't waste any more time before getting started. If you're a fiction writer, yes, it will be a lesser concern, but a concern nonetheless. If you're a nonfiction writer or have self-published works that you'd like to sell, then a good media presence is by far your biggest chance of success. Start easy; smart small; but start today.

Leaping Into the Fray

How One Writer Got His First Book Published

by Robert Hicks

I am the son of an optimist. Every night when I was young, just before my father turned out the light and left the room, he would stand at the door and whisper his oft-repeated mantra to my brother and me: "Never forget all things are possible."

I tell you this because it is at the bedrock of why I decided, in my mid-40s, after many years as a music publisher in Nashville, that I would write a novel. I made this choice despite never having taken a creative writing course or written so much as a sentence of fiction, unless, of course, you count tax returns. What followed this decision were years of struggle and frustration and, ultimately, joy, as I journeyed from there to here and leaped into the fray.

A story that needs to be told

Unlike most of you, I had given up any and all aspirations of being a novelist sometime after the eighth grade. It was *worry* that would eventually bring those aspirations back. I was afraid that a story dear to my heart—a story that needed to live on—would be forgotten. Twelve years ago, I was collecting donations to support the Carnton Plantation in Franklin, Tenn., a non-profit historical site commemorating the Battle of Franklin in the Civil War and the extraordinary efforts of Carrie McGavock, the plantation owner. I found myself trying to figure out how this little house-museum and Carrie's tale was going to survive after I left. We never received any public funding and the day was going to come when I wouldn't be around any longer to solicit donations. Then what?

That's when I decided someone needed to publish her story: *Widow of the South*. Not a pamphlet or a Web site, mind you—a *book*. If I had any clue as to how impossible this goal would be, I can pretty much assure you I would have given up before I started. Yet, born out of the same ignorance, that seems to have driven humanity forward since the beginning of time, I was filled with both hope and confidence as I sat down and outlined Carrie's story—my story—that afternoon in my office on Music Row in Nashville.

An accidental connection

The next several years were spent trying to get others interested in writing the story themselves. I wasn't looking for a ghostwriter; I was looking for a *writer*—someone willing to use my outline as a starting point and take the reins. I pitched my non-novel that I wasn't really

ROBERT HICKS is the author of *The Widow of the South* (Hachette). He and Jeff Kleinman have now sold two more novels. In addition, they also have sold *A Guitar and a Pen*, a collection of short stories by Nashville songwriters Robert co-edited with John Bohlinger and Justin Stelter, released May 2008.

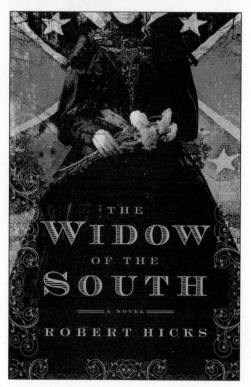

writing to just about anyone who might listen. Problem was, few *were* listening. Of course, now that I know a bit more about the business, I understand why folks sounded so confused on the few occasions I was even able to make my pitch.

Good fortune finally came when I met, via a cold call, a wonderfully kind nonfiction editor named P.J. Dempsey. She listened to my story and gave some helpful feedback but explained that she didn't publish fiction. Before she hung up, she told me that I should call Jeff Kleinman, a "great" literary agent in D.C. who seemed to have a passion for lost causes. Now, this may not seem like much encouragement, but beggars can't be choosers and it was direction, and direction meant momentum, and for that I will forever thank P.J. Within minutes, I called Jeff's office and somehow (this part neither of us have ever figured out) my call went straight to him. Sounding both a bit confused and annoyed, he gave me a chance to lay out Carrie's story, and before I had finished, he seemed genuinely moved.

Throughout the next couple of years, though we never met face to face, Jeff stayed in touch and slowly convinced me that if this was truly *my* story, I needed to be the author. Following his advice, I went back to my original outline and started building from there.

That's when I realized what all writers already know: sitting down to write is far harder than simply pitching a story. I guess that's why bars are filled with more folks who will gladly pitch you a yarn than with published authors. I had yet to see if Jeff was truly a "great" agent, but I soon realized he was a great editor. He read my early chapters and redlined my scribbling with question marks and words of disbelief, yet always pushing me forward.

When the first third of the book was more or less completed, Jeff told me he wanted to shop it as a "partial." Until that point, the only "partials" I had ever heard of were in the mouths of elderly relatives. Jeff explained that he would shop it to his favorite 12 editors. His plan was to give them time to read over it, and if and when they all passed on it, he would then shop it to a dozen more. (Only later would I find out that both attracting an agent and selling a manuscript using only a partial was extremely rare. Usually, the whole manuscript should be complete and polished before starting the process.)

A few weeks later, one Monday morning, while standing in line at a taco stand in Santa Barbara, waiting to place my order, Jeff called to tell me that the partial had sold to Warner Books. In disbelief, I remember asking him if he had shopped it.

"Yes, of course—on Friday!" he said.

"Which Friday?"

"Last Friday. Three days ago!"

P.J. was right; Jeff really was a great agent.

An addiction to editing

With a phone call, I met my editor, Amy Einhorn. We became friends during the next year as she guided me through the rest of the book, always reminding me to stay true to my passion for the story yet be sure to draw readers into that passion. When the manuscript was finished, I came to New York and finally met Amy in person. I also got to have breakfast with the entire editorial team at Warner with whom I'd be working.

Now that the writing was done, it was time for editing and revising and then more editing. Surprisingly, I found myself hooked on the process of editing. Finally, I realized it really was an *addiction*, much like folks who get hooked on plastic surgery. Editing is a key part of writing, of course, but too much can cut out your literary voice as sure as Michael Jackson lost his nose. So one day, I handed Amy my only copy of the manuscript and told her though I would ask to go over it again in the future, not to let me. Three days later, I called her and said I needed to look it over just one more time. She said no. I not only had a great agent, but a great editor, too.

From start to finish, the whole process was new to me, and I accomplished it thanks to help from other individuals who were as passionate about the story as I was. Without Jeff or Amy, I would have stopped in my tracks long before the finish line. And if all this is beginning to sound like my own one-man roast of my agent and my editor, it's only right that it should. Thanks to them, I was prepared for what was to follow with the publication.

The mantra come true

Three days after an amazing book launch back at Carnton (where my story began so many years before), I found myself alone in a hotel room in Cincinnati, waiting for my ride to Joseph-Beth Booksellers for a signing. Amy called to tell me that the book—Carrie's story—made the *New York Times* Best Seller List. As I stood there, listening, I was awash in thought. So rarely in our lives is the end result as we envisioned it. So rarely are we given the chance to live out our dreams. It all began with that optimist who stood in the doorway and whispered to my brother and me. He always told us that we make our own luck, but everything in life is a gift. I think he was right on both counts.

Luck or not, it's my profound belief (and my father's) that all things really are possible, despite all the "no's" that come our way in life. And to that I would add, if you're allowed to live out your dreams, never forget that despite all the work and frustration, as well as the rewrites and the no's, in the end, it all really was a gift. So, my fellow scribblers, leap into the fray. I can't tell you how it will turn out, but never forget it really is possible.

Perspectives

For the Self-Published

The Low Down on Dealing With Agents

by W.E. Reinka

Self-publishing is a complex and contentious topic. Bring it up at any writers' conference and you're bound to start a discussion, with novice writers and accomplished publishing pros all chiming in with their two cents. Some preach against the practice, while others praise it.

If you've already self-published a book and want to see it in stores across the country, you're past any discussion about the pros and cons of the practice; instead, you want to hear about how to get an agent to rep your book. Is it possible? Sure. Is it likely? That depends. Some self-published books have broke out with success thanks to agents, while many have stayed in the shadows. Here are some success stories and candid thoughts from agents on taking your book from boxes in the garage to the big bookstore chains across America.

THE GOOD NEWS: SUCCESS STORIES

One individual who took the leap from self-published scribe to successful author was Tama Kieves. Heeding her parents' advice ("You write, you'll starve"), Kieves dutifully followed her childhood conditioning. Go to college. Get a good job. Make money. Conditioning in hand, she excelled at Harvard Law School before joining a Denver law firm. She epitomized success, except for one thing: She wasn't happy.

Hang the money and prestige, she boldly decided; it was time to follow her heart's path, not the life others had laid out for her. It took her 12 years to write *This Time I Dance! Trusting The Journey Of Creating The Work You Love*. After her searches for publishers and agents fell short, she went on her own. "I decided to skip all that and self-publish a book I'd take straight to the public. At my reading at Tattered Cover Book Store (in Denver), 200 people attended as I'd already built a platform through my seminars on following your heart in your career."

"Platform" is not a word one finds in many manuals about the craft of writing, but it inevitably comes up when chatting with authors who have gone from self-publishing to agency representation. Demonstrating that a self-published book stands on a solid sales platform is the surest way for a self-published author to secure representation to traditional publishers. Kieves got a boost when a former publishing executive who was undergoing her own career transition discovered the book and found it so helpful she brought it to the attention of her former colleagues in New York. Soon Kieves had an agent and a contract with Tarcher/Penguin. Sure, she was fortunate, but she also put herself in position to score. "I took a lot of initiative. *This Time I Dance* made *The Denver Post*'s bestseller list before I had an agent."

W.E. REINKA has published more than 1,000 articles, essays and stories. He often writes about books and authors.

A writer's platform is not limited to nonfiction. Kieves' fellow Coloradan, Dom Testa, is passionate about helping adolescents and teens resist peer pressure in the expected areas—drugs, alcohol and sex, but with the added notion of combating pressure not to excel academically (to resist the notion that being stupid is cool). He uses his celebrity as a morning drive radio personality to visit schools and promote his Big Brain Club. To enhance his zealous cause, he wrote a sci-fi novel with teen heroes, which he self-published and eventually turned into a series. A few years later, TOR Books phoned to say they were interested in his writing. After several conversations, Testa and his new agent, Jacques de Spoelberch, decided to work together. Soon after, Spoelberch secured Testa a six-book contract.

It sounds like an overnight success story, but the above paragraph compresses years of writing and overseeing painstaking publishing details. "You don't want to get so overwhelmed that quality starts to dissipate people," Testa says. "I coach people to take one baby step at a time."

THE BAD NEWS: SLUSH PILES AND STIGMAS

Self-publishing, though more popular than ever, remains a touchy subject with many agents, publicists and reviewers. Agents' and editors' concern regarding the inconsistent quality of self-published books is nothing new. The stigma stems from their thinking that many self-published books are self-published for one of two reasons—either they're not of high enough quality, or there's no market for book. Some memoirs, for example, may be compelling, but publishers know that the book's audience is too limited for them ever to turn a profit.

Agent Katharine Sands of the Sarah Jane Freymann Literary Agency says she's hesitant to rep self-published books for several reasons. "Number one: Your ISBN number and sales record are tracked, and the numbers will not be as high as a trade publisher would like to see," she says. "Secondly, a book from five years ago looks like what the Japanese call 'old cake.' It does not look as fresh or current as it might have done when it was published. Lastly, I have to presume 158 agents have declined the project prior to the author's decision to self-publish and pay to have books printed. Even though we know it may well be untrue, this is a pop-up thought in an agent's mind."

Agent Jody Rein, who is no longer in business, discovered several gems among the stacks of self-published books and sold them to big-name publishers. Still, Rein candidly tells us that "when a self-published book crosses an agent's desk, the agent has to ask: Why did this person go to the trouble of publishing this book him or herself? The obvious answer: because he or she couldn't sell it to a larger publisher. So, immediately, the self-published book sends the message 'I'm not good enough' to be published by a big house and my author is the kind of person who just doesn't know when to quit."

Sometimes, a self-published book may not take off, but can lead to other things. Kathy Sanborn of Sacramento published her first book, *Grow Your Own Love*, as an e-book through www.Booklocker.com as she slowly built up an excellent platform through her Web site. When she finished her second book, *The Seasons Of Your Career*, the tremendous Internet exposure she generated with her first self-published first effort gave her greater credibility in attracting agent Joelle Delbourgo, who was convinced Sanborn had perseverance and assertiveness enough to market her work successfully. *The Seasons Of My Career* was eventually sold to McGraw-Hill and sold 15,000 copies sold in China alone. No, Sanborn's wasn't an easy path, but then one of the tenets of Sanborn's career counseling is: "Avoid taking shortcuts to success. They almost always backfire!"

Also, there is the concern that everyone who will have bought the book has already done so. For example, let's say you self-publish a book about the role of Lake Erie in the War of 1812 and sell 5,000 copies among the lake region to history buffs, your relatives and other enthusiasts. Finding a big publisher for the book likely won't lead to high sales because the book has already reached its limited target audience, for the most part. It's virtually impossible to build a platform on a passé or esoteric topic, and agents and mainstream publishers are not interested in limited markets.

The good news for self-published authors, regardless of the ultimate fate of their books, is that they show the perseverance to see the project through. Everyone wants to be a writer but only a miniscule percentage shows the guts and determination to see it through. Even if your quest to see a self-published book reach greater heights never comes to fruition, you've already proven you have the discipline to write a book, so think about writing another book and starting from scratch there.

Literary Agents

gents listed in this section generate 98-100 percent of their income from commission on sales. They do not charge for reading, critiquing or editing your manuscript or book proposal. It's the goal of an agent to find salable manuscripts: Her income depends on finding the best publisher for your manuscript.

Since an agent's time is better spent meeting with editors, she will have little or no time to critique your writing. Agents who don't charge fees must be selective and often prefer to work with established authors, celebrities or those with professional credentials in a particular field.

Some agents in this section may charge clients for office expenses such as photocopying, foreign postage, long-distance phone calls or express mail services. Make sure you have a clear understanding of what these expenses are before signing any agency agreement.

SUBHEADS

Each agency listing is broken down into subheads to make locating specific information easier. In the first section, you'll find contact information for each agency. You'll also learn if the agents within the agency belong to any professional organizations; membership in these organizations can tell you a lot about an agency. For example, members of the Association of Authors' Representatives (AAR) are prohibited from charging reading or evaluating fees. Additional information in this section includes the size of each agency, its willingness to work with new or unpublished writers, and its general areas of interest.

Member Agents: Agencies comprised of more than one agent list member agents and their individual specialties. This information will help you determine the appropriate person to whom you should send your query letter.

Represents: This section allows agencies to specify what nonfiction and fiction subjects they represent. Make sure you query only those agents who represent the type of material you write.

⚿ Look for the key icon to quickly learn an agent's areas of specialization. In this portion of the listing, agents mention the specific subject areas they're currently seeking, as well as those subject areas they do not consider.

How to Contact: Most agents open to submissions prefer an initial query letter that briefly describes your work. While some agents may ask for an outline and a specific number of sample chapters, most don't. You should send these items only if the agent requests them. In this section, agents also mention if they accept queries by fax or e-mail, if they consider simultaneous submissions, and how they prefer to obtain new clients.

Recent Sales: To give you a sense of the types of material they represent, the agents list specific titles they've sold, as well as a sampling of clients' names. Note that some agents consider their client list confidential and may only share client names once they agree to represent you.

Terms: Provided here are details of an agent's commission, whether a contract is offered and for how long, and what additional office expenses you might have to pay if the agent agrees to represent you. Standard commissions range from 10-15 percent for domestic sales and 15-20 percent for foreign or dramatic sales (with the difference going to the co-agent who places the work).

Writers' Conferences: A great way to meet an agent is at a writers' conference. Here agents list the conferences they usually attend. For more information about a specific conference, check the Conferences section starting on page 234.

Tips: In this section, agents offer advice and additional instructions for writers.

SPECIAL INDEXES

Literary Agents Specialties Index: This index (page 268) organizes agencies according to the subjects they are interested in receiving. This index should help you compose a list of agents specializing in your areas. Cross-referencing categories and concentrating on agents interested in two or more aspects of your manuscript might increase your chances of success.

Agents Index: This index (page 338) provides a list of agents' names in alphabetical order, along with the name of the agency for which they work. Find the name of the person you would like to contact, and then check the agency listing.

General Index: This index (page 356) lists all agencies and conferences appearing in the book.

Quick Reference Icons

At the beginning of some listings, you will find one or more of the following symbols:

N   Agency new to this edition

   Canadian agency

   International agency

   Agency actively seeking clients

   Agency seeking both new and established writers

   Agency seeking mostly established writers through referrals

   Agency specializing in certain types of work

   Agency not currently seeking new clients

Find a pull-out bookmark with a key to symbols on the inside cover of this book.

◉ A + B WORKS

E-mail: amy@aplusbworks.com. Website: www.aplusbworks.com. **Contact:** Amy Jameson. Estab. 2004.
- Prior to her current position, Ms. Jameson worked at Janklow & Nesbit Associates.

Represents Nonfiction books, novels. **Considers these fiction areas:** Young adult; women's.
- ⊶ This agency specializes in middle grade and YA fiction, women's fiction and some adult nonfiction. "We are only interested in established writers at this time." Does not want to receive thrillers or science fiction.

How to Contact Query with SASE. Query via e-mail only. Send queries to query@aplusbworks.com. No fax queries.

Recent Sales *Sun and Moon, Ice and Snow,* by Jessica Day George (Bloomsbury); *River Secrets,* by Shannon Hale (Bloomsbury); *Tall Tales,* by Karen Day (Wendy Lamb Books).

◔ DOMINICK ABEL LITERARY AGENCY, INC.

146 W. 82nd St., #1B, New York NY 10024. (212)877-0710. Fax: (212)595-3133. E-mail: agency@dalainc.com. Estab. 1975. Member of AAR. Represents 100 clients. Currently handles: adult nonfiction books; adult novels.
How to Contact Query with SASE.
Terms Agent receives 15% commission on domestic sales; 20% commission on foreign sales.

✣ ◔ ACACIA HOUSE PUBLISHING SERVICES, LTD.

62 Chestnut Ave., Brantford ON N3T 4C2 Canada. (519)752-0978. **Contact:** (Ms.) Frances Hanna or Bill Hanna. Estab. 1985. Represents 100 clients. Currently handles: 30% nonfiction books; 70% novels.
- Ms. Hanna has been in the publishing business for 30 years, first in London as a fiction editor with Barrie & Jenkins and Pan Books, and as a senior editor with a packager of mainly illustrated books. She was condensed books editor for 6 years for *Reader's Digest* in Montreal and senior editor and foreign rights manager for William Collins & Sons (now HarperCollins) in Toronto. Mr. Hanna has more than 40 years of experience in the publishing business.

Member Agents Frances Hanna; Bill Hanna, vice president (self-help, modern history, military history).
Represents Nonfiction books, novels. **Considers these nonfiction areas:** Animals; biography/autobiography; language/literature/criticism; memoirs; military/war; music/dance; nature/environment; theater/film; travel. **Considers these fiction areas:** Action/adventure; detective/police/crime; literary; mainstream/contemporary; mystery/suspense; thriller.
- ⊶ This agency specializes in contemporary fiction—literary or commercial. Actively seeking outstanding first novels with literary merit. Does not want to receive horror, occult or science fiction.

How to Contact Query with outline, SASE. *No unsolicited mss.* No phone queries. No e-mail or fax queries. Responds in 6 weeks to queries. Returns materials only with SASE.
Recent Sales This agency prefers not to share information on specific sales.
Terms Agent receives 15% commission on English language sales; 20% commission on dramatic sales; 25% commission on foreign sales. Charges clients for photocopying, postage, courier.
Tips "We prefer that writers be previously published, with at least a few short stories or articles to their credit. Strongest consideration will be given to those with three or more published books. However, we would take on an unpublished writer of outstanding talent."

◔ ADAMS LITERARY

7845 Colony Road C4, #215, Charlotte NC 28226. (704)542-1440. Fax: (704)542-1450. E-mail: info@adamsliterary.com. Website: www.adamsliterary.com. **Contact:** Tracey Adams, Josh Adams. Estab. 2004. Member of AAR; SCBWI.
Member Agents Tracey Adams; Josh Adams.
- ⊶ Adams Literary is a full-service literary agency exclusively representing children's book authors and artists. "Although we remain absolutely dedicated to finding new talent, we must announce that, until further notice, we can no longer accept unsolicited manuscripts. We also cannot accept queries or submissions via e-mail."

◖ THE AGENCY GROUP, LLC

1880 Century Park E., Suite 711, Los Angeles CA, 90068. (310)385-2800. E-mail: marcgerald@theagencygroup.com. Website: www.theagencygroup.com. **Contact:** Marc Gerald, Caroline Greeven. Estab. 2002. Represents 50 clients. 10% of clients are new/unpublished writers. Currently handles: 60% nonfiction books; 30% novels; 10% multimedia.
- Prior to becoming an agent, Mr. Gerald owned and ran an independent publishing and entertainment agency.

Member Agents Marc Gerald; Caroline Greeven; Sarah Stephens.

Represents Nonfiction books, novels. **Considers these nonfiction areas:** Anthropology/archaeology; art/architecture/design; biography/autobiography; business/economics; child guidance/parenting; cooking/foods/nutrition; ethnic/cultural interests; government/politics/law; health/medicine; history; how-to; humor/satire; memoirs; money/finance; music/dance; nature/environment; popular culture; psychology; self-help/personal improvement; sports; true crime/investigative; interior design/decorating. **Considers these fiction areas:** All subjects except science fiction/fantasy.

> ⊶ "While we admire beautiful writing, we largely represent recording artists, celebrities, authors, and pop culture and style brands with established platforms. When we represent fiction, we work almost exclusively in genre and in areas of expertise. We tend to take a non-linear approach to content—many of our projects ultimately have a TV/film or digital component." This agency is only taking on new clients through referrals.

How to Contact Considers simultaneous queries. Responds in 1 month to queries; 3 months to mss. Obtains most new clients through recommendations from others.

Recent Sales Sold 40 titles in the last year. *50 by 50*, by 50 Cent (Pocket); *Sew U*, by Wendy Mullin (Bullfinch); *Little Things*, by Jeffrey Brown (Fireside); *The Hustler's Wife #2*, by Nikki Turner (Random House); *One Red Paperclip*, by Kyle MacDonald (Three Rivers Press). Other clients include Tim McGraw, Eminem, Project Alabama, Wahida Clark, Steve Rinella, Meta Smith, Joy King, Merlin Bronques, Jim Limburgh, Chris Jericho.

Terms Agent receives 15% commission on domestic sales; 20% commission on foreign sales. Offers written contract. Charges clients for office fees (only for mss that have been sold).

⊘ THE AHEARN AGENCY, INC.

2021 Pine St., New Orleans LA 70118. E-mail: pahearn@aol.com. **Contact:** Pamela G. Ahearn. Estab. 1992. Member of MWA, RWA, ITW. Represents 35 clients. 20% of clients are new/unpublished writers. Currently handles: 10% nonfiction books; 90% novels.

> ● Prior to opening her agency, Ms. Ahearn was an agent for 8 years and an editor with Bantam Books.

Considers these nonfiction areas: Animals; child guidance/parenting; current affairs; ethnic/cultural interests; gay/lesbian issues; health/medicine; history; popular culture; self-help/personal improvement; theater/film; true crime/investigative; women's issues/studies. **Considers these fiction areas:** Action/adventure; contemporary issues; detective/police/crime; ethnic; family saga; feminist; glitz; historical; humor/satire; literary; mainstream/contemporary; mystery/suspense; psychic/supernatural; regional; romance; thriller.

> ⊶ This agency specializes in historical romance and is also very interested in mysteries and suspense fiction. Does not want to receive category romance, science fiction or fantasy.

How to Contact Query with SASE. Accepts e-mail queries (no attachments). Considers simultaneous queries. Responds in 8 weeks to queries; 10 weeks to mss. Obtains most new clients through recommendations from others, solicitations, conferences.

Recent Sales *Red Chrysanthemum*, by Laura Joh Rowland; *Only a Duke Will Do*, by Sabrina Jeffries; *The Alexandria Link*, by Steve Berry.

Terms Agent receives 15% commission on domestic sales; 20% commission on foreign sales. Offers written contract, binding for 1 year; renewable by mutual consent.

Writers' Conferences Moonlight & Magnolias; RWA National Conference; Thriller Fest; Florida Romance Writers; Bouchercon; Malice Domestic.

Tips "Be professional! Always send in exactly what an agent/editor asks for—no more, no less. Keep query letters brief and to the point, giving your writing credentials and a very brief summary of your book. If one agent rejects you, keep trying—there are a lot of us out there!"

⊕ ⊘ AITKEN ALEXANDER ASSOCIATES

18-21 Cavaye Place, London England SW10 9PT, United Kingdom. (44)(207)373-8672. Fax: (44)(207)373-6002. E-mail: reception@aitkenalexander.co.uk. Website: www.aitkenalexander.co.uk. **Contact:** Submissions Department. Estab. 1977. Represents 300+ clients. 10% of clients are new/unpublished writers.

Member Agents Gillon Aitken, agent; Clare Alexander, agent; Kate Shaw, children's; Ayesha Karim, agent; Lesley Thorne, film/television.

Represents Nonfiction books, novels, novellas, movie scripts, TV scripts. **Considers these nonfiction areas:** Current affairs; government/politics/law; history; memoirs; popular culture. **Considers these fiction areas:** Historical; literary.

> ⊶ "We specialize in literary fiction and nonfiction."

How to Contact Query with SASE. Submit synopsis, first 30 pages. Send screenplay submissions to Lesley Thorne. Responds in 6-8 weeks to queries. Returns materials only with SASE. Obtains most new clients through recommendations from others, solicitations.

Recent Sales Sold 35+ titles and sold 4+ scripts in the last year. *My Life With George*, by Judith Summers

(Voice); *The Separate Hearth*, by Simon Robson (Cape); *The Fall of the House of Wittynstein*, by Alexander Vaugh (Bloomsbury); *Shakespeare's Life*, by Germane Greer; *Occupational Hazards*, by Rory Stewart.

Terms Agent receives 10% commission on domestic sales; 20% commission on foreign sales. Offers written contract; 28-day notice must be given to terminate contract. Charges for photocopying and postage.

Tips "Before submitting to us, we advise you to look at our existing client list to establish whether your work will be of interest. Equally, you should consider whether the material you have written is ready to submit to a literary agency. If you feel your work qualifies, then send us a letter introducing yourself: Keep it relevant to your writing (e.g., tell us about any previously published work, be it a short story or journalism; you may be studying or have completed a post-graduate qualification in creative writing; when it comes to nonfiction, we would want to know what qualifies you to write about the subject)."

ALIVE COMMUNICATIONS, INC.

7680 Goddard St., Suite 200, Colorado Springs CO 80920. (719)260-7080. Fax: (719)260-8223. Website: www.alivecom.com. Estab. 1989. Member of AAR, Authors Guild. Represents 100+ clients. 5% of clients are new/unpublished writers. Currently handles: 50% nonfiction books; 35% novels; 5% novellas; 10% juvenile books.

Member Agents Rick Christian, president (blockbusters, bestsellers); Lee Hough (popular/commercial nonfiction and fiction, thoughtful spirituality, children's); Beth Jusino (thoughtful/inspirational nonfiction, women's fiction/nonfiction, Christian living).

Represents Nonfiction books, novels, short story collections, novellas. **Considers these nonfiction areas:** Biography/autobiography; business/economics; child guidance/parenting; how-to; memoirs; religious/inspirational; self-help/personal improvement; women's issues/studies. **Considers these fiction areas:** Action/adventure; contemporary issues; detective/police/crime; family saga; historical; humor/satire; literary; mainstream/contemporary; mystery/suspense; religious/inspirational; thriller.

> ○→ This agency specializes in fiction, Christian living, how-to and commercial nonfiction. Actively seeking inspirational, literary and mainstream fiction, and work from authors with established track records and platforms. Does not want to receive poetry, young adult paperbacks, scripts or dark themes.

How to Contact Query with SASE. Be advised that this agency works primarily with well-established, bestselling, and career authors. Returns materials only with SASE. Obtains most new clients through recommendations from others.

Recent Sales Sold 300+ titles in the last year. A spiritual memoir, by Eugene Peterson (Viking); A biography of Rwandan president Paul Kagame, by Stephen Kinzer; *Ever After*, by Karen Klingsbury (Zondervan).

Terms Agent receives 15% commission on domestic sales; 15% commission on foreign sales. Offers written contract; 2-month notice must be given to terminate contract.

Tips "Rewrite and polish until the words on the page shine. Endorsements and great connections may help, provided you can write with power and passion. Network with publishing professionals by making contacts, joining critique groups, and attending writers' conferences in order to make personal connections and to get feedback. Alive Communications, Inc., has established itself as a premiere literary agency. We serve an elite group of authors who are critically acclaimed and commercially successful in both Christian and general markets."

ALLEN O'SHEA LITERARY AGENCY

615 Westover Road, Stamford CT 06902. (203)359-9965. Fax: (203)357-9909. E-mail: ma615@aol.com. **Contact:** Marilyn Allen. Estab. 2002. Represents 100 clients. 20% of clients are new/unpublished writers. Currently handles: 100% nonfiction books.

• Prior to becoming agents, both Ms. Allen and Ms. O'Shea held senior positions in publishing.

Member Agents Marilyn Allen; Coleen O'Shea.

Represents Nonfiction books. **Considers these nonfiction areas:** Animals (pet books); biography/autobiography; business/economics; cooking/foods/nutrition; current affairs; health/medicine; history; how-to; humor/satire; military/war; money/finance; popular culture; psychology; self-help/personal improvement; sports; interior design/decorating.

> ○→ This agency specializes in practical nonfiction including health, cooking, sports, business, pop culture, etc. "We look for clients with strong marketing platforms and new ideas coupled with strong writing." Actively seeking narrative nonfiction, craft, health and history writers. Does not want to receive fiction, poetry, textbooks or children's.

How to Contact Query with SASE, submit outline, author bio, marketing page. No phone or fax queries. Considers simultaneous queries. Responds in 1 week to queries; 1-2 months to mss. Returns materials only with SASE. Obtains most new clients through recommendations from others, conferences.

Recent Sales Sold 45 titles in the last year. This agency prefers not to share information about specific sales.

Terms Agent receives 15% commission on domestic sales. Offers written contract, binding for 2 years; 1-

month notice must be given to terminate contract. Charges for photocopying large mss, and overseas postage—"typically minimal costs."

Writers' Conferences ASJA, Publicity Submit for Writers, Connecticut Authors and Publishers, Willamette Writers' Conference.

Tips "Prepare a strong overview, with competition, marketing and bio."

☑ MIRIAM ALTSHULER LITERARY AGENCY

53 Old Post Road N., Red Hook NY 12571. (845)758-9408. Website: www.miriamaltshulerliteraryagency.com. **Contact:** Miriam Altshuler. Estab. 1994. Member of AAR. Represents 40 clients. Currently handles: 45% nonfiction books; 45% novels; 5% story collections; 5% juvenile books.

   • Ms. Altshuler has been an agent since 1982.

Represents Nonfiction books, novels, short story collections, juvenile books. **Considers these nonfiction areas:** Biography/autobiography; ethnic/cultural interests; history; language/literature/criticism; memoirs; multicultural; music/dance; nature/environment; popular culture; psychology; sociology; theater/film; women's issues/studies. **Considers these fiction areas:** Literary; mainstream/contemporary; multicultural.

   ○→ Does not want self-help, mystery, how-to, romance, horror, spiritual, fantasy, poetry, screenplays, science fiction or techno-thriller.

How to Contact Query with SASE, submit contact info with e-mail address. Prefers to read materials exclusively. No e-mail or fax queries. Considers simultaneous queries. Responds in 3 weeks to mss. Returns materials only with SASE. Obtains most new clients through recommendations from others.

Terms Agent receives 15% commission on domestic sales; 20% commission on foreign sales. Charges clients for overseas mailing, photocopies, overnight mail when requested by author.

Writers' Conferences Bread Loaf Writers' Conference; Washington Independent Writers Conference; North Carolina Writers' Network Conference.

Tips See the Web site for specific submission details.

☑ AMBASSADOR LITERARY AGENCY

P.O. Box 50358, Nashville TN 37205. (615)370-4700. E-mail: Wes@AmbassadorAgency.com. Website: www.AmbassadorAgency.com. **Contact:** Wes Yoder. Estab. 1997. Represents 25-30 clients. 10% of clients are new/unpublished writers. Currently handles: 95% nonfiction books; 5% novels.

   • Prior to becoming an agent, Mr. Yoder founded a music artist agency in 1973; he established a speakers bureau division of the company in 1984.

Represents Nonfiction books, novels. **Considers these nonfiction areas:** Biography/autobiography; child guidance/parenting; current affairs; education; ethnic/cultural interests; government/politics/law; health/medicine; history; how-to; memoirs; money/finance; popular culture; religious/inspirational; self-help/personal improvement; women's issues/studies. **Considers these fiction areas:** Action/adventure; ethnic; family saga; literary; mainstream/contemporary; religious/inspirational.

   ○→ This agency specializes in religious market publishing and has excellent national media relationships, dealing primarily with A-level publishers. Actively seeking popular nonfiction themes, including the following: practical living; Christian spirituality; literary fiction. Does not want to receive short stories, children's books, screenplays or poetry.

How to Contact Query with SASE, submit proposal package, outline, synopsis, 6 sample chapter(s), author bio. Accepts e-mail queries. No fax queries. Considers simultaneous queries. Responds in 2-4 weeks to queries. Obtains most new clients through recommendations from others.

Recent Sales Sold 20 titles in the last year. *The Death and Life of Gabriel Phillips*, by Stephen Baldwin (Hachette); *Amazing Grace: William Wilberforce and the Heroic Campaign to End Slavery*, by Eric Mataxas (Harper San Francisco); *Life@The Next Level*, by Courtney McBath (Simon & Schuster); *Women, Take Charge of Your Money*, by Carolyn Castleberry (Random House/Multnomah).

Terms Agent receives 15% commission on domestic sales; 20% commission on foreign sales. Offers written contract.

☑ BETSY AMSTER LITERARY ENTERPRISES

P.O. Box 27788, Los Angeles CA 90027-0788. **Contact:** Betsy Amster. Estab. 1992. Member of AAR. Represents more than 65 clients. 35% of clients are new/unpublished writers. Currently handles: 65% nonfiction books; 35% novels.

   • Prior to opening her agency, Ms. Amster was an editor at Pantheon and Vintage for 10 years, and served as editorial director for the Globe Pequot Press for 2 years.

Represents Nonfiction books, novels. **Considers these nonfiction areas:** Biography/autobiography; child guidance/parenting; ethnic/cultural interests; gardening; health/medicine; history; money/finance; psychology;

sociology; women's issues/studies. **Considers these fiction areas:** Ethnic; literary; mystery/suspense (quirky); thriller (quirky); women's (high quality).

O— Actively seeking strong narrative nonfiction, particularly by journalists; outstanding literary fiction (the next Richard Ford or Jhumpa Lahiri); witty, intelligent commerical women's fiction (the next Elinor Lipman or Jennifer Weiner); mysteries that open new worlds to us; and high-profile self-help and psychology, preferably research based. Does not want to receive poetry, children's books, romances, Western, science fiction or action/adventure.

How to Contact For fiction, send query, first 3 pages, SASE. For nonfiction, send query or proposal with SASE. No e-mail or fax queries. Considers simultaneous queries. Responds in 1 month to queries; 2 months to mss. Obtains most new clients through recommendations from others, solicitations, conferences.

Recent Sales *The Blessing of a B Minus*, by Dr. Wendy Mogel (Scribner); *Winners and Lovers: Balancing Love and Power in All Your Relationships*, by Dr. Elaine N. Aron (Little, Brown); *Wild Indigo and Wild Inferno*, by Sandi Ault (Berkley Prime Crime); *Mona Lisa in Camelot: Jacqueline Kennedy and the True Story of the Painting's High-Stakes Journey to America*, by Margaret Leslie Davis (DaCapo); *The Girl I Left Behind: A Narrative History of the Sixties*, by Judith Nies (HarperCollins); *The Battle for Wine and Love (Or How I Saved the World from Parkerization)*, by Alice Feiring (Harcourt); *Mutts*, by Sharon Montrose (Stewart, Tabori & Chang); *A Vicky Hill Exclusive!*, by Hannah Dennison (Berkley Prime Crime); *100 Trees and How They Got Their Names*, by Diana Wells (Algonquin). Other clients include Dr. Linda Acredolo and Dr. Susan Goodwyn, Dwight Allen, Barbara DeMarco-Barrett, Robin Chotzinoff, Rob Cohen & David Wollock, Phil Doran, Ruth Andrew Ellenson, Maria Amparo Escandon, Paul Mandelbaum, Joy Nicholson, Christopher Noxon, Edward Schneider and R.J. Smith.

Terms Agent receives 15% commission on domestic sales; 20% commission on foreign sales. Offers written contract, binding for 1 year; 3-month notice must be given to terminate contract. Charges for photocopying, postage, long distance phone calls, messengers, galleys/books used in submissions to foreign and film agents and to magazines for first serial rights.

Writers' Conferences Squaw Valley Writers' Workshop; San Diego State University Writers' Conference; UCLA Extension Writers' Program; The Loft Literary Center.

◙ MARCIA AMSTERDAM AGENCY

41 W. 82nd St., Suite 9A, New York NY 10024-5613. (212)873-4945. **Contact:** Marcia Amsterdam. Estab. 1970. Signatory of WGA. Currently handles: 15% nonfiction books; 70% novels; 5% movie scripts; 10% TV scripts.

• Prior to opening her agency, Ms. Amsterdam was an editor.

Represents Novels, feature film, sitcom. **Considers these fiction areas:** Action/adventure; detective/police/ crime; horror; mainstream/contemporary; mystery/suspense; romance (contemporary, historical); science fiction; thriller; young adult. **Considers these script subject areas:** Comedy; romantic comedy.

How to Contact Query with SASE. No e-mail or fax queries. Responds in 1 month to queries.

Recent Sales *Hidden Child*, by Isaac Millman (FSG); *Lucky Leonardo*, by Jonathan Canter (Sourcebooks).

Terms Agent receives 15% commission on domestic sales; 20% commission on foreign sales; 10% commission on dramatic rights sales. Offers written contract, binding for 1 year. Charges clients for extra office expenses, foreign postage, copying, legal fees (when agreed upon).

Tips "We are always looking for interesting literary voices."

◙ THE ANDERSON LITERARY AGENCY

435 Convent Ave., Suite 5, New York NY 10031. (212)234-0692. E-mail: gilesa@rcn.com. **Contact:** Giles Anderson.

Represents Nonfiction books. **Considers these nonfiction areas:** Biography; memoir; religion; science; true crime.

How to Contact Send brief query via e-mail.

◙ ANDERSON LITERARY MANAGEMENT, LLC

12 W. 19th St., New York NY 10011. (212)645-6045. Fax: (212)741-1936. E-mail: kathleen@andersonliterary. com; info@andersonliterary.com. Website: www.andersonliterary.com/. **Contact:** Kathleen Anderson. Estab. 2006. Member of AAR. Represents 100+ clients. 20% of clients are new/unpublished writers. Currently handles: 50% nonfiction books; 50% novels.

• Prior to her current position, Ms. Anderson was with Grinberg Literary. She has more than two decades of publishing experience.

Represents Nonfiction books, novels, short story collections, juvenile books. **Considers these nonfiction areas:** Anthropology/archaeology; art/architecture/design; biography/autobiography; current affairs; education; ethnic/cultural interests; gay/lesbian issues; government/politics/law; history; memoirs; music/dance; nature/ environment; psychology; women's issues/studies. **Considers these fiction areas:** Action/adventure; ethnic;

family saga; feminist; gay/lesbian; historical; literary; mystery/suspense; thriller; westerns/frontier; young adult; women's.

> O⭠ Specializes in commercial fiction (literary, women's, thriller, historical, young adult) and commercial nonfiction (investigative journalism, women's studies, biography, environmental studies, history, philosophy and religious studies) Does not want to receive genre fantasy, sci-fi or romance.

How to Contact Query with SASE, submit synopsis, first 3 sample chapter(s), proposal (for nonfiction). Accepts e-mail queries. No fax queries. Considers simultaneous queries. Responds in 12 weeks to queries; 12 weeks to mss. Returns materials only with SASE. Obtains most new clients through recommendations from others, solicitations, conferences.

Recent Sales Sold 20+ titles in the last year. *Vibes*, by Amy Ryan (Houghton Mifflin); *Another Faust*, by Daniel and Dina Nayeri (Candlewick); *The Assassins' Gate*, by George Packer; *17 Huntley Gardens*, by Richard Mason (Knopf); *The Reindeer People*, by Piers Vitebsky (Houghton Mifflin); *Maps for Lost Lovers*, by Nadeem Aslam (Knopf). Other clients include Emma Donoghue, Charles Bowden, Rafi Zabor, Marcia Willett, Jane Shaw, Molly Peacock, Anna Oliver, Conn Iggulden, Bella Bathurst, Kerry Hardie, Anna Beer, Janet Todd, Glen Hirshberg, Deanne Stillman, Chuck Wachtel, Barry Lyga, Craig Childs, Sarah Bilston.

Terms Agent receives 15% commission on domestic sales. Offers written contract.

Writers' Conferences Squaw Valley Conference.

◢ APPLESEEDS MANAGEMENT

200 E. 30th St., Suite 302, San Bernardino CA 92404. (909)882-1667. **Contact:** S. James Foiles. Estab. 1988. 40% of clients are new/unpublished writers. Currently handles: 15% nonfiction books; 85% novels.

Represents Nonfiction books, novels. **Considers these nonfiction areas:** True crime/investigative. **Considers these fiction areas:** Detective/police/crime; mystery/suspense.

How to Contact Query with SASE. Responds in 2 weeks to queries; 2 months to mss.

Recent Sales This agency prefers not to share information on specific sales.

Terms Agent receives 10-15% commission on domestic sales; 20% commission on foreign sales. Offers written contract, binding for 1-7 years.

Tips "Because readership of mysteries is expanding, Appleseeds specializes in mysteries with a detective who could be in a continuing series."

◢ ARCADIA

31 Lake Place N., Danbury CT 06810. E-mail: pryor@arcadialit.com. **Contact:** Victoria Gould Pryor. Member of AAR.

Represents Nonfiction books, literary and commercial fiction. **Considers these nonfiction areas:** Biography/autobiography; business/economics; current affairs; health/medicine; history; memoirs; psychology; science/technology; true crime/investigative; women's issues/studies; investigative journalism; culture; classical music; life transforming self-help.

> O⭠ "I'm a very hands-on agent, which is necessary in this competitive marketplace. I work with authors on revisions until whatever we present to publishers is as perfect as it can be. I represent talented, dedicated, intelligent and ambitious writers who are looking for a long-term relationship based on professional success and mutual respect." Does not want to receive science fiction/fantasy, horror, humor or children's/YA. "We are only able to read fiction submissions from previously published authors."

How to Contact Query with SASE. This agency accepts e-queries (no attachments).

Recent Sales This agency prefers not to share information on specific sales.

N EDWARD ARMSTRONG LITERARY AGENCY

PO Box 3343, Fayville MA 01745. (401)569-7099. **Contact:** Edward Armstrong. Estab. 2006. Currently handles: 100% fiction.

> • Prior to becoming an agent, Mr. Armstrong was a business professional specializing in quality and regulatory compliance.

Represents Novels, short story collections, novellas. **Considers these fiction areas:** Mainstream/contemporary; romance; science fiction; thriller; suspense.

> O⭠ **Does not want to receive nonfiction or textbooks.**

How to Contact Query with SASE, submit synopsis, 3 sample chapter(s), author bio. Accepts e-mail queries. No fax queries. Considers simultaneous queries. Responds in 2-4 weeks to queries; 3 months to mss. Returns materials only with SASE. Obtains most new clients through solicitations.

Terms Agent receives 5% commission on domestic sales; 5% commission on foreign sales. This agency charges for photocopying and postage.

◪ ARTISTS AND ARTISANS INC.

104 W. 29th St., 11th Floor, New York NY 10001. Fax: (212)931-8377. E-mail: adam@artistsandartisans.com. Website: www.artistsandartisans.com. **Contact:** Adam Chromy. Estab. 2002. Represents 40 clients. 80% of clients are new/unpublished writers. Currently handles: 63% nonfiction books; 35% novels; 2% scholarly books.

• Prior to becoming an agent, Mr. Chromy was an entrepreneur in the technology field for nearly a decade.

Represents Nonfiction books, novels. **Considers these nonfiction areas:** Biography/autobiography; business/economics; child guidance/parenting; cooking/foods/nutrition; current affairs; ethnic/cultural interests; health/medicine; how-to; humor/satire; language/literature/criticism; memoirs; money/finance; music/dance; popular culture; religious/inspirational; science/technology; self-help/personal improvement; sports; theater/film; true crime/investigative; women's issues/studies; fashion/style. **Considers these fiction areas:** Confession; family saga; humor/satire; literary; mainstream/contemporary.

O→ "My education and experience in the business world ensure that my clients' enterprise as authors gets as much attention and care as their writing." Actively seeking working journalists for nonfiction books. Does not want to receive scripts.

How to Contact Query with SASE. Considers simultaneous queries. Responds in 2 weeks to queries; 2 weeks to mss. Returns materials only with SASE. Obtains most new clients through recommendations from others, solicitations, conferences.

Recent Sales Sold 12 titles in the last year. *Dr. Z on Scoring*, by Victoria Zdrok (Touchstone Fireside); *Winning Points with Your Woman*, by Jaci Rae (Touchstone); *From Binge to Blackout*, by Chris Volkmann and Toren Volkmann (NAL Penguin Group); *Modest Mouse*, by Alan Goldsher (Thomas Dunne Books); *Jewtopia*, by Brian Fogel and Sam Wolfson (Warner Books).

Terms Agent receives 15% commission on domestic sales; 25% commission on foreign sales. Offers written contract; 1-month notice must be given to terminate contract. "We only charge for extraordinary expenses (e.g., client requests check via FedEx instead of regular mail)."

Writers' Conferences ASJA Writers Conference.

Tips "Please make sure you are ready before approaching us or any other agent. If you write fiction, make sure it is the best work you can do and get objective criticism from a writing group. If you write nonfiction, make sure the proposal exhibits your best work and a comprehensive understanding of the market."

◪ ROBERT ASTLE AND ASSOCIATES LITERARY MANAGEMENT, INC.

820 West End Ave., Suite 15F, New York 10025, NY. (646)682-7864. E-mail: robert@astleliterary.com. Website: www.astleliterary.com. **Contact:** Robert Astle.

• Prior to becoming an agent, Mr. Astle spent 25 years in theater.

Represents Nonfiction books, novels.

O→ "We are especially interested in receiving nonfiction projects with a wide range of topics, including narrative nonfiction, popular culture, arts and culture, theater and performance, sports, travel, celebrity, biography, politics, memoir, history, new media and multi-ethnic. We are actively seeking writers of literary fiction and commercial fiction—mysteries and suspense, thrillers, mainstream literary fiction, historical fiction, women's fiction, humor/satire and graphic novels. We will also seek writers in the genre of young audiences: middle grade and teen."

How to Contact Use the online form to query. Specifications for nonfiction and fiction submissions are online. No e-mail or fax queries. Returns materials only with SASE. Obtains most new clients through recommendations from others, solicitations.

Tips "Please read the submission guidelines carefully, and make sure your query letter is the best it can be."

◪ THE AUGUST AGENCY, LLC

E-mail: submissions@augustagency.com. Website: www.augustagency.com. **Contact:** Cricket Pechstein, Jeffery McGraw. Estab. 2004. Represents 25-40 clients. 50% of clients are new/unpublished writers. Currently handles: 75% nonfiction books; 20% novels; 5% other.

• Before opening The August Agency, Ms. Pechstein was a freelance writer, magazine editor and independent literary agent; Mr. McGraw worked as an editor for HarperCollins and publicity manager for Abrams.

Member Agents Jeffery McGraw (politics/current affairs, entertainment, business, psychology, self-help, narrative nonfiction, contemporary women's fiction, literary fiction); Cricket Pechstein (mystery/crime fiction, chick lit, thrillers).

Represents Nonfiction books, novels. **Considers these nonfiction areas:** Biography/autobiography; business/economics; child guidance/parenting; cooking/foods/nutrition; current affairs; ethnic/cultural interests; gay/lesbian issues; government/politics/law; health/medicine; history; how-to; humor/satire; interior design/decorating; memoirs; military/war; money/finance; music/dance; popular culture; psychology; self-help/personal improvement; sociology; sports; theater/film; true crime/investigative; women's issues/studies; inspirational.

Considers these fiction areas: Action/adventure; detective/police/crime; ethnic; family saga; gay/lesbian; historical; humor/satire; literary; mainstream/contemporary; mystery/suspense; psychic/supernatural; thriller; smart chick lit (non-genre romance).

O⌐ "We actively pursue an array of fiction and nonfiction writers to represent, with an emphasis in media (seasoned journalists receive special favor here), popular culture/entertainment, political science, diet/fitness, health, cookbooks, psychology, business, memoir, highly creative nonfiction, accessible literary fiction, women's fiction, and high-concept mysteries and thrillers. When it comes to nonfiction, we favor persuasive and prescriptive works with a full-bodied narrative command and an undeniable contemporary relevance. Our favorite novelists are as eclectic as our minds are broad, yet they all share one common denominator that might explain a peculiar predisposition for what we prefer to call 'emotional fiction'—a brand of storytelling defined not so much by a novel's category as by its extraordinary power to resonate universally on a deeply emotional level." Does not want to receive academic textbooks, children's books, cozy mysteries, horror, poetry, science fiction/fantasy, short story collections, Western's, screenplays, genre romance or previously self-published works.

How to Contact Submit book summary (1-2 paragraphs), chapter outline (nonfiction only), first 1,000 words or first chapter, total page/word count, brief paragraph on why you have chosen to write the book. Send via e-mail only (no attachments). Responds in 2-3 weeks to queries; 3 months to mss. Obtains most new clients through recommendations from others, solicitations, conferences.

Terms Agent receives 15% commission on domestic sales; 20% commission on foreign sales. Offers written contract; 1-month notice must be given to terminate contract.

Writers' Conferences Surrey International Writers' Conference; Southern California Writers' Conference; Naples Writers' Conference, et al.

◖ AUTHENTIC CREATIONS LITERARY AGENCY

911 Duluth Hwy., Suite D3-144, Lawrenceville GA 30043. (770)339-3774. Fax: (770)339-7126. E-mail: ron@authenticcreations.com. Website: www.authenticcreations.com. **Contact:** Mary Lee Laitsch. Estab. 1993. Member of AAR, Authors Guild. Represents 70 clients. 30% of clients are new/unpublished writers. Currently handles: 60% nonfiction books; 40% novels.

Member Agents Mary Lee Laitsch; Ronald Laitsch; Jason Laitsch.

Represents Nonfiction books, novels, scholarly books. **Considers these nonfiction areas:** Anthropology/archaeology; biography/autobiography; child guidance/parenting; crafts/hobbies; current affairs; history; how-to; science/technology; self-help/personal improvement; sports; true crime/investigative; women's issues/studies. **Considers these fiction areas:** Action/adventure; detective/police/crime; family saga; literary; mainstream/contemporary; mystery/suspense; romance; sports; thriller.

How to Contact Query with SASE. No e-mail or fax queries. Considers simultaneous queries. Responds in 2 weeks to queries; 2 months to mss.

Recent Sales Sold 20 titles in the last year. *Secret Agent*, by Robyn Spizman and Mark Johnston (Simon & Schuster); *Beauchamp Beseiged*, by Elaine Knighton (Harlequin); *Visible Differences*, by Dominic Pulera (Continuum).

Terms Agent receives 15% commission on domestic sales; 15% commission on foreign sales. This agency charges clients for photocopying.

◖ AVENUE A LITERARY

419 Lafayette St., Third Floor, New York NY 10003. (212)624-5859. Fax: (212)228-6149. E-mail: submissions@avenuealiterary.com. Website: www.avenuealiterary.com. **Contact:** Jennifer Cayea. Estab. 2006. Represents 20 clients. 75% of clients are new/unpublished writers. Currently handles: 40% nonfiction books; 45% novels; 5% story collections; 10% juvenile books.

● Prior to opening her agency, Ms. Cayea was an agent and director of foreign rights for Nicholas Ellison, Inc., a division of Sanford J. Greenburger Associates. She was also an editor in the audio and large print divisions of Random House.

Represents Nonfiction books, novels, short story collections, juvenile books. **Considers these nonfiction areas:** Cooking/foods/nutrition; current affairs; ethnic/cultural interests; health/medicine; history; memoirs; music/dance; popular culture; self-help/personal improvement; sports; theater/film. **Considers these fiction areas:** Family saga; feminist; historical; literary; mainstream/contemporary; thriller; young adult; women's/chick lit.

O⌐ "Our authors are dynamic and diverse. We seek strong new voices in fiction and nonfiction, and are fiercely dedicated to our authors."

How to Contact Query with SASE, submit synopsis, publishing history, author bio, full contact info. Paste info in e-mail body. No attachments. Accepts e-mail queries. No fax queries. Considers simultaneous queries. Responds in 8 weeks to queries. Returns materials only with SASE. Obtains most new clients through recommendations from others, solicitations, conferences.

Recent Sales Two young adult novels, by Sofia Quintero (Knopf). Other clients include K.L. Cook, Dr. Raeleen D'Agostino, Elisha Miranda, Mario Bosquez, Jennifer Calderon, Daniel Serrano, Yasmin Davidds.
Terms Agent receives 15% commission on domestic sales; 15% commission on foreign sales. Offers written contract; 30-day notice must be given to terminate contract.
Tips ''Build a résumé by publishing short stories if you are a fiction writer.''

THE AXELROD AGENCY

55 Main St., P.O. Box 357, Chatham NY 12037. (518)392-2100. Fax: (518)392-2944. E-mail: steve@axelrodagenc y.com. **Contact:** Steven Axelrod. Estab. 1983. Member of AAR. Represents 20-30 clients. 1% of clients are new/unpublished writers. Currently handles: 5% nonfiction books; 95% novels.

  • Prior to becoming an agent, Mr. Axelrod was a book club editor.

Represents Nonfiction books, novels. **Considers these fiction areas:** Mystery/suspense; romance; women's.
How to Contact Query with SASE. Considers simultaneous queries. Responds in 3 weeks to queries; 6 weeks to mss. Returns materials only with SASE. Obtains most new clients through recommendations from others.
Recent Sales This agency prefers not to share information on specific sales.
Terms Agent receives 15% commission on domestic sales; 20% commission on foreign sales. No written contract.
Writers' Conferences RWA National Conference.

BAKER'S MARK LITERARY AGENCY

P.O. Box 8382, Portland OR 97207. (503)432-8170. E-mail: info@bakersmark.com. Website: www.Bakersmark. com. **Contact:** Bernadette Baker or Gretchen Stelter. Estab. 2005. Currently handles: 35% nonfiction books; 25% novels; 40% graphic novels.

  • Prior to becoming an agent, Ms. Baker received an M.S. in professional writing and publishing from Portland State University. She was the marketing director for Beyond Words Publishing—where she headed up marketing campaigns for two *New York Times* bestsellers. Ms. Stelter has worked as a freelance editor and writer for several Australian newspapers and Bond University; she also worked for Ooligan Press.

Represents Nonfiction books, novels, novellas, scholarly books, animation, anthologies, graphic novels (preferably with art). **Considers these nonfiction areas:** Anthropology/archaeology; biography/autobiography; business/economics; ethnic/cultural interests; gay/lesbian issues; government/politics/law; how-to; humor/satire; popular culture; true crime/investigative; women's issues/studies. **Considers these fiction areas:** Comic books/cartoon; detective/police/crime; erotica; ethnic; experimental; fantasy; feminist; gay/lesbian; glitz; historical; horror; humor/satire; literary; mainstream/contemporary; mystery/suspense; psychic/supernatural; regional (Pacific Northwest); thriller; women's; chick lit.

  ○→ ''Baker's Mark specializes in graphic novels and popular nonfiction with an extremely selective taste in commercial fiction.'' Actively seeking graphic novels, nonfiction, fiction. Does not want to receive Western, poetry, sci-fi or children's.

How to Contact Query with SASE, submit proposal package, synopsis, 5 sample chapter(s), author bio, sample art and script for graphic novels. No fax queries. Considers simultaneous queries. Returns materials only with SASE. Obtains most new clients through recommendations from others, solicitations.
Recent Sales *City of Readers: A Book Lover's Guide to Portland, Oregon*, by Gabriel Boehmer (Tall Grass Press); *Unaffordable Nation: Searching for a Decent Life in America*, by Jeffrey D. Jones (Prometheus Books); *German Town* and *The Fielding Course*, both graphic novels, by Laurence Klavan and Susan Kim (:01 First Second Books); *The Wrenchies*, by Farel Dalrymple (:01 First Second Books).
Terms Agent receives 15% commission on domestic sales; 20% commission on foreign sales. Offers written contract, binding for 18 months; 30-day notice must be given to terminate contract.
Writers' Conferences New York Comic Convention, BookExpo of America, San Diego Comic Con, Stumptown Comics Fest, Emerald City Comic Con.

BALKIN AGENCY, INC.

P.O. Box 222, Amherst MA 01004. (413)548-9835. Fax: (413)548-9836. E-mail: rick62838@crocker.com. **Contact:** Rick Balkin, president. Estab. 1972. Member of AAR. Represents 50 clients. 10% of clients are new/unpublished writers. Currently handles: 90% nonfiction books; 5% scholarly books; 5% reference books.

  • Prior to opening his agency, Mr. Balkin served as executive editor with Bobbs-Merrill Company.

Represents Nonfiction books, scholarly books. **Considers these nonfiction areas:** Animals; anthropology/archaeology; current affairs; health/medicine; history; how-to; nature/environment; popular culture; science/technology; sociology; translation; biography.

  ○→ This agency specializes in adult nonfiction. Does not want to receive fiction, poetry, screenplays or computer books.

How to Contact Query with SASE, submit proposal package, outline. Accepts e-mail queries. No fax queries.

Responds in 1 week to queries; 2 weeks to mss. Returns materials only with SASE. Obtains most new clients through recommendations from others.

Recent Sales Sold 30 titles in the last year. *The Many Faces of God*, by (W.W. Norton Co.); *A Perfect Mess*, by Eric Abrahamson and David H. Freedman (Little Brown); *Playing God*, by Noah Efron (Harvard Univ. Press).

Terms Agent receives 15% commission on domestic sales; 20% commission on foreign sales. Offers written contract, binding for 1 year. This agency charges clients for photocopying and express or foreign mail.

Tips "I do not take on books described as bestsellers or potential bestsellers. Any nonfiction work that is either unique, paradigmatic, a contribution, truly witty, or a labor of love is grist for my mill."

✪ THE PAULA BALZER AGENCY

55 Eastern Parkway, #5H, Brooklyn NY 11238. (347)787-4131. E-mail: info@pbliterary.com. Website: www.pbli terary.com. **Contact:** Paula Balzer. Member of AAR. Represents 35 clients. 50% of clients are new/unpublished writers. Currently handles: 50% nonfiction books; 50% novels.

• Prior to her current position, Ms. Balzer was with Carlisle & Company, as well as Sarah Lazin Books.

Represents Nonfiction books, novels. **Considers these nonfiction areas:** Biography/autobiography; child guidance/parenting; cooking/foods/nutrition; current affairs; education; gay/lesbian issues; government/politics/law; history; how-to; humor/satire; memoirs; popular culture; psychology; science/technology; self-help/personal improvement; women's issues/studies. **Considers these fiction areas:** Erotica; family saga; gay/lesbian; glitz; historical; horror; humor/satire; literary; mainstream/contemporary; mystery/suspense; thriller; women's.

○┱ Humor and popular culture.

How to Contact Query with SASE, submit proposal package, author bio, 50 sample pages. Accepts e-mail queries. No fax queries. Responds in 3 weeks to queries; 4-6 weeks to mss. Returns materials only with SASE. Obtains most new clients through recommendations from others.

Recent Sales *Separated*, by Sheldon Rusch (Berkley); *Pledged: The Secret Life of Sororities*, by Alexandra Robbins (Hyperion); *Quarterlife Crisis: The Unique Challenges of Life in Your Twenties*, by Alexandra Robbins (Penguin Putnam); *Dear Mrs. Lindbergh: A Novel*, by Kathleen Hughes (W.W. Norton & Company).

Terms Agent receives 15% commission on domestic sales; 20% commission on foreign sales. Offers written contract.

✪ BARER LITERARY, LLC

270 Lafayette St., Suite 1504, New York NY 10012. Website: www.barerliterary.com. **Contact:** Julie Barer. Member of AAR.

Represents Nonfiction books, novels, short story collections. **Considers these nonfiction areas:** Biography/autobiography; ethnic/cultural interests; history; memoirs; popular culture; women's issues/studies. **Considers these fiction areas:** Ethnic; family saga; historical; literary; mainstream/contemporary.

○┱ This agency no longer accepts young adult submissions.

How to Contact Query with SASE.

Recent Sales *A Ticket to Ride*, by Paula McLain (Ecco); *What You Have Left*, by Will Allison (Free Press); *Still Life With Husband*, by Lauren Fox (Knopf); *Then We Came to the End*, by Joshua Ferris (Little, Brown); *Frenemies*, by Megan Crane (Warner Books); *The Time It Takes to Fall*, by Margaret Lazarus Dean (Simon & Schuster).

Terms Agent receives 15% commission on domestic sales; 20% commission on foreign sales. Offers written contract. Charges for photocopying and books ordered.

✪ LORETTA BARRETT BOOKS, INC.

101 Fifth Ave., New York NY 10003. (212)242-3420. Fax: (212)807-9579. E-mail: query@lorettabarrettbooks.c om. Website: www.lorettabarrettbooks.com. **Contact:** Loretta A. Barrett, Nick Mullendore. Estab. 1990. Member of AAR. Currently handles: 50% nonfiction books; 50% novels.

• Prior to opening her agency, Ms. Barrett was vice president and executive editor at Doubleday and editor-in-chief of Anchor Books.

Member Agents Loretta A. Barrett; Nick Mullendore; Gabriel Davis.

Represents Nonfiction books, novels. **Considers these nonfiction areas:** Biography/autobiography; child guidance/parenting; current affairs; ethnic/cultural interests; government/politics/law; health/medicine; history; memoirs; money/finance; multicultural; nature/environment; popular culture; psychology; religious/inspirational; science/technology; self-help/personal improvement; sociology; spirituality; sports; women's issues/studies; nutrition; creative nonfiction. **Considers these fiction areas:** Action/adventure; contemporary issues; detective/police/crime; ethnic; family saga; historical; literary; mainstream/contemporary; mystery/suspense; psychic/supernatural; thriller.

O-π This agency specializes in general interest books. No children's, juvenile, science fiction, or fantasy.
How to Contact Query with SASE. Accepts e-mail queries. No fax queries. Considers simultaneous queries. Responds in 2-3 weeks to queries. Returns materials only with SASE.
Recent Sales *Spiritual Progress*, by Thomas D. Williams (Hachette); *The Hazards of Space Travel*, by Neil Comins (Ballantine); *Mother Angelica's Little Book of Life Lessons*, by Raymond Arroyo (Doubleday) and more.
Terms Agent receives 15% commission on domestic sales; 20% commission on foreign sales. Offers written contract. Charges clients for shipping and photocopying.

◑ BARRON'S LITERARY MANAGEMENT

4615 Rockland Drive, Arlington TX 76016. E-mail: barronsliterary@sbcglobal.net. **Contact:** Adele Barron-Brooks, president.
Represents Nonfiction books, novels. **Considers these nonfiction areas:** Cooking/foods/nutrition; government/politics/law; health/medicine; history; science/technology; business, investing, small business marketing, cook books, dating and relationships. **Considers these fiction areas:** Detective/police/crime; mystery/suspense; romance; science fiction; medical and legal thrillers, historical, chick lit, contemporary suspense, paranormal.

O-π "Barron's Literary Management is a small Dallas/Fort Worth-based agency with good contacts in New York and London." Actively seeking tightly written, fast moving fiction, as well as authors with a significant platform or subject area expertise for nonfiction book concepts.
How to Contact Contact by e-mail initially. Send only a brief synopsis of your story or a proposal for nonfiction. Accepts e-mail queries. No fax queries. Obtains most new clients through recommendations from others, solicitations.
Tips "I strongly favor a e-mail queries. Have your book tightly edited, polished and ready to be seen before contacting agents. I respond quickly and if interested may request an electronic or hard copy mailing."

◎ VIVIAN BECK AGENCY

124 Zandra Ave., Lyons GA 30436-4006. Fax: (912)526-6112. Website: www.vivianbeck.com. **Contact:** Vivian Beck. Estab. 2005. Member of RWA; adheres to AAR canon of ethics. Currently handles: 100% novels.
● Prior to her current position, Ms. Beck took an apprenticeship with the Ferguson Literary Agency. She has more than 21 years combined professional experience as a literary agent, editor, writer and bookseller.
Represents Novels. **Considers these fiction areas:** Romance; science fiction; thriller; women's.

O-π Does not want to receive short stories, novellas, poetry, autobiographies, nonfiction, self-help or erotica.
How to Contact As of early 2008, this agency was not taking unsolicited queries. Check the Web site for more info. Responds in 1 month to queries. Obtains most new clients through recommendations from others, solicitations.
Recent Sales *Tempted by Innocence*, by Linda Raper (Harlequin Mills & Boon); *Warrior or Wife*, by Linda Raper (Mills & Boon); *Maidensong*, by Diana Groe (Leisure).

⊕ ◐ LORELLA BELLI LITERARY AGENCY

54 Hartford House, 35 Tavistock Crescent, Notting Hill, London England W11 1AY, United Kingdom. (44)(207)727-8547. Fax: (44)(870)787-4194. E-mail: info@lorellabelliagency.com. Website: www.lorellabelliagency.com. **Contact:** Lorella Belli. Estab. 2002. Member of AAA.
Represents Nonfiction books, novels. **Considers these nonfiction areas:** Business/economics; current affairs; history; science/technology; self-help/personal improvement; travel; women's issues/studies; politics; food/wine; popular music; lifestyle. **Considers these fiction areas:** Historical; literary; genre fiction; women's; crime.

O-π "We are interested in first-time novelists, journalists, multicultural and international writing, and books about Italy." Does not want children's books, fantasy, science fiction, screenplays, short stories, or poetry.
How to Contact For fiction, send query letter, first 3 chapters, synopsis, brief CV, SASE. For nonfiction, send query letter, full proposal, chapter outline, 2 sample chapters, SASE. Accepts initial query letters via e-mail. Send all submissions via postal mail.
Terms Agent receives 15% commission on domestic sales; 20% commission on foreign sales.

◐ FAYE BENDER LITERARY AGENCY

337 W. 76th St., #E1, New York NY 10023. E-mail: info@fbliterary.com. Website: www.fbliterary.com. **Contact:** Faye Bender. Estab. 2004. Member of AAR.
Represents Nonfiction books, novels, juvenile books. **Considers these nonfiction areas:** Memoirs; popular culture; women's issues/studies; young adult; narrative; health; biography; popular science. **Considers these fiction areas:** Literary; young adult (middle-grade); women's; commercial.

○➤ "I choose books based on the narrative voice and strength of writing. I work with previously published and first-time authors." Does not want to receive genre fiction (Western, romance, horror, fantasy, science fiction).

How to Contact Query with SASE and 10 sample pages via mail or e-mail. No fax queries.

Recent Sales *Science Experiments*, by Karen Romano Young (National Geographic Society); *The Last Beach Bungalow*, by Jennie Nash (Berkley).

Tips "Please keep your letters to the point, include all relevant information, and have a bit of patience."

◢ BENNETT & WEST LITERARY AGENCY

1004 San Felipe Lane, The Villages FL 32159. (352)751-2314. E-mail: joanpwest@comcast.net. Website: www.bennettwestlit.com. **Contact:** Joan West or Lois Bennett. Estab. 2005; adheres to AAR canon of ethics. Represents 80 clients. 60% of clients are new/unpublished writers. Currently handles: 30% nonfiction books; 65% novels; 5% juvenile books.

● Prior to becoming an agent, Ms. West was a college professor and editor; Ms. Bennett was a psychologist and writer.

Member Agents Joan West (fiction, nonfiction, no juvenile or YA); Lois Bennett (YA and fiction, no nonfiction).

Represents Nonfiction books, novels, juvenile books (YA). **Considers these nonfiction areas:** Biography/autobiography; memoirs; military/war; New Age/metaphysics; self-help/personal improvement; sociology; sports; true crime/investigative; women's issues/studies. **Considers these fiction areas:** Action/adventure; detective/police/crime; family saga; fantasy; historical; juvenile; literary; mainstream/contemporary; mystery/suspense; psychic/supernatural; regional; romance; science fiction; sports; thriller; young adult.

○➤ "We are sensitive to the writer's needs and friendly to new writers." Does not want to receive erotica, horror, screenplays, picture books or academic.

How to Contact Query with SASE, submit proposal package, outline/proposal, synopsis, 3 sample chapter(s), author bio, indication whether a reply via e-mail is acceptable. Query only, if contacting by e-mail. Submit all YA to Ms. Bennett and all nonfiction to Ms. West. Accepts e-mail queries. No fax queries. Considers simultaneous queries. Responds in 2-4 weeks to queries. Returns materials only with SASE. Obtains most new clients through recommendations from others.

Recent Sales *From the Depths*, by Gerry Doyle; *Into the Woods*, by RR Smythe; *Marie Antoinette, Diana and Alexandra: The Third*, by Alexandra Levin; *The Flame of Learning: The Life of Louise Pound*, by Marie Krohn.

Terms Agent receives 15% commission on domestic sales; 20% commission on foreign sales. Offers written contract, binding for 1 year; 30-day notice must be given to terminate contract. Charges for postage and copying fees (five cents per page) for material sent to publishers.

Writers' Conferences The Villages Literary Festival; Gulf Coast Writers' Conference; Florida First Coast Writers' Conference.

Tips "Proofread and edit your material. Be sure you have your submission in the proper format. Please reference our guidelines for format. Nonfiction writers must have appropriate credentials."

◢ BENREY LITERARY

P.O. Box 812, Columbia MD 21044. (443)545-5620. Fax: (886)297-9483. E-mail: query@benreyliterary.com. Website: www.benreyliterary.com. **Contact:** Janet Benrey. Estab. 2006. Represents 35 clients. 20% of clients are new/unpublished writers. Currently handles: 50% nonfiction books; 50% novels.

● Prior to her current position, Ms. Benrey was with the Hartline Literary Agency.

Represents Nonfiction books, novels, scholarly books (narrow focus). **Considers these nonfiction areas:** How-to; religious/inspirational; self-help/personal improvement; true crime/investigative. **Considers these fiction areas:** Action/adventure; detective/police/crime; family saga; literary; mainstream/contemporary; mystery/suspense; religious/inspirational; romance; thriller; women's.

○➤ This agency's specialties include romance, women's fiction, mystery, true crime, thriller (secular and Christian), as well as Christian living, church resources, inspirational. Actively seeking women's fiction, romance, mystery, suspense, Christian living, church resources. Does not want to receive fantasy, science fiction, Christian speculative fiction, erotica or paranormal.

How to Contact Query with SASE, submit proposal package, synopsis, 3 sample chapter(s), author bio. More submission details available online. Accepts e-mail queries. No fax queries. Considers simultaneous queries. Responds in 6 weeks to queries; 3 months to mss. Returns materials only with SASE. Obtains most new clients through recommendations from others, solicitations, conferences.

Recent Sales Sold 30 titles in the last year. *Hunt Club*, by Lisa Landolt (Avon); *Soldier on the Porch*, by Sharon Wildwind (Five Star); *In the Dead of Winter*, by Nancy Mehl (Barbour); *A Bird in the Hand*, by Nancy Mehl (Barbour). Agent receives 15% commission on domestic sales; 20% commission on foreign sales. Offers written contract; 30-day notice must be given to terminate contract. "We pass on the out-of-pocket costs of copying and shipping manuscripts for new clients until we have made their first sales."

Tips "Understand the market as best you can. Attend conferences and network. Don't create a new genre."

◙ MEREDITH BERNSTEIN LITERARY AGENCY

2095 Broadway, Suite 505, New York NY 10023. (212)799-1007. Fax: (212)799-1145. Estab. 1981. Member of AAR. Represents 85 clients. 20% of clients are new/unpublished writers. Currently handles: 50% nonfiction books; 50% fiction.

• Prior to opening her agency, Ms. Bernstein served at another agency for 5 years.

Represents Nonfiction books, novels. **Considers these nonfiction areas:** Any area of nonfiction in which the author has an established platform. **Considers these fiction areas:** Literary; mystery/suspense; romance; thriller; women's.

O⌐ This agency does not specialize. It is very eclectic.

How to Contact Query with SASE. No e-mail or fax queries. Considers simultaneous queries. Obtains most new clients through recommendations from others, conferences, developing/packaging ideas.

Recent Sales Three untitled thrillers, by Jordan Dane (Avon); Three untitled House of Night spinoff books, by PC Cast and Kristen Cast (St. Martin's Press); Untitled work, by Susan Shapiro (St. Martin's); *Home from the Honeymoon*, by Sharon Naylor (Stewart, Tabori & Chang).

Terms Agent receives 15% commission on domestic sales; 20% commission on foreign sales. Charges clients $75 disbursement fee/year.

Writers' Conferences Southwest Writers' Conference; Rocky Mountain Fiction Writers' Colorado Gold; Pacific Northwest Writers' Conference; Willamette Writers' Conference; Surrey International Writers' Conference; San Diego State University Writers' Conference.

◙ VICKY BIJUR LITERARY AGENCY

333 West End Ave., Apt. 5B, New York NY 10023. E-mail: assistant@vickybijuragency.com. Member of AAR.

Represents Nonfiction books, novels. **Considers these nonfiction areas:** Cooking/foods/nutrition; government/politics/law; health/medicine; history; psychology (psychiatry); science/technology; self-help/personal improvement; sociology; biography; child care/development; environmental studies; journalism; social sciences.

O⌐ Does not want science fiction, fantasy, horror, romance, poetry, children's or YA.

How to Contact Accepts e-mail queries.

◙ DAVID BLACK LITERARY AGENCY

156 Fifth Ave., Suite 608, New York NY 10010-7002. (212)242-5080. Fax: (212)924-6609. **Contact:** David Black, owner. Estab. 1990. Member of AAR. Represents 150 clients. Currently handles: 90% nonfiction books; 10% novels.

Member Agents David Black; Susan Raihofer (general nonfiction, literary fiction); Gary Morris (commercial fiction, psychology); Joy E. Tutela (general nonfiction, literary fiction); Leigh Ann Eliseo; Linda Loewenthal (general nonfiction, health, science, psychology, narrative).

Represents Nonfiction books, novels. **Considers these nonfiction areas:** Biography/autobiography; business/economics; government/politics/law; health/medicine; history; memoirs; military/war; money/finance; multicultural; psychology; religious/inspirational; sports; women's issues/studies. **Considers these fiction areas:** Literary; mainstream/contemporary; commercial.

O⌐ This agency specializes in business, sports, politics, and novels.

How to Contact Query with SASE, outline. No e-mail or fax queries. Considers simultaneous queries. Responds in 2 months to queries. Returns materials only with SASE.

Recent Sales *Body for Life*, by Bill Phillips with Mike D'Orso (HarperCollins); *Devil in the White City*, by Erik Larson; The Don't Know Much About series by Ken Davis; *Tuesdays with Morrie*, by Mitch Albom.

Terms Agent receives 15% commission on domestic sales. Charges clients for photocopying and books purchased for sale of foreign rights.

◙ BLISS LITERARY AGENCY INTERNATIONAL, INC.

1601 N. Sepulveda Blvd, #389, Manhattan Beach CA 90266. E-mail: query@blissliterary.com. Website: www.blissliterary.com. **Contact:** Jenoyne Adams. Estab. 2007.

Member Agents Prior to her current position, Ms. Adams was with Levine Greenberg Literary Agency.

Represents Nonfiction books, novels, juvenile books. **Considers these nonfiction areas:** Narrative nonfiction, women's, parenting. **Considers these fiction areas:** Literary; multicultural; commercial.

O⌐ "Middle grade, YA fiction and nonfiction, young reader? Bring it on. We absolutely adore these categories. We are interested in developing and working on projects that run the gamut—fantasy, urban/edgy, serious, bling-blingy? SURE. We love it all. And we haven't found it yet, but with a deep appreciation for anime and martial arts flicks, we are looking for the perfect graphic novel."

How to Contact Query via e-mail or snail mail. Send query, synopsis, one chapter. No attachments. Responds in 8 weeks to queries.

Tips Non-query related matters can be addressed by e-mailing info@blissliterary.com.

☑ THE BLUMER LITERARY AGENCY, INC.

350 Seventh Ave., Suite 2003, New York NY 10001-5013. (212)947-3040. **Contact:** Olivia B. Blumer. Estab. 2002. Member of AAR. Represents 34 clients. 60% of clients are new/unpublished writers. Currently handles: 67% nonfiction books; 33% novels.

- Prior to becoming an agent, Ms. Blumer spent 25 years in publishing (subsidiary rights, publicity, editorial).

Represents Nonfiction books, novels. **Considers these nonfiction areas:** Agriculture/horticulture; animals; anthropology/archaeology; art/architecture/design; biography/autobiography; business/economics; cooking/foods/nutrition; ethnic/cultural interests; health/medicine; how-to; humor/satire; language/literature/criticism; memoirs; money/finance; nature/environment; photography; popular culture; psychology; religious/inspirational; self-help/personal improvement; true crime/investigative; women's issues/studies; New Age/metaphysics; crafts/hobbies; interior design/decorating. **Considers these fiction areas:** Detective/police/crime; ethnic; family saga; feminist; historical; humor/satire; literary; mainstream/contemporary; mystery/suspense; regional; thriller.

- ⚲ Actively seeking quality fiction, practical nonfiction, and memoir with a larger purpose.

How to Contact Query with SASE. No e-mail or fax queries. Responds in 3 weeks to queries; 4-6 weeks to mss. Returns materials only with SASE. Obtains most new clients through recommendations from others, but significant exceptions have come from the slush pile.

Recent Sales *The Color of Law*, by Mark Gimenez; *Still Life with Chickens*, by Catherine Goldhammer; *Demolition Desserts*, by Elizabeth Falkner; *Fat* by Jennifer McLagan; *Carpool Diem*, by Nancy Star. Other clients include Joan Anderson, Marialisa Calta, Ellen Rolfes, Laura Karr, Liz McGregor, Lauri Ward, Susann Cokal, Dennis L. Smith, Sharon Pywell, Sarah Turnbull, Naomi Duguid, Jeffrey Alford.

Terms Agent receives 15% commission on domestic sales; 20% commission on foreign sales. Charges for photocopying, overseas shipping, FedEx/UPS.

☑ THE BLYTHE AGENCY

25 Washington St., Ste 614, Brooklyn NY 11201. (718)781-6489. Website: www.blythe-agency.com. **Contact:** Rolph Blythe. Estab. 2006. Member of AAR.

- Prior to his current position, Mr. Blythe was an agent with Dunow, Carlson & Lerner Literary Agency.

Represents Nonfiction books, novels. **Considers these nonfiction areas:** Biography/autobiography; history; memoirs; narrative nonfiction. **Considers these fiction areas:** Detective/police/crime; literary; mystery/suspense; thriller.

- ⚲ This agency is currently closed to new submissions. Keep checking the Web site to learn more.

How to Contact No e-mail or fax queries.

Recent Sales *Four-Letter Words and Other Secrets of Crossword Puzzle Champions*, by Michelle Arnot (Perigee); *Madly*, by William Benton.

Terms Agent receives 15% commission on domestic sales; 20% commission on foreign sales.

☑ BOND LITERARY AGENCY

Denver CO. **Contact:** Sandra Bond.

- Prior to her current position, Ms. Bond worked with agent Jody Rein.

Represents Nonfiction books, novels. **Considers these nonfiction areas:** Business/economics; health/medicine; history; science/technology; narrative nonfiction. **Considers these fiction areas:** Literary; general fiction, mystery, juvenile fiction.

- ⚲ "Unfortunately, my client list is currently closed and I am not considering any new submissions. Please check back later."

How to Contact Do not send queries or materials to this agent until she opens her client list.

Recent Sales *Her Story: A Timeline of the Women Who Changed America*, by Charlotte Waisman and Jill Tietjen (HarperCollins); *Write Tight*, by William Brohaugh (Sourcebooks); *Everything You Know About English is Wrong*, by William Brouhaugh; *The Football Uncyclopedia*, by Michael Kun and Adam Hoff (Clerisy Press).

Ⓝ ☑ BOOK CENTS LITERARY AGENCY, LLC

2011 Quarrier Street, Charleston WV 25311. (304)347-2330, ext. 1105. E-mail: cwitthohn@hotmail.com. Website: www.bookcentsliteraryagency.com. **Contact:** Christine Witthohn. Estab. 2006.

- ⚲ Actively seeking Single Title Romance (Contemporary, Romantic Comedy, Women's Lit, Paranormal, Mystery/Suspense), Mainstream Mystery/Suspense, Medical or Legal Fiction, Espionage. Does not want to receive Category Romance, Erotica, Inspirational, Historical, Sci-fi/Fantasy, Horror/Dark Thrillers, Screenplays.

🔒 BOOKENDS, LLC

136 Long Hill Rd., Gillette NJ 07933. Website: www.bookends-inc.com; bookendslitagency.blogspot.com. **Contact:** Jessica Faust, Jacky Sach, Kim Lionetti. Estab. 1999. Member of AAR. Represents 50+ clients. 10% of clients are new/unpublished writers. Currently handles: 50% nonfiction books; 50% novels.
Member Agents Jessica Faust (fiction: romance, erotica, chick lit, women's fiction, mysterious and suspense; nonfiction: business, finance, career, parenting, psychology, women's issues, self-help, health, sex); Jacky Sach (mysteries, women's fiction, suspense, self-help, spirituality, alternative and mainstream health, business and career, addiction, chick-lit nonfiction).
Represents Nonfiction books, novels. **Considers these nonfiction areas:** Business/economics; child guidance/parenting; ethnic/cultural interests; gay/lesbian issues; health/medicine; how-to; money/finance; New Age/metaphysics; psychology; religious/inspirational; self-help/personal improvement; sex; spirituality; true crime/investigative; women's issues/studies. **Considers these fiction areas:** Detective/police/crime (cozies); mainstream/contemporary; mystery/suspense; romance; thriller; women's; chick lit.
- ⚷ BookEnds does not want to receive children's books, screenplays, science fiction, poetry, or technical/military thrillers.

How to Contact Review Web site for guidelines, as they change. Accepts e-mail queries. No fax queries.
Recent Sales *1,000 Wine Secrets*, by Carolyn Hammond (Sourcebooks); *Wolf Tales III*, by Kate Douglas (Kensington Aphrodisia); *Women at Ground Zero*, by Mary Carouba and Susan Hagen (Alpha Books).

🔒 BOOKS & SUCH LITERARY AGENCY

52 Mission Circle, Suite 122, PMB 170, Santa Rosa CA 95409. E-mail: (agentfirstname)@booksandsuch.biz. Website: www.booksandsuch.biz. **Contact:** Janet Kobobel Grant, Wendy Lawton. Estab. 1996. Member of CBA (associate), American Christian Fiction Writers. Represents 80 clients. 5% of clients are new/unpublished writers. Currently handles: 50% nonfiction books; 50% novels.
- Prior to becoming an agent, Ms. Grant was an editor for Zondervan and managing editor for *Focus on the Family*; Ms. Lawton was an author, sculptor and designer of porcelein dolls.

Represents Nonfiction books, novels. **Considers these nonfiction areas:** Child guidance/parenting; humor/satire; religious/inspirational; self-help/personal improvement; women's issues/studies. **Considers these fiction areas:** Contemporary issues; family saga; historical; mainstream/contemporary; religious/inspirational; romance; African American adult.
- ⚷ This agency specializes in general and inspirational fiction, romance, and in the Christian booksellers market. Actively seeking well-crafted material that presents Judeo-Christian values, if only subtly.

How to Contact Query with SASE. Considers simultaneous queries. Responds in 1 month to queries; 2 months to mss. Returns materials only with SASE. Obtains most new clients through recommendations from others, conferences.
Recent Sales Sold 112 titles in the last year. *Awaken My Heart*, by Diann Mills (Avon Inspire); *My Life As a Doormat (In Three Acts)*, by Rene Gutteridge; *Having a Mary Spirit*, by Joanna Weaver; *Finding Father Christmas*, by Robin Jones Gunn; *No More Mr. Christian Nice Guy*, by Paul Coughlin. Other clients include Janet McHenry, Jane Orcutt, Gayle Roper, Stephanie Grace Whitson, Dale Cramer, Patti Hill, Gayle Roper, Sara Horn.
Terms Agent receives 15% commission on domestic sales; 15% commission on foreign sales. Offers written contract; 2-month notice must be given to terminate contract. Charges clients for postage, photocopying, telephone calls, fax, express mail.
Writers' Conferences Mount Hermon Christian Writers' Conference; Wrangling With Writing; Glorieta Christian Writers' Conference; Writing for the Soul; Blue Ridge Mountains Christian Writers' Conference; American Christian Fiction Writers' Conference; Sandy Cove Christian Writers' Conference; San Francisco Writers' Conference.
Tips "The heart of our agency's motivation is to develop relationships with the authors we serve, to do what we can to shine the light of success on them, and to help be a caretaker of their gifts and time."

🔒 GEORGES BORCHARDT, INC.

136 E. 57th St., New York NY 10022. Estab. 1967. Member of AAR.
Member Agents Anne Borchardt; Georges Borchardt; Valerie Borchardt.
- ⚷ This agency specializes in literary fiction and outstanding nonfiction.

How to Contact *No unsolicited mss.* Obtains most new clients through recommendations from others.
Terms Agent receives 15% commission on domestic sales; 20% commission on foreign sales. Offers written contract.

🔒 THE BARBARA BOVA LITERARY AGENCY

P.O. Box 770365, Naples FL 34107. (941)649-7237. Fax: (239)649-7263. E-mail: barbarabova@barbarabovaliteraryagency.com. Website: www.barbarabovaliteraryagency.com. **Contact:** Barbara Bova, Marlene Stringer, Michael Burke. Estab. 1974. Represents 30 clients. Currently handles: 20% nonfiction books; 80% novels.

Represents Nonfiction books, novels. **Considers these nonfiction areas:** Biography/autobiography; history; science/technology; self-help/personal improvement; true crime/investigative; women's issues/studies; social sciences. **Considers these fiction areas:** Action/adventure; detective/police/crime; mystery/suspense; science fiction; thriller; young adult; women's; teen lit.

O→ This agency specializes in fiction and nonfiction, hard and soft science.

How to Contact Query through website. Obtains most new clients through recommendations from others.

Recent Sales Sold 24 titles in the last year. *The Green Trap* and *The Aftermath*, by Ben Bova; *Empire* and *A War of Gifts*, by Orson Scott Card; *Radioman*, by Carol E. Hipperson.

Terms Agent receives 15% commission on domestic sales; 20% commission on foreign sales.

Tips "We also handle foreign, movie, television, and audio rights."

BRADFORD LITERARY AGENCY

5694 Mission Center Road, #347, San Diego CA 92108. (619)521-1201. E-mail: laura@bradfordlit.com. Website: www.bradfordlit.com. **Contact:** Laura Bradford. Estab. 2001. Represents 23 clients. 20% of clients are new/ unpublished writers. Currently handles: 10% nonfiction books; 90% novels.

• Ms. Bradford started with her first literary agency straight out of college and has 13 years of experience as a bookseller in parallel.

Represents Nonfiction books, novels, novellas (within a single author's collection), anthology. **Considers these nonfiction areas:** Business/economics; child guidance/parenting; current affairs; government/politics/law; health/medicine; history; how-to; memoirs; money/finance; popular culture; psychology; religious/inspirational; self-help/personal improvement; women's issues/studies. **Considers these fiction areas:** Action/adventure; detective/police/crime; erotica; ethnic; family saga; historical; humor/satire; mainstream/contemporary; mystery/suspense; religious/inspirational; romance; thriller; young adult; women's (and chick lit); psychic/supernatural.

O→ Actively seeking romance (including category), romantica, women's fiction, mystery, thrillers and young adult. Does not want to receive poetry, short stories, children's books (juvenile) or screenplays.

How to Contact Query with SASE, submit cover letter, first 30 pages of completed ms., synopsis and SASE. Send no attachments via e-mail; only send a query. Accepts e-mail queries. No fax queries. Considers simultaneous queries. Responds in 10 weeks to queries; 10 weeks to mss. Returns materials only with SASE. Obtains most new clients through solicitations.

Recent Sales Sold 8 titles in the last year. *Witch Heart*, by Anya Bast (Berkley Sensation); *Hotter After Midnight*, by Cynthia Eden (Kensington Brava); *Sweet and Sinful*, by Jodi Lynn Copeland; *Every Night I'm Yours*, by Christia Kelley; *Grimspace*, by Ann Aguirre (Ace); *Hawk's Talons*, by Vonna Harper.

Terms Agent receives 15% commission on domestic sales; 25% commission on foreign sales. Offers written contract, binding for 2 years; 45-day notice must be given to terminate contract. Charges for photocopies, postage, extra copies of books for submissions.

Writers' Conferences RWA National Conference; Romantic Times Booklovers Convention.

BRANDS-TO-BOOKS, INC.

419 Lafayette St., New York NY 10003. Website: www.brandstobooks.com. **Contact:** Kathleen Spinelli, Robert Allen. Estab. 2004. 70% of clients are new/unpublished writers. Currently handles: 100% nonfiction books.

• Prior to co-founding Brands-to-Books, Mr. Allen was president and publisher of the Random House Audio Division; Ms. Spinelli was vice president/director of marketing for Ballantine Books.

Member Agents Kathleen Spinelli, kspinelli@brandstobooks.com (lifestyle, design, business, personal finance, health, pop culture, sports, travel, cooking, crafts, how-to, reference); Robert Allen, rallen@brandstobooks.com (business, motivation, psychology, how-to, pop culture, self-help/personal improvement, narrative nonfiction).

Represents Nonfiction books, ghostwriters. **Considers these nonfiction areas:** Anthropology/archaeology; art/architecture/design; biography/autobiography; business/economics; child guidance/parenting; computers/ electronic; cooking/foods/nutrition; crafts/hobbies; current affairs; ethnic/cultural interests; gay/lesbian issues; government/politics/law; health/medicine; history; how-to; humor/satire; interior design/decorating; language/literature/criticism; memoirs; money/finance; music/dance; photography; popular culture; psychology; self-help/personal improvement; sports; theater/film; books based from brands.

O→ "We concentrate on brand-name businesses, products, and personalities whose platform, passion, and appeal translate into successful publishing ventures. We offer more than literary representation—we provide clients a true marketing partner, pursuing and maximizing every opportunity for promotion and sales within the publishing process." Actively seeking nonfiction proposals supported by strong media platforms and experienced ghostwriters—especially those who have worked with brands/personalities. Does not want fiction or poetry.

How to Contact E-Query with book overview, résumé/platform. Accepts e-mail queries. No fax queries. Considers simultaneous queries. Responds in 3 weeks to queries. Obtains most new clients through recommendations from others, outreach to brand managers and the licensing industry.

Recent Sales *The Travel Mom's Ultimate Book of Family Travel*, by Emily Kaufman (Broadway Books); *TV Guide: TV on DVD 2006*, by the editors of *TV Guide* (St. Martin's Press); *Signature Weddings: Creating a Day Uniquely Your Own*, by Michelle Rago (Gotham Books); *A Passion for Jewelry*, by Temple St. Clair (Regan Books).

Terms Agent receives 15% commission on domestic sales; 20% commission on foreign sales. Offers written contract; 3-month written notice must be given to terminate contract. Charges for office expenses (copying, messengers, express mail).

Tips "In your query, clearly show your passion for the subject and why you are the best person to write this book. Establish your media experience and platform. Indicate you have done your market research and demonstrate how this book is different from what is already on the shelves."

BRANDT & HOCHMAN LITERARY AGENTS, INC.

1501 Broadway, Suite 2310, New York NY 10036. (212)840-5760. Fax: (212)840-5776. **Contact:** Gail Hochman. Estab. 1913. Member of AAR. Represents 200 clients.

Member Agents Carl Brandt; Gail Hochman; Marianne Merola; Charles Schlessiger; Bill Contardi.

Represents Nonfiction books, novels, short story collections, juvenile books, journalism. **Considers these nonfiction areas:** Biography/autobiography; current affairs; ethnic/cultural interests; government/politics/law; history; women's issues/studies. **Considers these fiction areas:** Contemporary issues; ethnic; historical; literary; mainstream/contemporary; mystery/suspense; romance; thriller; young adult.

How to Contact Query with SASE. No e-mail or fax queries. Considers simultaneous queries. Responds in 1 month to queries. Returns materials only with SASE. Obtains most new clients through recommendations from others.

Recent Sales *Season of Betrayal*, by Margaret Lowrie Robertson (Harcourt); *The Misremembered Man*, by Christina McKenna (Toby Press). Other clients include Scott Turow, Carlos Fuentes, Ursula Hegi, Michael Cunningham, Mary Pope Osborne, Julia Glass.

Terms Agent receives 15% commission on domestic sales; 20% commission on foreign sales. Charges clients for ms duplication or other special expenses agreed to in advance.

Tips "Write a letter which will give the agent a sense of you as a professional writer—your long-term interests as well as a short description of the work at hand."

THE JOAN BRANDT AGENCY

788 Wesley Drive, Atlanta GA 30305-3933. (404)351-8877. **Contact:** Joan Brandt. Estab. 1980.

• Prior to her current position, Ms. Brandt was with Sterling Lord Literistic.

Represents Nonfiction books, novels, short story collections. **Considers these nonfiction areas:** True crime/investigative. **Considers these fiction areas:** Family saga; historical; literary; mystery/suspense; thriller; women's.

How to Contact Query with SASE. No e-mail or fax queries. Considers simultaneous queries. Returns materials only with SASE.

Recent Sales This agency prefers not to share information on specific sales.

Terms Agent receives 15% commission on domestic sales; 20% commission on foreign sales. No written contract.

THE HELEN BRANN AGENCY, INC.

94 Curtis Road, Bridgewater CT 06752. Fax: (860)355-2572. Member of AAR.

How to Contact Query with SASE.

BARBARA BRAUN ASSOCIATES, INC.

151 West 19th St/, 4th floor, New York NY 10011. Fax: (212)604-9041. E-mail: bba230@earthlink.net. Website: www.barbarabraunagency.com. **Contact:** Barbara Braun. Member of AAR.

Member Agents Barbara Braun; John F. Baker.

Represents Nonfiction books, novels.

• "Our fiction is strong on women's stories, historical and multicultural stories, as well as mysteries and thrillers. We're interested in narrative nonfiction and books by journalists. We do not represent poetry, science fiction, fantasy, horror, or screenplays." Look online for more details.

How to Contact Query with SASE. Mail queries via snail mail.

Recent Sales *Luncheon of the Boating Party*, by Susan Vreeland (Viking/Penguin); *Looking for Salvation at the Dairy Queen* and a second novel, by Susan Gregg Gilmore (Shaye Areheart/Crown); *Vivaldi's Girls*, by Laurel Corona (Hyperion); *Heartbreak Town* and a sequel, by Marsha Moyer (Three Rivers/Crown); *The Lost Van*

Gogh, by A.J. Zerries (Tor/Forge); *Terror in Michigan*, by Arnie Bernstein (Univ. of Michigan Press); *A Strand of Corpses* and *A Friend of Need*, by J.R. Benn (Soho Press).

Terms Agent receives 15% commission on domestic sales; 20% commission on foreign sales.

Tips "Fiction submissions: One-page synopsis and two sample chapters. Nonfiction submissions: Send proposal with overview, chapter outline, author biography, two sample chapters and short profile of competition."

◙ PAUL BRESNICK LITERARY AGENCY, LLC

115 W. 29th St., Third Floor, New York NY 10001. (212)239-3166. Fax: (212)239-3165. E-mail: paul@bresnickag ency.com. **Contact:** Paul Bresnick.

- Prior to becoming an agent, Mr. Bresnick spent 25 years as a trade book editor.

Represents Nonfiction books, novels. **Considers these nonfiction areas:** Biography/autobiography; health/ medicine; history; humor/satire; memoirs; multicultural; popular culture; sports; travel; true crime/investigative; celebrity-branded books, narrative nonfiction, pop psychology, relationship issues. **Considers these fiction areas:** Quality commercial fiction.

How to Contact For fiction, submit query/SASE and 2 chapters. For nonfiction, submit query/SASE with proposal. No e-mail or fax queries.

Recent Sales *West of Jesus*, by Steven Kotler (Bloomsbury); *Jeans: A Cultural History of an American Icon*, by James Sullivan (Gotham); *Sons of Providence: The Brown Brothers, the Slave Trade and the American Revolution*, by Charles Rappleye (Simon & Schuster); *Awesome: A Novel*, by Jack Pendarvis (McAdam Cage); *How to Raise a Jewish Dog*, by Ellis Weiner and Barbara Devilman (Little, Brown); *Burning Book: A Visual History of Burning Man*, by Jessica Buder (Simon & Schuster); *Sing Me Back Home: Love, Death and Country Music*, by Dina Jennings (Farrar Straus).

Ⓝ ◯ BRESSLER SCOGGINS LITERARY AGENCY

338 N. Elm St., Suite 308, Greensboro NC 27401. (336)553-3982; NY phone (646)688-5043. Fax: (336)553-0959. E-mail: becky@amplify-comm.com. Website: www.bresslerscoggins.com. **Contact:** Becky Scoggins. Estab. 2007. 80% of clients are new/unpublished writers. Currently handles: 10% nonfiction books; 70% novels; 20% juvenile books.

- Prior to becoming an agent, Ms. Scoggins spent several years in corporate sales and marketing for Borders Group.

Member Agents Becky Scoggins (fiction, juvenile, children's, picture); Jordan Bressler (fiction: romance, Southern, literary, mystery).

Represents Nonfiction books, novels, juvenile books. **Considers these nonfiction areas:** Child guidance/parenting; humor/satire; memoirs. **Considers these fiction areas:** Action/adventure; humor/satire; juvenile; literary; mainstream/contemporary; mystery/suspense; picture books; regional; romance; young adult; women's.

- ⊶ "We specialize in romance, Southern and literary fiction. We are an energetic and fun agency that acts as your advocate and team in the publishing industry." Actively seeking romance, Southern lit, juvenile and young adult/ Does not want to receive poetry, business, historical nonfiction or short stories.

How to Contact Query with SASE, submit synopsis, 3 sample chapter(s). Accepts e-mail and fax queries. Considers simultaneous queries. Responds in 3 months to queries; 6 months to mss. Returns materials only with SASE. Obtains most new clients through recommendations from others, solicitations, conferences.

Terms Agent receives 15% commission on domestic sales; 20% commission on foreign sales. Offers written contract; 60-day notice must be given to terminate contract. This agency charges for copying of ms. and sometimes for shipping/postage.

Writers' Conferences South Carolina Book Festival; BookExpo America.

Tips "Read our submission guidelines carefully! Please be sure your manuscript is polished and completed. Have someone read it who can give you an honest opinion before sending it to an agent. In your query, be unique and eye-catching. Most of all, be patient."

◙ BRICK HOUSE LITERARY AGENTS

80 Fifth Ave., Suite 1101, New York NY 10011. Website: www.brickhouselit.com. **Contact:** Sally Wofford-Girand. Member of AAR.

Member Agents Sally Wofford-Girand; Jenni Ferrari-Adler; Melissa Sarver, assistant.

Represents Nonfiction books, novels. **Considers these nonfiction areas:** Ethnic/cultural interests; history; memoirs; women's issues/studies; biography; science; natural history. **Considers these fiction areas:** Literary.

- ⊶ Actively seeking history, memoir, women's issues, cultural studies, literary fiction and quality commerical fiction.

How to Contact Query via mail or e-mail.

🌐 ✒ CURTIS BROWN (AUST) PTY LTD

P.O. Box 19, Paddington NSW 2021, Australia. (61)(2)9361-6161. Fax: (61)(2)9360-3935. E-mail: info@curtisbrown.com.au. Website: www.curtisbrown.com.au. **Contact:** Submissions Department. Estab. 1967. Represents 350 clients. 10% of clients are new/unpublished writers. Currently handles: 30% nonfiction books; 30% novels; 25% juvenile books; 5% scholarly books; 5% textbooks; 5% other.

- "Prior to joining Curtis Brown, most of our agents worked in publishing or the film/theatre industries in Australia and the United Kingdom."

Member Agents Fiona Inglis, managing director; Fran Moore, agent/deputy managing director; Tara Wynne, agent; Pippa Masson, agent; Clare Forster, agent.

Represents Nonfiction books, novels, novellas, juvenile books.

- ⟶ "We are the oldest and largest literary agency in Australia and we look after a wide variety of clients." No poetry, short stories, film scripts, picture books or translations.

How to Contact Submit 3 sample chapters, cover letter with biographical information, synopsis (2-3 pages), SASE. No fax queries.

Recent Sales *The Book Thief*, by Marcus Zusak (Pan MacMillan); *Pip: The Story of Olive* (Allen and Unwin).

✒ BROWN LITERARY AGENCY

410 Seventh St. NW, Naples FL 34120. Website: www.brownliteraryagency.com. **Contact:** Roberta Brown. Estab. 1996. Member of AAR, RWA, Author's Guild. Represents 47 clients. 5% of clients are new/unpublished writers.

Represents Novels. **Considers these fiction areas:** Erotica; romance (single title and category); women's.

- ⟶ This agency is selectively reading material at this time.

How to Contact Responds in 2 weeks to queries.

Terms Agent receives 15% commission on domestic sales; 20% commission on foreign sales. Offers written contract; 30-day notice must be given to terminate contract.

Writers' Conferences RWA National Conference; Romantic Times Convention.

Tips "Polish your manuscript. Be professional."

✒ ANDREA BROWN LITERARY AGENCY, INC.

1076 Eagle Drive, Salinas CA 93905. E-mail: andrea@andreabrownlit.com. Website: www.andreabrownlit.com. **Contact:** Andrea Brown, president. Estab. 1981. 10% of clients are new/unpublished writers.

- Prior to opening her agency, Ms. Brown served as an editorial assistant at Random House and Dell Publishing and as an editor with Knopf.

Member Agents Andrea Brown; Laura Rennert; April Eberhardt, Michelle Andelman; Caryn Wiseman; Jennifer Jaeger; Jennifer Laughran, associate agent; and Jamie Weiss, associate agent.

Represents Nonfiction books, novels. **Considers these nonfiction areas:** Juvenile nonfiction; memoirs; young adult; narrative. **Considers these fiction areas:** Juvenile; literary; picture books; thriller; young adult; women's.

How to Contact For picture books, submit complete ms, SASE. For fiction, submit short synopsis, SASE, first 3 chapters. For nonfiction, submit proposal, 1-2 sample chapters. For illustrations, submit 4-5 color samples (no originals). We only accept queries via e-mail. Considers simultaneous queries. Obtains most new clients through referrals from editors, clients and agents.

Recent Sales *Chloe*, by Catherine Ryan Hyde (Knopf); Sasha Cohen Autobiography (HarperCollins); *The Five Ancestors*, by Jeff Stone (Random House).

Terms Agent receives 15% commission on domestic sales; 20% commission on foreign sales. Offers written contract. Charges clients for shipping costs.

Writers' Conferences SCBWI; Asilomar; Maui Writers' Conference; Southwest Writers' Conference; San Diego State University Writers' Conference; Big Sur Children's Writing Workshop; William Saroyan Writers' Conference; Columbus Writers' Conference; Willamette Writers' Conference; La Jolla Writers' Conference; San Francisco Writers' Conference; Hilton Head Writers' Conference.

Ⓝ ✒ TRACY BROWN LITERARY AGENCY

P.O. Box 88, Scarsdale NY 10583. (914)400-4147. Fax: (914)931-1746. E-mail: tracy@brownlit.com. **Contact:** Tracy Brown. Estab. 2006. Represents 35 clients. Currently handles: 75% nonfiction books; 25% novels.

- Prior to becoming an agent, Ms. Brown was a book editor for 25 years.

Represents Nonfiction books, novels, short story collections, anthologies. **Considers these nonfiction areas:** Animals; biography/autobiography; business/economics; cooking/foods/nutrition; current affairs; government/politics/law; health/medicine; history; how-to; humor/satire; memoirs; military/war; money/finance; music/dance; nature/environment; popular culture; psychology; religious/inspirational; science/technology; self-help/personal improvement; sociology; sports; women's issues/studies. **Considers these fiction areas:** Feminist; literary; mainstream/contemporary; women's.

O—🔈 Specializes in thorough involvement with clients' books at every stage of the process from writing to proposals to publication. Actively seeking serious nonfiction and fiction. Does not want to receive YA, sci-fi or romance.

How to Contact Submit outline/proposal, synopsis, 1 sample chapter(s), author bio. Accepts e-mail queries. No fax queries. Considers simultaneous queries. Responds in 2 weeks to queries; 3 weeks to mss. Obtains most new clients through recommendations from others, solicitations.

Recent Sales *Supergirl: A Novel*, by Daphne Uviller (Bantam); *Perfect Girls*; *Starving Daughters*, by Courtney E. Martin; *Mating in Captivity*, by Esther Perel; *Losing It*, by Jessica Valenti.

Terms Agent receives 15% commission on domestic sales; 20% commission on foreign sales. Offers written contract.

🌀 BROWNE & MILLER LITERARY ASSOCIATES

410 S. Michigan Ave., Suite 460, Chicago IL 60605-1465. (312)922-3063. E-mail: mail@browneandmiller.com. **Contact:** Danielle Egan-Miller. Estab. 1971. Member of AAR, RWA, MWA, Author's Guild. Represents 150 clients. 2% of clients are new/unpublished writers. Currently handles: 25% nonfiction books; 75% novels.

Represents Nonfiction books, novels. **Considers these nonfiction areas:** Agriculture/horticulture; animals; anthropology/archaeology; biography/autobiography; business/economics; child guidance/parenting; cooking/foods/nutrition; crafts/hobbies; current affairs; ethnic/cultural interests; health/medicine; how-to; humor/satire; memoirs; money/finance; nature/environment; popular culture; psychology; religious/inspirational; science/technology; self-help/personal improvement; sociology; sports; true crime/investigative; women's issues/studies. **Considers these fiction areas:** Detective/police/crime; ethnic; family saga; glitz; historical; literary; mainstream/contemporary; mystery/suspense; religious/inspirational; romance (contemporary, gothic, historical, regency); sports; thriller; paranormal, erotica.

O—🔈 "We are partial to talented newcomers and experienced authors who are seeking hands-on career management, highly personal representation, and who are interested in being full partners in their books' successes. We are editorially focused and work closely with our authors through the whole publishing process, from proposal to after publication." Actively seeking highly commercial mainstream fiction and nonfiction. Does not represent poetry, short stories, plays, screenplays, articles, or children's books.

How to Contact Query with SASE. *No unsolicited mss.* Prefers to read material exclusively. Put "submission" in the subject line. Send no attachments. Responds in 6 weeks to queries. Returns materials only with SASE. Obtains most new clients through referrals, queries by professional/marketable authors.

Terms Agent receives 15% commission on domestic sales; 20% commission on foreign sales. Offers written contract, binding for 2 years. Charges clients for photocopying, overseas postage, faxes, phone calls.

Writers' Conferences BookExpo America; Frankfurt Book Fair; RWA National Conference; CBA National Conference; London Book Fair; Bouchercon, regional writers conferences.

Tips "If interested in agency representation, be well informed."

🌀 PEMA BROWNE, LTD.

11 Tena Place, Valley Cottage NY 10989. E-mail: ppbltd@optonline.net. Website: www.pemabrowneltd.com. **Contact:** Pema Browne. Estab. 1966. Member of SCBWI, RWA; signatory of WGA. Represents 30 clients. Currently handles: 25% nonfiction books; 50% novels/romance novels; 25% juvenile books.

• Prior to opening her agency, Ms. Browne was an artist and art buyer.

Represents Nonfiction books, novels, juvenile books, reference books. **Considers these nonfiction areas:** Business/economics; child guidance/parenting; cooking/foods/nutrition; ethnic/cultural interests; gay/lesbian issues; health/medicine; how-to; juvenile nonfiction; money/finance; New Age/metaphysics; popular culture; psychology; religious/inspirational; self-help/personal improvement; spirituality; women's issues/studies; reference. **Considers these fiction areas:** Action/adventure; contemporary issues; feminist; gay/lesbian; glitz; historical; juvenile; literary; mainstream/contemporary (commercial); mystery/suspense; picture books; religious/inspirational; romance (contemporary, gothic, historical, regency); young adult.

O—🔈 "We are not accepting any new projects or authors until further notice."

How to Contact Query with SASE. No attachments for e-mail.

Recent Sales *The Champion*, by Heather Grothaus (Kensington/Zebra); *The Highlander's Bride*, by Michele Peach (Kensington/Zebra); *Whispers*, by Samatha Garver (Kensington/Zebra); *Yellowstone Park*, by Linda Cargill (Cora Verlag); *The Daring Harriet Quimby*, by Suzane Whitaker (Holiday House); *One Night to Be Sinful*, by Samantha Garver (Kensington); *Point Eyes of the Dragon*, by Linda Cargill (Cora Verlag).

Terms Agent receives 20% commission on domestic sales; 20% commission on foreign sales.

Tips "We do not review manuscripts that have been sent out to publishers. If writing romance, be sure to receive guidelines from various romance publishers. In nonfiction, one must have credentials to lend credence to a proposal. Make sure of margins, double-space, and use clean, dark type."

⚡ ◎ THE BUKOWSKI AGENCY

14 Prince Author Ave., Suite 202, Toronto Ontario M5R 1A9, Canada. (416)928-6728. Fax: (416)963-9978. E-mail: assistant@thebukowskiagency.com. Website: www.thebukowskiagency.com. **Contact:** Denise Bukowski. Estab. 1986. Represents 70 clients.

- Prior to becoming an agent, Ms. Bukowski was a book editor.

Represents Nonfiction books, novels.

- ☞ "The Bukowski Agency specializes in international literary fiction and up-market nonfiction for adults. Bukowski looks for Canadian writers whose work can be marketed in many media and territories, and who have the potential to make a living from their work." Actively seeking nonfiction and fiction works from Canadian writers. Does not want submissions from American authors, as well as genre fiction, poetry, children's literature, picture books, film scripts or television scripts.

How to Contact Query with SASE, submit proposal package, outline/proposal, synopsis, publishing history, author bio. Send submissions by snail mail only. See online guidelines for nonfiction and fiction specifics. Responds in 6 weeks to queries.

Recent Sales *The Girls*, by Lori Lansens (Little, Brown); *Holding My Breath*, by Sidura Ludwig (Shaye Areheart Books); *The Rules of Engagement*, by Catherine Bush (Farrar, Straus & Giroux); *Night Watch*, stories by Kevin Armstrong (Harcourt Brace). Other clients include A full list of this agency's clients is online.

◉ SHEREE BYKOFSKY ASSOCIATES, INC.

PO Box 706, Brigantine NJ 08203. E-mail: submitbee@aol.com. Website: www.shereebee.com. **Contact:** Sheree Bykofsky. Estab. 1984, incorporated 1991. Member of AAR, ASJA, WNBA. Currently handles: 80% nonfiction books; 20% novels.

- Prior to opening her agency, Ms. Bykofsky served as executive editor of The Stonesong Press and managing editor of Chiron Press. She is also the author or co-author of more than 20 books, including *The Complete Idiot's Guide to Getting Published*. Ms. Bykofsky teaches publishing at NYU and SEAK, Inc.

Member Agents Janet Rosen, associate.

Represents Nonfiction books, novels. **Considers these nonfiction areas:** Americana; animals; art/architecture/ design; biography/autobiography; business/economics; child guidance/parenting; cooking/foods/nutrition; crafts/hobbies; current affairs; education; ethnic/cultural interests; gardening; gay/lesbian issues; government/ politics/law; health/medicine; history; how-to; humor/satire; interior design/decorating; language/literature/ criticism; memoirs; military/war; money/finance (personal finance); multicultural; music/dance; nature/environment; New Age/metaphysics; philosophy; photography; popular culture; psychology; recreation; regional; religious/inspirational; science/technology; self-help/personal improvement; sex; sociology; spirituality; sports; theater/film; translation; travel; true crime/investigative; women's issues/studies; anthropolgy; creative nonfiction. **Considers these fiction areas:** Literary; mainstream/contemporary; mystery/suspense.

- ☞ This agency specializes in popular reference nonfiction, commercial fiction with a literary quality, and mysteries. "I have wide-ranging interests, but it really depends on quality of writing, originality, and how a particular project appeals to me (or not). I take on fiction when I completely love it—it doesn't matter what area or genre." Does not want to receive poetry, material for children, screenplays, westerns, horror, science fiction, or fantasy.

How to Contact Query with SASE. No unsolicited mss, e-mail queries, or phone calls. Considers simultaneous queries. Responds in 3 weeks to queries with SASE. Responds in 1 month to requested mss. Returns materials only with SASE. Obtains most new clients through recommendations from others.

Recent Sales Sold 100 titles in the last year. *Self-Esteem Sickness*, by Albert Ellis (Prometheus); *When the Ghost Screams*, by Leslie Rule (Andrews McMeel); *225 Squares*, by Matt Gaffney (Avalon).

Terms Agent receives 15% commission on domestic sales; 20% commission on foreign sales. Offers written contract, binding for 1 year. Charges for postage, photocopying, fax.

Writers' Conferences ASJA Writers Conference; Asilomar; Florida Suncoast Writers' Conference; Whidbey Island Writers' Conference; Florida First Coast Writers' Festibal; Agents and Editors Conference; Columbus Writers' Conference; Southwest Writers' Conference; Willamette Writers' Conferece; Dorothy Canfield Fisher Conference; Maui Writers' Conference; Pacific Northwest Writers' Conference; IWWG.

Tips "Read the agent listing carefully and comply with guidelines."

◉ CANTON SMITH AGENCY

E-mail: cantonsmithagency@cantonsmithagency.com. Website: www.cantonsmithagency.com. **Contact:** Eric Smith, senior partner (esmith@cantonsmithagency.com); Chamein Canton, partner (chamein@cantonsmithagency.com); Netta Beckford, associate (nettab@cantonsmithagency.com). Estab. 2001. Represents 28 clients. 100% of clients are new/unpublished writers.

- Prior to becoming agents, Mr. Smith was in advertising and bookstore retail; Ms. Canton was a writer and a paralegal.

Member Agents Chamein Canton, managing partner, chamein@cantonsmithagency (women's fiction, chick-lit, business, how to, fashion, romance, erotica, African American, Latina, women's issues, health, relationships, decorating, cookbooks, lifestyle, literary novels, astrology, numerology, New Age) Eric Smith, senior partner, ericsmith@cantonsmithagency.com (science fiction, sports, literature); James Weil, reviewer, jamesw@canton smithagency.com.

Represents Nonfiction books, novels, juvenile books, scholarly books, textbooks, movie scripts. **Considers these nonfiction areas:** Art/architecture/design; business/economics; child guidance/parenting; cooking/foods/nutrition; education; ethnic/cultural interests; health/medicine; history; how-to; humor/satire; language/literature/criticism; memoirs; military/war; music/dance; photography; psychology; sports; translation; women's issues/studies. **Considers these fiction areas:** Fantasy; humor/satire; juvenile; multicultural; romance; young adult; Latina fiction; chick lit; African-American fiction; entertainment. **Considers these script subject areas:** Action/adventure; comedy; romantic comedy; romantic drama; science fiction.

> O— "We specialize in helping new and established writers expand their marketing potential for prospective publishers. We are currently focusing on women's fiction (chick lit), Latina fiction, African American fiction, multicultural, romance, memoirs, humor and entertainment, in addition to more nonfiction titles (cooking, how to, fashion, home improvement, etc)."

How to Contact Only accepts e-queries. Send a query, not sample chapters and/or proposals, unless specifically requested. Considers simultaneous queries. Responds in 5 months to queries; 5 months to mss. Obtains most new clients through recommendations from others.

Recent Sales Sold 7 titles in the last year. Clients include Robert Koger, Olivia, Jennifer DeWit, Sheila Smestad, James Weil, Jaime Nava, JC Miller, Diana Smith, Robert Beers, Marcy Gannon, Keith Maxwell, Dawn Jackson, Jeannine Carney, Mark Barlow, Robert Marsocci, Anita Ballard Jones, Deb Mohr, Seth Ahonen, Melissa Graf, Robert Zavala, Cliff Webb, John and Carolyn Osborne.

Terms Agent receives 15% commission on domestic sales; 20% commission on foreign sales. Offers written contract; 2-month notice must be given to terminate contract.

Tips "Know your market. Agents, as well as publishers, are keenly interested in writers with their finger on the pulse of their market."

🖉 CARNICELLI LITERARY MANAGEMENT

30 Bond St., New York NY 10012. (212)979-0101. E-mail: matthew@carnicellilit.com. Website: www.carnecellilit.com. **Contact:** Matthew Carnicelli. Estab. 2004. Represents 40 clients. 20% of clients are new/unpublished writers. Currently handles: 75% nonfiction books; 25% novels.

> • Prior to opening his agency, Mr. Carnicelli held senior editorial positions at the Penguin Group, Contemporary Books and McGraw-Hill.

Represents Nonfiction books, novels. **Considers these nonfiction areas:** Biography/autobiography; business/economics; child guidance/parenting; current affairs; education; ethnic/cultural interests; gay/lesbian issues; government/politics/law; health/medicine; history; memoirs; money/finance; popular culture; psychology; religious/inspirational; science/technology; sociology; sports. **Considers these fiction areas:** Literary; mainstream/contemporary.

How to Contact Query with SASE or via e-mail (no attachments). Considers simultaneous queries. Returns materials only with SASE. Obtains most new clients through referrals from other writers.

Recent Sales Sold 20 titles in the last year. *Goldrush in the Jungle*, by Daniel Drollette (Harmony); *April 16th: Virginia Tech Remembers*, by Roland Lazenby (Plume); *Life Disrupted*, by Laurie Edwards (Walker).

Terms Agent receives 15% commission on domestic sales; 20% commission on foreign sales. Offers written contract; 30-day notice must be given to terminate contract. Charges for photocopying/messenger and express mail services.

Tips "It's very important that authors present themselves to agents in a formal, professional, and specific way. I simply ignore mass e-mails and most queries, though I will pay more attention if it's clear the author has actually researched the types of books I represent. It's also very important for authors to be as focused and as specific as possible about their writing. Ask yourself: Why am I the only one who can write this book? What are my unique credentials? How will my book be different from the many other books already published on this subject? What is my big idea, why is it relevant, and why will people want to read about it?"

🖉 MARIA CARVAINIS AGENCY, INC.

1270 Avenue of the Americas, Suite 2320, New York NY 10019. (212)245-6365. Fax: (212)245-7196. E-mail: mca@mariacarvainisagency.com. **Contact:** Maria Carvainis, Donna Bagdasarian. Estab. 1977. Member of AAR, Authors Guild, Women's Media Group, ABA, MWA, RWA; signatory of WGA. Represents 75 clients. 10% of clients are new/unpublished writers. Currently handles: 35% nonfiction books; 65% novels.

> • Prior to opening her agency, Ms. Carvainis spent more than 10 years in the publishing industry as a senior editor with Macmillan Publishing, Basic Books, Avon Books, and Crown Publishers. Ms. Carvainis has served as a member of the AAR Board of Directors and AAR Treasurer, as well as serving as chair of the

AAR Contracts Committee. She presently serves on the AAR Royalty Committee. Ms. Bagdasarian began her career as an academic at Boston University, then spent 5 years with Addison Wesley Longman as an acquisitions editor before joining the William Morris Agency in 1998. She has represented a breadth of projects, ranging from literary fiction to celebrity memoir.

Member Agents Maria Carvainis, president/literary agent; Donna Bagdasarian, literary agent; Moira Sullivan, literary associate/subsidiary rights manager; Christopher Jaskot, literary assistant.

Represents Nonfiction books, novels. **Considers these nonfiction areas:** Biography/autobiography; business/ economics; history; memoirs; science/technology (pop science); women's issues/studies. **Considers these fiction areas:** Historical; literary; mainstream/contemporary; mystery/suspense; thriller; young adult; women's; middle grade.

O— Does not want to receive science fiction or children's picture books.

How to Contact Query with SASE. Responds in up to 3 to mss. Obtains most new clients through recommendations from others, conferences, query letters.

Recent Sales *Simply Magic*, by Mary Balogh (Bantam Dell); *Save Your Own*, by Elizabeth Brink (Houghton Mifflin); *Ricochet*, by Sandra Brown (Simon & Schuster); *The Marriage Wager*, by Candace Camp (Mira); *Jeb: America's Next Bush*, by S.V. Date (Penguin Group/Tarcher Imprint); *A Widow's Curse*, by Phillip DePoy (St. Martin's Press); *A Falconer's Voice*, by Tim Gallagher (Houghton Mifflin); *Into the Dark*, by Cindy Gerard (St. Martin's Press); *Picture Perfect*, by D. Anne Love (Simon & Schuster Children's Publishing). Other clients include Sue Erikson Bloland, David Bottoms, Pam Conrad, John Faunce, Samantha James, Lucy Lehrer, Dushan Zaric and Jason Kosmas.

Terms Agent receives 15% commission on domestic sales; 20% commission on foreign sales. Offers written contract. Charges clients for foreign postage and bulk copying.

Writers' Conferences BookExpo America; Frankfurt Book Fair; London Book Fair; Mystery Writers of America; Thrillerfest; Romance Writers of America.

◙ CASTIGLIA LITERARY AGENCY

1155 Camino Del Mar, Suite 510, Del Mar CA 92014. (858)755-8761. Fax: (858)755-7063. Website: home.earthlink.net/~mwgconference/id22.html. Estab. 1993. Member of AAR, PEN. Represents 50 clients. Currently handles: 55% nonfiction books; 45% novels.

Member Agents Julie Castiglia; Winifred Golden; Sally Van Haitsma; Deborah Ritchken.

Represents Nonfiction books, novels. **Considers these nonfiction areas:** Animals; anthropology/archaeology; biography/autobiography; business/economics; child guidance/parenting; cooking/foods/nutrition; current affairs; ethnic/cultural interests; health/medicine; history; language/literature/criticism; money/finance; nature/ environment; psychology; religious/inspirational; science/technology; self-help/personal improvement; women's issues/studies. **Considers these fiction areas:** Ethnic; literary; mainstream/contemporary; mystery/suspense; women's.

O— Does not want to receive horror, screenplays, poetry or academic nonfiction.

How to Contact Query with SASE. No fax queries. Returns materials only with SASE. Obtains most new clients through recommendations from others, solicitations, conferences.

Recent Sales Sold 29 titles in the last year. *Opium Season*, by Joel Havferstein (Lyons); *Bride of Casa Dracula*, by Marta Acosta (S&S); *Forever*, by Doug Keister (Gibbs Smith); *Orphan's Alliance*, by Robert Buettner (Little, Brown); *Waiting for the Apocalypse*, by Veronica Chater (Norton).

Terms Agent receives 15% commission on domestic sales; 25% commission on foreign sales. Offers written contract; 6-week notice must be given to terminate contract.

Writers' Conferences Santa Barbara Writers' Conference; Southern California Writers' Conference; Surrey International Writers' Conference; San Diego State University Writers' Conference; Willamette Writers' Conference.

Tips ''Be professional with submissions. Attend workshops and conferences before you approach an agent.''

◙ JANE CHELIUS LITERARY AGENCY

548 Second St., Brooklyn NY 11215. (718)499-0236. Fax: (718)832-7335. E-mail: queries@janechelius.com. Website: www.janechelius.com. Member of AAR.

Represents Nonfiction books, novels. **Considers these nonfiction areas:** Humor/satire; women's issues/studies; popular science; parenting; medicine; biography; natural history; narrative. **Considers these fiction areas:** Literary; mystery/suspense; women's; men's adventure.

O— Does not want to receive fantasy, science fiction, children's books, stage plays, screenplays, or poetry.

How to Contact Submission details are in flux; please see Web site for all info.

⊙ ◎ ELYSE CHENEY LITERARY ASSOCIATES, LLC

270 Lafayette St., Suite 1504, New York NY 10012. Website: www.cheneyliterary.com. **Contact:** Elyse Cheney.
• Prior to her current position, Ms. Cheney was an agent with Sanford J. Greenburger Associates.

Represents Nonfiction books, novels. **Considers these nonfiction areas:** Biography/autobiography; history; multicultural; sports; women's issues/studies; narrative. **Considers these fiction areas:** Historical; horror; literary; romance; thriller.

How to Contact Query this agency with a referral. Snail mail queries only. Include SASE or IRC. No e-mail or fax queries.

Recent Sales *Moonwalking With Einstein: A Journey into Memory and the Mind*, by Joshua Foer; *The Coldest Winter Ever*, by Sister Souljah (Atria); *A Heartbreaking Work of Staggering Genius*, by Dave Eggers (Simon & Schuster).

⊙ ◎ THE CHUDNEY AGENCY

72 North State Road, Suite 501, Briarcliff Manor NY 10510. (914)488-5008. E-mail: mail@thechudneyagency.com. Website: www.thechudneyagency.com. **Contact:** Steven Chudney. Estab. 2002. Member of SCBWI. 90% of clients are new/unpublished writers.
• Prior to becoming an agent, Mr. Chudney held various sales positions with major publishers.

Represents Novels, juvenile books. **Considers these nonfiction areas:** Juvenile nonfiction. **Considers these fiction areas:** Historical; juvenile; literary; mystery/suspense; young adult.

0➡ This agency specializes in children's books, and wants to find authors who are illustrators as well. Actively seeking children's books. Does not want to receive Board books or lift-the flap books, Fables, folklore, or traditional fairytales, Poetry or "mood pieces", Stories for "all ages" (as these ultimately are too adult oriented), Message-driven stories that are heavy-handed, didactic or pedantic.

How to Contact Query with SASE, submit proposal package, 4-6 sample chapter(s). For children's, submit full text and 3-5 illustrations. Accepts e-mail and fax queries. Considers simultaneous queries. Responds in 2-3 weeks to queries; 3-4 weeks to mss.

Recent Sales Sold 25+ titles in the last year. The Youngest Templar trilogy, by Michael Spradlin (Putnam); Do the Math series, by Wendy Lichtman (Greenwillow/HarperCollins); *Sir Ryan's Quest*, by Jason Deeble (Roaring Books Press); *Braless in Wonderland*, by Debbie Reed Fischer (Dutton Books/Penguin). Other clients include Barry Varela, Linda Johns, Dorian Cirrone, Leda Scubert, Deborah Lynn Jacobs, Shirley Harazin, Julie Sitegemeyer, Carol Baicker-McKee.

Terms Agent receives 15% commission on domestic sales; 20% commission on foreign sales. Offers written contract, binding for 1 year; 30-day notice must be given to terminate contract.

Tips "If an agent has a Web site, review it carefully to make sure your material is appropriate for that agent. Read lots of books within the genre you are writing; work hard on your writing; don't follow trends—most likely, you'll be too late."

⊙ EDWARD B. CLAFLIN LITERARY AGENCY, LLC

128 High Ave., Suite #4, Nyack NY 10960. (845)358-1084. E-mail: edclaflin@aol.com. **Contact:** Edward Claflin. Estab. 2004. Represents 30 clients. 10% of clients are new/unpublished writers.
• Prior to opening his agency, Mr. Claflin worked at Banbury Books, Rodale and Prentice Hall Press. He is the co-author of 13 books.

Represents Nonfiction books. **Considers these nonfiction areas:** Business/economics; cooking/foods/nutrition; current affairs; health/medicine; history; how-to; military/war; money/finance; psychology; sports.

0➡ This agency specializes in consumer health, narrative history, psychology/self-help and business. Actively seeking compelling and authoritative nonfiction for specific readers. Does not want to receive fiction.

How to Contact Query with synopsis, bio, SASE or e-mail attachment in Word. Responds in 1 month to queries. Obtains most new clients through recommendations from others.

Terms Agent receives 15% commission on domestic sales.

⊙ WM CLARK ASSOCIATES

154 Christopher St., Suite 3C, New York NY 10014. (212)675-2784. Fax: (646)349-1658. E-mail: query@wmclark.com. Website: www.wmclark.com. Estab. 1997. Member of AAR. 50% of clients are new/unpublished writers. Currently handles: 50% nonfiction books; 50% novels.
• Prior to opening WCA, Mr. Clark was an agent at the William Morris Agency.

Represents Nonfiction books, novels. **Considers these nonfiction areas:** Art/architecture/design; biography/autobiography; current affairs; ethnic/cultural interests; history; memoirs; music/dance; popular culture; religious/inspirational (Eastern philosophy only); science/technology; sociology; theater/film; translation. **Consid-**

ers these fiction areas: Contemporary issues; ethnic; historical; literary; mainstream/contemporary; Southern fiction.

○→ "Building on a reputation for moving quickly and strategically on behalf of his clients, and offering individual focus and a global presence, William Clark practices an aggressive, innovative, and broad-ranged approach to the representation of content and the talent that creates it. His clients range from authors of first fiction and award-winning bestselling narrative nonfiction, to international authors in translation, musicians, and artists."

How to Contact E-mail queries only. Prefers to read requested materials exclusively. No attachments. Responds in 1-2 months to queries.

Recent Sales Sold 25 titles in the last year. *Fallingwater Rising: E.J. Kaufman and Frank Lloyd Wright Create the Most Exciting House in the World*, by Franklin Toker (Alfred A. Knopf); *The Balthazar Cookbook*, by Riad Nasr, Lee Hanson, and Keith McNally (Clarkson Potter); *The Book of 'Exodus': The Making and Meaning of Bob Marley's Album of the Century*, by Vivien Goldman (Crown/Three Rivers Press); *Hungry Ghost*, by Keith Kachtick (HarperCollins). Other clients include Russell Martin, Daye Haddon, Bjork, Mian Mian, Jonathan Stone, Jocko Weyland, Peter Hessler, Rev. Billy (a.k.a. Billy Talen).

Terms Agent receives 15% commission on domestic sales; 20% commission on foreign sales. Offers written contract.

Tips "WCA works on a reciprocal basis with Ed Victor Ltd. (UK) in representing select properties to the US market and vice versa. Translation rights are sold directly in the German, Italian, Spanish, Portuguese, Latin American, French, Dutch, and Scandinavian territories in association with Andrew Nurnberg Associates Ltd. (UK); through offices in China, Bulgaria, Czech Republic, Latvia, Poland, Hungary, and Russia; and through corresponding agents in Japan, Greece, Israel, Turkey, Korea, Taiwan, and Thailand."

☑ COLCHIE AGENCY, GP

324 85th St., Brooklyn NY 11209. (718)921-7468. E-mail: ColchieLit@earthlink.net. **Contact:** Thomas or Elaine Colchie. Currently handles: 100% fiction.

Represents Novels.

○→ Does not want to receive nonfiction.

How to Contact This listing does not take or respond to unsolicited queries or submissions.

Recent Sales *Contract With God*, by Juan Gomez-Jurado (Atria); *The Story of a Widow*, by Musharraf Ali Farooqi (Knopf); *Reclaiming Paris*, by Fabiola Santiago (Atria); *The Killer's Wife*, by Bill Floyd (St. Martin's); *Twilight*, by Azhar Abidi (Penguin).

☑ FRANCES COLLIN, LITERARY AGENT

P.O. Box 33, Wayne PA 19087-0033. Website: www.francescollin.com. **Contact:** Sarah Yake. Member of AAR. Represents 90 clients. 1% of clients are new/unpublished writers. Currently handles: 50% nonfiction books; 48% novels; 1% textbooks; 1% poetry.

Represents Nonfiction books, fiction.

○→ "We are accepting almost no new clients unless recommended by publishing professionals or current clients." Does not want to receive cookbooks, crafts, children's books, software, or original screenplays.

How to Contact Query with SASE, brief proposal. No phone, fax, or e-mail inquiries. Enclose sufficient IRCs if outside the US. Considers simultaneous queries.

Terms Agent receives 15% commission on domestic sales; 20% commission on foreign sales. Offers written contract. Charges clients for overseas postage for books mailed to foreign agents; photocopying of mss, books, proposals; copyright registration fees; registered mail fees; passes along cost of any books purchased.

☑ DON CONGDON ASSOCIATES INC.

156 Fifth Ave., Suite 625, New York NY 10010-7002. (212)645-1229. Fax: (212)727-2688. E-mail: dca@doncongd on.com. **Contact:** Don Congdon, Michael Congdon, Susan Ramer, Cristina Concepcion. Estab. 1983. Member of AAR. Represents 100 clients. Currently handles: 60% nonfiction books; 40% fiction.

Represents Nonfiction books, fiction. **Considers these nonfiction areas:** Anthropology/archaeology; biography/autobiography; child guidance/parenting; cooking/foods/nutrition; current affairs; government/politics/law; health/medicine; history; humor/satire; language/literature/criticism; memoirs; military/war; music/dance; nature/environment; popular culture; psychology; science/technology; theater/film; travel; true crime/investigative; women's issues/studies; creative nonfiction. **Considers these fiction areas:** Action/adventure; detective/police/crime; literary; mainstream/contemporary; mystery/suspense; short story collections; thriller; women's.

○→ Especially interested in narrative nonfiction and literary fiction.

How to Contact Query with SASE or via e-mail (no attachments). Responds in 3 weeks to queries; 1 month to mss. Obtains most new clients through recommendations from other authors.

Terms Agent receives 15% commission on domestic sales; 19% commission on foreign sales. Charges client for extra shipping costs, photocopying, copyright fees, book purchases.

Tips "Writing a query letter with a self-addressed stamped envelope is a must. We cannot guarantee replies to foreign queries via standard mail. No phone calls. We never download attachments to e-mail queries for security reasons, so please copy and paste material into your e-mail."

◨ THE DOE COOVER AGENCY

P.O. Box 668, Winchester MA 01890. (781)721-6000. Fax: (781)721-6727. E-mail: info@doecooveragency.com. Website: doecooveragency.com. Estab. 1985. Represents more than 100 clients. Currently handles: 80% nonfiction books; 20% novels.

Member Agents Doe Coover (general nonfiction, cooking); Colleen Mohyde (literary and commercial fiction, general and narrative nonfiction); Amanda Lewis (children's books); Frances Kennedy, associate. **Considers these nonfiction areas:** Biography/autobiography; business/economics; cooking/foods/nutrition; gardening; history; science/technology; social issues, narrative nonfiction. **Considers these fiction areas:** Literary; commercial.

> ○➝ This agency specializes in nonfiction, particularly books on history, popular science, biography, social issues, and narrative nonfiction, as well as cooking, gardening, and literary and commercial fiction. Does not want romance, fantasy, science fiction, poetry or screenplays.

How to Contact Query with SASE, outline. No e-mail or fax queries. Considers simultaneous queries. Returns materials only with SASE. Obtains most new clients through recommendations from others, solicitations.

Recent Sales Sold 25-30 titles in the last year. *More Fast Food My Way*, by Jacques Pepin (Houghton Mifflin); *Entertaining Simple*, by Matthew Mead (John Wiley & Sons); *International Grilling*, by Chris Schlesinger and John Willoughby (Dorling Kindersley); *The Setpoint Solution*, by George Blackburn (HarperCollins Publishers); *You're Never Too Old To Start Something New*, by Martha Manglesdorf (Ten Speed Press); *Openwork*, by Adria Bernardi (SMU Press); *See What You Can Be*, by Liz Suneby and Diane Heiman (American Girl). *Movie/TV MOW script(s) optioned/sold: A Crime in the Neighborhood*, by Suzanne Berne; *Mr. White's Confession*, by Robert Clark. Other clients include WGBH, New England Aquarium, Blue Balliett, Deborah Madison, Rick Bayless, Molly Stevens, David Allen, Adria Bernardi, Paula Poundstone.

Terms Agent receives 15% commission on domestic sales; 10% of original advance commission on foreign sales.

◨ CORNERSTONE LITERARY, INC.

4525 Wilshire Blvd., Ste. 208, Los Angeles CA 90010. (323)930-6037. Fax: (323)930-0407. E-mail: info@cornerstoneliterary.com. Website: www.cornerstoneliterary.com. **Contact:** Helen Breitwieser. Estab. 1998. Member of AAR, Author's Guild, MWA, RWA, PEN, Poets & Writers. Represents 40 clients. 30% of clients are new/unpublished writers.

> • Prior to founding her own boutique agency, Ms. Breitwieser was a literary agent at The William Morris Agency.

Represents Novels. **Considers these fiction areas:** Detective/police/crime; erotica; ethnic; family saga; glitz; historical; literary; mainstream/contemporary; multicultural; mystery/suspense; romance; thriller; women's.

> ○➝ "We are not taking new clients at this time. We do not respond to unsolicited e-mail inquiries. All unsolicited manuscripts will be returned unopened." Does not want to receive science fiction, Western, poetry, screenplays, fantasy, gay/lesbian, horror, self-help, psychology, business or diet.

How to Contact Obtains most new clients through recommendations from others.

Recent Sales Sold 37 titles in the last year. *The Bright Side of Disaster*, by Katherine Center (Random House); *The Archangel Project*, by Steven Graham; *How to Kill a Guy in Ten Days*, by Kayla Perrin (HarperCollins); *When Mermaids Sing*, by C.S. Harris (Nal). Other clients include Catherine O'Connell, Judi McCoy, Rachel Lee, Pam Rosenthal, Tracy Ann Warren, Ahmet Zappa.

Terms Agent receives 15% commission on domestic sales; 20% commission on foreign sales. Offers written contract, binding for 1 year; 2-month notice must be given to terminate contract.

◨ THE CREATIVE CULTURE, INC.

72 Spring St., Suite 304, New York NY 10012. (212)680-3510. Fax: (212)680-3509. Website: www.thecreativeculture.com. **Contact:** Debra Goldstein. Estab. 1998. Member of AAR.

> • Prior to opening her agency, Ms. Goldstein and Ms. Gerwin were agents at the William Morris Agency; Ms. Naples was a senior editor at Simon & Schuster.

Member Agents Debra Goldstein (self-help, creativity, fitness, inspiration, lifestyle); Mary Ann Naples (health/nutrition, lifestyle, narrative nonfiction, practical nonfiction, literary fiction, animals/vegetarianism); Laura Nolan (literary fiction, parenting, self-help, psychology, women's studies, current affairs, science); Karen Gerwin; Emmanuelle Alspaugh (romance, general nonfiction, fiction).

Represents Nonfiction books, novels.

○→ Does not want to receive children's, poetry, screenplays or science fiction.

How to Contact Query with bio, book description, 5-7 sample pages (fiction only), SASE. ''We only reply if interested.'' Accepts e-mail queries. No fax queries. Responds in 2 months to queries.

Recent Sales *Dr. Neal Barnard's Program for Reversing Diabetes*, by Neil Barnard (Rodale); *The Power of Patience: How to Slow the Rush and Enjoy More Happiness, Success, and Peace of Mind Every Day*, by M.J. Ryan (Broadway Books); *The Secret Lives of Curious Virgins: My Life as a Reluctant Good Girl*, by Carlene Bauer (HarperCollins). Other clients include David Awbrey, Tom Hughes, Brenda McClain, Paula Chaffee Scardamalia.

◐ CRICHTON & ASSOCIATES

6940 Carroll Ave., Takoma Park MD 20912. (301)495-9663. Fax: (202)318-0050. E-mail: cricht1@aol.com. Website: www.crichton-associates.com. **Contact:** Sha-Shana Crichton. Estab. 2002. 90% of clients are new/unpublished writers. Currently handles: 20% nonfiction books; 80% novels.

• Prior to becoming an agent, Ms. Crichton did commercial litigation for a major law firm.

Represents Nonfiction books, novels. **Considers these nonfiction areas:** Child guidance/parenting; ethnic/cultural interests; gay/lesbian issues; government/politics/law; true crime/investigative; women's issues/studies; Caribbean, Hispanic and Latin-American studies, African-American studies. **Considers these fiction areas:** Ethnic; feminist; literary; mainstream/contemporary; mystery/suspense; religious/inspirational; romance.

○→ Actively seeking women's fiction, romance, and chick lit. Looking also for multicultural fiction and nonfiction. Does not want to receive poetry.

How to Contact For fiction, include short synopsis and first 3 chapters with query. Send no e-attachments. For nonfiction, send a book proposal. Accepts e-mail queries. No fax queries. Responds in 3-5 weeks to queries. Returns materials only with SASE.

Recent Sales *Driven*, by Eve Kenin (Dorchester); *His Dark Prince*, by Eve Silver (Kensington); *Demon Kiss*, by Eve Silver (Warner); *Wish Club*, by Kim Strickland (Crown); *How to Salsa In a Sari*, by Dona Sakar (Kimani TRU); *My Soul Cries Out*, by Sherri Lewis (Urban Christian); *Dead Broke*, by Trista Russell (Simon & Schuster); *Give Me More*, by PJ Mellor (Kensington); *Spirit of Our Ancestors*, by Natalie Robertson (Praeger). Other clients include Dirk Gibson, Kimberley White, Beverly Long, Jessica Trap, Altonya Washington, Ann Christopher.

Terms Agent receives 15% commission on domestic sales; 20% commission on foreign sales. Offers written contract, binding for 45 days. Only charges fees for postage and photocopying.

Writers' Conferences Silicon Valley RWA; BookExpo America.

⊕ ☑ THE MARY CUNNANE AGENCY

PO Box 336, Bermagui, NSW 2546, Australia. Website: www.cunnaneagency.com.

Member Agents Mary Cunnane: mary@cunnaneagency.com; Isobel Wightman: isobel@cunnaneagency.com.

○→ This agency does not work with North American authors.

Recent Sales *Diamond Dove*, by Adrian Hyland (Soho Press).

◐ RICHARD CURTIS ASSOCIATES, INC.

171 E. 74th St., New York NY 10021. (212)772-7363. Fax: (212)772-7393. Website: www.curtisagency.com. Estab. 1979. Member of RWA, MWA, SFWA; signatory of WGA. Represents 100 clients. 1% of clients are new/unpublished writers. Currently handles: 50% nonfiction books; 50% genre fiction.

• Prior to opening his agency, Mr. Curtis was an agent with the Scott Meredith Literary Agency for seven years. He has also authored more than 50 published books. **Considers these nonfiction areas:** Biography/autobiography; business/economics; health/medicine; history; science/technology.

How to Contact Send 1-page query letter and no more than a 5-page synopsis. Don't send ms unless specifically requested. If requested, submission must be accompanied by a SASE. No e-mail or fax queries. Responds in 6 weeks to queries. Returns materials only with SASE.

Recent Sales Sold 100 titles in the last year. *Pendragon*, by DJ MacHale; *City at the End of Time*, by Greg Bear; *For a Few Demons More*, by Kim Harrison; *Crave*, by Cynthia Bulik.

Terms Agent receives 15% commission on domestic sales; 25% commission on foreign sales. Offers written contract. Charges for photocopying, express mail, international freight, book orders.

Writers' Conferences SFWA Conference; HWA Conference; RWA National Conference.

◎ JAMES R. CYPHER, THE CYPHER AGENCY

816 Wolcott Ave., Beacon NY 12508-4261. Phone/Fax: (845)831-5677. E-mail: jim@jimcypher.com. Website: www.jimcypher.com. **Contact:** James R. Cypher. Estab. 1993. Member of AAR, Authors Guild. Represents 23 clients. 56% of clients are new/unpublished writers. Currently handles: 100% nonfiction books.

• Prior to opening his agency, Mr. Cypher worked as a corporate public relations manager for a Fortune 500 multi-national computer company for 28 years.

Represents Nonfiction books. **Considers these nonfiction areas:** Current affairs; health/medicine; history;

memoirs; popular culture; science/technology; sports (NASCAR, golf, baseball); true crime/investigative; biography.

    O⇥ This agent is semi-retired, and taking on few new clients. Does not want to receive humor, sewing, computer books, children's, gardening, cookbooks, spiritual, religious, or New Age topics.

How to Contact Query with SASE, submit proposal package. Accepts e-mail queries, though proposals should be sent snail mail with envelope/postage. No fax queries. Considers simultaneous queries. Responds in 2 weeks to queries; 6 weeks to mss. Obtains most new clients through recommendations from others, conferences, networking on online computer service.

Recent Sales Sold 9 titles in the last year. *Courting the Media: Public Relations for the Accused and the Accuser*, by Margaret A. Mackenzie (Praeger Publishers); *The Great Sex Secret: What Satisfied Women and Men Know That No One Talks About*, by Kim Marshall (Sourcebooks, Inc.); *Terrorism on American Soil: A Concise History of Plots and Perpetrators from the Famous to the Forgotten*, by Joseph T. McCann (Sentient Publications); *The National Wrestling Alliance: The Untold Story of the Monopoly That Controlled Pro Wrestling*, by Timothy M. Hornbaker (ECW Press). Other clients include Walter Harvey, Mark Horner, Charles Hustmyre, Glenn Puit, Robert L. Snow.

Terms Agent receives 15% commission on domestic sales; 20% commission on foreign sales. Offers written contract; 1-month notice must be given to terminate contract. 100% of business is derived from commissions on ms sales.

⬛ LAURA DAIL LITERARY AGENCY, INC.

350 Seventh Ave., Suite 2003, New York NY 10010. (212)239-7477. Fax: (212)947-0460. E-mail: queries@ldlainc .com. Website: www.ldlainc.com. Member of AAR.

Member Agents Talia Rosenblatt Cohen; Laura Dail; Tamar Ellman.

Represents Nonfiction books, novels.

    O⇥ "Due to the volume of queries and manuscripts received, we apologize for not answering every e-mail and letter." Specializes in historical, literary and some young adult fiction, as well as both practical and idea-driven nonfiction.

How to Contact Query with SASE. This agency prefers e-queries.

Recent Sales *This Year's Model*, by Carol Alt and Nina Malkin (Regan); *Skinny Bitch in the Kitch and Skinny Mama*, by Rory Freedman and Kim Barnoin (Running Press); *The Lost Memoirs of Jane Austin: A Novel*, by Syrie James (Avon).

⬛ ⬛ DANIEL LITERARY GROUP

1701 Kingsbury Drive, Suite 100, Nashville TN 37215. (615)730-8207. E-mail: submissions@danielliterarygroup. com. Website: www.danielliterarygroup.com. **Contact:** Greg Daniel. Estab. 2007. Represents 45 clients. 30% of clients are new/unpublished writers. Currently handles: 85% nonfiction books; 15% novels.

    ● Prior to becoming an agent, Mr. Daniel spent 10 years in publishing—six at the executive level at Thomas Nelson Publishers.

Represents Nonfiction books, novels. **Considers these nonfiction areas:** Biography/autobiography; business/economics; child guidance/parenting; current affairs; health/medicine; history; how-to; humor/satire; memoirs; nature/environment; popular culture; religious/inspirational; self-help/personal improvement; sports; theater/film; women's issues/studies. **Considers these fiction areas:** Action/adventure; contemporary issues; detective/police/crime; family saga; historical; humor/satire; literary; mainstream/contemporary; mystery/suspense; religious/inspirational; thriller; The agency currently accepts all fiction topics, except for children's, romance and sci-fi.

    O⇥ "We take pride in our ability to come alongside our authors and help strategize about where they want their writing to take them in both the near and long term. Forging close relationships with our authors, we help them with such critical factors as editorial refinement, branding, audience, and marketing." Actively seeking nonfiction. The agency is open to submissions in almost every popular category of nonfiction, especially if authors are recognized experts in their fields. Does not want to receive screenplays, poetry or short stories.

How to Contact Query with SASE, submit publishing history, author bio, brief synopsis of work, key selling points. E-queries only. Send no attachments. For fiction, send first 5 pages pasted in e-mail. Accepts e-mail queries. No fax queries. Responds in 1-6 weeks to queries. Returns materials only with SASE.

Recent Sales Sold 25 titles in the last year. *Wild Things*, by Stephen James and David Thomas (Tyndale); *My Life as a Holy Roller*, by Julie Lyons (WaterBrook Multnomah); *40 Days Living the Jesus Creed*, by Scot McKnight (Paraclete); *The Sacredness of Questioning Everything*, by David Dark (Zondervan); *The Preacher*, by Darren Dillman (David C. Cook); *A New Kind of Human*, by Alex McManus (Zondervan).

◑ DARHANSOFF, VERRILL, FELDMAN LITERARY AGENTS

236 W. 26th St., Suite 802, New York NY 10001. (917)305-1300. Fax: (917)305-1400. Website: www.dvagency.c om. Estab. 1975. Member of AAR. Represents 120 clients. 10% of clients are new/unpublished writers. Currently handles: 25% nonfiction books; 60% novels; 15% story collections.

Member Agents Liz Darhansoff; Charles Verrill; Leigh Feldman.

Represents Nonfiction books, novels, short story collections.

How to Contact Obtains most new clients through recommendations from others.

⊕ ◑ CAROLINE DAVIDSON LITERARY AGENCY

5 Queen Anne's Gardens, London England W4 ITU, United Kingdom. (44)(208)995-5768. Fax: (44)(208)994-2770. E-mail: caroline@cdla.co.uk. Website: www.cdla.co.uk. **Contact:** Caroline Davidson. Estab. 1988.

Represents Nonfiction books (serious material only), novels.

   Oⁿ Does not consider autobiographies, chick lit, children's, crime, erotica, fantasy, horror, local history, murder mysteries, occult, self-help, short stories, sci-fi, thrillers, individual short stories, or memoir.

How to Contact Query with SASE. Query by mail with SAE/IRC. No fax queries. Responds in 2 weeks to queries. Obtains most new clients through recommendations from others, solicitations.

Recent Sales *The Islamist*, by Ed Husain; *The Light Revolution*, by Richard Hobday; *Doorway*, by Simon Unwin.

Tips ''Visit our Web site before submitting any work to us.''

Ⓝ ◑ DAVIS WAGER LITERARY AGENCY

419 N. Larchmont Blvd., #317, Los Angeles CA 90004. (323)962-7741. E-mail: timothy@daviswager.com. Website: www.daviswager.com/. **Contact:** Timothy Wager. Estab. 2004.

   ● Prior to his current position, Mr. Wager was with the Sandra Dijkstra Literary Agency, where he worked as a reader and associate agent.

Represents Nonfiction books, novels. **Considers these fiction areas:** Literary.

   Oⁿ Actively seeking: ''literary fiction and general-interest nonfiction.''

How to Contact Query with SASE, submit author bio, synopsis for fiction, book proposal or outline for nonfiction. Query via e-mail. No fax queries.

◑ LIZA DAWSON ASSOCIATES

350 Seventh Ave., Ste. 2003, New York NY 10001. (212)465-9071. Fax: (212)947-0460. Website: www.lizadawso nassociates.com. Member of AAR, MWA, Women's Media Group. Represents 50 + clients. 15% of clients are new/unpublished writers. Currently handles: 60% nonfiction books; 40% novels.

   ● Prior to becoming an agent, Ms. Dawson was an editor for 20 years, spending 11 years at William Morrow as vice president and 2 years at Putnam as executive editor. Ms. Bladell was a senior editor at HarperCollins and Avon. Ms. Miller is an *Essence*-bestselling author and niche publisher. Ms. Olswanger is an author.

Member Agents Liza Dawson (plot-driven literary fiction, historicals, thrillers, suspense, parenting books, history, psychology—both popular and clinical—politics, narrative nonfiction and memoirs) Caitlin Blasdell (science fiction, fantasy—both adult and young adult—parenting, business, thrillers and women's fiction) Anna Olswanger (gift books for adults, young adult fiction and nonfiction, children's illustrated books, and Judaica) Havis Dawson (business books, how-to and practical books, spirituality, fantasy, Southern-culture fiction and military memoirs); David Austern (fiction and nonfiction, with an interest in young adult, pop culture, sports, and male-interest works).

Represents Nonfiction books, novels, novels and gift books (Olswanger only). **Considers these nonfiction areas:** Biography/autobiography; health/medicine; history; memoirs; psychology; sociology; women's issues/ studies; politics; business; parenting. **Considers these fiction areas:** Fantasy (Blasdell only); historical; literary; mystery/suspense; regional; science fiction (Blasdell only); thriller; African-American (Miller only).

   Oⁿ This agency specializes in readable literary fiction, thrillers, mainstream historicals, women's fiction, academics, historians, business, journalists and psychology.

How to Contact Query with SASE. Individual query e-mails are query[agentfirstname] izadawsonassociates.com. Responds in 3 weeks to queries; 6 weeks to mss. Obtains most new clients through recommendations from others, conferences.

Recent Sales Sold 40 titles in the last year. *Going for It*, by Karen E. Quinones Miller (Warner); *Mayada: Daughter of Iraq*, by Jean Sasson (Dutton); *It's So Much Work to Be Your Friend: Social Skill Problems at Home and at School*, by Richard Lavoie (Touchstone); *WORDCRAFT: How to Write Like a Professional*, by Jack Hart (Pantheon); . . .*And a Time to Die: How Hospitals Shape the End of Life Experience*, by Dr. Sharon Kaufman (Scribner); *Zeus: A Biography*, by Tom Stone (Bloomsbury).

Terms Agent receives 15% commission on domestic sales; 20% commission on foreign sales. Offers written contract. Charges clients for photocopying and overseas postage.

☑ THE JENNIFER DECHIARA LITERARY AGENCY

31 East 32nd St., Suite 300, New York NY 10016. (212)481-8484. E-mail: jenndec@aol.com. Website: www.jdlit. com. **Contact:** Jennifer DeChiara. Estab. 2001. Represents 100 clients. 50% of clients are new/unpublished writers. Currently handles: 50% nonfiction books; 25% novels; 25% juvenile books.

- Prior to becoming an agent, Ms. DeChiara was a writing consultant, freelance editor at Simon & Schuster and Random House, and a ballerina and an actress.

Represents Nonfiction books, novels, juvenile books. **Considers these nonfiction areas:** Biography/autobiography; child guidance/parenting; cooking/foods/nutrition; crafts/hobbies; current affairs; education; ethnic/cultural interests; gay/lesbian issues; government/politics/law; health/medicine; history; how-to; humor/satire; interior design/decorating; juvenile nonfiction; language/literature/criticism; memoirs; military/war; money/finance; music/dance; nature/environment; photography; popular culture; psychology; science/technology; self-help/personal improvement; sociology; sports; theater/film; true crime/investigative; women's issues/studies. **Considers these fiction areas:** Confession; detective/police/crime; ethnic; family saga; fantasy; feminist; gay/lesbian; historical; horror; humor/satire; juvenile; literary; mainstream/contemporary; mystery/suspense; picture books; regional; sports; thriller; young adult; chick lit; psychic/supernatural; glitz.

- ☞ "We represent both children's and adult books in a wide range of ages and genres. We are a full-service agency and fulfill the potential of every book in every possible medium—stage, film, television, etc. We help writers every step of the way, from creating book ideas to editing and promotion. We are passionate about helping writers further their careers, but are just as eager to discover new talent, regardless of age or lack of prior publishing experience. This agency is committed to managing a writer's entire career. For us, it's not just about selling books, but about making dreams come true. We are especially attracted to the downtrodden, the discouraged, and the downright disgusted." Actively seeking literary fiction, chick lit, young adult fiction, self-help, pop culture, and celebrity biographies. Does not want westerns, poetry, or short stories.

How to Contact Query with SASE. Considers simultaneous queries. Responds in 3-6 months to queries; 3-6 months to mss. Returns materials only with SASE. Obtains most new clients through recommendations from others, conferences, query letters.

Recent Sales Sold 30 titles in the last year. *I Was a Teenage Popsicle*, by Bev Katz Rosenbaum (Berkley/JAM); *Hazing Meri Sugarman*, by M. Apostolina (Simon Pulse); *The 10-Minute Sexual Solution* and *Virgin Sex: A Guy's Guide to Sex*, by Dr. Darcy Luadzers (Hatherleigh Press). *Movie/TV MOW script(s) optioned/sold: Geography Club*, by Brent Hartinger (East of Doheny). Other clients include Adam Meyer, Herbie J. Pilato, Chris Demarest, Jeff Lenburg, Joe Cadora, Tiffani Amber Thiessen, Bonnie Neubauer.

Terms Agent receives 15% commission on domestic sales; 20% commission on foreign sales. Offers written contract.

☑ DEFIORE & CO.

72 Spring St., Suite 304, New York NY 10012. (212)925-7744. Fax: (212)925-9803. E-mail: info@defioreandco.c om. Website: www.defioreandco.com. **Contact:** Lauren Gilchrist. Estab. 1999. Member of AAR. Represents 75 clients. 50% of clients are new/unpublished writers. Currently handles: 70% nonfiction books; 30% novels.

- Prior to becoming an agent, Mr. DeFiore was publisher of Villard Books (1997-1998), editor-in-chief of Hyperion (1992-1997), and editorial director of Delacorte Press (1988-1992).

Member Agents Brian DeFiore (popular nonfiction, business, pop culture, parenting, commercial fiction); Laurie Abkemeier (memoir, parenting, business, how-to/self-help, popular science); Kate Garrick (literary fiction, crime, pop culture, politics, history, psychology, narrative nonfiction); Randi Murray (literary fiction, mystery, historical fiction, chick lit, memoir, history, biography, business, current affairs, women's issues, sports, psychology, humor).

Represents Nonfiction books, novels. **Considers these nonfiction areas:** Biography/autobiography; business/economics; child guidance/parenting; cooking/foods/nutrition; money/finance; multicultural; popular culture; psychology; religious/inspirational; self-help/personal improvement; sports; young adult (and middle grade). **Considers these fiction areas:** Ethnic; literary; mainstream/contemporary; mystery/suspense; thriller.

How to Contact Query with SASE. Considers simultaneous queries. Responds in 3 weeks to queries; 2 months to mss. Returns materials only with SASE. Obtains most new clients through recommendations from others.

Recent Sales Sold 35 titles in the last year. *Marley: A Dog Like No Other* and *Bad Dog Marley!*, by John Grogan; *A Lifetime of Secrets* and *The Secret Lives of Men and Women*, by Frank Warren; *Mary Modern*, by Camille DeAngelis; *The Baby Name Bible*, by Pam Satran and Linda Rosenkrantz; *The Follower*, by Jason Starr; *Bright Lights, Big Ass*, by Jen Lancaster; *A Circle is a Balloon and Compass Both*, by Ben Greenman.

Terms Agent receives 15% commission on domestic sales; 20% commission on foreign sales. Offers written contract; 10-day notice must be given to terminate contract. Charges clients for photocopying and overnight delivery (deducted only after a sale is made).

Writers' Conferences Maui Writers Conference; Pacific Northwest Writers Conference; North Carolina Writers' Network Fall Conference.

☺ JOELLE DELBOURGO ASSOCIATES, INC.

516 Bloomfield Ave., Suite 5, Montclair NJ 07042. (973)783-6800. Fax: (973)783-6802. E-mail: info@delbourgo.com. Website: www.delbourgo.com. **Contact:** Joelle Delbourgo, Molly Lyons. Estab. 2000. Represents 80 clients. 40% of clients are new/unpublished writers. Currently handles: 75% nonfiction books; 25% novels.

• Prior to becoming an agent, Ms. Delbourgo was an editor and senior publishing executive at HarperCollins and Random House.

Member Agents Joelle Delbourgo (parenting, self-help, psychology, business, serious nonfiction, narrative nonfiction, quality fiction); Molly Lyons (practical and narrative nonfiction, memoir, quality fiction).

Represents Nonfiction books, novels, short story collections. **Considers these nonfiction areas:** Biography/autobiography; business/economics; child guidance/parenting; cooking/foods/nutrition; current affairs; education; ethnic/cultural interests; gay/lesbian issues; government/politics/law; health/medicine; history; how-to; money/finance; nature/environment; popular culture; psychology; religious/inspirational; science/technology; self-help/personal improvement; sociology; true crime/investigative; women's issues/studies; New Age/metaphysics, interior design/decorating. **Considers these fiction areas:** Historical; literary; mainstream/contemporary; mystery/suspense.

○━ "We are former publishers and editors, with deep knowledge and an insider perspective. We have a reputation for individualized attention to clients, strategic management of authors' careers, and creating strong partnerships with publishers for our clients." Actively seeking history, narrative nonfiction, science/medicine, memoir, literary fiction, psychology, parenting, biographies, current affairs, politics, young adult fiction and nonfiction. Does not want to receive genre fiction or screenplays.

How to Contact Query with SASE. No e-mail or fax queries. Considers simultaneous queries. Responds in 3 weeks to queries; 2 months to mss. Returns materials only with SASE.

Recent Sales Sold 23 titles in the last year. *Amen, Amen,* by Abby Sker (Scribner/Simon & Schuster); *Standing By: The Making of an Unlikely Military Family,* by Alison Buckholtz (Penguin); *Mother and Adult Daughters,* by Linda Gordon and Susan Shaffer (New American Library/Penguin); *Brainstorms: Diagnosing, Treating and Living with Traumatic Brain Injury,* by John W. Cassidy (Da Capo) *The Sneaky Chef 2: How to Cheat on Your Man in the Kitchen,* by Missy Chase Lapine (Running Press).

Terms Agent receives 15% commission on domestic sales; 20% commission on foreign sales. Offers written contract. Charges clients for postage and photocopying.

Tips "Do your homework. Do not cold call. Read and follow submission guidelines before contacting us. Do not call to find out if we received your material. No e-mail queries. Treat agents with respect, as you would any other professional, such as a doctor, lawyer or financial advisor."

☻ DH LITERARY, INC.

P.O. Box 805, Nyack NY 10960-0990. E-mail: dhendin@aol.com. **Contact:** David Hendin. Estab. 1993. Member of AAR. Represents 10 clients. Currently handles: 80% nonfiction books; 10% novels; 10% scholarly books.

• Prior to opening his agency, Mr. Hendin served as president and publisher for Pharos Books/World Almanac, as well as senior VP and COO at sister company United Feature Syndicate.

○━ **"We are not accepting new clients. Please do not send queries or submissions."**

Recent Sales *No Vulgar Hotel,* by Judith Martin (Norton); *Murder Between the Covers,* by Elaine Viets (Penguin/Putnam); *Coined by God,* by Jeffrey McQuain and Stanley Malless (Norton).

Terms Agent receives 15% commission on domestic sales; 20% commission on foreign sales. Offers written contract, binding for 1 year. Charges for out-of-pocket expenses for overseas postage specifically related to the sale.

☺ DHS LITERARY, INC.

10711 Preston Road, Suite 100, Dallas TX 75230. (214)363-4422. Fax: (214)363-4423. E-mail: submissions@dhsliterary.com. Website: www.dhsliterary.com. **Contact:** David Hale Smith, president. Estab. 1994. Represents 35 clients. 15% of clients are new/unpublished writers. Currently handles: 60% nonfiction books; 40% novels.

• Prior to opening his agency, Mr. Smith was an agent at Dupree/Miller & Associates.

Represents Nonfiction books, novels. **Considers these nonfiction areas:** Biography/autobiography; business/economics; child guidance/parenting; cooking/foods/nutrition; current affairs; ethnic/cultural interests; popular culture; sports; true crime/investigative. **Considers these fiction areas:** Detective/police/crime; ethnic; literary; mainstream/contemporary; mystery/suspense; thriller; westerns/frontier.

○━ This agency is not actively seeking clients and usually takes clients on by referral only.

How to Contact Only responds if interested. *No unsolicited mss.* No fax queries.

Recent Sales *Officer Down*, by Theresa Schwegel; *Private Wars*, by Greg Rucka; *The Lean Body Promise*, by Lee Labrada.

Terms Agent receives 15% commission on domestic sales; 25% commission on foreign sales. Offers written contract; 10-day notice must be given to terminate contract. This agency charges for postage and photocopying.

Tips "Remember to be courteous and professional, and to treat marketing your work and approaching an agent as you would any formal business matter. If you have a referral, always query first via e-mail. Sorry, but we cannot respond to queries sent via mail, even with a SASE. Visit our Web site for more information."

☑ SANDRA DIJKSTRA LITERARY AGENCY

1155 Camino del Mar, PMB 515, Del Mar CA 92014. (858)755-3115. Fax: (858)794-2822. E-mail: sdla@dijkstraagency.com. **Contact:** Taryn Fagerness. Estab. 1981. Member of AAR, Authors Guild, PEN West, Poets and Editors, MWA. Represents 100+ clients. 30% of clients are new/unpublished writers. Currently handles: 50% nonfiction books; 45% novels; 5% juvenile books.

Member Agents Sandra Dijkstra; Jill Marsal; Kevan Lyon; Taryn Fagerness; Elise Capron; Kelly Sonnack.

Represents Nonfiction books, novels. **Considers these nonfiction areas:** Americana; animals (pets); anthropology/archaeology; business/economics; child guidance/parenting; cooking/foods/nutrition; ethnic/cultural interests; gay/lesbian issues; government/politics/law; health/medicine; history; juvenile nonfiction; language/literature/criticism; memoirs; military/war; money/finance; nature/environment; psychology; regional; religious/inspirational; science/technology; self-help/personal improvement; sociology; travel; women's issues/studies; Asian studies; art; accounting; biography; environmental studies; technology; transportation. **Considers these fiction areas:** Erotica; ethnic; fantasy; juvenile (YA middle grade and picture books); literary; mainstream/contemporary; mystery/suspense; picture books; science fiction; thriller; graphic novels.

➝ Does not want to receive Western, screenplays, short story collections or poetry.

How to Contact Submit for fiction, send brief synopsis and 50 sample pages double-spaced and single-sided, SASE. No e-mail or fax queries. Responds in 6 weeks to queries. Obtains most new clients through recommendations from others, solicitations, conferences.

Recent Sales

Terms Agent receives 15% commission on domestic sales; 20% commission on foreign sales. Offers written contract. Charges clients for expenses for foreign postage and copying costs if a client requests a hard copy submission to publishers.

Tips "Be professional and learn the standard procedures for submitting your work. Be a regular patron of bookstores, and study what kind of books are being published and will appear on the shelves next to yours. Read! Check out your local library and bookstores—you'll find lots of books on writing and the publishing industry that will help you. At conferences, ask published writers about their agents. Don't believe the myth that an agent has to be in New York to be successful. We've already disproved it!"

◐ THE JONATHAN DOLGER AGENCY

49 E. 96th St., Suite 9B, New York NY 10128. Fax: (212)369-7118. Estab. 1980. Member of AAR.

Represents Nonfiction books, novels. **Considers these nonfiction areas:** Biography/autobiography; history; women's issues/studies; cultural/social. **Considers these fiction areas:** Women's; commercial.

How to Contact Query with SASE. No e-mail queries.

Recent Sales This agency prefers not to share information on specific sales.

Terms Agent receives 15% commission on domestic sales; 25% commission on foreign sales.

Tips "Writers must have been previously published if submitting fiction. We prefer to work with published/established authors, and work with a small number of new/previously unpublished writers."

◎ DONADIO & OLSON, INC.

121 W. 27th St., Suite 704, New York NY 10001. (212)691-8077. Fax: (212)633-2837. E-mail: mail@donadio.com. Member of AAR.

Member Agents Neil Olson (no queries); Ira Silverberg (query via snail mail for general fiction, history, biography, pop culture); Edward Hibbert (no queries); Darren Web (query via snail mail).

Represents Nonfiction books, novels.

➝ This agency represents mostly fiction, and is very selective.

How to Contact Query by snail mail is preferred; only send submissions to open agents. No fax queries. Obtains most new clients through recommendations from others.

Recent Sales *Kings of Infinite Space*, by James Hynes (St. Martin's Press); *Shifting Through Neutral*, by Bridgett M. Davis (Amistad); *The Faithful Narrative of a Pastor's Disappearance: A Novel*, by Benjamin Anastas (Straus Giroux).

✪ JANIS A. DONNAUD & ASSOCIATES, INC.

525 Broadway, Second Floor, New York NY 10012. (212)431-2664. Fax: (212)431-2667. E-mail: jdonnaud@aol.com; donnaudassociate@aol.com. **Contact:** Janis A. Donnaud. Member of AAR; signatory of WGA. Represents 40 clients. 5% of clients are new/unpublished writers. Currently handles: 100% nonfiction books.

- Prior to opening her agency, Ms. Donnaud was vice president and associate publisher of Random House Adult Trade Group.

Represents Nonfiction books. **Considers these nonfiction areas:** Biography/autobiography; child guidance/parenting; cooking/foods/nutrition; current affairs; health/medicine; humor/satire; psychology (pop); women's issues/studies; lifestyle.

- ☞ This agency specializes in health, medical, cooking, humor, pop psychology, narrative nonfiction, biography, parenting, and current affairs. "We give a lot of service and attention to clients." Does not want to receive fiction, poetry, mysteries, juvenile books, romances, science fiction, young adult, religious or fantasy.

How to Contact Query with SASE, submit description of book, 2-3 pages of sample material. Prefers to read materials exclusively. No phone calls. Accepts e-mail queries. No fax queries. Responds in 1 month to queries; 1 month to mss. Obtains most new clients through recommendations from others.

Recent Sales Sold 25 titles in the last year. *Inventing the Rest of Our Lives*, by Suzanne Braun Levine; *Southern Fried Divorce: A Woman Unleashes Her Hound and His Dog in the Big Easy*, by Judy Conner (Light of New Orleans Publishing); *Inventing The Rest Of Our Lives: Women In Second Adulthood*, by Susanne Braun Levine (Viking Books).

Terms Agent receives 15% commission on domestic sales; 20% commission on foreign sales; 20% commission on dramatic rights sales. Offers written contract; 1-month notice must be given to terminate contract. Charges clients for messengers, photocopying and purchase of books.

✪ ◎ JIM DONOVAN LITERARY

4515 Prentice St., Suite 109, Dallas TX 75206. E-mail: jdlqueries@sbcglobal.net. **Contact:** Melissa Shultz, agent. Estab. 1993. Represents 30 clients. 10% of clients are new/unpublished writers. Currently handles: 75% nonfiction books; 25% novels.

Member Agents Jim Donovan (history—particularly American, military and Western; biography; sports; popular reference; popular culture; fiction—literary, thrillers and mystery); Melissa Shultz (chick lit, parenting, women's issues, memoir).

Represents Nonfiction books, novels. **Considers these nonfiction areas:** Biography/autobiography; business/economics; child guidance/parenting; current affairs; government/politics/law; health/medicine; history; how-to; memoirs; military/war; money/finance; music/dance; nature/environment; popular culture; sports; true crime/investigative; women's issues/studies. **Considers these fiction areas:** Action/adventure; detective/police/crime; literary; mainstream/contemporary; mystery/suspense; thriller; women's.

- ☞ This agency specializes in commercial fiction and nonfiction. Does not want to receive poetry, children's, short stories, inspirational or anything else not listed above.

How to Contact For nonfiction, send query letter and SASE. For fiction, send 3 sample chapters, synopsis, SASE. Responds to e-queries only if interested. Accepts e-mail queries. No fax queries. Considers simultaneous queries. Responds in 3 weeks to queries; 1 month to mss. Returns materials only with SASE. Obtains most new clients through recommendations from others.

Recent Sales Sold 24 titles in the last year. *Born to be Hurt*, by Sam Staggs (St. Martin's Press); *The Last Great Season*, by Mike Shropshire (Grand Central); *To Hell on a Fast Horse*, by Mark Gardner (Morrow); *Live Fast, Die Young*, by Jeff Guinn (Simon and Schuster).

Terms Agent receives 15% commission on domestic sales; 20% commission on foreign sales. Offers written contract, binding for 1 year; 30-day notice must be given to terminate contract. This agency charges for things such as overnight delivery and manuscript copying. Charges are discussed beforehand.

Tips "Get published in short form—magazine reviews, journals, etc.—first. This will increase your credibility considerably, and make it much easier to sell a full-length book."

✪ DOYEN LITERARY SERVICES, INC.

1931 660th St., Newell IA 50568-7613. (712)272-3300. Website: www.barbaradoyen.com. **Contact:** (Ms.) B.J. Doyen, president. Estab. 1988. Represents over 100 clients. 20% of clients are new/unpublished writers. Currently handles: 95% nonfiction books; 5% novels.

- Prior to opening her agency, Ms. Doyen worked as a published author, teacher, guest speaker, and wrote and appeared in her own weekly TV show airing in 7 states. She is also the co-author of *The Everything Guide to Writing a Book Proposal* (Adams 2005) and *The Everything Guide to Getting Published* (Adams 2006).

Represents Nonfiction books, novels. **Considers these nonfiction areas:** Agriculture/horticulture; americana;

animals; anthropology/archaeology; art/architecture/design; biography/autobiography; business/economics; child guidance/parenting; computers/electronic; cooking/foods/nutrition; crafts/hobbies; current affairs; education; ethnic/cultural interests; gardening; government/politics/law; health/medicine; history; how-to; interior design/decorating; language/literature/criticism; memoirs; military/war; money/finance; multicultural; music/dance; nature/environment; New Age/metaphysics; philosophy; photography; popular culture; psychology; recreation; regional; religious/inspirational; science/technology; self-help/personal improvement; sex; sociology; software; spirituality; theater/film; travel; true crime/investigative; women's issues/studies; young adult; creative nonfiction. **Considers these fiction areas:** Family saga; historical; literary; mainstream/contemporary.

> ⊶ This agency specializes in nonfiction and occasionally handles mainstream fiction for adults. Actively seeking business, health, how-to, self-help—all kinds of adult nonfiction suitable for the major trade publishers. Does not want to receive pornography, children's books, or poetry.

How to Contact Query with SASE. Snail mail queries preferred, but you can submit a query on the Web site as well. Include bio/background info. Send no unsolicited samples. No e-mail or fax queries. Considers simultaneous queries. Responds in 3 weeks to mss. Responds immediately to queries. Returns materials only with SASE.

Recent Sales *The Good Marriage*, by Isaacson/Schneider (Adams); *1,000 Best Casino Tips*, by Bill Burton (Sourcebooks).

Terms Agent receives 15% commission on domestic sales; 20% commission on foreign sales. Offers written contract, binding for 2 years.

Tips "Our authors receive personalized attention. We market aggressively, undeterred by rejection. We get the best possible publishing contracts. We are very interested in nonfiction book ideas at this time and will consider most topics. Many writers come to us from referrals, but we also get quite a few who initially approach us with query letters. Do not call us regarding queries. It is best if you do not collect editorial rejections prior to seeking an agent, but if you do, be upfront and honest about it. Do not submit your manuscript to more than 1 agent at a time—querying first can save you (and us) much time. We're open to established or beginning writers—just send us a terrific letter!"

🄳 DUNHAM LITERARY, INC.

156 Fifth Ave., Suite 625, New York NY 10010-7002. (212)929-0994. Website: www.dunhamlit.com. **Contact:** Jennie Dunham. Estab. 2000. Member of AAR. Represents 50 clients. 15% of clients are new/unpublished writers. Currently handles: 25% nonfiction books; 25% novels; 50% juvenile books.

> • Prior to opening her agency, Ms. Dunham worked as a literary agent for Russell & Volkening. The Rhoda Weyr Agency is now a division of Dunham Literary, Inc.

Represents Nonfiction books, novels, short story collections, juvenile books. **Considers these nonfiction areas:** Anthropology/archaeology; biography/autobiography; ethnic/cultural interests; government/politics/law; health/medicine; history; language/literature/criticism; nature/environment; popular culture; psychology; science/technology; women's issues/studies. **Considers these fiction areas:** Ethnic; juvenile; literary; mainstream/contemporary; picture books; young adult.

How to Contact Query with SASE. No e-mail or fax queries. Responds in 1 week to queries; 2 months to mss. Obtains most new clients through recommendations from others, solicitations.

Recent Sales *America the Beautiful*, by Robert Sabuda; *Dahlia*, by Barbara McClintock; *Living Dead Girl*, by Tod Goldberg; *In My Mother's House*, by Margaret McMulla; *Black Hawk Down*, by Mark Bowden; *Look Back All the Green Valley*, by Fred Chappell; *Under a Wing*, by Reeve Lindbergh; *I Am Madame X*, by Gioia Diliberto.

Terms Agent receives 15% commission on domestic sales; 20% commission on foreign sales.

🄳 DUNOW, CARLSON, & LERNER AGENCY

27 W. 20th St., #1107, New York NY 10011. E-mail: mail@dclagency.com. Website: www.dclagency.com/. **Contact:** Jennifer Carlson, Henry Dunow, Betsy Lerner. Member of AAR.

Member Agents Jennifer Carlson (young adult and middle grade, some fiction and nonfiction); Henry Dunow (quality fiction—literary, historical, strongly written commercial—and with voice-driven nonfiction across a range of areas—narrative history, biography, memoir, current affairs, cultural trends and criticism, science, sports); Erin Hosier (nonfiction: popular culture, music, sociology and memoir); Betsy Lerner (nonfiction writers in the areas of psychology, history, cultural studies, biography, current events, business; fiction: literary, dark, funny, voice driven; Jeff Moores (quality contemporary fiction and literature, narrative nonfiction, memoir, politics, current affairs, journalism, graphic novels, gay & lesbian, popular culture and popular science).

Represents Nonfiction books, novels, juvenile books.

How to Contact Query with SASE.

Recent Sales *Black Olives*, by Martha Tod Dudman (Simon & Schuster).

Tips "Query letters are also welcome via e-mail (mail@dclagency.com). Please do not send attachments. Due to the volume of inquiries the agency receives, we are unable to respond to all e-mailed queries. We apologize in advance for this inconvenience."

◎ DUPREE/MILLER AND ASSOCIATES INC. LITERARY

100 Highland Park Village, Suite 350, Dallas TX 75205. (214)559-BOOK. Fax: (214)559-PAGE. E-mail: jan@dupr eemiller.com. **Contact:** Submissions Department. Estab. 1984. Member of ABA. Represents 200 clients. 20% of clients are new/unpublished writers. Currently handles: 90% nonfiction books; 10% novels.

Member Agents Jan Miller, president/CEO; Shannon Miser-Marven, senior executive VP; Annabelle Baxter; Nena Madonia; Cheri Gillis.

Represents Nonfiction books, novels, scholarly books, syndicated material (1), religious.inspirational/spirituality. **Considers these nonfiction areas:** Americana; animals; anthropology/archaeology; art/architecture/design; biography/autobiography; business/economics; child guidance/parenting; cooking/foods/nutrition; crafts/hobbies; creative nonfiction (1); current affairs; education; ethnic/cultural interests; gardening; government/politics/law; health/medicine; history; how-to; humor/satire; interior design/decorating; language/literature/criticism; memoirs; money/finance; multicultural; music/dance; nature/environment; New Age/metaphysics; philosophy; photography; popular culture; psychology; recreation; regional; science/technology; self-help/personal improvement; sex; sociology; sports; theater/film; translation; true crime/investigative; women's issues/studies. **Considers these fiction areas:** Action/adventure; detective/police/crime; ethnic; experimental; family saga; feminist; glitz; historical; humor/satire; literary; mainstream/contemporary; mystery/suspense; picture books; psychic/supernatural; religious/inspirational; sports; thriller.

 ⊙┓ This agency specializes in commercial fiction and nonfiction.

How to Contact Submit 1-page query, outline, SASE. Obtains most new clients through recommendations from others, conferences, lectures.

Recent Sales Sold 30 titles in the last year. *It's All About You: Get the Life You're Craving*, by Mary Goulet and Heather Reider (Free Press). Other clients include Dr. Phil Mcgraw, Robin Mcgraw, Maria Shriver, Catherine Crier, Anthony Robbins, Dr. Stephen Covey, Pastor Joel Osteen, Deborah Norville, Dr. Creflo Dollar, Dr. Frank Lawlis, Dr. Bill Dorfman.

Terms Agent receives 15% commission on domestic sales. Offers written contract.

Writers' Conferences Aspen Summer Words Literary Festival.

Tips "If interested in agency representation, it is vital to have the material in the proper working format. As agents' policies differ, it is important to follow their guidelines. The best advice I can give is to work on establishing a strong proposal that provides sample chapters, an overall synopsis (fairly detailed), and some biographical information on yourself. Do not send your proposal in pieces; it should be complete upon submission. Remember you are trying to sell your work, and it should be in its best condition."

◎ DWYER & O'GRADY, INC.

Agents for Writers & Illustrators of Children's Books, P.O. Box 790, Cedar Key FL 32625-0790. (352)543-9307. Fax: (603)375-5373. Website: www.dwyerogrady.com. **Contact:** Elizabeth O'Grady. Estab. 1990. Member of SCBWI. Represents 30 clients. Currently handles: 100% juvenile books.

 ● Prior to opening their agency, Mr. Dwyer and Ms. O'Grady were booksellers and publishers.

Member Agents Elizabeth O'Grady; Jeff Dwyer.

Represents Juvenile books. **Considers these nonfiction areas:** Juvenile nonfiction. **Considers these fiction areas:** Juvenile; picture books; young adult.

 ⊙┓ "We are not accepting new clients at this time." This agency represents only writers and illustrators of children's books. No juvenile books.

How to Contact *No unsolicited mss.* Obtains most new clients through recommendations from others, direct approach by agent to writer whose work they've read.

Recent Sales Other clients include Kim Ablon Whitney, Jay Allison, Nancy Antle, Mary Azarian, Tom Bodett, Odds Bodkin, Matthew Faulkner, Maxine Kumin, E.B. Lewis, Steve Schuch, Virginia Stroud, Natasha Tarpley, Zong-Zhou Wang, Rich Michelson, Barry Moser, James Rumford, Clemence McLaren, Nat Tripp, Lita Judge, Geoffrey Norman, Stan Fellows, Irving Toddy, Howard Mansfield, Matt Collins, Birgitta Sif, Kelly Starling-Lyons.

Terms Agent receives 15% commission on domestic sales; 20% commission on foreign sales. Offers written contract; 1-month notice must be given to terminate contract. This agency charges clients for photocopying of longer mss or mutually agreed upon marketing expenses.

Writers' Conferences BookExpo America; American Library Association Annual Conference; SCBWI.

Tips This agency previously had an address in New Hampshire. Mail all materials to the new Florida address.

◎ DYSTEL & GODERICH LITERARY MANAGEMENT

1 Union Square W., Suite 904, New York NY 10003. (212)627-9100. Fax: (212)627-9313. E-mail: miriam@dystel. com. Website: www.dystel.com. **Contact:** Miriam Goderich. Estab. 1994. Member of AAR. Represents 300 clients. 50% of clients are new/unpublished writers. Currently handles: 65% nonfiction books; 25% novels; 10% cookbooks.

• Dystel & Goderich Literary Management recently acquired the client list of Bedford Book Works.

Member Agents Stacey Glick; Jane Dystel; Miriam Goderich; Michael Bourret; Jim McCarthy; Lauren Abramo; Adina Kahn.

Represents Nonfiction books, novels, cookbooks. **Considers these nonfiction areas:** Animals; anthropology/archaeology; biography/autobiography; business/economics; child guidance/parenting; cooking/foods/nutrition; current affairs; education; ethnic/cultural interests; gay/lesbian issues; government/politics/law; health/medicine; history; humor/satire; military/war; money/finance; New Age/metaphysics; popular culture; psychology; religious/inspirational; science/technology; true crime/investigative; women's issues/studies. **Considers these fiction areas:** Action/adventure; detective/police/crime; ethnic; family saga; gay/lesbian; literary; mainstream/contemporary; mystery/suspense; thriller.

O━ This agency specializes in cookbooks and commercial and literary fiction and nonfiction.

How to Contact Query with SASE. Considers simultaneous queries. Responds in 1 month to queries; 6 weeks to mss. Obtains most new clients through recommendations from others, solicitations, conferences.

Terms Agent receives 15% commission on domestic sales; 19% commission on foreign sales. Offers written contract. Charges for photocopying. Galley charges and book charges from the publisher are passed on to the author.

Writers' Conferences Whidbey Island Writers' Conference; Backspace Writers' Conference; Iowa Summer Writing Festival; Pacific Northwest Writers' Association; Pike's Peak Writers' Conference; Santa Barbara Writers' Conference; Harriette Austin Writers' Conference; Sandhills Writers' Conference; Denver Publishing Institute; Love Is Murder.

Tips "Work on sending professional, well-written queries that are concise and addressed to the specific agent the author is contacting. No dear Sirs/Madam."

⊕ ☑ TOBY EADY ASSOCIATES

Third Floor, 9 Orme Court, London England W2 4RL, United Kingdom. (44)(207)792-0092. Fax: (44)(207)792-0879. E-mail: Jamie@tobyeady.demon.co.uk. Website: www.tobyeadyassociates.co.uk. **Contact:** Jamie Coleman. Estab. 1968. Represents 53 clients. 13% of clients are new/unpublished writers. Currently handles: 50% nonfiction books; 50% novels.

Member Agents Toby Eady (China, the Middle East, Africa, politics of a Swiftian nature); Laetitia Rutherford (fiction and nonfiction from around the world).

Represents Nonfiction books, novels, short story collections, novellas, anthologies. **Considers these nonfiction areas:** Art/architecture/design; cooking/foods/nutrition; current affairs; ethnic/cultural interests; government/politics/law; health/medicine; history; memoirs; popular culture. **Considers these fiction areas:** Action/adventure; confession; historical; literary; mainstream/contemporary.

O━ "We handle fiction and nonfiction for adults and we specialize in China, the Middle East and Africa." Actively seeking stories that demand to be heard. Does not want to receive poetry, screenplays or children's books.

How to Contact Send the first 50 pages of your work, double-spaced and unbound, with a synopsis and a brief bio. Considers simultaneous queries. Responds in 2 weeks to queries; 2 weeks to mss. Returns materials only with SASE. Obtains most new clients through recommendations from others, solicitations, conferences.

Recent Sales *My Name Is Salma*, by Fadia Faquir (Doubleday); *Speaking to the Heart*, by Sister Wendy Beckett (Constable & Robinson); *February Flowers*, by Fan Wu (Picador Asia). Other clients include Bernard Cornwell, Chris Cleave, Rana Dasgupta, Julia Lovell and Rachel Seiffert.

Terms Agent receives 15% commission on domestic sales; 20% commission on foreign sales. Offers written contract; 3-month notice must be given to terminate contract.

Writers' Conferences City Lit; Winchester Writers' Festival.

Tips Send submissions to this address: Jamie Coleman, Third Floor, 9 Orme Court, London W2 4RL.

Ⓝ ◯ EAMES LITERARY SERVICES

4117 Hillsboro Road, Suite 251, Nashville TN 37215. Fax: (615)463.9361. E-mail: info@eamesliterary.com; John@eamesliterary.com; Ahna@eamesliterary.com. Website: www.eamesliterary.com. **Contact:** John Eames.

Member Agents John Eames, Ahna Phillips.

Represents Nonfiction books, novels. **Considers these nonfiction areas:** Memoirs; religious/inspirational; young adult. **Considers these fiction areas:** Religious/inspirational; young adult.

O━ This agency specializes in the Christian marketplace. Actively seeking adult and young adult fiction that sparks the imagination, illuminates some angle of truth about the human condition, causes the reader to view the world with fresh eyes, and supports a Christian perspective on life in all its complexities. Stories might be redemptive, or tragic. Characters might be noble, or flawed. Situations might be humorous, or dark. And many manuscripts might contain some combination of all of the above. We also seek adult and young adult nonfiction that is anecdotal as well as instructional, utilizes a "show, don't tell" philosophy of writing, and offers a unique and biblically sound perspective on a given topic. If the submission is a nonfiction narrative (or memoir), the work should follow most of the same recommendations for a work of fiction, as listed above.

Recent Sales *Less is More Leadership: 8 Secrets to How to Lead and Still Have a Life*, by H. Dale Bourke (Harvest House Publishers); *Lessons from Lucy*, by Wendy Murray Zoba (NavPress).

N ⓒ EAST/WEST AGENCY

1158 26th St., Suite 462, Santa Monica CA 90403. (310)573-9303. Fax: (310)453-9008. E-mail: creativeideaz@roa drunner.com. **Contact:** Deborah Warren, founder. Estab. 2000; adheres to AAR canon of ethics. Represents 100 clients. 70% of clients are new/unpublished writers. Currently handles: 25% nonfiction books; 75% juvenile books.

Member Agents Deborah Warren; Lisa Rojany Buccieri; Susan B. Katz (writers/illustrators in the Latino market, representing Spanish-speaking clients).

Represents Nonfiction books, juvenile books. **Considers these nonfiction areas:** Art/architecture/design; crafts/hobbies; how-to; humor/satire; interior design/decorating; juvenile nonfiction; language/literature/criticism; music/dance; photography; popular culture; religious/inspirational; self-help/personal improvement. **Considers these fiction areas:** Comic books/cartoon; ethnic; juvenile; picture books; young adult.

> 🔾 "EWA is, purposefully, a niche agency, to facilitate hands-on, personalized service and attention to our authors, authorial illustrators, illustrators and their books. EWA provides career management for established and first time authors and our breadth of experience in many genres enables us to meet the demands of a diverse clientele. Understanding the in-depth process of acquisitions, sales and marketing helps Ms. Warren and her co-agents attain the stated goals for each of the agency's clients: to close the best possible deal with the best possible editor at the best possible publishing house." Actively seeking clients by referral only. This agency works with board books, illustrated picture books and bilingual (Spanish-speaking) authors frequently.

How to Contact Query with SASE, submit first 3 sample chapter(s), table of contents (2 pages or fewer), synopsis (1 page). For picture books, submit entire ms. For chapter books/novels. Responds in 2 months to mss. Obtains most new clients through recommendations from others.

Recent Sales Sold 30 titles in the last year.

Terms Agent receives 15% commission on domestic sales; 25% commission on foreign sales. Offers written contract; 30-day notice must be given to terminate contract. Charges for out-of-pocket expenses, such as postage and copying.

Tips "Send submissions to CreativeIdeaz@roadrunner.com, or snail mail to Requested Materials, EWA, 1543 Sycamore Canyon Drive, Westlake Village, CA 91361. Submit the manuscript as a Word document in Courier, 12-point, double-spaced, with 1.20 inch margin on left, ragged right text, 25 lines per page, continuously paginated, with all your contact info on the first page. Include an SASE and a manila envelope with appropriate postage to expedite our response."

ⓒ EBELING AND ASSOCIATES

P.O. Box 790267, Pala HI 96779. (808)579-6414. Fax: (808)579-9294. Website: www.ebelingagency.com. **Contact:** Michael Ebeling or Kristina Holmes. Estab. 2003. Represents 6 clients. 50% of clients are new/unpublished writers. Currently handles: 100% nonfiction books.

> • Prior to becoming an agent, Mr. Ebeling established a career in the publishing industry through long-term author management. He has expertise in sales, platforms, publicity and marketing. Ms. Holmes joined the agency in 2005, and considers many types of projects. She is interested in books that take a stand, bring an issue to light or help readers.

Member Agents Michael Ebeling, ebothat@yahoo.com; Kristina Holmes, kristina@ebelingagency.com.

Represents Nonfiction books. **Considers these nonfiction areas:** Animals; anthropology/archaeology; art/architecture/design; biography/autobiography; business/economics; child guidance/parenting; computers/electronic; cooking/foods/nutrition; current affairs; education; ethnic/cultural interests; gay/lesbian issues; government/politics/law; health/medicine; history; how-to; humor/satire; memoirs; money/finance; music/dance; nature/environment; photography; popular culture; psychology; religious/inspirational; science/technology; self-help/personal improvement; sports; travel; women's issues/studies; food/fitness.

> 🔾 "We accept very few clients for representation. We represent nonfiction authors, most predominantly in the areas of business and self-help. We are very committed to our authors and their messages, which is a main reason we have such a high placement rate. We are always looking at new ways to help our authors gain the exposure they need to not only get published, but develop a successful literary career." Actively seeking well written nonfiction material with fresh perspectives written by writers with established platforms. Does not want to receive fiction.

How to Contact E-mail query and proposal to either Michael or Kristina. E-queries only. Considers simultaneous queries. Responds in 2-4 weeks to queries. Obtains most new clients through recommendations from others, solicitations.

Recent Sales Sold 10 titles in the last year. *Defenders of the Heart: 12 Strategies for a Richer, Satisying and Fulfilling Life*, by Marilyn Kagan and Neil Einbund (Hay House); *Don't Get Lucky, Get Smart: Why Your Love Life Sucks and What You Can Do About It*, by Alan Cohen; *Shiny Marketing Objects*, by Dave Labonte (Wiley).

Terms Agent receives 15% commission on domestic sales; 15% commission on foreign sales. Offers written contract; 60-day notice must be given to terminate contract. There is a charge for normal out-of-pocket fees, not to exceed $200 without client approval.

Writers' Conferences BookExpo America; San Francisco Writers' Conference.

Tips "Approach agents when you're already building your platform, you have a well written book, you have a firm understanding of the publishing process, and have come up with a complete competitive proposal. Know the name of the agent you are contacting. You're essentially selling a business plan to the publisher. Make sure you've made a convincing pitch throughout your proposal, as ultimately, publishers are taking a financial risk by investing in your project."

ANNE EDELSTEIN LITERARY AGENCY

20 W. 22nd St., Suite 1603, New York NY 10010. (212)414-4923. Fax: (212)414-2930. E-mail: info@aeliterary.com. Website: www.aeliterary.com. Estab. 1990. Member of AAR.

Member Agents Anne Edelstein; Krista Ingebretson.

Represents Nonfiction books, Fiction. **Considers these nonfiction areas:** History; memoirs; psychology; religious/inspirational; Buddhist thought. **Considers these fiction areas:** Literary.

O→ This agency specializes in fiction and narrative nonfiction.

How to Contact Query with SASE; submit 25 sample pages. No e-mail or fax queries.

Recent Sales *Confessions of a Buddhist Athlete*, by Stephen Batchelor (Spiegel & Grau); *April & Oliver*, by Tess Callahan (Doubleday).

EDUCATIONAL DESIGN SERVICES, LLC

5750 Bou Ave., Suite 1508, Bethesda MD MD 20852. (561)739-9402. Fax: (561)739-9402. E-mail: blinder@educationaldesignservices.com. Website: www.educationaldesignservices.com. **Contact:** Bertram L. Linder, president. Estab. 1981. Represents 14 clients. 95% of clients are new/unpublished writers. Currently handles: 100% textbooks and professional materials for education.

• Prior to becoming an agent, Mr. Linder was an author and a teacher.

Member Agents Bertram Linder (textbooks and professional materials for education).

Represents Scholarly books, textbooks.

O→ "We are one of the few agencies that specialize exclusively in materials for the education market. We handle text materials for grades preK-12, text materials for college/university use, and materials for professionals in the field of education, staff development and education policy." Does not want to receive children's fiction and nonfiction, or picture books.

How to Contact Query with SASE, submit proposal package, outline, outline/proposal, 2-3 sample chapter(s), SASE. Accepts e-mail queries. No fax queries. Considers simultaneous queries. Responds in 3-4 weeks to queries; 3-4 weeks to mss. Returns materials only with SASE. Obtains most new clients through recommendations from others, solicitations, conferences.

Recent Sales Sold 4 titles in the last year. *No Parent Left Behind*, by P. Petrosino and L. Spiegel (Rowman & Littlefield Education); *Preparing for the 8th Grade Test in Social Studies*, by E. Farran and A. Paci (Amsco Book Company); *Teaching Test-Taking Skills by G. Durham* (Rowman & Littlefield Education); *Teachers's Quick Guide to Communicating*, by G. Sundem (Corwin Press).

Terms Agent receives 15% commission on domestic sales; 25% commission on foreign sales. Offers written contract; 30 days notice must be given to terminate contract. Charges clients for extraordinary expenses in postage and shipping, as well as long distance telephone calls.

JUDITH EHRLICH LITERARY MANAGEMENT, LLC

880 Third Ave., Eighth Floor, New York NY 10022. (646)505-1570. E-mail: jehrlich@JudithEhrlichLiterary.com. Website: www.judithehrlichliterary.com. Estab. 2002. Member of Author's Guild, the American Society of Journalists and Authors.

• Prior to her current position, Ms. Ehrlich was an award-winning journalist; she is the co-author of *The New Crowd: The Changing of the Jewish Guard on Wall Street* (Little, Brown). Ms. Hoffman worked at Harold Matson Company and as a freelance editor.

Member Agents Judith Ehrlich, jehrlich@judithehrlichliterary.com; Sophia Seidner, sseidner@judithehrlichliterary.com; Martha Hoffman, mhoffman@judithehrlichliterary.com (psychology, cultural commentary, and historical work that ties unique perspectives to strong narrative).

Represents Nonfiction books, novels.

O⇥ "Special areas of interest include compelling narrative nonfiction, outstanding biographies and memoirs, lifestyle books, works that reflect our changing culture, women's issues, psychology, science, social issues, current events, parenting, health, history, business, and prescriptive books offering fresh information and advice." Does not want to receive children's or young adult books, novellas, poetry, textbooks, plays or screenplays.

How to Contact Query with SASE. Queries should include a synopsis and some sample pages. Send e-queries to jehrlich@judithehrlichliterary.com. The agency will respond only if interested. Accepts e-mail queries. No fax queries. Returns materials only with SASE.

Recent Sales *Up and Running: The Jami Goldman Story*, by Andrea Cagan (Pocket Books); *Forewarned: Why the Government Is Failing to Protect Us—and What Can We Do to Protect Ourselves*, by Michael Cherkasky (Ballantine); *Let the Baby Drive: Navigating the Road of New Motherhood*, by Lu Hanessian (St. Martin's); *Marriage from the Heart: Eight Commitments of a Spiritually Fulfilling Life Together*, by Lois Kellerman and Nelly Bly (Viking).

THE LISA EKUS GROUP, LLC

57 North St., Hatfield MA 01038. (413)247-9325. Fax: (413)247-9873. E-mail: LisaEkus@lisaekus.com. Website: www.lisaekus.com. **Contact:** Lisa Ekus-Saffer. Estab. 1982. Member of AAR.

Represents Nonfiction books. **Considers these nonfiction areas:** Cooking/foods/nutrition; occasionally health/well-being and women's issues.

How to Contact Submit a one-page query via e-mail or submit your complete hard copy proposal with title page, proposal contents, concept, bio, marketing, TOC, etc. No fax queries.

Recent Sales Please see the regularly updated client listing at www.lisaekus.com.

Tips "Please do not call. No phone queries."

ETHAN ELLENBERG LITERARY AGENCY

548 Broadway, #5-E, New York NY 10012. (212)431-4554. Fax: (212)941-4652. E-mail: agent@ethanellenberg.com. Website: www.ethanellenberg.com. **Contact:** Ethan Ellenberg. Estab. 1983. Represents 80 clients. 10% of clients are new/unpublished writers. Currently handles: 25% nonfiction books; 75% novels.

● Prior to opening his agency, Mr. Ellenberg was contracts manager of Berkley/Jove and associate contracts manager for Bantam.

Represents Nonfiction books, novels, children's books. **Considers these nonfiction areas:** Current affairs; health/medicine; history; military/war; science/technology; narrative, biography. **Considers these fiction areas:** Commerical fiction—specializing in romance/fiction for women, science fiction and fantasy, thrillers, suspense and mysteries, children's books (all types: picture books, middle grade and YA).

O⇥ This agency specializes in commercial fiction—especially thrillers, romance/women's, and specialized nonfiction. "We also do a lot of children's books." Actively seeking commercial fiction as noted above—romance/fiction for women, science fiction and fantasy, thrillers, suspense and mysteries. Our other two main areas of interest are children's books and narrative nonfiction. We are actively seeking clients, follow the directions on our Web site. Does not want to receive poetry, short stories, Western's, autobiographies or screenplays.

How to Contact For fiction, send introductory letter, outline, first 3 chapters, SASE. For nonfiction, send query letter, proposal, 1 sample chapter, SASE. For children's books, send introductory letter, up to 3 picture book mss, outline, first 3 chapters, SASE. No fax queries. Accepts e-mail queries (no attachments). Will only respond to e-mail queries if interested. Considers simultaneous queries. Responds in 4-6 weeks to mss. Returns materials only with SASE.

Recent Sales *Sleeping With the Fishes and Dead and Loving It*, by Maryjanice Davidson (Berkley); *The Summoner*, by Gail Martin (Solaris); *Empress of Mijak*, by Karen Miller (Harper Australia); *Hellgate: London*, by Mel Odom (Pocket Books); *The Last Colony* and *Android's Dream*, by John Scalzi (Tor Books); *General Winston's Daughter*, by Sharon Shinn (Ace Books); *Dead Sexy*, by Amanda Ashley (Kensington); *A Kitten Tale*, by Eric Rohmann (Knopf); *Howl at the Moon*, by Christine Warren. Other clients include Mel Odom, MaryJanice Davidson, Amanda Ashley, Rebecca York, Bertrice Small, Eric Rohmann.

Terms Agent receives 15% commission on domestic sales; 10% commission on foreign sales. Offers written contract. Charges clients (with their consent) for direct expenses limited to photocopying and postage.

Writers' Conferences RWA National Conference; Novelists, Inc; and other regional conferences.

Tips "We do consider new material from unsolicited authors. Write a good, clear letter with a succinct description of your book. We prefer the first 3 chapters when we consider fiction. For all submissions, you must include a SASE or the material will be discarded. It's always hard to break in, but talent will find a home. Check our Web site for complete submission guidelines. We continue to see natural storytellers and nonfiction writers with important books."

⬛ ANN ELMO AGENCY, INC.

60 E. 42nd St., New York NY 10165. (212)661-2880. Fax: (212)661-2883. **Contact:** Lettie Lee. Estab. 1959. Member of AAR, Authors Guild.

Member Agents Lettie Lee; Mari Cronin (plays); A.L. Abecassis (nonfiction).

Represents Nonfiction books, novels. **Considers these nonfiction areas:** Biography/autobiography; current affairs; health/medicine; history; how-to; popular culture; science/technology. **Considers these fiction areas:** Ethnic; family saga; mainstream/contemporary; romance (contemporary, gothic, historical, regency); thriller; women's.

How to Contact Only accepts mailed queries with SASE. Do not send full ms unless requested. No e-mail or fax queries. Responds in 3 months to queries. Obtains most new clients through recommendations from others.

Recent Sales This agency prefers not to share information on specific sales.

Terms Agent receives 15% commission on domestic sales; 20% commission on foreign sales. Offers written contract.

Tips "Query first, and **only** when asked send a double-spaced, readable manuscript. Include a SASE, of course."

⬛ THE ELAINE P. ENGLISH LITERARY AGENCY

4701 41st St. NW, Suite D, Washington DC 20016. (202)362-5190. Fax: (202)362-5192. E-mail: elaine@elaineeng lish.com. Website: www.elaineenglish.com. **Contact:** Elaine English. Member of AAR. Represents 16 clients. 25% of clients are new/unpublished writers. Currently handles: 100% novels.

● Ms. English has been working in publishing for more than 20 years. She is also an attorney specializing in media and publishing law.

Represents Novels. **Considers these fiction areas:** Historical; multicultural; mystery/suspense; romance (single title, historical, contemporary, romantic, suspense, chick lit, erotic); thriller; general women's fiction. The agency is slowly but steadily acquiring in all mentioned areas.

O→ Actively seeking women's fiction, including single-title romances. Does not want to receive any science fiction, time travel, children's, or young adult.

How to Contact Prefers e-queries sent to queries@elaineenglish.com. If requested, submit synopsis, first 3 chapters, SASE. Accepts e-mail queries. No fax queries. Responds in 6-12 weeks to queries; 6 months to requested ms. Returns materials only with SASE. Obtains most new clients through recommendations from others, conferences, submissions.

Recent Sales *The Blue-Eyed Devil*, by Diane Whiteside (Kensington).

Terms Agent receives 15% commission on domestic sales; 20% commission on foreign sales. Offers written contract; 30-day notice must be given to terminate contract. Charges only for copying and postage; generally taken from proceeds.

Writers' Conferences RWA National Conference; SEAK Medical & Legal Fiction Writing Conference; Novelists, Inc; Malice Domestic; Washington Romance Writers Retreat, among others.

⬛ THE EPSTEIN LITERARY AGENCY

P.O. Box 356, Avon MA 02368. (781)718-4025. E-mail: kate@epsteinliterary.com. Website: www.epsteinliterary .com. **Contact:** Kate Epstein. Estab. 2005. Represents 30 clients. 70% of clients are new/unpublished writers. Currently handles: 100% nonfiction books.

● Prior to opening her literary agency, Ms. Epstein was an acquisitions editor at Adams Media.

Represents Nonfiction books. **Considers these nonfiction areas:** Animals; biography/autobiography; business/economics; child guidance/parenting; cooking/foods/nutrition; current affairs; health/medicine; how-to; humor/satire; memoirs; popular culture; psychology; self-help/personal improvement; sociology; women's issues/studies; New Age/metaphysics.

O→ "My background as an editor means that I'm extremely good at selling to them. It also means I'm a careful and thorough line editor. I'm particularly skilled at hardening concepts to make them salable and proposing the logical follow-up for any book. Most of my list is practical nonfiction, and I have a particular affinity for pets." Actively seeking commercial nonfiction for adults. Does not want scholarly works.

How to Contact Query via e-mail (no attachments). Considers simultaneous queries. Responds in 2 months to queries. Returns materials only with SASE. Obtains most new clients through solicitations.

Recent Sales *Pets and the Planet*, by Carol Frischmann (Wiley); *Green Stable*, by Heather Cook (Storey); *Christmas Traditions*, edited by Helen Polaski (Adams); *Your 401(canine) Plan*, by Mary Jane Checchi (TFH); *Rock Star Mommy*, by Judy Davids (Citadel). Other clients include Jeff Alexander, Peter Allison, Tena Bastian, Jennifer Keene, Mary Beth Temple, Drew Emborksky.

Terms Agent receives 15% commission on domestic sales; 20% commission on foreign sales. Offers written contract; 30-day notice must be given to terminate contract.

🔲 FELICIA ETH LITERARY REPRESENTATION

555 Bryant St., Suite 350, Palo Alto CA 94301-1700. (650)375-1276. Fax: (650)401-8892. E-mail: feliciaeth@aol.c om. **Contact:** Felicia Eth. Estab. 1988. Member of AAR. Represents 25-35 clients. Currently handles: 85% nonfiction books; 15% adult novels.

Represents Nonfiction books, novels. **Considers these nonfiction areas:** Animals; anthropology/archaeology; biography/autobiography; business/economics; child guidance/parenting; current affairs; ethnic/cultural interests; gay/lesbian issues; government/politics/law; health/medicine; history; nature/environment; popular culture; psychology; science/technology; sociology; true crime/investigative; women's issues/studies. **Considers these fiction areas:** Literary; mainstream/contemporary; thriller.

    O— This agency specializes in high-quality fiction (preferably mainstream/contemporary) and provocative, intelligent, and thoughtful nonfiction on a wide array of commercial subjects.

How to Contact Query with SASE, outline. Considers simultaneous queries. Responds in 3 weeks to queries; 4-6 weeks to mss.

Recent Sales Sold 7-10 titles in the last year. *My Mercedes is Not For Sale*, by Jereon Van Bergeijk; *Boys Adrift*, by Leonard Sax (Basic Books); *Anna Maria Violina*, by Barbara Quick (HarperCollins); *The Porn Trap*, by Wendy and Larry Maltz.

Terms Agent receives 15% commission on domestic sales; 20% commission on foreign sales; 20% commission on dramatic rights sales. Charges clients for photocopying and express mail service.

Writers' Conferences National Coalition of Independent Scholars Conference.

Tips "For nonfiction, established expertise is certainly a plus—as is magazine publication—though not a prerequisite. I am highly dedicated to those projects I represent, but highly selective in what I choose."

🔲 MARY EVANS INC.

242 E. Fifth St., New York NY 10003. (212)979-0880. Fax: (212)979-5344. Website: www.maryevansinc.com. Member of AAR.

Member Agents Mary Evans (no unsolicited queries); Tanya McKinnon, tanya@maryevansinc.com (children's, humor, journalism, multicultural, graphic novels, African-American fiction and nonfiction); Devin McIntyre, devin@maryevansinc.com (commericial and literary fiction, narrative nonfiction, pop culture, graphic novels, multicultural, pop science, sports, food).

Represents Nonfiction books, novels.

How to Contact Query with SASE. Query with SASE. Query by snail mail. Non-query correspondence can be sent to info(at)maryevansinc.com. No fax queries. Obtains most new clients through recommendations from others, solicitations.

🔲 FAIRBANK LITERARY REPRESENTATION

199 Mount Auburn St., Suite 1, Cambridge MA 02138-4809. (617)576-0030. Fax: (617)576-0030. E-mail: queries @fairbankliterary.com. Website: www.fairbankliterary.com. **Contact:** Sorche Fairbank. Estab. 2002. Represents 40 clients. 20% of clients are new/unpublished writers. Currently handles: 60% nonfiction books; 22% novels; 3% story collections; 15% illustrated.

Member Agents Sorche Fairbank; Matthew Frederick (sports, nonfiction, architecture, design).

Represents Nonfiction books, novels, short story collections. **Considers these nonfiction areas:** Agriculture/ horticulture; art/architecture/design; biography/autobiography; cooking/foods/nutrition; crafts/hobbies; current affairs; ethnic/cultural interests; gay/lesbian issues; government/politics/law; how-to; interior design/ decorating; memoirs; nature/environment; photography; popular culture; science/technology; sociology; sports; true crime/investigative; women's issues/studies. **Considers these fiction areas:** Action/adventure; feminist; gay/lesbian; literary; mainstream/contemporary; mystery/suspense; sports; thriller; women's; Southern voices.

    O— "I have a small agency in Harvard Square, where I tend to gravitate toward literary fiction and narrative nonfiction, with a strong interest in women's issues and women's voices, international voices, class and race issues, and projects that simply teach me something new about the greater world and society around us. We have a good reputation for working closely and developmentally with our authors and love what we do." Actively seeking literary fiction, international and culturally diverse voices, narrative nonfiction, topical subjects (politics, current affairs), history, sports, architecture/design and pop culture. Does not want to receive romance, poetry, science fiction, young adult or children's works.

How to Contact Query with SASE, submit author bio. Accepts e-mail queries. No fax queries. Considers simultaneous queries. Responds in 6 weeks to queries; 10 weeks to mss. Returns materials only with SASE. Obtains most new clients through recommendations from others, solicitations, conferences, ideas generated in-house.

Recent Sales Sold 19 titles in the last year. *Tale of Two Subs*, by Jonathan J. McCullough (Grand Central); *101 Things I Learned in Architecture School*, by Matthew Frederick (MIT Press); *Invisible Sisters*, by Jessica Handler (Public Affairs); *Bent Objects*, by Terry Border (Running Press); *To Full Term: A Mother's Triumph Over Miscar-

riage, by Darci Hamilton-Klein (Berkley/Penguin); *Spirit of Summer: At Home in the Thousand Islands*, by Kathleen Quigley (Rizzoli); *The Uncommon Quilter*, by Jeanne Williamson (Potter Craft/Crown); *Solar Revolution*, by Travis Bradford (The MIT Press).

Terms Agent receives 15% commission on domestic sales; 20% commission on foreign sales. Offers written contract, binding for 12 months; 30-day notice must be given to terminate contract.

Writers' Conferences San Francisco Writers' Conference, Muse and the Marketplace/Grub Street Conference, Washington Independent Writers' Conference, Murder in the Grove, Surrey International Writers' Conference.

Tips "Be professional from the very first contact. There shouldn't be a single typo or grammatical flub in your query. Have a reason for contacting me about your project other than I was the next name listed on some Web site. Please do not use form query software! Believe me, we can get a dozen or so a day that look identical—we know when you are using a form. Show me that you know your audience—and your competition. Have the writing and/or proposal at the very, very best it can be before starting the querying process. Don't assume that if someone likes it enough they'll 'fix' it. The biggest mistake new writers make is starting the querying process before they—and the work—are ready. Take your time and do it right."

◢ FARRIS LITERARY AGENCY, INC.

P.O. Box 570069, Dallas TX 75357. (972)203-8804. E-mail: farris1@airmail.net. Website: www.farrisliterary.com. **Contact:** Mike Farris, Susan Morgan Farris. Estab. 2002. Represents 30 clients. 60% of clients are new/unpublished writers.

 • Both Mr. Farris and Ms. Farris are attorneys.

Represents Nonfiction books, novels. **Considers these nonfiction areas:** Biography/autobiography; business/economics; child guidance/parenting; cooking/foods/nutrition; current affairs; government/politics/law; health/medicine; history; how-to; humor/satire; memoirs; military/war; music/dance; popular culture; religious/inspirational; self-help/personal improvement; sports; women's issues/studies. **Considers these fiction areas:** Action/adventure; detective/police/crime; historical; humor/satire; mainstream/contemporary; mystery/suspense; religious/inspirational; romance; sports; thriller; westerns/frontier.

 ◻━ "We specialize in both fiction and nonfiction books. We are particularly interested in discovering unpublished authors. We adhere to AAR guidelines." Does not want to receive science fiction, fantasy, gay and lesbian, erotica, young adult or children's.

How to Contact Query with SASE. Considers simultaneous queries. Responds in 2-3 weeks to queries; 4-8 weeks to mss. Returns materials only with SASE. Obtains most new clients through recommendations from others, solicitations, conferences.

Recent Sales Sold 4 titles in the last year. *The Show Must Go On*, by Doug Snauffer (McFarland).

Terms Agent receives 15% commission on domestic sales; 20% commission on foreign sales. Offers written contract; 30-day notice must be given to terminate contract. Charges clients for postage and photocopying.

Writers' Conferences Oklahoma Writers Federation Conference; The Screenwriting Conference in Santa Fe; Pikes Peak Writers Conference; Women Writing the West Annual Conference.

◢ THE FIELDING AGENCY, LLC

269 S. Beverly Drive, No. 341, Beverly Hills CA 90212. (323)461-4791. E-mail: wlee@fieldingagency.com. Website: www.fieldingagency.com. **Contact:** Whitney Lee. Estab. 2003. Currently handles: 25% nonfiction books; 35% novels; 35% juvenile books; 5% other.

 • Prior to her current position, Ms. Lee worked at other agencies in different capacities.

Represents Nonfiction books, novels, short story collections, juvenile books. **Considers these nonfiction areas:** Animals; anthropology/archaeology; art/architecture/design; biography/autobiography; business/economics; child guidance/parenting; cooking/foods/nutrition; crafts/hobbies; current affairs; education; ethnic/cultural interests; gay/lesbian issues; government/politics/law; health/medicine; history; how-to; humor/satire; interior design/decorating; juvenile nonfiction; language/literature/criticism; memoirs; military/war; money/finance; nature/environment; popular culture; psychology; science/technology; self-help/personal improvement; sociology; sports; translation; true crime/investigative; women's issues/studies. **Considers these fiction areas:** Action/adventure; comic books/cartoon; detective/police/crime; ethnic; family saga; fantasy; feminist; gay/lesbian; glitz; historical; horror; humor/satire; juvenile; literary; mainstream/contemporary; mystery/suspense; picture books; romance; thriller; young adult; women's.

 ◻━ "We specialize in representing books published abroad and have strong relationships with foreign co-agents and publishers. For books we represent in the U.S., we have to be head-over-heels passionate about it because we are involved every step of the way." Does not want to receive scripts for TV or film.

How to Contact Query with SASE, submit synopsis, author bio. Accepts queries by e-mail and snail mail. No fax queries. Considers simultaneous queries. Returns materials only with SASE. Obtains most new clients through recommendations from others.

Recent Sales *The Crows of Pearblossom*, by Aldous Huxley (Abrams); *It's Vintage, Darling!*, by Christa Weil (Hodder & Stoughton); *Thugs and Kisses*, by Sue Ann Jaffarian (Midnight Ink); *The Fine Art of Confident Conversation*, by Debra Fine (Piatkus/LB).

Terms Agent receives 15% commission on domestic sales; 20% commission on foreign sales. Offers written contract, binding for 9-12 months.

Writers' Conferences London Book Fair; Frankfurt Book Fair.

🖉 DIANA FINCH LITERARY AGENCY

116 W. 23rd St., Suite 500, New York NY 10011. (646)375-2081. E-mail: diana.finch@verizon.net. **Contact:** Diana Finch. Estab. 2003. Member of AAR. Represents 45 clients. 20% of clients are new/unpublished writers. Currently handles: 65% nonfiction books; 25% novels; 5% juvenile books; 5% multimedia.

• Prior to opening her agency, Ms. Finch worked at Ellen Levine Literary Agency for 18 years.

Represents Nonfiction books, novels, scholarly books. **Considers these nonfiction areas:** Biography/autobiography; business/economics; child guidance/parenting; computers/electronic; current affairs; ethnic/cultural interests; government/politics/law; health/medicine; history; how-to; humor/satire; juvenile nonfiction; memoirs; military/war; money/finance; music/dance; nature/environment; photography; popular culture; psychology; science/technology; self-help/personal improvement; sports; theater/film; translation; true crime/investigative; women's issues/studies. **Considers these fiction areas:** Action/adventure; detective/police/crime; ethnic; historical; literary; mainstream/contemporary; thriller; young adult.

🔾 Actively seeking narrative nonfiction, popular science, and health topics. Does not want romance, mysteries, or children's picture books.

How to Contact Query with SASE or via e-mail (no attachments). No phone or fax queries. Considers simultaneous queries. Returns materials only with SASE. Obtains most new clients through recommendations from others.

Recent Sales *Armed Madhouse*, by Greg Palast (Penguin US/UK); *The Bush Agenda*, by Antonia Juhasz; *Journey of the Magi*, by Tudor Parfitt (Farrar, Straus & Giroux); *Radiant Days*, by Michael FitzGerald (Shoemaker & Hoard); *The Queen's Soprano*, by Carol Dines (Harcourt Young Adult); *Was the 2004 Election Stolen?*, by Steven Freeman and Joel Bleifuss (Seven Stories); *An Iranian Memoir*, by Azadeh Moaveni (Random House); *Great Customer Connections*, by Rich Gallagher (Amacom). Other clients include Daniel Duane, Thomas Goltz, Hugh Pope, Owen Matthews, Dr. Robert Marion, Loretta Napoleoni.

Terms Agent receives 15% commission on domestic sales; 20% commission on foreign sales. Offers written contract. "I charge for photocopying, overseas postage, galleys, and books purchased, and try to recap these costs from earnings received for a client, rather than charging outright."

Tips "Do as much research as you can on agents before you query. Have someone critique your query letter before you send it. It should be only 1 page and describe your book clearly—and why you are writing it—but also demonstrate creativity and a sense of your writing style."

🖉 FINEPRINT LITERARY MANAGEMENT

240 West 35th St., Suite 500, New York NY 10001. (212)279-1282. E-mail: (agentfirstname)@fineprintlit.com. Website: www.fineprintlit.com. Estab. 2007. Member of AAR.

Member Agents Peter Rubie, CEO (nonfiction interests include narrative nonfiction, popular science, spirituality, history, biography, pop culture, business, technology, parenting, health, self help, music, and food; fiction interests include literate thrillers, crime fiction, science fiction and fantasy, military fiction and literary fiction); Stephany Evans, president (nonfiction interests include health and wellness—especially women's health, spirituality, lifestyle, home renovating/decorating, entertaining, food and wine, popular reference, and narrative nonfiction; fiction interests include stories with a strong and interesting female protagonist, both literary and upmarket commercial—including chick lit, romance, mystery, and light suspense); June Clark (nonfiction: entertainment, self-help, parenting, reference/how-to books, teen books, food and wine, style/beauty, and prescriptive business titles); Diane Freed (nonfiction: health/fitness, women's issues, memoir, baby boomer trends, parenting, popular culture, self-help, humor, young adult, and topics of New England regional interest); Meredith Hays (both fiction and nonfiction: commercial and literary; she is interested in sophisticated women's fiction such as urban chick lit, pop culture, lifestyle, animals, and absorbing nonfiction accounts); Gary Heidt (history, science, true crime, pop culture, psychology, business, military and some literary fiction); Janet Reid (mysteries and offbeat literary fiction); Amy Tipton (edgy fiction—gritty and urban, women's fiction, nonfiction/memoir, and YA).

Represents Nonfiction books, novels. **Considers these nonfiction areas:** Business/economics; child guidance/parenting; cooking/foods/nutrition; government/politics/law; health/medicine; history; how-to; humor/satire; interior design/decorating; memoirs; music/dance; psychology; science/technology; self-help/personal improvement; spirituality; true crime/investigative; women's issues/studies; young adult; narrative nonfiction, popular science. **Considers these fiction areas:** Detective/police/crime; fantasy; literary; military/war; mystery/suspense; romance; science fiction; young adult; women's.

How to Contact Query with SASE, submit synopsis and first two chapters for fiction; proposal for nonfiction. Do not send attachments or manuscripts without a request. Accepts e-mail queries. No fax queries. Returns materials only with SASE. Obtains most new clients through recommendations from others, solicitations.

Recent Sales *Baby Proof*, by Emily Giffin (St. Martin's Press); *Crossing Into Medicine Country*, by David Carson (Arcade); *Rollergirl: Totally True Tales From the Track*, by Melissa Joulwan (Simon & Schuster); *The Pirate Primer*, by George Choundras (Writer's Digest Books).

Terms Agent receives 15% commission on domestic sales; 20% commission on foreign sales.

✪ FIREBRAND LITERARY

701 President St., #4, Brooklyn NY 11215. (347)689-4762. Fax: (347)689-4762. E-mail: info@firebrandliterary.com. Website: www.firebrandliterary.com. **Contact:** Nadia Cornier. Estab. 2005. Represents 30 clients. 50% of clients are new/unpublished writers. Currently handles: 10% nonfiction books; 85% novels; 5% novellas.

- Before becoming an agent, Ms. Cornier started her own publicity firm and currently channels her interest and skill in marketing into her work with authors.

Member Agents Nadia Cornier, nadia@firebrandliterary.com (young adult, adult commercial, adult genre romance, nonfiction, some middle grade); Ted Malawar.

Represents Nonfiction books, novels, novellas, juvenile books. **Considers these nonfiction areas:** Business/economics; how-to; humor/satire; juvenile nonfiction; language/literature/criticism; money/finance. **Considers these fiction areas:** Erotica; fantasy; historical; juvenile; literary; mainstream/contemporary; romance; young adult; women's.

- "Firebrand endeavors to be a perfect fit for a few authors rather than a good fit for every author—we do so by working with our writers with editing and marketing direction alongside the usual responsibilities of selling their properties. Most of all, we want the author to be excited about what they're doing and what they're writing. While we in turn want to be excited to work with them. That kind of enthusiasm is contagious and we feel it is an important foundation to have when it comes to pitching an author's ideas not only to publishers and the industry, but to the world." Does not want to receive children's books, screenplays, poetry or anything about terrorists.

How to Contact This agency prefers its submissions made through the Web site form. See the site for all details. Send ms only by request. No e-mail or fax queries. Considers simultaneous queries. Responds in 2 weeks to queries; 2 months to mss. Returns materials only with SASE. Obtains most new clients through recommendations from others, solicitations.

Recent Sales *Austenland*, by Shannon Hale (Bloomsbury); *How To Get Suspended & Influence People*, by Adam Selzer (Random House/Delacorte); *Bitterwood*, by James Maxey (Solaris); Salem Witch Tryouts (series), by Kelly McClymer (Simon & Schuster).

Terms Agent receives 15% commission on domestic sales; 20% commission on foreign sales. Offers written contract; 30-day notice must be given to terminate contract.

Tips "Send a short query letter and let the work stand on its own."

✪ JAMES FITZGERALD AGENCY

80 E. 11th St., Suite 301, New York NY. (212)308-1122. E-mail: submissions@jfitzagency.com. Website: www.jfitzagency.com. **Contact:** James Fitzgerald. Estab. 2003.

- Prior to his current position, Mr. Fitzgerald was an editor at St. Martin's Press and Doubleday. Ms. Garrett held positions at Cambridge University Press and Seven Stories Press.

Member Agents James Fitzgerald; Anne Garrett.

Represents Nonfiction books, novels,

- Does not want to receive poetry or screenplays.

How to Contact Query with SASE, submit proposal package, outline/proposal, publishing history, author bio, overview. Accepts e-mail queries. No fax queries.

Recent Sales A biography of film director David Lynch, by Dennis Lim (Wiley); *But Princes Don't Moonwalk: Essays on Rock, Pop, Country, and Rap's Most Famous, Infamous, Underappreciated, and Unthought-of Rivalries*, by Sean Manning (Three Rivers Press); *To the End of East Bay*, by Jack Boulware and Silke Tudor's (Viking Penguin); *Pocket Karaoke*, by Sarah Lewitinn (Simon Spotlight Entertainment); *The Art of the Creche: Folk Art Nativities from Around the World*, by James L. Govan (Merrell). Other clients include Dennis Hopper, Sonny Barger, Andy Greenwald, Osho, Ed Sanders, David Carradine, Blair Tindall, Dale Maharidge, Nat Finkelstein, Legs McNeil, Marc Spitz.

Tips "As an agency, we primarily represent books that reflect the popular culture of today being in the forms of fiction, nonfiction, graphic and packaged books. Please submit all information in English, even if your manuscript is in Spanish."

FLAMING STAR LITERARY ENTERPRISES

320 Riverside Drive, New York NY 10025. E-mail: flamingstarlit@aol.com; janvall@aol.com. Website: flamingst arlit.com for Joseph Vallely; www.janisvallely.com for Janis Vallely. **Contact:** Joseph B. Vallely, Janis C. Vallely. Estab. 1985. Represents 100 clients. 25% of clients are new/unpublished writers. Currently handles: 100% nonfiction books.

- Prior to opening the agency, Mr. Vallely served as national sales manager for Dell; Ms. Vallely was vice president of Doubleday.

Represents Nonfiction books. **Considers these nonfiction areas:** Current affairs; government/politics/law; health/medicine; memoirs; psychology; self-help/personal improvement; sports.

○➡ This agency specializes in upscale commercial nonfiction.

How to Contact E-mail only (no attachments). Obtains most new clients through recommendations from others, solicitations.

Recent Sales *His and Hers*, by Daniel Monti and Anthony Bazzan (Collins).

Terms Agent receives 15% commission on domestic sales; 20% commission on foreign sales. Offers written contract. Charges clients for photocopying and postage only.

FLANNERY LITERARY

1155 S. Washington St., Suite 202, Naperville IL 60540. (630)428-2682. Fax: (630)428-2683. E-mail: FlanLit@aol. com. **Contact:** Jennifer Flannery. Estab. 1992. Represents 40 clients. 50% of clients are new/unpublished writers. Currently handles: 100% juvenile books.

○➡ This agency specializes in children's and young adult fiction and nonfiction. It also accepts picture books.

How to Contact Query with SASE. No fax or e-mail queries. Responds in 2 weeks to queries; 1 month to mss. Obtains most new clients through recommendations from others, submissions.

Recent Sales Sold 50 titles in the last year. This agency prefers not to share information on specific sales.

Terms Agent receives 15% commission on domestic sales; 20% commission on foreign sales. Offers written contract, binding for life of book in print; 1-month notice must be given to terminate contract. 100% of business is derived from commissions on ms sales.

Tips "Write an engrossing, succinct query describing your work. We are always looking for a fresh new voice."

PETER FLEMING AGENCY

P.O. Box 458, Pacific Palisades CA 90272. (310)454-1373. E-mail: peterfleming@earthlink.net. **Contact:** Peter Fleming. Estab. 1962. Currently handles: 100% nonfiction books.

○➡ This agency specializes in nonfiction books that unearth innovative and uncomfortable truths with bestseller potential. Greatly interested in journalists in the free press (the Internet).

How to Contact Query with SASE. Obtains most new clients through "a different, one-of-a-kind idea for a book often backed by the writer's experience in that area of expertise."

Recent Sales *Rulers of Evil*, by F. Tupper Saussy (HarperCollins); *Why Is It Always About You—Saving Yourself from the Narcissists in Your Life*, by Sandy Hotchkiss (Free Press).

Terms Agent receives 15% commission on domestic sales; 25% commission on foreign sales. Offers written contract, binding for 1 year. Charges clients only those fees agreed to in writing.

Tips "You can begin by starting your own Web site."

FLETCHER & PARRY

78 Fifth Ave., 3rd Floor, New York NY 10011. (212)614-0778. Fax: (212)614-0728. E-mail: mail@fletcherparry.c om. Website: www.fletcherparry.com/. **Contact:** Christy Fletcher, Emma Parry. Estab. 2003. Member of AAR.

Represents Nonfiction books, novels. **Considers these nonfiction areas:** Current affairs; history; memoirs; sports; travel; African American; narrative; science; biography; business; health; lifestyle. **Considers these fiction areas:** Literary; young adult; commercial.

○➡ Does not want genre fiction.

How to Contact Query with SASE. Responds in 6 weeks to queries.

Recent Sales *Let Them In: The Case for Open Borders*, by Jason Riley (Gotham); *The Vanishing Act of Esme Lennox*, by Maggie O'Farrell (Harcourt).

THE FOLEY LITERARY AGENCY

34 E. 38th St., New York NY 10016-2508. (212)686-6930. **Contact:** Joan Foley, Joseph Foley. Estab. 1961. Represents 10 clients. Currently handles: 75% nonfiction books; 25% novels.

Represents Nonfiction books, novels.

How to Contact Query with letter, brief outline, SASE. Responds promptly to queries. Obtains most new clients through recommendations from others (rarely taking on new clients).

Recent Sales This agency prefers not to share information on specific sales.

Terms Agent receives 10% commission on domestic sales; 15% commission on foreign sales. 100% of business is derived from commissions on ms sales.

☑ FOLIO LITERARY MANAGEMENT, LLC

505 Eighth Ave., Suite 603, New York NY 10018. Website: www.foliolit.com. Alternate address: 1627 K St. NW, Suite 1200, Washington DC 20006. Estab. 2006. Member of AAR. Represents 100+ clients.

• Prior to creating Folio Literary Management, Mr. Hoffman worked for several years at another agency; Mr. Kleinman was an agent at Graybill & English; Ms. Wheeler was an agent at Creative Media Agency; Ms. Fine was an agent at Vigliano Associates and Trident Media Group; Ms. Cartwright-Niumata was an editor at Simon & Schuster, HarperCollins, and Avalon Books; Ms. Becker worked as a copywriter, journalist and author.

Member Agents Scott Hoffman; Jeff Kleinman; Paige Wheeler; Celeste Fine; Erin Cartwright-Niumata, Laney K. Becker; Rachel Vater (fantasy, young adult, women's fiction).

Represents Nonfiction books, novels, short story collections. **Considers these nonfiction areas:** Animals (equestrian); business/economics; child guidance/parenting; history; how-to; humor/satire; memoirs; military/war; nature/environment; popular culture; psychology; religious/inspirational; science/technology; self-help/personal improvement; women's issues/studies; narrative nonfiction; art; espionage; biography; crime; politics; health/fitness; lifestyle; relationship; culture; cookbooks. **Considers these fiction areas:** Erotica; fantasy; literary; mystery/suspense; religious/inspirational; romance; science fiction; thriller (psychological); young adult; women's; Southern; legal; edgy crime.

How to Contact Query with SASE or via e-mail (no attachments). Read agent bios online for specific submission guidelines. Responds in 1 month to queries.

Recent Sales Sold more than 100 titles in the last year. *Finn*, by Jon Clinch (Random House); *A Killing Tide*, by P.J. Alderman (Dorchester); *The Inn on Half Moon Bay*, by Diane Tyrrel (Berkley); *The Biography of Kenny Chesney*, by Holly Gleason (Center Street); *Color of the Sea*, by John Hamamura (Thomas Dunne Books/St. Martin's Press); *The 30-Day Diabetes Miracle* (Perigee); *Meow Is for Murder*, by Linda O. Johnston (Berkley Prime Crime); *Wildlife's Scotland Yard*, by Laurel Neme (Joseph Henry Press); *Mockingbird*, by Charles J. Shields (Henry Holt); *Under the Mask*, by Heidi Ardizzone (Norton); *The Culture Code*, by Dr. Clotaire Rapaille (Doubleday).

Tips "Please do not submit simultaneously to more than one agent at Folio. If you're not sure which of us is exactly right for your book, don't worry. We work closely as a team, and if one of our agents gets a query that might be more appropriate for someone else, we'll always pass it along. Keep in mind, however, that although we do work closely together, we are all individuals, with specific tastes and preferences ' as well as our own unique working styles. So it's important that you check each agent's bio page for clear directions as to how to submit, as well as when to expect feedback."

☑ ◎ FOX CHASE AGENCY, INC.

701 Lee Road, Suite 102, Chesterbrook Corporate Center, Chesterbrook PA 19087. Estab. 1972. Member of AAR.

Member Agents A.L. Hart; Jo C. Hart.

Represents Nonfiction books, novels.

How to Contact Query with SASE.

☑ JEANNE FREDERICKS LITERARY AGENCY, INC.

221 Benedict Hill Road, New Canaan CT 06840. (203)972-3011. Fax: (203)972-3011. E-mail: jeanne.fredericks@gmail.com. Website: jeannefredericks.com/. **Contact:** Jeanne Fredericks. Estab. 1997. Member of AAR, Authors Guild. Represents 90 clients. 10% of clients are new/unpublished writers. Currently handles: 100% nonfiction books.

• Prior to opening her agency, Ms. Fredericks was an agent and acting director with the Susan P. Urstadt, Inc. Agency.

Represents Nonfiction books. **Considers these nonfiction areas:** Animals; biography/autobiography; child guidance/parenting; cooking/foods/nutrition; gardening; health/medicine (alternative health); history; how-to; interior design/decorating; money/finance; nature/environment; photography; psychology; self-help/personal improvement; sports (not spectator sports); women's issues/studies.

○━ This agency specializes in quality adult nonfiction by authorities in their fields. Does not want to receive children's books or fiction.

How to Contact Query first with SASE, then send outline/proposal, 1-2 sample chapters, SASE. No fax queries. Accepts short e-mail queries (no attachments). Considers simultaneous queries. Responds in 3-5 weeks to queries; 2-4 months to mss. Returns materials only with SASE. Obtains most new clients through recommendations from others, solicitations, conferences.

Recent Sales *American Quilts*, by Robert Shaw (Sterling); *Lilias! Yoga Gets Better with Age*, by Lilias Folan (Rodale); *Homescaping*, by Anne Halpin (Rodale); *The Big Steal*, by Emyl Jenkins (Algonquin); *Creating Optimism in Your Child*, by Bob Murray, PhD, and Alice Fortinberry, MS (McGraw-Hill); *Waking the Warrior Goddess*, by Christine Horner, MD (Basic Health); *Healing the Heart with EECP*, by Debra Braverman, MD (Celestial Arts).

Terms Agent receives 15% commission on domestic sales; 25% commission on foreign sales with co-agent; without co-agent receives 20% commission on foreign sales. Offers written contract, binding for 9 months; 2-month notice must be given to terminate contract. Charges client for photocopying of whole proposals and mss, overseas postage, priority mail, express mail services.

Writers' Conferences Connecticut Press Club Biennial Writer's Conference; ASJA Writers' Conference; BookExpo America; Garden Writers' Association Annual Symposium.

Tips ''Be sure to research competition for your work and be able to justify why there's a need for your book. I enjoy building an author's career, particularly if he/she is professional, hardworking, and courteous. Aside from 17 years of agenting experience, I've had 10 years of editorial experience in adult trade book publishing that enables me to help an author polish a proposal so that it's more appealing to prospective editors. My MBA in marketing also distinguishes me from other agents.''

GRACE FREEDSON'S PUBLISHING NETWORK

375 North Broadway, Suite 102, Jericho NY 11753. (516)931-7757. Fax: (516)931-7759. E-mail: gfreedson@worl d.att.net. **Contact:** Grace Freedson. Estab. 2000. Represents 100 clients. 10% of clients are new/unpublished writers. Currently handles: 90% nonfiction books; 10% juvenile books.

• Prior to becoming an agent, Ms. Freedson was a managing editor and director of acquisition for Barron's Educational Series.

Represents Nonfiction books, juvenile books. **Considers these nonfiction areas:** Animals; business/economics; cooking/foods/nutrition; current affairs; education; health/medicine; history; how-to; humor/satire; money/finance; nature/environment; popular culture; psychology; science/technology; self-help/personal improvement; sports; craft/hobbies.

O→ ''In addition to representing many qualified authors, I work with publishers as a packager of unique projects—mostly series.'' Does not want to receive fiction.

How to Contact Query with SASE, submit synopsis, SASE. Responds in 2-6 weeks to queries. Returns materials only with SASE. Obtains most new clients through recommendations from others.

Recent Sales Sold 50 titles in the last year. *Maybe Baby*, by Matt Miller (HCI); *Brainsense*, by Faith Brynie (Amacom); *Buzz Marketing 101*, by Susan Benjamin (Adams Media). *Women Who Launch*, by Karin Abarbival and Bruce Freeman (Ten Speed Press); *Privacy Lost*, by David Holtzman (Jossey-Bass/Wiley); *The Connected Father*, by Carl Pickhacer (Palgrave-MacMillan).

Terms Agent receives 15% commission on domestic sales. Offers written contract; 30-day notice must be given to terminate contract.

Writers' Conferences BookExpo of America.

Tips ''At this point, I am only reviewing proposals on nonfiction topics by credentialed authors with platforms.''

FRESH BOOKS LITERARY AGENCY

231 Diana St., Placerville CA 95667. E-mail: matt@fresh-books.com. Website: www.fresh-books.com. **Contact:** Matt Wagner. Estab. 2005. Represents 30+ clients. 5% of clients are new/unpublished writers. Currently handles: 95% nonfiction books; 5% multimedia.

• Prior to becoming an agent, Mr. Wagner was with Waterside Productions for 15 years.

Represents Nonfiction books. **Considers these nonfiction areas:** Animals; anthropology/archaeology; art/architecture/design; business/economics; child guidance/parenting; computers/electronic; cooking/foods/nutrition; crafts/hobbies; current affairs; education; ethnic/cultural interests; gay/lesbian issues; government/politics/law; health/medicine; history; how-to; humor/satire; military/war; money/finance; music/dance; nature/environment; photography; popular culture; psychology; science/technology; sports.

O→ ''I specialize in tech and how-to. I love working with books and authors, and I've repped many of my clients for upwards of 15 years now.'' Actively seeking popular science, natural history, adventure, how-to, business, education and reference. Does not want to receive fiction, children's books or poetry.

How to Contact Query with SASE. No phone calls. Accepts e-mail queries. No fax queries. Considers simultaneous queries. Responds in 1-4 weeks to queries; 1-4 weeks to mss. Returns materials only with SASE. Obtains most new clients through recommendations from others.

Recent Sales Sold 30+ titles in the last year. *iPhone for Dummies*, by Edward Baig (Wiley); *How To Do Everything with Second Life*, by Richard Mansfield (McGraw-Hill Professional); *Diary of a Real Estate Rookie*, by Alison Rogers (Kaplan); *Anthropology for Dummies*, by Cameron Smith (Wiley). Other clients include Dan Gookin, Andy Rathbone, Gary Bouton, Harold Davis, Taz Tally, Christopher Spencer, Kevin Epstein.

Terms Agent receives 15% commission on domestic sales; 20% commission on foreign sales.

Tips "Do your research. Find out what sorts of books and authors an agent represents. Go to conferences. Make friends with other writers—most of my clients come from referrals."

◑ SARAH JANE FREYMANN LITERARY AGENCY

59 W. 71st St., Suite 9B, New York NY 10023. (212)362-9277. E-mail: sarah@sarahjanefreymann.com; Submissi ons@SarahJaneFreymann.com. Website: www.sarahjanefreymann.com. **Contact:** Sarah Jane Freymann, Steve Schwartz. Represents 100 clients. 20% of clients are new/unpublished writers. Currently handles: 75% nonfic tion books; 23% novels; 2% juvenile books.

Member Agents Sarah Jane Freymann; Steve Schwartz, steve@sarahjanefreymann.com (historical novels, thril lers, crime, sports, humor, food, travel); Katharine Sands.

Represents Nonfiction books, novels, illustrated books. **Considers these nonfiction areas:** Animals; anthropol ogy/archaeology; art/architecture/design; biography/autobiography; business/economics; child guidance/par enting; cooking/foods/nutrition; current affairs; ethnic/cultural interests; health/medicine; history; interior design/decorating; memoirs (narrative); nature/environment; psychology; religious/inspirational; self-help/ personal improvement; women's issues/studies; lifestyle. **Considers these fiction areas:** Ethnic; literary; main stream/contemporary.

How to Contact Query with SASE. Responds in 2 weeks to queries; 6 weeks to mss. Obtains most new clients through recommendations from others.

Recent Sales *Girl Stories*, by Lauren Weinstein (Henry Holt); *The Good, Good Pig*, by Sy Montgomery (Ballan tine/Random House); *The Man Who Killed the Whale*, by Linda Hogan (W.W. Norton); *Writing the Fire! Yoga and the Art of Making Your Words Come Alive*, by Gail Sher (Harmoney/Bell Tower); *Mexicocina*, by Melba Levick and Betsy McNair (Chronicle); *Holy Play*, by Kirk Byron Jones (Jossey Bass).

Terms Agent receives 15% commission on domestic sales; 20% commission on foreign sales. Offers written contract. Charges clients for long distance, overseas postage, photocopying. 100% of business is derived from commissions on ms sales.

Tips "I love fresh, new, passionate works by authors who love what they are doing and have both natural talent and carefully honed skill."

◑ FREDRICA S. FRIEDMAN AND CO., INC.

136 E. 57th St., 14th Floor, New York NY 10022. (212)829-9600. Fax: (212)829-9669. E-mail: info@fredricafried man.com; submissions@fredricafriedman.com. Website: fredricafriedman.com/. **Contact:** Lee Bacon. Estab. 2001. Represents 75+ clients. 50% of clients are new/unpublished writers. Currently handles: 95% nonfiction books; 5% novels.

Represents Nonfiction books, novels, anthologies. **Considers these nonfiction areas:** Art/architecture/design; biography/autobiography; business/economics; child guidance/parenting; cooking/foods/nutrition; current af fairs; education; ethnic/cultural interests; gay/lesbian issues; government/politics/law; health/medicine; his tory; how-to; humor/satire; language/literature/criticism; memoirs; money/finance; music/dance; photogra phy; popular culture; psychology; self-help/personal improvement; sociology; theater/film; true crime/ investigative; women's issues/studies; interior design/decorating. **Considers these fiction areas:** Literary.

> ○— "We represent a select group of outstanding nonfiction and fiction writers. We are particularly interested in helping writers expand their readership and develop their careers." Does not want poetry, plays, screenplays, children's books, sci-fi/fantasy, or horror.

How to Contact Submit e-query, synopsis. Considers simultaneous queries. Responds in 2-4 weeks to queries; 4-6 weeks to mss. Obtains most new clients through recommendations from others.

Recent Sales Sold 30-40 titles in the last year. *Just This Once*, by Frances Kuffel (Basic Books); *Footpaths in the Painted City*, by Sadia Shepard (Penguin Press); *China Ghosts*, by Jeff Gammage (William Morrow); *Seducing the Boys' Club*, by Nina DiSesa (Random House).

Terms Agent receives 15% commission on domestic sales; 25% commission on foreign sales. Offers written contract. Charges for photocopying and messenger/shipping fees for proposals.

Tips "Spell the agent's name correctly on your query letter."

◑ FULL CIRCLE LITERARY, LLC

7676 Hazard Center Dr., Suite 500, San Diego CA 92108. E-mail: info@fullcircleliterary.com. Website: www.fullc ircleliterary.com. **Contact:** Lilly Ghahremani, Stefanie Von Borstel. Estab. 2004. Represents 40 clients. 60% of clients are new/unpublished writers. Currently handles: 70% nonfiction books; 10% novels; 20% juvenile books.

> • Before forming Full Circle, Ms. Von Borstel worked in both marketing and editorial capacities at Penguin and Harcourt; Ms. Ghahremani received her law degree from UCLA, and has experience in representing authors on legal affairs.

Member Agents Lilly Ghahremani (young adult, pop culture, crafts, useful humor, how-to, narrative nonfiction, cookbooks, business, relationships, health, Middle Eastern interest, performing arts, multicultural); Stefanie Von Borstel (Latino interest, crafts, parenting, wedding/relationships, how-to, self help, middle grade/teen fiction/YA, green living, multicultural/bilingual picture books).

Represents Nonfiction books, juvenile books. **Considers these nonfiction areas:** Animals; biography/autobiography; business/economics; child guidance/parenting; cooking/foods/nutrition; crafts/hobbies; current affairs; ethnic/cultural interests; health/medicine; how-to; humor/satire; juvenile nonfiction; music/dance; popular culture; self-help/personal improvement; sports; translation; women's issues/studies. **Considers these fiction areas:** Ethnic; literary; young adult.

 ○─ "Our full-service boutique agency, representing a range of nonfiction and children's books (limited fiction), provides a one-stop resource for authors. Our extensive experience in the realms of law and marketing provide Full Circle clients with a unique edge." Actively seeking nonfiction by authors with a unique and strong platform, projects that offer new and diverse viewpoints, and literature with a global or multicultural perspective. "We are particularly interested in books with a Latino or Middle Eastern angle and books related to pop culture." Does not want to receive screenplays, poetry, commercial fiction or genre fiction (horror, thriller, mystery, Western, sci-fi, fantasy, romance, historical fiction).

How to Contact Agency accepts e-queries. See Web site for fiction guidelines, as they are in flux. For nonfiction, send full proposal. Considers simultaneous queries. Responds in 1-2 weeks to queries; 4-6 weeks to mss. Returns materials only with SASE. Obtains most new clients through recommendations from others, solicitations, conferences.

Recent Sales Sold 30 titles in the last year.

Terms Agent receives 15% commission on domestic sales; 20% commission on foreign sales. Offers written contract; up to 30-day notice must be given to terminate contract. Charges for copying and postage.

Tips "Put your best foot forward. Contact us when you simply can't make your project any better on your own, and please be sure your work fits with what the agent you're approaching represents. Little things count, so copyedit your work. Join a writing group and attend conferences to get objective and constructive feedback before submitting. Be active about building your platform as an author before, during, and after publication. Remember this is a business and your agent is a business partner."

◎ NANCY GALLT LITERARY AGENCY

273 Charlton Ave., South Orange NJ 07079. (973)761-6358. Fax: (973)761-6318. E-mail: ngallt@aol.com. **Contact:** Nancy Gallt. Estab. 2000. Represents 40 clients. 30% of clients are new/unpublished writers. Currently handles: 100% juvenile books.

 • Prior to opening her agency, Ms. Gallt was subsidiary rights director of the children's book division at Morrow, Harper and Viking.

Member Agents Nancy Gallt, Craig Virden.

Represents Juvenile books.

 ○─ "I only handle children's books." Actively seeking middle-grade and young adult novels. Does not want to receive rhyming picture book texts.

How to Contact Query with 3 sample chapters, SASE. If an author wants the ms returned, include a large SASE. Considers simultaneous queries. Responds in 3 months to queries; 3 months to mss. Obtains most new clients through recommendations from others, solicitations.

Recent Sales Sold 50 titles in the last year. Percy Jackson series, by Rick Riordan (Hyperion); A-Z Mysteries Super-Edition, by Ron Roy (Random House Books for Young Readers); *Little Gnome* (Simon & Schuster); *My Bar Mitzvah* (Simon & Schuster).

Terms Agent receives 10% commission on domestic sales; 20% commission on foreign sales. Offers written contract; 30-day notice must be given to terminate contract.

Tips "A book stands on its own, so a submission should be as close to perfect as the author can make it."

🔳 ◎ THE GARAMOND AGENCY, INC.

12 Horton St., Newburyport MA 01950. E-mail: query@garamondagency.com. Website: www.garamondagency.com. Estab. 1998; Author's Guild.

Member Agents Lisa Adams; David Miller.

Represents Nonfiction books. **Considers these nonfiction areas:** Business/economics; government/politics/law; history; psychology; science/technology; social science, narrative nonfiction.

 ○─ "We work closely with our authors through each stage of the publishing process, first in developing their books and then in presenting themselves and their ideas effectively to publishers and to readers. We represent our clients throughout the world in all languages, media, and territories through an extensive network of subagents." Does not want to receive "proposals for children's or young adult books, fiction, poetry, or memoir."

How to Contact See Web site.

Recent Sales *The Breakthrough Imperative*, by Mark Gottfredson and Steven Schaubert (HarperCollins); *Loneliness*, by John Capioppo and William Patrick (Norton); *The Virtue of Vice*, by Arthur Brooks (Basic). Other clients include See Web site.

Tips "Query us first if you have any questions about whether we are the right agency for your work."

⬤ GELFMAN SCHNEIDER LITERARY AGENTS, INC.

250 W. 57th St., Suite 2122, New York NY 10107. (212)245-1993. Fax: (212)245-8678. E-mail: mail@gelfmansch neider.com. **Contact:** Jane Gelfman, Deborah Schneider. Estab. 1981. Member of AAR. Represents 300+ clients. 10% of clients are new/unpublished writers.

Represents Nonfiction books, novels. **Considers these nonfiction areas:** Biography; health; lifestyle; politics; science. **Considers these fiction areas:** Literary; mainstream/contemporary; mystery/suspense; women's.

⊶ Does not want to receive romance, science fiction, westerns, or children's books.

How to Contact Query with SASE. Send queries via snail mail only. No e-mail or fax queries. Responds in 1 month to queries; 2 months to mss.

Terms Agent receives 15% commission on domestic sales; 20% commission on foreign sales; 15% commission on dramatic rights sales. Offers written contract. Charges clients for photocopying and messengers/couriers.

⬤ THE GERNERT COMPANY

136 East 57th St., 18th Floor, New York NY 10022. (212)838-7777. Fax: (212)838-6020. E-mail: info@thegernertc o.com. **Contact:** Sarah Burnes.

● Prior to her current position, Ms. Burnes was with Burnes & Clegg, Inc.

Member Agents Sarah Burnes, sburnes@thegernertco.com (commercial fiction, adventure and true story); Stephanie Cabot (literary fiction, commercial fiction, historical fiction); Chris Parris-Lamb, clamb@thegernertco .com.

Represents Nonfiction books, novels.

How to Contact Query with SASE. E-query with cover letter and first sample chapter. Queries should be addressed to a specific agent via the email subject line. See company Web site for more instructions. No fax queries. Obtains most new clients through recommendations from others, solicitations.

Recent Sales *House of Joy*, by Sarah-Kate Lynch (Plume); *Mudbound*, by Hillary Jordan (Algonquin); *The Reluctant Diplomat: Peter Paul Rubens and His Secret Mission to Save Europe from Itself*, by Mark Lamster (Talese).

⬤ THE GISLASON AGENCY

219 Main St. SE, Suite 506, Minneapolis MN 55414-2160. (612)331-8033. Fax: (612)331-8115. Website: www.the gislasonagency.com/default.html. **Contact:** Barbara J. Gislason. Estab. 1992. Member of Minnesota State Bar Association, American Bar Association, Art & Entertainment Law Section, Animal Law, Minnesota Intellectual Property Law Association Copyright Committee; Icelandic Association of Minnesota, American Academy of Acupuncture and Oriental Medicine. 80% of clients are new/unpublished writers. Currently handles: 10% nonfiction books; 90% novels.

● Ms. Gislason became an attorney in 1980, and continues to practice art and entertainment law. She has been nationally recognized as a Leading American Attorney and a Super Lawyer.

Represents Nonfiction books, novels. **Considers these nonfiction areas:** Animals; companion animals/pets, feral animals, working and service animals, domestic and farm animals, laboratory animals, caged animals and wild animals. **Considers these fiction areas:** Animals (companion animals/pets, feral animals, working and service animals, domestic and farm animals, laboratory animals, caged animals and wild animals).

⊶ This agency is not taking submissions at this time. Check the Web site for updates.

How to Contact No e-mail or fax queries. Responds in 1 months to queries; 6 months to mss. Obtains most new clients through recommendations from others, conferences, *Guide to Literary Agents, Literary Market Place*, other reference books.

Terms Agent receives 15% commission on domestic sales; 20% commission on foreign sales. Offers written contract, binding for 1 year with option to renew. Charges clients for photocopying and postage.

Writers' Conferences Southwest Writers Conference; Willamette Writers Conference; Wrangling with Writing; other state and regional conferences.

Tips "We are looking for manuscripts for adults that express ideas and tell stories powerful enough to change people's views about animals, without overt sentimentality. Your cover letter should be well written and include a detailed synopsis (fiction) or proposal (nonfiction), the first 3 chapters, and author bio. Appropriate SASE required. If submitting nonfiction work, explain how the submission differs from and adds to previously published works in the field. Remember to proofread. If the work was written with a specific publisher in mind, this should be communicated."

BARRY GOLDBLATT LITERARY, LLC

320 Seventh Ave., #266, Brooklyn NY 11215. Fax: (718)360-5453. Website: www.bgliterary.com/contactme.ht ml. **Contact:** Barry Goldblatt. Member of AAR.

Represents Juvenile books. **Considers these fiction areas:** Picture books; young adult; middle grade.

How to Contact Query with SASE.

Recent Sales The Chasing Yesterday trilogy, by Robin Wasserman (Scholastic); *Rabbit and Squirrel*, by Kara LaReau (Harcourt); *Go Go Gorillas*, by Julia Durango (Simon & Schuster Children's).

FRANCES GOLDIN LITERARY AGENCY, INC.

57 E. 11th St., Suite 5B, New York NY 10003. (212)777-0047. Fax: (212)228-1660. E-mail: agency@goldinlit.com. Website: www.goldinlit.com. Estab. 1977. Member of AAR. Represents over 100 clients.

Member Agents Frances Goldin, principal/agent; Ellen Geiger, agent (commercial and literary fiction and non-fiction, cutting-edge topics of all kinds); Matt McGowan, agent/rights director (innovative works of fiction and nonfiction); Sam Stoloff, agent (literary fiction, memoir, history, accessible sociology and philosophy, cultural studies, serious journalism, narrative and topical nonfiction with a progressive orientation); Josie Schoel, agent/office manager (literary fiction and nonfiction).

Represents Nonfiction books, novels. **Considers these nonfiction areas:** Serious, controversial nonfiction with a progressive political orientation. **Considers these fiction areas:** Adult literary.

> ⌒ "We are hands on and we work intensively with clients on proposal and manuscript development." Does not want anything that is racist, sexist, agist, homophobic, or pornographic. No screenplays, children's books, art books, cookbooks, business books, diet books, self-help, or genre fiction.

How to Contact Query with SASE. No unsolicited mss or work previously submitted to publishers. Prefers hard-copy queries. Responds in 6 weeks to queries.

Recent Sales *Skin Deep*, by Dalton Conley (Pantheon); *Conned: How Millions Have Lost the Right to Vote*, by Sasha Abramsky (New Press); *Gotham II*, by Mike Wallace; *Animal, Vegetable, Miracle*, by Barbara Kingslover; an untitled memoir by Staceyann Chin.

THE SUSAN GOLOMB LITERARY AGENCY

875 Avenue of the Americas, Suite 2302, New York NY 10001. Fax: (212)239-9503. E-mail: susan@sgolombagen cy.com. **Contact:** Susan Golumb. Estab. 1991. Represents 100 clients. 20% of clients are new/unpublished writers. Currently handles: 50% nonfiction books; 40% novels; 10% story collections.

Represents Nonfiction books, novels, short story collections, novellas. **Considers these nonfiction areas:** Animals; anthropology/archaeology; biography/autobiography; business/economics; current affairs; government/politics/law; health/medicine; history; memoirs; military/war; money/finance; nature/environment; popular culture; psychology; science/technology; sociology; women's issues/studies. **Considers these fiction areas:** Ethnic; historical; humor/satire; literary; mainstream/contemporary; thriller; young adult; women's/chick lit.

> ⌒ "We specialize in literary and upmarket fiction and nonfiction that is original, vibrant and of excellent quality and craft. Nonfiction should be edifying, paradigm-shifting, fresh and entertaining." Actively seeking writers with strong voices. Does not want to receive genre fiction.

How to Contact Query with SASE, submit outline/proposal, synopsis, 1 sample chapter(s), author bio, SASE. Query via mail or e-mail. Accepts e-mail queries. No fax queries. Responds in 2 week to queries; 8 weeks to mss. Returns materials only with SASE. Obtains most new clients through recommendations from others, solicitations.

Recent Sales Sold 20 titles in the last year. *Sunnyside*, by Glen David Gold (Knopf); *A Book for Charley*, by Tanya Egan Gibson (Dutton); *Telex to Cuba*, by Rachel Kushner (Scribner).

Terms Agent receives 15% commission on domestic sales; 20% commission on foreign sales. Offers written contract.

GOLVAN ARTS MANAGEMENT

P.O. Box 766, Kew VIC 3101 Australia. E-mail: golvan@ozemail.com.au. Website: www.golvanarts.com.au. **Contact:** Colin Golvan.

Represents Nonfiction books, novels, juvenile books, poetry books, movie scripts, TV scripts, stage plays.

How to Contact Query with author bio, SASE.

Recent Sales *The Runaway Circus*, by Gordon Reece (Lothian Books); *Two for the Road*, by Shirly Hardy-Rix and Brian Rix (Macmillan); *The Catch*, by Marg Vandeleur (Penguin).

Terms Agent receives 11% commission on domestic sales.

⊚ GOODMAN ASSOCIATES

500 West End Ave., New York NY 10024-4317. (212)873-4806. Estab. 1976. Member of AAR.
  O→ Accepting new clients by recommendation only.
Recent Sales *Urban Preservation*, by Eugenia Bone (Clarkson Potter).

⊿ IRENE GOODMAN LITERARY AGENCY

80 Fifth Ave., Suite 1101, New York NY 10011. E-mail: queries@irenegoodman.com. Website: www.irenegood
man.com. **Contact:** Irene Goodman, Miriam Kriss. Member of AAR.
Member Agents Irene Goodman; Miriam Kriss; Barbara Poelle.
Represents Nonfiction books, novels. **Considers these nonfiction areas:** History; parenting, social issues,
francophilia, anglophilia, Judaica, lifestyles, cooking, memoir. **Considers these fiction areas:** Historical; literary; mystery/suspense; romance; thriller; young adult; women's; chick lit; modern urban fantasies.
  O→ Specializes in "the finest in commercial fiction and nonfiction. We have a strong background in women's
    voices, including mysteries, romance, women's fiction, thrillers, suspense, and chick lit. Historical
    fiction is one of Irene's particular passions and Miriam is fanatical about modern urban fantasies. We
    are also very interested in young adult fiction, both literary and those with an edgy, chick-litty voice. In
    nonfiction, Irene is looking for topics on narrative history, social issues and trends, education, Judaica,
    Francophilia, Anglophilia, other cultures, animals, food, crafts, and memoir."
How to Contact Query with SASE, submit synopsis, first 10 pages. E-mail queries only! See the Web site
submission page. No e-mail attachments. Responds in 2 months to queries.
Recent Sales *Beg For Mercy*, by Toni Andrews; *The Devil Inside*, by Jenna Black; *Hooking Up or Holding Out*,
by Jamie Callan; *Seducing The Spy*, by Celeste Bradley.
Tips "We are receiving an unprecedented amount of e-mail queries. If you find that the mailbox is full, please
try again in two weeks. E-mail queries to our personal addresses will not be answered."

⊞ ◻ GRAHAM MAW LITERARY AGENCY

19 Thornhill Square, London England N1 1BJ, United Kingdom. (44)(207)812-9937. E-mail: enquiries@graham
mawagency.com. Website: www.grahammawagency.com. Estab. 2005. Represents 20 clients. 30% of clients
are new/unpublished writers. Currently handles: 100% nonfiction books.
  • Prior to opening her agency, Ms. Graham Maw was a publishing director at HarperCollins and worked in
    rights, publicity and editorial. She has ghostwritten several nonfiction books, which gives her an insider's
    knowledge of both the publishing industry and the pleasures and pitfalls of authorships. Ms. Christie has a
    background in advertising and journalism.
Member Agents Jane Graham Maw; Jennifer Christie.
Represents Nonfiction books. **Considers these nonfiction areas:** Biography/autobiography; child guidance/
parenting; cooking/foods/nutrition; health/medicine; how-to; memoirs; popular culture; psychology; self-help/
personal improvement.
  O→ "We aim to make the publishing process easier and smoother for authors. We work hard to ensure that
    publishing proposals are watertight before submission. We aim for collaborative relationships with
    publishers so that we provide the right books to the right editor at the right time. We represent ghostwrit-
    ers as well as authors." Actively seeking work from UK writers only. Does not want to receive fiction,
    poetry, plays or e-mail submissions.
How to Contact Query with synopsis, chapter outline, bio, SASE. No e-mail or fax queries. Responds in 2 weeks
to queries. Returns materials only with SASE. Obtains most new clients through recommendations from others.
Recent Sales Sold 6 titles in the last year. *Jack Osbourne: 21 Years Gone*, by Jack Osbourne (Macmillan);
Nourish, by Jennifer Harper-Deacon (Rodale); *For the Love of My Son*, by Margaret Davis (Hodder).
Terms Agent receives 15% commission on domestic sales; 20% commission on foreign sales. Offers written
contract; 30-day notice must be given to terminate contract.
Writers' Conferences London Book Fair, Frankfurt Book Fair.
Tips "UK clients only!"

⊠ GRAND STREET LITERARY AGENCY

66 Grand Street, Suite 1, New York NY 10013. (212)226-1936. Fax: (212)226-1398. E-mail: mecoy@grandstreetlit
erary.com. Website: www.grandstreetliterary.com. **Contact:** Bob Mecoy.
Member Agents Bob Mecoy.
Recent Sales *Crimson Verses*, by Adrian McKinty; Fahrenheit 451 graphic novel adaptation, by Tim Hamilton;
Inside Out, by Maria Snyder; *Knife Skills Illustrated*, by Peter Hertzmann; *Hidden Noon*, by James Church.

⊿ THE GRANT AGENCY

3621 Huntwick Drive, Orange TX 77632. E-mail: query@thegrantagency.com. Website: www.thegrantagency.c
om. **Contact:** Steven Grant; adheres to AAR canon of ethics.

Represents Novels. **Considers these fiction areas:** Erotica; romance (all sub-genres).

O➡ Romance. Romance **only**. Does not want to receive self-help, poetry, nonfiction or children's books.

How to Contact E-query with first 5 pages pasted in e-mail. No attachments. No snail mail queries. No fax queries. Responds in 4 weeks to queries; 12 weeks to mss. Obtains most new clients through recommendations from others, solicitations.

Recent Sales Three inspirational romances by Renee Ryan (Harlequin); an erotic romance novella, by Donna Grant (Kensington); *The Druid's Glen 5: Highland Magic*, by Donna Grant; *Project Daddy*, by Kate Perry (Kensington). Other clients include Renee Halverson w/a Renee Field, Judith Leger, Marcy O'Connor, Georgia Ward.

Terms Agent receives 15% commission on domestic sales; 20% commission on foreign sales. Offers written contract.

Tips "If you are concerned as to receipt of your material, please inquire through e-mail. Only send one project at a time. Do not send unsolicited mss. Please put 'query' or 'submission' in the subject heading of the e-mail."

☺ ASHLEY GRAYSON LITERARY AGENCY

1342 18th St., San Pedro CA 90732. Fax: (310)514-1148. E-mail: graysonagent@earthlink.net. Estab. 1976. Member of AAR. Represents 100 clients. 5% of clients are new/unpublished writers. Currently handles: 20% nonfiction books; 50% novels; 30% juvenile books.

Member Agents Ashley Grayson (fantasy, mystery, thrillers, young adult); Carolyn Grayson (chick lit, mystery, children's, nonfiction, women's fiction, romance, thrillers); Denise Dumars (mind/body/spirit, women's fiction, dark fantasy/horror); Lois Winston (women's fiction, chick lit, mystery).

Represents Nonfiction books, novels. **Considers these nonfiction areas:** Business/economics; computers/electronic; history; popular culture; science/technology; self-help/personal improvement; sports; true crime/investigative; mind/body/spirit; health; lifestyle. **Considers these fiction areas:** Fantasy; juvenile; multicultural; mystery/suspense; romance; science fiction; young adult; women's; chick lit.

O➡ "We prefer to work with published (traditional print), established authors. We will give first consideration to authors who come recommended to us by our clients or other publishing professionals. We accept a very small number of new, previously unpublished authors."

How to Contact As of early 2008, the agency was only open to fiction authors with publishing credits (no self-published). For nonfiction, only writers with great platforms will be considered.

Recent Sales *Ball Don't Lie*, by Matt de la Pena (Delacorte); *Heaven*, by Jack Cohen and Ian Stewart (Warner Books); *I Wish I Never Met You*, by Denise Wheatley (Touchstone/Simon & Schuster). Other clients include Isaac Adamson, John Barnes, Andrew Fox, Barb and J.C. Hendee, Geoffrey Landis, Bruce Coville, J.B. Cheaney, David Lubar and Christopher Pike.

Terms Agent receives 15% commission on domestic sales; 20% commission on foreign sales.

☺ KATHRYN GREEN LITERARY AGENCY, LLC

250 West 57th St., Suite 2302, New York NY 10107. (212)245-2445. Fax: (212)245-2040. E-mail: query@kgreenagency.com. **Contact:** Kathy Green. Estab. 2004. Member of Women's Media Group. Represents 20 clients. 50% of clients are new/unpublished writers. Currently handles: 50% nonfiction books; 25% novels; 25% juvenile books.

• Prior to becoming an agent, Ms. Green was a book and magazine editor.

Represents Nonfiction books, novels, short story collections, juvenile books (middle grade and young adult only). **Considers these nonfiction areas:** Biography/autobiography; business/economics; child guidance/parenting; cooking/foods/nutrition; current affairs; education; history; how-to; humor/satire; memoirs; popular culture; psychology; self-help/personal improvement; sports; true crime/investigative; women's issues/studies; interior design, juvenile. **Considers these fiction areas:** Detective/police/crime; family saga; historical; humor/satire; juvenile (middle grade and young adult only); literary; mainstream/contemporary; mystery/suspense; romance; thriller; young adult; women's.

O➡ "Keeping the client list small means that writers receive my full attention throughout the process of getting their project published." Does not want to receive science fiction or fantasy.

How to Contact Query with SASE. Query first. Send no samples unless requested. Accepts e-mail queries. No fax queries. Considers simultaneous queries. Responds in 1-2 months to mss. Returns materials only with SASE. Obtains most new clients through recommendations from others, solicitations, conferences.

Recent Sales The Touch series, by Laurie Srolarz; *A Common Bond*, by Donigan Merritt; *The Contrarian Effect*, by Michael Port; *Waiting to Score*, by J.E. Macleod.

Terms Agent receives 15% commission on domestic sales; 20% commission on foreign sales. No written contract.

Tips This agency offers a written agreement.

☺ SANFORD J. GREENBURGER ASSOCIATES, INC.

55 Fifth Ave., New York NY 10003. (212)206-5600. Fax: (212)463-8718. E-mail: firstinitiallastname@sjga.com. Website: www.greenburger.com. Estab. 1932. Member of AAR. Represents 500 clients.

Member Agents Heide Lange; Faith Hamlin; Dan Mandel; Matthew Bialer; Jeremy Katz; Tricia Davey.

Represents Nonfiction books, novels. **Considers these nonfiction areas:** Agriculture/horticulture; americana; animals; anthropology/archaeology; art/architecture/design; biography/autobiography; business/economics; child guidance/parenting; computers/electronic; cooking/foods/nutrition; crafts/hobbies; current affairs; education; ethnic/cultural interests; gardening; gay/lesbian issues; government/politics/law; health/medicine; history; how-to; humor/satire; interior design/decorating; juvenile nonfiction; language/literature/criticism; memoirs; military/war; money/finance; multicultural; music/dance; nature/environment; New Age/metaphysics; philosophy; photography; popular culture; psychology; recreation; regional; religious/inspirational; science/technology; self-help/personal improvement; sex; sociology; software; sports; theater/film; translation; travel; true crime/investigative; women's issues/studies; young adult. **Considers these fiction areas:** Action/adventure; detective/police/crime; ethnic; family saga; feminist; gay/lesbian; glitz; historical; humor/satire; literary; mainstream/contemporary; mystery/suspense; psychic/supernatural; regional; sports; thriller.

    O→ No romances or Westerns.

How to Contact Submit query, first 3 chapters, synopsis, brief bio, SASE. Accepts e-mail and fax queries. Considers simultaneous queries. Responds in 2 months to queries and mss. Returns materials only with SASE. Obtains most new clients through recommendations from others.

Recent Sales Sold 200 titles in the last year. This agency prefers not to share information on specific sales.

Terms Agent receives 15% commission on domestic sales; 20% commission on foreign sales. Charges for photocopying and books for foreign and subsidiary rights submissions.

Ⓝ Ⓔ Ⓒ THE GREENHOUSE LITERARY AGENCY

11308 Lapham Drive, Oakton VA 22124. (703)865-4990. E-mail: sarahd@greenhouseliterary.com. Website: www.greenhouseliterary.com. **Contact:** Sarah Davies. Estab. 2008; SCBWI. Represents 4 clients. 100% of clients are new/unpublished writers. Currently handles: 100% juvenile books.

    • Prior to becoming an agent, Ms. Davies was the publishing director of MacMillan Children's Books in London.

Represents Juvenile books. **Considers these fiction areas:** Juvenile; young adult.

    O→ "We exclusively represent authors writing fiction for children and teens. The agency has offices in both the USA and UK, and Sarah Davies (who is British) personally represents authors to both markets. The agency's commission structure reflects this—taking 15% for sales to both US and UK, thus treating both as 'domestic' market." All genres of children's and YA fiction—ages 5 + . Does not want to receive nonfiction, poetry, picture books (text or illustration) or work aimed at adults.

How to Contact Query with SASE, submit one-paragraph synopsis, one-paragraph bio, 3 sample chapters. Accepts queries by e-mail and snail mail. Responds in 6 week to queries. Returns materials only with SASE. Obtains most new clients through recommendations from others, solicitations, conferences.

Terms Agent receives 15% commission on domestic sales; 25% commission on foreign sales. Offers written contract. This agency charges for copies for overseas submissions.

Writers' Conferences Bologna Children's Book Fair, SCBWI conferences, BookExpo America.

Tips "Before submitting material, authors should read the Greenhouse's 'Top 10 Tips for Authors of Children's Fiction,' which can be found on our Web site."

Ⓜ Ⓔ GREGORY & CO. AUTHORS' AGENTS

3 Barb Mews, Hammersmith, London W6 7PA, England. (44)(207)610-4676. Fax: (44)(207)610-4686. E-mail: info@gregoryandcompany.co.uk. Website: www.gregoryandcompany.co.uk. **Contact:** Mary Jones. Estab. 1987. Member of AAA. Represents 60 clients. Currently handles: 10% nonfiction books; 90% novels.

Represents Nonfiction books, novels. **Considers these nonfiction areas:** Biography/autobiography; history. **Considers these fiction areas:** Detective/police/crime; historical; literary; mainstream/contemporary; thriller; contemporary women's fiction.

    O→ "As a British agency, we do not generally take on American authors." Actively seeking well-written, accessible modern novels. Does not want to receive horror, science fiction, fantasy, mind/body/spirit, children's books, screenplays, plays, short stories or poetry.

How to Contact Query with SASE, submit outline, 3 (or fewer than 10 pages if sending by e-mail) sample chapter(s), publishing history, author bio. Send submissions to Mary Jones, submissions editor. Considers simultaneous queries. Returns materials only with SASE. Obtains most new clients through recommendations from others, conferences.

Recent Sales *Tokyo*, by Mo Hayder (Bantam UK/Gove Atlantic); *The Torment of Others*, by Val McDermid (HarperCollins UK/St. Martin's Press); *Disordered Minds*, by Minette Walters (MacMillan UK/Putnam USA); *The Lover*, by Laura Wilson (Orion UK/Bantam USA); *Gagged & Bound*, by Natasha Cooper (Simon & Schuster UK/St. Martin's Press); *Demon of the Air*, by Simon Levack (Simon & Schuster/St. Martin's Press).

Terms Agent receives 15% commission on domestic sales; 20% commission on foreign sales. Offers written

contract; 3-month notice must be given to terminate contract. Charges clients for photocopying of whole type-scripts and copies of book for submissions.
Writers' Conferences CWA Conference; Bouchercon.

⊘ GREGORY LITERARY AGENCY, LLC

Birmingham AL 35242. (205)799-0380. Fax: (205)278-8572. E-mail: gregoryliteraryagency@yahoo.com. **Contact:** Steven P. Gregory. Estab. 2006. Currently handles: 50% nonfiction books; 50% novels.

• Prior to becoming an agent, Mr. Gregory was an attorney.

Represents Nonfiction books, novels. **Considers these nonfiction areas:** Biography/autobiography; current affairs; ethnic/cultural interests; government/politics/law; memoirs; military/war; money/finance; New Age/metaphysics; religious/inspirational; sports. **Considers these fiction areas:** Action/adventure; detective/police/crime; ethnic; glitz; literary; mainstream/contemporary; mystery/suspense; sports; thriller; women's.

     O━ Actively seeking mainstream fiction, mystery/thriller, memoir, biography, African-American fiction/nonfiction, military history, money/finance/economics, law/government/politics, economics/current affairs, New Age/Buddhist. Does not want children's, science fiction, cookbooks, how-to, general nonfiction, humor or religious/inspirational.

How to Contact Query with SASE. Send no unsolicited mss of any kind. Accepts e-mail queries. No fax queries. Considers simultaneous queries. Responds in 1 month to queries; 2 months to mss. Obtains most new clients through recommendations from others, solicitations. Agent receives 15% commission on domestic sales; 20% commission on foreign sales. Offers written contract. This agency charges for postage, overnight delivery and travel; costs are charged against advance after sales.

Tips "Write the best book you can then polish and edit the final version. Do not waste money on a 'professional editor.' Edit the manuscript yourself. If you write in first person, the narrator must exhibit a compelling and unique voice. My agency strongly prefers to receive queries and requested samples by e-mail and by pdf attachments."

◓ BLANCHE C. GREGORY, INC.

2 Tudor City Place, New York NY 10017. (212)697-0828. E-mail: info@bcgliteraryagency.com; query@bcgliteraryagency.com. Website: www.bcgliteraryagency.com. Member of AAR.

Represents Nonfiction books, novels, juvenile books.

     O━ This agency specializes in adult fiction and nonfiction; children's literature is also considered. Does not want to receive screenplays, stage plays or teleplays.

How to Contact Submit query, brief synopsis, bio, SASE. No e-mail queries. No fax queries. Obtains most new clients through recommendations from others.

Recent Sales *Chilly Scenes of Winter Distortions*, a short story collection by Ann Beattie; *Loose Ends*, by Neal Bowers; *It Happened in Boston*, by Russell H. Greenan.

◻ JILL GRINBERG LITERARY AGENCY

244 Fifth Ave., Floor 11, New York NY 10011. (212)620-5883. Fax: (212)627-4725. E-mail: jillgrin@aol.com. Website: www.grinbergliterary.com.

     • Prior to her current position, Ms. Grinberg was at Anderson Grinberg Literary Management.

Member Agents Jill Grinberg; Kirsten Wolf (foreign rights).

Represents Nonfiction books, novels. **Considers these nonfiction areas:** Biography/autobiography; business/economics; current affairs; government/politics/law; health/medicine; history; multicultural; psychology; science/technology; spirituality; travel; women's issues/studies. **Considers these fiction areas:** Fantasy; historical; romance; science fiction; young adult; women's; literary fiction, commercial fiction, children's, middle grade.

How to Contact Query with SASE, submit Send a proposal and author bio for nonfiction; send a query, synopsis and the first 50 pages for fiction. No e-mail or fax queries.

Recent Sales *Red Sky in Mourning*, by Jill Grinberg (Hyperion); *Strange Angel*, by George Pendle (Harcourt); *Jesse James: Last Rebel of the Civil War*, by T.J. Stiles (Vintage); *Searching for El Dorado*, by Marc Herman (Nan A. Talese).

Tips "We prefer submissions by mail."

⊘ JILL GROSJEAN LITERARY AGENCY

1390 Millstone Road, Sag Harbor NY 11963-2214. (631)725-7419. Fax: (631)725-8632. E-mail: jill6981@aol.com. **Contact:** Jill Grosjean. Estab. 1999. Represents 40 clients. 100% of clients are new/unpublished writers. Currently handles: 100% novels.

     • Prior to becoming an agent, Ms. Grosjean was manager of an independent bookstore. She has also worked in publishing and advertising.

Represents Novels. **Considers these fiction areas:** Historical; literary; mainstream/contemporary; mystery/suspense; regional; romance.

O→ This agency offers some editorial assistance (i.e., line-by-line edits). Actively seeking literary novels and mysteries.

How to Contact Query with SASE. No cold calls, please. Considers simultaneous queries. Responds in 1 week to queries; 1 month to mss. Returns materials only with SASE. Obtains most new clients through recommendations from others, solicitations.

Recent Sales *On the Wings of the Morning* and *Comfort and Joy*, by Marie Bostwick (Kensington); *Beating the Babushka, by Tim Maleeny (Midnight Ink); Whispers Within*, by Don Locke (Nav Press); *Rivers Edge*, by Marie Bostwick (Kensington Publishing); *Stealing the Dragon*, by Tim Maleeny (Midnight Ink); *I Love You Like a Tomato*, by Marie Giordano (Forge Books); *Nectar*, by David C. Fickett (Forge Books); *Cycling* and *Sanctuary*, by Greg Garrett (Kensington); *The Smoke*, by Tony Broadbent (St. Martin's Press/Minotaur); *Fields of Gold*, by Marie Bostwick (Kensington); *Spectres in the Smoke*, by Tony Broadbent (St. Martin's Press/Minotaur).

Terms Agent receives 15% commission on domestic sales; 20% commission on foreign sales. No written contract. Charges clients for photocopying and mailing expenses.

Writers' Conferences Book Passage's Mystery Writers' Conference; Agents and Editors Conference; Texas Writers' and Agents' Conference.

Ⓝ Ⓥ LAURA GROSS LITERARY AGENCY

75 Clinton Place, Newton MA 02459. (617)964-2977. Fax: (617)964-3023. E-mail: LGLitAg@aol.com. **Contact:** Laura Gross. Estab. 1988. Represents 30 clients. 75% of clients are new/unpublished writers. Currently handles: 40% nonfiction books; 50% novels; 10% scholarly books.

• Prior to becoming an agent, Ms. Gross was an editor.

Represents Nonfiction books, novels. **Considers these nonfiction areas:** Biography/autobiography; child guidance/parenting; current affairs; ethnic/cultural interests; government/politics/law; health/medicine; history; memoirs; popular culture; psychology; sports; women's issues/studies. **Considers these fiction areas:** Historical; literary; mainstream/contemporary; mystery/suspense; thriller.

How to Contact Query with SASE, submit author bio. Accepts e-mail queries. No fax queries. Responds in several to queries; several to mss. Obtains most new clients through recommendations from others.

Recent Sales Sold 10+ titles in the last year. This agency prefers not to share information on specific sales.

Terms Agent receives 15% commission on domestic sales; 20% commission on foreign sales. Offers written contract.

Ⓥ REECE HALSEY NORTH

98 Main St., #704, Tiburon CA 94920. Fax: (415)789-9177. E-mail: info@reecehalseynorth.com. Website: www.reecehalseynorth.com. **Contact:** Kimberley Cameron. Estab. 1957 (Reece Halsey Agency); 1993 (Reece Halsey North). Member of AAR. Represents 40 clients. 30% of clients are new/unpublished writers. Currently handles: 75% fiction, 25% nonfiction.

• The Reece Halsey Agency has had an illustrious client list of established writers, including the estate of Aldous Huxley, and has represented Upton Sinclair, William Faulkner, and Henry Miller.

Member Agents Kimberley Cameron, Elizabeth Evans; Phil Lang.

Represents Nonfiction books, novels. **Considers these nonfiction areas:** Biography/autobiography; current affairs; history; language/literature/criticism; popular culture; science/technology; true crime/investigative; women's issues/studies. **Considers these fiction areas:** Action/adventure; contemporary issues; detective/police/crime; ethnic; family saga; historical; horror; literary; mainstream/contemporary; mystery/suspense; science fiction; thriller; women's.

O→ "We are looking for a unique and heartfelt voice that conveys a universal truth."

How to Contact Query with SASE, first 50 pages of novel. Please do not fax queries. Responds in 3-6 weeks to queries; 1 month to mss. Obtains most new clients through recommendations from others, solicitations.

Terms Agent receives 15% commission on domestic sales; 10% commission on dramatic rights sales. Offers written contract, binding for 1 year. Requests 6 copies of ms if representing an author.

Writers' Conferences Maui Writers Conference; Aspen Summer Words Literary Festival; Willamette Writers Conference, numerous others.

Tips "Always send a polite, well-written query and please include a SASE with it."

Ⓝ Ⓥ HALSTON FREEMAN LITERARY AGENCY, INC.

140 Broadway, 46th Floor, New York NY 10005. E-mail: queryhalstonfreemanliterary@hotmail.com. **Contact:** Molly Freeman, Betty Halston. Estab. 2007. Currently handles: 65% nonfiction books; 35% novels.

• Prior to becoming an agent, Ms. Halston was a marketing and promotion director for a local cable affiliate; Ms. Freeman was a television film editor and ad agency copywriter.

Member Agents Molly Freeman, Betty Halston.

Represents Nonfiction books, novels. **Considers these nonfiction areas:** Agriculture/horticulture; biography/

autobiography; business/economics; child guidance/parenting; current affairs; ethnic/cultural interests; gay/lesbian issues; government/politics/law; health/medicine; history; how-to; humor/satire; memoirs; New Age/metaphysics; psychology; self-help/personal improvement; true crime/investigative; women's issues/studies. **Considers these fiction areas:** Action/adventure; detective/police/crime; ethnic; feminist; historical; horror; humor/satire; literary; mainstream/contemporary; mystery/suspense; romance; science fiction; thriller; westerns/frontier; women's.

> O—¬ "We are a hands-on agency specializing in quality nonfiction and fiction. As a new agency, it is imperative that we develop relationships with good writers who are smart, hardworking and understand what's required of them to promote their books." Does not want to receive children's books, textbooks or poetry. Send no e-mail attachments.

How to Contact Query with SASE. For nonfiction, include sample chapters, synopsis, platform, bio and competitive titles. For fiction, include synopsis, bio and three sample chapters. No e-mail attachments. Accepts e-mail queries. No fax queries. Considers simultaneous queries. Responds in 2-6 weeks to queries; 1-2 months to mss. Obtains most new clients through recommendations from others, solicitations, conferences.

Terms Agent receives 15% commission on domestic sales; 20% commission on foreign sales. This agency charges clients for copying and postage directly related to the project.

◖ HALYARD LITERARY AGENCY

Chicago IL. E-mail: submissions@halyardagency.com; agrayson@halyardagency.com (general info). Website: www.halyardagency.com. **Contact:** Alaina Grayson.

Member Agents Alaina Grayson.

Represents Nonfiction books, novels. **Considers these nonfiction areas:** Biography/autobiography; history; science/technology. **Considers these fiction areas:** Fantasy; historical; juvenile; science fiction; young adult; general, paranormal.

> O—¬ "Based out of Chicago, Halyard Literary Agency is a new agency on the lookout for authors who have the same passion for innovation that we do. Halyard is small, but provides assistance through every stage of book production. We're dedicated to building relationships with our authors, not just for one book or one year, but throughout their publishing life."

How to Contact Query with SASE. E-mail queries only. Send requested materials as e-mail attachments. No fax queries.

◖ THE JOY HARRIS LITERARY AGENCY, INC.

156 Fifth Ave., Suite 617, New York NY 10010. (212)924-6269. Fax: (212)924-6609. **Contact:** Joy Harris. Member of AAR. Represents more than 100 clients. Currently handles: 50% nonfiction books; 50% novels.

Represents Nonfiction books, novels. **Considers these fiction areas:** Ethnic; experimental; family saga; feminist; gay/lesbian; glitz; hi-lo; historical; humor/satire; literary; mainstream/contemporary; multicultural; multimedia; mystery/suspense; regional; short story collections; spiritual; translation; young adult; women's.

> O—¬ No screenplays.

How to Contact Query with sample chapter, outline/proposal, SASE. No e-mail or fax queries. Considers simultaneous queries. Responds in 2 months to queries. Returns materials only with SASE. Obtains most new clients through recommendations from clients and editors.

Recent Sales This agency prefers not to share information on specific sales.

Terms Agent receives 15% commission on domestic sales; 20% commission on foreign sales. Charges clients for some office expenses.

◖ HARTLINE LITERARY AGENCY

123 Queenston Dr., Pittsburgh PA 15235-5429. (412)829-2483. Fax: (412)829-2432. E-mail: joyce@hartlineliterary.com. Website: www.hartlineliterary.com. **Contact:** Joyce A. Hart. Estab. 1990. Represents 40 clients. 20% of clients are new/unpublished writers. Currently handles: 40% nonfiction books; 60% novels.

Member Agents Joyce A. Hart, principal agent; Andrea Boeshaar; Terry Burns; Tamela Hancock Murray; Diana Flegal; Erik Schmidgal.

Represents Nonfiction books, novels. **Considers these nonfiction areas:** Business/economics; child guidance/parenting; cooking/foods/nutrition; money/finance; religious/inspirational; self-help/personal improvement; women's issues/studies. **Considers these fiction areas:** Action/adventure; contemporary issues; family saga; historical; literary; mystery/suspense (amateur sleuth, cozy); regional; religious/inspirational; romance (contemporary, gothic, historical, regency); thriller.

> O—¬ This agency specializes in the Christian bookseller market. Actively seeking adult fiction, self-help, nutritional books, devotional, and business. Does not want to receive erotica, gay/lesbian, fantasy, horror, etc.

How to Contact Submit summary/outline, author bio, 3 sample chapters. Accepts e-mail and fax queries.

Considers simultaneous queries. Responds in 2 months to queries; 3 months to mss. Returns materials only with SASE. Obtains most new clients through recommendations from others.

Recent Sales *A Tendering in the Storm* and *A Mending at the Edge*, by Jane Kirkpatrick, (Waterbrook); *Jillian Dare*, by Melanie Jeschke, (Revell); *Gone to Glory*, by Ron & Janet Benrey (Steeple Hill); *A Candle in the Darkness* and *Through the Eyes of Love*, by Dorothy Clark (Steeple Hill); *A Cowboy Worth Marrying*, by Deborah Clopton (Steeple Hill); *Melodies for Murder*, Donn Taylor; *Right from the Start*, by Brenda Nixon (Revell).

Terms Agent receives 15% commission on domestic sales. Offers written contract.

ANTONY HARWOOD LIMITED

103 Walton St., Oxford OX2 6EB, England. (44)(186)555-9615. Fax: (44)(186)531-0660. E-mail: mail@antonyharwood.com. Website: www.antonyharwood.com. **Contact:** Antony Harwood, James Macdonald Lockhart. Estab. 2000. Represents 52 clients.

• Prior to starting this agency, Mr. Harwood and Mr. Lockhart worked at publishing houses and other literary agencies.

Represents Nonfiction books, novels. **Considers these nonfiction areas:** Agriculture/horticulture; americana; animals; anthropology/archaeology; art/architecture/design; biography/autobiography; business/economics; child guidance/parenting; computers/electronic; cooking/foods/nutrition; creative nonfiction (1); current affairs; education; ethnic/cultural interests; gardening; gay/lesbian issues; government/politics/law; health/medicine; history; how-to; humor/satire; language/literature/criticism; memoirs; military/war; money/finance; multicultural; music/dance; nature/environment; philosophy; photography; popular culture; psychology; recreation; regional; religious/inspirational; science/technology; self-help/personal improvement; sex; sociology; software; spirituality; sports; theater/film; translation; travel; true crime/investigative; women's issues/studies. **Considers these fiction areas:** Action/adventure; comic books/cartoon; confession; detective/police/crime; erotica; ethnic; experimental; family saga; fantasy; feminist; gay/lesbian; gothic; hi-lo; historical; horror; humor/satire; literary; mainstream/contemporary; military/war; multicultural; multimedia; mystery/suspense; occult; picture books; plays; regional; religious/inspirational; romance; science fiction; spiritual; sports; thriller; translation; westerns/frontier; young adult.

○→ "We accept every genre of fiction and nonfiction except for children's fiction for readers ages 10 and younger." No poetry or screenplays.

How to Contact Submit outline, 2-3 sample chapters via e-mail or postal mail (include SASE or IRC). No fax queries. Responds in 2 months to queries.

Terms Agent receives 15% commission on domestic sales; 20% commission on foreign sales.

JOHN HAWKINS & ASSOCIATES, INC.

71 W. 23rd St., Suite 1600, New York NY 10010. (212)807-7040. Fax: (212)807-9555. E-mail: jha@jhalit.com. Website: www.jhalit.com. **Contact:** Moses Cardona (moses@jhalit.com). Estab. 1893. Member of AAR. Represents over 100 clients. 5-10% of clients are new/unpublished writers. Currently handles: 40% nonfiction books; 40% novels; 20% juvenile books.

Member Agents Moses Cardona; Warren Frazier; Anne Hawkins; John Hawkins; William Reiss.

Represents Nonfiction books, novels, young adult. **Considers these nonfiction areas:** Agriculture/horticulture; americana; anthropology/archaeology; art/architecture/design; biography/autobiography; business/economics; current affairs; education; ethnic/cultural interests; gardening; gay/lesbian issues; government/politics/law; health/medicine; history; how-to; interior design/decorating; language/literature/criticism; memoirs; money/finance; multicultural; nature/environment; philosophy; popular culture; psychology; recreation; science/technology; self-help/personal improvement; sex; sociology; software; theater/film; travel; true crime/investigative; young adult; music, creative nonfiction. **Considers these fiction areas:** Action/adventure; detective/police/crime; ethnic; experimental; family saga; feminist; gay/lesbian; glitz; gothic; hi-lo; historical; literary; mainstream/contemporary; military/war; multicultural; multimedia; mystery/suspense; psychic/supernatural; religious/inspirational; short story collections; sports; thriller; translation; westerns/frontier; young adult; women's.

How to Contact Submit query, proposal package, outline, SASE. Considers simultaneous queries. Responds in 1 month to queries. Returns materials only with SASE. Obtains most new clients through recommendations from others.

Recent Sales *Tears of Pearl*, by Tasha Alexander; *Butterfly Mosque*, by Willow Wilson; *Tarnished Beauty*, by Cecilia Samartin.

Terms Agent receives 15% commission on domestic sales; 20% commission on foreign sales. Charges clients for photocopying.

HEACOCK LITERARY AGENCY, INC.

West Coast Office, 11740 Big Tujunga Canyon Road, Tujunga CA 91042. E-mail: catt@heacockliteraryagency.com. Website: www.heacockliteraryagency.com. **Contact:** Catt LeBaigue. Estab. 1978. Member of AAR, SCBWI.

- Prior to becoming an agent, Ms. LeBaigue spent 18 years with Sony Pictures and Warner Bros.

Member Agents Rosalie Grace Heacock Thompson (semi-retired, no queries at this time); Catt LeBaigue (juvenile fiction, adult nonfiction including arts, crafts, anthropolgy, astronomy, nature studies, ecology, body/mind/spirit, humanities, self-help).

Represents Nonfiction books, juvenile books.

How to Contact Query with SASE. E-mail queries only. No unsolicited manuscripts. No e-mail attachments. Returns materials only with SASE. Obtains most new clients through recommendations from others, solicitations.

Recent Sales Other clients include Don and Audrey Wood, Stephen Cosgrove, Larry Dane Brimner, Elliot Abravanel, E.A. King, E. Joseph Cossman, Joseph Bark. Offers written contract.

Tips "Take time to write an informative e-query letter expressing your book idea, the market for it, your qualifications to write the book, the 'hook' that would make a potential reader buy the book."

⚏ HELEN HELLER AGENCY INC.

892 Avenue Road, Toronto Ontario M5P 2K6, Canada. (416)631-0968. E-mail: info@helenhelleragency.com. Website: www.helenhelleragency.com. **Contact:** Helen Heller. Estab. 1988. Represents 30+ clients.

- Prior to her current position, Ms. Heller worked for Cassell & Co. (England), was an editor for Harlequin Books, a senior editor for Avon Books, and editor-in-chief for Fitzhenry & Whiteside.

Member Agents Helen Heller, helen@helenhelleragency.com; Daphne Hart, daphne.hart@sympatico.ca; Sarah Heller, sarah@helenhelleragency.com.

Represents Nonfiction books, novels.

    ○→ Actively seeking adult fiction and nonfiction (excluding children's literature, screenplays or genre fiction). Does not want to receive children's literature, screenplays or genre fiction such as fantasy and science fiction.

How to Contact Query with SASE, submit synopsis, publishing history, author bio. Obtains most new clients through recommendations from others, solicitations.

Recent Sales *Break on Through*, by Jill Murray (Doubleday Canada); *Womankind: Faces of Change Around the World*, by Donna Nebenzahl (Raincoast Books); *One Dead Indian: The Premier, The Police and the Ipperwash Crisis*, by Peter Edwards (McClelland & Stewart); a full list of deals is available online.

Tips "Whether you are an author searching for an agent, or whether an agent has approached you, it is in your best interest to first find out who the agent represents, what publishing houses has that agent sold to recently and what foreign sales have been made. You should be able to go to the bookstore, or search online and find the books the agent refers to. Many authors acknowledge their agents in the front or back or their books."

⚏ RICHARD HENSHAW GROUP

22 West 23rd St., Fifth Floor, New York NY 10010. (212)414-1172. Fax: (212)414-1182. E-mail: submissions@henshaw.com. Website: www.rich.henshaw.com. **Contact:** Rich Henshaw. Estab. 1995. Member of AAR, SinC, MWA, HWA, SFWA, RWA. Represents 35 clients. 20% of clients are new/unpublished writers. Currently handles: 35% nonfiction books; 65% novels.

- Prior to opening his agency, Mr. Henshaw served as an agent with Richard Curtis Associates, Inc.

Represents Nonfiction books, novels. **Considers these nonfiction areas:** Animals; biography/autobiography; business/economics; child guidance/parenting; computers/electronic; cooking/foods/nutrition; current affairs; gay/lesbian issues; government/politics/law; health/medicine; how-to; humor/satire; military/war; money/finance; music/dance; nature/environment; New Age/metaphysics; popular culture; psychology; science/technology; self-help/personal improvement; sociology; sports; true crime/investigative; women's issues/studies. **Considers these fiction areas:** Action/adventure; detective/police/crime; ethnic; family saga; fantasy; glitz; historical; horror; humor/satire; literary; mainstream/contemporary; mystery/suspense; psychic/supernatural; romance; science fiction; sports; thriller.

    ○→ This agency specializes in thrillers, mysteries, science fiction, fantasy and horror.

How to Contact Query with SASE. Responds in 3 weeks to queries; 6 weeks to mss. Obtains most new clients through recommendations from others, solicitations, conferences.

Recent Sales *Prepared For Rage*, By Dana Stabenow (St. Martin's Press); *The Girl With The Braided Hair*, by Margaret Coel (Berkley); *The History Of The Ancient World*, by Susan Wise Bauer (Norton); *The Art Of The Public Grovel*, By Susan Wise Bauer (Princeton University Press); *Three Sisters*, by James D. Doss (St. Martin's Press); *The Serpent Prince*, by Elizabeth Hoyt (Grand Central Publishing); *Hot*, by Julia Harper (Grand Central Publishing); *Dog Leg: Alternative Therapies For Animals*, by Lisa Preston (Alpine Publishing). Other clients include Jessie Wise, Peter van Dijk, Jay Caselberg, Judith Laik.

Terms Agent receives 15% commission on domestic sales; 20% commission on foreign sales. No written contract. 100% of business is derived from commissions on ms sales. Charges clients for photocopying and book orders.

Tips "While we do not have any reason to believe that our submission guidelines will change in the near future, writers can find up-to-date submission policy information on our Web site. Always include a SASE with correct return postage."

☑ THE JEFF HERMAN AGENCY, LLC

P.O. Box 1522, Stockbridge MA 01262. (413)298-0077. Fax: (413)298-8188. E-mail: jeff@jeffherman.com. Website: www.jeffherman.com. **Contact:** Jeffrey H. Herman. Estab. 1985. Represents 100 clients. 10% of clients are new/unpublished writers. Currently handles: 85% nonfiction books; 5% scholarly books; 5% textbooks.

  • Prior to opening his agency, Mr. Herman served as a public relations executive.

Member Agents Deborah Levine, vice president (nonfiction book doctor); Jeff Herman.

Represents Nonfiction books. **Considers these nonfiction areas:** Business/economics; government/politics/law; health/medicine (recovery issues); history; how-to; self-help/personal improvement; spirituality; popular reference; technology; popular psychology.

  ⟲ This agency specializes in adult nonfiction.

How to Contact Query with SASE. Accepts e-mail and fax queries. Considers simultaneous queries.

Recent Sales Sold 35 titles in the last year. This agency prefers not to share information on specific sales.

Terms Agent receives 15% commission on domestic sales. Offers written contract. Charges clients for copying and postage.

☑ HIDDEN VALUE GROUP

1240 E. Ontario Ave., Ste. 102-148, Corona CA, 92881. (951)549-8891. Fax: (951)549-8891. E-mail: bookquery@hiddenvaluegroup.com. Website: www.hiddenvaluegroup.com. **Contact:** Nancy Jernigan. Estab. 2001. Represents 40 clients. 20% of clients are new/unpublished writers.

Member Agents Jeff Jernigan, jjernigan@hiddenvaluegroup.com (men's nonfiction, fiction, Bible studies/curriculum, marriage and family); Nancy Jernigan, njernigan@hiddenvaluegroup.com (nonfiction, women's issues, inspiration, marriage and family, fiction).

Represents Nonfiction books, novels, juvenile books. **Considers these nonfiction areas:** Biography/autobiography; business/economics; child guidance/parenting; history; how-to; juvenile nonfiction; language/literature/criticism; memoirs; money/finance; psychology; religious/inspirational; self-help/personal improvement; women's issues/studies. **Considers these fiction areas:** Action/adventure; detective/police/crime; fantasy; literary; religious/inspirational; thriller; westerns/frontier; women's.

  ⟲ "The Hidden Value Group specializes in helping authors throughout their publishing career. We believe that every author has a special message to be heard and we specialize in getting that message heard." Actively seeking established fiction authors, and authors who are focusing on women's issues. Does not want to receive poetry or short stories.

How to Contact Query with SASE, submit synopsis, 3 sample chapter(s), author bio. Accepts queries to bookquery@hiddenvaluegroup.com. Accepts e-mail queries. No fax queries. Considers simultaneous queries. Responds in 1 month to queries; 1 month to mss. Returns materials only with SASE. Obtains most new clients through recommendations from others, solicitations.

Recent Sales *Tilt*, by Erik Rees (Group Publishing); *Character Makeover*, by Katie Brazelton (Zondervan); *More Than a Match*, by Michael and Amy Smalley (Waterbrook Press); *Body, Beauty, Boys*, by Sarah Bragg; *The DNA of Relationships*, by Gary Smalley; *A Happier, Healthier You*, by Lorraine Bosse Smith.

Terms Agent receives 15% commission on domestic sales; 15% commission on foreign sales. Offers written contract.

Writers' Conferences Glorieta Christian Writers' Conference; CLASS Publishing Conference.

☑ FREDERICK HILL BONNIE NADELL, INC.

1842 Union St., San Francisco CA 94123. (415)921-2910. Fax: (415)921-2802. **Contact:** Elise Proulx. Estab. 1979. Represents 100 clients.

Member Agents Bonnie Nadell; Elise Proulx, associate.

Represents Nonfiction books, novels. **Considers these nonfiction areas:** Current affairs; health/medicine; history; language/literature/criticism; nature/environment; popular culture; science/technology; biography; government/politics, narrative. **Considers these fiction areas:** Literary; mainstream/contemporary.

How to Contact Query with SASE. Keep your query to one page. Send via snail mail. No e-mail or fax queries. Considers simultaneous queries. Returns materials only with SASE.

Recent Sales *It Might Have Been What He Said*, by Eden Collinsworth; *Consider the Lobster and Other Essays*, by David Foster Wallace; *The Underdog*, by Joshua Davis.

Terms Agent receives 15% commission on domestic sales; 20% commission on foreign sales; 15% commission on dramatic rights sales. Charges clients for photocopying and foreign mailings.

◉ HILL MEDIA

1155 Camino Del Mar, #530, Del Mar CA 92014. (858)259-2595. Fax: (858)259-2777. **Contact:** Julie Hill. Estab. 1994. Represents 50 clients. 20% of clients are new/unpublished writers. Currently handles: 90% nonfiction books; 5% story collections; 5% books that accompany films.

Member Agents Julie Hill, agent/publicist; Anette Farrell, agent.

Represents Nonfiction books, short story collections, anthologies. **Considers these nonfiction areas:** Art/architecture/design; biography/autobiography; cooking/foods/nutrition; ethnic/cultural interests; health/medicine; history; how-to; interior design/decorating; language/literature/criticism; memoirs; music/dance; New Age/metaphysics; popular culture; psychology; religious/inspirational; self-help/personal improvement; women's issues/studies.

    ○⊸ "Check your ego at the door. If we love your book, we mean it. If we are so-so, we also mean that. If we cannot place it, we tell you ASAP." Actively seeking nonfiction: travel, health, media tie-ins. Does not want to receive horror, juvenile, sci-fi, thrillers or autobiographies of any kind.

How to Contact Query with SASE, submit outline/proposal, SASE. Send all submissions via snail mail. See the Web site for more instructions. Never send a complete ms unless requested. No e-mail or fax queries. Considers simultaneous queries. Responds in 4-6 weeks to queries. Obtains most new clients through recommendations from others, solicitations, conferences.

Recent Sales Sold 20 titles in the last year. *Sunshines, The Astrology of Happiness*, by Michael Lutin (Simon and Schuster); *Images from the Film: Memoirs of a Geisha* (Newmarket Press); *Return to Naples*, by Robert Zweig (Dusty Spark).

◉ BARBARA HOGENSON AGENCY

165 West End Ave., Suite 19-C, New York NY 10023. (212)874-8084. Fax: (212)362-3011. E-mail: bhogenson@aol.com. **Contact:** Barbara Hogenson, Nicole Verity. Member of AAR.

How to Contact Query with SASE. No e-mail or fax queries. Obtains most new clients through recommendations from other clients.

◉ HORNFISCHER LITERARY MANAGEMENT

P.O. Box 50544, Austin TX 78763. E-mail: queries@hornfischerlit.com. Website: www.hornfischerlit.com. **Contact:** James D. Hornfischer, president. Estab. 2001. Represents 45 clients. 10% of clients are new/unpublished writers. Currently handles: 98% nonfiction books; 2%.

    ● Prior to opening his agency, Mr. Hornfischer was an agent with Literary Group International and held editorial positions at HarperCollins and McGraw-Hill. "My New York editorial background working with a variety of bestselling authors, such as Erma Bombeck, Jared Diamond, and Erica Jong, is useful in this regard. In 14 years as an agent, I've handled eight *New York Times* nonfiction bestsellers, including two No. 1's."

Represents Nonfiction books. **Considers these nonfiction areas:** Anthropology/archaeology; biography/autobiography; business/economics; child guidance/parenting; current affairs; government/politics/law; health/medicine; history; how-to; humor/satire; memoirs; military/war; money/finance; multicultural; nature/environment; popular culture; psychology; religious/inspirational; science/technology; self-help/personal improvement; sociology; sports; true crime/investigative.

    ○⊸ Actively seeking the best work of terrific writers. Does not want poetry or genre fiction.

How to Contact Submit proposal package, outline, 2 sample chapters. Considers simultaneous queries. Responds in 8 weeks to queries. Returns materials only with SASE. Obtains most new clients through referrals from clients, reading books and magazines, pursuing ideas with New York editors.

Recent Sales *Cosmotopia: The Shaping of American Thought and Culture*, by William H. Goetzmann (Basic); see this agency's Web site for more sales information.

Terms Agent receives 15% commission on domestic sales; 25% commission on foreign sales. Offers written contract. Reasonable expenses deducted from proceeds after book is sold.

Tips "When you query agents and send out proposals, present yourself as someone who's in command of his material and comfortable in his own skin. Too many writers have a palpable sense of anxiety and insecurity. Take a deep breath and realize that—if you're good—someone in the publishing world will want you."

◉ ANDREA HURST LITERARY MANAGEMENT

P.O. Box 19010, Sacramento CA 95819. E-mail: (agentfirstname)@andreahurst.com. Website: www.andreahurst.com. **Contact:** Andrea Hurst, president; Judy Mikalonis, associate agent. Estab. 2002. Represents 50+ clients. 50% of clients are new/unpublished writers. Currently handles: 75% nonfiction books; 10% novels; 15% juvenile books.

    ● Prior to becoming an agent, Ms. Hurst was an acquisitions editor as well as a freelance editor and published writer; Ms. Mikalonis was in marketing and branding consulting.

Member Agents Andrea Hurst, andrea@andreahurst.com (nonfiction—including personal growth, health and wellness, science, business, parenting, relationships, women's issues, animals, spirituality, women's issues, metaphysical, psychological, cookbooks and self help; fiction interests include adult fiction); Judy Mikalonis, judy@andreahurst.com (YA fiction, Christian fiction, Christian nonfiction); Verna Dreisbach (Commercial & literary fiction, mystery, suspense, thriller, commercial women's fiction, young adult, Native American Indian, horsemanship, Adult nonfiction: Travel writing, self-help, parenting, business, pets, health, true crime).

Represents Nonfiction books, novels, juvenile books. **Considers these nonfiction areas:** Animals; art/architecture/design; biography/autobiography; business/economics; child guidance/parenting; cooking/foods/nutrition; crafts/hobbies; education; health/medicine; how-to; humor/satire; interior design/decorating; juvenile nonfiction; memoirs; military/war; money/finance; music/dance; nature/environment; New Age/metaphysics; photography; popular culture; psychology; religious/inspirational; science/technology; self-help/personal improvement; sociology; true crime/investigative; women's issues/studies; gift books. **Considers these fiction areas:** Juvenile; literary; mainstream/contemporary; psychic/supernatural; religious/inspirational; romance; thriller; young adult; women's.

> O— "We work directly with our signed authors to help them polish their work and their platform for optimum marketability. Our staff is always available to answer phone calls and e-mails from our authors and we stay with a project until we have exhausted all publishing avenues." Actively seeking well written nonfiction by authors with a strong platform; superbly crafted fiction with depth that touches the mind and heart and all of our listed subjects. Does not want to receive sci-fi, mystery, horror, Western, poetry or screenplays.

How to Contact Query with SASE, submit outline/proposal, synopsis, 2 sample chapter(s), author bio. Accepts e-mail queries. No fax queries. Considers simultaneous queries. Obtains most new clients through recommendations from others, solicitations, conferences.

Recent Sales Sold 20 titles in the last year. *The Hope and Joy,* by Bernie Siegel (Rodale); *The Lazy Dog's Guide to Enlightenment,* by Andrea Hurst and Beth Wilson (New World Library); *Best Recipes from Italy's Food Festivals,* by James Fraioli (Penguin); *True Self—True Wealth,* by Peter Cole and Daisy Reese.

Terms Agent receives 15% commission on domestic sales; 20% commission on foreign sales. Offers written contract, binding for 6 to 12 months; 30-day notice must be given to terminate contract. This agency charges for postage.

Writers' Conferences San Francisco Writers' Conference; Willamette Writers' Conference; Santa Barbara Writers' Conference; Surrey International; PNWA; Whidbey Island Writers Conference.

Tips "Do your homework and submit a professional package. Get to know the agent you are submitting to by researching their Web site or meeting them at a conference. Perfect your craft: Write well and edit ruthlessly over and over again before submitting to an agent. Be realistic: Understand that publishing is a business and be prepared to prove why your book is marketable and how you will market it on your own. Be Persistent!"

INKWELL MANAGEMENT, LLC

521 Fifth Ave., 26th Floor, New York NY 10175. (212)922-3500. Fax: (212)922-0535. E-mail: submissions@inkwellmanagement.com. Website: www.inkwellmanagement.com. Estab. 2004. Represents 500 clients. Currently handles: 60% nonfiction books; 40% novels.

Member Agents Michael Carlisle; Richard Pine; Kimberly Witherspoon; George Lucas; Catherine Drayton; David Forrer; Susan Arellano; Alexis Hurley; Patricia Burke, Susan Hobson; Nat Jacks; Ethan Bassoff, Julie Schilder, Libby O'Neill; Elisa Petrini, Mairead Duffy.

Represents Nonfiction books, novels.

How to Contact Query with SASE or via e-mail. Obtains most new clients through recommendations from others.

Recent Sales Sold 100 titles in the last year.

Terms Agent receives 15% commission on domestic sales; 20% commission on foreign sales. Offers written contract.

Tips "We will not read manuscripts before receiving a letter of inquiry."

INTERNATIONAL CREATIVE MANAGEMENT

825 Eighth Ave., New York NY 10019. (212)556-5600. Website: www.icmtalent.com. **Contact:** Literary Department. Member of AAR; signatory of WGA.

Member Agents Christine Earle, cearle@icmtalent.com(fiction interests include: young adult, children's, middle grade; nonfiction interests include: dating/relationships, pop culture); Lisa Bankoff, lbankoff@icmtalent.com (fiction interests include: literary fiction, family saga, historical fiction, offbeat/quirky; nonfiction interests include: history, biography, parenting, memoirs, narrative, humor); Sam Cohn; Patrick Herold, pherold@icmtalent.com; Jennifer Joel, jjoel@icmtalent.com (fiction interests include: literary fiction, commercial fiction, historical fiction, thrillers/suspense; nonfiction interests include: history, sports, art, adventure/true story, pop culture); Esther Newberg; Sloan Harris; Amanda "Binky" Urban; Mitch Douglas; Heather Schroder; Kristine Dahl;

Andrea Barzvi, abarzvi@icmtalent.com (fiction interests include: chick lit, commercial fiction, women's fiction, thrillers/suspense; nonfiction interests include: sports, celebrity, self-help, dating/relationships, women's issues, pop culture, health and fitness); Tina Dubois Wexler, twexler@icmtalent.com (literary fiction, chick lit, young adult, middle grade, memoir, narrative nonfiction); Katharine Cluverius; Kate Lee, klee@icmtalent.com (mystery, commercial fiction, short stories, memoir, dating/relationships, pop culture, humor, journalism). **Represents** Nonfiction books, novels.

○━ "We do not accept unsolicited submissions."

How to Contact Query with SASE. Send queries via snail mail and include an SASE. Target a specific agent. No fax queries. Obtains most new clients through recommendations from others.

Terms Agent receives 15% commission on domestic sales; 20% commission on foreign sales.

◑ INTERNATIONAL LITERARY ARTS

RR 5, Box 5391 A, Moscow PA, 18444. E-mail: query@InternationalLiteraryArts.com. Website: www.InternationalLiteraryArts.com. **Contact:** Pamela K. Brodowsky. Estab. 2000.

● Prior to her current position, Ms. Fazio worked at Prentice Hall, Random House, M.E. Sharpe and Baker & Taylor; Ms. Brodowsky is a public speaker, as well as the author of *Secrets of Successful Query Letters* and *Bulletproof Book Proposals*.

Member Agents Pamela K. Brodowsky; Evelyn Fazio.

Represents Nonfiction books, movie scripts. **Considers these nonfiction areas:** Biography/autobiography; business/economics; cooking/foods/nutrition; current affairs; health/medicine; history; humor/satire; money/finance; science/technology; self-help/personal improvement; sports; travel; reference, parenting, lifestyle.

○━ "ILA is a full service literary property agency representing authors in all areas of nonfiction across the creative spectrum. The agency is committed to the clients it represents and to the publishers with whom we match our talent. Our goal is to provide for our publishers talented authors with long-term career goals. Our mission is to create the continuance of the discovery of new talent and thriving careers for our represented clients." Does not want to receive fiction at this time.

How to Contact Query with SASE. For nonfiction, send an e-mail cover letter, contact info, proposal and sample chapter. Send no e-attachments. Accepts e-mail queries. No fax queries. Responds in 4-6 weeks to queries.

Recent Sales *Planning for Disaster*, by William Ramroth (Kaplan); *PR on a Budget*, by Leonard Saffir (Dearborn Trade); *The Five Jerks You Meet on Earth*, by Ray Zardetto (Andrews McMeel); *How to Raise Kids You Want to Keep*, by Jerry Day (Sourcebooks).

Writers' Conferences BookExpo America.

Tips "If you are inquiring about a nonfiction book project, please address your material to the attention of the Book Department. For screenplays, please address your material to the attention of the Motion Picture Department. Due to the enormous amount of submissions we receive, we will only respond to queries that we feel are a good fit for our agency."

◑ INTERNATIONAL TRANSACTIONS, INC.

P.O. Box 97, Gila NM 88038-0097. (845)373-9696. Fax: (845)373-7868. E-mail: info@intltrans.com. Website: www.intltrans.com; www.itincusa.com. **Contact:** Peter Riva. Estab. 1975. Represents 40+ clients. 10% of clients are new/unpublished writers. Currently handles: 60% nonfiction books; 25% novels; 5% story collections; 5% juvenile books; 5% scholarly books.

Member Agents Peter Riva (nonfiction, fiction, illustrated; television and movie rights placement); Sandra Riva (fiction, juvenile, biographies); JoAnn Collins (fiction, women's fiction, medical fiction).

Represents Nonfiction books, novels, short story collections, juvenile books, scholarly books, illustrated books, anthologies. **Considers these nonfiction areas:** Anthropology/archaeology; art/architecture/design; biography/autobiography; computers/electronic; cooking/foods/nutrition; current affairs; ethnic/cultural interests; gay/lesbian issues; government/politics/law; health/medicine; history; humor/satire; language/literature/criticism; memoirs; military/war; music/dance; nature/environment; photography; science/technology; self-help/personal improvement; sports; translation; true crime/investigative; women's issues/studies. **Considers these fiction areas:** Action/adventure; detective/police/crime; erotica; experimental; family saga; feminist; gay/lesbian; historical; humor/satire; literary; mainstream/contemporary; mystery/suspense; sports; thriller; young adult; women's/chick lit.

○━ "We specialize in large and small projects, helping qualified authors perfect material for publication." Actively seeking intelligent, well-written innovative material that breaks new ground. Does not want to receive material influenced by TV (too much dialogue); a rehash of previous successful novels' themes or poorly prepared material.

How to Contact First, e-query with an outline or synopsis. E-queries only!. No fax queries. Responds in 3 weeks to queries; 5 weeks to mss. Obtains most new clients through recommendations from others, solicitations.

Recent Sales Sold 12 titles in the last year. *Colt*, by Dennis Adler (Book Sales Inc.); *Penguins*, by Brutus Ostling

(HarperCollins); *Road to Damascus*, by Lena Einhorn (Lyons Press); *Tao of Daily Life*, by Derek Lin (Penguin). **Terms** Agent receives 15% (25% on illustrated books) commission on domestic sales; 5% commission on foreign sales. Offers written contract; 180-day notice must be given to terminate contract.

Tips " 'Book'—a published work of literature. That last word is the key. Not a string of words, not a book of (TV or film) 'scenes,' and never a stream of consciousness unfathomable by anyone outside of the writer's coterie. A writer should only begin to get 'interested in getting an agent' if the work is polished, literate and ready to be presented to a publishing house. Anything less is either asking for a quick rejection or is a thinly disguised plea for creative assistance—which is often given but never fiscally sound for the agents involved. Writers, even published authors, have difficulty in being objective about their own work. Friends and family are of no assistance in that process either. Writers should attempt to get their work read by the most unlikely and stern critic as part of the editing process, months before any agent is approached."

JABBERWOCKY LITERARY AGENCY

P.O. Box 4558, Sunnyside NY 11104-0558. (718)392-5985. Website: www.awfulagent.com. **Contact:** Joshua Bilmes. Estab. 1994. Member of SFWA. Represents 40 clients. 15% of clients are new/unpublished writers. Currently handles: 15% nonfiction books; 75% novels; 5% scholarly books; 5% other.

Represents Nonfiction books, novels, scholarly books. **Considers these nonfiction areas:** Biography/autobiography; business/economics; cooking/foods/nutrition; current affairs; gay/lesbian issues; government/politics/law; health/medicine; history; humor/satire; language/literature/criticism; military/war; money/finance; nature/environment; popular culture; science/technology; sociology; sports; theater/film; true crime/investigative; women's issues/studies. **Considers these fiction areas:** Action/adventure; contemporary issues; detective/police/crime; ethnic; family saga; fantasy; gay/lesbian; glitz; historical; horror; humor/satire; literary; mainstream/contemporary; psychic/supernatural; regional; science fiction; sports; thriller.

> ⊶ This agency represents quite a lot of genre fiction and is actively seeking to increase the amount of nonfiction projects. It does not handle juvenile or young adult. Book-length material only—no poetry, articles, or short stories.

How to Contact Query with SASE. Do not send mss unless requested. No e-mail or fax queries. Considers simultaneous queries. Responds in 3 weeks to queries. Returns materials only with SASE. Obtains most new clients through solicitations, recommendation by current clients.

Recent Sales Sold 30 US and 100 foreign titles in the last year. *From Dead to Worse*, by Charlaine Harris; *Victory Conditions*, by Elizabeth Moon; *Underground*, by Kat Richardson; Mistborn & Alcatraz series by Brandon Sanderson. Other clients include Simon Green, Tanya Huff, Tobias Buckell.

Terms Agent receives 15% commission on domestic sales; 20% commission on foreign sales. Offers written contract, binding for 1 year. Charges clients for book purchases, photocopying, international book/ms mailing.

Writers' Conferences Malice Domestic (May 2009); World Sci-Fi Convention (August 2008); full schedule on Web site.

Tips "In approaching with a query, the most important things to me are your credits and your biographical background to the extent it's relevant to your work. I (and most agents) will ignore the adjectives you may choose to describe your own work."

JAMES PETER ASSOCIATES, INC.

P.O. Box 358, New Canaan CT 06840. (203)972-1070. E-mail: gene_brissie@msn.com. **Contact:** Gene Brissie. Estab. 1971. Represents 75 individual and 6 corporate clients. 15% of clients are new/unpublished writers. Currently handles: 100% nonfiction books.

Represents Nonfiction books. **Considers these nonfiction areas:** Anthropology/archaeology; art/architecture/design; biography/autobiography; business/economics; child guidance/parenting; current affairs; ethnic/cultural interests; gay/lesbian issues; government/politics/law; health/medicine; history; language/literature/criticism; memoirs (political, business); military/war; money/finance; music/dance; popular culture; psychology; self-help/personal improvement; theater/film; travel; women's issues/studies.

> ⊶ "We are especially interested in general, trade and reference nonfiction." Does not want to receive children's/young adult books, poetry or fiction.

How to Contact Submit proposal package, outline, SASE. Prefers to read materials exclusively. No e-mail or fax queries. Responds in 1 month to queries. Returns materials only with SASE. Obtains most new clients through recommendations from others, solicitations, contact with people who are doing interesting things.

Recent Sales Sold 50 titles in the last year. *Nothing to Fear*, by Alan Axelrod (Prentice-Hall); *The Right Way*, by Mark Smith (Regnery); *Churchill's Folly*, by Christopher Catherwood (Carroll & Graf); *The Encyclopedia of Cancer*, by Carol Turkington (Facts on File); *The Lazy Person's Guide to Investing*, by Paul Farrell (Warner Books); *The Subject Is Left-Handed*, by Barney Rosset (Algonquin Books); *It's OK to Be Neurotic*, by Frank Bruno (Adams Media).

Terms Agent receives 15% commission on domestic sales; 20% commission on foreign sales. Offers written contract.

🖉 JANKLOW & NESBIT ASSOCIATES

445 Park Ave., New York NY 10022. (212)421-1700. Fax: (212)980-3671. **Contact:** Morton L. Janklow, Lynn Nesbit. Estab. 1989.

Represents Commercial and literary nonfiction and novels.

   0┐ Does not want to receive unsolicited submissions or queries.

How to Contact Obtains most new clients through recommendations from others.

Recent Sales *Operation Redwood*, by Susannah French (Amulet).

🖉 JCA LITERARY AGENCY

174 Sullivan St., New York NY 10012. (212)807-0888. E-mail: mel@jcalit.com. Website: www.jcalit.com. Tony's mailing address: Midpoint Trade Books, 27 West 20th Street, New York, NY 10011; (212)727-0190 **Contact:** Melanie Meyers Cushman. Estab. 1978. Member of AAR. Represents 100 clients.

Member Agents Tom Cushman; Melanie Meyers Cushman; Tony Outhwaite.

Represents Nonfiction books, novels. **Considers these nonfiction areas:** Biography/autobiography; current affairs; government/politics/law; history; language/literature/criticism; memoirs; popular culture; sociology; sports; theater/film; translation; true crime/investigative. **Considers these fiction areas:** Action/adventure; contemporary issues; detective/police/crime; family saga; historical; literary; mainstream/contemporary; mystery/suspense; sports; thriller.

   0┐ Does not want to receive screenplays, poetry, children's books, science fiction/fantasy or genre romance.

How to Contact Query with SASE. No unsolicited mss. Materials not returned without proper envelope/postage. Agent receives 15% commission on domestic sales; 20% commission on foreign sales. No written contract.

🖉 JELLINEK & MURRAY LITERARY AGENCY

HI 96822. E-mail: r.jellinek@verizon.net; jellinek@lava.net. **Contact:** Roger Jellinek. Estab. 1995. Represents 75 clients. 90% of clients are new/unpublished writers. Currently handles: 70% nonfiction books; 30% novels.

   ● Prior to becoming an agent, Mr. Jellinek was deputy editor, *New York Times Book Review* (1966-1974); editor-in-chief, New York Times Book Co. (1975-1981); editor/packager of book/TV projects (1981-1995); editorial director, Inner Ocean Publishing (2000-2003).

Member Agents Roger Jellinek; Eden Lee Murray. Literary Associates: Grant Ching; Lavonne Leong; Jeremy Colvin.

Represents Nonfiction books, novels, textbooks, movie scripts (from book clients), TV scripts (from book clients). **Considers these nonfiction areas:** Animals; anthropology/archaeology; art/architecture/design; biography/autobiography; business/economics; child guidance/parenting; computers/electronic; cooking/foods/nutrition; current affairs; ethnic/cultural interests; gay/lesbian issues; government/politics/law; health/medicine; history; how-to; memoirs; military/war; money/finance; nature/environment; New Age/metaphysics; popular culture; psychology; religious/inspirational; science/technology; self-help/personal improvement; travel; true crime/investigative; women's issues/studies. **Considers these fiction areas:** Action/adventure; confession; contemporary issues; detective/police/crime; erotica; ethnic; family saga; feminist; gay/lesbian; glitz; historical; horror; humor/satire; literary; mainstream/contemporary; multicultural; mystery/suspense; New Age; picture books; psychic/supernatural; regional (specific to Hawaii); thriller.

   0┐ "Half our clients are based in Hawaii and half are from all over the world. We prefer submissions (after query) via e-mail attachment. We only send out fully-edited proposals and manuscripts." Actively seeking first-rate writing.

How to Contact Outline. Query with SASE, outline, author bio, 2 sample chapters, credentials/platform. Accepts e-mail and fax queries. Considers simultaneous queries. Responds in 2-3 weeks to queries; 2 months to mss. Returns materials only with SASE. Obtains most new clients through recommendations from others, solicitations, conferences.

Recent Sales Sold 10 titles and 1 script in the last year.

Terms Agent receives 15% commission on domestic sales; 25% commission on foreign sales. Offers written contract, binding for indefinite period; 30-day notice must be given to terminate contract. Charges clients for photocopies and postage. May refer to editing services if author asks for recommendation. "We derive no income from our referrals. Referrals to editors do not imply representation."

Writers' Conferences Mr. Jellinek manages the publishing program at the Maui Writers Conference.

Tips "Would-be authors should be well read and knowledgeable about their field and genre."

🖉 JET LITERARY ASSOCIATES

2570 Camino San Patricio, Santa Fe NM 87505. (505)474-9139. Fax: (505)474-9139. E-mail: etp@jetliterary.com. Website: www.jetliterary.com. **Contact:** Liz Trupin-Pulli. Estab. 1975. Represents 75 clients. 35% of clients are new/unpublished writers.

Member Agents Liz Trupin-Pulli (adult and YA fiction/nonfiction; romance, mysteries, parenting); Jim Trupin (adult fiction/nonfiction, military history, pop culture).

Represents Nonfiction books, novels, short story collections. **Considers these nonfiction areas:** Biography/autobiography; business/economics; child guidance/parenting; current affairs; ethnic/cultural interests; gay/lesbian issues; government/politics/law; humor/satire; memoirs; military/war; popular culture; sports; true crime/investigative; women's issues/studies. **Considers these fiction areas:** Action/adventure; detective/police/crime; erotica; ethnic; gay/lesbian; glitz; historical; humor/satire; literary; mainstream/contemporary; mystery/suspense; romance; thriller; young adult; women's.

> O→ "JET was founded in New York in 1975, so we bring a wealth of knowledge and contacts, as well as quite a bit of expertise to our representation of writers." Actively seeking women's fiction, mysteries and narrative nonfiction. Does not want to receive sci-fi, fantasy, horror, poetry, children's or religious.

How to Contact An e-query is preferred; if sending by snail mail, include an SASE. No fax queries. Responds in 1 week to queries; 8 weeks to mss. Returns materials only with SASE. Obtains most new clients through recommendations from others, solicitations, conferences.

Recent Sales Sold 20 titles in the last year. *Virtually His*, by Gennita Lowe (MIRA/Harlequin); *Uncontrollable*, by Charlotte Mede (Kensington/BRAVA); *Over Exposéd*, by Joanna Campbell Slan (Midnight Ink); *For Thine Is the Kingdom*, by Sarah Posner (Polipoint Press).

Terms Agent receives 15% commission on domestic sales; 10% commission on foreign sales. Offers written contract, binding for 3 years. This agency charges for reimbursement of mailing and any photocopying.

Writers' Conferences Ozark Creative Writers; Women Writing the West.

Tips "Do not write 'cute' queries—stick to a straightforward message that includes the title and what your book is about, why you are suited to write this particular book, and what you have written in the past (if anything), along with a bit of a bio."

⬤ CAREN JOHNSON LITERARY AGENCY

132 East 43rd St., No. 216, New York NY 10017. Fax: (718)228-8785. E-mail: cjohnson@johnsonlitagency.com. Website: www.carenjohnson.com. **Contact:** Caren Johnson. Estab. 2006. Represents 20 clients. 50% of clients are new/unpublished writers. Currently handles: 10% nonfiction books; 70% novels; 20% juvenile books.

> • Prior to her current position, Ms. Johnson was with Firebrand Literary and the Peter Rubie Agency.

Represents Nonfiction books, novels. **Considers these nonfiction areas:** History; popular culture; science/technology. **Considers these fiction areas:** Detective/police/crime; erotica; ethnic; mainstream/contemporary; mystery/suspense; romance; young adult; women's.

> O→ Does not want to receive picture books, plays or screenplays/scripts.

How to Contact Query with SASE. Query via e-mail only, with query and up to one chaoter in the body of the e-mail. Considers simultaneous queries. Responds in 4-6 weeks to queries; 6-8 weeks to mss. Obtains most new clients through recommendations from others.

Recent Sales Sold 15 titles in the last year. This agency prefers not to share information on specific sales. Other clients include A.E. Roman, Kelley St. John, Dianna Love Snell, Caridad Pineiro, Barbara Ferrer, Irene Peterson, Karen Anders, Rob Preece, Stephanie Kuehnert, L. Faye Hughes, Anne Elizabeth, Terri Molina, Lori Avocato, Kelsey Timmerman, Marelene Wagman-Geller and Jennifer Echols.

Terms Agent receives 15% commission on domestic sales; 20% commission on foreign sales. Offers written contract; 30-day notice must be given to terminate contract. This agency charges for postage and photocopying, though the author is consulted before any charges are incurred.

Writers' Conferences RWA National; Romantic Times Conference; Backspace; BookExpo America; Moonlight and Magnolias.

⬤ ◎ KELLER MEDIA INC.

23852 West Pacific Coast Hwy., Suite 701, Malibu CA 90265. (310)857-6828. Fax: (310)857-6373. E-mail: query @KellerMedia.com. Website: www.KellerMedia.com. **Contact:** Wendy Keller, senior agent. Estab. 1989. Member of National Speakers Association. 25% of clients are new/unpublished writers. Currently handles: 100% nonfiction books.

> • Prior to becoming an agent, Ms. Keller was an award-winning journalist and worked for PR Newswire and several newspapers.

Represents Nonfiction books, scholarly books. **Considers these nonfiction areas:** Anthropology/archaeology; biography/autobiography; business/economics; child guidance/parenting; current affairs; government/politics/law; health/medicine; history; language/literature/criticism; money/finance; nature/environment; New Age/metaphysics; popular culture; psychology; science/technology; self-help/personal improvement; sociology; women's issues/studies.

> O→ "We focus a great deal of attention on authors who want to also become paid professional speakers, and speakers who want to become authors." Actively seeking nonfiction by highly credible experts,

who have or want a significant platform in media, academia, politics, paid professional speaking, syndicated columns or regular appearances on radio/TV. Does not want (and absolutely will not respond to) to fiction, scripts, teleplays, poetry, juvenile, anything Christian, picture books, illustrated books, first-person stories of mental or physical illness, wrongful incarceration, or abduction by aliens, books channeled by aliens/demons/the dead ("I wish I was kidding!").

How to Contact Query with SASE, submit proposal package, author bio, the first chapter and whatever is most prescriptive in the book. Include marketing plans. Accepts e-mail and fax queries. Considers simultaneous queries. Responds in 7 days to queries; 2 weeks to mss. Returns materials only with SASE. Obtains most new clients through recommendations from others.

Recent Sales Sold 16 titles in the last year. *Our Own Worst Enemy: Fighting Terrorism From the Oval Office to Your Kitchen Table*, by Col. Randall J. Larsen (Warner Books); *The Top Ten Distinctions Between Millionaires and the Middle Class*, by Keith Cameron Smith (Random House); *Inner Wisdom: Trusting Your Own Intuition in Life, Love and Business*, by Char Margolis (Simon & Schuster); *The Confident Millionaire*, by Kelvin Boston (Wiley).

Terms Agent receives 15% commission on domestic sales; 20% commission on foreign sales.

Tips "Don't send a query to an agent unless you're certain they handle the type of book you're writing. 80% of what we reject is because it doesn't fit our established, advertised, printed, touted guidelines. Be organized! Have your proposal in order. Never make apologies for 'bad writing' or sloppy content—get it right before you waste your one shot with us. Write a solid proposal with something new, different or interesting to say."

NATASHA KERN LITERARY AGENCY

P.O. Box 1069, White Salmon WA 98672. (509)493-3803. E-mail: queries@natashakern.com. Website: www.natashakern.com. **Contact:** Natasha Kern. Estab. 1986. Member of RWA, MWA, SinC.

- Prior to opening her agency, Ms. Kern worked as an editor and publicist for Simon & Schuster, Bantam, and Ballantine. "This agency has sold more than 700 books."

Represents Adult commercial nonfiction and fiction. **Considers these nonfiction areas:** Animals; child guidance/parenting; current affairs; ethnic/cultural interests; gardening; health/medicine; nature/environment; New Age/metaphysics; popular culture; psychology; religious/inspirational; self-help/personal improvement; spirituality; women's issues/studies; investigative journalism. **Considers these fiction areas:** Women's; chick lit; lady lit; romance (contemporary, historical); historical; mainstream/contemporary; multicultural; mystery/suspense; religious/inspirational; thriller.

- This agency specializes in commercial fiction and nonfiction for adults. "We are a full-service agency." Does not represent sports, true crime, scholarly works, coffee table books, war memoirs, software, scripts, literary fiction, photography, poetry, short stories, children's, horror, fantasy, genre science fiction, stage plays, or traditional westerns.

How to Contact See submission instructions online. Query with submission history, writing credits and length of ms. Don't include SASE. Considers simultaneous queries. Responds in 3 weeks to queries.

Recent Sales Sold 56 titles in the last year. *China Dolls*, by Michelle Yu and Blossom Kan (St. Martin's); *Bastard Tongues*, by Derek Bickerton (Farrar Strauss); *Bone Rattler*, by Eliot Pattison; *Wicked Pleasure*, by Nina Bangs (Berkley); *Inviting God In*, by David Aaron (Shambhala); *Perfect Killer*, by Lewis Perdue (Tor); *Unlawful Contact*, by Pamela Clare (Berkley); *Dead End Dating*, by Kimberly Raye (Ballantine); *A Scent of Roses*, by Nikki Arana (Baker Book House); *The Sexiest Man Alive*, by Diana Holquist (Warner Books).

Terms Agent receives 15% commission on domestic sales; 20% commission on foreign sales; 15% commission on dramatic rights sales.

Writers' Conferences RWA National Conference; MWA National Conference; ACFW Conference; and many regional conferences.

Tips "Your chances of being accepted for representation will be greatly enhanced by going to our website first. Our idea of a dream client is someone who participates in a mutually respectful business relationship, is clear about needs and goals, and communicates about career planning. If we know what you need and want, we can help you achieve it. A dream client has a storytelling gift, a commitment to a writing career, a desire to learn and grow, and a passion for excellence. We want clients who are expressing their own unique voice and truly have something of their own to communicate. This client understands that many people have to work together for a book to succeed and that everything in publishing takes far longer than one imagines. Trust and communication are truly essential."

LOUISE B. KETZ AGENCY

1485 First Ave., Suite 4B, New York NY 10021-1363. (212)535-9259. Fax: (212)249-3103. E-mail: ketzagency@aol.com. **Contact:** Louise B. Ketz. Estab. 1983. Represents 25 clients. 15% of clients are new/unpublished writers. Currently handles: 100% nonfiction books.

Represents Nonfiction books. **Considers these nonfiction areas:** Current affairs; history; military/war; science/technology; economics.

O— This agency specializes in science, history and reference.

How to Contact Query with SASE, submit outline, 1 sample chapter, author bio (with qualifications for authorship of work). Responds in 6 weeks to mss. Obtains most new clients through recommendations from others, idea development.

Terms Agent receives 15% commission on domestic sales.

VIRGINIA KIDD AGENCY, INC.

538 E. Harford St., P.O. Box 278, Milford PA 18337. (570)296-6205. Fax: (570)296-7266. Website: www.vk-agency.com. Estab. 1965. Member of SFWA, SFRA. Represents 80 clients.

Member Agents Christine Cohen; Vaughne Hansen.

Represents Novels. **Considers these fiction areas:** Fantasy; historical; mystery/suspense; science fiction; women's; speculative; mainstream.

O— This agency specializes in science fiction and fantasy.

How to Contact Query with SASE, submit synopsis (1-3 pages), cover letter, first chapter, SASE. Snail mail queries only. Responds in 6 weeks to queries.

Recent Sales *Sagramanda*, by Alan Dean Foster (Pyr); *Incredible Good Fortune*, by Ursula K. Le Guin (Shambhala); *The Wizard* and *Soldier of Sidon*, by Gene Wolfe (Tor); *Voices* and *Powers*, by Ursula K. Le Guin (Harcourt); *Galileo's Children*, by Gardner Dozois (Pyr); *The Light Years Beneath My Feet* and *Running From the Deity*, by Alan Dean Foster (Del Ray); *Chasing Fire*, by Michelle Welch. Other clients include Eleanor Arnason, Ted Chiang, Jack Skillingstead, Daryl Gregory, Nick DiChario, Patricia Briggs, and the estates for James Tiptree Jr., Murray Leinster, E.E. "Doc" Smith, R.A. Lafferty.

Terms Agent receives 15% commission on domestic sales; 20-25% commission on foreign sales; 20% commission on dramatic rights sales. Offers written contract; 2-month notice must be given to terminate contract. Charges clients occasionally for extraordinary expenses.

Tips "If you have a completed novel that is of extraordinary quality, please send us a query."

KIRCHOFF/WOHLBERG, INC., AUTHORS' REPRESENTATION DIVISION

866 United Nations Plaza, #525, New York NY 10017. (212)644-2020. Fax: (212)223-4387. E-mail: lford@kirchoffwohlberg.com. **Contact:** Liza Pulitzer Voges. Estab. 1930s. Member of AAR, AAP, Society of Illustrators, SPAR, Bookbuilders of Boston, New York Bookbinders' Guild, AIGA. Represents 50 clients. 10% of clients are new/unpublished writers. Currently handles: 5% nonfiction books; 25% novels; 5% young adult; 65% picture books.

● Kirchoff/Wohlberg has been in business for over 60 years.

O— This agency specializes in only juvenile through young adult trade books.

How to Contact For novels, query with SASE, outline, a few sample chapters. For picture books, send entire ms, SASE. No e-mail or fax queries. Considers simultaneous queries. Responds in 1 month to queries; 2 months to mss. Returns materials only with SASE. Obtains most new clients through recommendations from authors, illustrators, and editors.

Recent Sales Sold more than 50 titles in the last year. *Dizzy*, by Jonah Winter (Scholastic); *Homework Machine*, by Dan Gutman (Simon and Schuster); Princess Power series, by Suzanne Williams (HarperCollins); My Weird School series, by Dan Gutman (HarperCollins); *Biscuit*, by Alyssa Capucilli (HarperCollins).

Terms Offers written contract, binding for at least 1 year. Agent receives standard commission, depending upon whether it is an author only, illustrator only, or an author/illustrator book.

KLEINWORKS AGENCY

2814 Brooks Ave., No. 635, Missoula MT 59801. E-mail: judyklein@kleinworks.com. Website: www.kleinworks.com. **Contact:** Judy Klein. Estab. 2005. Represents 10 clients. Currently handles: 50% nonfiction books; 40% novels; 10% juvenile books.

● Prior to becoming an agent, Ms. Klein spent a dozen years with Farrar, Straus & Giroux; she also held the position of editor-in-chief at The Literary Guild Book Club and later, at Booksonline.com.

Represents Nonfiction books, novels. **Considers these nonfiction areas:** Biography/autobiography; business/economics; health/medicine; how-to; memoirs; money/finance; nature/environment; popular culture; self-help/personal improvement. **Considers these fiction areas:** Ethnic; experimental; humor/satire; literary; young adult; women's/chick lit.

O— "Kleinworks Agency may be geographically removed from the red-hot center of New York publishing, but our credentials and connections keep us close to New York's best publishers and editors. As a publishing veteran with two decades of book experience, intimate knowledge of the industry and expertise in domestic and international negotiations, I provide my clients with an edge in getting their books published well. Kleinworks offers dedicated services to a very small, select group of writers and publishers so that we can guarantee spirited and undivided attention.''

How to Contact Query with SASE, submit proposal package, outline/proposal, synopsis, author bio, sample chapters. No phone queries. Accepts e-mail and fax queries. Considers simultaneous queries. Responds in 4 weeks to queries; 1-2 months to mss. Returns materials only with SASE. Obtains most new clients through recommendations from others.

Recent Sales This agency prefers not to share information on specific sales.

Terms Agent receives 15% commission on domestic sales; 20% commission on foreign sales. Offers written contract, binding for optional, for 1 year; 3-month notice must be given to terminate contract. Charges for postage and photocopying fees after six months.

Writers' Conferences Montana Festival of the Book, Yellowstone Nature Writers' Field Conference.

⬛ HARVEY KLINGER, INC.

300 W. 55th St., Suite 11V, New York NY 10019. (212)581-7068. E-mail: queries@harveyklinger.com. Website: www.harveyklinger.com. **Contact:** Harvey Klinger. Estab. 1977. Member of AAR. Represents 100 clients. 25% of clients are new/unpublished writers. Currently handles: 50% nonfiction books; 50% novels.

Member Agents David Dunton (popular culture, music-related books, literary fiction, crime novels, thrillers); Sara Crowe (children's and young adult authors, adult fiction and nonfiction, foreign rights sales); Andrea Somberg (literary fiction, commercial fiction, romance, sci-fi/fantasy, mysteries/thrillers, young adult, middle grade, quality narrative nonfiction, popular culture, how-to, self-help, humor, interior design, cookbooks, health/fitness); Anna Corey Watson (contemporary fiction, both literary and commercial, particularly plot and narrative driven literary fiction, issue driven women's fiction, thrillers, memoir, popular science, psychology and sociology).

Represents Nonfiction books, novels. **Considers these nonfiction areas:** Biography/autobiography; cooking/foods/nutrition; health/medicine; psychology; science/technology; self-help/personal improvement; spirituality; sports; true crime/investigative; women's issues/studies. **Considers these fiction areas:** Action/adventure; detective/police/crime; family saga; glitz; literary; mainstream/contemporary; mystery/suspense; thriller.

    O⫞ This agency specializes in big, mainstream, contemporary fiction and nonfiction.

How to Contact Query with SASE. No phone or fax queries. Don't send unsolicited manuscripts or e-mail attachments. Accepts e-mail queries. No fax queries. Responds in 2 months to queries and mss. Obtains most new clients through recommendations from others.

Recent Sales *Breakable You*, By Brian Morton; *The Money In You!*, by Julie Stav; *The Mercy Seller*, by Brenda Vantrease; *A Country Music Christmas*, by Edie Hand and Buddy Killen; *Keep Climbing*, by Sean Swarner; *The Cubicle Survival Guide*, by James F. Thomspon; *Cookie Sensations*, by Meaghan Mountford; *Stranger*, by Justine Musk; *Laird Of The Mist*, by Paula Quinn. Other clients include Barbara Wood, Terry Kay, Barbara De Angelis, Jeremy Jackson.

Terms Agent receives 15% commission on domestic sales; 25% commission on foreign sales. Offers written contract. Charges for photocopying mss and overseas postage for mss.

⬛ KNEERIM & WILLIAMS AT FISH & RICHARDSON

225 Franklin St., Boston MA 02110. (617)542-5070. Fax: (617)542-8906. Website: http://www.fr.com/practice/agents.cfm. **Contact:** Cara Krenn. Estab. 1990. Represents 200 clients. 5% of clients are new/unpublished writers. Currently handles: 80% nonfiction books; 15% novels; 5% movie scripts.

    ● Prior to becoming an agent, Mr. Williams was a lawyer; Ms. Kneerim was a publisher and editor; Mr. Wasserman was an editor and journalist; Ms. Grosvenor was an editor.

Member Agents John Taylor Williams; Jill Kneerim; Steve Wasserman; Bretthe Bloom; Deborah C. Grosvenor.

Represents Nonfiction books, novels. **Considers these nonfiction areas:** Anthropology/archaeology; biography/autobiography; business/economics; child guidance/parenting; current affairs; government/politics/law; health/medicine; history; language/literature/criticism; memoirs; nature/environment; popular culture; psychology; religious/inspirational; science/technology; sociology; sports; women's issues/studies. **Considers these fiction areas:** Historical; literary; mainstream/contemporary.

    O⫞ This agency specializes in narrative nonfiction, history, science, business, women's issues, commercial and literary fiction, film, and television. "We have 5 agents and 4 scouts in Boston, New York, Washington DC and Santa Fe." Actively seeking distinguished authors, experts, professionals, intellectuals, and serious writers. Does not want to receive blanket multiple submissions, genre fiction or original screenplays.

How to Contact Query with SASE. Responds in 2 weeks to queries; 2 months to mss. Returns materials only with SASE. Obtains most new clients through recommendations from others.

Recent Sales *First Family*, by Joseph J. Ellis; *Superorganism*, by Edward O. Wilson; *Little Boy Burning*, by Joey

Kramer; *Frank Gehry and the Bilbao Museum*, by Nicolai Ouroussoff (Basic); *Nuclear Terrorism*, by Graham Allison (Times Books); *Beggar at the Gate*, by Thalassa Ali (Bantam).

🌑 LINDA KONNER LITERARY AGENCY

10 W. 15th St., Suite 1918, New York NY 10011-6829. (212)691-3419. E-mail: ldkonner@cs.com. **Contact:** Linda Konner. Estab. 1996. Member of AAR, ASJA; signatory of WGA. Represents 85 clients. 30-35% of clients are new/unpublished writers. Currently handles: 100% nonfiction books.

Represents Nonfiction books. **Considers these nonfiction areas:** Biography/autobiography (celebrity); gay/lesbian issues; health/medicine (diet/nutrition/fitness); how-to; money/finance (personal finance); popular culture; psychology (pop psychology); self-help/personal improvement; women's issues; African American and Latino issues; business; parenting; relationships.

> O➝ This agency specializes in health, self-help, and how-to books. Authors/co-authors must be top experts in their field with a substantial media platform.

How to Contact Query with SASE, synopsis, author bio, sufficient return postage. Prefers to read materials exclusively for 2 weeks. Considers simultaneous queries. Obtains most new clients through recommendations from others, occasional solicitation among established authors/journalists.

Recent Sales Sold 30 titles in the last year. *Run Faster: From the 5K to the Marathon*, by Brad Hudson and Matt Fitzgerald (Doubleday Broadway); *The Whole Food Cure*, by Andrew Larson and Ivy Larson (Gibbs Smith); *How to Cheat at Gardening and Yard Work*, by Jeff Bredenberg (Rodale); *Stop Self-Sabotage!*, by Pat Pearson (McGraw-Hill).

Terms Agent receives 15% commission on domestic sales; 25% commission on foreign sales. Offers written contract. Charges one-time fee for domestic expenses; additional expenses may be incurred for foreign sales.

Writers' Conferences ASJA Writers Conference.

🌑 ELAINE KOSTER LITERARY AGENCY, LLC

55 Central Park W., Suite 6, New York NY 10023. (212)362-9488. Fax: (212)712-0164. **Contact:** Elaine Koster, Stephanie Lehmann. Member of AAR, MWA; Author's Guild, Women's Media Group. Represents 40 clients. 10% of clients are new/unpublished writers. Currently handles: 30% nonfiction books; 70% novels.

> • Prior to opening her agency in 1998, Ms. Koster was president and publisher of Dutton-NAL, part of the Penguin Group.

Represents Nonfiction books, novels. **Considers these nonfiction areas:** Biography/autobiography; business/economics; child guidance/parenting; cooking/foods/nutrition; current affairs; ethnic/cultural interests; health/medicine; history; how-to; money/finance; nature/environment; popular culture; psychology; self-help/personal improvement; spirituality; women's issues/studies. **Considers these fiction areas:** Contemporary issues; detective/police/crime; ethnic; family saga; feminist; historical; literary; mainstream/contemporary; mystery/suspense; regional; thriller; young adult; chick lit.

> O➝ This agency specializes in quality fiction and nonfiction. Does not want to receive juvenile, screenplays, or science fiction.

How to Contact Query with SASE, outline, 3 sample chapters. Prefers to read materials exclusively. No e-mail or fax queries. Responds in 3 weeks to queries; 1 month to mss. Returns materials only with SASE. Obtains most new clients through recommendations from others.

Recent Sales *Stalking Susan*, by Julie Kramer (Doubleday); *Takeover*, by Lisa Black (Morrow); *One in a Million*, by Kimberla Lawson Roby.

Terms Agent receives 15% commission on domestic sales. Bills back specific expenses incurred doing business for a client.

Tips "We prefer exclusive submissions. Don't e-mail or fax submissions. Please include biographical information and publishing history."

🌑 KRAAS LITERARY AGENCY

E-mail: irenekraas@sbcglobal.net. Website: www.kraasliteraryagency.com. **Contact:** Irene Kraas. Estab. 1990. Represents 35 clients. 75% of clients are new/unpublished writers. Currently handles: 2% nonfiction books; 98% novels.

Member Agents Irene Kraas, principal.

Represents Novels. **Considers these fiction areas:** Literary; thriller; young adult.

> O➝ This agency is interested in working with published writers, but that does not mean self-published writers. Actively seeking psychological thrillers, medical thrillers, some literary fiction and young adult. "With each of these areas, I want something new. No Da Vinci Code or Harry Potter ripoffs. I am especially not interested in storylines that include the Mafia or government. Not interested in personal stories of growth, stories about generation hangups and stories about drugs, incest, etc." Does not want

to receive short stories, plays or poetry. This agency no longer represents adult fantasy or science fiction.

How to Contact Query and e-mail the first 10 pages of a completed ms. Requires exclusive read on mss. No fax queries. Considers simultaneous queries. Returns materials only with SASE. Offers written contract.

Tips "I am interested in material—in any genre—that is truly, truly unique."

☑ BERT P. KRAGES

6665 SW Hampton St., Suite 200, Portland OR 97223. (503)597-2525. E-mail: krages@onemain.com. Website: www.krages.com. **Contact:** Bert Krages. Estab. 2001. Represents 10 clients. 80% of clients are new/unpublished writers. Currently handles: 95% nonfiction books; 5% scholarly books.

  • Mr. Krages is also an attorney.

Represents Nonfiction books. **Considers these nonfiction areas:** Agriculture/horticulture; animals; anthropology/archaeology; art/architecture/design; biography/autobiography; business/economics; child guidance/parenting; computers/electronic; current affairs; education; ethnic/cultural interests; health/medicine; history; memoirs; military/war; nature/environment; psychology; science/technology; self-help/personal improvement; sociology.

  ⚷ "I handle a small number of literary clients and concentrate on trade nonfiction (science, history)." No fiction submissions until further notified—check the Web site.

How to Contact Keep queries to one page—nonfiction only. Considers simultaneous queries. Responds in 1-6 weeks to queries. Obtains most new clients through solicitations. Sold 2 titles in the last year.

Terms Agent receives 15% commission on domestic sales; 20% commission on foreign sales. Offers written contract, binding for 1 year; 60-day notice must be given to terminate contract. Charges for photocopying and postage only if the book is placed.

Tips "Read at least 2 books on how to prepare book proposals before sending material. An extremely well-prepared proposal will make your material stand out."

☑ STUART KRICHEVSKY LITERARY AGENCY, INC.

381 Park Ave. S., Suite 914, New York NY 10016. (212)725-5288. Fax: (212)725-5275. E-mail: query@skagency.com. Member of AAR.

Member Agents Stuart Krichevsky; Shana Cohen (science fiction, fantasy); Kathryne Wick.

Represents Nonfiction books, novels.

How to Contact Submit query, synopsis, 1 sample page via e-mail (no attachments). Snail mail queries also acceptable. No fax queries. Obtains most new clients through recommendations from others, solicitations.

Recent Sales Untitled, by C.J. Chivers (Simon & Schuster); *American Islam*, by Paul M. Barrett (Farrar, Straus and Giroux); *The Nabokov's Nutcracker: Knowing and Loving the Parts of Speech*, by Ben Yagoda (Broadway Books).

ᴺ ◯ KT LITERARY

9249 S. Broadway, #200-543, Highlands Ranch CO 80129. (720)344-4728. Fax: (720)344-4728. E-mail: queries@ktliterary.com. Website: www.ktliterary.com/about.html. **Contact:** Kate Schafer. Estab. 2008; SCBWI. Represents 12 clients. 60% of clients are new/unpublished writers. Currently handles: 5% nonfiction books; 5% novels; 90% juvenile books.

  • Prior to her current position, Ms. Schafer was an agent with Janklow & Nesbit.

Represents Nonfiction books, novels, juvenile books. **Considers these nonfiction areas:** Popular culture. **Considers these fiction areas:** Action/adventure; fantasy; historical; juvenile; romance; science fiction; young adult; women's.

  ⚷ "I'm bringing my years of experience in the New York publishing scene, as well as my lifelong love of reading, to a vibrant area for writers, proving that great work can be found, and sold, from anywhere." Actively seeking brilliant, funny, original middle grade and young adult fiction, both literary and commercial; witty women's fiction (chick lit); and pop-culture, narrative nonfiction. Quirky is good. Does not want picture books, serious nonfiction, and adult literary fiction.

How to Contact Query with SASE, submit author bio, 2-3 sample pages. Absolutely no attachments. Paste text in e-mail body. E-mail queries only. Accepts e-mail queries. No fax queries. Responds in 2 weeks to queries; 1 month to mss. Obtains most new clients through recommendations from others, solicitations, conferences. Other clients include Maureen Johnson, Alyson Noël, Ellen Booraem, Susannah French, Daniel J. Blau, Josie Bloss, and Matthew Cody.

Terms Agent receives 15% commission on domestic sales; 20% commission on foreign sales. Offers written contract; 30-day notice must be given to terminate contract.

Writers' Conferences Various SCBWI conferences, BookExpo America.

Tips "If we like your query, we'll ask for (more). Continuing advice is offered regularly on my blog 'Ask Daphne', which can be accessed from my Web site."

KT PUBLIC RELATIONS & LITERARY SERVICES

1905 Cricklewood Cove, Fogelsville PA 18051. (610)395-6298. Fax: (610)395-6299. Website: www.ktpublicrelati ons.com. **Contact:** Jon Tienstra. Estab. 2005. Represents 12 clients. 75% of clients are new/unpublished writers. Currently handles: 50% nonfiction books; 50% novels.
- Prior to becoming an agent, Kae Tienstra was publicity director for Rodale, Inc. for 13 years and then founded her own publicity agency; Mr. Tienstra joined the firm in 1995 with varied corporate experience and a master's degree in library science.

Member Agents Kae Tienstra (health, parenting, psychology, how-to, crafts, foods/nutrition, beauty, women's fiction, general fiction); Jon Tienstra (nature/environment, history, cooking/foods/nutrition, war/military, automotive, health/medicine, gardening, general fiction, science fiction/contemporary fantasy, popular fiction).

Represents Nonfiction books, novels. **Considers these nonfiction areas:** Agriculture/horticulture; animals; child guidance/parenting; cooking/foods/nutrition; crafts/hobbies; health/medicine; history; how-to; military/war; nature/environment; popular culture; psychology; science/technology; self-help/personal improvement; interior design/decorating. **Considers these fiction areas:** Action/adventure; detective/police/crime; family saga; fantasy (contemporary—no swords or dragons); historical; literary; mainstream/contemporary; mystery/suspense; romance; science fiction; thriller.
- "We have worked with a variety of authors and publishers over the years and have learned what individual publishers are looking for in terms of new acquisitions. We are both mad about books and authors and we look forward to finding publishing success for all our clients." Specializes in parenting, history, cooking/foods/nutrition, crafts, beauty, war, health/medicine, psychology, how-to, gardening, science fiction, fantasy, women's fiction, and popular fiction. Does not want to see unprofessional material.

How to Contact Query with SASE. Prefers snail mail queries. Will accept e-mail queries. Responds in 3 months to chapters; 6-9 months for mss. No fax queries. Considers simultaneous queries. Responds in 2 weeks to queries. Returns materials only with SASE.

Terms Agent receives 15% commission on domestic sales; 20% commission on foreign sales. Offers written contract. Charges clients for long-distance phone calls, fax, postage, photocopying (only when incurred). No advance payment for these out-of-pocket expenses.

THE LA LITERARY AGENCY

P.O. Box 46370, Los Angeles CA 90046. (323)654-5288. E-mail: laliteraryag@aol.com. **Contact:** Ann Cashman, Eric Lasher. Estab. 1980.
- Prior to becoming an agent, Mr. Lasher worked in publishing in New York and Los Angeles.

Represents Nonfiction books, novels. **Considers these nonfiction areas:** Animals; anthropology/archaeology; art/architecture/design; biography/autobiography; business/economics; child guidance/parenting; cooking/foods/nutrition; current affairs; ethnic/cultural interests; government/politics/law; health/medicine; history; how-to; nature/environment; popular culture; psychology; science/technology; self-help/personal improvement; sociology; sports; true crime/investigative; women's issues/studies; narrative nonfiction. **Considers these fiction areas:** Action/adventure; detective/police/crime; family saga; feminist; historical; literary; mainstream/contemporary; sports; thriller.

How to Contact Query with SASE, outline, 1 sample chapter. No e-mail or fax queries.

Recent Sales *Full Bloom: The Art and Life of Georgia O'Keeffe*, by Hunter Drohojowska-Philp (Norton); *And the Walls Came Tumbling Down*, by H. Caldwell (Scribner); *Italian Slow & Savory*, by Joyce Goldstein (Chronicle); *A Field Guide to Chocolate Chip Cookies*, by Dede Wilson (Harvard Common Press); *Teen Knitting Club* (Artisan); *The Framingham Heart Study*, by Dr. Daniel Levy (Knopf).

LADNERBOND LITERARY MANAGEMENT

12A Longfellow Ave., Brunswick ME 04011. (207)841-9634. Website: ladnerbondlm.com. **Contact:** Christopher Ladner. Estab. 2002; adheres to AAR canon of ethics.
- Prior to his current position, Mr. Ladner began his career in publishing as an associate at Writers House.

Represents Nonfiction books, novels. **Considers these nonfiction areas:** Biography/autobiography; health/medicine; history; memoirs; popular culture; sports; lifestyle.

How to Contact Query with SASE. As of early 2008, this agency was closed to queries. Check the Web site for more info. Accepts e-mail queries. No fax queries. Responds in 4 weeks to queries; 6-8 weeks to mss. Returns materials only with SASE. Obtains most new clients through recommendations from others, solicitations.

Recent Sales *Smart Moves: Career Lessons from Liberal Arts Graduates*, by Sheila Curran and Suzanne Greenwald (Ten Speed Press); *Summer Snow*, by William Hathaway (Avatar Publications).

❂ ALBERT LaFARGE LITERARY AGENCY

Fax: (270)512-5179. E-mail: lafargeliterary@gmail.com. **Contact:** Albert LaFarge. Estab. 2003. Represents 24 clients. 50% of clients are new/unpublished writers. Currently handles: 90% nonfiction books; 10% novels.

• Prior to becoming an agent, Mr. LaFarge was an editor.

Represents Nonfiction books, novels. **Considers these nonfiction areas:** Art/architecture/design; biography/autobiography; current affairs; health/medicine; history; memoirs; music/dance; nature/environment; photography; psychology; sports. **Considers these fiction areas:** Literary.

☛ This agency specializes in helping clients to develop nonfiction.

How to Contact Query with SASE, submit outline and sample chapters. Accepts e-mail queries. No fax queries. Obtains most new clients through recommendations from others.

Recent Sales This agency prefers not to share information on specific sales.

Terms Agent receives 15% commission on domestic sales; 20% commission on foreign sales. Offers written contract. Charges for photocopying.

❂ PETER LAMPACK AGENCY, INC.

551 Fifth Ave., Suite 1613, New York NY 10176-0187. (212)687-9106. Fax: (212)687-9109. E-mail: alampack@verizon.net. **Contact:** Andrew Lampack. Estab. 1977. Represents 50 clients. 10% of clients are new/unpublished writers. Currently handles: 20% nonfiction books; 80% novels.

Member Agents Peter Lampack (president); Rema Delanyan (foreign rights); Andrew Lampack (new writers).

Represents Nonfiction books, novels. **Considers these fiction areas:** Action/adventure; detective/police/crime; family saga; literary; mainstream/contemporary; mystery/suspense; thriller; contemporary relationships.

☛ This agency specializes in commercial fiction and nonfiction by recognized experts. Actively seeking literary and commercial fiction, thrillers, mysteries, suspense, and psychological thrillers. Does not want to receive horror, romance, science fiction, westerns, historical literary fiction or academic material.

How to Contact Query with SASE. *No unsolicited mss.* Accepts e-mail queries. No fax queries. Responds in 2 months to queries. Obtains most new clients through referrals made by clients.

Recent Sales *Diary of a Bad Year*, by J.M. Coetzee; *The Chase*, by Clive Cussler and Dick Cussler; *Plague Ship*, by Clive Cussler and Jack Du Brul; *The Navigator*, by Clive Cussler with Paul Kemprecos; *Dust*, by Martha Grimes; *Bloodthirsty Bitches and Pious Pimps of Power*, by Gerry Spence; *Tsar*, by Ted Bell.

Terms Agent receives 15% commission on domestic sales; 20% commission on foreign sales.

Writers' Conferences BookExpo America.

Tips "Submit only your best work for consideration. Have a very specific agenda of goals you wish your prospective agent to accomplish for you. Provide the agent with a comprehensive statement of your credentials—educational and professional."

❂ LAURA LANGLIE, LITERARY AGENT

239 Carroll St., Garden Apartment, Brooklyn NY 11231. (718)855-8102. Fax: (718)855-4450. E-mail: laura@lauralanglie.com. **Contact:** Laura Langlie. Estab. 2001. Represents 25 clients. 50% of clients are new/unpublished writers. Currently handles: 25% nonfiction books; 48% novels; 2% story collections; 25% juvenile books.

• Prior to opening her agency, Ms. Langlie worked in publishing for 7 years and as an agent at Kidde, Hoyt & Picard for 6 years.

Represents Nonfiction books, novels, short story collections, novellas, juvenile books. **Considers these nonfiction areas:** Animals (not how-to); biography/autobiography; current affairs; ethnic/cultural interests; government/politics/law; history; humor/satire; memoirs; nature/environment; popular culture; psychology; theater/film; women's issues/studies; history of medicine and science; language/literature. **Considers these fiction areas:** Detective/police/crime; ethnic; feminist; historical; humor/satire; juvenile; literary; mystery/suspense; romance; thriller; young adult; mainstream.

☛ "I love working with first-time authors. I'm very involved with and committed to my clients. I also employ a publicist to work with all my clients to make the most of each book's publication. Most of my clients come to me via recommendations from other agents, clients and editors. I've met very few at conferences. I've often sought out writers for projects, and I still find new clients via the traditional query letter." Does not want to receive children's picture books, science fiction, poetry, men's adventure or erotica.

How to Contact Query with SASE. Accepts queries via fax. Considers simultaneous queries. Responds in 1 week to queries; 1 month to mss. Returns materials only with SASE. Obtains most new clients through recommendations, submissions.

Recent Sales Sold 30 titles in the last year. *The Broken Teaglass*, by Emily Arsenault (Delacorte); *Ms. Taken Identity*, by Dan Begley (Grand Central); Allie Finke's Rules for Girls series, by Meg Cabot (Scholastic); *Mating Rituals of the North American Wasp*, by Lauren Lipton (Grand Central); *Boys are Dogs*, by Leslie Margolis (Bloomsbury). Other clients include Renee Ashley, Mignon F. Ballard, Jessica Benson, Joan Druett, Jack El-

Hai, Sarah Elliott, Fiona Gibson, Robin Hathaway, Melanie Lynne Hauser, Mary Hogan, Jonathan Neale, Eric Pinder, Delia Ray, Cheryl L. Reed, Jennifer Sturman.

Terms Agent receives 15% commission on domestic sales; 20% commission on foreign sales. No written contract.

Tips "Be complete, forthright and clear in your communications. Do your research as to what a particular agent represents."

MICHAEL LARSEN/ELIZABETH POMADA, LITERARY AGENTS

1029 Jones St., San Francisco CA 94109-5023. (415)673-0939. E-mail: larsenpoma@aol.com. Website: www.lar sen-pomada.com. **Contact:** Mike Larsen, Elizabeth Pomada. Estab. 1972. Member of AAR, Authors Guild, ASJA, PEN, WNBA, California Writers Club, National Speakers Association. Represents 100 clients. 40-45% of clients are new/unpublished writers. Currently handles: 70% nonfiction books; 30% novels.

- Prior to opening their agency, Mr. Larsen and Ms. Pomada were promotion executives for major publishing houses. Mr. Larsen worked for Morrow, Bantam and Pyramid (now part of Berkley); Ms. Pomada worked at Holt, David McKay and The Dial Press. Mr. Larsen is the author of the third editions of *How to Write a Book Proposal* and *How to Get a Literary Agent* as well as the coauthor of *Guerilla Marketing for Writers: 100 Weapons for Selling Your Work.*

Member Agents Michael Larsen (nonfiction); Elizabeth Pomada (fiction, narrative nonfiction, nonfiction for women); Laurie McLean, laurie@agentsavant.com (fantasy, science, romance, middle-grade and YA fiction).

Represents Adult book-length fiction and nonfiction that will interest New York publishers or are irresistibly written or conceived. **Considers these nonfiction areas:** Anthropology/archaeology; art/architecture/design; biography/autobiography; business/economics; cooking/foods/nutrition; current affairs; ethnic/cultural interests; gay/lesbian issues; government/politics/law; health/medicine; history; how-to; humor/satire; memoirs; money/finance; music/dance; nature/environment; New Age/metaphysics; popular culture; psychology; religious/inspirational; science/technology; self-help/personal improvement; sociology; sports; theater/film; travel; true crime/investigative; women's issues/studies; futurism. **Considers these fiction areas:** Action/adventure; contemporary issues; detective/police/crime; ethnic; experimental; family saga; fantasy; feminist; gay/lesbian; glitz; historical; humor/satire; literary; mainstream/contemporary; mystery/suspense; religious/inspirational; romance (contemporary, gothic, historical); chick lit.

- "We have diverse tastes. We look for fresh voices and new ideas. We handle literary, commercial and genre fiction, and the full range of nonfiction books." Actively seeking commercial, genre and literary fiction. Does not want to receive children's books, plays, short stories, screenplays, pornography, poetry or stories of abuse.

How to Contact Query with SASE. Accepts e-mail queries. No fax queries. Responds in 2 weeks to queries. Responds in 8 weeks to pages or submissions.

Recent Sales Sold at least 15 titles in the last year. *Dangerous Touch*, by Jill Sorenson (Silhouette); *The Soul and the Scalpel: Surgery as a Path to Spiritual Transformation for Patients and Physicians*, by Allan Hamilton, M.D.(Tarcher/Penguin); *The Perfect SalesForce: The 6 Best Practices of the World's Best Sales Teams* by Derek Gatehouse (Portfolio/Penguin); *The Solemn Lantern Maker*, by Merlinda Bobis (Bantam); *Bitten to Death*, the fourth book in an urban fantasy series by J.D. Rardin (Laurie McLean) (Orbit/Grand Central).

Terms Agent receives 15% commission on domestic sales; 20% (30% for Asia) commission on foreign sales. May charge for printing, postage for multiple submissions, foreign mail, foreign phone calls, galleys, books, legal fees.

Writers' Conferences This agency organizes the annual San Francisco Writers' Conference (www.sfwriters.org).

Tips "We love helping writers get the rewards and recognition they deserve. If you can write books that meet the needs of the marketplace and you can promote your books, now is the best time ever to be a writer. We must find new writers to make a living, so we are very eager to hear from new writers whose work will interest large houses, and nonfiction writers who can promote their books. For a list of recent sales, helpful info, and three ways to make yourself irresistible to any publisher, please visit our Web site."

THE STEVE LAUBE AGENCY

5025 N. Central Ave., #635, Phoenix AZ 85012. (602)336-8910. E-mail: krichards@stevelaube.com. Website: www.stevelaube.com. **Contact:** Steve Laube. Estab. 2004. Member of CBA. Represents 60+ clients. 5% of clients are new/unpublished writers. Currently handles: 48% nonfiction books; 48% novels; 2% novellas; 2% scholarly books.

- Prior to becoming an agent, Mr. Laube worked 11 years as a Christian bookseller and 11 years as editorial director of nonfiction with Bethany House Publishers.

Represents Nonfiction books, novels. **Considers these nonfiction areas:** Religious/inspirational. **Considers these fiction areas:** Religious/inspirational.

o— "We primarily serve the Christian market (CBA)." Actively seeking Christian fiction and religious nonfiction. Does not want to receive children's picture books, poetry or cookbooks.

How to Contact Submit proposal package, outline, 3 sample chapters, SASE. No e-mail submissions. Consult Web site for guidelines. Considers simultaneous queries. Responds in 6-8 weeks to queries. Returns materials only with SASE. Obtains most new clients through recommendations from others, solicitations, conferences.

Recent Sales Sold 80 titles in the last year. *Day With a Perfect Stranger*, by David Gregory (Kelly's Filmworks). Other clients include Deborah Raney, Bright Media, Allison Bottke, H. Norman Wright, Ellie Kay, Jack Cavanaugh, Karen Ball, Tracey Bateman, Clint Kelly, Susan May Warren, Lisa Bergren, John Rosemond, David Gregory, Cindy Woodsmall, Alton Gansky, Karol Ladd, Judith Pella.

Terms Agent receives 15% commission on domestic sales; 20% commission on foreign sales. Offers written contract; 30-day notice must be given to terminate contract.

Writers' Conferences Mount Hermon Christian Writers' Conference; American Christian Fiction Writers' Conference; Glorieta Christian Writers' Conference.

☐ ☑ LAUNCHBOOKS LITERARY AGENCY

566 Sweet Pea Place, Encinitas CA 92024. (760)944-9909. E-mail: david@launchbooks.com. Website: www.launchbooks.com. **Contact:** David Fugate. Estab. 2005. Represents 35 clients. 35% of clients are new/unpublished writers. Currently handles: 85% nonfiction books; 5% novels; 10% multimedia.

• Prior to his current position, Mr. Fugate was hired by the Margret McBride Agency to handle its submissions. In 1994, he moved to Waterside Productions, Inc., where he served as an agent for 11 years and successfully represented more than 600 book titles before leaving to form LaunchBooks.

Represents Nonfiction books, novels, textbooks. **Considers these nonfiction areas:** Anthropology/archaeology; biography/autobiography; business/economics; child guidance/parenting; computers/electronic; cooking/foods/nutrition; current affairs; education; ethnic/cultural interests; government/politics/law; health/medicine; history; how-to; humor/satire; memoirs; military/war; money/finance; music/dance; nature/environment; popular culture; science/technology; sociology; sports; true crime/investigative. **Considers these fiction areas:** Action/adventure; humor/satire; mainstream/contemporary; science fiction; thriller.

o— Actively seeking a wide variety of nonfiction, including business, technology, adventure, popular culture, creative nonfiction, current events, history, politics, reference, memoirs, health, how-to, lifestyle, parenting and more. Mr. Fugate is also interested in hard science fiction.

How to Contact Query with SASE, submit outline/proposal, synopsis, 1 sample chapter(s), author bio. Accepts e-mail queries. No fax queries. Considers simultaneous queries. Responds in 1 week to queries; 4 weeks to mss. Returns materials only with SASE. Obtains most new clients through recommendations from others, solicitations.

Recent Sales Sold 49 titles in the last year. *When A Billion Chinese Jump*, By Jonathan Watts (Scribner); *Everyday Edisons*, By Louis Foreman And Jill Gilbert Welytok (Workman); *The Making Of Second Life*, By Wagner James Au (Harpercollins); *The Ghost Train*, By John Jeter (W.W. Norton); *Branding Only Works On Cows*, By Jonathan Baskin (Grand Central); *Upgrade Your Life*, By Gina Trapani (John Wiley & Sons); *Truth, Lies, And Kevin Mitnick* (Little, Brown)]; *The Cure For Alcoholism*, By Roy David Eskapa, Ph.D. (Benbella Books). Other clients include Kevin Mitnick, Molly Holzschlag, Eric Meyer, Jill Gilbert Welytok, Paul Nielsen.

Terms Agent receives 15% commission on domestic sales; 25% commission on foreign sales. Offers written contract; 30-day notice must be given to terminate contract. Charges occur very seldom and typically only if the author specifically requests overnight or something of that nature. This agency's agreement limits any charges to $50 unless the author gives a written consent.

☑ LAZEAR AGENCY GROUP, INC.

431 Second St., Suite 300, Hudson WI 54016. (715)531-0012. Fax: (715)531-0016. E-mail: admin@lazear.com; info@lazear.com. Website: www.lazear.com. **Contact:** Editorial Board. Estab. 1984. 20% of clients are new/unpublished writers. Currently handles: 65% nonfiction books; 30% novels; 5% juvenile books.

• The Lazear Agency opened a New York office in September 1997.

Member Agents Jonathon Lazear; Christi Cardenas; Darrick Kline; Julie Mayo; Anne Blackstone; director of digital media Nate Roen.

Represents Nonfiction books, novels, short story collections, novellas, juvenile books, graphic novels. **Considers these nonfiction areas:** Agriculture/horticulture; americana; animals; anthropology/archaeology; art/architecture/design; biography/autobiography; business/economics; child guidance/parenting; computers/electronic; cooking/foods/nutrition; current affairs; education; ethnic/cultural interests; gardening; gay/lesbian issues; government/politics/law; health/medicine; history; how-to; humor/satire; interior design/decorating; juvenile nonfiction; language/literature/criticism; memoirs; military/war; money/finance; multicultural; music/dance; nature/environment; New Age/metaphysics; philosophy; photography; popular culture; psychology; recreation; regional; religious/inspirational; science/technology; self-help/personal improvement; sex; sociology; software; spirituality; sports; theater/film; travel; true crime/investigative; women's issues/studies; young adult; creative nonfiction. **Considers these fiction areas:** Action/adventure; confession; detective/police/crime; ethnic; family saga; fantasy; feminist; gay/lesbian; gothic; hi-lo; historical; humor/satire; juvenile; literary; mainstream/contemporary; military/war; multicultural; multimedia; mystery/suspense; New Age; occult; picture books; plays; poetry; poetry in translation; psychic/supernatural; religious/inspirational; romance; science fiction; short story collections; spiritual; sports; thriller; translation; westerns/frontier; young adult; women's.

> O→ Actively seeking new voices in commercial fiction and nonfiction. "It's all in the writing, no matter the subject matter." Does not want to receive horror, poetry, scripts and/or screenplays.

How to Contact Query with SASE, submit outline/proposal, synopsis, author bio, SASE. No phone calls or faxes. We prefer snail mail queries. Responds in 2 weeks to queries; 3 weeks to mss. Returns materials only with SASE. Obtains most new clients through recommendations from others, solicitations.

Recent Sales Sold more than 50 titles in the last year. *Dragonships*, by Margaret Weis and Tracy Hickman (Tor); Motorhead YA series, by Will Weaver (FSG); Untitled Book, by Henry Alford (Twelve); Untitled Book, by Jane Goodall and Thane Maynard (Hachette); *Gastroanomalies: Questionable Culinary Creations from the Golden Age of American Cookery*, by James Lileks (Crown).

Terms Agent receives 15% commission on domestic sales; 20% commission on foreign sales. Offers written contract. Charges clients for photocopying, international express mail, bound galleys, books used for subsidiary rights sales. No fees charged if book is not sold.

Tips "The writer should first view himself as a salesperson in order to obtain an agent. Sell yourself, your idea, your concept. Do your homework. Notice what is in the marketplace. Be sophisticated about the arena in which you are writing. Please note that we also have a New York office, but the primary office remains in Hudson, Wis., for the receipt of any material."

☑ SARAH LAZIN BOOKS

126 Fifth Ave., Suite 300, New York NY 10011. (212)989-5757. Fax: (212)989-1393. Member of AAR. Represents 75+ clients. Currently handles: 80% nonfiction books; 20% novels.

Member Agents Sarah Lazin; Shawn Mitchell.

Represents Nonfiction books, novels. **Considers these nonfiction areas:** Biography/autobiography; ethnic/cultural interests; gay/lesbian issues; history; music/dance; popular culture; religious/inspirational.

How to Contact Query with SASE. No e-mail queries.

Recent Sales *Weird Like Us*; *Pledged: The Secret Life of Sororities*, by Alexandra Robbins.

Terms Agent receives 15% commission on domestic sales; 20% commission on foreign sales.

◎ THE NED LEAVITT AGENCY

70 Wooster St., Suite 4F, New York NY 10012. (212)334-0999. Website: www.nedleavittagency.com. **Contact:** Ned Leavitt. Member of AAR. Represents 40+ clients.

Member Agents Ned Leavitt, founder and agent; Britta Alexander, agent; Jill Beckman, editorial assistant.

Represents Nonfiction books, novels.

> O→ "We are small in size, but intensely dedicated to our authors and to supporting excellent and unique writing."

How to Contact This agency now only takes queries/submissions through referred clients. Do *not* cold query. No fax queries.

Recent Sales *In Time of War*, by Allen Appel (Carroll & Graf); *From Father to Son*, by Allen Appel (St. Martin's); *The Way of Song*, by Shawna Carol (St. Martin's); *Alchemy of Illness*, by Kat Duff (Pantheon); *Are You Getting Enlightened or Losing Your Mind?*, by Dennis Gersten (Harmony).

Tips Look online for this agency's recently changed submission guidelines.

⬍ ☑ ROBERT LECKER AGENCY

4055 Melrose Ave., Montreal QC H4A 2S5 Canada. (514)830-4818. Fax: (514)483-1644. E-mail: leckerlink@aol.com. Website: www.leckeragency.com. **Contact:** Robert Lecker. Estab. 2004. Represents 15 clients. 20% of clients are new/unpublished writers. Currently handles: 80% nonfiction books; 10% novels; 10% scholarly books.

> ● Prior to becoming an agent, Mr. Lecker was the co-founder and publisher of ECW Press and professor of English literature at McGill University. He has 30 years of experience in book and magazine publishing.

Member Agents Robert Lecker (popular culture, music); Mary Williams (travel, food, popular science).

Represents Nonfiction books, novels, scholarly books, syndicated material. **Considers these nonfiction areas:** Biography/autobiography; cooking/foods/nutrition; ethnic/cultural interests; how-to; language/literature/criticism; music/dance; popular culture; science/technology; theater/film. **Considers these fiction areas:** Action/adventure; detective/police/crime; erotica; literary; mainstream/contemporary; mystery/suspense; thriller.

O— RLA specializes in books about popular culture, music, entertainment, food and travel. The agency responds to articulate, innovative proposals within 2 weeks. Actively seeking original book mss only after receipt of outlines and proposals.

How to Contact Query first. Only responds to queries of interest. Discards the rest. Accepts e-mail queries. No fax queries. Considers simultaneous queries. Responds in 2 weeks to queries; 1 month to mss. Obtains most new clients through recommendations from others, conferences, interest in Web site.

Terms Agent receives 15% commission on domestic sales; 15-20% commission on foreign sales. Offers written contract, binding for 1 year; 6-month notice must be given to terminate contract.

⬤ LESCHER & LESCHER, LTD.

47 E. 19th St., New York NY 10003. (212)529-1790. Fax: (212)529-2716. **Contact:** Robert Lescher, Susan Lescher. Estab. 1966. Member of AAR. Represents 150 clients. Currently handles: 80% nonfiction books; 20% novels.
Represents Nonfiction books, novels. **Considers these nonfiction areas:** Current affairs; history; memoirs; popular culture; biography; cookbooks/wines; law; contemporary issues; narrative nonfiction. **Considers these fiction areas:** Literary; mystery/suspense; commercial.

O— Does not want to receive screenplays, science fiction or romance.

How to Contact Query with SASE. Obtains most new clients through recommendations from others.

Recent Sales Sold 35 titles in the last year. This agency prefers not to share information on specific sales. Clients include Neil Sheehan, Madeleine L'Engle, Calvin Trillin, Judith Viorst, Thomas Perry, Anne Fadiman, Frances FitzGerald, Paula Fox, Robert M. Parker Jr.

Terms Agent receives 15% commission on domestic sales; 20% commission on foreign sales.

◎ LEVELFIVEMEDIA, LLC

130 W. 42nd St., Suite 1901-02, New York NY 10036. (212)575-3096. Fax: (212)575-7797. E-mail: levelfivemedia @l5m.net; submissions@l5m.net. Website: www.l5m.net. **Contact:** Stephen Hanselman. Estab. 2005.

● Prior to becoming an agent, Ms. Hemming served as president and publisher of HarperCollins General Books. Mr. Hanselman served as senior VP and publisher of HarperBusiness, HarperResource and HarperSanFrancisco.

Member Agents Stephen Hanselman; Cathy Hemming.

Represents Nonfiction books, novels. **Considers these nonfiction areas:** Business/economics; cooking/foods/nutrition; health/medicine; history; money/finance; psychology; religious/inspirational; self-help/personal improvement; fitness/exercise, inspiration, popular science, investigative journalism, lifestyle, how-to, popular reference, parenting, cultural studies. **Considers these fiction areas:** Commercial, literary, children's.

O— "Our commitment is to focus on fewer authors and to provide more of these missing services, including media development and marketing consultation, by building their benefits into each project that is offered to publishers. Given this choice of focus, we are not accepting submissions except from published authors, credentialed speakers, established journalists, media personalities, leading scholars and religious figures, prominent science and health professionals, and high-level business consultants."

How to Contact Query with SASE, submit synopsis, publishing history, author bio, cover letter. No snail mail queries. Qualified fiction authors must have a previously published book or be referred. Accepts e-mail queries. No fax queries. Obtains most new clients through recommendations from others.

Recent Sales *The Message*, by William Griffin (NavPress); *The Saint & The Sultan*, by Paul Moses; *On the Night You Were Born*, by Nancy Tillman (Feiwel & Friends).

▣ PAUL S. LEVINE LITERARY AGENCY

1054 Superba Ave., Venice CA 90291-3940. (310)450-6711. Fax: (310)450-0181. E-mail: pslevine@ix.netcom.c om. Website: www.paulslevine.com. **Contact:** Paul S. Levine. Estab. 1996. Member of the State Bar of California. Represents over 100 clients. 75% of clients are new/unpublished writers. Currently handles: 30% nonfiction books; 30% novels; 10% movie scripts; 30% TV scripts.

Represents Nonfiction books, novels, movie scripts, feature film, TV scripts, TV movie of the week, episodic drama, sitcom, animation, documentary, miniseries, syndicated material. **Considers these nonfiction areas:** Art/architecture/design; biography/autobiography; business/economics; child guidance/parenting; computers/electronic; cooking/foods/nutrition; crafts/hobbies; current affairs; education; ethnic/cultural interests; gay/lesbian issues; government/politics/law; health/medicine; history; how-to; humor/satire; interior design/decorating; language/literature/criticism; memoirs; military/war; money/finance; music/dance; nature/environment; New Age/metaphysics; photography; popular culture; psychology; religious/inspirational; science/technology; self-help/personal improvement; sociology; sports; theater/film; true crime/investigative; women's issues/studies; creative nonfiction. **Considers these fiction areas:** Action/adventure; comic books/cartoon; confession; detective/police/crime; erotica; ethnic; experimental; family saga; feminist; gay/lesbian; glitz; historical; humor/satire; literary; mainstream/contemporary; mystery/suspense; regional; religious/inspirational;

Literary Agents

romance; sports; thriller; westerns/frontier. **Considers these script subject areas:** Action/adventure; biography/autobiography; cartoon/animation; comedy; contemporary issues; detective/police/crime; erotica; ethnic; experimental; family saga; feminist; gay/lesbian; glitz; historical; horror; juvenile; mainstream; multimedia; mystery/suspense; religious/inspirational; romantic comedy; romantic drama; sports; teen; thriller; western/frontier.

O— Actively seeking commercial fiction and nonfiction. Also handles children's and young adult fiction and nonfiction. Does not want to receive science fiction, fantasy, or horror.

How to Contact Query with SASE. Accepts e-mail and fax queries. Considers simultaneous queries. Responds in 1 day to queries; 2 months to mss. Returns materials only with SASE. Obtains most new clients through conferences, referrals, listings on various websites and in directories.

Recent Sales Sold 25 titles in the last year. This agency prefers not to share information on specific sales.

Terms Agent receives 15% commission on domestic sales; 20% commission on foreign sales. Offers written contract. Charges clients for messengers, long distance calls, postage (only when incurred). No advance payment necessary.

Writers' Conferences California Lawyers for the Arts Workshops; Selling to Hollywood Conference; Willamette Writers Conference; and many others.

ROBERT LIEBERMAN ASSOCIATES

400 Nelson Rd., Ithaca NY 14850-9440. (607)273-8801. Fax: (801)749-9682. E-mail: rhl10@cornell.edu. Website: www.people.cornell.edu/pages/rhl10. **Contact:** Robert Lieberman. Estab. 1993. Represents 30 clients. 50% of clients are new/unpublished writers. Currently handles: 20% nonfiction books.

Represents Nonfiction books (trade), scholarly books, textbooks (college/high school/middle school). **Considers these nonfiction areas:** Agriculture/horticulture; anthropology/archaeology; art/architecture/design; business/economics; computers/electronic; education; health/medicine; memoirs (by authors with high public recognition); money/finance; music/dance; nature/environment; psychology; science/technology; sociology; theater/film.

O— This agency only accepts nonfiction ideas and specializes in university/college-level textbooks, CD-ROM/software for the university/college-level textbook market, and popular trade books in math, engineering, economics, and other subjects. Does not want to receive fiction, self-help, or screenplays.

How to Contact Query with SASE or by e-mail. Prefers to read materials exclusively. Prefers e-mail queries. Responds in 2 weeks to queries; 1 month to mss. Returns materials only with SASE. Obtains most new clients through referrals.

Recent Sales Sold 15 titles in the last year. *The Theory of Almost Everything*, by Robert Oerter (Plume Press); *Fundamentals in Voice Quality Engineering in Wireless Networks*, by Avi Perry (Cambridge University Press); *C++ Programming*, by John Mason (Prentice Hall); *College Physics*, by Giambattist and Richardson (McGraw-Hill); *Conflict Resolution*, by Baltos and Weir (Cambridge University Press).

Terms Agent receives 15% commission on domestic sales; 20% commission on foreign sales. Offers written contract; 1-month notice must be given to terminate contract. 100% of business is derived from commissions on ms sales. Fees are sometimes charged to clients for shipping and when special reviewers are required.

Tips "The trade books we handle are by authors who are highly recognized in their fields of expertise. Our client list includes Nobel Prize winners and others with high name recognition, either by the public or within a given area of expertise."

LIMELIGHT MANAGEMENT

33 Newman St., London W1T 1PY England. (44)(207)637-2529. E-mail: mary@limelightmanagement.com; Submissions@limelightmanagement.com. Website: www.limelightmanagement.com. **Contact:** Fiona Lindsay. Estab. 1990. Member of AAA. Represents 70 clients. Currently handles: 100% nonfiction books; multimedia.

• Prior to becoming an agent, Ms. Lindsay was a public relations manager at the Dorchester and was working on her law degree.

Represents Nonfiction books. **Considers these nonfiction areas:** Art/architecture/design; cooking/foods/nutrition; crafts/hobbies; gardening (agriculture/horticulture); health/medicine; interior design/decorating; nature/environment; New Age/metaphysics; photography; self-help/personal improvement; sports; travel.

O— "We are celebrity agents for TV celebrities, broadcasters, writers, journalists, celebrity speakers and media personalities, after dinner speakers, motivational speakers, celebrity chefs, TV presenters and TV chefs." This agency will consider women's fiction, as well.

How to Contact Prefers to read materials exclusively. Query with SASE/IRC via e-mail. Agents will be in contact if they want to see more. No attachments to e-mails. Accepts e-mail queries. No fax queries. Responds in 1 week to queries. Returns materials only with SASE. Obtains most new clients through recommendations from others.

Recent Sales This agency prefers not to share information on specific sales. Clients include Oz Clarke, Antony Worrall Thompson, David Stevens, Linda Barker, James Martin.

Terms Agent receives 15% commission on domestic sales; 20% commission on foreign sales. Offers written contract; 2-month notice must be given to terminate contract.

LINDSTROM LITERARY MANAGEMENT, LLC

871 N. Greenbrier St., Arlington VA 22205. Fax: (703)527-7624. E-mail: lindstromlit@aol.com. Website: www.li ndstromliterary.com. **Contact:** Kristin Lindstrom. Estab. 1993. Member of Author's Guild. Represents 9 clients. 50% of clients are new/unpublished writers. Currently handles: 30% nonfiction books; 70% novels.

● Prior to her current position, Ms. Lindstrom was an editor of a monthly magazine in the energy industry, and an independent marketing and publicity consultant.

Represents Nonfiction books, novels. **Considers these nonfiction areas:** Animals; biography/autobiography; business/economics; current affairs; history; memoirs; popular culture; science/technology; true crime/investigative. **Considers these fiction areas:** Action/adventure; detective/police/crime; erotica; mainstream/contemporary; mystery/suspense; religious/inspirational; thriller; women's.

Oー "In 2006, I decided to add my more specific promotion/publicity skills to the mix in order to support the marketing efforts of my published clients." Actively seeking commercial fiction and narrative nonfiction. Does not want to receive juvenile or children's books.

How to Contact Query with SASE, submit author bio, synopsis and first four chapters if submitting fiction. For nonfiction, send the first 4 chapters, synopsis, proposal, outline and mission statement. Accepts e-mail queries. No fax queries. Considers simultaneous queries. Responds in 5 weeks to queries; 8 weeks to mss. Returns materials only with SASE. Obtains most new clients through recommendations from others, solicitations.

Recent Sales Sold 7 titles in the last year. *Perfect Circle* and *Prisoner*, by Carlos J. Cortes (Bantam Spectra); *Rain Song* and *Evening Peace*, by Alice Wisler (Bethany House); *Beach Trip* and a second book, by Cathy Holton (Ballantine); *7th Son: Descent*, by JC Hutchins (St. Martin's).

Terms Agent receives 15% commission on domestic sales; 20% commission on foreign sales. Offers written contract. This agency charges for postage, UPS, copies and other basic office expenses.

Tips "Do your homework on accepted practices; make sure you know what kind of book the agent handles."

WENDY LIPKIND AGENCY

120 E. 81st St., New York NY 10028. (212)628-9653. Fax: (212)585-1306. E-mail: lipkindag@aol.com. **Contact:** Wendy Lipkind. Estab. 1977. Member of AAR. Represents 50 clients. Currently handles: 100% nonfiction books.

Represents Nonfiction books. **Considers these nonfiction areas:** Biography/autobiography; current affairs; health/medicine; history; science/technology; women's issues/studies; social history; narrative nonfiction.

Oー This agency specializes in adult nonfiction.

How to Contact Prefers to read materials exclusively. Accepts e-mail queries only (no attachments). Obtains most new clients through recommendations from others.

Recent Sales Sold 10 titles in the last year. *Lost at School*, by Ross Greene (Scribner); *Professional Wedding Cakes*, by Toba Garrett (Wiley); *One Small Step*, by Robert Mauner (Workman); *Kingdom of Strangers: A Muslim Woman's Journey Through Fear and Faith in Saudi Arabia*, by Dr. Qanta Amhed (Sourcebooks).

Terms Agent receives 15% commission on domestic sales; 20% commission on foreign sales. Sometimes offers written contract. Charges clients for foreign postage, messenger service, photocopying, transatlantic calls, faxes.

Tips "Send intelligent query letter first. Let me know if you've submitted to other agents."

LIPPINCOTT MASSIE MCQUILKIN

80 Fifth Ave., Suite 1101, New York NY 10011. (212)337-2044. Fax: (212)352-2059. E-mail: info@lmqlit.com. Website: www.lmqlit.com. **Contact:** Molly Lindley, assistant. Estab. 2003. Represents 90 clients. 30% of clients are new/unpublished writers. Currently handles: 40% nonfiction books; 40% novels; 10% story collections; 5% scholarly books; 5% poetry.

Member Agents Maria Massie (fiction, memoir, cultural criticism); Will Lippincott (politics, current affairs, history); Rob McQuilkin (fiction, history, psychology, sociology, graphic material).

Represents Nonfiction books, novels, short story collections, scholarly books, graphic novels. **Considers these nonfiction areas:** Animals; anthropology/archaeology; art/architecture/design; biography/autobiography; business/economics; child guidance/parenting; current affairs; ethnic/cultural interests; gay/lesbian issues; government/politics/law; health/medicine; history; language/literature/criticism; memoirs; military/war; money/finance; music/dance; nature/environment; popular culture; psychology; religious/inspirational; science/technology; self-help/personal improvement; sociology; theater/film; true crime/investigative; women's issues/studies. **Considers these fiction areas:** Action/adventure; comic books/cartoon; confession; family saga; feminist; gay/lesbian; historical; humor/satire; literary; mainstream/contemporary; regional.

LMQ focuses on bringing new voices in literary and commercial fiction to the market, as well as popularizing the ideas and arguments of scholars in the fields of history, psychology, sociology, political science, and current affairs. Actively seeking fiction writers who already have credits in magazines and quarterlies, as well as nonfiction writers who already have a media platform or some kind of a university affiliation. Does not want to receive romance, genre fiction or children's material.

How to Contact Send query via e-mail. Only send additional materials if requested. Considers simultaneous queries. Responds in 1 week to queries; 1 month to mss. Obtains most new clients through recommendations from others, solicitations, conferences.

Recent Sales Sold 27 titles in the last year. *The Abstinence Teacher*, by Tom Perrotta (St. Martins); *Queen of Fashion*, by Caroline Weber (Henry Holt); *Whistling Past Dixie*, by Tom Schaller (Simon & Schuster); *Pretty Little Dirty*, by Amanda Boyden (Vintage). Other clients include Peter Ho Davies, Kim Addonizio, Don Lee, Natasha Trethewey, Anatol Lieven, Sir Michael Marmot, Anne Carson, Liza Ward, David Sirota, Anne Marie Slaughter, Marina Belozerskaya, Kate Walbert.

Terms Agent receives 15% commission on domestic sales; 20% commission on foreign sales. Offers written contract; 30-day notice must be given to terminate contract. Only charges for reasonable business expenses upon successful sale.

LITERARY AGENCY FOR SOUTHERN AUTHORS

2123 Paris Metz Road, Chattanooga TN 37421. E-mail: southernlitagent@aol.com. **Contact:** Lantz Powell. Estab. 2001. Represents 20 clients. 60% of clients are new/unpublished writers. Currently handles: 50% nonfiction books; 50% novels.

• Prior to becoming an agent, Mr. Powell was in sales and contract negotiation.

Represents Nonfiction books, novels, juvenile books (for ages 14 and up). **Considers these nonfiction areas:** Art/architecture/design; biography/autobiography; business/economics; crafts/hobbies; current affairs; education; ethnic/cultural interests; government/politics/law; history; how-to; humor/satire; interior design/decorating; language/literature/criticism; military/war; New Age/metaphysics; photography; popular culture; religious/inspirational; self-help/personal improvement; true crime/investigative. **Considers these fiction areas:** Comic books/cartoon; horror; humor/satire; literary; mainstream/contemporary; regional (Southern); religious/inspirational; young adult.

"We focus on authors that live in the Southern United States. We have the ability to translate and explain complexities of publishing for the Southern author." Actively seeking quality projects by authors with a vision of where they want to be in 10 years and a plan of how to get there. Does not want to receive unfinished, unedited projects that do not follow the standard presentation conventions of the trade. No romance.

How to Contact Query via e-mail first and include a synopsis. Accepts e-mail queries. No fax queries. Considers simultaneous queries. Responds in 2-3 days to queries; 1 week to mss. Obtains most new clients through recommendations from others.

Recent Sales Sold 10+ titles in the last year. List of other clients and books sold will be available to authors pre-signing, but is not for public knowledge.

Terms Agent receives 15% commission on domestic sales; 25% commission on foreign sales. Offers written contract. "We charge when a publisher wants a hard copy overnight or the like. The client always knows this beforehand."

Writers' Conferences Conference for Southern Literature; Tennessee Book Fair.

Tips "If you are an unpublished author, join a writers group, even if it is on the Internet. You need good honest feedback. Don't send a manuscript that has not been read by at least five people. Don't send a manuscript cold to any agent without first asking if they want it. Try to meet the agent face to face before signing. Make sure the fit is right."

LITERARY AND CREATIVE ARTISTS, INC.

3543 Albemarle St. NW, Washington DC 20008-4213. (202)362-4688. Fax: (202)362-8875. E-mail: query@lcadc. com; lca9643@lcadc.com. Website: www.lcadc.com. **Contact:** Muriel Nellis. Estab. 1981. Member of AAR, Authors Guild, American Bar Association. Represents 75 clients. Currently handles: 70% nonfiction books; 30% novels.

Member Agents Muriel Nellis; Jane Roberts.

Represents Nonfiction books, novels. **Considers these nonfiction areas:** Biography/autobiography; business/economics; cooking/foods/nutrition; government/politics/law; health/medicine; how-to; memoirs; philosophy; human drama; lifestyle.

How to Contact Query with SASE. *No unsolicited mss.* Send no e-mail attachments. Accepts e-mail queries. No fax queries. Responds in 3 months to queries.

Recent Sales *Lady Cottington's Pressed Fairy Book*, by Brian Froud and Terry Jones (Pavilion); *The New*

Feminine Brain, by Mona Lisa Schulz (Free Press); *Al Qaeda in Europe*, by Lorenzo Vidino (Prometheus Books); *What Type of Leader Am I?*, by Ginger Lapid-Bogda (McGraw-Hill); *The Longest Ride*, by Emilio Scotto (MBI Publishing).

Terms Agent receives 15% commission on domestic sales; 20% commission on foreign sales; 25% commission on dramatic rights sales. Charges clients for long-distance phone/fax, photocopying, shipping.

Tips "While we prefer published writers, publishing credits are not required if the proposed work has great merit."

◙ THE LITERARY GROUP INTERNATIONAL

51 E. 25th St., Suite 401, New York NY 10010. (212)274-1616. Fax: (212)274-9876. E-mail: fweimann@theliterarygroup.com. Website: www.theliterarygroup.com. **Contact:** Frank Weimann. Estab. 1985. 65% of clients are new/unpublished writers. Currently handles: 50% nonfiction books; 50% fiction.

Member Agents Frank Weimann; acquisitions editor Jaimee Garbacik.

Represents Nonfiction books, novels, graphic novels. **Considers these nonfiction areas:** Animals; anthropology/archaeology; biography/autobiography; business/economics; child guidance/parenting; crafts/hobbies; current affairs; education; ethnic/cultural interests; government/politics/law; health/medicine; history; how-to; humor/satire; juvenile nonfiction; language/literature/criticism; memoirs; military/war; money/finance; multicultural; music/dance; nature/environment; popular culture; psychology; religious/inspirational; science/technology; self-help/personal improvement; sociology; sports; theater/film; true crime/investigative; women's issues/studies; creative nonfiction. **Considers these fiction areas:** Action/adventure; contemporary issues; detective/police/crime; ethnic; family saga; fantasy; feminist; horror; humor/satire; mystery/suspense; psychic/supernatural; romance (contemporary, gothic, historical, regency); sports; thriller; westerns/frontier; young adult; experimental.

    ○— This agency specializes in nonfiction (memoir, military, history, biography, sports, how-to).

How to Contact Query with SASE, outline, 3 sample chapters. Prefers to read materials exclusively. Only responds if interested. Returns materials only with SASE. Obtains most new clients through referrals, writers' conferences, query letters.

Recent Sales Sold 90 titles in the last year. *The Magician*, by Michael Scott; *Dog & Bear: Two's Company*, by Laura Vaccaro Seeger; *101 Erotic Dares*, by Laura Corn; *Why Men Die First*, by Marianne Legato; *Bean's Books*, by Chudney Ross.

Terms Agent receives 15% commission on domestic sales; 20% commission on foreign sales. Offers written contract; 30-day notice must be given to terminate contract.

Writers' Conferences San Diego State University Writers' Conference; Maui Writers' Conference; Agents and Editors Conference, among others.

◓ LITERARY MANAGEMENT GROUP, INC.

(615)812-4445. E-mail: brucebarbour@literarymanagementgroup.com; brb@brucebarbour.com. Website: www.literarymanagementgroup.com; www.brucebarbour.com. **Contact:** Bruce Barbour. Estab. 1995.

    ● Prior to becoming an agent, Mr. Barbour held executive positions at several publishing houses, including Revell, Barbour Books, Thomas Nelson, and Random House.

Represents Nonfiction books, novels. **Considers these nonfiction areas:** Biography/autobiography; Christian living; spiritual growth; women's and men's issues; prayer; devotional; meditational; Bible study; marriage; business; family/parenting. **Considers these fiction areas:** Accepts a few works of adult fiction each year.

    ○— Does not want to receive gift books, poetry, children's books, short stories, or juvenile/young adult fiction. No unsolicited mss or proposals from unpublished authors.

How to Contact Query with SASE. E-mail proposal as an attachment.

Terms Agent receives 15% commission on domestic sales.

◙ LITERARY SERVICES, INC.

P.O. Box 888, Barnegat NJ 08005. (609)698-7162. Fax: (609)698-7163. E-mail: john@LiteraryServicesInc.com. Website: www.LiteraryServicesInc.com. **Contact:** John Willig. Estab. 1991. Member of Author's Guild. Represents 85 clients. 25% of clients are new/unpublished writers. Currently handles: 100% nonfiction books.

Member Agents John Willig (business, personal growth, narratives, history, health); Cynthia Zigmund (personal finance, investments, entrepreneurship); Joel Margulis (business).

Represents Nonfiction books. **Considers these nonfiction areas:** Art/architecture/design; biography/autobiography; business/economics; child guidance/parenting; cooking/foods/nutrition; crafts/hobbies; health/medicine; history; how-to; humor/satire; language/literature/criticism; money/finance; New Age/metaphysics; popular culture; psychology; science/technology; self-help/personal improvement; sports; true crime/investigative.

    ○— "Our publishing experience and 'inside' knowledge of how companies and editors really work sets us apart from many agencies; our specialties are noted above, but we are open to unique presentations in all nonfiction topic areas.'' Actively seeking business, work/life topics, story-driven narratives. Does not want to receive fiction, children's books, science fiction, religion or memoirs.

How to Contact Query with SASE. For starters, a one-page outline sent via e-mail is acceptable. See our Web site to learn more. Accepts e-mail queries. No fax queries. Considers simultaneous queries. Responds in 2 weeks to queries; 4 weeks to mss. Returns materials only with SASE. Obtains most new clients through recommendations from others, solicitations, conferences.

Recent Sales Sold 22 titles in the last year. *The Energy Cure: How to Recharge Your Life Every Day*, by Kimberly Kinsley (New Page Books); A full list of new books are noted on the Web site.

Terms Agent receives 15% commission on domestic sales; 20% commission on foreign sales. Offers written contract. This agency charges fees for copying, postage, etc.

Writers' Conferences Author 101; Mega Book Marketing; Publicity Summit.

Tips ''Be focused. In all likelihood, your work is not going to be of interest to 'a very broad audience' or 'every parent,' so I appreciate when writers put aside their passion and do some homework, i.e. positioning, special features and benefits of your work. Be a marketer. How have you tested your ideas and writing (beyond your inner circle of family and friends)? Have you received any key awards for your work or endorsements from influential persons in your field? What steps have you taken to increase your presence in the market?''

LJK LITERARY MANAGEMENT

708 Third Ave., 16th Floor, New York NY 10018. (212)221-8797. Fax: (212)221-8722. E-mail: submissions@ljklit erary.com. Website: www.ljkliterary.com. Represents 20+ clients.

• Prior to becoming an agent, Mr. Laghi worked for ICM; Mr. Kirshbaum worked for Random House; Ms. Einstein was a senior executive at Maria Campbell Associates.

Member Agents Larry Kirshbaum; Susanna Einstein (contemporary fiction, literary fiction, romance, suspense, historical fiction, middle grade, young adult, crime fiction, narrative nonfiction, memoir and biography); Jud Laghi (celebrity, pop culture, humor, journalism).

Represents Nonfiction books, novels.

○→ ''We are not considering picture books at this time.''

How to Contact Query with SASE. E-mail queries are preferred. The only attachment should be the writing sample. No fax queries. Responds in 8 weeks to queries; 8 weeks to mss.

Recent Sales *Think Big and Kick Ass*, by Donald Trump and Bill Zanker; *In Secret Service*, by Mitch Silver; *The Christmas Pearl*, by Dorothea Benton Frank; *Eye of the Beholder*, by David Ellis; *Brainiac: Adventures in the Curious, Competitive, Compulsive World of Trivia*, by Ken Jennings; *Found II*, by Davy Rothbart; *Amberville*, by Tim Davys.

Tips ''All submissions will receive a response from us if they adhere to our submission guidelines. Please do not contact us to inquire about your submission unless 10 weeks have passed since you submitted it.''

JULIA LORD LITERARY MANAGEMENT

38 W. Ninth St., #4, New York NY 10011. (212)995-2333. Fax: (212)995-2332. E-mail: julialordliterary@nyc.rr.c om. Estab. 1999. Member of AAR.

Member Agents Julia Lord, owner; Riley Kellogg, subagent.

Represents Fiction and nonfiction. **Considers these nonfiction areas:** Biography/autobiography; history; humor/satire; nature/environment; science/technology; sports; travel (and adventure); African-American; lifestyle; narrative nonfiction. **Considers these fiction areas:** Action/adventure; historical; literary; mainstream/contemporary.

How to Contact Query with SASE or via e-mail. Obtains most new clients through recommendations from others, solicitations.

STERLING LORD LITERISTIC, INC.

65 Bleecker St., 12th Floor, New York NY 10012. (212)780-6050. Fax: (212)780-6095. E-mail: info@sll.com. Website: www.sll.com. Estab. 1952. Member of AAR; signatory of WGA. Represents 600 clients. Currently handles: 50% nonfiction books; 50% novels.

Member Agents Sterling Lord; Peter Matson; Phillippa Brophy (represents journalists, nonfiction writers and novelists, and is most interested in current events, memoir, science, politics, biography, and women's issues); Chris Calhoun; Claudia Cross (a broad range of fiction and nonfiction, from literary fiction to commercial women's fiction and romance novels, to cookbooks, lifestyle titles, memoirs, serious nonfiction on religious and spiritual topics, and books for the CBA marketplace); Rebecca Friedman (memoir, reportorial nonfiction, history, current events, literary, international and commerical fiction); Robert Guinsler (literary and commercial fiction, journalism, narrative nonfiction with an emphasis on pop culture, science and current events, memoirs and biographies); Laurie Liss (commercial and literary fiction and nonfiction whose perspectives are well developed and unique); Judy Heiblum (fiction and non-fiction writers, looking for distinctive voices that challenge the reader, emotionally or intellectually. She works with journalists, academics, memoirists, and essayists, and is particularly interested in books that explore the intersections of science, culture, history and philosophy. In addition, she is always looking for writers of literary fiction with fresh, uncompromising voices); Neeti Madan (memoir, journalism, history, pop culture, health, lifestyle, women's issues, multicultural books and virtually any intelligent writing on intriguing topics. Neeti is looking for smart, well-written commercial novels, as well as compelling and provocative literary works); George Nicholson (writers and illustrators for children); Marcy Posner (commercial women's fiction, historical fiction, and mystery to biography, history, health, and lifestyle); Paul Rodeen (picture books by artists that both write and illustrate, but he is actively seeking writers of fiction and nonfiction for young adult and middle grade readers; different address: 3501 N. Southport #497, Chicago, IL 60657); Jim Rutman; Charlotte Sheedy; Ira Silverberg; Douglas Stewart (literary fiction, narrative nonfiction, and young adult fiction).

Represents Nonfiction books, novels.

How to Contact Query with SASE. Query by snail mail. No e-mail or fax queries. Responds in 1 month to mss. Obtains most new clients through recommendations from others.

Recent Sales This agency prefers not to share information on specific sales. Other clients include Kent Haruf, Dick Francis, Mary Gordon, Sen. John McCain, Simon Winchester, James McBride, Billy Collins, Richard Paul Evans, Dave Pelzer.

Terms Agent receives 15% commission on domestic sales; 20% commission on foreign sales. Offers written contract. Charges clients for photocopying.

☑ NANCY LOVE LITERARY AGENCY

250 E. 65th St., New York NY 10065-6614. (212)980-3499. Fax: (212)308-6405. E-mail: nloveag@aol.com. **Contact:** Nancy Love. Estab. 1984. Member of AAR. Represents 60-80 clients. 25% of clients are new/unpublished writers. Currently handles: 100% nonfiction books.

• This agency is not taking on any new fiction writers at this time.

Represents Nonfiction books. **Considers these nonfiction areas:** Biography/autobiography; child guidance/parenting; cooking/foods/nutrition; current affairs; ethnic/cultural interests; government/politics/law; health/medicine; history; how-to; nature/environment; popular culture; psychology; religious/inspirational; science/technology; self-help/personal improvement; sociology; spirituality; travel (armchair only, no how-to); true crime/investigative; women's issues/studies.

○━ This agency specializes in adult nonfiction. Actively seeking narrative nonfiction.

How to Contact Query with SASE. No fax queries. Considers simultaneous queries. Responds in 3 weeks to queries; 6 weeks to mss. Returns materials only with SASE. Obtains most new clients through recommendations from others, solicitations.

Recent Sales Sold 18 titles in the last year. *The Monster in the Corner Office*, by Patricia King (Adams); *Building Better Brains*, by Judy Willis (Sourcebooks); *The New Native American Cuisine*, by Marian Betancourt (Globe Pequot); *Addiction Proof Your Child*, by Stanton Peele (Random House); *Murder in the Silver City*, by Annamaria Alfieri (St. Martin's); *Germ Proof Your Kids*, by Harey Rotbart (ASM Press).

Terms Agent receives 15% commission on domestic sales; 20% commission on foreign sales. Offers written contract. Charges clients for photocopying if it runs more than $20.

Tips "Nonfiction authors and/or collaborators must be an authority in their subject area and have a platform. Send an SASE if you want a response."

☑ LOWENSTEIN-YOST ASSOCIATES

121 W. 27th St., Suite 601, New York NY 10001. (212)206-1630. Fax: (212)727-0280. Website: www.lowensteiny ost.com. **Contact:** Barbara Lowenstein or Nancy Yost. Estab. 1976. Member of AAR. Represents 150 clients. 20% of clients are new/unpublished writers. Currently handles: 60% nonfiction books; 40% novels.

Member Agents Barbara Lowenstein, president (nonfiction interests include narrative nonfiction, health, money, finance, travel, multicultural, popular culture and memoir; fiction interests include literary fiction and women's fiction); Nancy Yost, vice president (mainstream/contemporary fiction, mystery, suspense, contemporary/historical romance, thriller, women's fiction); Norman Kurz, business affairs; Zoe Fishman, foreign rights (young adult, literary fiction, narrative nonfiction); Natanya Wheeler (narrative nonfiction, literary fiction, historical, women's fiction, birds).

Represents Nonfiction books, novels. **Considers these nonfiction areas:** Animals; anthropology/archaeology; biography/autobiography; business/economics; child guidance/parenting; current affairs; education; ethnic/cultural interests; government/politics/law; health/medicine; history; how-to; language/literature/criticism; memoirs; money/finance; multicultural; nature/environment; popular culture; psychology; self-help/personal improvement; sociology; travel; women's issues/studies; music; narrative nonfiction; science; film. **Considers these fiction areas:** Detective/police/crime; erotica; ethnic; feminist; historical; literary; mainstream/contemporary; mystery/suspense; romance (contemporary, historical, regency); thriller; women's; fantasy, young adult.

O—➤ This agency specializes in health, business, creative nonfiction, literary fiction and commercial fiction—especially suspense, crime and women's issues. ''We are a full-service agency, handling domestic and foreign rights, film rights and audio rights to all of our books.''

How to Contact Query with SASE. Prefers to read materials exclusively. For fiction, send outline and first chapter. *No unsolicited mss.* No e-mail or fax queries. Responds in 4 weeks to queries. Returns materials only with SASE. Obtains most new clients through recommendations from others, solicitations, conferences.

Recent Sales *Body After Baby*, by Jackie Keller (Avery); *Creating Competitive Advantage*, by Jaynie Smith & Bill Flanagan (Doubleday); *To Keep a Husband*, by Lindsay Graves (Ballantine); *The Notorious Mrs. Winston*, by Mary Mackey (Berkley); *Gleason's Gym Total Body Boxing Workout for Women*, by Hector Roca & Bruce Silverglade (Fireside); *More Than A Champion: A Biography of Mohammed Ali*, by Ishmael Reed (Shaye Areheart); *Dreams of A Caspian Rain*, by Gina Nahai; *House of Dark Delights*, by Louisa Burton (Bantam); a new thriller by Perri O'Shaugnessy (Pocket); the debut thriller by N.P.R. writer Susan Arnout Smith (St. Martin's); *Sworn to Silence*, by Linda Castillo; *Thinner or Pretty on the Outside*, by Valerie Frankel; *In the Stars*, by Eileen Cook; *The Dark Lantern*, by Gerri Brightwell. Other clients include Stephanie Laurens, Dr. Ro, Penny McFall, Deborah Crombie, Liz Carlyle, Suzanne Enoch, Gaelen Foley, Tamar Myers, Sandi K. Shelton, Kathryn Smith, Cheyenne McCray, Barbara Keesling.

Terms Agent receives 15% commission on domestic sales; 20% commission on foreign sales. Offers written contract. Charges for large photocopy batches, messenger service, international postage.

Writers' Conferences Malice Domestic; Bouchercon; RWA National Conference.

Tips ''Know the genre you are working in and read! Also, please see our Web site for details on which agent to query for your project.''

🌐 🙂 ANDREW LOWNIE LITERARY AGENCY, LTD.

36 Great Smith St., London SW1P 3BU, England. (44)(207)222-7574. Fax: (44)(207)222-7576. E-mail: lownie@gl obalnet.co.uk. Website: www.andrewlownie.co.uk. **Contact:** Andrew Lownie. Estab. 1988. Member of AAA. Represents 130 clients. 20% of clients are new/unpublished writers. Currently handles: 90% nonfiction books; 10% novels.

• Prior to becoming an agent, Mr. Lownie was a journalist, bookseller, publisher, author of 12 books and director of the Curtis Brown Agency.

Represents Nonfiction books. **Considers these nonfiction areas:** Biography/autobiography; current affairs; government/politics/law; history; memoirs; military/war; popular culture; true crime/investigative.

O—➤ This agent has wide publishing experience, extensive journalistic contacts, and a specialty in showbiz/celebrity memoir. Showbiz memoirs, narrative histories, and biographies. No poetry, short stories, children's fiction, academic or scripts.

How to Contact Query with SASE and/or IRC. Submit outline, 1 sample chapter. Accepts e-mail and fax queries. Considers simultaneous queries. Responds in 1 week to queries; 1 month to mss. Returns materials only with SASE. Obtains most new clients through recommendations from others.

Recent Sales Sold 50 titles in the last year. *Avenging Justice*, by David Stafford (Time Warner); *Shadow of Solomon*, by Laurence Gardner; David Hasselhoff's autobiography. Other clients include Norma Major, Guy Bellamy, Joyce Cary estate, Lawrence James, Juliet Barker, Patrick McNee, Sir John Mills, Peter Evans, Desmond Seward, Laurence Gardner, Richard Rudgley, Timothy Good, Tom Levine.

Terms Agent receives 15% commission on domestic sales; 15% commission on foreign sales. Offers written contract; 30-day notice must be given to terminate contract.

🙂 LYONS LITERARY, LLC

116 West 23rd St., Suite 500, New York NY 10011. (212)851-8428. Fax: (212)851-8405. E-mail: info@lyonsliterar y.com. Website: www.lyonsliterary.com. **Contact:** Jonathan Lyons. Estab. 2007. Member of AAR, The Author's Guild, American Bar Association, New York State Bar Associaton, New York State Intellectual Property Law Section. Represents 42 clients. 15% of clients are new/unpublished writers. Currently handles: 60% nonfiction books; 40% novels.

Represents Nonfiction books, novels. **Considers these nonfiction areas:** Animals; biography/autobiography; cooking/foods/nutrition; crafts/hobbies; current affairs; ethnic/cultural interests; gay/lesbian issues; government/politics/law; health/medicine; history; how-to; humor/satire; memoirs; military/war; money/finance; multicultural; nature/environment; popular culture; psychology; science/technology; sociology; sports; translation; travel; true crime/investigative; women's issues/studies. **Considers these fiction areas:** Detective/police/crime; fantasy; feminist; gay/lesbian; historical; humor/satire; literary; mainstream/contemporary; mystery/suspense; psychic/supernatural; regional; science fiction; sports; thriller; women's; chick lit.

O—➤ ''With my legal expertise and experience selling domestic and foreign language book rights, paperback reprint rights, audio rights, film/TV rights and permissions, I am able to provide substantive and personal guidance to my clients in all areas relating to their projects. In addition, with the advent of new publishing technology, Lyons Literary, LLC is situated to address the changing nature of the industry while concurrently handling authors' more traditional needs.''

How to Contact Query with SASE. Submit outline, synopsis, author bio. Accepts e-queries through online submission form. No fax queries. Considers simultaneous queries. Responds in 8 weeks to queries; 12 weeks to mss. Returns materials only with SASE. Obtains most new clients through recommendations from others. This agency prefers not to share information on specific sales.

Terms Agent receives 15% commission on domestic sales; 20% commission on foreign sales. Offers written contract.

Writers' Conferences Agents and Editors Conference.

Tips ''Please submit electronic queries through our Web site submission form.''

🌐 DONALD MAASS LITERARY AGENCY

121 W. 27th St., Suite 801, New York NY 10001. (212)727-8383. E-mail: info@maassagency.com. Website: www.maassagency.com. Estab. 1980. Member of AAR, SFWA, MWA, RWA. Represents more than 100 clients. 5% of clients are new/unpublished writers. Currently handles: 100% novels.

- Prior to opening his agency, Mr. Maass served as an editor at Dell Publishing (New York) and as a reader at Gollancz (London). He also served as the president of AAR.

Member Agents Donald Maass (mainstream, literary, mystery/suspense, science fiction); Jennifer Jackson (commercial fiction, romance, science fiction, fantasy, mystery/suspense); Cameron McClure (literary, mystery/suspense, urban, fantasy, narrative nonfiction and projects with multicultural, international, and environmental themes, gay/lesbian); Stephen Barbara (literary fiction, young adult novels, middle grade, narrative nonfiction, historical nonfiction, mainstream, genre).

Represents Novels. **Considers these nonfiction areas:** Young adult. **Considers these fiction areas:** Detective/police/crime; fantasy; historical; horror; literary; mainstream/contemporary; mystery/suspense; psychic/supernatural; romance (historical, paranormal, time travel); science fiction; thriller; women's.

- ☛ This agency specializes in commercial fiction, especially science fiction, fantasy, mystery and suspense. Actively seeking to expand in literary fiction and women's fiction. Does not want to receive nonfiction, picture books, prescriptive nonfiction, or poetry.

How to Contact Query with SASE, synopsis, first 5 pages. Returns material only with SASE. Considers simultaneous queries. Responds in 2 weeks to queries; 3 months to mss.

Recent Sales *Afternoons With Emily*, by Rose MacMurray (Little, Brown); *Denial: A Lew Fonesca Mystery*, by Stuart Kaminsky (Forge); *The Shifting Tide*, by Anne Perry (Ballantine); *Midnight Plague*, by Gregg Keizer (G.P. Putnam's Sons); *White Night: A Novel of The Dresden Files*, by Jim Butcher (Roc).

Terms Agent receives 15% commission on domestic sales; 20% commission on foreign sales.

Writers' Conferences Donald Maass: World Science Fiction Convention; Frankfurt Book Fair; Pacific Northwest Writers Conference; Bouchercon. Jennifer Jackson: World Science Fiction Convention; RWA National Conference.

Tips ''We are fiction specialists, also noted for our innovative approach to career planning. Few new clients are accepted, but interested authors should query with a SASE. Works with subagents in all principle foreign countries and Hollywood. No prescriptive nonfiction, picture books or poetry will be considered.''

🌐 GINA MACCOBY LITERARY AGENCY

P.O. Box 60, Chappaqua NY 10514. (914)238-5630. **Contact:** Gina Maccoby. Estab. 1986. Represents 25 clients. Currently handles: 33% nonfiction books; 33% novels; 33% juvenile books; illustrators of children's books.

Represents Nonfiction books, novels, juvenile books. **Considers these nonfiction areas:** Biography/autobiography; current affairs; ethnic/cultural interests; history; juvenile nonfiction; popular culture; women's issues/studies. **Considers these fiction areas:** Juvenile; literary; mainstream/contemporary; mystery/suspense; thriller; young adult.

How to Contact Query with SASE. Considers simultaneous queries. Responds in 3 months to queries. Returns materials only with SASE. Obtains most new clients through recommendations from clients and publishers.

Recent Sales Sold 21 titles in the last year.

Terms Agent receives 15% commission on domestic sales; 25% commission on foreign sales. Charges clients for photocopying. May recover certain costs, such as legal fees or the cost of shipping books by air to Europe or Japan.

🌐 MACGREGOR LITERARY

2373 N.W. 185th Ave., Suite 165, Hillsboro OR 97214. (503)277-8308. E-mail: submissions@macgregorliterary.com. Website: www.macgregorliterary.com. **Contact:** Chip MacGregor. Signatory of WGA. Represents 40 clients. 10% of clients are new/unpublished writers. Currently handles: 40% nonfiction books; 60% novels.

- Prior to his current position, Mr. MacGregor was the senior agent with Alive Communications. Most recently, he was associate publisher for Time-Warner Book Group's Faith Division, and helped put together their Center Street imprint.

Represents Nonfiction books, novels. **Considers these nonfiction areas:** Business/economics; current affairs; history; how-to; humor/satire; popular culture; religious/inspirational; self-help/personal improvement; sports; marriage, parenting. **Considers these fiction areas:** Detective/police/crime; historical; mainstream/contemporary; mystery/suspense; religious/inspirational; romance; thriller; women's/chick lit.

- ⚬ "My specialty has been in career planning with authors—finding commercial ideas, then helping authors bring them to market, and in the midst of that assisting the authors as they get firmly established in their writing careers. I'm probably best known for my work with Christian books over the years, but I've done a fair amount of general market projects as well." Actively seeking authors with a Christian worldview and a growing platform. Does not want to receive fantasy, sci-fi, children's books, poetry or screenplays.

How to Contact Query with SASE. Accepts e-mail queries. No fax queries. Considers simultaneous queries. Responds in 3 weeks to queries. Obtains most new clients through recommendations from others.

Recent Sales *Pop Culture Mom*, by Lynne Spears (Thomas Nelson); *Never Say Diet*, by Chantel Hobbs (Random House); The Amanda Bell Browne series, by Claudia Mair Burney (Simon & Schuster).

Terms Agent receives 15% commission on domestic sales; 15% commission on foreign sales. Offers written contract; 30-day notice must be given to terminate contract. Charges for "exceptional fees" after receiving authors' permission.

Writers' Conferences Blue Ridge Christian Writers' Conference; Write to Publish.

Tips "Seriously consider attending a good writers' conference. It will give you the chance to be face-to-face with people in the industry. Also, if you're a novelist, consider joining one of the national writers' organizations. The American Christian Fiction Writers (ACFW) is a wonderful group for new as well as established writers. And if you're a Christian writer of any kind, check into The Writers View, an online writing group. All of these have proven helpful to writers."

🖉 GILLIAN MACKENZIE AGENCY

544 Cottage Road, South Portland ME 04106-5038. E-mail: query@gillianmackenzieagency.com. Website: www .gillianmackenzieagency.com. **Contact:** Gillian MacKenzie.

- Prior to her current position, Ms. MacKenzie was vice president of Jane Startz Productions, Inc. She began her literary career at Curtis Brown.

Represents Nonfiction books, juvenile books.

- ⚬ Actively seeking adult nonfiction and select children's titles.

How to Contact Query with SASE. Query via e-mail. No fax queries. Obtains most new clients through recommendations from others, solicitations.

Recent Sales *Eight Pieces of Empire*, by Lawrence Scott Sheets (Crown); *The Last Single Woman in America*, by Cindy Guidry (Dutton); The Go Pop series, by Bob Staake (LB Kids).

🖉 RICIA MAINHARDT AGENCY (RMA)

612 Argyle Road, #L5, Brooklyn NY 11230. (718)434-1893. Fax: (718)434-2157. E-mail: ricia@ricia.com. Website: www.ricia.com. **Contact:** Ricia Mainhardt. Estab. 1986. Represents 10 clients. 50% of clients are new/unpublished writers. Currently handles: 40% nonfiction books; 50% novellas; 10% juvenile books.

Represents Nonfiction books, novels, juvenile books. **Considers these nonfiction areas:** Any area of nonfiction that seems commercial enough to sell. **Considers these fiction areas:** Action/adventure; confession; detective/police/crime; erotica; ethnic; family saga; fantasy; feminist; gay/lesbian; glitz; historical; horror; humor/satire; juvenile; literary; mainstream/contemporary; mystery/suspense; psychic/supernatural; regional; romance; science fiction; sports; thriller; westerns/frontier; young adult; women's.

- ⚬ "We are a small boutique agency that provides hands-on service and attention to clients." Actively seeking adult and young adult fiction, nonfiction, picture books for early readers. Does not want to receive poetry, children's books or screenplays.

How to Contact Query with SASE, submit first 2 sample chapter(s), publishing history, author bio, No attachments or diskettes. Accepts e-mail queries. No fax queries. Considers simultaneous queries. Responds in 1 month to queries; 4 months to mss. Returns materials only with SASE. Obtains most new clients through recommendations from others, solicitations.

Recent Sales A full list of this agency's sales is available online.

Terms Agent receives 15% commission on domestic sales. Offers written contract; 90-day notice must be given to terminate contract.

Writers' Conferences Science Fiction Worldcon; Lunacon.

Tips "Be professional; be patient. It takes a long time for me to evaluate all the submissions that come through the door. Pestering phone calls and e-mails are not appreciated. Write the best book you can in your own style and keep an active narrative voice.''

KIRSTEN MANGES LITERARY AGENCY

115 West 29th St., Third Floor, New York NY 10001. E-mail: kirsten@mangeslit.com. Website: www.mangeslit.com. **Contact:** Kirsten Manges.

- • Prior to her current position, Ms. Manges was an agent at Curtis Brown.

Represents Nonfiction books, novels. **Considers these nonfiction areas:** Cooking/foods/nutrition; history; memoirs; multicultural; psychology; science/technology; spirituality; sports; travel; women's issues/studies; journalism, narrative. **Considers these fiction areas:** Women's; commercial, chick lit.

- o— This agency has a focus on women's issues. Actively seeking high quality fiction and nonfiction. ''I'm looking for strong credentials, an original point of view and excellent writing skills. With fiction, I'm looking for well written commercial novels, as well as compelling and provocative literary works.''

How to Contact Query with SASE. Accepts e-mail queries. No fax queries. Obtains most new clients through recommendations from others, solicitations.

Recent Sales *A Rose for the Crown*, by Anne Easter Smith (Touchstone); *Flip-Flopped*, by Jill Smolinski (Griffin); *Financial Identity*, by Bonnie Eaker Weil (Hudson Street Press/Plume). Other clients include Jennifer Vandever, Olympia Vernon.

CAROL MANN AGENCY

55 Fifth Ave., New York NY 10003. (212)206-5635. Fax: (212)675-4809. E-mail: will@carolmannagency.com. Website: www.carolmannagency.com/. **Contact:** Will Sherlin. Estab. 1977. Member of AAR. Represents roughly 200 clients. 15% of clients are new/unpublished writers. Currently handles: 90% nonfiction books; 10% novels.

Member Agents Carol Mann (health/medical, religion, spirituality, self-help, parenting, narrative nonfiction); Laura Yorke; Nicole Bergstrom; Urvashi Chakravarty.

Represents Nonfiction books, novels. **Considers these nonfiction areas:** Anthropology/archaeology; art/architecture/design; biography/autobiography; business/economics; child guidance/parenting; current affairs; ethnic/cultural interests; government/politics/law; health/medicine; history; money/finance; popular culture; psychology; self-help/personal improvement; sociology; sports; women's issues/studies; music. **Considers these fiction areas:** Literary; commercial.

- o— This agency specializes in current affairs, self-help, popular culture, psychology, parenting, and history. Does not want to receive genre fiction (romance, mystery, etc.).

How to Contact Keep initial query/contact to no more than two pages. Responds in 4 weeks to queries.

Recent Sales Clients include novelists Paul Auster and Marita Golden; National Book Award Winner Tim Egan, Hannah Storm, and Willow Bay; Pulitzer Prize-winner Fox Butterfield; bestselling essayist Shelby Steele; sociologist Dr. William Julius Wilson; economist Thomas Sowell; bestselling diet doctors Mary Dan and Michael Eades; ACLU president Nadine Strossen; pundit Mona Charen; memoirist Lauren Winner; photography project editors Rick Smolan and David Cohen (*America 24/7*); Kevin Liles, executive vice president of Warner Music Group and former president of Def Jam Records; and Jermaine Dupri.

Terms Agent receives 15% commission on domestic sales; 20% commission on foreign sales. Offers written contract.

SARAH MANSON LITERARY AGENT

6 Totnes Walk, London N2 0AD United Kingdom. (44)(208)442-0396. E-mail: info@sarahmanson.com. Website: www.sarahmanson.com. **Contact:** Sarah Manson. Estab. 2002. Currently handles: 100% juvenile books.

- • Prior to opening her agency, Ms. Manson worked in academic and children's publishing for 10 years and was a chartered school librarian for 8 years.
- o— This agency specializes in fiction for children and young adults. No picture books. Does not want to receive submissions from writers outside the United Kingdom and the Republic of Ireland.

How to Contact See Web site for full submission guidelines.

Recent Sales This agency prefers not to give information on specific sales.

Terms Agent receives 10% commission on domestic sales; 20% commission on foreign sales. Offers written contract, binding for 1-month.

MANUS & ASSOCIATES LITERARY AGENCY, INC.

425 Sherman Ave., Suite 200, Palo Alto CA 94306. (650)470-5151. Fax: (650)470-5159. E-mail: manuslit@manuslit.com. Website: www.manuslit.com. 445 Park Ave., New York NY 10022. (212)644-8020. Fax (212)644-3374. **Contact:** Janet Manus. **Contact:** Jillian Manus, Jandy Nelson, Stephanie Lee, Donna Levin, Penny Nelson. Estab. 1985. Member of AAR. Represents 75 clients. 30% of clients are new/unpublished writers. Currently handles: 70% nonfiction books; 30% novels.

• Prior to becoming an agent, Ms. Manus was associate publisher of two national magazines and director of development at Warner Bros. and Universal Studios; she has been a literary agent for 20 years.

Member Agents Jandy Nelson, jandy@manuslit.com (self-help, health, memoirs, narrative nonfiction, women's fiction, literary fiction, multicultural fiction, thrillers); Stephanie Lee, slee@manuslit.com (self-help, narrative nonfiction, commercial literary fiction, quirky/edgy fiction, pop culture, pop science); Jillian Manus, jillian @manuslit.com (political, memoirs, self-help, history, sports, women's issues, Latin fiction and nonfiction, thrillers); Penny Nelson, penny@manuslit.com (memoirs, self-help, sports, nonfiction); Dena Fischer (literary fiction, mainstream/commercial fiction, chick lit, women's fiction, historical fiction, ethnic/cultural fiction, narrative nonfiction, parenting, relationships, pop culture, health, sociology, psychology).

Represents Nonfiction books, novels. **Considers these nonfiction areas:** Biography/autobiography; business/ economics; child guidance/parenting; current affairs; ethnic/cultural interests; health/medicine; how-to; memoirs; money/finance; nature/environment; popular culture; psychology; science/technology; self-help/personal improvement; women's issues/studies; Gen X and Gen Y issues; creative nonfiction. **Considers these fiction areas:** Literary; mainstream/contemporary; multicultural; mystery/suspense; thriller; women's; quirky/edgy fiction.

O⚼ "Our agency is unique in the way that we not only sell the material, but we edit, develop concepts, and participate in the marketing effort. We specialize in large, conceptual fiction and nonfiction, and always value a project that can be sold in the TV/feature film market." Actively seeking high-concept thrillers, commercial literary fiction, women's fiction, celebrity biographies, memoirs, multicultural fiction, popular health, women's empowerment and mysteries. No horror, romance, science fiction, fantasy, Western, young adult, children's, poetry, cookbooks or magazine articles.

How to Contact Query with SASE. If requested, submit outline, 2-3 sample chapters. All queries should be sent to the California office. Accepts e-mail queries. No fax queries. Considers simultaneous queries. Responds in 3 months to queries; 3 months to mss. Returns materials only with SASE. Obtains most new clients through recommendations from others, solicitations, conferences.

Recent Sales *Nothing Down for the 2000s* and *Multiple Streams of Income for the 2000s*, by Robert Allen; *Missed Fortune* and *Missed Fortune 101*, by Doug Andrew; *Cracking the Millionaire Code*, by Mark Victor Hansen and Robert Allen; *Stress Free for Good*, by Dr. Fred Luskin and Dr. Ken Pelletier; *The Mercy of Thin Air*, by Ronlyn Domangue; *The Fine Art of Small Talk*, by Debra Fine; *Bone Man of Bonares*, by Terry Tarnoff.

Terms Agent receives 15% commission on domestic sales; 20-25% commission on foreign sales. Offers written contract, binding for 2 years; 60-day notice must be given to terminate contract. Charges for photocopying and postage/UPS.

Writers' Conferences Maui Writers' Conference; San Diego State University Writers' Conference; Willamette Writers' Conference; BookExpo America; MEGA Book Marketing University.

Tips "Research agents using a variety of sources."

◐ MARCH TENTH, INC.

4 Myrtle St., Haworth NJ 07641-1740. (201)387-6551. Fax: (201)387-6552. E-mail: hchoron@aol.com; schoron @aol.com. Website: www.marchtenthinc.com. **Contact:** Harry Choron, vice president. Estab. 1982. Represents 40 clients. 30% of clients are new/unpublished writers. Currently handles: 100% nonfiction books.

Represents Nonfiction books, novels. **Considers these nonfiction areas:** Biography/autobiography; current affairs; health/medicine; history; humor/satire; language/literature/criticism; music/dance; popular culture; theater/film.

O⚼ "We prefer to work with published/established writers." Does not want to receive children's or young adult novels, plays, screenplays or poetry.

How to Contact Query with SASE. Include your genre, bio, qualifications, short synopsis and 10 pages if submitting fiction. Considers simultaneous queries. Responds in 1 month to queries. Returns materials only with SASE.

Recent Sales Sold 24 titles in the last year. *Bruce Springsteen on Tour*, by Dave Marsh (Bloomsbury); *Art of the Chopper*, by Tom Zimberoff; *Bruce Springstein Live*, by Dave Marsh; *Complete Annotated Grateful Dead Lyrics*, by David Dodd.

Terms Agent receives 15% commission on domestic sales; 20% commission on foreign sales; 20% commission on dramatic rights sales. Charges clients for postage, photocopying, overseas phone expenses. Does not require expense money upfront.

◉ THE DENISE MARCIL LITERARY AGENCY, INC.

156 Fifth Ave., Suite 625, New York NY 10010. (212)337-3402. Fax: (212)727-2688. Website: www.DeniseMarcil Agency.com. **Contact:** Denise Marcil, Maura Kye-Casella. Estab. 1977. Member of AAR.

- Prior to opening her agency, Ms. Marcil served as an editorial assistant with Avon Books and as an assistant editor with Simon & Schuster.

Member Agents Denise Marcil (women's commercial fiction, thrillers, suspense, popular reference, how-to, self-help, health, business, and parenting.

O→ This agency is currently not taking on new authors.

Recent Sales Sold 43 titles in the last year. *Welcome to Serenity*, by Sherryl Woods; *The Potable Pediatrician*; *Super Seniors*, by William Sears and Peter Sears; *In High Gear*, by Gina Wilkins; *The Anti-Alzheimers' Prescription*, by Vincent Fortanasce.

Terms Agent receives 15% commission on domestic sales; 20% commission on foreign sales. Offers written contract, binding for 2 years; 100% of business is derived from commissions on ms sales. Charges $100/year for postage, photocopying, long-distance calls, etc.

Writers' Conferences Pacific Northwest Writers' Conference; RWA National Conference.

N ◻ SUSAN MARLANE LITERARY AGENCY

P.O. Box 4, Simi Valley CA 93062. Website: www.susanmarlaneliteraryagency.com. **Contact:** Susan Marlane. Estab. 2006. 80% of clients are new/unpublished writers. Currently handles: 90% nonfiction books; 10% novels.

Member Agents Prior to becoming an agent, Ms. Marlane was a freelance editor.

Represents Nonfiction books, novels. **Considers these nonfiction areas:** Biography/autobiography; business/economics; child guidance/parenting; cooking/foods/nutrition; crafts/hobbies; current affairs; education; government/politics/law; health/medicine; how-to; humor/satire; interior design/decorating; memoirs; music/dance; nature/environment; popular culture; psychology; religious/inspirational; science/technology; self-help/personal improvement; true crime/investigative; women's issues/studies; entertainment/film/celebrity; weight loss. **Considers these fiction areas:** Action/adventure; confession; detective/police/crime; family saga; historical; humor/satire; literary; mainstream/contemporary; mystery/suspense; religious/inspirational; romance; thriller; women's.

O→ Actively seeking nonfiction: self help, current affairs, popular culture, money/finance, weight loss and Christian works. Does not want to receive short stories, sexually explicit materials, fantasy or poetry.

How to Contact Query with SASE, submit a one-page query letter or book proposal. Include your plans for promoting the work. Snail mail queries only. Considers simultaneous queries. Responds in 4-8 weeks to queries; 1-3 months to mss. Returns materials only with SASE. Obtains most new clients through recommendations from others, solicitations.

Terms Agent receives 15% commission on domestic sales; 20% commission on foreign sales. Offers written contract; 30-day notice must be given to terminate contract.

Tips "Carefully proofread your work before sending. Make sure it's the best it can be. Be professional."

⊕ THE MARSH AGENCY, LTD

50 Albemarle Street, London England W1S 4BD, United Kingdom. (44)(207)399-2800. Fax: (44)(207)399-2801. Website: www.marsh-agency.co.uk. Estab. 1994.

Member Agents Caroline Hardman, rights executive and junior agent (caroline@marsh-agency.co.uk); Jessica Woollard, agent (jessica@marsh-agency.co.uk, specialties: literary fiction, narrative nonfiction, international literature—especially from the Far East); Geraldine Cooke, agent (geraldine@marsh-agency.co.uk); Leyla Moghadam, agent (leyla@marsh-agency.co.uk; she is concentrating on English-language sales).

Represents Novels.

O→ This agency was founded "as an international rights specialist for literary agents and publishers in the United Kingdom, the U.S., Canada and New Zealand, for whom we sell foreign rights on a commission basis. We work directly with publishers in all the major territories and in the majority of the smaller ones; sometimes in conjunction with local representatives." Actively seeking crime novels.

How to Contact Query with SASE. No fax queries. Obtains most new clients through recommendations from others, solicitations.

Recent Sales A full list of clients and sales is available online.

Tips Use this agency's online form to send a generic e-mail message.

♥ THE EVAN MARSHALL AGENCY

Six Tristam Place, Pine Brook NJ 07058-9445. (973)882-1122. Fax: (973)882-3099. E-mail: evanmarshall@thenovelist.com. **Contact:** Evan Marshall. Estab. 1987. Member of AAR, MWA, RWA, Sisters in Crime. Currently handles: 100% novels.

Represents Novels. **Considers these fiction areas:** Action/adventure; erotica; ethnic; historical; horror; humor/satire; literary; mainstream/contemporary; mystery/suspense; religious/inspirational; romance (contemporary, gothic, historical, regency); science fiction; westerns/frontier.

How to Contact Query first with SASE; do not enclose material. No e-mail queries. Responds in 1 week to queries; 3 months to mss. Obtains most new clients through recommendations from others.

Recent Sales *Last Known Victim*, by Erica Spindler (Mira); *Julia's Chocolates*, by Cathy Lamb (Kensington); *Maverick*, by Joan Hohl (Silhouette).

Terms Agent receives 15% commission on domestic sales; 20% commission on foreign sales. Offers written contract.

◙ THE MARTELL AGENCY

545 Madison Ave., Seventh Floor, New York NY 10022-4219. Fax: (212)317-2676. E-mail: afmartell@aol.com. **Contact:** Alice Martell.

Represents Nonfiction books, novels. **Considers these nonfiction areas:** Business/economics; health/medicine (fitness); history; memoirs; multicultural; psychology; self-help/personal improvement; women's issues/studies. **Considers these fiction areas:** Mystery/suspense; thriller (espionage); women's; suspense, commercial.

> O⊸ Actively seeking mysteries.

How to Contact Query with SASE, submit sample chapters, SASE. Submit via snail mail. No e-mail or fax queries.

Recent Sales *Peddling Peril: The Secret Nuclear Arms Trade*, by David Albright and Joel Wit (Free Press); *Hunger Point: A Novel*, by Jillian Medoff (Harpercollins); *America's Women: Four Hundred Years of Dolls, Drudges, Helpmates, and Heroines*, by Gail Collins (William Morrow). Other clients include Serena Bass, Thomas E. Ricks, Janice Erlbaum.

◙ MARTIN LITERARY MANAGEMENT

17328 Ventura Blvd., Suite 138, Encino (LA) CA 91316. (818)595-1130. Fax: (818)715-0418. E-mail: sharlene@martinliterarymanagement.com. Website: www.MartinLiteraryManagement.com. Ronnie's address: 37 West 20th St., Suite 804 , New York, NY 10011; Ginny's address: 2511 West Schaumburg Road, No. 217, Schaumburg, IL 60184 (312) 480-5754 **Contact:** Sharlene Martin. Estab. 2002. Member of AAR. 75% of clients are new/unpublished writers.

• Prior to becoming an agent, Ms. Martin worked in film/TV production and acquisitions.

Member Agents Sharlene Martin (nonfiction); Ronnie Gramazio (literary, historical, mass market/commercial, and fantasy, children's, true crime, and select nonfiction); Ginny Weissman (writers with a developed platform and a book that fits the Mind, Body, Spirit genre, including health, spirituality, religion, diet, exercise, psychology, relationships, and metaphysics).

Represents Nonfiction books, novels. **Considers these nonfiction areas:** Biography/autobiography; business/economics; child guidance/parenting; current affairs; health/medicine; history; how-to; humor/satire; memoirs; popular culture; psychology; religious/inspirational; self-help/personal improvement; true crime/investigative; women's issues/studies. **Considers these fiction areas:** Fantasy; historical; juvenile; literary.

> O⊸ This agency has strong ties to film/TV. Actively seeking nonfiction that is highly commercial and that can be adapted to film.

How to Contact Query with SASE, submit outline, 2 sample chapters. Prefers e-mail queries. Will request supporting materials if interested. No phone queries. Do not send materials unless requested. Submission guidelines defined on Web site. Accepts e-mail queries. No fax queries. Considers simultaneous queries. Responds in 1 week to queries; 3-4 weeks to mss. Returns materials only with SASE. Obtains most new clients through recommendations from others.

Recent Sales *Prince of Darkness—Richard Perle: The Kingdom, The Power, and the End of Empire in America*, by Alan Weisman (Union Square Press/Sterling); *Truth At Last: The Real Story of James Earl Ray*, by John Larry Ray with Lyndon Barsten (Lyons Press).

Terms Agent receives 15% commission on domestic sales; 25% commission on foreign sales. Offers written contract, binding for 1 year; 1-month notice must be given to terminate contract. Charges author for postage and copying if material is not sent electronically. 99 percent of materials are sent electronically to minimize charges to author for postage and copying.

Tips "Have a strong platform for nonfiction. Please don't call. I welcome e-mail. I'm very responsive when I'm interested in a query and work hard to get my clients materials in the best possible shape before submissions. Do your homework prior to submission and only submit your best efforts. Please review our Web site carefully to make sure we're a good match for your work."

◙ HAROLD MATSON CO. INC.

276 Fifth Ave., New York NY 10001. (212)679-4490. Fax: (212)545-1224. **Contact:** Jonathan Matson. Estab. 1937. Member of AAR.

Member Agents Jonathan Matson (literary, adult); Ben Camardi (literary, adult, dramatic).

Represents Novels.

Recent Sales *The Unwalled City*, by Xu Xi (Chameleon Press); *The Mermaid That Came Between Them*, by Carol Ann Sima (Coffee House Press); *The Zen Commandments*, by Dean Sluyter (Penguin Putnam).

MAX AND CO., A LITERARY AGENCY AND SOCIAL CLUB

115 Hosea Ave., Cincinnati OH, 45220. (201)704-2483. E-mail: mmurphy@maxlit.com. Website: www.maxliter ary.org. **Contact:** Michael Murphy. Estab. 2007.

- Prior to his current position, Mr. Murphy was with Queen Literary Agency. He has been in book publishing since 1981. His first 13 years were with Random House, where he was a vice president. Later, he ran William Morrow as their publisher, up until the company's acquisition & merger into HarperCollins. **Considers these nonfiction areas:** Humor/satire; memoirs; narrative nonfiction. **Considers these fiction areas:** Literary.
- Actively seeking narrative nonfiction, memoir, literary fiction, humor, and visual books. Does not want to receive genre fiction nor YA and children's books.

How to Contact E-queries preferred. Include brief synopsis, author bio and sample writing.

Recent Sales *Down and Out on Murder Mile*, by Tony O'Neill (HarperCollins);*Family Sentence*, by Jeanine Cornillot (Beacon Press); *Hero of the Underground*, by Jason Peter (St. Martin's); *Familial Ground* (Princeton Architectural)

MARGRET MCBRIDE LITERARY AGENCY

7744 Fay Ave., Suite 201, La Jolla CA 92037. (858)454-1550. Fax: (858)454-2156. E-mail: staff@mcbridelit.com. Website: www.mcbrideliterary.com. **Contact:** Michael Daley, submissions manager. Estab. 1980. Member of AAR, Authors Guild. Represents 55 clients.

- Prior to opening her agency, Ms. McBride worked at Random House, Ballantine Books, and Warner Books.

Represents Nonfiction books, novels. **Considers these nonfiction areas:** Biography/autobiography; business/ economics; cooking/foods/nutrition; current affairs; ethnic/cultural interests; government/politics/law; health/ medicine; history; how-to; money/finance; music/dance; popular culture; psychology; science/technology; self-help/personal improvement; sociology; women's issues/studies; style. **Considers these fiction areas:** Action/ adventure; detective/police/crime; ethnic; historical; humor/satire; literary; mainstream/contemporary; mystery/suspense; thriller; westerns/frontier.

- This agency specializes in mainstream fiction and nonfiction. Does not want to receive screenplays, romance, poetry, or children's/young adult.

How to Contact Query with synopsis, bio, SASE. No e-mail or fax queries. Considers simultaneous queries. Responds in 4-6 weeks to queries; 6-8 weeks to mss. Returns materials only with SASE.

Terms Agent receives 15% commission on domestic sales; 25% commission on foreign sales. Charges for overnight delivery and photocopying.

ANNE MCDERMID & ASSOCIATES, LTD

83 Willcocks St., Toronto ON M5S 1C9, Canada. (416)324-8845. Fax: (416)324-8870. E-mail: info@mcdermidage ncy.com. Website: www.mcdermidagency.com. **Contact:** Anne McDermid. Estab. 1996. Represents 60+ clients.

Member Agents Lise Henderson, Anne McDermid.

Represents Nonfiction books, novels. **Considers these nonfiction areas:** Biography/autobiography; history; memoirs; science/technology; travel; true crime/investigative.

- Does not want to receive children's writing, self-help, business or computer books, gardening and cookery, fantasy, science fiction or romance.

How to Contact Submission instructions online. Obtains most new clients through recommendations from others.

Recent Sales *La-La Joy*, by Michelle Kim Mossop (Groundwood Books); *Empress of Asia*, by Adam Lewis Schroeder (Thomas Dunne Books); *Radiance*, by Shaena Lambert; *The Horseman's Graves*, by Jacqueline Baker.

MCINTOSH & OTIS

353 Lexington Ave., 15th Floor, New York NY 10016. E-mail: info@mcintoshandotis.com. Website: www.mcint oshandotis.net/. Member of AAR.

Member Agents Eugene H. Winick; Elizabeth Winick (literary fiction, women's fiction, historical fiction, and mystery/suspense, along with narrative nonfiction, spiritual/self-help, history and current affairs. Elizabeth represents numerous New York T); Edward Necarsulmer IV; Rebecca Strauss (nonfiction, literary and commercial fiction, women's fiction, memoirs, and pop culture); Cate Martin; Ina Winick (psychology, self-help, and mystery/suspense); Ian Polonsky (Film/TV/Stage/Radio).

Represents Nonfiction books, novels, movie scripts, feature film. **Considers these script subject areas:** General.

How to Contact Send a query, synopsis, two sample chapters, and SASE by regular mail. For nonfiction, include bio and outline. For screenplays, send a query letter, synopsis, and SASE by regular mail. Responds in 8 weeks to queries.

Recent Sales Paperback rights to Donald J. Sobol's Encyclopedia Brown series (Puffin).

Tips "Please send a query letter, synopsis, two sample chapters, and SASE by regular mail. For non-fiction, please include a biography and outline as well. For screenplays, please send a query letter, synopsis, and SASE by regular mail. No phone calls please."

MENDEL MEDIA GROUP, LLC

115 West 30th St., Suite 800, New York NY 10001. (646)239-9896. Fax: (212)685-4717. E-mail: scott@mendelme dia.com. Website: www.mendelmedia.com. Estab. 2002. Member of AAR. Represents 40-60 clients.

- Prior to becoming an agent, Mr. Mendel was an academic. "I taught American literature, Yiddish, Jewish studies, and literary theory at the University of Chicago and the University of Illinois at Chicago while working on my PhD in English. I also worked as a freelance technical writer and as the managing editor of a healthcare magazine. In 1998, I began working for the late Jane Jordan Browne, a long-time agent in the book publishing world."

Represents Nonfiction books, novels, scholarly books (with potential for broad/popular appeal). **Considers these nonfiction areas:** Americana; animals; anthropology/archaeology; art/architecture/design; biography/ autobiography; business/economics; child guidance/parenting; cooking/foods/nutrition; current affairs; education; ethnic/cultural interests; gardening; gay/lesbian issues; government/politics/law; health/medicine; history; how-to; humor/satire; language/literature/criticism; memoirs; military/war; money/finance; multicultural; music/dance; nature/environment; philosophy; popular culture; psychology; recreation; regional; religious/inspirational; science/technology; self-help/personal improvement; sex; sociology; software; spirituality; sports; true crime/investigative; women's issues/studies; Jewish topics; creative nonfiction. **Considers these fiction areas:** Action/adventure; contemporary issues; detective/police/crime; erotica; ethnic; feminist; gay/lesbian; glitz; historical; humor/satire; juvenile; literary; mainstream/contemporary; mystery/suspense; picture books; religious/inspirational; romance; sports; thriller; young adult; Jewish fiction.

- "I am interested in major works of history, current affairs, biography, business, politics, economics, science, major memoirs, narrative nonfiction, and other sorts of general nonfiction. Actively seeking new, major or definitive work on a subject of broad interest, or a controversial, but authoritative, new book on a subject that affects many people's lives. I also represent more light-hearted nonfiction projects, such as gift or novelty books, when they suit the market particularly well." Does not want queries about projects written years ago that were unsuccessfully shopped to a long list of trade publishers by either the author or another agent. "I am specifically not interested in reading short, category romances (regency, time travel, paranormal, etc.), horror novels, supernatural stories, poetry, original plays, or film scripts."

How to Contact Query with SASE. Do not e-mail or fax queries. For nonfiction, include a complete, fully-edited book proposal with sample chapters. For fiction, include a complete synopsis and no more than 20 pages of sample text. Responds in 2 weeks to queries; 4-6 weeks to mss. Returns materials only with SASE. Obtains most new clients through recommendations from others.

Terms Agent receives 15% commission on domestic sales; 20% commission on foreign sales. Offers written contract, binding for 2 years; 1-month notice must be given to terminate contract. Charges clients for ms duplication, expedited delivery services (when necessary), any overseas shipping, telephone calls/faxes necessary for marketing the author's foreign rights.

Writers' Conferences BookExpo America; Frankfurt Book Fair; London Book Fair; RWA National Conference; Modern Language Association Convention; Jerusalem Book Fair.

Tips "While I am not interested in being flattered by a prospective client, it does matter to me that she knows why she is writing to me in the first place. Is one of my clients a colleague of hers? Has she read a book by one of my clients that led her to believe I might be interested in her work? Authors of descriptive nonfiction should have real credentials and expertise in their subject areas, either as academics, journalists, or policy experts, and authors of prescriptive nonfiction should have legitimate expertise and considerable experience communicating their ideas in seminars and workshops, in a successful business, through the media, etc."

SCOTT MEREDITH LITERARY AGENCY

200 W. 57th St., Suite 904, New York NY 10019. (646)274-1970. Fax: (212)977-5997. E-mail: aklebanoff@rosetta books.com. Website: www.scottmeredith.com. **Contact:** Arthur Klebanoff, CEO. Estab. 1946; adheres to the AAR canon of ethics. Represents 20 clients. 0% of clients are new/unpublished writers. Currently handles: 90% nonfiction books; 5% novels; 5% textbooks.

- Prior to becoming an agent, Mr. Klebanoff was a lawyer.

Represents Nonfiction books, textbooks. **Considers these nonfiction areas:** Any category leading entry.

- This agency's specialty lies in category nonfiction publishing programs. Actively seeking category leading nonfiction. Does not want to receive first fiction projects.

How to Contact Query with SASE, submit proposal package, author bio. Accepts e-mail queries. No fax queries. Considers simultaneous queries. Responds in 1 week to queries; 2 weeks to mss. Returns materials only with SASE. Obtains most new clients through recommendations from others.

Recent Sales Sold 10 titles in the last year. *Positively American*, by U.S. Sen. Chuck Schumer (Rodale); *The New American Story*, by Bill Bradley (Random House); *The Conscience of a Liberal*, by Paul Krugman (Norton); *The Silver Palate Cookbook: 25th Anniversary Edition*, by Julee Rosso and Sheila Lukins (Workman); *Michel Thomas Language Program*, by Michel Thomas (Hodder and Stoughton McGraw Hill); *Roots: 30th Anniversary Edition*, by Alex Haley (Vanguard Press/Perseus). Other clients include Paul Krugman, Mayo Clinic, Roger Tory Peterson, Linda Goodman, Janson Family (Janson's History of Art), Michael Steinhardt.

Terms Agent receives 15% commission on domestic sales; 25% commission on foreign sales. Offers written contract.

⊘ JENNY MEYER LITERARY AGENCY

115 W 29th St., New York NY 10001. (212)564-9898. Fax: (212)564-6044. **Contact:** Jenny Meyer.

● Prior to her current position, Ms. Meyer was a former associate at the Agnes Krup Literary Agency.

Member Agents Jenny Meyer; Aaron Rich (aaron@meyerlit.com).

Represents Foreign rights.

o→ This agency specializes in selling foreign rights.

How to Contact Do not query this agency.

Recent Sales Foreign rights to *The Fifth Postulate*, by Jason Socrates Bardi (Wiley).

⊙ DORIS S. MICHAELS LITERARY AGENCY, INC.

1841 Broadway, Suite 903, New York NY 10023. (212)265-9474. Fax: (212)265-9480. E-mail: query@dsmagency .com. Website: www.dsmagency.com. **Contact:** Doris S. Michaels, president. Estab. 1994. Member of AAR, WNBA.

Represents Novels. **Considers these fiction areas:** Literary (with commercial appeal and strong screen potential).

How to Contact Query by e-mail; see submission guidelines on Web site. Obtains most new clients through recommendations from others, conferences.

Recent Sales *Cheap and Easy: Fast Food for Fast Girls*, by Sandra Bark and Alexis Kanfer; *Why Did I Marry You Anyway?*, by Barbara Bartlein; *You Look Too Young to be a Mom*, by Deborah Davis.

Terms Agent receives 15% commission on domestic sales; 20% commission on foreign sales. Offers written contract, binding for 1 year; 1-month notice must be given to terminate contract. 100% of business is derived from commissions on ms sales. Charges clients for office expenses, not to exceed $150 without written permission.

Writers' Conferences BookExpo America; Frankfurt Book Fair; London Book Fair; Maui Writers Conference.

⊙ MARTHA MILLARD LITERARY AGENCY

50 W. 67th St., #1G, New York NY 10023. (212)787-7769. Fax: (212)787-7867. **Contact:** Martha Millard. Estab. 1980. Member of AAR, SFWA. Represents 50 clients. Currently handles: 25% nonfiction books; 65% novels; 10% story collections.

● Prior to becoming an agent, Ms. Millard worked in editorial departments of several publishers and was vice president at another agency for more than four years.

Represents Nonfiction books, novels. **Considers these nonfiction areas:** Art/architecture/design; biography/autobiography; business/economics; child guidance/parenting; cooking/foods/nutrition; current affairs; education; ethnic/cultural interests; health/medicine; history; how-to; juvenile nonfiction; memoirs; money/finance; music/dance; New Age/metaphysics; photography; popular culture; psychology; self-help/personal improvement; theater/film; true crime/investigative; women's issues/studies. **Considers these fiction areas:** Fantasy; mystery/suspense; romance; science fiction.

How to Contact No unsolicited queries. **Referrals only.** No e-mail or fax queries. Returns materials only with SASE. Obtains most new clients through recommendations from others.

Recent Sales *The Dragons of Babel*, by Michael Swanwick (Tor); *Nazi Art: The Secret of Post-War History*, by Gregory Maertz (Yale University Press); *Playing With the HP Way*, by Peter Burrows (John Wiley & Sons); *Restore Yourself*, by James Simm and Victoria Houston (Berkley).

Terms Agent receives 15% commission on domestic sales; 20% commission on foreign sales. Offers written contract.

⊙ THE MILLER AGENCY

Film Center, 630 Ninth Ave., Suite 1102, New York NY 10036. (212) 206-0913. Fax: (212) 206-1473. E-mail: angela@milleragency.net. Website: www.milleragency.net. **Contact:** Angela Miller, Sharon Bowers, Jennifer Griffin. Estab. 1990. Represents 100 clients. 5% of clients are new/unpublished writers.

Represents Nonfiction books. **Considers these nonfiction areas:** Anthropology/archaeology; art/architecture/design; biography/autobiography; business/economics; child guidance/parenting; cooking/foods/nutrition; current affairs; ethnic/cultural interests; gay/lesbian issues; health/medicine; language/literature/criticism; New Age/metaphysics; psychology; self-help/personal improvement; sports; women's issues/studies.

O→ This agency specializes in nonfiction, multicultural arts, psychology, self-help, cookbooks, biography, travel, memoir, and sports. Fiction is considered selectively.

How to Contact Query with SASE, outline, a few sample chapters. Considers simultaneous queries. Responds in 1 week to queries. Obtains most new clients through referrals.

Recent Sales Sold 25 titles in the last year.

Terms Agent receives 15% commission on domestic sales; 20-25% commission on foreign sales. Offers written contract, binding for 2 years; 2-month notice must be given to terminate contract. 100% of business is derived from commissions on ms sales. Charges clients for postage (express mail or messenger services) and photocopying.

◐ PATRICIA MOOSBRUGGER LITERARY AGENCY

165 Bennet Ave., #6M, New York NY 10040. Website: www.pmagency.net. **Contact:** Patricia Moosbrugger. Member of AAR.

Represents Nonfiction books.

How to Contact Query with SASE.

Recent Sales *Indiana, Indiana*, by Laird Hunt (Coffee House Press); *Surrendered Child: A Birth Mother's Journey*, by Karen Salyer McElmurray (University of Georgia Press).

◐ HOWARD MORHAIM LITERARY AGENCY

30 Pierrepont St., Brooklyn NY 11201. (718)222-8400. Fax: (718)222-5056. Website: www.morhaimliterary.com/. Member of AAR.

Member Agents Howard Morhaim, Kate McKean, Brandi Bowles, Katie Menick.

Represents Fiction, young adult fiction, nonfiction.

O→ Actively seeking fiction, nonfiction and young-adult novels.

How to Contact Query via e-mail with cover letter and three sample chapters.

◐ WILLIAM MORRIS AGENCY, INC.

1325 Avenue of the Americas, New York NY 10019. (212)586-5100. Fax: (212)246-3583. Website: www.wma.com. Alternate address: One William Morris Place, Beverly Hills CA 90212. (310)859-4000. Fax: (310)859-4462. **Contact:** Literary Department Coordinator. Member of AAR.

Member Agents Owen Laster; Jennifer Rudolph Walsh; Suzanne Gluck; Joni Evans; Tracy Fisher; Mel Berger; Jay Mandel; Peter Franklin; Lisa Grubka; Jonathan Pecursky.

Represents Nonfiction books, novels, feature film, TV scripts.

O→ Does not want to receive screenplays.

How to Contact Query with synopsis, publication history, SASE. Send book queries to the NYC address. Considers simultaneous queries.

Recent Sales This agency prefers not to share information on specific sales.

Terms Agent receives 15% commission on domestic sales; 20% commission on foreign sales.

Tips "If you are a prospective writer interested in submitting to the William Morris Agency in **London**, please follow these guidelines: For all queries, please send a cover letter, synopsis, and the first three chapters (up to 50 pages) by e-mail only to: ldnsubmissions@wma.com."

◐ HENRY MORRISON, INC.

105 S. Bedford Road, Suite 306A, Mt. Kisco NY 10549. (914)666-3500. Fax: (914)241-7846. **Contact:** Henry Morrison. Estab. 1965. Signatory of WGA. Represents 53 clients. 5% of clients are new/unpublished writers. Currently handles: 5% nonfiction books; 95% novels.

Represents Nonfiction books, novels. **Considers these nonfiction areas:** Anthropology/archaeology; biography/autobiography; government/politics/law; history. **Considers these fiction areas:** Action/adventure; detective/police/crime; family saga; historical.

How to Contact Query with SASE. Responds in 2 weeks to queries; 3 months to mss. Obtains most new clients through recommendations from others.

Recent Sales Sold 15 titles in the last year. *The Bourne Sanction*, by Eric Lustbader (Grand Central); *The Vampire of New York*, by R.L. Stevens (Signet); *The Cortez Mask*, by Paul Christopher (Signet); *City of God*, by Beverly Swerling (S&S); *Cold Plague*, by Dan Kalla (Forge); *Mausoleum*, by Justin Scott (Poisoned Press); *Spade & Archer*, by Joe Gores (Knopf); *Ghosts*, by Charles W. Henderson. Other clients include Daniel Cohen, Joel N. Ross, Dan Kalla, Christopher Hyde, Charles W. Henderson.

Terms Agent receives 15% commission on domestic sales; 25% commission on foreign sales. Charges clients for ms copies, bound galleys, finished books for submissions to publishers, movie producers and foreign publishers.

◉ MORTIMER LITERARY AGENCY

52645 Paui Road, Aguanga CA 92536. (951)763-2600. E-mail: kellymortimer@mortimerliterary.com. Website: www.mortimerliterary.com. **Contact:** Kelly L. Mortimer. Estab. 2006. Member of American Christian Fiction Writers. Represents 15 clients. 70% of clients are new/unpublished writers. Currently handles: 5% nonfiction books; 90% novels; 5% juvenile books.

 • Prior to becoming an agent, Ms. Mortimer was a freelance writer and the CFO of Microvector, Inc. She has a degree in contract law, and was nominated for the ACGW "Agent of the Year" award.

Represents Nonfiction books, novels, novellas, juvenile books (young adult and middle grade). **Considers these nonfiction areas:** Religious/inspirational; self-help/personal improvement; relationship advice, finance. **Considers these fiction areas:** Action/adventure; detective/police/crime; historical; mainstream/contemporary; mystery/suspense; religious/inspirational; romance; thriller; young adult; middle grade.

 ⟳ "I keep a short client list to give my writers personal attention. I edit my clients' manuscripts as necessary. I send manuscripts out to pre-selected editors in a timely fashion, and send my clients monthly reports. I am not seeking new clients now, but will be in the future."

How to Contact Query with SASE. Check the Web site for current submission info. E-queries and partials only. Considers simultaneous queries. Responds in 4 months to mss. Returns materials only with SASE. Obtains most new clients through recommendations from others, solicitations, conferences.

Recent Sales Sold 9 titles in the last year. *Bayou Justice*, by Robin Caroll; *Courting Miss Adelaide*, by Janey Dean; *Creating Your Own Destiny: How to Get Exactly What You Want Out of Life*, by Patrick Snow.

Terms Agent receives 15% commission on domestic sales; 20% commission on foreign sales. Offers written contract. "I charge for postage—only the amount I pay and it comes out of the author's advance. The writer provides me with copies of their manuscripts."

Writers' Conferences RWA, ACFW.

Tips "Follow submission guidelines on the Web site, submit your best work and don't query unless your manuscript is finished. Don't send material or mss that I haven't requested."

◉ DEE MURA LITERARY

269 West Shore Drive, Massapequa NY 11758-8225. (516)795-1616. Fax: (516)795-8797. E-mail: query@deemur aliterary.com. **Contact:** Dee Mura, Karen Roberts, Bobbie Sokol, David Brozain. Estab. 1987. Signatory of WGA. 50% of clients are new/unpublished writers.

 • Prior to opening her agency, Ms. Mura was a public relations executive with a roster of film and entertainment clients and worked in editorial for major weekly news magazines. **Considers these nonfiction areas:** Agriculture/horticulture; animals; anthropology/archaeology; biography/autobiography; business/economics; child guidance/parenting; computers/electronic; current affairs; education; ethnic/cultural interests; gay/lesbian issues; government/politics/law; health/medicine; history; how-to; humor/satire; juvenile nonfiction; memoirs; military/war; money/finance; nature/environment; science/technology; self-help/personal improvement; sociology; sports; travel; true crime/investigative; women's issues/studies. **Considers these fiction areas:** Action/adventure; contemporary issues; detective/police/crime (and espionage); ethnic; experimental; family saga; fantasy; feminist; gay/lesbian; glitz; historical; humor/satire; juvenile; literary; mainstream/contemporary; mystery/suspense; psychic/supernatural; regional; romance (contemporary, gothic, historical, regency); science fiction; sports; thriller; westerns/frontier; young adult; political. **Considers these script subject areas:** Action/adventure; cartoon/animation; comedy; contemporary issues; detective/police/crime (and espionage); family saga; fantasy; feminist; gay/lesbian; glitz; historical; horror; juvenile; mainstream; mystery/suspense; psychic/supernatural; religious/inspirational; romantic comedy; romantic drama; science fiction; sports; teen; thriller; western/frontier.

 ⟳ "Some of us have special interests and some of us encourage you to share your passion and work with us." Does not want to receive ideas for sitcoms, novels, films, etc., or queries without SASEs.

How to Contact Query with SASE. Accepts e-mail queries (no attachments). If via e-mail, put "query" and your genre in subject line. If via snail mail, include first few chapters or full proposal. No fax queries. Considers simultaneous queries. Only responds if interested; responds as soon as possible. Returns materials only with SASE. Obtains most new clients through recommendations from others, queries.

Recent Sales Sold more than 40 titles and sold 35 scripts in the last year.

Terms Agent receives 15% commission on domestic sales; 20% commission on foreign sales. Offers written contract. Charges clients for photocopying, mailing expenses, overseas/long distance phone calls/faxes.

Tips "Please include a paragraph on your background, even if you have no literary background, and a brief synopsis of the project."

❷ ERIN MURPHY LITERARY AGENCY

2700 Woodlands Village, #300-458, Flagstaff AZ 86001-7172. (928)525-2056. Fax: (928)525-2480. **Contact:** Erin Murphy.

> **O─** This agency only represents children's books. "We do not accept unsolicited manuscripts or queries. We consider new clients by referral or personal contact only."

❷ MUSE LITERARY MANAGEMENT

189 Waverly Place, #4, New York NY 10014. (212)925-3721. E-mail: museliterarymgmt@aol.com. Website: www.museliterary.com/. **Contact:** Deborah Carter. Estab. 1998. Member of MediaBistro, Author's Guild, SC-BWI, International Thriller Writers. Represents 10 clients. 80% of clients are new/unpublished writers.

> • Prior to starting her agency, Ms. Carter trained with an AAR literary agent and worked in the music business and as a talent scout for record companies in artist management. She has a BA in English and music from Washington Square University College at NYU.

Represents Novels, short story collections, novellas, juvenile books. **Considers these nonfiction areas:** Narrative-only nonfiction (memoir, outdoors, music, writing). Please query other narrative nonfiction subjects. **Considers these fiction areas:** Action/adventure; detective/police/crime; picture books; young adult; espionage; middle-grade novels; literary short story collections, literary fiction with popular appeal, mystery/suspense/thriller (no cozies).

> **O─** Specializes in manuscript development, the sale and administration of print, performance, and foreign rights to literary works, and post-publication publicity and appearances. Actively seeking progressive, African-American, and multicultural fiction for adults and children in the U.S. market. Does not want to receive category fiction (romance, chick lit, fantasy, science fiction, horror), or fiction/nonfiction with religious/spiritual matter, illness or victimhood.

How to Contact Query with SASE. Query via e-mail (no attachments). Discards unwanted queries. Responds in 2 weeks to queries; 2-3 weeks to mss. Obtains most new clients through recommendations from others, conferences.

Recent Sales Sold 2 titles in the last year. Untitled children's folktale collection, by Anne Shelby (UNC Press); foreign rights sales: *The Fund*, by Wes DeMott in Russian. Other clients include various new writers.

Terms Agent receives 15% commission on domestic sales; 20% commission on foreign sales. Offers written contract, binding for 1 year; 1-day notice must be given to terminate contract. Sometimes charges for postage and photocopying. All expenses are subject to client approval.

❷ JEAN V. NAGGAR LITERARY AGENCY, INC.

216 E. 75th St., Suite 1E, New York NY 10021. (212)794-1082. E-mail: jvnla@jvnla.com. Website: www.jvnla.com. **Contact:** Jean Naggar. Estab. 1978. Member of AAR, PEN, Women's Media Group, Women's Forum. Represents 80 clients. 20% of clients are new/unpublished writers. Currently handles: 35% nonfiction books; 45% novels; 15% juvenile books; 5% scholarly books.

> • Ms. Naggar has served as president of AAR.

Member Agents Jean Naggar (mainstream fiction, nonfiction); Jennifer Weltz, director (subsidiary rights, children's books); Alice Tasman, senior agent (commercial and literary fiction, thrillers, narrative nonfiction); Mollie Glick, agent and director of contracts (specializes in literary fiction as well as narrative and practical nonfiction); Jessica Regel, agent (young adult fiction and nonfiction).

Represents Nonfiction books, novels. **Considers these nonfiction areas:** Biography/autobiography; child guidance/parenting; current affairs; government/politics/law; health/medicine; history; juvenile nonfiction; memoirs; New Age/metaphysics; psychology; religious/inspirational; self-help/personal improvement; sociology; travel; women's issues/studies. **Considers these fiction areas:** Action/adventure; detective/police/crime; ethnic; family saga; feminist; historical; literary; mainstream/contemporary; mystery/suspense; psychic/supernatural; thriller.

> **O─** This agency specializes in mainstream fiction and nonfiction and literary fiction with commercial potential.

How to Contact Query with SASE. Prefers to read materials exclusively. No e-mail or fax queries. Responds in 1 day to queries; 2 months to mss. Returns materials only with SASE. Obtains most new clients through recommendations from others.

Recent Sales *An Absolute Gentleman*, by Rose Marie Kinder; *Scot On The Rocks*, by Brenda Janowitz; *The Deporter*, by Ames Holbrook; *Love And Sex With Robots*, by David Levy, *You Must Be This Happy To Enter* By Elizabeth Crane; *Night Navigation*, by Ginnah Howard; *After Hours At The Almost Home*, by Tara Yelen, *An Entirely Synthetic Fish: A Biography Of Rainbow Trout*, by Anders Halverson; *The Patron Saint Of Butterflies, by Cecilia Galante, 6 Sick Hipsters* By Rayo Casablanca; *Enola Holmes And The Case Of The Bizarre Bouquets*, by Nancy Springer; *Skin And Bones*, by Teri Coyne; *Dark Angels*, by Karleen Koen, *Wild Girls*, by Pat Murphy;

Executive Privilege, by Phillip Margolin; *The Last Queen*, by C.W. Gortner; *Donkey-Donkey*, by Roger Duvoisin; *The Elephant Quilt*, by Susan Lowell; *Rhymes With Rufus*, by Iza Trapani.

Terms Agent receives 15% commission on domestic sales; 20% commission on foreign sales. Offers written contract. Charges for overseas mailing, messenger services, book purchases, long-distance telephone, photocopying—all deductible from royalties received.

Writers' Conferences Willamette Writers Conference; Pacific Northwest Writers Conference; Bread Loaf Writers Conference; Marymount Manhattan Writers Conference; SEAK Medical & Legal Fiction Writing Conference.

Tips "Use a professional presentation. Because of the avalanche of unsolicited queries that flood the agency every week, we have had to modify our policy. We will now only guarantee to read and respond to queries from writers who come recommended by someone we know. Our areas are general fiction and nonfiction—no children's books by unpublished writers, no multimedia, no screenplays, no formula fiction, and no mysteries by unpublished writers. We recommend patience and fortitude: the courage to be true to your own vision, the fortitude to finish a novel and polish it again and again before sending it out, and the patience to accept rejection gracefully and wait for the stars to align themselves appropriately for success."

◙ NANCY COFFEY LITERARY & MEDIA REPRESENTATION

240 W. 35th St., Suite 500, New York NY 10001. Fax: (212)279-0927. **Contact:** Nancy Coffey. Member of AAR. Currently handles: 5% nonfiction books; 90% novels; 5% juvenile books.

Represents Nonfiction books, novels, juvenile books (young adult, from cutting edge material to fantasy). **Considers these fiction areas:** Family saga; fantasy; military/war (espionage); mystery/suspense; romance; science fiction; thriller; young adult; women's.

How to Contact Query with SASE.

Recent Sales *The Gardens of Covington*, by Joan A. Medlicott (Thomas Dunne Books); *The Sixth Fleet*, by David E. Meadows (Berkley).

◙ NAPPALAND LITERARY AGENCY

A Division of Nappaland Communications, Inc., P.O. Box 1674, Loveland CO 80539-1674. Fax: (970)635-9869. E-mail: Literary@nappaland.com. Website: www.nappaland.com/literary.htm. **Contact:** Mike Nappa, senior agent. Estab. 1995. Represents 8 clients. 0% of clients are new/unpublished writers. Currently handles: 45% nonfiction books; 50% novels; 5% scholarly books.

- Prior to becoming an agent, Mr. Nappa served as an acquisition editor for three major Christian publishing houses.

Represents Nonfiction books, novels. **Considers these nonfiction areas:** Child guidance/parenting; current affairs; popular culture; religious/inspirational; women's issues/studies. **Considers these fiction areas:** Action/adventure; detective/police/crime; literary; mainstream/contemporary; religious/inspirational; thriller.

- ❍━ This agency will not consider any new authors unless they come with a recommendation from a current Nappaland client. All queries without such a recommendation are immediately rejected. Interested in thoughtful, vivid, nonfiction works on religious and cultural themes. Also, fast-paced, well-crafted fiction (suspense, literary, women's) that reads like a work of art. Established authors only; broad promotional platform preferred. Does not want to receive children's books, movie or television scripts, textbooks, short stories, stage plays or poetry.

How to Contact Query with SASE, submit author bio. Include the name of the person referring you to us. Do *not* send entire proposal unless requested. Send query and bio only. E-queries preferred and given first priority. No attachments please. Accepts e-mail and fax queries. Considers simultaneous queries. Responds in 1 month to queries; 3 months to mss.

Recent Sales Sold 3 titles in the last year. *Unpretty*, by Sharon Carter Rogers (Howard); *Creative Family Prayer Times*, by Mike and Amy Nappa (NavPress); *Misquoting Truth*, by Timothy Paul Jones (InterVarsity Press); *Zachary's Zoo*, by Mike and Amy Nappa (Zondervan); *The Christ Conspiracies*, by Timothy Paul Jones (Strang Book Group).

Terms Agent receives 15% commission on domestic sales; 20% commission on foreign sales. Offers written contract; 30-day notice must be given to terminate contract.

Writers' Conferences Colorado Christian Writers' Conference in Estes Park.

◙ THE NASHVILLE AGENCY

P.O. Box 110909, Nashville TN 37222. (615)263-4143. Fax: (866)333-8663. E-mail: info@nashvilleagency.com; submissions@nashvilleagency.com. Website: www.nashvilleagency.com. **Contact:** Taylor Joseph. Estab. 2002. Represents 18 clients. 50% of clients are new/unpublished writers. Currently handles: 40% nonfiction books; 15% novels; 5% novellas; 40% juvenile books.

Member Agents Tim Grable (business books); Jonathan Clements (nonfiction, juvenile); Taylor Joseph (fiction, novels, memoirs).

Represents Nonfiction books, novels, novellas, juvenile books, scholarly books, movie scripts, documentary. **Considers these nonfiction areas:** Biography/autobiography; business/economics; child guidance/parenting; cooking/foods/nutrition; crafts/hobbies; current affairs; education; history; how-to; humor/satire; juvenile nonfiction; memoirs; military/war; music/dance; popular culture; religious/inspirational; self-help/personal improvement; sports; true crime/investigative; women's issues/studies. **Considers these fiction areas:** Action/adventure; fantasy; historical; humor/satire; juvenile; literary; mainstream/contemporary; mystery/suspense; regional; religious/inspirational; thriller; young adult; women's. **Considers these script subject areas:** Action/adventure; contemporary issues.

> O⊸ "Our agency looks not as much for specific genres or stylings. Rather, we look for far-reaching potentials (i.e., brands, properties) to branch outside a token specific market." Actively seeking novels, nonfiction, religious/spiritual material. Does not want to receive poetry, stage plays or textbooks.

How to Contact Query with SASE, submit proposal package, synopsis, publishing history, author bio, Description of how your relationship with The Nashville Agency was initiated. Query via e-mail. No fax queries. Considers simultaneous queries. Responds in 3 weeks to queries; 3 months to mss. Returns materials only with SASE. Obtains most new clients through recommendations from others.

Recent Sales This agency prefers not to share information on specific sales.

Terms Agent receives 15% commission on domestic sales; 20% commission on foreign sales. Offers written contract, binding for 5 years; 30-day notice must be given to terminate contract. This agency charges for standard office fees.

Writers' Conferences Blue Ridge Writers' Conference.

◪ NELSON LITERARY AGENCY

1732 Wazee St., Suite 207, Denver CO 80202. (303)292-2805. E-mail: query@nelsonagency.com. Website: www.nelsonagency.com. **Contact:** Kristin Nelson. Estab. 2002. Member of AAR.

> • Prior to opening her own agency, Ms. Nelson worked as a literary scout and subrights agent for agent Jody Rein.

Represents Novels, select nonfiction. **Considers these nonfiction areas:** Memoirs; narrative nonfiction. **Considers these fiction areas:** Literary; romance (includes fantasy with romantic elements, science fiction, fantasy, young adult); women's; chick lit (includes mysteries); commercial/mainstream.

> O⊸ NLA specializes in representing commercial fiction and high caliber literary fiction. Actively seeking Latina writers who tackle contemporary issues in a modern voice (think *Dirty Girls Social Club*). Does not want short story collections, mysteries (except chick lit), thrillers, Christian, horror, or children's picture books.

How to Contact Query by e-mail only.

Recent Sales *Schemes of Love*, by Sherry Thomas (Bantam Dell); *The Camelot Code*, by Mari Mancusi (Dutton Children's); *Magic Lost, Trouble Found*, by Lisa Shearin (Ace); *Magellan's Witch*, by Carolyn Jewel (Hachette/Warner); *No Place Safe*, by Kim Reid (Kensington); *Plan B*, by Jennifer O'Connell (MTV/Pocket Books); *Code of Love*, by Cheryl Sawyer (NAL/Penguin Group); *Once Upon Stilettos*, by Shanna Swendson (Ballantine); *I'd Tell You I Love You But Then I'd Have to Kill You*, by Ally Carter (Hyperion Children's); *An Accidental Goddess*, by Linnea Sinclair (Bantam Spectra). Other clients include Paula Reed, Becky Motew, Jack McCallum, Jana Deleon.

◪ THE NEVILLE AGENCY

E-mail: info@nevilleagency.com. Website: www.nevilleagency.com. **Contact:** Barret Neville. Currently handles: 90% nonfiction books; 10% novels.

> • Prior to his current position, Mr. Neville was an editor, and spent 10 years acquiring and developing books, including several national and *New York Times* bestsellers, for publishers such as Penguin, St. Martin's Press and McGraw-Hill. He is also the author, with John Salka, of *First In, Last Out: Leadership Lessons of the New York Fire Department*.

Represents Nonfiction books, novels. **Considers these nonfiction areas:** Biography/autobiography; business/economics; health/medicine; history; humor/satire; popular culture; self-help/personal improvement; narrative, parenting. **Considers these fiction areas:** Historical; mystery/suspense; thriller.

> O⊸ "The Neville Agency is a boutique literary agency specializing in nonfiction. We seek out authors who are experts in their fields; who have a unique voice or vision; and who are poised to contribute something new or provocative to the cultural dialogue. We also handle a select number of mysteries and thrillers."

How to Contact Send a brief e-query with a bio and any relevant publishing history. No snail mail queries or phone calls. No fax queries. Responds in 3 days to queries.

Recent Sales *Run Less, Run Faster: Become a Faster, Stronger Runner with the Revolutionary FIRST Training Program*, by William Pierce, et al (Rodale); *Adoption 101: Secrets to a Fast, Safe and Affordable Adoption*, by

Randall Hicks (Penguin/Perigee); *Flipping the Switch*, by John Miller; *The Dictionary of Corporate Bullshit*, by Lois Beckwith; *The Baby Game*, by Randall Hicks.

Tips "For mysteries and thrillers, our ideal partners are authors who have a clear understanding of their book's appeal (for example, it's a cozy, a police procedural, romantic suspense, etc.) and who are bringing something new to the genre, be it an unusual protagonist, unique setting or unforgettable voice."

◙ NEW BRAND AGENCY GROUP, LLC

E-mail: mark@literaryagent.net. Website: www.literaryagent.net. **Contact:** Mark Ryan. Estab. 1994. Represents 3 clients. Currently handles: 33% nonfiction books; 33% novels; 33% juvenile books.

Represents Nonfiction books, novels, juvenile books. **Considers these nonfiction areas:** Biography/autobiography; business/economics; juvenile nonfiction; memoirs; popular culture; psychology; religious/inspirational; self-help/personal improvement; sex; spirituality; women's issues/studies; body and soul; health; humor; family; finance; fitness; gift/novelty; leadership; men's issues; parenting; relationships; success. **Considers these fiction areas:** Fantasy; historical; horror; juvenile; literary; mainstream/contemporary; mystery/suspense; romance (mainstream); science fiction; thriller; cross-genre; magical realism; supernatural.

    O➤ New Brand Agency is currently closed to submissions. Check the Web site for more details. "We only work with authors we are passionate about."

Recent Sales *Black Valley*, by Jim Brown (Ballantine); *The Marriage Plan*, by Aggie Jordan (Broadway/Bantam); *Mother to Daughter*, by Harry Harrison (Workman); *The She*, by Carol Plum-Ucci (Harcourt).

Terms Agent receives 15% commission on domestic sales. Offers written contract, binding for 6 months; 1-month notice must be given to terminate contract. Charges for postage and phone costs after sale of the project.

◎ NEW ENGLAND PUBLISHING ASSOCIATES, INC.

P.O. Box 361, Chester CT 06412-0645. (860)345-READ or (860)345-4976. Fax: (860)345-3660. E-mail: nepa@nepa.com. Website: www.nepa.com. **Contact:** Edward W. Knappman, Victoria Harlow. Estab. 1983. Member of AAR. Represents 125-150 clients. Currently handles: 100% nonfiction books.

Member Agents Ed Knappman.

Represents Nonfiction books (for adults, no juvenile). **Considers these nonfiction areas:** Biography/autobiography; business/economics; child guidance/parenting; government/politics/law; health/medicine; history; language/literature/criticism; military/war; money/finance; nature/environment; psychology; science/technology; self-help/personal improvement; sports; true crime/investigative; women's issues/studies; reference.

    O➤ This agency specializes in adult nonfiction of serious purpose. Currently, this agency is only taking on 2-3 new clients per year.

How to Contact Send outline/proposal, SASE. Accepts e-mail and fax queries. Considers simultaneous queries. Responds in 1 month to queries; 5 weeks to mss. Returns materials only with SASE.

Recent Sales Sold 20 titles in the last year. *When Your Parent Moves In*, by David Horgan & Shira Block (Adams); *Baptism by Fire: Eight Presidents Inaugurated in a Time of Crisis*, by Mark Updegrove (St. Martin); *Obsessive Compulsive Disorder for Dummies*, by Charles Elliot & Laura Smith (Wiley); *Conquering Post Traumatic Stress*, by John Arden and Victoria Beckner (Fair Winds); *The Finest Hours*, by Michael Tougias and Casey Sherman (Scribner); *Be a Recruiting Superstar*, by Mary & Wane Christensen (Amacom).

Terms Agent receives 15% commission on domestic sales; 20% commission on foreign sales. Offers written contract, binding for 6 months. Charges clients for copying.

Writers' Conferences BookExpo America; London Book Fair.

Tips "Send us a well-written proposal that clearly identifies your audience—who will buy this book and why. Check our website for tips on proposals and advice on how to market your books."

Ⓝ ◙ NOBLE LITERARY AGENCY

450 Geary St., #200, San Francisco CA 94102. E-mail: mikenoble@nobleliteraryagency.com. Website: www.nobleliteraryagency.com. **Contact:** Mike Noble.

Represents Nonfiction books, novels, juvenile books. **Considers these nonfiction areas:** Humor/satire (and gift books); reference digests. **Considers these fiction areas:** Young adult.

    O➤ Adult nonfiction (all good ideas are encouraged); reference books (we supply professional illustration and photography if you can't); humor (short books, requiring either illustration or photography; books for that last-minute gift). Does not want to receive fantasy or science fiction.

How to Contact Query with SASE. Accepts e-mail queries. No fax queries. Obtains most new clients through solicitations.

Terms Agent receives 15% commission on domestic sales.

◙ NORTHERN LIGHTS LITERARY SERVICES, LLC

306 North Center Valley Road, Sandpoint ID 83864. (888)558-4354. Fax: (208)265-1948. E-mail: agent@northernlightsls.com. Website: www.northernlightsls.com. **Contact:** Sammie Justesen. Estab. 2005. Represents 25 cli-

ents. 35% of clients are new/unpublished writers. Currently handles: 90% nonfiction books; 10% novels.
Member Agents Sammie Justesen (fiction and nonfiction); Vorris Dee Justesen (business and current affairs).
Represents Nonfiction books, novels. **Considers these nonfiction areas:** Animals; biography/autobiography; business/economics; child guidance/parenting; cooking/foods/nutrition; crafts/hobbies; current affairs; ethnic/cultural interests; health/medicine; how-to; memoirs; nature/environment; New Age/metaphysics; popular culture; psychology; religious/inspirational; self-help/personal improvement; sports; true crime/investigative; women's issues/studies. **Considers these fiction areas:** Action/adventure; detective/police/crime; ethnic; family saga; feminist; glitz; historical; mainstream/contemporary; mystery/suspense; psychic/supernatural; regional; religious/inspirational; romance; thriller; women's.

> O➤ "Our goal is to provide personalized service to clients and create a bond that will endure throughout the writer's career. We seriously consider each query we receive and will accept hardworking new authors who are willing to develop their talents and skills. We enjoy working with healthcare professionals and writers who clearly understand their market and have a platform." Actively seeking general nonfiction—especially if the writer has a platform. Does not want to receive fantasy, horror, erotica, children's books, screenplays, poetry or short stories.

How to Contact Query with SASE, submit outline/proposal, synopsis, 3 sample chapter(s), author bio. E-queries preferred. No phone queries. All queries considered, but the agency only replies if interested. No fax queries. Considers simultaneous queries. Responds in 2 months to queries; 2 months to mss. Returns materials only with SASE. Obtains most new clients through solicitations, conferences.
Recent Sales *The Mouth Trap*, by Gary Siegel (Career Press); *SuperStar Selling*, by Paul M McCord (Moragn James); *The Power of Purrs* and *The Power of Paws*, by Gary Sheibler (Lyons).
Terms Agent receives 15% commission on domestic sales; 20% commission on foreign sales. Offers written contract; 30-day notice must be given to terminate contract.
Tips "If you're fortunate enough to find an agent who answers your query and asks for a printed manuscript, always include a letter and cover page containing your name, physical address, e-mail address and phone number. Be professional!"

❤ HAROLD OBER ASSOCIATES

425 Madison Ave., New York NY 10017. (212)759-8600. Fax: (212)759-9428. **Contact:** Craig Tenney. Estab. 1929. Member of AAR. Represents 250 clients. 10% of clients are new/unpublished writers. Currently handles: 35% nonfiction books; 50% novels; 15% juvenile books.

• Mr. Elwell was previously with Elwell & Weiser.

Member Agents Phyllis Westberg; Pamela Malpas; Craig Tenney (few new clients, mostly Ober backlist); Jake Elwell.
Represents Nonfiction books, novels, juvenile books.

> O➤ "We consider all subjects/genres of fiction and nonfiction."

How to Contact Submit query letter only with SASE. No e-mail or fax queries. Responds as promptly as possible. Obtains most new clients through recommendations from others.
Terms Agent receives 15% commission on domestic sales; 20% commission on foreign sales. Charges clients for photocopying and express mail/package services.

Ⓝ ❤ ◎ OBJECTIVE ENTERTAINMENT

265 Canal St., Suite 603 B, New York NY, 10013. (212)431-5454. Fax: (917)464.6394. E-mail: ej@objectiveent.com. Website: www.objectiveent.com. **Contact:** Elizabeth Joté.
Member Agents Jarred Weisfeld; Ian Kleinert, IK@objectiveent.com; Brendan Deneen. Brendan@objectiveent.com (novelists and screenwriters for publishing & film/television, as well as producing select feature film and television projects); Fred Borden, Fred@objectiveent.com (fiction and nonfiction related to Middle Eastern politics, sports—especially mixed martial arts—popular culture, and film); Elizabeth Jote, ej@objectiveent.com (commercial fiction (women's fiction, lad lit, thrillers, mysteries, young adult, urban fiction and multicultural books, narrative nonfiction, pop culture, current events, lifestyle books and graphic novels).
Represents Nonfiction books, novels, movie scripts, feature film, TV scripts.
How to Contact Query via e-mail. Send query only unless more information or materials are requested.
Recent Sales *Little T Learns to Share*, by Terrell Owens; *The Blackgloom Bounty*, by Jon Baxley; *Cash & Carry*, by Tim Broderick; *Relics*, by Darren Speegle.

❤ FIFI OSCARD AGENCY, INC.

110 W. 40th St., 21st Floor, New York NY 10018. (212)764-1100. Fax: (212)840-5019. E-mail: agency@fifioscard.com. Website: www.fifioscard.com. **Contact:** Literary Department. Estab. 1978. Signatory of WGA.
Member Agents Peter Sawyer; Carmen La Via; Kevin McShane; Carolyn French.
Represents Nonfiction books, novels, stage plays. **Considers these nonfiction areas:** Business/economics

(finance); history; religious/inspirational; science/technology; sports; women's issues/studies; African American; biography; body/mind/spirit; health; lifestyle; cookbooks. **Considers these fiction areas:** Literary fiction or something else that catches our eye.

How to Contact Query through online submission form preferred, though snail mail queries are acceptable. *No unsolicited mss.* Responds in 2 weeks to queries.

Recent Sales *Ralph Ellison: A Biography* by Arnold Rampersad (Knopf); *On the Brink: An Insider's Account of How the White House Compromised American Intelligence* (Carroll & Graf); *Thumbs, Toes and Tears & Other Traits that Make Us Human*, By Chip Walter (Walker); *Beating Around the Bush*, by Art Buchwald (Seven Stories); *To the Mountaintop*, by Stewart Burns (HarperSanFrancisco); *Perfect . . . I'm Not*, by David Wells and Chris Kreski (Wm. Morrow). Other clients include This agency's client list is available online.

Terms Agent receives 15% commission on domestic sales; 20% commission on foreign sales; 10% commission on dramatic rights sales. Charges clients for photocopying expenses.

ⓝ OSHUN LITERARY ASSOCIATES

E-mail: oshunlit@comcast.net. Website: www.oshunliterary.com/. **Contact:** Karen E. Quinones Miller.

● Prior to her current position, Karen was with Liza Dawson Associates. She is also an author.

Member Agents Karen E. Quinones Miller

Represents Nonfiction books, novels. **Considers these nonfiction areas:** Self-help/personal improvement. **Considers these fiction areas:** Literary; multicultural.

    ○→ This agency is brand new, and is still forming its Web site and submission guidelines, as of publication of this book. Check the Web site for updated information.

How to Contact Query via e-mail.

ⓓ PARK LITERARY GROUP, LLC

270 Lafayette St., Suite 1504, New York NY 10012. (212)691-3500. Fax: (212)691-3540. E-mail: info@parkliterary.com. Website: www.parkliterary.com. Estab. 2005.

● Prior to their current positions, Ms. Park and Ms. O'Keefe were literary agents at Sanford J. Greenburger Associates. Prior to 1994, she was a practicing attorney.

Member Agents Theresa Park (plot-driven fiction and serious nonfiction); Abigail Koons (quirky, edgy and commercial fiction, as well as superb thrillers and mysteries; adventure and travel narrative nonfiction, exceptional memoirs, popular science, history, politics and art).

Represents Nonfiction books, novels.

    ○→ "The Park Literary Group represents fiction and nonfiction with a boutique approach: an emphasis on servicing a relatively small number of clients, with the highest professional standards and focused personal attention." Does not want to receive poetry or screenplays.

How to Contact Query with SASE, submit synopsis, 1-3 sample chapter(s), SASE. Send all submissions through the mail. No e-mail or fax queries. Responds in 4-6 weeks to queries.

Recent Sales

ⓦ THE RICHARD PARKS AGENCY

Box 693, Salem NY 12865. (518)854-9466. Fax: (518)854-9466. E-mail: rp@richardparksagency.com. Website: www.richardparksagency.com. **Contact:** Richard Parks. Estab. 1988. Member of AAR. Currently handles: 55% nonfiction books; 40% novels; 5% story collections.

Represents Nonfiction books, novels. **Considers these nonfiction areas:** Animals; anthropology/archaeology; art/architecture/design; biography/autobiography; business/economics; child guidance/parenting; cooking/foods/nutrition; crafts/hobbies; current affairs; ethnic/cultural interests; gardening; gay/lesbian issues; government/politics/law; health/medicine; history; how-to; humor/satire; language/literature/criticism; memoirs; military/war; money/finance; music/dance; nature/environment; popular culture; psychology; science/technology; self-help/personal improvement; sociology; theater/film; travel; women's issues/studies.

    ○→ Actively seeking nonfiction. Considers fiction by referral only. Does not want to receive unsolicited material.

How to Contact Query with SASE. No e-mail or fax queries. Considers simultaneous queries Responds in 2 weeks to queries. Returns materials only with SASE. Obtains most new clients through recommendations/referrals.

Terms Agent receives 15% commission on domestic sales; 20% commission on foreign sales. Charges clients for photocopying or any unusual expense incurred at the writer's request.

ⓦ KATHI J. PATON LITERARY AGENCY

P.O. Box 2240 Radio City Station, New York NY 10101. (212)265-6586. E-mail: kjplitbiz@optonline.net. **Contact:** Kathi Paton. Estab. 1987. Currently handles: 85% nonfiction books; 15% novels.

Represents Nonfiction books, novels, short story collections, book-based film rights. **Considers these nonfiction areas:** Business/economics; child guidance/parenting; humor/satire; money/finance (personal investing); nature/environment; psychology; religious/inspirational; personal investing. **Considers these fiction areas:** Literary; mainstream/contemporary; multicultural; short stories.

O→ This agency specializes in adult nonfiction.

How to Contact Accepts e-mail queries only. Considers simultaneous queries. Obtains most new clients through recommendations from current clients.

Recent Sales *Zero Day Threat* by Byron Acohido and Jon Swartz (Union Square and Sterling); *Unraveling the Mystery of Autism*, by Karyn Seroussi (Simon & Schuster); *Bury My Heart at Cooperstown*, by Frank Russo and Gene Racz (Triumph/Random House).

Terms Agent receives 15% commission on domestic sales; 20% commission on foreign sales. Offers written contract. Charges clients for photocopying.

Writers' Conferences Attends major regional panels, seminars and conferences.

◎ PAVILION LITERARY MANAGEMENT

660 Massachusetts Ave., Suite 4, Boston MA 02118. (617)792-5218. E-mail: query@pavilionliterary.com. Website: www.pavilionliterary.com. **Contact:** Jeff Kellogg.

● Prior to his current position, Mr. Kellogg was a literary agent with The Stuart Agency, and an acquiring editor with HarperCollins.

Represents Nonfiction books, novels, memoir. **Considers these nonfiction areas:** Biography/autobiography; computers/electronic; health/medicine; history; military/war; multicultural; nature/environment; psychology; science/technology; sports; travel; neuroscience, medicine, physics/astrophysics. **Considers these fiction areas:** Action/adventure; fantasy; juvenile; mystery/suspense; thriller; general fiction, genre-blending fiction.

O→ "We are presently accepting fiction submissions only from previously published authors and/or by client referral. Nonfiction projects, specifically narrative nonfiction and cutting-edge popular science from experts in their respective fields, are most welcome."

How to Contact Query first by e-mail (no attachments). Your subject line should specify fiction or nonfiction and include the title of the work. If submitting nonfiction, include a book proposal (no longer than 75 pages), with sample chapters. No fax queries.

Recent Sales *I'm With Stupid.* by Elaine Szewczyk (Warner 5 Spot); *Grievances*, by Mark Ethridge (New South Books); *The Other Brain*, by R. Douglas Fields (S&S); *The Fourth Horseman*, by Robert Koenig (Public Affairs); *Knowing: The Deceptive Biology of Convinction*, by Robert Burton, (SMP). Other clients include Steve Almond, Mark Ethridge, R. Douglas Fields, Juliana Hatfield, Robert Koenig, George Rabasa, Dennis Drayna.

◙ PEARSON, MORRIS & BELT

3000 Connecticut Ave., NW, Suite 317, Washington DC 20008. (202)723-6088. E-mail: dpm@morrisbelt.com; llb@morrisbelt.com. Website: www.morrisbelt.com.

● Prior to their current positions, Ms. Belt and Ms. Morris were agents with Adler & Robin Books, Inc.

Member Agents Laura Belt (nonfiction and computer books); Djana Pearson Morris (fiction, nonfiction, and computer books. Her favorite subjects are self-help, narrative nonfiction, African-American fiction and nonfiction, health and fitness, women's fiction, technology and parenting).

Represents Nonfiction books, novels, computer books.

O→ This agency specializes in nonfiction, computer books and exceptional fiction. Does not want to receive poetry, children's literature or screenplays. Regarding fiction, this agency does not accept science fiction, thrillers or mysteries.

How to Contact Query with SASE, submit proposal (nonfiction); detailed synopsis and 2-3 sample chapters (fiction). Only query with a finished ms. No e-mail attachments. Accepts e-mail queries. No fax queries. Responds in 6-8 weeks to queries. Returns materials only with SASE. Obtains most new clients through recommendations from others, solicitations.

Recent Sales *The New Color of Success*, by Niki Butler-Michell (Prima Publishing); *Mid-Life Motherhood*, by Jann Blackstone Ford (St. Martin's Press); *Hour to Hour*, by Shelly Marshall (Pocket Books); *Fried, Dyed, and Laid to the Side*, by Michele Collison (Amistad/HarperCollins); *It's All Good*, by Michele Collison (Amistad/HarperCollins); *Everything Monsters*, by Shannon Turlington (Adams Media).

Tips "Many of our books come from ideas and proposals we generate in-house. We retain a proprietary interest in and control of all ideas we create and proposals we write."

◙ PELHAM LITERARY AGENCY

2451 Royal St. James Drive, El Cajon CA, 92019-4408. (619)447-4468. E-mail: jmeals@pelhamliterary.com. Website: pelhamliterary.com. **Contact:** Jim Meals. Estab. 1993. Currently handles: 10% nonfiction books; 90% novels.

● Before becoming agents, both Mr. Pelham and Mr. Meals were writers.

Member Agents Howard Pelham; Jim Meals.

Represents Nonfiction books, novels.

O⌐ "Every manuscript that comes to our agency receives a careful reading and assessment. When a writer submits a promising manuscript, we work extensively with the author until the work is ready for marketing."

How to Contact Query by mail or e-mail first; do not send unsolicited mss. No fax queries.

Recent Sales *The Complete Guide to Foreign Adoption*, by Barbara Bascom and Carole McKelvey; *The General*, by Patrick A. Davis; *The Highest Bidder*, by B.H.B. Harper.

Terms Agent receives 15% commission on domestic sales. Offers written contract. Charges for photocopying and postage.

Tips "Only phone if it's necessary."

Ⓝ ◯ ELLEN PEPUS LITERARY AGENCY

4200 Wisconsin Avenue, NW, #106-233, Washington DC 20016. (301)896-0185. Fax: (301)896-0185. E-mail: ellen@epliterary.com. Website: www.epliterary.com. **Contact:** Ellen Pepus; adheres to AAR canon of ethics. Represents 9 clients. 90% of clients are new/unpublished writers. Currently handles: 30% nonfiction books; 70% novels.

● Prior to her current position, Ms. Pepus was employed at Graybill & English Literary Agency. She worked in foreign rights as well.

Represents Nonfiction books, novels. **Considers these nonfiction areas:** Animals; anthropology/archaeology; art/architecture/design; biography/autobiography; child guidance/parenting; cooking/foods/nutrition; crafts/hobbies; current affairs; ethnic/cultural interests; gay/lesbian issues; government/politics/law; health/medicine; history; how-to; humor/satire; interior design/decorating; language/literature/criticism; memoirs; military/war; money/finance; music/dance; nature/environment; New Age/metaphysics; photography; popular culture; psychology; science/technology; self-help/personal improvement; sociology; translation; true crime/investigative; women's issues/studies. **Considers these fiction areas:** Action/adventure; detective/police/crime; erotica; ethnic; family saga; fantasy; feminist; gay/lesbian; historical; literary; mainstream/contemporary; mystery/suspense; psychic/supernatural; romance; thriller; women's.

O⌐ This agency specializes in fiction—both genre and literary. Narrative nonfiction is sought out, though Ms. Pepus will consider other nonfiction. Actively seeking literary and commercial fiction, narrative nonfiction. Does not want to receive children's, young adult, poetry, short stories, screenplays, science fiction or horror.

How to Contact Query with SASE, submit first 5 pages. E-queries are preferred. No fax queries. Considers simultaneous queries. Responds in 2 weeks to queries; 8 weeks to mss. Returns materials only with SASE. Obtains most new clients through recommendations from others, solicitations, conferences.

Terms Agent receives 15% commission on domestic sales; 20% commission on foreign sales. Offers written contract; 30-day notice must be given to terminate contract.

Writers' Conferences Washington Independent Writers, Society of Southwestern Authors, North Carolina Writers Network, Southern California Writers Conference, Space Coast Writers Guild Conference.

Ⓩ L. PERKINS ASSOCIATES

5800 Arlington Ave., Riverdale NY 10471. (718)543-5344. Fax: (718)543-5354. E-mail: lperkinsagency@yahoo.com. **Contact:** Lori Perkins, Amy Stout (jrlperkinsagency@yahoo.com). Estab. 1990. Member of AAR. Represents 90 clients. 10% of clients are new/unpublished writers.

● Ms. Perkins has been an agent for 20 years. She is also the author of *The Insider's Guide to Getting an Agent* (Writer's Digest Books), as well as three other nonfiction books. She has also edited two anthologies.

Represents Nonfiction books, novels. **Considers these nonfiction areas:** Popular culture. **Considers these fiction areas:** Erotica; fantasy; horror; literary (dark); science fiction.

O⌐ Most of Ms. Perkins' clients write both fiction and nonfiction. "This combination keeps my clients publishing for years. I am also a published author, so I know what it takes to write a good book." Actively seeking a Latino *Gone With the Wind* and *Waiting to Exhale*, and urban ethnic horror. Does not want to receive anything outside of the above categories (westerns, romance, etc.).

How to Contact Query with SASE. Considers simultaneous queries. Responds in 12 weeks to queries; 3-6 months to mss. Returns materials only with SASE. Obtains most new clients through recommendations from others, solicitations, conferences.

Recent Sales Sold 100 titles in the last year. *How to Make Love Like a Porn Star: A Cautionary Tale*, by Jenna Jameson (Reagan Books); *Everything But ...?*, by Rachel Krammer Bussel (Bantam); *Dear Mom, I Always Wanted You to Know*, by Lisa Delman (Perigee Books); *The Illustrated Ray Bradbury*, by Jerry Weist (Avon); *The Poet* *in Exile*, by Ray Manzarek (Avalon); *Behind Sad Eyes: The Life of George Harrison*, by Marc Shapiro (St. Martin's Press).

Terms Agent receives 15% commission on domestic sales; 20% commission on foreign sales. No written contract. Charges clients for photocopying.

Writers' Conferences San Diego State University Writers' Conference; NECON; BookExpo America; World Fantasy Convention.

Tips "Research your field and contact professional writers' organizations to see who is looking for what. Finish your novel before querying agents. Read my book, *An Insider's Guide to Getting an Agent*, to get a sense of how agents operate. Read agent blogs—litsoup.blogspot.com and missnark.blogspot.com.

⊘ STEPHEN PEVNER, INC.

382 Lafayette St., Eighth Floor, New York NY 10003. (212)674-8403. Fax: (212)529-3692. E-mail: spevner@aol.com. **Contact:** Stephen Pevner.

Represents Nonfiction books, novels, feature film, TV scripts, TV movie of the week, episodic drama, animation, documentary, miniseries. **Considers these nonfiction areas:** Biography/autobiography; ethnic/cultural interests; gay/lesbian issues; history; humor/satire; language/literature/criticism; memoirs; music/dance; New Age/metaphysics; photography; popular culture; religious/inspirational; sociology; travel. **Considers these fiction areas:** Comic books/cartoon; erotica; ethnic; experimental; gay/lesbian; glitz; horror; humor/satire; literary; mainstream/contemporary; psychic/supernatural; thriller; urban. **Considers these script subject areas:** Comedy; contemporary issues; detective/police/crime; gay/lesbian; glitz; horror; romantic comedy; romantic drama; thriller.

 ⊶ This agency specializes in motion pictures, novels, humor, pop culture, urban fiction, and independent filmmakers.

How to Contact Query with SASE, submit outline/proposal. Prefers to read materials exclusively. No e-mail or fax queries. Responds in 2 weeks to queries; 1 month to mss. Obtains most new clients through recommendations from others.

Terms Agent receives 15% commission on domestic sales; 20% commission on foreign sales. Offers written contract, binding for 1 year; 6-week notice must be given to terminate contract. 100% of business is derived from commissions on ms sales.

Tips "Be persistent, but civilized."

⊙ PFD NEW YORK

373 Park Ave. S, Fifth Floor, New York NY 10016. (917)256-0707. Fax: (212)685-9635. E-mail: email@pfdny.com. Website: www.pfdny.com. **Contact:** Submissions Department. Estab. 2003 (NYC office).

 • Prior to his current position, Mr. Reiter worked at IMG; Ms. Pagnamenta was with the Wylie Agency.

Member Agents Zoe Pagnamenta (U.S. authors), ajump@pfdgroup.com; Mark Reiter (U.S. authors), mreiter@pfdgroup.com.

Represents Nonfiction books, novels, short story collections (if the author has other written works), poetry books.

 ⊶ This agency has offices in New York as well as the United Kingdom.

How to Contact Query with SASE, submit proposal package, synopsis, 2-3 sample chapter(s), publishing history, author bio, cover letter. Submit via snail mail. See online submission guidelines for more information. No e-mail or fax queries. Responds in 1 month to queries. Returns materials only with SASE. Obtains most new clients through recommendations from others, solicitations.

Recent Sales *Seize the Fire*, by Adam Nicolson; *Have Glove, Will Travel*, by Bill "Spaceman" Lee and Richard Lally; *Crippen*, by John Boyne; *The First Scientific American: Benjamin Franklin and the Pursuit of Genius*, by Joyce Chaplin.

N ◯ PHENOMENON BOOKS AGENCY

10324 West 44th Ave., #3A, Wheat Ridge CO 80033. (720)210-3373. E-mail: phenomenonbooks@yahoo.com. Website: www.phenomenonbooks.com. **Contact:** Pamela Trayser. Estab. 2006. Currently handles: 2% nonfiction books; 98% novels.

 • Prior to becoming an agent, Ms. Trayser was a writer.

Represents Novels. **Considers these fiction areas:** Fantasy; horror; juvenile (picture books to young adult); literary; thriller; young adult; psychic/supernatural; Christian, when dealing with marked genres.

 ⊶ Actively seeking picture books, middle grade fiction, political thrillers and literary work of the highest quality.

How to Contact Query with SASE, submit synopsis, 3 sample chapter(s). Consider submissions only from October to December, and March to May. Accepts e-mail queries. No fax queries. Considers simultaneous

queries. Responds in 10 weeks to queries; 3 months to mss. Obtains most new clients through solicitations.
Terms Agent receives 15% commission on domestic sales; 20% commission on foreign sales.

☑ ALISON J. PICARD, LITERARY AGENT
P.O. Box 2000, Cotuit MA 02635. Phone/Fax: (508)477-7192. E-mail: ajpicard@aol.com. **Contact:** Alison Picard.
Estab. 1985. Represents 48 clients. 30% of clients are new/unpublished writers. Currently handles: 40% nonfiction books; 40% novels; 20% juvenile books.
- • Prior to becoming an agent, Ms. Picard was an assistant at a literary agency in New York.
Represents Nonfiction books, novels, juvenile books. **Considers these nonfiction areas:** Animals; biography/
autobiography; business/economics; child guidance/parenting; cooking/foods/nutrition; current affairs; education; ethnic/cultural interests; gay/lesbian issues; government/politics/law; health/medicine; history; how-to;
humor/satire; juvenile nonfiction; memoirs; military/war; money/finance; multicultural; nature/environment;
New Age/metaphysics; popular culture; psychology; religious/inspirational; science/technology; self-help/personal improvement; travel; true crime/investigative; women's issues/studies; young adult. **Considers these
fiction areas:** Action/adventure; contemporary issues; detective/police/crime; erotica; ethnic; family saga; feminist; gay/lesbian; glitz; historical; horror; humor/satire; juvenile; literary; mainstream/contemporary; multicultural; mystery/suspense; New Age; picture books; psychic/supernatural; romance; sports; thriller; young adult.
- ⊶ "Many of my clients have come to me from big agencies, where they felt overlooked or ignored. I
communicate freely with my clients and offer a lot of career advice, suggestions for revising manuscripts,
etc. If I believe in a project, I will submit it to a dozen or more publishers, unlike some agents who
give up after four or five rejections." No science fiction/fantasy, Western, poetry, plays or articles.
How to Contact Query with SASE. Considers simultaneous queries. Responds in 2 weeks to queries; 4 months
to mss. Returns materials only with SASE. Obtains most new clients through recommendations from others,
solicitations.
Recent Sales Two untitled mysteries, by David Housewright (St. Martin's Press); *Simply Scandalous* and two
untitled romances by Tamara Lejeune (Kensington Publishing Corp.); two untitled erotic novels by Fiona Zedde
(Kensington Publishing Corp.); *The Right Kind of People*, by Daniel Kimmel (Ivan R. Dee); *The Merchants of
Fear*, by Christopher Catherwood and Joe Divanna (Lyons Press); *Hoops of Steel* and *Running With the Wind*,
by John Foley (Llewellyn/Flux); *A Habit of Death* and *Ice in His Veins*, by Charles Zito (Llewellyn/Midnight
Ink); four mysteries by Richard Schwartz (Llewellyn/Midnight Ink); *Breathing Underwater*, by Lu Vickers
(Alyson); *One Size Fits All*, by Ben Patrick Johnson (Alyson). Other clients include Theresa Alan, Tom Eslick,
Nancy Means Wright, Dina Friedman and Margi Preus.
Terms Agent receives 15% commission on domestic sales; 20% commission on foreign sales. Offers written
contract, binding for 1 year; 1-week notice must be given to terminate contract.
Tips "Please don't send material without sending a query first via mail or e-mail. I don't accept phone or fax
queries. Always enclose an SASE with a query."

◖ PINDER LANE & GARON-BROOKE ASSOCIATES, LTD.
159 W. 53rd St., Suite 14C, New York NY 10019. Member of AAR; signatory of WGA.
Member Agents Robert Thixton, pinderl@rcn.com; Dick Duane, pinderl@rcn.com.
- ⊶ This agency specializes in mainstream fiction and nonfiction. Does not want to receive screenplays, TV
series teleplays, or dramatic plays.
How to Contact Query with SASE. *No unsolicited mss.* Obtains most new clients through referrals.
Terms Agent receives 15% commission on domestic sales; 30% commission on foreign sales. Offers written
contract.

◎ PIPPIN PROPERTIES, INC.
155 E. 38th St., Suite 2H, New York NY 10016. (212)338-9310. Fax: (212)338-9579. E-mail: info@pippinpropertie
s.com. Website: www.pippinproperties.com. **Contact:** Holly McGhee. Estab. 1998. Represents 40 clients. Currently handles: 100% juvenile books.
- • Prior to becoming an agent, Ms. McGhee was an editor for 7 years and in book marketing for 4 years.
Prior to becoming an agent, Ms. van Beek worked in children's book editorial for 4 years.
Member Agents Holly McGhee; Emily van Beek; Samantha Cosentino.
Represents Juvenile books.
- ⊶ "We are strictly a children's literary agency devoted to the management of authors and artists in all
media. We are small and discerning in choosing our clientele." Actively seeking middle-grade and
young-adult novels.
How to Contact Query with SASE. Accepts e-mail queries. Considers simultaneous queries. Responds in 8
weeks to queries; 10 weeks to mss. Obtains most new clients through recommendations from others.
Terms Agent receives 15% commission on domestic sales; 25% commission on foreign sales. Offers written

contract; 30-day notice must be given to terminate contract. Charges for color copying and UPS/FedEx.
Tips "Please do not start calling after sending a submission."

ALICKA PISTEK LITERARY AGENCY, LLC
302A W. 12th St., #124, New York NY 10014. E-mail: info@apliterary.com. Website: www.apliterary.com.
Contact: Alicka Pistek. Estab. 2003. Represents 15 clients. 50% of clients are new/unpublished writers. Currently handles: 60% nonfiction books; 40% novels.
• Prior to opening her agency, Ms. Pistek worked at ICM and as an agent at Nicholas Ellison, Inc.
Represents Nonfiction books, novels. **Considers these nonfiction areas:** Animals; anthropology/archaeology; biography/autobiography; child guidance/parenting; current affairs; government/politics/law; health/medicine; history; how-to; language/literature/criticism; memoirs; military/war; money/finance; nature/environment; psychology; science/technology; self-help/personal improvement; travel; creative nonfiction. **Considers these fiction areas:** Detective/police/crime; ethnic; family saga; historical; literary; mainstream/contemporary; mystery/suspense; romance; thriller.
O– Does not want to receive fantasy, science fiction or Western's.
How to Contact Send e-query to info@apliterary.com. The agency will only respond if interested. Accepts e-mail queries. No fax queries. Considers simultaneous queries. Responds in 2 months to queries; 8 weeks to mss. Returns materials only with SASE.
Recent Sales *The Animal Girl*, by John Fulton; *Elephants on Acid*, by Alex Boese; *Living on the Fly*, by Amanda Switzer and Daniel A. Shaw. Other clients include Matthew Zapruder, Steven R. Kinsella, Julie Tilsner, Michael Christopher Carroll, Quinton Skinner, Erin Grady.
Terms Agent receives 15% commission on domestic sales; 20% commission on foreign sales. Offers written contract. This agency charges for photocopying more than 40 pages and international postage.
Tips "Be sure you are familiar with the genre you are writing in and learn standard procedures for submitting your work. A good query will go a long way."

PLAINSMART PUBLISHING AGENCY
520 Kerr St., #20033, Oakville ON L6K 3C7, Canada. E-mail: query@plainsmart.com; info@plainsmart.com. Website: www.plainsmart.com/contactinfo.html. **Contact:** Curtis Russell. Estab. 2005. Represents 8 clients. 25% of clients are new/unpublished writers. Currently handles: 50% nonfiction books; 50% novels.
Represents Nonfiction books, novels, juvenile books. **Considers these nonfiction areas:** Biography/autobiography; business/economics; child guidance/parenting; cooking/foods/nutrition; current affairs; government/politics/law; health/medicine; how-to; humor/satire; memoirs; military/war; money/finance; nature/environment; popular culture; science/technology; self-help/personal improvement; sports; true crime/investigative; women's issues/studies. **Considers these fiction areas:** Action/adventure; detective/police/crime; erotica; ethnic; family saga; historical; horror; humor/satire; juvenile; literary; mainstream/contemporary; mystery/suspense; picture books; romance; sports; thriller; young adult; women's.
O– "We take on a very small number of clients per year in order to provide focused, hands-on representation. We pride ourselves in providing industry leading client service." Does not want to receive poetry or screenplays.
How to Contact Query with SASE, submit synopsis, author bio. Accepts e-mail queries. No fax queries. Considers simultaneous queries. Responds in 6 weeks to queries; 6 weeks to mss. Obtains most new clients through solicitations.
Recent Sales *World Famous*, by David Tyreman (AMACOM); *What Burns Within* and *The Frailty of Flesh*, by Sandra Ruttan; *The Road to a Nuclear al-qaeda*, by Al J. Venter (Potomac).
Terms Agent receives 15% commission on domestic sales; 25% commission on foreign sales. Offers written contract; 30-day notice must be given to terminate contract. This agency charges for postage/messenger services only if a project is sold.
Tips "Please review our Web site for the most up-to-date submission guidelines."

PMA LITERARY AND FILM MANAGEMENT, INC.
45 West 21st St., Suite 4SW, New York NY 10010. (212)929-1222. Fax: (212)206-0238. E-mail: queries@pmalitfilm.com. Website: www.pmalitfilm.com. Address for packages is P.O. Box 1817, Old Chelsea Station, New York NY 10113 **Contact:** Kelly Skillen. Represents more than 100 clients. 50% of clients are new/unpublished writers. Currently handles: 40% nonfiction books; 30% novels; 5% juvenile books; 25% movie scripts.
• In his time in the literary world, Mr. Miller has successfully managed more than 1,000 books and dozens of motion picture and television properties. He is the author of *Author! Screenwriter!*; Ms. Skillen was previously in the restaurant and nightclub industry.
Member Agents Peter Miller ("big" nonfiction, business, true crime, religion); Kelly Skillen, kelly@pmalitfilm.

com (literary fiction, narrative nonfiction, pop culture); Adrienne Rosado (literary and commercial fiction, young adult).

Represents Nonfiction books, novels, juvenile books, movie scripts, TV scripts, TV movie of the week. **Considers these nonfiction areas:** Biography/autobiography; business/economics; child guidance/parenting; cooking/foods/nutrition; current affairs; ethnic/cultural interests; humor/satire; memoirs; money/finance; popular culture; religious/inspirational; self-help/personal improvement; sports; true crime/investigative. **Considers these fiction areas:** Action/adventure; detective/police/crime; erotica; ethnic; experimental; gay/lesbian; historical; humor/satire; juvenile; literary; mainstream/contemporary; mystery/suspense; psychic/supernatural; religious/inspirational; romance; thriller; young adult; women's. **Considers these script subject areas:** Action/adventure; comedy; mainstream; romantic comedy; romantic drama; thriller.

O— "PMA believes in long-term relationships with professional authors. We manage an author's overall career—hence the name—and have strong connections to Hollywood." Actively seeking new ideas beautifully executed. Does not want to receive poetry, stage plays, picture books and clichés.

How to Contact Query with SASE, submit publishing history, author bio. Send no attachments or mss of any kind unless requested. Accepts e-mail queries. No fax queries. Considers simultaneous queries. Responds in 4-6 weeks to mss. 5-7 days for e-mail queries; six months for paper submissions Returns materials only with SASE. Obtains most new clients through recommendations from others, solicitations, conferences.

Recent Sales *For the Sake of Liberty*, by M. William Phelps (Thomas Dunne Books); *The Haunting of Cambria*, by Richard Taylor (Tor); *Cover Girl Confidential*, by Beverly Bartlett (5 Spot); *Ten Prayers God Always Says Yes To!*, by Anthony DeStefano (Doubleday); *Miss Fido Manners: The Complete Book of Dog Etiquette*, by Charlotte Reed (Adams Media); film rights to *Murder in the Heartland*, by M. William Phelps (Mathis Entertainment); film rights to *The Killer's Game*, by Jay Bonansinga (Andrew Lazar/Mad Chance, Inc.).

Terms Agent receives 15% commission on domestic sales; 25% commission on foreign sales. Offers written contract; 30-day notice must be given to terminate contract. This agency charges for approved expenses, such as photocopies and overnight delivery.

Writers' Conferences A full list of Mr. Miller's speaking engagements is available online.

Tips "Don't approach agents before your work is ready, and always approach them as professionally as possible. Don't give up."

⊘ THE POYNOR GROUP

444 East 82nd St., Suite 28C, New York NY 10028. (212)734-5909. Fax: (212)734-5909. E-mail: jpoynor@nyc.rr.com. **Contact:** Jay Poynor, president. Estab. 1995. Represents 30 clients. **Considers these nonfiction areas:** Biography/autobiography; business/economics; cooking/foods/nutrition; ethnic/cultural interests; health/medicine; multicultural; religious/inspirational. **Considers these fiction areas:** Juvenile; mystery/suspense; romance.

How to Contact Query with SASE.

Recent Sales This agency prefers not to share information about specific sales.

⊘ HELEN F. PRATT INC.

1165 Fifth Ave., New York NY 10029. (212)722-5081. Fax: (212)722-8569. E-mail: hfpratt@verizon.net. **Contact:** Helen F. Pratt. Member of AAR. Currently handles: 100% illutsrated books and nonfiction.

Member Agents Helen Pratt (illustrated books, fashion/decorative design nonfiction).

Represents Nonfiction books.

How to Contact Query with SASE. Include illustrations if possible. Accepts e-mail queries. No fax queries.

⊘ PROSPECT AGENCY LLC

285 Fifth Ave., PMB 445, Brooklyn NY 11215. (718)788-3217. E-mail: esk@prospectagency.com. Website: www.prospectagency.com. **Contact:** Emily Sylvan Kim. Estab. 2005. Represents 15 clients. 50% of clients are new/unpublished writers. Currently handles: 66% novels; 33% juvenile books.

• Prior to starting her agency, Ms. Kim briefly attended law school and worked for another literary agency.

Member Agents Emily Sylvan Kim; Becca Stumpf (adult and YA literary, mainstream fiction; nonfiction interests include narrative nonfiction, journalistic perspectives, fashion, film studies, travel, art, and informed analysis of cultural phenomena. She has a special interest in aging in America and environmental issues); Rachel Orr (fiction and nonfiction, particularly picture books, beginning readers, chapter books, middle-grade, YA novels).

Represents Nonfiction books, novels, juvenile books. **Considers these nonfiction areas:** Memoirs; science/technology; juvenile. **Considers these fiction areas:** Action/adventure; detective/police/crime; erotica; ethnic; family saga; juvenile; literary; mainstream/contemporary; mystery/suspense; picture books; romance; science fiction; thriller; westerns/frontier; young adult.

O— "We are currently looking for the next generation of writers to shape the literary landscape. Our clients receive professional and knowledgeable representation. We are committed to offering skilled editorial advice and advocating our clients in the marketplace.'' Actively seeking romance, literary fiction, and young adult submissions. Does not want to receive poetry, short stories, textbooks, or most nonfiction. **How to Contact** Upload outline and 3 sample chapters to the Web site. Considers simultaneous queries. Responds in 3 weeks to queries; 1 month to mss. Obtains most new clients through recommendations from others, conferences, unsolicited mss. **Recent Sales** *Love Potion #10*, by Janice Maynard (NAL); *Spectacular Now*, by Tim Tharp (Knopf Children). Other clients include Diane Perkins, Opal Carew, Marissa Doyle, Meagan Brothers, Elizabeth Scott, Bonnie Edwards, Susan Lyons, Rose Kent, Catherine Stine. **Terms** Agent receives 15% commission on domestic sales; 20% commission on foreign sales. Offers written contract. **Writers' Conferences** SCBWI Annual Winter Conference; Pikes Peak Writers Conference; RWA National Conference.

SUSAN ANN PROTTER, LITERARY AGENT

110 W. 40th St., Suite 1408, New York NY 10018. Website: SusanAnnProtter.com. **Contact:** Susan Protter. Estab. 1971. Member of AAR, Authors Guild.

- Prior to opening her agency, Ms. Protter was associate director of subsidiary rights at Harper & Row Publishers.
- O﹣ Writers must have a book-length project or ms that is ready to sell. Actively seeking for a limited number of quality new clients writing mysteries, health, science and medical. Nonfiction must be by authors with a platform and be new and original concepts by established professionals. Does not want westerns, romance, children's books, young adult novels, screenplays, plays, poetry, Star Wars, or Star Trek.

How to Contact Query by snail mail are preferable; include SASE.
Terms
Tips Charges 15% commission on all sales.

⬛ PSALTIS LITERARY

Post Office: Park West Finance, P.O. Box 20736, New York NY 10025. E-mail: psaltisliterary@mpsaltis.com. Website: www.mpsaltis.com/psaltisliterary.htm. **Contact:** Michael Psaltis. Member of AAR. Represents 30-40 clients. **Represents** Nonfiction books, novels. **Considers these nonfiction areas:** Biography/autobiography; business/economics; cooking/foods/nutrition; health/medicine; history; memoirs; popular culture; psychology; science/technology. **Considers these fiction areas:** Mainstream/contemporary. **How to Contact** Query only, and query by e-mail. Unrequested manuscripts will not be read. No fax queries. **Recent Sales** *Hometown Appetites*, by Kelly Alexander and Cindy Harris (Gotham Books); *A Life in Twilight*, by Mark Wolverton (Joseph Henry Press); *Cooked*, by Jeff Henderson (William Morrow). **Terms** Agent receives 15% commission on domestic sales; 20% commission on foreign sales. Offers written contract.

◯ JOANNA PULCINI LITERARY MANAGEMENT

E-mail: info@jplm.com. Website: www.jplm.com. **Contact:** Joanna Pulcini.

- O﹣ "JPLM is not accepting submissions at this time; however, I do encourage those seeking representation to read the 'Advice to Writers' essay on our Web site for some guidance on finding an agent.''

How to Contact Do not query this agency until they open their client list.
Recent Sales Other clients include Jennifer Weiner, Nick Clooney, John Searles and Megan McCafferty.

◗ QUEEN LITERARY AGENCY

850 Seventh Ave., Suite 704, New York NY 10019. (212)974-8333. Fax: (212)974-8347. Website: www.queenliterary.com. **Contact:** Lisa Queen. Estab. 2006.

- Prior to her current position, Ms. Queen was a former publishing executive and most recently head of IMG Worldwide's literary division; Mr. Murphy was a vice president at Random House and has 26 years experience in book publishing.

Represents Nonfiction books, novels.

- O﹣ Ms. Queen's specialties: "While our agency represents a wide range of nonfiction titles, we have a particular interest in business books, food writing, science and popular psychology, as well as books by well-known chefs, radio and television personalities and sports figures.''

How to Contact Query with SASE. No fax queries.
Recent Sales *Hero of the Underground*, by Jason Peter (St. Martin's); *Change Your Life in Seven Days*, by Paul McKenna; *Pig Perfect*, by Peter Kaminsky.

◢ QUICKSILVER BOOKS: LITERARY AGENTS

508 Central Park Ave., #5101, Scarsdale NY 10583. Phone/Fax: (914)722-4664. E-mail: QBONLINE@ARTSNET. NET. Website: www.quicksilverbooks.com. **Contact:** Bob Silverstein. Estab. 1973 as packager; 1987 as literary agency. Represents 50 clients. 50% of clients are new/unpublished writers. Currently handles: 75% nonfiction books; 25% novels.

- Prior to opening his agency, Mr. Silverstein served as senior editor at Bantam Books and Dell Books/ Delacorte Press.

Represents Nonfiction books, novels. **Considers these nonfiction areas:** Anthropology/archaeology; biography/autobiography; business/economics; child guidance/parenting; cooking/foods/nutrition; current affairs; ethnic/cultural interests; health/medicine; history; how-to; language/literature/criticism; memoirs; nature/environment; New Age/metaphysics; popular culture; psychology; religious/inspirational; science/technology; self-help/personal improvement; sociology; sports; true crime/investigative; women's issues/studies. **Considers these fiction areas:** Action/adventure; glitz; mystery/suspense; thriller.

- ⊶ This agency specializes in literary and commercial mainstream fiction and nonfiction, especially psychology, New Age, holistic healing, consciousness, ecology, environment, spirituality, reference, self-help, cookbooks and narrative nonfiction. Does not want to receive science fiction, pornography, poetry or single-spaced mss.

How to Contact Query with SASE. Authors are expected to supply SASE for return of ms and for query letter responses. No fax queries. Considers simultaneous queries. Responds in 2 weeks to queries; 1 month to mss. Returns materials only with SASE. Obtains most new clients through recommendations, listings in sourcebooks, solicitations, workshop participation.

Recent Sales Sold more than 20 titles in the last year. *God Without Religion*, by Sankara Saranam (BenBella); *Mr. Jefferson Goes to Paris*, by Charles Cerami (Wiley); *The Ultimate Guide to Home Workouts for Women*, by Brad Schoenfeld; *See Jane Lead*, by Lois Frankel (Warner); *28-Day Shapeover*, by Brad Schoenfeld (Human Kinetics); *Don't Sabotage Your Career*, by Lois Frankel (Warner); *Beyond the Indigo Children*, by P.M.H. Atwater (Bear & Company); *Dinner at Mr. Jefferson's*, by Charles Cerami (Wiley); *Nice Girls Don't Get Rich*, by Lois P. Frankel (Warner Books); *The Young Patriots*, by Charles Cerami (Sourcebooks); *The Coming of the Beatles*, by Martin Goldsmith (Wiley); *The Real Food Daily Cookbook*, by Ann Gentry (Ten Speed Press); *The Complete Book of Vinyasa Yoga*, by Srivatsa Ramaswami (Marlowe & Co.).

Terms Agent receives 15% commission on domestic sales; 20% commission on foreign sales. Offers written contract.

Writers' Conferences National Writers Union.

Tips "Write what you know. Write from the heart. Publishers print, authors sell."

◢ SUSAN RABINER, LITERARY AGENCY, INC.

315 W. 39th St., Suite 1501, New York NY 10018. (212)279-0316. Fax: (212)279-0932. Website: www.rabinerlit.c om. **Contact:** Susan Rabiner.

- Prior to becoming an agent, Ms. Rabiner was editorial director of Basic Books. She is also the co-author of *Thinking Like Your Editor: How to Write Great Serious Nonfiction and Get it Published* (W.W. Norton).

Member Agents Susan Rabiner; Sydelle Kramer; Helena Schwarz; Holly Bemiss. See the Web site for individual agent e-mails.

Represents Nonfiction books, novels, textbooks. **Considers these nonfiction areas:** Biography/autobiography; business/economics; education; government/politics/law; health/medicine; history; philosophy; psychology; religious/inspirational; science/technology; sociology; sports; biography, law/politics.

How to Contact Query by e-mail only, with cover letter and proposal for nonfiction. Considers simultaneous queries. Responds in 3 weeks to queries. Returns materials only with SASE. Obtains most new clients through recommendations from others.

Recent Sales *The Middle East by Vali Nasr* (The Free Press); *Madness: A Life*, by Marya Hornbacher (Houghton-Mifflin); *Love Life: A Case Study*, by Allison Bechdel (Houghton-Mifflin); *The Sino-Japanese War*, by Rana Mitter (Houghton-Mifflin); *Shop Craft as Soul Craft*, by Matthew Crawford (Penguin Press); *French Milk*, a graphic novel by Lucy Knisley (Touchstone/Fireside).

Terms Agent receives 15% commission on domestic sales; 20% commission on foreign sales. Offers written contract; 1-month notice must be given to terminate contract.

◢ ◉ LYNNE RABINOFF AGENCY

72-11 Austin St., No. 201, Forest Hills NY 11375. (718)459-6894. E-mail: Lynne@lynnerabinoff.com. **Contact:** Lynne Rabinoff. Estab. 1991. Represents 50 clients. 50% of clients are new/unpublished writers. Currently handles: 99% nonfiction books; 1% novels.

- Prior to becoming an agent, Ms. Rabinoff was in publishing and dealt with foreign rights.

Represents Nonfiction books. **Considers these nonfiction areas:** Anthropology/archaeology; biography/autobiography; business/economics; current affairs; ethnic/cultural interests; government/politics/law; history;

memoirs; military/war; popular culture; psychology; religious/inspirational; science/technology; women's issues/studies.

o→ This agency specializes in history, political issues, current affairs and religion.

How to Contact Query with SASE, submit proposal package, synopsis, 1 sample chapter(s), author bio. Accepts e-mail queries. No fax queries. Responds in 3 weeks to queries; 1 month to mss. Obtains most new clients through recommendations from others.

Recent Sales *The Confrontation*, by Walid Phares (Palgrave); *Flying Solo*, by Robert Vaughn (Thomas Dunne); *Thugs*, by Micah Halpern (Thomas Nelson); *Cleared for Charge*, by James Lacey (St. Martin's Press); *Now They Call Me Infidel*, by Nonie Darwish (Sentinel/Penguin); *34 Days*, by Avid Issacharoff (Palgrave).

Terms Agent receives 15% commission on domestic sales; 20% commission on foreign sales. Offers written contract; 60-day notice must be given to terminate contract. This agency charges for postage.

⬤ RAINES & RAINES

103 Kenyon Road, Medusa NY 12120. (518)239-8311. Fax: (518)239-6029. **Contact:** Theron Raines (member of AAR); Joan Raines; Keith Korman. Represents 100 clients.

Represents Nonfiction books, novels. **Considers these nonfiction areas:** All subjects. **Considers these fiction areas:** Action/adventure; detective/police/crime; fantasy; historical; mystery/suspense; picture books; science fiction; thriller; westerns/frontier.

How to Contact Query with SASE. Responds in 2 weeks to queries.

Terms Agent receives 15% commission on domestic sales; 20% commission on foreign sales. Charges for photocopying.

⬤ CHARLOTTE CECIL RAYMOND, LITERARY AGENT

32 Bradlee Rd., Marblehead MA 01945. E-mail: raymondliterary@comcast.net. **Contact:** Charlotte Cecil Raymond. Estab. 1983. Currently handles: 90% nonfiction books; 10% novels.

Represents Nonfiction books. **Considers these nonfiction areas:** Current affairs; ethnic/cultural interests; history; nature/environment; psychology; sociology; biography, gender interests.

o→ Does not want to receive self-help/personal improvement, science fiction, fantasy, young adult, juvenile, poetry, or screenplays.

How to Contact Query with SASE, proposal package, outline. Responds in 2 weeks to queries; 6 weeks to mss.

Terms Agent receives 15% commission on domestic sales. 100% of business is derived from commissions on ms sales.

Ⓝ ⬤ ◎ RED SOFA LITERARY

2163 Grand Avenue, #2, St. Paul MN 55105. (651)224-6670. E-mail: dawn@redsofaliterary.com. Website: www.redsofaliterary.com/. **Contact:** Dawn Frederick, Associate Agent. Estab. 2008. Represents 10 clients. 50% of clients are new/unpublished writers. Currently handles: 97% nonfiction books; 2% novels; 1% story collections.

• Prior to her current position, Ms. Frederick spent five years at Sebastian Literary Agency.

Represents Nonfiction books. **Considers these nonfiction areas:** Animals; anthropology/archaeology; cooking/foods/nutrition; crafts/hobbies; current affairs; ethnic/cultural interests; gay/lesbian issues; government/politics/law; health/medicine; history; humor/satire; popular culture; sociology; true crime/investigative; women's issues/studies.

How to Contact Query with SASE, submit proposal package, synopsis, 3 sample chapter(s), author bio. Accepts e-mail queries. No fax queries. Considers simultaneous queries. Responds in 3 weeks to queries; 6 weeks to mss. Returns materials only with SASE. Obtains most new clients through recommendations from others, solicitations.

Terms Agent receives 15% commission on domestic sales; 20% commission on foreign sales. Offers written contract. Recoups some office costs (postage, copying) if sale is made.

Writers' Conferences SDSU Writers' Conference.

Tips "Truly research us. Don't just email or snail mail blast us w/ your book idea. We receive so many, that it can become tedious reading queries we'd never represent to begin with. Look at the websites, guides like this one, online directories and more, before assuming every literary agent is wanting your book idea. Each agent has a vision of what he/she wants to represent, we're waiting for those specific book ideas to come our direction."

🌐 ⬤ REDHAMMER MANAGEMENT, LTD.

186 Bickenhall Mansions, London England W1U 6BX, United Kingdom. (44)(207)487-3465. E-mail: info@redhammer.info. Website: www.redhammer.info. **Contact:** Peter Cox, managing director. Estab. 1999. Represents

24 clients. 65% of clients are new/unpublished writers. Currently handles: 40% nonfiction books; 10% novels; 30% juvenile books; 10% movie scripts; 10% TV scripts.

- Prior to becoming an agent, Mr. Cox was a bestselling author. He was also the managing director of an advertising agency.

Represents Nonfiction books, novels, juvenile books, movie scripts, TV scripts, TV movie of the week, documentary. **Considers these nonfiction areas:** Biography/autobiography; business/economics; current affairs; gay/lesbian issues; government/politics/law; health/medicine; history; how-to; humor/satire; language/literature/criticism; memoirs; military/war; money/finance; music/dance; nature/environment; popular culture; psychology; religious/inspirational; science/technology; self-help/personal improvement; sociology; sports; true crime/investigative. **Considers these fiction areas:** Action/adventure; erotica; family saga; feminist; gay/lesbian; historical; horror; humor/satire; juvenile; literary; mainstream/contemporary; mystery/suspense; romance; science fiction; sports; thriller; young adult; women's/chick lit. **Considers these script subject areas:** Action/adventure; biography/autobiography; comedy; contemporary issues; detective/police/crime; fantasy; glitz; historical; horror; juvenile; mainstream; mystery/suspense; romantic comedy; romantic drama; science fiction; thriller.

- ⚬⇥ "We handle a small number of clients and give them unparalleled attention, help them plan their writing careers, fulfill their goals and dreams, and leverage maximum value out of all aspects of their creative output." Actively seeking committed, top-flight authors with distinctive voices and extraordinary talent. Does not want to receive bulk e-mail submissions. "Read our Web site if you are serious about submitting work to us."

How to Contact See the Web site for submission information. Considers simultaneous queries. Responds in 6 weeks to queries; 6 weeks to mss. Returns materials only with SASE.

Recent Sales Sold 20 titles and sold 4 scripts in the last year. *Jack Flint and the Redthorn Sword*, by Joe Donnelly (Orion Children's Books); *Perfect Hostage*, by Justin Wintle (Hutchinson); *Dave Allen: The Biography*, by Carolyn Soutar (Orion); *The God Effect*, by Brian Clegg (St. Martin's Press). Other clients include Martin Bell, Nicolas Booth, John Brindley, Audrey Eyton, Maria Harris, U.S. Sen. Orrin Hatch, Amanda Lees, Nicholas Monson, Michelle Paver, Donald Trelford, David Yelland.

Terms Agent receives 17.5% commission on domestic sales; 20% commission on foreign sales. Offers written contract; 90-day notice must be given to terminate contract. "We charge reimbursement for couriers and FedEx but these fees are applied only once the writer has started earning royalty."

⬛ THE REDWOOD AGENCY

474 Wellesley Ave., Mill Valley CA, 94941. (415)381-2269 ext. 2. Fax: (415)381-2719. E-mail: info@redwoodagency.com. Website: www.redwoodagency.com. **Contact:** Catherine Fowler, founder; adheres to AAR canon of ethics. Currently handles: 100% nonfiction books.

- Prior to becoming an agent, Ms. Fowler was an editor, subsidiary rights director and associate publisher for Doubleday, Simon & Schuster and Random House.

Represents Nonfiction books. **Considers these nonfiction areas:** Business/economics; cooking/foods/nutrition; health/medicine; humor/satire; memoirs; nature/environment; popular culture; psychology; self-help/personal improvement; women's issues/studies; narrative, parenting, aging, reference, lifestyle, cultural technology.

- ⚬⇥ "Along with our love of books and publishing, we have the desire and commitment to work with fun, interesting and creative people, to do so with respect and professionalism, but also with a sense of humor." Actively seeking high-quality, nonfiction works created for the general consumer market, as well as projects with the potential to become book series. Does not want to receive fiction. Do not send packages that require signature for delivery.

How to Contact Query with SASE. You can also submit through the agency's online form. Accepts e-mail queries. No fax queries. Obtains most new clients through recommendations from others, solicitations.

Recent Sales *The Absent Savior*, by Sandra Kring (Bantam Dell); *The Girl & the Fig Cookbook: More than 100 Recipes from the Acclaimed California Wine Country Restaurant*, by Sondra Bernstein (Simon & Schuster); Students Helping Students series (Perigee). Offers written contract. Charges for copying and delivery charges as specified in author/agency agreement.

⬛ HELEN REES LITERARY AGENCY

376 North St., Boston MA 02113-2013. (617)227-9014. Fax: (617)227-8762. E-mail: reesagency@reesagency.com. **Contact:** Joan Mazmanian, Ann Collette, Helen Rees, Lorin Rees. Estab. 1983. Member of AAR, PEN. Represents more than 100 clients. 50% of clients are new/unpublished writers. Currently handles: 60% nonfiction books; 40% novels.

Member Agents Ann Collette (literary fiction, women's studies, health, biography, history); Helen Rees (business, money/finance/economics, government/politics/law, contemporary issues, literary fiction); Lorin Rees

(business, money/finance, management, history, narrative nonfiction, science, literary fiction, memoir).
Represents Nonfiction books, novels. **Considers these nonfiction areas:** Biography/autobiography; business/economics; current affairs; government/politics/law; health/medicine; history; money/finance; women's issues/studies. **Considers these fiction areas:** Historical; literary; mainstream/contemporary; mystery/suspense; thriller.
How to Contact Query with SASE, outline, 2 sample chapters. No unsolicited e-mail submissions. No multiple submissions. No e-mail or fax queries. Responds in 3-4 weeks to queries. Obtains most new clients through recommendations from others, conferences, submissions.
Recent Sales Sold more than 35 titles in the last year. *Get Your Shipt Together*, by Capt. D. Michael Abrashoff; *Overpromise and Overdeliver*, by Rick Berrara; *Opacity*, by Joel Kurtzman; *America the Broke*, by Gerald Swanson; *Murder at the B-School*, by Jeffrey Cruikshank; *Bone Factory*, by Steven Sidor; *Father Said*, by Hal Sirowitz; *Winning*, by Jack Welch; *The Case for Israel*, by Alan Dershowitz; *As the Future Catches You*, by Juan Enriquez; *Blood Makes the Grass Grow Green*, by Johnny Rico; *DVD Movie Guide*, by Mick Martin and Marsha Porter; *Words That Work*, by Frank Luntz; *Stirring It Up*, by Gary Hirshberg; *Hot Spots*, by Martin Fletcher; *Andy Grove: The Life and Times of an American*, by Richard Tedlow; *Girls Most Likely To*, by Poonam Sharma.
Terms Agent receives 15% commission on domestic sales; 20% commission on foreign sales.

☑ REGAL LITERARY AGENCY

1140 Broadway, Penthouse, New York NY 10001. (212)684-7900. Fax: (212)684-7906. E-mail: Shannon@regal-literary.com. Website: www.regal-literary.com. **Contact:** Shannon Firth, Marcus Hoffmann. Estab. 2002. Member of AAR. Represents 100 clients. 20% of clients are new/unpublished writers. Currently handles: 48% nonfiction books; 46% novels; 6% poetry.

- Prior to becoming agents, Mr. Regal was a musician; Mr. Steinberg was a filmmaker and screenwriter; Ms. Reid and Ms. Schott Pearson were magazine editors; Mr. Hoffman worked in the publishing industry in London.

Member Agents Joseph Regal (literary fiction, science, history, memoir); Peter Steinberg (literary and commercial fiction, history, humor, memoir, narrative nonfiction, young adult); Bess Reed (literary fiction, narrative nonfiction, self-help); Lauren Schott Pearson (literary fiction, commercial fiction, memoir, narrative nonfiction, thrillers, mysteries); Markus Hoffmann (foreign rights manager, literary fiction, mysteries, thrillers, international fiction, science, music). Michael Psaltis of Psaltis Literary also works with Regal Literary agents to form the Culinary Cooperative—a joint-venture agency dedicated to food writing, cookbooks, and all things related to cooking. Recent sales include *Cooked* (William Morrow); *Carmine's Family Style* (St. Martin's Press); *Fish On a First-Name Basis* (St. Martin's Press); *The Reverse Diet* (John Wiley & Sons); and *The Seasoning of a Chef* (Doubleday/Broadway).
Represents Nonfiction books, novels, short story collections, novellas. **Considers these nonfiction areas:** Anthropology/archaeology; art/architecture/design; biography/autobiography; business/economics; cooking/foods/nutrition; current affairs; ethnic/cultural interests; gay/lesbian issues; history; humor/satire; language/literature/criticism; memoirs; military/war; music/dance; nature/environment; photography; popular culture; psychology; religious/inspirational; science/technology; sports; translation; women's issues/studies. **Considers these fiction areas:** Comic books/cartoon; detective/police/crime; ethnic; historical; literary; mystery/suspense; thriller; contemporary.

- ○┅ "We have discovered more than a dozen successful literary novelists in the last 5 years. We are small, but are extraordinarily responsive to our writers. We are more like managers than agents, with an eye toward every aspect of our writers' careers, including publicity and other media." Actively seeking literary fiction and narrative nonfiction. Does not want romance, science fiction, horror, or screenplays.

How to Contact Query with SASE, 5-15 sample pages. No phone calls. No e-mail or fax queries. Considers simultaneous queries. Responds in 2-3 weeks to queries; 4-12 to mss. Returns materials only with SASE. Obtains most new clients through recommendations from others, unsolicited submissions.
Recent Sales Sold 20 titles in the last year. *The Stolen Child*, by Keith Donohue (Nan Talese/Doubleday); *What Elmo Taught Me*, by Kevin Clash (HarperCollins); *The Affected Provincial's Companion*, by Lord Breaulove Swells Whimsy (Bloomsbury); *The Three Incestuous Sisters*, by Audrey Niffenegger (Abrams); *The Traveler*, by John Twelve Hawks (Doubleday). Other clients include James Reston Jr., Tony Earley, Dennie Hughes, Mark Lee, Jake Page, Cheryl Bernard, Daniel Wallace, John Marks, Keith Scribner, Cathy Day, Alicia Erian, Gregory David Roberts, Dallas Hudgens, Tim Winton, Ian Spiegelman, Brad Barkley, Heather Hepler, Gavin Edwards, Sara Voorhees, Alex Abella.
Terms Agent receives 15% commission on domestic sales; 20% commission on foreign sales. No written contract. Charges clients for typical/major office expenses, such as photocopying and foreign postage.

⊘ JODY REIN BOOKS, INC.

7741 S. Ash Ct., Centennial CO 80122. (303)694-4430. Fax: (303)694-0687. Website: www.jodyreinbooks.com. **Contact:** Winnefred Dollar. Estab. 1994. Member of AAR, Authors' Guild. Currently handles: 70% nonfiction books; 30% novels.

• Prior to opening her agency, Ms. Rein worked for 13 years as an acquisitions editor for Contemporary Books and as executive editor for Bantam/Doubleday/Dell and Morrow/Avon.

Represents Nonfiction books, novels. **Considers these nonfiction areas:** Business/economics; child guidance/ parenting; current affairs; ethnic/cultural interests; government/politics/law; history; humor/satire; music/ dance; nature/environment; popular culture; psychology; science/technology; sociology; theater/film; women's issues/studies. **Considers these fiction areas:** Literary; mainstream/contemporary.

○━ This agency specializes in commercial and narrative nonfiction and literary/commercial fiction. Actively seeking Narrative nonfiction, Commercial nonfiction (business, health, psychology, inspiration, parenting, science, relationships, history and sociology), Memoir, Literary Fiction, Commercial Fiction (no romance, no boy books, no Westerns, no horror, no true crime). Does not want to receive poetry, romance, horror, children's books, science fiction, fantasy, or men's adventure.

How to Contact Send one page query via snail mail with SASE. Further detailed instructions online. No e-mail or fax queries.

Recent Sales *How to Remodel a Man*, by Bruce Cameron (St. Martin's Press); *8 Simple Rules for Dating My Teenage Daughter*, by Bruce Cameron (ABC/Disney); *Skeletons on the Zahara*, by Dean King (Little, Brown); *The Big Year*, by Mark Obmascik (The Free Press).

Terms Agent receives 15% commission on domestic sales; 25% commission on foreign sales; 20% commission on dramatic rights sales. Offers written contract. Charges clients for express mail, overseas expenses, photocopying mss.

Tips "Do your homework before submitting. Make sure you have a marketable topic and the credentials to write about it. We want well-written books on fresh and original nonfiction topics that have broad appeal, as well as novels written by authors who have spent years developing their craft. Authors must be well established in their fields and have strong media experience."

◐ THE AMY RENNERT AGENCY

98 Main St., #302, Tiburon CA 94920. E-mail: queries@amyrennert.com. Website: www.amyrennert.com. **Contact:** Amy Rennert.

Represents Nonfiction books, novels. **Considers these nonfiction areas:** Biography/autobiography; health/ medicine; history; memoirs; sports; lifestyle, narrative nonfiction. **Considers these fiction areas:** General fiction, mystery.

○━ "The Amy Rennert Agency specializes in books that matter. We provide career management for established and first-time authors, and our breadth of experience in many genres enables us to meet the needs of a diverse clientele."

How to Contact Query via e-mail. For nonfiction, send cover letter and attach a Word file with proposal/first chapter. For fiction, send cover letter and attach file with 10-20 pages.

Recent Sales *A Salty Piece of Land*, by Jimmy Buffett; *Maisie Dobbs*, by Jacqueline Winspear; *The Prize Winner of Defiance, Ohio*, by Terry Ryan; *The Travel Detective*, by Peter Greenberg; *Offer of Proof*, by Robert Heilbrun; *No Place to Hide*, by Robert O'Harrow; *The Poet of Tolstoy Park*, by Sonny Brewer. Other clients include Elliot Jaspin, Beth Kephart, Kris Kristofferson, Adam Phillips, Don Lattin, Kathryn Shevelow, Cynthia Kaplan, Frank Viviano, Amy Krouse Rosenthal, Kim Severson, Pat Walsh, John Shannon, Brian Copeland, Tony Broadbent, Janis Cooke Newman.

Tips "Due to the high volume of submissions, it is not possible to respond to each and every one. Please understand that we are only able to respond to queries that we feel may be a good fit with our agency."

◐ JODIE RHODES LITERARY AGENCY

8840 Villa La Jolla Drive, Suite 315, La Jolla CA 92037-1957. **Contact:** Jodie Rhodes, president. Estab. 1998. Member of AAR. Represents 65 clients. 60% of clients are new/unpublished writers. Currently handles: 45% nonfiction books; 35% novels; 20% juvenile books.

• Prior to opening her agency, Ms. Rhodes was a university-level creative writing teacher, workshop director, published novelist, and vice president/media director at the N.W. Ayer Advertising Agency.

Member Agents Jodie Rhodes; Clark McCutcheon (fiction); Bob McCarter (nonfiction).

Represents Nonfiction books, novels. **Considers these nonfiction areas:** Biography/autobiography; child guidance/parenting; ethnic/cultural interests; government/politics/law; health/medicine; history; memoirs; military/war; science/technology; women's issues/studies. **Considers these fiction areas:** Ethnic; family saga; historical; literary; mainstream/contemporary; mystery/suspense; thriller; young adult; women's.

Actively seeking witty, sophisticated women's books about career ambitions and relationships; edgy/trendy YA and teen books; narrative nonfiction on groundbreaking scientific discoveries, politics, economics, military and important current affairs by prominent scientists and academic professors. Does not want to receive erotica, horror, fantasy, romance, science fiction, religious/inspirational, or children's books (does accept young adult/teen).

How to Contact Query with brief synopsis, first 30-50 pages, SASE. Do not call. Do not send complete ms unless requested. This agency does not return unrequested material weighing a pound or more that requires special postage. Include e-mail address with query. No e-mail or fax queries. Considers simultaneous queries. Responds in 3 weeks to queries. Returns materials only with SASE. Obtains most new clients through recommendations from others, agent sourcebooks.

Recent Sales Sold 40 titles in the last year. *The Ring*, By Kavita Daswani (HarperCollins); *Train To Trieste*, By Domnica Radulescu; *A Year With Cats And Dogs*, by Margaret Hawkins (Permanent Press); *Silence And Silhouettes*, by Ryan Smithson (Harpercollins); *Internal Affairs*, by Constance Dial (Permanent Press); *How Math Rules The World*, by James Stein (Harpercollins).

Terms Agent receives 15% commission on domestic sales; 20% commission on foreign sales. Offers written contract; 1-month notice must be given to terminate contract. Charges clients for fax, photocopying, phone calls, postage. Charges are itemized and approved by writers upfront.

Tips "Think your book out before you write it. Do your research, know your subject matter intimately, and write vivid specifics, not bland generalities. Care deeply about your book. Don't imitate other writers. Find your own voice. We never take on a book we don't believe in, and we go the extra mile for our writers. We welcome talented, new writers."

RICHARDS LITERARY AGENCY

P.O. Box 31 240, Milford Auckland 1309 New Zealand. (64)(9)410-0209. E-mail: rla.richards@clear.net.nz. **Contact:** Ray Richards. Estab. 1977. Member of NZALA. Represents 100 clients. 20% of clients are new/unpublished writers. Currently handles: 20% nonfiction books; 15% novels; 5% story collections; 40% juvenile books; 5% scholarly books; 15% movie rights.

- Prior to opening his agency, Mr. Richards was a book publisher, managing director and vice chairman.
- "We offer a high quality of experience, acceptances and client relationships." Does not want to receive short stories, articles or poetry.

How to Contact Submit outline/proposal. Do not send full ms until requested. Responds in 1 week to queries; 1 month to mss. Returns materials only with SASE. Obtains most new clients through referrals.

Recent Sales *Blindsight*, by Maurice Gee (Penguin/Faber); *The Whale Rider*, by Witi Ihimaera (Reed Publishing); *Margaret Mahy: A Writer's Life*, by Tessa Duder (HarperCollins); Wild Cards: *New Zealand Eccentrics*, by John Dunmore (New Holland).

Terms Agent receives 15% commission on domestic sales; 20% commission on foreign sales. Offers written contract. Charges clients for overseas postage and photocopying.

Tips "We first need a full book proposal, outline of 2-10 pages, author statement of experience and published works."

ANGELA RINALDI LITERARY AGENCY

P.O. Box 7877, Beverly Hills CA 90212-7877. (310)842-7665. Fax: (310)837-8143. E-mail: amr@rinaldiliterary.com. Website: www.rinaldiliterary.com. **Contact:** Angela Rinaldi. Estab. 1994. Member of AAR. Represents 50 clients. Currently handles: 50% nonfiction books; 50% novels.

- Prior to opening her agency, Ms. Rinaldi was an editor at NAL/Signet, Pocket Books and Bantam, and the manager of book development for *The Los Angeles Times*.

Represents Nonfiction books, novels, TV and motion picture rights (for clients only). **Considers these nonfiction areas:** Biography/autobiography; business/economics; health/medicine; money/finance; self-help/personal improvement; true crime/investigative; women's issues/studies; books by journalists and academics. **Considers these fiction areas:** Literary; commercial; upmarket women's fiction; suspense.

- Actively seeking commercial and literary fiction. Does not want to receive scripts, poetry, category romances, children's books, Western's, science fiction/fantasy, technothrillers or cookbooks.

How to Contact For fiction, send first 3 chapters, brief synopsis, SASE. For nonfiction, query with SASE or send outline/proposal, SASE. Do not send certified or metered mail. Brief e-mail inquiries are OK (no attachments). Considers simultaneous queries. Please advise if it is a multiple submission. Responds in 6 weeks to queries. Returns materials only with SASE.

Recent Sales *Mother Love*, by Drusilla Campbell (Grand Central Publishing); *Put It in Writing*, by Deborah Hutchison (Sterling); *Global Warming Is Good for Business* (Quill Driver Books); *Zen Putting*, by Dr. Joseph Parent (Gotham Books).

Terms Agent receives 15% commission on domestic sales; 20% commission on foreign sales. Offers written contract. Charges clients for photocopying.

◐ ANN RITTENBERG LITERARY AGENCY, INC.

30 Bond St., New York NY 10012. (212)684-6936. Fax: (212)684-6929. Website: www.rittlit.com. **Contact:** Ann Rittenberg, president. Estab. 1992. Member of AAR. Currently handles: 50% nonfiction books; 50% novels.
Represents Nonfiction books, novels. **Considers these nonfiction areas:** Biography/autobiography; history (social/cultural); memoirs; women's issues/studies. **Considers these fiction areas:** Literary.

  O— This agent specializes in literary fiction and literary nonfiction. Does not want to receive Screenplays, genre fiction, Poetry, Self-help.

How to Contact Query with SASE, submit outline, 3 sample chapter(s), SASE. Query via snail mail *only*. No e-mail or fax queries. Considers simultaneous queries. Responds in 6 weeks to queries; 2 months to mss. Obtains most new clients through referrals from established writers and editors.
Recent Sales *Bad Cat*, by Jim Edgar (Workman); *A Certain Slant of Light*, by Laura Whitcomb (Houghton Mifflin); *New York Night*, by Mark Caldwell (Scribner); *In Plain Sight*, by C.J. Box (Putnam); *Improbable*, by Adam Fawer; *Colleges That Change Lives*, by Loren Pope.
Terms Agent receives 15% commission on domestic sales; 20% commission on foreign sales. Offers written contract. This agency charges clients for photocopying only.

Ⓝ ◑ LESLIE RIVERS, INTERNATIONAL (LRI)

P.O. Box 940772, Houston TX 77094-7772. (281)493'5822. Fax: (281)493'5835. E-mail: LRivers@LeslieRivers.com. Website: www.leslierivers.com. **Contact:** Judith Bruni. Estab. 2005; adheres to AAR's canon of ethics. Represents 20 clients. 80% of clients are new/unpublished writers. Currently handles: 25% nonfiction books; 70% novels; 5% scholarly books.
Member Agents Judith Bruni, literary agent and founder; Mark Bruni, consulting editor.
Represents Nonfiction books, novels, scholarly books, movie scripts, TV scripts, stage plays. **Considers these nonfiction areas:** Open to all genres, as long as the author is established with a platform. **Considers these fiction areas:** All fiction genres, but no children's fiction. **Considers these script subject areas:** Considers all script genres.

  O— LRI collaborates with creative professionals and offers a customized, boutique service, based on the client's individual requirements. Send only your finest work. Actively seeking fiction—all subgenres. Does not want to receive children's books or poetry.

How to Contact Query with SASE, submit synopsis, author bio, 3 chapters or 50 pages, whichever is longer. Prefers an exclusive read, but will consider simultaneous queries. Accepts e-mail queries. No fax queries. Responds in 2 months to queries; 2 months to mss. Returns materials only with SASE. Obtains most new clients through recommendations from others, solicitations.
Terms Agent receives 15% commission on domestic sales; 25% commission on foreign sales. Offers written contract; 90-day notice must be given to terminate contract. This agency charges for postage, printing, copying, etc. If no sale is made, no charges are enforced.

◑ RLR ASSOCIATES, LTD.

Literary Department, 7 W. 51st St., New York NY 10019. (212)541-8641. Fax: (212)262-7084. E-mail: sgould@rlr associates.net. Website: www.rlrliterary.net. **Contact:** Jennifer Unter, Scott Gould. Member of AAR. Represents 50 clients. 25% of clients are new/unpublished writers. Currently handles: 70% nonfiction books; 25% novels; 5% story collections.
Represents Nonfiction books, novels, short story collections, scholarly books. **Considers these nonfiction areas:** Animals; anthropology/archaeology; art/architecture/design; biography/autobiography; business/economics; child guidance/parenting; cooking/foods/nutrition; current affairs; education; ethnic/cultural interests; gay/lesbian issues; government/politics/law; health/medicine; history; humor/satire; interior design/decorating; language/literature/criticism; memoirs; money/finance; multicultural; music/dance; nature/environment; photography; popular culture; psychology; religious/inspirational; science/technology; self-help/personal improvement; sociology; sports; translation; travel; true crime/investigative; women's issues/studies. **Considers these fiction areas:** Action/adventure; comic books/cartoon; detective/police/crime; ethnic; experimental; family saga; feminist; gay/lesbian; historical; horror; humor/satire; literary; mainstream/contemporary; multicultural; mystery/suspense; sports; thriller.

  O— "We provide a lot of editorial assistance to our clients and have connections." Actively seeking fiction, current affairs, history, art, popular culture, health and business. Does not want to receive science fiction, fantasy, screenplays or illustrated children's stories.

How to Contact Query with SASE. Considers simultaneous queries. Responds in 4-8 weeks to queries. Returns materials only with SASE. Obtains most new clients through recommendations from others.

Recent Sales Other clients include Shelby Foote, The Grief Recovery Institute, Don Wade, Don Zimmer, The Knot.com, David Plowden, PGA of America, Danny Peary, Goerge Kalinsky, Peter Hyman, Daniel Parker, Lee Miller, Elise Miller, Nina Planck, Karyn Bosnak.

Terms Agent receives 15% commission on domestic sales; 20% commission on foreign sales. Offers written contract.

Tips "Please check out our Web site for more details on our agency."

⦿ B.J. ROBBINS LITERARY AGENCY

5130 Bellaire Ave., North Hollywood CA 91607-2908. (818)760-6602. E-mail: robbinsliterary@aol.com. **Contact:** (Ms.) B.J. Robbins. Estab. 1992. Member of AAR. Represents 40 clients. 50% of clients are new/unpublished writers. Currently handles: 50% nonfiction books; 50% novels.

Represents Nonfiction books, novels. **Considers these nonfiction areas:** Biography/autobiography; current affairs; ethnic/cultural interests; health/medicine; how-to; humor/satire; memoirs; music/dance; popular culture; psychology; self-help/personal improvement; sociology; sports; theater/film; travel; true crime/investigative; women's issues/studies. **Considers these fiction areas:** Detective/police/crime; ethnic; literary; mainstream/contemporary; mystery/suspense; sports; thriller.

How to Contact Query with SASE, submit outline/proposal, 3 sample chapters, SASE. Accepts e-mail queries (no attachments). No fax queries. Considers simultaneous queries. Responds in 2-6 weeks to queries; 6-8 weeks to mss. Returns materials only with SASE. Obtains most new clients through conferences, referrals.

Recent Sales Sold 15 titles in the last year. *Getting Stoned with Savages*, by J. Maarten Troost (Broadway); *Hot Water*, by Kathryn Jordan (Berkley); *Between the Bridge and the River*, by Craig Ferguson (Chronicle); *I'm Proud of You*, by Tim Madigan (Gotham); *Man of the House*, by Chris Erskine (Rodale); *Bird of Another Heaven*, by James D. Houston (Knopf); *Tomorrow They Will Kiss*, by Eduardo Santiago (Little, Brown); *A Terrible Glory*, by James Donovan (Little, Brown); *The Writing on My Forehead*, by Nafisa Haji (Morrow); *Carry Me Home*, by John Hour Jr. (Simon & Schuster); *Lost on Planet China*, by J. Maarten Troost (Braodway).

Terms Agent receives 15% commission on domestic sales; 20% commission on foreign sales. Offers written contract; 3-month notice must be given to terminate contract. 100% of business is derived from commissions on ms sales. This agency charges clients for postage and photocopying (only after sale of ms).

Writers' Conferences Squaw Valley Writers Workshop; San Diego State University Writers' Conference; Santa Barbara Writers' Conference.

⊕ ⦿ ROGERS, COLERIDGE & WHITE

20 Powis Mews, London England W11 1JN, United Kingdom. (44)(207)221-3717. Fax: (44)(207)229-9084. E-mail: info@rcwlitagency.co.uk. Website: www.rcwlitagency.co.uk. Estab. 1987.

- Prior to opening the agency, Ms. Rogers was an agent with Peter Janson-Smith; Ms. Coleridge worked at Sidgwick & Jackson, Chatto & Windus, and Anthony Sheil Associates; Ms. White was an editor and rights director for Simon & Schuster; Mr. Straus worked at Hodder and Stoughton, Hamish Hamilton, and Macmillan; Mr. Miller worked as Ms. Rogers' assistant and was treasurer of the AAA; Ms. Waldie worked with Carole Smith.

Member Agents Deborah Rogers; Gill Coleridge; Pat White (illustrated and children's books); Peter Straus; David Miller; Zoe Waldie (fiction, biography, current affairs, narrative history); Laurence Laluyaux (foreign rights); Stephen Edwards (foreign rights).

Represents Nonfiction books, novels, juvenile books. **Considers these nonfiction areas:** Cooking/foods/nutrition; current affairs; history (narrative); humor/satire; sports; biography. **Considers these fiction areas:** Most fiction categories.

    O— Does not want to receive plays, screenplays, technical books or educational books.

How to Contact Submit synopsis, proposal, sample chapters, bio, SAE by mail. Responds in 6-8 weeks to queries. Obtains most new clients through recommendations from others, solicitations, conferences.

Recent Sales *Where They Were Missed*, by Lucy Caldwell (Viking); *Theft: A Love Story*, by Peter Carey (Faber); *Nefertiti*, by Nick Drake (Transworld); *Kept: A Victorian Mystery*, by D.J. Taylor (Chatto).

Terms Agent receives 15% commission on domestic sales; 20% commission on foreign sales. Offers written contract.

⦿ LINDA ROGHAAR LITERARY AGENCY, LLC

133 High Point Drive, Amherst MA 01002. (413)256-1921. Fax: (413)256-2636. E-mail: contact@lindaroghaar.com. Website: www.lindaroghaar.com. **Contact:** Linda L. Roghaar. Estab. 1996. Represents 50 clients. 10% of clients are new/unpublished writers. Currently handles: 100% nonfiction books.

- Prior to opening her agency, Ms. Roghaar worked in retail bookselling for 5 years and as a publishers' sales rep for 15 years.

Represents Nonfiction books. **Considers these nonfiction areas:** Animals; anthropology/archaeology; biography/autobiography; education; history; nature/environment; popular culture; religious/inspirational; self-help/personal improvement; women's issues/studies.

How to Contact Query with SASE. Accepts e-mail queries. No fax queries. Considers simultaneous queries. Responds in 2 months to queries; 4 months to mss.

Recent Sales *Poetry as Spiritual Practice*, by Robert McDowell (FreePress); *Growing Up Dead*, by Peter Conners (DaCapo/Perseus); *Free-Range Knitter*, by Stephanie Pearl-McPhee (Andrews McMeel); *Awakened Writer*, by Laraine Herring (Shambhala); *Starting From Scratch*, by Pam Johnson Bennett (Penguin); *Knitting Yarn and The Truth About How Things Are*, by Stephanie Pearl-McPhee (Andrews McMeel).

Terms Agent receives 15% commission on domestic sales; negotiable commission on foreign sales. Offers written contract.

THE ROSENBERG GROUP

23 Lincoln Ave., Marblehead MA 01945. (781)990-1341. Fax: (781)990-1344. Website: www.rosenberggroup.com. **Contact:** Barbara Collins Rosenberg. Estab. 1998. Member of AAR, recognized agent of the RWA. Represents 25 clients. 15% of clients are new/unpublished writers. Currently handles: 30% nonfiction books; 30% novels; 10% scholarly books; 30% college textbooks.

- Prior to becoming an agent, Ms. Rosenberg was a senior editor for Harcourt.

Represents Nonfiction books, novels, textbooks (college textbooks only). **Considers these nonfiction areas:** Current affairs; popular culture; psychology; sports; women's issues/studies; women's health; food/wine/beverages. **Considers these fiction areas:** Romance; women's.

- Ms. Rosenberg is well-versed in the romance market (both category and single title). She is a frequent speaker at romance conferences. Actively seeking romance category or single title in contemporary chick lit, romantic suspense, and the historical subgenres. Does not want to receive inspirational or spiritual romances.

How to Contact Query with SASE. No e-mail or fax queries. Responds in 2 weeks to queries; 4-6 weeks to mss. Returns materials only with SASE. Obtains most new clients through recommendations from others, solicitations, conferences.

Recent Sales Sold 21 titles in the last year.

Terms Agent receives 15% commission on domestic sales; 15% commission on foreign sales. Offers written contract; 1-month notice must be given to terminate contract. Charges maximum of $350/year for postage and photocopying.

Writers' Conferences RWA National Conference; BookExpo America.

RITA ROSENKRANZ LITERARY AGENCY

440 West End Ave., Suite 15D, New York NY 10024-5358. (212)873-6333. **Contact:** Rita Rosenkranz. Estab. 1990. Member of AAR. Represents 35 clients. 30% of clients are new/unpublished writers. Currently handles: 99% nonfiction books; 1% novels.

- Prior to opening her agency, Ms. Rosenkranz worked as an editor in major New York publishing houses.

Represents Nonfiction books. **Considers these nonfiction areas:** Animals; anthropology/archaeology; art/architecture/design; biography/autobiography; business/economics; child guidance/parenting; computers/electronic; cooking/foods/nutrition; crafts/hobbies; current affairs; ethnic/cultural interests; gay/lesbian issues; government/politics/law; health/medicine; history; how-to; humor/satire; interior design/decorating; language/literature/criticism; military/war; money/finance; music/dance; nature/environment; New Age/metaphysics; photography; popular culture; psychology; religious/inspirational; science/technology; self-help/personal improvement; sports; theater/film; women's issues/studies.

- This agency focuses on adult nonfiction, stresses strong editorial development and refinement before submitting to publishers, and brainstorms ideas with authors. Actively seeking authors who are well paired with their subject, either for professional or personal reasons.

How to Contact Submit proposal package, outline, SASE. No e-mail or fax queries. Considers simultaneous queries. Responds in 2 weeks to queries. Obtains most new clients through solicitations, conferences, word of mouth.

Recent Sales Sold 30 titles in the last year. *By Any Means Necessary: Love, Lawsuits, Con Artists and Voodoo Queens on the Underground Railroad*, by Betty DeRamus (Atria Books); *A Survival Guide for Landlocked Mermaids*, by Margot Datz (Beyond Words); *Straight Talk about Cosmetic Surgery*, by Arthur W. Perry (Yale University Press); *Voice for Hire*, by Randy Thomas and Peter Rofe (Billboard Books); *The Wines and Wineries of the North Fork and the Hamptons*, by Jane Taylor Starwood and Bruce Curtis (Globe Pequot Press); *Baseball Hall of Fame Museum*, by Bert Sugar (Running Press).

Terms Agent receives 15% commission on domestic sales; 20% commission on foreign sales. Offers written contract, binding for 3 years; 3-month written notice must be given to terminate contract. 100% of business is

derived from commissions on ms sales. Charges clients for photocopying. Makes referrals to editing services.
Tips "Identify the current competition for your project to make sure the project is valid. A strong cover letter is very important."

N̄ ◘ ANDY ROSS LITERARY AGENCY

797 San Diego Road, Berkeley CA 94707. (510)525-0685. E-mail: andyrossagency@hotmail.com. Website: www .andyrossagency.com. **Contact:** Andy Ross. Estab. 2007. Represents 5 clients. 20% of clients are new/unpublished writers. Currently handles: 100% nonfiction books.
Represents Nonfiction books, scholarly books. **Considers these nonfiction areas:** Anthropology/archaeology; biography/autobiography; child guidance/parenting; current affairs; education; ethnic/cultural interests; government/politics/law; history; language/literature/criticism; military/war; nature/environment; popular culture; psychology; science/technology; sociology.

> **O₋** This agency specializes in general nonfiction, politics and current events, history, biography, journalism and contemporary culture. Actively seeking narrative nonfiction. Does not want to receive personal memoir, fiction, poetry, juvenile books.

How to Contact Query with SASE. Considers simultaneous queries. Responds in 1 week to queries.
Terms Agent receives 15% commission on domestic sales; 25% commission on foreign sales. Offers written contract.

◘ THE GAIL ROSS LITERARY AGENCY

1666 Connecticut Ave. NW, #500, Washington DC 20009. (202)328-3282. Fax: (202)328-9162. E-mail: jennifer@ gailross.com. Website: www.gailross.com. **Contact:** Jennifer Manguera. Estab. 1988. Member of AAR. Represents 200 clients. 75% of clients are new/unpublished writers. Currently handles: 95% nonfiction books.
Represents Nonfiction books. **Considers these nonfiction areas:** Anthropology/archaeology; biography/autobiography; business/economics; education; ethnic/cultural interests; gay/lesbian issues; government/politics/law; health/medicine; money/finance; nature/environment; psychology; religious/inspirational; science/technology; self-help/personal improvement; sociology; sports; true crime/investigative.

> **O₋** This agency specializes in adult trade nonfiction.

How to Contact Query with SASE. Considers simultaneous queries. Responds in 1 month to queries. Obtains most new clients through recommendations from others.
Recent Sales Sold 50 titles in the last year.
Terms Agent receives 15% commission on domestic sales; 25% commission on foreign sales. Charges for office expenses.

◙ CAROL SUSAN ROTH, LITERARY & CREATIVE

P.O. Box 620337, Woodside CA 94062. (650)323-3795. E-mail: carol@authorsbest.com. Website: www.authors best.com. **Contact:** Carol Susan Roth. Estab. 1995. Represents 50 clients. 15% of clients are new/unpublished writers. Currently handles: 100% nonfiction books.

> • Prior to becoming an agent, Ms. Roth was trained as a psychotherapist and worked as a motivational coach, conference producer, and promoter for best-selling authors (e.g., Scott Peck, Bernie Siegal, John Gray) and the 1987 Heart of Business conference (the first business and spirituality conference).

Represents Nonfiction books. **Considers these nonfiction areas:** Business/economics; health/medicine (wellness); history; humor/satire; money/finance (personal finance/investing); popular culture; religious/inspirational; science/technology; self-help/personal improvement; spirituality; Buddhism, yoga, humor, real estate, entrepreneurship, beauty, social action, wellness.

> **O₋** This agency specializes in health, science, pop culture, spirituality, personal growth, personal finance, entrepreneurship and business. Actively seeking previously published, media saavy journalists, authors, and experts with an established audience in pop culture, history, the sciences, health, spirituality, personal growth, and business. Does not want to receive fiction or children's books.

How to Contact Submit proposal package, media kit, promotional video, SASE. Accepts e-mail queries (no attachments). Considers simultaneous queries. Responds in 2 days to queries. Returns materials only with SASE. Obtains most new clients through recommendations from others, solicitations.
Recent Sales Sold 17 titles in the last year. *The Immortals and Confessions of an Alien Hunter*, by Seth Shostak; *How Life Begins*, by David Deamer; *The Magic Dictionary*, by Craig Conley; *Way of the Fertile Soul*, by Randine Lewis (Atria/S&S); *Teachings of the Adventure Rabbi*, by Rabbi Jamie Korngold (Doubleday); *Seven Stones That Rocked the World*, by Patrick Hunt (University of California Press); *Ten Discoveries That Rewrote History*, by Patrick Hunt (Penguin Plume); *Snooze or Lose!*, by Helene Emsellem (Joseph Henry Press).
Terms Agent receives 15% commission on domestic sales; 15% commission on foreign sales. Offers written contract, binding for 3 years (only for work with the acquiring publisher); 60-day notice must be given to

terminate contract. This agency asks the client to provide postage (FedEx airbills) and do copying. Refers to book doctor for proposal development and publicity service on request.

Writers' Conferences Stanford Professional Publishing Course, MEGA Book Marketing University, Maui Writers Conference, Jack London Writers' Conference, San Francisco Writers' Conference.

Tips "Have charisma, content, and credentials—solve an old problem in a new way. I prefer experts with an Internet blog presence as well as extensive teaching and speaking experience."

☑ JANE ROTROSEN AGENCY LLC

318 E. 51st St., New York NY 10022. (212)593-4330. Fax: (212)935-6985. E-mail: firstinitiallastname@janerotros en.com. Estab. 1974. Member of AAR, Authors Guild. Represents over 100 clients. Currently handles: 30% nonfiction books; 70% novels.

Member Agents Jane R. Berkey; Andrea Cirillo; Annelise Robey; Margaret Ruley; Kelly Harms; Christina Hogrebe; Peggy Gordijn, director of translation rights.

Represents Nonfiction books, novels. **Considers these nonfiction areas:** Biography/autobiography; business/ economics; child guidance/parenting; cooking/foods/nutrition; current affairs; health/medicine; how-to; humor/satire; money/finance; nature/environment; popular culture; psychology; self-help/personal improvement; sports; true crime/investigative; women's issues/studies. **Considers these fiction areas:** Action/adventure; detective/police/crime; family saga; historical; horror; mainstream/contemporary; mystery/suspense; romance; thriller; women's.

How to Contact Query with SASE. No e-mail or fax queries. Responds in 2 months to mss. Responds in 2 weeks to writers who have been referred by a client or colleague. Returns materials only with SASE. Obtains most new clients through referrals.

Recent Sales This agency prefers not to share information on specific sales.

Terms Agent receives 15% commission on domestic sales; 20% commission on foreign sales. Offers written contract, binding for 3-5 years; 2-month notice must be given to terminate contract. Charges clients for photocopying, express mail, overseas postage, book purchase.

☑ THE DAMARIS ROWLAND AGENCY

5 Cooper Rd., Apt. 13H, New York NY 10010. **Contact:** Damaris Rowland. Estab. 1994. Member of AAR.

Represents Nonfiction books, novels.

• This agency specializes in women's fiction, literary fiction and nonfiction, and pop fiction.

How to Contact Query with SASE. Obtains most new clients through recommendations from others, solicitations, conferences.

Terms Agent receives 15% commission on domestic sales; 20% commission on foreign sales. Offers written contract.

☑ ◎ THE RUDY AGENCY

825 Wildlife Lane, Estes Park CO 80517. (970)577-8500. Fax: (970)577-8600. E-mail: mak@rudyagency.com. Website: www.rudyagency.com. **Contact:** Maryann Karinch. Estab. 2003; adheres to AAR canon of ethics. Represents 15 clients. 50% of clients are new/unpublished writers. Currently handles: 100% nonfiction books.

• Prior to becoming an agent, Ms. Karinch was, and continues to be, an author of nonfiction books—covering the subjects of health/medicine and human behavior. Prior to that, she was in public relations and marketing: areas of expertise she also applies in her practice as an agent.

Member Agents Maryann Karinch (nonfiction: health/medicine, culture/values, history, biography, memoir, science/technology, military/intelligence).

Represents Nonfiction books, textbooks (with consumer appeal). **Considers these nonfiction areas:** Anthropology/archaeology; biography/autobiography; business/economics; child guidance/parenting; computers/electronic; current affairs; education; ethnic/cultural interests; gay/lesbian issues; government/politics/law; health/ medicine; history; how-to; language/literature/criticism; memoirs; military/war; money/finance; music/dance; nature/environment; popular culture; psychology; science/technology; self-help/personal improvement; sociology; sports; true crime/investigative; women's issues/studies.

• "We support authors from the proposal stage through promotion of the published work. We work in partnership with publishers to promote the published work and coach authors in their role in the marketing and public relations campaigns for the book." Actively seeking projects with social value, projects that open minds to new ideas and interesting lives, and projects that entertain through good storytelling. Does not want to receive poetry, children's/juvenile books, screenplays/plays, art/photo books, novels/novellas, religion books, and joke books or books that fit in to the impulse buy/gift book category.

How to Contact Query us. If we like the query, we will invite a complete proposal. No phone queries. Accepts e-mail and fax queries. Considers simultaneous queries. Responds in 8 weeks to mss. Returns materials only with SASE. Obtains most new clients through recommendations from others, solicitations.

Recent Sales Sold 11 titles in the last year. *Live from Jordan: Letters Home from My Journal Through the Middle East*, by Benjamin Orbach (Amacom); *Finding Center: Strategies to Build Strong Girls & Women*, by Maureen Mack (New Horizon Press); *Crossing Fifth Avenue to Bergdorf Goodman: An Insider's Account on the Rise of Luxury Retailing*, by Ira Neimark (SPI Books); *Hamas vs. Fatah: The Struggle for Palestine*, by Jonathan Schanzer (Palgrave Macmillan); *The First American: The Suppressed Story of the People Who Discovered the New World*, by Christopher Hardaker (Career Press/New Page Books). Other clients include Gregory Hartley, Peter Earnest, Curtrise Garner, Mary Branson, Martina Sprague, Michael Kagan, Guy Smith, Matt Hilfer, Joy Carlough, Lea-Rachel Kosnik, Fred Pushies, Sunil Singh, Pat Lechault, David Marshall, Richard Killblane, Savo Heleta, Vanessa Vega.

Terms Agent receives 15% commission on domestic sales. Offers written contract, binding for 1 year.

Writers' Conferences BookExpo of America; industry events.

Tips "Present yourself professionally. I tell people all the time: Subscribe to *Writer's Digest* (I do), because you will get good advice about how to approach an agent."

⊙ MARLY RUSOFF & ASSOCIATES, INC.

P.O. Box 524, Bronxville NY 10708. (914)961-7939. E-mail: mra_queries@rusoffagency.com. Website: www.rusoffagency.com. **Contact:** Marly Rusoff.

- Prior to her current position, Ms. Rusoff held positions at Houghton Mifflin, Doubleday and William Morrow. Ms. Hansen worked for Crown, Simon & Schuster and Doubleday.

Member Agents Marly Rusoff; Judith Hansen.

Represents Nonfiction books, novels. **Considers these nonfiction areas:** Art/architecture/design; biography/autobiography; business/economics; health/medicine; history; memoirs; money/finance; popular culture; psychology. **Considers these fiction areas:** Historical; literary; commercial.

> "While we take delight in discovering new talent, we are particularly interested in helping established writers expand readership and develop their careers."

How to Contact Query with SASE, submit synopsis, publishing history, author bio, contact information. For e-queries, include no attachments or pdf files. This agency only responds if interested. No fax queries. Obtains most new clients through recommendations from others.

Recent Sales *Ellington Boulevard*, by Adam Langer (Spiegel & Grau); *Confessions of a Jane Austen Addict*, by Laurie Viera Rigler; *My Father's Bonus March*, by Adam Langer; *The Decency Rules and Regulations*, by Susan and Frank Fuller.

⊙ RUSSELL & VOLKENING

50 W. 29th St., #7E, New York NY 10001. (212)684-6050. Fax: (212)889-3026. Website: www.randvinc.com. **Contact:** Timothy Seldes, Jesseca Salky. Estab. 1940. Member of AAR. Represents 140 clients. 20% of clients are new/unpublished writers. Currently handles: 45% nonfiction books; 50% novels; 3% story collections; 2% novellas.

Represents Nonfiction books, novels, short story collections. **Considers these nonfiction areas:** Anthropology/archaeology; art/architecture/design; biography/autobiography; business/economics; cooking/foods/nutrition; current affairs; education; ethnic/cultural interests; gay/lesbian issues; government/politics/law; health/medicine; history; language/literature/criticism; military/war; money/finance; music/dance; nature/environment; photography; popular culture; psychology; science/technology; sociology; sports; theater/film; true crime/investigative; women's issues/studies; creative nonfiction. **Considers these fiction areas:** Action/adventure; detective/police/crime; ethnic; literary; mainstream/contemporary; mystery/suspense; picture books; sports; thriller.

> This agency specializes in literary fiction and narrative nonfiction.

How to Contact Query with SASE, submit synopsis, several pages. No e-mail or fax queries. Responds in 4 weeks to queries.

Recent Sales *Digging to America*, by Anne Tyler (Knopf); *Get a Life*, by Nadine Gardiner; *The Franklin Affair*, by Jim Lehrer (Random House).

Terms Agent receives 15% commission on domestic sales; 20% commission on foreign sales. Charges clients for standard office expenses relating to the submission of materials.

Tips "If the query is cogent, well written, well presented, and is the type of book we'd represent, we'll ask to see the manuscript. From there, it depends purely on the quality of the work."

⊙ REGINA RYAN PUBLISHING ENTERPRISES, INC.

251 Central Park W., 7D, New York NY 10024. (212)787-5589. E-mail: queryreginaryanbooks@rcn.com. **Contact:** Regina Ryan. Estab. 1976. Currently handles: 100% nonfiction books.

• Prior to becoming an agent, Ms. Ryan was an editor at Alfred A. Knopf, editor-in-chief of Macmillan Adult Trade, and a book producer.

Represents Nonfiction books. **Considers these nonfiction areas:** Gardening; government/politics/law; history; psychology; travel; women's issues/studies; narrative nonfiction; natural history (especially birds and birding); popular science; parenting; adventure; architecture, lifestyle.

How to Contact Query by e-mail or mail with SASE. No telephone queries. Does not accept queries for juvenile or fiction. Considers simultaneous queries. Tries to respond in 1 month to queries. Returns materials only with SASE. Obtains most new clients through recommendations from others.

Recent Sales *Gilded Mansions*, by Wayne Craven (WW Norton); *The Commonsense Book of Death*, by Edwin Schneidman; *Mortality Bites*, by Kairol Rosenthal (Wiley); *Tightrope: Six Centuries of a Jewish Dynasty*, by Michael Karpin (Wiley); *The Secret of Success is No Secret*, by Darcy Andries (Sellers).

Terms Agent receives 15% commission on domestic sales; 15% commission on foreign sales. Offers written contract. Charges clients for all out-of-pocket expenses (e.g., long distance calls, messengers, freight, copying) if it's more than just a nominal amount.

Tips "An analysis of why your proposed book is different and better than the competition is essential; a sample chapter is helpful."

☑ THE SAGALYN AGENCY

4922 Fairmont Ave., Suite 200, Bethesda MD 20814. (301)718-6440. Fax: (301)718-6444. E-mail: query@sagalyn .com. Website: www.sagalyn.com. Estab. 1980. Member of AAR. Currently handles: 85% nonfiction books; 5% novels; 10% scholarly books.

Member Agents Raphael Sagalyn; Bridget Wagner.

Represents Nonfiction books. **Considers these nonfiction areas:** Biography/autobiography; business/economics; history; memoirs; popular culture; religious/inspirational; science/technology; journalism.

    O→ Does not want to receive stage plays, screenplays, poetry, science fiction, fantasy, romance, children's books or young adult books.

How to Contact Please send e-mail queries only (no attachments). Include 1 of these words in the subject line: query, submission, inquiry. Accepts e-mail queries. No fax queries.

Tips "We receive 1,000-1,200 queries a year, which in turn lead to 2 or 3 new clients. Query via e-mail only. See our Web site for sales information and recent projects."

☑ SALKIND LITERARY AGENCY

Part of Studio B, 734 Indiana St., Lawrence KS 66044. (913)538-7113. Fax: (516)706-2369. E-mail: neil@studiob. com. Website: www.salkindagency.com. **Contact:** Neil Salkind. Estab. 1995. Represents 100 clients. 25% of clients are new/unpublished writers. Currently handles: 60% nonfiction books; 20% scholarly books; 20% textbooks.

    • Prior to becoming an agent, Mr. Salkind authored numerous trade textbooks.

Represents Nonfiction books, scholarly books, textbooks. **Considers these nonfiction areas:** Business/economics; child guidance/parenting; computers/electronic; cooking/foods/nutrition; crafts/hobbies; education; ethnic/cultural interests; gay/lesbian issues; health/medicine; how-to; money/finance; photography; popular culture; psychology; religious/inspirational; science/technology; self-help/personal improvement; sports.

    O→ Actively seeking distinct nonfiction that takes risks and explores new ideas from authors who have, or can establish, a significant platform. Does not want to receive book proposals based on ideas where potential authors have not yet researched what has been published.

How to Contact Query with SASE, submit publishing history, author bio. Accepts e-mail queries. No fax queries. Responds in 1 week to queries; 1 week to mss. Obtains most new clients through recommendations from others.

Recent Sales Sold 120 titles in the last year. *Googlinaire*, by Anthony Boreilli (Wiley); *Clinical Psychology*, by Dean McKay (Blackwell); *The American Dream*, by Ralph Roberts (Kaplan); *Microsoft 2007 Exchange Admin Companion*, by Walter Glenn (Microsoft Press).

Terms Agent receives 15% commission on domestic sales; 15% commission on foreign sales.

Tips "Present a unique idea based on a thorough knowledge of the market, be it a trade or textbook."

☑ VICTORIA SANDERS & ASSOCIATES

241 Avenue of the Americas, Suite 11 H, New York NY 10014. (212)633-8811. Fax: (212)633-0525. E-mail: queriesvsa@hotmail.com. Website: www.victoriasanders.com. **Contact:** Victoria Sanders, Diane Dickensheid. Estab. 1993. Member of AAR; signatory of WGA. Represents 135 clients. 25% of clients are new/unpublished writers. Currently handles: 30% nonfiction books; 70% novels.

Represents Nonfiction books, novels. **Considers these nonfiction areas:** Biography/autobiography; current affairs; ethnic/cultural interests; gay/lesbian issues; government/politics/law; history; humor/satire; language/ literature/criticism; music/dance; popular culture; psychology; theater/film; translation; women's issues/studies. **Considers these fiction areas:** Action/adventure; contemporary issues; ethnic; family saga; feminist; gay/lesbian; literary; thriller.

How to Contact Query by e-mail only.

Recent Sales Sold 20+ titles in the last year.

Terms Agent receives 15% commission on domestic sales; 20% commission on foreign sales. Offers written contract. Charges for photocopying, messenger, express mail. If in excess of $100, client approval is required.

Tips "Limit query to letter (no calls) and give it your best shot. A good query is going to get a good response."

◗ SANDUM & ASSOCIATES

144 E. 84th St., New York NY 10028-2035. (212)737-2011. **Contact:** Howard E. Sandum. Estab. 1987.

   Oᴦ This agency specializes in general nonfiction and occasionally literary fiction.

How to Contact Query with synopsis, bio, SASE. Do not send full ms unless requested.

Terms Agent receives 15% commission on domestic sales. Charges clients for photocopying, air express, long-distance telephone/fax.

◗ SCHIAVONE LITERARY AGENCY, INC.

236 Trails End, West Palm Beach FL 33413-2135. (561)966-9294. Fax: (561)966-9294. E-mail: profschia@aol.com. New York office: 3671 Hudson Manor Terrace, No. 11H, Bronx, NY, 10463-1139, phone: (718)548-5332; fax: (718)548-5332; e-mail: jendu77@aol.com **Contact:** Dr. James Schiavone. CEO, corporate offices in Florida; Jennifer DuVall, president, New York office. Estab. 1996. Member of National Education Association. Represents 60+ clients. 2% of clients are new/unpublished writers. Currently handles: 50% nonfiction books; 49% novels; 1% textbooks.

   ● Prior to opening his agency, Dr. Schiavone was a full professor of developmental skills at the City University of New York and author of 5 trade books and 3 textbooks. Jennifer DuVall has many years of combined experience in office management and agenting.

Represents Nonfiction books, novels, juvenile books, scholarly books, textbooks. **Considers these nonfiction areas:** Animals; anthropology/archaeology; biography/autobiography; child guidance/parenting; current affairs; education; ethnic/cultural interests; gay/lesbian issues; government/politics/law; health/medicine; history; how-to; humor/satire; juvenile nonfiction; language/literature/criticism; military/war; nature/environment; popular culture; psychology; science/technology; self-help/personal improvement; sociology; spirituality (mind and body); true crime/investigative. **Considers these fiction areas:** Ethnic; family saga; historical; horror; humor/satire; juvenile; literary; mainstream/contemporary; science fiction; young adult.

   Oᴦ This agency specializes in celebrity biography and autobiography and memoirs. Does not want to receive poetry.

How to Contact Query with SASE. Do not send unsolicited materials or parcels requiring a signature. Send no e-attachments. Accepts e-mail queries. No fax queries. Considers simultaneous queries. Responds in 2 weeks to queries; 6 weeks to mss. Returns materials only with SASE. Obtains most new clients through recommendations from others, solicitations, conferences.

Terms Agent receives 15% commission on domestic sales; 20% commission on foreign sales. Offers written contract. Charges clients for postage only.

Writers' Conferences Key West Literary Seminar; South Florida Writers' Conference; Tallahassee Writers' Conference, Million Dollar Writers' Conference; Alaska Writers Conference.

Tips "We prefer to work with established authors published by major houses in New York. We will consider marketable proposals from new/previously unpublished writers."

◖ ◗ ◎ SUSAN SCHULMAN LITERARY AGENCY

454 West 44th St., New York NY 10036. (212)713-1633. Fax: (212)581-8830. E-mail: schulman@aol.com. Website: www.schulmanagency.com. **Contact:** Susan Schulman. Estab. 1980. Member of AAR, Dramatists Guild; signatory of WGA. 10% of clients are new/unpublished writers. Currently handles: 50% nonfiction books; 25% novels; 15% juvenile books; 10% stage plays.

Member Agents Linda Kiss, director of foreign rights; Katherine Stones, theater; Emily Uhry, submissions editor.

Represents Adult nonfiction and fiction as well as children's books. **Considers these nonfiction areas:** Anthropology/archaeology; biography/autobiography; business/economics; child guidance/parenting; cooking/foods/nutrition; current affairs; education; ethnic/cultural interests; gay/lesbian issues; government/politics/law; health/medicine; history; how-to; language/literature/criticism; memoirs; money/finance; music/dance; nature/environment; popular culture; psychology; religious/inspirational; self-help/personal improvement; sociology; sports; true crime/investigative; women's issues/studies. **Considers these fiction areas:** Action/adventure; detective/police/crime; feminist; historical; humor/satire; juvenile; literary; mainstream/contemporary; mystery/suspense; picture books; religious/inspirational; young adult; women's.

O─ "We specialize in books for, by and about women and women's issues including nonfiction self-help books, fiction and theater projects. We also handle the film, television and allied rights for several agencies as well as foreign rights for several publishing houses." Actively seeking new nonfiction. Considers plays. Does not want to receive poetry, television scripts or concepts for television.

How to Contact Query with SASE, submit outline, synopsis, author bio, 3 sample chapters, SASE. Accepts e-mail queries. No fax queries. Considers simultaneous queries. Responds in 6 weeks to queries; 6 weeks to mss. Returns materials only with SASE. Obtains most new clients through recommendations from others, solicitations, conferences.

Recent Sales Sold 50 titles in the last year.

Terms Agent receives 15% commission on domestic sales; 20% commission on foreign sales. Offers written contract; 30-day notice must be given to terminate contract.

Writers' Conferences Geneva Writers' Conference (Switzerland); Columbus Writers' Conference; Skidmore Conference of the Independent Women's Writers Group.

Tips "Keep writing!"

JONATHAN SCOTT, INC

933 West Van Buren, Suite 510, Chicago IL 60607. (847)557-2365. Fax: (847)557-8408. E-mail: jon@jonathansco tt.us; scott@jonathanscott.us. Website: www.jonathanscott.us. **Contact:** Jon Malysiak, Scott Adlington. Estab. 2005. Represents 40 clients. 75% of clients are new/unpublished writers. Currently handles: 90% nonfiction books; 10% novels.

Member Agents Scott Adlington (narrative nonfiction, sports, health, wellness, fitness, environmental issues); Jon Malysiak (narrative nonfiction and fiction, current affairs, history, memoir, business).

Represents Nonfiction books. **Considers these nonfiction areas:** Biography/autobiography; business/economics; current affairs; ethnic/cultural interests; gay/lesbian issues; government/politics/law; health/medicine; history; humor/satire; memoirs; military/war; nature/environment; popular culture; self-help/personal improvement; sociology; sports; true crime/investigative.

O─ "We are very hands-on with our authors in terms of working with them to develop their proposals and manuscripts. Since both of us come from publishing backgrounds—editorial and sales—we are able to give our authors a perspective of what goes on within the publishing house from initial consideration through the entire development, publication, marketing and sales processes."

How to Contact Query with SASE, submit proposal package, synopsis, 2-3 sample chapter(s), author bio. Accepts e-mail queries. No fax queries. Considers simultaneous queries. Responds in 1-2 weeks to queries; 4-6 weeks to mss. Obtains most new clients through recommendations from others, solicitations, contacting good authors for representation.

Recent Sales Sold 12 titles in the last year. *101 Wines to Inspire, Delight and Bring Thunder to Your World*, by Gary Vaynerchuk (Rodale 2008); *America's Best Girl*, by Tim Dahlberg (St. Martin's Press 2008); *The Search for the Perfect Shot*, by Kate Hopkins (St. Martin's Press, 2009); *Make More, Worry Less* by Wes Moss (Prentice Hall 2008); *The Phoenix Principle*, by Adam Hartung (Prentice Hall 2008); *F Wall Street*, by Joe Ponzio (Adams Media 2009); *It's Not About the Babe*, by Jerry Gutlon (Skyhorse Publishing 2008); *The Offsite* by Robert Thompson (Jossey-Bass 2008).

Terms Agent receives 15% commission on domestic sales; 20% commission on foreign sales. Offers written contract; 30-day notice must be given to terminate contract.

Tips "Platform, platform, platform. We can't emphasize this enough. Without a strong national platform, it is nearly impossible to get the interest of a publisher. Also, be organized in your thoughts and your goals before contacting an agent. Think of the proposal as your business plan. What do you hope to achieve by publishing your book. How can your book change the world?"

SCOVIL CHICHAK GALEN LITERARY AGENCY

276 Fifth Ave., Suite 708, New York NY 10001. (212)679-8686. Fax: (212)679-6710. E-mail: info@scglit.com. Website: www.scglit.com. **Contact:** Russell Galen. Estab. 1992. Member of AAR. Represents 300 clients. Currently handles: 60% nonfiction books; 40% novels.

Member Agents Jack Scovil, jackscovil@scglit.com; Russell Galen, russellgalen@scglit.com (fiction novels that stretch the bounds of reality; strong, serious nonfiction books on almost any subject that teach something new; no books that are merely entertaining, such as diet or pop psych books; serious interests include science, history, journalism, biography, business, memoir, nature, politics, sports, contemporary culture, literary nonfiction, etc.); Anna Ghosh, annaghosh@scglit.com (strong nonfiction proposals on all subjects as well as adult commercial and literary fiction by both unpublished and published authors; serious interests include investigative journalism, literary nonfiction, history, biography, memoir, popular culture, science, adventure, art, food, religion, psychology, alternative health, social issues, women's fiction, historical novels and literary fiction);

Ann Behar, annbehar@scglit.com (juvenile books for all ages); Danny Baror, dannybaror@scglit.com (foreign rights).

Represents Nonfiction books, novels.

How to Contact E-mail queries preferred. Considers simultaneous queries.

Recent Sales *Nefertiti: A Novel*, by Michelle Moran (Crown); *The Making of the Fittest: DNA and the Record of Evolution*, by Sean B. Carroll; *Why Marines Fight*, by James Brady.

Terms

☺ SCRIBBLERS HOUSE, LLC LITERARY AGENCY

P.O. Box 1007, Cooper Station, New York NY 10276-1007. (212)714-7744. E-mail: query@scribblershouse.net. Website: www.scribblershouse.net. **Contact:** Stedman Mays, Garrett Gambino. Estab. 2003. 25% of clients are new/unpublished writers.

Represents Nonfiction books, novels (occasionally). **Considers these nonfiction areas:** Business/economics; health/medicine; history; how-to; language/literature/criticism; memoirs; popular culture; psychology; self-help/personal improvement; sex; spirituality; diet/nutrition; the brain; personal finance; biography; politics; writing books; relationships; gender issues; parenting. **Considers these fiction areas:** Historical; literary; women's; suspense; crime; thrillers.

How to Contact Query via e-mail. Put "nonfiction query" or "fiction query" in the subject line followed by the title of your project. Considers simultaneous queries.

Recent Sales *Perfect Balance: Dr. Robert Greene's Breakthrough Program for Getting the Hormone Health You Deserve*, by Robert Greene and Leah Feldon (Clarkson Potter/Random House); *Age-Proof Your Mind*, by Zaldy Tan (Warner); *The Okinawa Program* and *The Okinawa Diet Plan*, by Bradley Willcox, Craig Willcox and Makoto Suzuki (Clarkson Potter/Random House); *The Emotionally Abusive Relationship*, by Beverly Engel (Wiley); *Help Your Baby Talk*, by Dr. Robert Owens with Leah Feldon (Perigee).

Terms Agent receives 15% commission on domestic sales. Charges clients for postage, shipping and copying.

Tips "We prefer e-mail queries, but if you must send by snail mail, we will return material or respond to a United States Postal Service-accepted SASE. (No international coupons or outdated mail strips, please.) Presentation means a lot. A well-written query letter with a brief author bio and your credentials is important. For query letter models, go to the bookstore or online and look at the cover copy and flap copy on other books in your general area of interest. Emulate what's best. Have an idea of other notable books that will be perceived as being in the same vein as yours. Know what's fresh about your project and articulate it in as few words as possible. Consult our Web site for the most up-to-date information on submitting."

◯ SCRIBE AGENCY, LLC

5508 Joylynne Dr., Madison WI 53716. E-mail: queries@scribeagency.com. Website: www.scribeagency.com. **Contact:** Kristopher O'Higgins. Estab. 2004. Represents 8 clients. 50% of clients are new/unpublished writers. Currently handles: 95% novels; 4% story collections; 1% novellas.

- "We have 17 years of experience in publishing and have worked on both agency and editorial sides in the past, with marketing expertise to boot. We love books as much or more than anyone you know. Check our website to see what we're about and to make sure you jive with the Scribe vibe."

Member Agents Kristopher O'Higgins; Jesse Vogel.

Represents Nonfiction books, novels, short story collections, novellas. **Considers these nonfiction areas:** Cooking/foods/nutrition; ethnic/cultural interests; gay/lesbian issues; humor/satire; memoirs; music/dance; popular culture; true crime/investigative; women's issues/studies. **Considers these fiction areas:** Action/adventure; comic books/cartoon; detective/police/crime; erotica; ethnic; experimental; fantasy; feminist; gay/lesbian; horror; humor/satire; literary; mainstream/contemporary; mystery/suspense; psychic/supernatural; science fiction; thriller; young adult.

O─ Actively seeking excellent writers with ideas and stories to tell.

How to Contact E-queries only. See the Web site for submission info, as it may change. Responds in 3-4 weeks to queries; 5 months to mss.

Recent Sales Sold 3 titles in the last year.

Terms Agent receives 15% commission on domestic sales; 20% commission on foreign sales. Offers written contract. Charges for postage and photocopying.

Writers' Conferences BookExpo America; The Writer's Institute; Spring Writer's Festival; WisCon; Wisconsin Book Festival; World Fantasy Convention.

N ☺ SEBASTIAN LITERARY AGENCY

2160 Kenwood Way, Wayzata MN, 55391. (952)471-9300. Fax: (952)314-4858. E-mail: laurie@sebastianagency.com. Website: www.sebastianagency.com. **Contact:** Laurie Harper Markusen. Estab. 1982. Member of Author's

Guild. Represents 30 clients. 20% of clients are new/unpublished writers. Currently handles: 90% nonfiction books; 10% novels.
• Prior to forming the agency, Laurie ran a small regional publishing company in San Francisco.
Represents Nonfiction books. **Considers these nonfiction areas:** Business/economics; health/medicine; money/finance; psychology; self-help/personal improvement; sociology; women's issues/studies. **Considers these fiction areas:** Literary; mainstream/contemporary.
O—• Actively seeking strong narrative nonfiction from authors with strong matching credentials and platform—whether in the category of psychology, sociology, science, lifestyle, business, health, medicine or women's issues. Only authors with published book credits (not self-published) can query for fiction. Does not want to receive memoir, biography, poetry, humor, relationship books.
How to Contact Query with SASE, submit proposal package, outline, 3 sample chapter(s). Accepts e-mail queries. No fax queries. Considers simultaneous queries. Responds in 3 weeks to queries. Returns materials only with SASE. Obtains most new clients through recommendations from others.
Recent Sales Sold 10 titles in the last year. *The Modern Mom's Guides to Dads*, by Hogan Hilling and Jesse Rutherford (Cumberland); *Customer Loyalty Guaranteed*, by Chip Bell and John Patterson (Adams); *More Than You Know*, by Michael Mauboussin (Columbia Univ.).
Terms Agent receives 15% commission on domestic sales; 20% commission on foreign sales. Offers written contract; 30-day notice must be given to terminate contract. Author is charged for copying of ms, if preauthorized.

☑ SERENDIPITY LITERARY AGENCY, LLC

305 Gates Ave., Brooklyn NY 11216. (718)230-7689. Fax: (718)230-7829. E-mail: rbrooks@serendipitylit.com. Website: www.serendipitylit.com. **Contact:** Regina Brooks. Estab. 2000. Represents 50 clients. 50% of clients are new/unpublished writers. Currently handles: 50% nonfiction books; 50% fiction.
• Prior to becoming an agent, Ms. Brooks was an acquisitions editor for John Wiley & Sons, Inc. and McGraw-Hill Companies.
Member Agents Regina Brooks; Guichard Cadet (sports, pop culture, fiction, Caribbean writers).
Represents Nonfiction books, novels, juvenile books, scholarly books, children's books. **Considers these nonfiction areas:** Business/economics; current affairs; education; ethnic/cultural interests; history; juvenile nonfiction; memoirs; money/finance; multicultural; New Age/metaphysics; popular culture; psychology; religious/inspirational; science/technology; self-help/personal improvement; sports; women's issues/studies; health/medical; narrative; popular science, biography; politics; crafts/design; food/cooking; contemporary culture. **Considers these fiction areas:** Action/adventure; confession; ethnic; historical; juvenile; literary; multicultural; picture books; thriller; suspense; mystery; romance.
O—• African-American nonfiction, commercial fiction, young adult novels with an urban flair and juvenile books. No stage plays, screenplays or poetry.
How to Contact Prefers to read materials exclusively. For nonfiction, submit outline, 1 sample chapter, SASE. Responds in 2 months to queries; 3 months to mss. Obtains most new clients through conferences, referrals.
Recent Sales This agency prefers not to share information on specific sales. Recent sales available upon request.
Terms Agent receives 15% commission on domestic sales; 20% commission on foreign sales. Offers written contract; 2-month notice must be given to terminate contract. Charges clients for office fees, which are taken from any advance.
Tips "We are eagerly looking for young adult books. We also represent illustrators."

☑ ☑ SEVENTH AVENUE LITERARY AGENCY

1663 West Seventh Ave., Vancouver British Columbia V6J 1S4, Canada. (604)734-3663. Fax: (604)734-8906. E-mail: info@seventhavenuelit.com. Website: www.seventhavenuelit.com. **Contact:** Robert Mackwood, director. Currently handles: 85% nonfiction books; 15% novels.
Represents Nonfiction books, novels. **Considers these nonfiction areas:** Biography/autobiography; business/economics; computers/electronic; health/medicine; history; science/technology; sports; travel; lifestyle.
O—• "Seventh Avenue Literary Agency is one of Canada's largest and most venerable literary and personal management agencies." (The agency was originally called Contemporary Management.) Actively seeking nonfiction. Does not want to receive poetry, screenplays, children's books, young adult titles, or genre writing such as science fiction, fantasy or erotica.
How to Contact Query with SASE, submit outline, synopsis, 1 (nonfiction) sample chapter(s), publishing history, author bio, table of contents with proposal or query. Send 1-2 chapters and submission history if sending fiction. No e-mail attachments. Provide full contact information. Accepts e-mail queries. No fax queries. Obtains most new clients through recommendations from others, solicitations.
Recent Sales *The Taxman is Watching*, by Paul DioGuardio and Philippe DioGuardio (Harper Canada); *Confes-*

sions of an Innocent Man: Torture and Survival in a Saudi Prison, by William Sampson; *Bud, Inc.*, by Ian Mulgrew; *The Rainbow Bridge*, by Adrian Raeside (Raincoast Books).

Tips "If you want your material returned, please include an SASE with adequate postage; otherwise, material will be recycled. (U.S. stamps are not adequate; they do not work in Canada.)"

THE SEYMOUR AGENCY

475 Miner St., Canton NY 13617. (315)386-1831. E-mail: marysue@slic.com. Website: www.theseymouragency .com. **Contact:** Mary Sue Seymour. Estab. 1992. Member of AAR, RWA, Authors Guild; signatory of WGA. Represents 50 clients. 5% of clients are new/unpublished writers. Currently handles: 50% nonfiction books; 50% fiction.

- Ms. Seymour is a retired New York State certified teacher.

Represents Nonfiction books, novels. **Considers these nonfiction areas:** Business/economics; health/medicine; how-to; self-help/personal improvement; Christian books; cookbooks; any well-written nonfiction that includes a proposal in standard format and 1 sample chapter. **Considers these fiction areas:** Religious/inspirational (Christian books); romance (any type).

How to Contact Query with SASE, synopsis, first 50 pages for romance. Accepts e-mail queries. No fax queries. Considers simultaneous queries. Responds in 1 month to queries; 3 months to mss. Returns materials only with SASE.

Recent Sales Three books, by Beth Wiseman (Thomas Nelson); *The Everything Triathalon Book*, by Brent Manley (Adams); *The Everything Self-Hypnosis Book*, by Rene Bastarache (Adams).

Terms Agent receives 12-15% commission on domestic sales.

THE ROBERT E. SHEPARD AGENCY

1608 Dwight Way, Berkeley CA 94703-1804. (510)849-3999. E-mail: mail@shepardagency.com. Website: www. shepardagency.com. **Contact:** Robert Shepard. Estab. 1994. Member of Authors Guild. Represents 70 clients. 15% of clients are new/unpublished writers. Currently handles: 90% nonfiction books; 10% scholarly books.

- Prior to opening his agency, Mr. Shepard was an editor and a sales and marketing manager in book publishing; he now writes, teaches courses for nonfiction authors, and speaks at many writers' conferences.

Represents Nonfiction books, scholarly books (appropriate for trade publishers). **Considers these nonfiction areas:** Business/economics; current affairs; gay/lesbian issues; government/politics/law; history; popular culture; psychology; sports; Judaica; narrative nonfiction; health; cultural issues; science for laypeople, parenting.

- This agency specializes in nonfiction, particularly key issues facing society and culture. Actively seeking works by experts recognized in their fields whether or not they're well-known to the general public, and books that offer fresh perspectives or new information even when the subject is familiar. Does not want to receive autobiographies, art books, memoir, spirituality or fiction.

How to Contact Query with SASE. E-mail queries encouraged. Fax and phone queries strongly discouraged. Considers simultaneous queries. Responds in 2-3 weeks to queries; 6 weeks to proposals or mss. Returns materials only with SASE. Obtains most new clients through recommendations from others, solicitations.

Recent Sales Sold 10 titles in the last year. *A Few Seconds of Panic*, by Stefan Fatsis (Penguin); *Big Boy Rules*, by Steve Fainaru (Da Capo Press); *American Band*, by Kristen Laine)Gotham).

Terms Agent receives 15% commission on domestic sales; 20% commission on foreign sales. Offers written contract, binding for term of project or until canceled; 30-day notice must be given to terminate contract. Charges clients for phone/fax, photocopying, postage (if and when the project sells).

Tips "We pay attention to detail. We believe in close working relationships between the author and agent, and in building better relationships between the author and editor. Please do your homework! There's no substitute for learning all you can about similar or directly competing books and presenting a well-reasoned competitive analysis in your proposal. Be sure to describe what's new and fresh about your work, why you are the best person to be writing on your subject, everything editors will need to know about your work, and how the book will serve the needs or interests of your intended readers. Don't work in a vacuum: Visit bookstores, talk to other writers about their experiences, and let the information you gather inform the work that you do as an author."

WENDY SHERMAN ASSOCIATES, INC.

450 Seventh Ave., Suite 2307, New York NY 10123. (212)279-9027. Fax: (212)279-8863. Website: www.wsherm an.com. **Contact:** Wendy Sherman. Estab. 1999. Member of AAR. Represents 50 clients. 30% of clients are new/unpublished writers. Currently handles: 50% nonfiction books; 50% novels.

- Prior to opening the agency, Ms. Sherman worked for The Aaron Priest agency and served as vice president, executive director, associate publisher, subsidary rights director, and sales and marketing director in the publishing industry.

Member Agents Wendy Sherman; Michelle Brower; Emmanuelle Alspaugh.

Represents Nonfiction books, novels. **Considers these nonfiction areas:** Psychology; narrative; practical. **Considers these fiction areas:** Literary; women's (suspense).

> O→ "We specialize in developing new writers, as well as working with more established writers. My experience as a publisher has proven to be a great asset to my clients."

How to Contact Query with SASE or send outline/proposal, 1 sample chapter. E-mail queries only for Ms. Brower and Ms. Alspaugh. Considers simultaneous queries. Responds in 1 month to queries. Returns materials only with SASE. Obtains most new clients through recommendations from others.

Recent Sales *The Measure of Brightness*, by Todd Johnson; *Supergirls Speak Out*, by Liz Funk; *Love in 90 Days*, by Diana Kirschner; *Pelican Road*, by Howard Bahr; *A Long, Long Time Ago and Essentially True*, by Brigid Pasulka; *Cooking and Screaming: A Memoir*, by Adrienne Kane.

Terms Agent receives 15% commission on domestic sales; 20% commission on foreign sales. Offers written contract.

Tips "The bottom line is: Do your homework. Be as well prepared as possible. Read the books that will help you present yourself and your work with polish. You want your submission to stand out."

☉ ROSALIE SIEGEL, INTERNATIONAL LITERARY AGENCY, INC.

1 Abey Dr., Pennington NJ 08543. (609)737-1007. Fax: (609)737-3708. **Contact:** Rosalie Siegel. Estab. 1977. Member of AAR. Represents 35 clients. 10% of clients are new/unpublished writers. Currently handles: 45% nonfiction books; 45% novels; 10% young adult books; short story collections for current clients.

How to Contact Obtains most new clients through referrals from writers and friends.

Terms Agent receives 15% commission on domestic sales; 20% commission on foreign sales. Offers written contract; 2-month notice must be given to terminate contract. Charges clients for photocopying.

Tips "I'm not looking for new authors in an active way."

⊕ ☉ JEFFREY SIMMONS LITERARY AGENCY

15 Penn House, Mallory St., London NW8 8SX England. (44)(207)224-8917. E-mail: jasimmons@btconnect.com. **Contact:** Jeffrey Simmons. Estab. 1978. Represents 43 clients. 40% of clients are new/unpublished writers. Currently handles: 65% nonfiction books; 35% novels.

> • Prior to becoming an agent, Mr. Simmons was a publisher. He is also an author.

Represents Nonfiction books, novels. **Considers these nonfiction areas:** Biography/autobiography; current affairs; government/politics/law; history; language/literature/criticism; memoirs; music/dance; popular culture; sociology; sports; theater/film; translation; true crime/investigative. **Considers these fiction areas:** Action/adventure; confession; detective/police/crime; family saga; literary; mainstream/contemporary; mystery/suspense; thriller.

> O→ This agency seeks to handle good books and promising young writers. "My long experience in publishing and as an author and ghostwriter means I can offer an excellent service all around, especially in terms of editorial experience where appropriate." Actively seeking quality fiction, biography, autobiography, showbiz, personality books, law, crime, politics, and world affairs. Does not want to receive science fiction, horror, fantasy, juvenile, academic books, or specialist subjects (e.g., cooking, gardening, religious).

How to Contact Submit sample chapter, outline/proposal, SASE (IRCs if necessary). Prefers to read materials exclusively. Responds in 1 week to queries; 1 month to mss. Obtains most new clients through recommendations from others, solicitations.

Terms Agent receives 10-15% commission on domestic sales; 15% commission on foreign sales. Offers written contract, binding for lifetime of book in question or until it becomes out of print.

Tips "When contacting us with an outline/proposal, include a brief biographical note (listing any previous publications, with publishers and dates). Preferably tell us if the book has already been offered elsewhere."

⊞ ☉ BEVERLEY SLOPEN LITERARY AGENCY

131 Bloor St. W., Suite 711, Toronto ON M5S 1S3 Canada. (416)964-9598. Fax: (416)921-7726. E-mail: beverly@slopenagency.ca. Website: www.slopenagency.ca. **Contact:** Beverley Slopen. Estab. 1974. Represents 70 clients. 20% of clients are new/unpublished writers. Currently handles: 60% nonfiction books; 40% novels.

> • Prior to opening her agency, Ms. Slopen worked in publishing and as a journalist.

Represents Nonfiction books, novels, scholarly books, textbooks (college). **Considers these nonfiction areas:** Anthropology/archaeology; biography/autobiography; business/economics; current affairs; psychology; sociology; true crime/investigative; women's issues/studies. **Considers these fiction areas:** Literary; mystery/suspense.

> O→ This agency has a strong bent toward Canadian writers. Actively seeking serious nonfiction that is accessible and appealing to the general reader. Does not want to receive fantasy, science fiction, or children's books.

How to Contact Query with SAE and IRCs. Returns materials only with SASE (Canadian postage only). Accepts short e-mail queries. Considers simultaneous queries. Responds in 2 months to queries.
Recent Sales Sold over 40 titles in the last year. *Court Lady* and *Country Wife*, by Lita-Rose Betcherman (HarperCollins Canada/Morrow/Wiley UK); *Vermeer's Hat*, by Timothy Brook (HarperCollins Canada); *Midnight Cab*, by James W. Nichol (Canongate US/Droemer); *Lady Franklin's Revenge*, by Ken McGoogan (HarperCollins Canada/Bantam UK); *Understanding Uncertainty*, by Jeffrey Rosenthal (HarperCollins Canada); *Damaged Angels*, by Bonnie Buxton (Carroll & Graf US); *Sea of Dreams*, by Adam Mayers (McClelland & Stewart Canada); *Memory Book*, by Howard Engel (Carroll & Graf); *Written in the Flesh*, by Edward Shorter (University of Toronto Press); *Punch Line*, by Joey Slinger. Other clients include Modris Eksteins, Michael Marrus, Robert Fulford, Morley Torgov, Elliott Leyton, Don Gutteridge, Joanna Goodman, Roberta Rich, Jennifer Welsh, Margaret Wente, Frank Wydra.
Terms Agent receives 15% commission on domestic sales; 10% commission on foreign sales. Offers written contract, binding for 2 years; 3-month notice must be given to terminate contract.
Tips ''Please, no unsolicited manuscripts.''

◎ SLW LITERARY AGENCY
4100 Ridgeland Ave., Northbrook IL 60062. (847)509-0999. Fax: (847)509-0996. E-mail: shariwenk@aol.com. **Contact:** Shari Wenk. Currently handles: 100% nonfiction books.
Represents Nonfiction books. **Considers these nonfiction areas:** Sports.
   O─┓ This agency specializes in representing books written by sports celebrities and sports writers.
How to Contact Query via e-mail, but note the agency's specific specialty.
Recent Sales *The NBA Crisis*, by Harvey Araton; *I'm Just Gettin' Started*, by Jack McKeon; *Buckeye Madness: Ohio State Football from Woody Hayes to a National Championship* (Simon & Schuster); Untitled, by Joe Menzer (Wiley). Other clients include Filip Bondy, Sam Smith, Skip Bayless, Ric Bucher, Earl Woods, Tiger Woods Foundation, Randy Johnson, Nolan Ryan, Jackie Joyner-Kersee, Joe Theismann, Terry Bradshaw, Joe Garagiola, Tony Gwynn, Mike Singletary, Jay Johnstone, Steve Garvey, Rickey Henderson.

▦ ◘ ROBERT SMITH LITERARY AGENCY, LTD.
12 Bridge Wharf, 156 Caledonian Rd., London NI 9UU England. (44)(207)278-2444. Fax: (44)(207)833-5680. E-mail: robertsmith.literaryagency@virgin.net. **Contact:** Robert Smith. Estab. 1997. Member of AAA. Represents 25 clients. 10% of clients are new/unpublished writers. Currently handles: 80% nonfiction books; 20% syndicated material.
   ● Prior to becoming an agent, Mr. Smith was a book publisher.
Represents Nonfiction books, syndicated material. **Considers these nonfiction areas:** Biography/autobiography; cooking/foods/nutrition; health/medicine; memoirs; music/dance; New Age/metaphysics; popular culture; self-help/personal improvement; theater/film; true crime/investigative.
   O─┓ This agency offers clients full management service in all media. Clients are not necessarily book authors. ''Our special expertise is in placing newspaper series internationally.'' Actively seeking autobiographies.
How to Contact Submit outline/proposal, SASE (IRCs if necessary). Prefers to read materials exclusively. Accepts e-mail and fax queries. Responds in 2 weeks to queries. Returns materials only with SASE. Obtains most new clients through recommendations from others, direct approaches to prospective authors.
Recent Sales Sold 25 titles in the last year. *Enter the Dragon*, by Theo Paphitis (Orion); Two untitled novels, by Roberta Kray (Little, Brown); *Destroyed*, by Jayne Sterne (Headline); *For Love of Julie*, by Ann Ming (HarperCollins) *Playing the Dark*, by Siobhan Kennedy-McGuinness; *For Better or Worse: Her Story*, by Christine Hamilton (Robson Books).
Terms Agent receives 15% commission on domestic sales; 20% commission on foreign sales. Offers written contract, binding for 3 months; 3-month notice must be given to terminate contract. Charges clients for couriers, photocopying, overseas mailings of mss (subject to client authorization).

◘ SPECTRUM LITERARY AGENCY
320 Central Park W., Suite 1-D, New York NY 10025. Fax: (212)362-4562. Website: www.spectrumliteraryagency.com. **Contact:** Eleanor Wood, president. Represents 90 clients. Currently handles: 10% nonfiction books; 90% novels.
Member Agents Lucienne Diver; Eleanor Wood.
Represents Nonfiction books, novels. **Considers these fiction areas:** Fantasy; historical; mainstream/contemporary; mystery/suspense; romance; science fiction.
How to Contact Query with SASE, submit author bio, publishing credits. No unsolicited mss will be read. Snail mail queries **only**. Eleanor and Lucienne have different addresses—see the Web site for full info. No e-mail or fax queries. Responds in 1-3 months to queries. Obtains most new clients through recommendations from authors.

Recent Sales Sold more than 100 titles in the last year. Sales available on this agency's Web site.

Terms Agent receives 15% commission on domestic sales. Deducts for photocopying and book orders.

Tips "Spectrum's policy is to read only book-length manuscripts that we have specifically asked to see. Unsolicited manuscripts are not accepted. The letter should describe your book briefly and include publishing credits and background information or qualifications relating to your work, if any."

◱ SPENCERHILL ASSOCIATES

P.O. Box 374, Chatham NY 12037. (518)392-9293. Fax: (518)392-9554. E-mail: ksolem@klsbooks.com; jennifer @klsbooks.com. **Contact:** Karen Solem or Jennifer Schober. Estab. 2001. Member of AAR. Represents 73 clients. 5% of clients are new/unpublished writers.

- Prior to becoming an agent, Ms. Solem was editor-in-chief at HarperCollins and an associate publisher.

Member Agents Karen Solem; Jennifer Schober.

Represents Novels. **Considers these fiction areas:** Detective/police/crime; historical; literary; mainstream/contemporary; religious/inspirational; romance; thriller; young adult.

- ◯╖ "We handle mostly commercial women's fiction, historical novels, romance (historical, contemporary, paranormal), thrillers, and mysteries. We also represent Christian fiction." No poetry, science fiction, children's picture books, or scripts.

How to Contact Query jennifer@klsbooks.com with synopsis and first three chapters. E-queries preferred. No fax queries. Responds in 1 month to queries. Returns materials only with SASE.

Terms Agent receives 15% commission on domestic sales; 20% commission on foreign sales. Offers written contract; 3-month notice must be given to terminate contract.

◲ THE SPIELER AGENCY

154 W. 57th St., Suite 135, New York NY 10019. E-mail: spieleragency@spieleragency.com. **Contact:** Katya Balter. Estab. 1981. Represents 160 clients. 2% of clients are new/unpublished writers.

- Prior to opening his agency, Mr. Spieler was a magazine editor.

Member Agents Joe Spieler; John Thornton (nonfiction); Lisa M. Ross (fiction, nonfiction); Deirdre Mullane (nonfiction); Eric Myers (nonfiction, fiction); Victoria Shoemaker (fiction, nonfiction).

Represents Nonfiction books, novels, children's books. **Considers these nonfiction areas:** Biography/autobiography; business/economics; child guidance/parenting; current affairs; gay/lesbian issues; government/politics/law; history; memoirs; money/finance; music/dance; nature/environment; religious/inspirational; sociology; spirituality; theater/film; travel; women's issues/studies. **Considers these fiction areas:** Detective/police/crime; feminist; gay/lesbian; literary; mystery/suspense.

How to Contact Query with SASE. Prefers to read materials exclusively. Returns materials only with SASE; otherwise materials are discarded when rejected. No fax queries. Considers simultaneous queries. Responds in 2 weeks to queries; 2 months to mss. Obtains most new clients through recommendations, listing in *Guide to Literary Agents*.

Recent Sales *Tilt-A-Whirl*, by Chris Grabenstein (Carroll and Graf); *What's the Matter with Kansas*, by Thomas Frank (Metropolitan/Holt); *Natural History of the Rich*, by Richard Conniff (W.W. Norton); *Juicing the Game*, by Howard Bryant (Viking).

Terms Agent receives 15% commission on domestic sales. Charges clients for messenger bills, photocopying, postage.

Writers' Conferences London Book Fair.

⬚ ◱ THE SPIRIDON LITERARY AGENCY

P.O. Box 47594, 946 Lawrence Ave. E., Unit 2, Toronto ON M3C 1P0, Canada. E-mail: spiridon@rogers.com. **Contact:** Alethea Spiridon. Estab. 2007. Currently handles: 20% nonfiction books; 40% novels; 10% story collections; 30% juvenile books.

- Prior to becoming an agent, Ms. Spiridon was an editor for Harlequin Books in Toronto.

Represents Nonfiction books, novels, short story collections, novellas, juvenile books. **Considers these nonfiction areas:** Business/economics; child guidance/parenting; cooking/foods/nutrition; current affairs; health/medicine; history; how-to; juvenile nonfiction; language/literature/criticism; memoirs; nature/environment; popular culture; self-help/personal improvement; women's issues/studies. **Considers these fiction areas:** Action/adventure; confession; experimental; family saga; fantasy; feminist; historical; humor/satire; juvenile; literary; mainstream/contemporary; mystery/suspense; picture books; romance; young adult.

- ◯╖ Actively seeking women's fiction, young adult, middle grade, nonfiction, literary fiction and commercial fiction.

How to Contact Submit outline/proposal, synopsis, author bio, 50 pages if submitting fiction, SASE. Query with IRC, not SASE! Accepts e-mail queries. No fax queries. Considers simultaneous queries. Responds in 8 weeks to queries; 10 weeks to mss. Obtains most new clients through recommendations from others, solicitations.

Terms Agent receives 15% commission on domestic sales; 20% commission on foreign sales. Offers written contract; 1-month notice must be given to terminate contract. This agency charges for office expenses, such as postage and photocopies.

Tips "Think of the agent as your first reader. Do a meticulous self-edit of your work to ensure you present your best possible writing. Observe how other books are marketed by reading tons of back cover copy and then write a blurb for your own book. If you're struggling, you might not have a clear sense of direction for your work. You need to have a solid sense of your manuscript so you can present it seamlessly to agents (and then editors). Be clear. Be concise."

◎ PHILIP G. SPITZER LITERARY AGENCY, INC

50 Talmage Farm Ln., East Hampton NY 11937. (631)329-3650. Fax: (631)329-3651. E-mail: spitzer516@aol.com. **Contact:** Philip Spitzer, Lukas Ortiz. Estab. 1969. Member of AAR. Represents 60 clients. 10% of clients are new/unpublished writers. Currently handles: 35% nonfiction books; 65% novels.

- Prior to opening his agency, Mr. Spitzer served at New York University Press, McGraw-Hill, and the John Cushman Associates literary agency.

Represents Nonfiction books, novels. **Considers these nonfiction areas:** Biography/autobiography; business/economics; current affairs; ethnic/cultural interests; government/politics/law; health/medicine; history; language/literature/criticism; military/war; music/dance; nature/environment; popular culture; psychology; sociology; sports; theater/film; true crime/investigative. **Considers these fiction areas:** Detective/police/crime; literary; mainstream/contemporary; mystery/suspense; sports; thriller.

- ☞ This agency specializes in mystery/suspense, literary fiction, sports and general nonfiction (no how-to).

How to Contact Query with SASE, outline, 1 sample chapter. Responds in 1 week to queries; 6 weeks to mss. Obtains most new clients through recommendations from others.

Recent Sales *Suitcase City*, by Michael Connelly; *Acts of Nature*, by Jonathon King; *Last Call*, by Alafair Burke; *The Tin Roof Blowdown*, by James Lee Burke.

Terms Agent receives 15% commission on domestic sales; 20% commission on foreign sales. Charges clients for photocopying.

Writers' Conferences BookExpo America.

⬚ ◨ ◎ P. STATHONIKOS AGENCY

146 Springbluff Heights SW, Calgary Alberta T3H 5E5, Canada. (403)245-2087. Fax: (403)245-2087. E-mail: pastath@telus.net. **Contact:** Penny Stathonikos.

- Prior to becoming an agent, Ms. Stathonikos was a bookstore owner and publisher's representative for 10 years.

Represents Nonfiction books, novels, juvenile books.

- ☞ Actively seeking children's literature, some young adult. Does not want to receive romance, fantasy, historical fiction, plays, movie scripts or poetry.

How to Contact Query with SASE, submit outline. Accepts e-mail queries. No fax queries. Responds in 1 month to queries; 2 months to mss.

Terms Agent receives 10% commission on domestic sales; 15% commission on foreign sales. Charges for postage, telephone, copying, etc.

Tips "Do your homework—read any of the Writer's Digest market books, join a writers' group and check out the local bookstore or library for similar books. Know who your competition is and why your book is different."

◎ NANCY STAUFFER ASSOCIATES

P.O. Box 1203, 1540 Boston Post Road, Darien CT 06820. (203)202-2500. Fax: (203)655-3704. E-mail: StaufferAssoc@optonline.net. **Contact:** Nancy Stauffer Cahoon. Estab. 1989. Member of Authors Guild. 5% of clients are new/unpublished writers. Currently handles: 15% nonfiction books; 85% novels. **Considers these nonfiction areas:** Current affairs; ethnic/cultural interests; creative nonfiction (narrative). **Considers these fiction areas:** Contemporary issues; literary; regional.

How to Contact Obtains most new clients through referrals from existing clients.

Recent Sales *The Absolutely True Diary of a Part-time Indian*, by Sherman Alexie; *West of Last Chance*, by Peter Brown and Kent Haruf.

Terms Agent receives 15% commission on domestic sales; 20% commission on foreign sales; 15% commission on dramatic rights sales.

STEELE-PERKINS LITERARY AGENCY

26 Island Ln., Canandaigua NY 14424. (585)396-9290. Fax: (585)396-3579. E-mail: pattiesp@aol.com. **Contact:** Pattie Steele-Perkins. Member of AAR, RWA. Currently handles: 100% novels.

Represents Novels. **Considers these fiction areas:** Romance, genre and women's fiction, including multicultural and inspirational.

How to Contact Submit outline, 3 sample chapters, SASE. Considers simultaneous queries. Responds in 6 weeks to queries. Returns materials only with SASE. Obtains most new clients through recommendations from others, queries/solicitations.

Recent Sales This agency prefers not to share information on specific sales.

Terms Agent receives 15% commission on domestic sales. Offers written contract, binding for 1 year; 1-month notice must be given to terminate contract.

Writers' Conferences RWA National Conference; BookExpo America; CBA Convention; Romance Slam Jam.

Tips "Be patient. E-mail rather than call. Make sure what you are sending is the best it can be."

STERNIG & BYRNE LITERARY AGENCY

2370 S. 107th St., Apt. #4, Milwaukee WI 53227-2036. (414)328-8034. Fax: (414)328-8034. E-mail: jackbyrne@h otmail.com. Website: www.sff.net/people/jackbyrne. **Contact:** Jack Byrne. Estab. 1950s. Member of SFWA, MWA. Represents 30 clients. 10% of clients are new/unpublished writers. Currently handles: 5% nonfiction books; 85% novels; 10% juvenile books.

Represents Nonfiction books, novels, juvenile books. **Considers these fiction areas:** Fantasy; horror; mystery/ suspense; science fiction.

O— "Our client list is comfortably full and our current needs are therefore quite limited." Actively seeking science fiction/fantasy and mystery by established writers. Does not want to receive romance, poetry, textbooks, or highly specialized nonfiction.

How to Contact Query with SASE. Prefers e-mail queries (no attachments); hard copy queries also acceptable. Accepts e-mail queries. No fax queries. Responds in 3 weeks to queries; 3 months to mss. Returns materials only with SASE.

Terms Agent receives 15% commission on domestic sales; 20% commission on foreign sales. Offers written contract; 2-month notice must be given to terminate contract.

Tips "Don't send first drafts, have a professional presentation (including cover letter), and know your field. Read what's been done—good and bad."

STIMOLA LITERARY STUDIO, LLC

306 Chase Court, Edgewater NJ 07020. Phone/Fax: (201)945-9353. E-mail: info@stimolaliterarystudio.com. Website: www.stimolaliterarystudio.com. **Contact:** Rosemary B. Stimola. Member of AAR.

Represents Preschool through young adult fiction and nonfiction.

How to Contact Query with SASE or via e-mail (no unsolicited attachments). Responds in 3 weeks to queries; 2 months to mss. Obtains most new clients through referrals. Unsolicited submissions are still accepted.

Recent Sales *Steinbeck's Ghost*, by Lewis Buzbee (Feiwel & Friends); B Mosnter Squad Series, by Laura Dower (Grosset & Dunlap); *Tom's Tweet*, by Jill Esbaum (Knopf); *Free Fall*, by Anna Levine (Greenwillow/Harper); *Sophomore Switch*, by Abby McDonald (Candlewick); *Road Trip*, by Mary Pearson (Holt); *Days of Little Texas*, by RA Nelson; *Hurricane Song*, by Paul Volponi (Viking).

Terms Agent receives 15% commission on domestic sales; 20% (if subagents are employed) commission on foreign sales.

STRACHAN LITERARY AGENCY

P.O. Box 2091, Annapolis MD 21404. E-mail: query@strachanlit.com. Website: www.strachanlit.com. **Contact:** Laura Strachan.

● Prior to becoming an agent, Ms. Strachan was (and still is) an attorney.

Represents Nonfiction books, novels. **Considers these nonfiction areas:** Cooking/foods/nutrition; gardening; interior design/decorating; memoirs; photography; psychology; self-help/personal improvement; travel; narrative, parenting, arts. **Considers these fiction areas:** Literary; mystery/suspense; legal and pyschological thrillers, children's.

O— This agency specializes in literary fiction and narrative nonfiction. Actively seeking new, fresh voices.

How to Contact Query with cover letter outlining your professional experience and a brief synopsis. Send no e-mail attachments. Accepts e-mail queries. No fax queries.

Recent Sales *Serpent Box*, by Vincent Carrella (HarperPerennial); *Swan Town: The Secret Journal of Susanna Shakespeare*, by Michael Ortiz (HarperCollins Children's); *Little Star of Bela Lua*, by Luana Monteiro (Delphinium Books); *The Good Man*, by Ed Jae-Suk Lee (Bridge Works Publishing).

⬤ ROBIN STRAUS AGENCY, INC.

229 E. 79th St., New York NY 10021. (212)472-3282. Fax: (212)472-3833. E-mail: info@robinstrausagency.com. Website: www.robinstrausagency.com/. **Contact:** Ms. Robin Straus. Estab. 1983. Member of AAR.

• Prior to becoming an agent, Robin Straus served as a subsidary rights manager at Random House and Doubleday and worked in editorial at Little, Brown.

Recent Sales

Terms Agent receives 15% commission on domestic sales; 20% commission on foreign sales. Offers written contract. Charges for "photocopying, express mail services, messenger and foreign postage, etc. as incurred."

⬤ PAM STRICKLER AUTHOR MANAGEMENT

1 Water St., New Paltz NY 12561. (845)255-0061. E-mail: pam302mail-aaaqueries@yahoo.com. Website: www. pamstrickler.com. **Contact:** Pamela Dean Strickler. Member of AAR.

• Prior to opening her agency, Ms. Strickler was senior editor at Ballantine Books.

☛ Specializes in romance, historical fiction and women's fiction. Does not want to receive nonfiction or children's books.

Recent Sales *Lady Dearing's Masquerade*, by Elena Greene (New American Library); *Her Body of Work*, by Marie Donovan (Harlequin/Blaze); *Deceived*, by Nicola Cornick (Harlequin/HQN).

⬤ THE STROTHMAN AGENCY, LLC

One Faneuil Hall Marketplace, Third Floor, Boston MA 02109. (617)742-2011. Fax: (617)742-2014. Website: www.strothmanagency.com. **Contact:** Wendy Strothman, Dan O'Connell. Estab. 2003. Member of AAR, Authors' Guild. Represents 50 clients. Currently handles: 70% nonfiction books; 10% novels; 20% scholarly books.

• Prior to becoming an agent, Ms. Strothman was head of Beacon Press (1983-1995) and executive vice president of Houghton Mifflin's Trade & Reference Division (1996-2002).

Member Agents Wendy Strothman; Dan O'Connell.

Represents Nonfiction books, novels, scholarly books. **Considers these nonfiction areas:** Current affairs; government/politics/law; history; language/literature/criticism; nature/environment. **Considers these fiction areas:** Literary.

☛ "Because we are highly selective in the clients we represent, we increase the value publishers place on our properties. We specialize in narrative nonfiction, memoir, history, science and nature, arts and culture, literary travel, current affairs, and some business. We have a highly selective practice in literary fiction and smart self-help. We are now opening our doors to more commercial fiction but ONLY from authors who have a platform. If you have a platform, please mention it in your query letter." Does not want to receive commercial fiction, romance, science fiction or self-help.

How to Contact Query with SASE. Snail mail queries only. Fax and e-queries not read. Considers simultaneous queries. Responds in 4 weeks to queries; 1 month to mss. Returns materials only with SASE. Obtains most new clients through recommendations from others.

Recent Sales Sold 25 titles in the last year. *Flights Against the Sunset*, by Kenn Kaufman (Houghton Mifflin); *Guantanamo Bay: A History*, by Jonathan Hansen (Random House); *Backcast: A Memoir of Fly Fishing, Fatherhood, and Divorce*, by Lou Ureneck (St. Martin's); *Model-Wives: Madame Cezanne, Madame Monet, Madame Rodin*, by Ruth Butler (Yale University Press); *Smithsonian Ocean*, by Deborah Cramer (Smithsonian Books); *Free Fall: The Rising Economic Risk Facing America's Working Families*, by Peter Gosselin (Basic Books).

Terms Agent receives 15% commission on domestic sales; 20% commission on foreign sales. Offers written contract; 30-day notice must be given to terminate contract.

Ⓝ KATHERINE A. SULKOWSKI LITERARY AGENCY

5141 Virginia Way, Suite 320, Brentwood TN 37027. E-mail: katie.sulkowski@creativetrust.com. Website: www .CreativeTrust.com. **Contact:** Katherine Sulkowski. Estab. 2003. Currently handles: 100% nonfiction books.

Represents Nonfiction books. **Considers these fiction areas:** Mystery/suspense; thriller; young adult.

Recent Sales *Me, Myself and Bob*, by Phil Vischer.

Tips "For Authors of nonfiction: Please send proposals that include an author bio, platform, market analysis (comparables), annotated chapter outline, and 3 or more sample chapters when applicable. For Authors of fiction: Please send proposals that include an author bio, platform, market analysis (comparables), annotated chapter outline, and 3 or more sample chapters when applicable for these designated genres: thriller/ crime/ mystery/ women's fiction/ southern fiction/ general fiction/ redemptive fiction. Please do not send chick lit or romance, thank you. Note: Creative Trust accepts proposals from previously published authors, we thank you for your interest and do our best to respond in a timely manner."

🌐 ◨ THE SUSIJN AGENCY

64 Great Titchfield St., London W1W 7QH England, United Kingdom. (44)(207)580-6341. Fax: (44)(207)580-8626. Website: www.thesusijnagency.com. **Contact:** Laura Susijn, Nicola Barr. Currently handles: 25% nonfiction books; 75% novels.

- Prior to becoming an agent, Ms. Susijn was a rights director at Sheil Land Associates and at Fourth Estate; Ms. Barr was a commissioning editor at Flamingo (literary imprint of HarperCollins).

Represents Nonfiction books, novels. **Considers these nonfiction areas:** Biography/autobiography; memoirs; multicultural; popular culture; science/technology; travel. **Considers these fiction areas:** Literary.

○ᗡ Does not want to receive romance, sagas, fantasy, children's/juvenile or screenplays.

How to Contact Submit outline, 2 sample chapters, SASE/IRC. Returns materials only with SASE. Obtains most new clients through recommendations from others.

Recent Sales Sold 120 titles in the last year. Clients include Dubravka Ugresic, Peter Ackroyd, Robin Baker, BI Feiyu, Jeffrey Moore, Podium, De Arbeiderspers, Van Oorschot.

Terms Agent receives 15% commission on domestic sales; 15-20% commission on foreign sales. Offers written contract; 6-week notice must be given to terminate contract. Charges clients for photocopying (only if sale is made).

◨ EMMA SWEENEY AGENCY, LLC

245 East 80th St., Suite 7E, New York NY 10021. E-mail: queries@emmasweeneyagency.com; info@emmasweeneyagency.com. Website: www.emmasweeneyagency.com. **Contact:** Eva Talmadge. Estab. 2006. Member of AAR, Women's Media Group. Represents 50 clients. 5% of clients are new/unpublished writers. Currently handles: 30% nonfiction books; 70% novels.

- Prior to becoming an agent, Ms. Sweeney was a subsidiary rights assistant at William Morrow. Since 1990, she has been a literary agent, and was most recently an agent with Harold Ober Associates.

Member Agents Emma Sweeney, president; Eva Talmadge, rights manager; Lauren Carnali, editorial assistant (lauren@emmasweeneyagency.com).

Represents Nonfiction books, novels. **Considers these nonfiction areas:** Agriculture/horticulture; animals; biography/autobiography; cooking/foods/nutrition; memoirs. **Considers these fiction areas:** Literary; mystery/suspense; thriller; women's.

○ᗡ "We specialize in quality fiction and non-fiction. Our primary areas of interest include literary and women's fiction, mysteries and thrillers; science, history, biography, memoir, religious studies and the natural sciences." Does not want to receive romance and westerns or screenplays.

How to Contact See Web site for submission and contact information. No snail mail queries. Query by e-mail. Send no attachments. Accepts e-mail queries. No fax queries.

Recent Sales *Water for Elephants*, by Sara Gruen (Algonquin); *The Joy of Living*, by Yongey Mingyur Rinpoche (Harmony Books); *The River Wife*, by Jonis Agee (Random House).

Terms Agent receives 15% commission on domestic sales; 10% commission on foreign sales.

Writers' Conferences Nebraska Writers' Conference; Words and Music Festival in New Orleans.

◨ THE SWETKY AGENCY

2150 Balboa Way, No. 29, St. George UT 84770. E-mail: fayeswetky@amsaw.org. Website: www.amsaw.org/swetkyagency/index.html. **Contact:** Faye M. Swetky. Estab. 2000. Member of American Society of Authors and Writers. Represents 40+ clients. 80% of clients are new/unpublished writers. Currently handles: 30% nonfiction books; 30% novels; 20% movie scripts; 20% TV scripts.

- Prior to becoming an agent, Ms. Swetky was an editor and corporate manager. She has also raised and raced thoroughbred horses.

Represents Nonfiction books, novels, short story collections, juvenile books, movie scripts, feature film, TV scripts, TV movie of the week, sitcom, documentary. **Considers these nonfiction areas:** All major nonfiction genres. **Considers these fiction areas:** All major fiction genres. **Considers these script subject areas:** Action/adventure; biography/autobiography; cartoon/animation; comedy; contemporary issues; detective/police/crime; erotica; ethnic; experimental; family saga; fantasy; feminist; gay/lesbian; glitz; historical; horror; juvenile; mainstream; multicultural; multimedia; mystery/suspense; psychic/supernatural; regional; religious/inspirational; romantic comedy; romantic drama; science fiction; sports; teen; thriller; western/frontier.

○ᗡ "We handle only book-length fiction and nonfiction and feature-length movie and television scripts. Please visit our Web site before submitting. All agency-related information is there, including a sample contract, e-mail submission forms, policies, clients, etc." Actively seeking young adult material. Do not send unprofessionally prepared mss and/or scripts.

How to Contact See Web site for submission instructions. Accepts e-mail queries only. Considers simultaneous queries. Response time varies. Obtains most new clients through queries.

Recent Sales *Zen and the Art of Pond Building*, by J.D. Herda (Sterling); *Solid Stiehl*, by D.J. Herda (Archebooks); *24/7*, by Susan Diplacido (Zumaya Publications); *House on the Road to Salisbury*, by Lisa Adams (Archebooks). ***Movie/TV MOW script(s) optioned/sold:*** *Demons 5*, by Jim O'Rear (Katzir Productions); *Detention* and *Instinct Vs. Reason*, by Garrett Hargrove (Filmjack Productions).

Terms Agent receives 15% commission on domestic sales; 20% commission on foreign sales; 20% commission on dramatic rights sales. Offers written contract, binding for 1 year; 30-day notice must be given to terminate contract.

Tips "Be professional. Have a professionally prepared product."

TALCOTT NOTCH LITERARY

276 Forest Road, Milford CT 06460. (203)877-1146. Fax: (203)876-9517. E-mail: editorial@talcottnotch.net. Website: www.talcottnotch.net. **Contact:** Gina Panettieri, president. Estab. 2003. Represents 25 clients. 30% of clients are new/unpublished writers.

• Prior to becoming an agent, Ms. Panettieri was a freelance writer and editor.

Member Agents Gina Panettieri (nonfiction, mystery); Rachel Dowen (children's fiction, mystery).

Represents Nonfiction books, novels, juvenile books, scholarly books, textbooks. **Considers these nonfiction areas:** Agriculture/horticulture; animals; anthropology/archaeology; art/architecture/design; biography/autobiography; business/economics; child guidance/parenting; computers/electronic; cooking/foods/nutrition; current affairs; education; ethnic/cultural interests; gay/lesbian issues; government/politics/law; health/medicine; history; how-to; memoirs; military/war; money/finance; music/dance; nature/environment; popular culture; psychology; science/technology; self-help/personal improvement; sociology; sports; true crime/investigative; women's issues/studies; New Age/metaphysics, interior design/decorating, juvenile nonfiction. **Considers these fiction areas:** Action/adventure; detective/police/crime; juvenile; mystery/suspense; thriller; young adult.

How to Contact Query via e-mail (preferred) or with SASE. Considers simultaneous queries. Responds in 1 week to queries; 2 weeks to mss. Returns materials only with SASE.

Recent Sales Sold 24 titles in the last year. *The Connected Child*, by Dr. Karyn Purvis, Dr. David Cross and Wendy Sunshine (Mcgraw-Hill); *Parenting Your Defiant Child*, by Dr. Philip Hall And Dr. Nancy Hall (Amacom); *Fall: The Rape and Murder of Innocence in a Small Town*, by Ron Franscell (New Horizon Press); *The New Supervisor's Handbook*, by Brette Sember and Terry Sember (Career Press); *The Executive's Guide To E-mail Correspondance*, by Dr. Dawn-Michelle Baude (Career Press). Other clients include Dr. Leslie Young, Moira Mccarthy, Corrie Lynne Player, David Evans Katz, Erik Lawrence, Dagmara Scalise, Nancy Whitney Reiter, A.E. Rought/Savannah Jordan.

Terms Agent receives 15% commission on domestic sales; 20% commission on foreign sales. Offers written contract, binding for 1 year.

Tips "Present your book or project effectively in your query. Don't include links to a Web page rather than a traditional query, and take the time to prepare a thorough but brief synopsis of the material. Make the effort to prepare a thoughtful analysis of comparison titles. How is your work different, yet would appeal to those same readers?"

PATRICIA TEAL LITERARY AGENCY

2036 Vista Del Rosa, Fullerton CA 92831-1336. Phone/Fax: (714)738-8333. **Contact:** Patricia Teal. Estab. 1978. Member of AAR. Represents 20 clients. Currently handles: 10% nonfiction books; 90% fiction.

Represents Nonfiction books, novels. **Considers these nonfiction areas:** Animals; biography/autobiography; child guidance/parenting; health/medicine; how-to; psychology; self-help/personal improvement; true crime/investigative; women's issues/studies. **Considers these fiction areas:** Glitz; mainstream/contemporary; mystery/suspense; romance (contemporary, historical).

• This agency specializes in women's fiction, commercial how-to, and self-help nonfiction. Does not want to receive poetry, short stories, articles, science fiction, fantasy, or regency romance.

How to Contact Published authors only may query with SASE. No e-mail or fax queries. Considers simultaneous queries. Responds in 10 days to queries; 6 weeks to mss. Returns materials only with SASE. Obtains most new clients through conferences, recommendations from authors and editors.

Recent Sales Sold 30 titles in the last year. *Texas Rose*, by Marie Ferrarella (Silhouette); *Watch Your Language*, by Sterling Johnson (St. Martin's Press); *The Black Sheep's Baby*, by Kathleen Creighton (Silhouette); *Man With a Message*, by Muriel Jensen (Harlequin).

Terms Agent receives 10-15% commission on domestic sales; 20% commission on foreign sales. Offers written contract, binding for 1 year. Charges clients for ms copies.

Writers' Conferences RWA Conferences; Asilomar; BookExpo America; Bouchercon; Maui Writers Conference.

Tips "Include SASE with all correspondence. I am taking on published authors only."

● TESSLER LITERARY AGENCY, LLC

27 W. 20th St., Suite 1003, New York NY 10011. (212)242-0466. Fax: (212)242-2366. Website: www.tessleragenc y.com. **Contact:** Michelle Tessler. Member of AAR.

- Prior to forming her own agency, Ms. Tessler worked at Carlisle & Co. (now a part of Inkwell Management). She has also worked at the William Morris Agency and the Elaine Markson Literary Agency.

Represents Nonfiction books. **Considers these nonfiction areas:** Business/economics; history; memoirs; popular culture; psychology; travel.

- ☞ The Tessler Agency is a full-service boutique agency that represents writers of literary fiction and high quality nonfiction in the following categories: popular science, reportage, memoir, history, biography, psychology, business and travel.

How to Contact Submit query through Web site only.

● THE TFS LITERARY AGENCY

P.O. Box 46-031, Lower Hutt 5044, New Zealand. E-mail: tfs@elseware.co.nz. Website: www.elseware.co.nz. **Contact:** Chris Else, Barbara Else. Estab. 1988. Member of NZALA.

- ☞ Seeks general fiction, nonfiction, and children's books from New Zealand authors only. No poetry, individual short stories, or articles.

How to Contact Send query and brief author bio via e-mail.

● 3 SEAS LITERARY AGENCY

P.O. Box 8571, Madison WI 53708. (608)221-4306. E-mail: queries@threeseaslit.com. Website: www.threeseasli t.com. **Contact:** Michelle Grajkowski, Cori Deyoe. Estab. 2000. Member of RWA, Chicago Women in Publishing. Represents 40 clients. 10% of clients are new/unpublished writers. Currently handles: 5% nonfiction books; 80% novels; 15% juvenile books.

- Prior to becoming an agent, Ms. Grajkowski worked in both sales and purchasing for a medical facility. She has a degree in journalism from the University of Wisconsin-Madison. Prior to joining the agency in 2006, Ms. Deyoe was a multi-published author. She is excited to be part of the agency and is actively building her client list.

Member Agents Michelle Grajkowski; Cori Deyoe.

Represents Nonfiction books, novels, juvenile books, scholarly books.

- ☞ 3 Seas focuses on romance (including category, historical, regency, Western, romantic suspense, paranormal), women's fiction, mysteries, nonfiction, young adult and children's stories. No poetry, screenplays or short stories.

How to Contact E-mail queries **only** For fiction and young adult, query with first 3 chapters, synopsis, bio, SASE. For nonfiction, query with complete proposal, first 3 chapters, SASE. For picture books, query with complete ms. Considers simultaneous queries. Responds in 1 month to queries. Responds in 3 months to partials. Returns materials only with SASE. Obtains most new clients through recommendations from others, conferences.

Recent Sales Sold 75 titles in the last year. *Even Vampires Get the Blues* and *Light My Fire*, by Katie MacAlister (NAL); *Vamps in the City*, by Kerrelyn Sparks (Avon); *Date Me Baby, One More Time* and *Must Love Dragons*, by Stephanie Rowe (Warner); *From the Dark*, by Michelle Hauf (Harlequin Nocturne); *The Runaway Daughter*, by Anna DeStefano; *Calamity Jayne Rides Again*, by Kathleen Bacus (Leisure); *Daddy Daycare*, by Laura Marie Altom (Harlequin American); *Dark Protector*, by Alexis Morgan (Pocket); *Seduced By the Night*, by Robin T. Popp (Warner); *What Happens In Paris*, by Nancy Robards Thompson (Harlequin NEXT). Other clients include Naomi Neale, Brenda Mott, Winnie Griggs, Barbara Jean Hicks, Cathy McDavid, Lisa Mondello, R. Barri Flowers, Dyanne Davis, Catherine Kean, Pat White, Mary Buckham.

Terms Agent receives 15% commission on domestic sales; 20% commission on foreign sales. Offers written contract.

◎ ANN TOBIAS: A LITERARY AGENCY FOR CHILDREN'S BOOKS

520 E. 84th St., Apt. 4L, New York NY 10028. **Contact:** Ann Tobias. Estab. 1988. Represents 25 clients. 10% of clients are new/unpublished writers. Currently handles: 100% juvenile books.

- Prior to opening her agency, Ms. Tobias worked as a children's book editor at Harper, William Morrow and Scholastic.

Represents Juvenile books. **Considers these nonfiction areas:** Juvenile nonfiction. **Considers these fiction areas:** Picture books; poetry (for children); young adult; illustrated mss; mid-level novels.

- ☞ This agency specializes in books for children.

How to Contact For all age groups and genres: Send a one-page letter of inquiry accompanied by a one-page writing sample, double-spaced. No e-mail or fax queries. Considers simultaneous queries, but requires 1-month exclusive on all requested mss. Responds in 2 months to mss. Returns materials only with SASE. Obtains most new clients through recommendations from editors.

Recent Sales This agency prefers not to share information on specific sales.

Terms Agent receives 15% commission on domestic sales; 20% commission on foreign sales. No written contract. This agency charges clients for photocopying, overnight mail, foreign postage, foreign telephone.

Tips "Read at least 200 children's books in the age group and genre in which you hope to be published. Follow this by reading another 100 children's books in other age groups and genres so you will have a feel for the field as a whole."

LYNDA TOLLS LITERARY AGENCY

P.O. Box 1884, Bend OR 97709. (541)388-3510. E-mail: LTLit@bendbroadband.com. **Contact:** Lynda Tolls Swarts. Estab. 1995. Represents 8 clients. 20% of clients are new/unpublished writers. Currently handles: 90% nonfiction books; 10% novels.

Represents Nonfiction books, novels. **Considers these nonfiction areas:** Education; ethnic/cultural interests; health/medicine; history; self-help/personal improvement; travel; biography; global interests; religious/spiritual. **Considers these fiction areas:** Mystery/suspense (and its subgenres).

How to Contact For nonfiction, query with book concept, market, competing titles, author expertise. For fiction, query with synopsis, first 10 pages.

Writers' Conferences Willamette Writers Conference; Surrey International Writers' Conference; Idaho Writers' Conference.

TRANSATLANTIC LITERARY AGENCY

72 Glengowan Road, Toronto Ontario M4N 1G4, Canada. E-mail: info@tla1.com. Website: www.tla1.com. **Contact:** Lynn Bennett. Estab. 1993. Represents 250 clients. 10% of clients are new/unpublished writers. Currently handles: 30% nonfiction books; 15% novels; 50% juvenile books; 5% textbooks.

Member Agents Lynn Bennett, Lynn@tla1.com, (juvenile and young adult fiction); Shaun Bradley, Shaun@tla1.com (literary fiction and narrative nonfiction); Marie Campbell, Marie@tla1.com (literary juvenile and young adult fiction); Andrea Cascardi, Andrea@tla1.com (literary juvenile and young adult fiction); Samantha Haywood, Sam@tla1.com (literary fiction, narrative nonfiction and graphic novels); Karen Klockner, Karen@tla1.com (juvenile nonfiction and illustration); Don Sedgwick, Don@tla1.com (literary fiction and narrative nonfiction).

Represents Nonfiction books, novels, juvenile books. **Considers these nonfiction areas:** Biography/autobiography; business/economics; current affairs; nature/environment. **Considers these fiction areas:** Juvenile; literary; mainstream/contemporary; mystery/suspense; young adult.

"In both children's and adult literature, we market directly into the United States, the United Kingdom and Canada." Actively seeking literary children's and adult fiction, nonfiction. Does not want to receive picture books, poetry, screenplays or stage plays.

How to Contact Submit E-query query with synopsis, 2 sample chapters, bio. Always refer to the Web site as guidelines will change. Accepts e-mail queries. No fax queries. Responds in 2 weeks to queries. Obtains most new clients through recommendations from others.

Recent Sales Sold 250 titles in the last year. *Denial of Service*, by Michael Calce and Craig Silverman (Penguin); *The Armageddon Factor*, by Marci McDonald (Random House); *Hot Art*, by Josh Knelman (Simon & Schuster); *The Perilous Realm*, by Thomas Wharton (Walker); *American Girl of the Year 2009*, by Mary Casanova (America Girl).

Terms Agent receives 15% commission on domestic sales; 20% commission on foreign sales. Offers written contract; 45-day notice must be given to terminate contract. This agency charges for photocopying and postage when it exceeds $100.

S©OTT TREIMEL NY

434 Lafayette St., New York NY 10003. (212)505-8353. Fax: (212)505-0664. E-mail: st.ny@verizon.net. **Contact:** John M. Cusick. Estab. 1995. Member of AAR, Authors Guild, SCBWI. 10% of clients are new/unpublished writers. Currently handles: 100% juvenile/teen books.

• Prior to becoming an agent, Mr. Treimel was an assistant to Marilyn E. Marlow at Curtis Brown, a rights agent for Scholastic, a book packager and rights agent for United Feature Syndicate, a freelance editor, a rights consultant for HarperCollins Children's Books, and the founding director of Warner Bros. Worldwide Publishing.

Represents Nonfiction books, novels, juvenile books (children's, picture books, young adult).

This agency specializes in tightly focused segments of the trade and institutional markets. Career clients.

How to Contact Send query/outline, SASE, sample chapters of no more than 30 pages. No multiple submissions. Queries without SASE will be recycled. No fax queries.

Recent Sales Sold 23 titles in the last year. *Dog Parade*, by Barbara Joosse (Harcourt); *Kitchen Dance*, by Maurice Manning (Clarion); *The Ninja Who Wanted to be Noticed*, by Julie Phillipps (Viking); *Roawr!*, by Barbara Joosse (Philomel); *Tickle Monster Illustrations*, by Kevan Atteberry (Compendi); *Kiki*, by Janie Bynum (Sterling).

Terms Agent receives 15% commission on domestic sales; 20% commission on foreign sales. Offers verbal or written contract. Charges clients for photocopying, express postage, messengers, and books needed to sell foreign, film and other rights.

Writers' Conferences SCBWI; The New School; Southwest Writers' Conference; Pikes Peak Writers' Conference.

☑ TRIADA U.S. LITERARY AGENCY, INC.

P.O. Box 561, Sewickley PA 15143. (412)401-3376. E-mail: uwe@triadaus.com. Website: www.triadaus.com. **Contact:** Dr. Uwe Stender. Estab. 2004. Represents 55 clients. 30% of clients are new/unpublished writers.

Member Agents Paul Hudson (science fiction, fantasy); Rebecca Post.

Represents Nonfiction books, novels, short story collections, juvenile books, scholarly books. **Considers these nonfiction areas:** Biography/autobiography; business/economics; child guidance/parenting; education; how-to; humor/satire; memoirs; popular culture; self-help/personal improvement; sports. **Considers these fiction areas:** Action/adventure; detective/police/crime; ethnic; fantasy; historical; horror; juvenile; literary; mainstream/contemporary; mystery/suspense; romance; science fiction; sports; thriller; young adult.

- ○━ "We are now focusing on self-help and how-to. Additionally, we specialize in literary novels and suspense. Education, business, popular culture, and narrative nonfiction are other strong suits. Our response time is fairly unique. We recognize that neither we nor the authors have time to waste, so we guarantee a 5-day response time. We usually respond within 24 hours." Actively looking for nonfiction, especially self-help, how-to, and prescriptive nonfiction. De-emphasizing fiction, although great writing will always be considered.

How to Contact E-mail queries preferred; otherwise query with SASE. Considers simultaneous queries. Responds in 1-5 weeks to queries; 2-6 weeks to mss. Returns materials only with SASE. Obtains most new clients through recommendations from others, conferences.

Recent Sales *The Sexual Solution*, by Joel Block and KD Neumann (Adams); *31 Days to Greatness*, by Kevin Elko and Bill Beausay (Amacom); *The Equation*, by Omar Tree (Wiley); *How to Survive Your Surgery*, by David Page and Pamela Rowland (Sterling).

Terms Agent receives 15% commission on domestic sales; 20% commission on foreign sales. Offers written contract; 30-day notice must be given to terminate contract.

Tips "I comment on all requested manuscripts that I reject."

☑ TRIDENT MEDIA GROUP

41 Madison Ave., 36th Floor, New York NY 10010. Website: www.tridentmediagroup.com. **Contact:** Ellen Levine. Member of AAR.

Member Agents Kimberly Whalen, whalen.assistant@tridentmediagroup (commercial fiction and nonfiction, women's fiction, suspense, paranormal and pop culture); Jenny Bent, jbent@tridentmediagroup.com (humor, literary fiction, women's commercial fiction, narrative nonfiction, biography, health, how-to); Eileen Cope, ecope@tridentmediagroup.comnarrative nonfiction, history, biography, pop culture, health, literary fiction and short story collections); Scott Miller, smiller@tridentmediagroup.com (thrillers, crime, mystery, young adult, children's, narrative nonfiction, current events, military, memoir, literary fiction, graohic novels, pop culture); Paul Fedorko, pfedorko@tridentmediagroup.com (commercial fiction, mysteries, thrillers, romantic suspense, business, sports, celebrity and pop culture); Alex Glass (aglass@tridentmediagroup, thrillers, literary fiction, crime, middle grade, pop culture, young adult, humor and narrative nonfiction); Melissa Flashman, mflashman-@tridentmediagroup.com (narrative nonfiction, serious nonfiction, pop culture, lifstyle); Alyssa Henkin, ahenkin@tridentmediagroup.com (juvenile, children's, YA).

Represents Nonfiction books, novels, short story collections, juvenile books. **Considers these nonfiction areas:** Biography/autobiography; current affairs; government/politics/law; humor/satire; memoirs; military/war; multicultural; popular culture; true crime/investigative; women's issues/studies; young adult. **Considers these fiction areas:** Detective/police/crime; humor/satire; juvenile; literary; military/war; multicultural; mystery/suspense; short story collections; thriller; young adult; women's.

- ○━ Actively seeking new or established authors in a variety of fiction and nonfiction genres.

How to Contact Query with SASE or via e-mail. Check Web site for more details.

☑ 2M COMMUNICATIONS, LTD.

121 W. 27 St., #601, New York NY 10001. (212)741-1509. Fax: (212)691-4460. E-mail: morel@bookhaven.com. Website: www.2mcommunications.com. **Contact:** Madeleine Morel. Estab. 1982. Member of AAR. Represents 100 clients. 20% of clients are new/unpublished writers. Currently handles: 100% nonfiction books.

● Prior to becoming an agent, Ms. Morel worked at a publishing company.

Represents Nonfiction books. **Considers these nonfiction areas:** Biography/autobiography; child guidance/parenting; ethnic/cultural interests; health/medicine; history; self-help/personal improvement; women's issues/studies; music; cookbooks.

    O→ This agency specializes in exclusively and non-exclusively representing professional ghostwriters and collaborators. This agency's writers have penned multiple bestsellers. They work closely with other leading literary agents and editors whose high-profile authors require confidential associations.

How to Contact Query with SASE, submit outline, 3 sample chapters. Considers simultaneous queries. Responds in 1 week to queries; 1 month to mss. Obtains most new clients through recommendations from others, solicitations.

Recent Sales Sold 25 titles in the last year. *How Do You Compare?*, by Andy Williams (Penguin Putnam); *Hormone Wisdom*, by Theresa Dale (John Wiley); *Irish Dessert Cookbook*, by Margaret Johnson (Chronicle).

Terms Agent receives 15% commission on domestic sales; 20% commission on foreign sales. Offers written contract, binding for 2 years. Charges clients for postage, photocopying, long-distance calls, faxes.

☑ THE RICHARD R. VALCOURT AGENCY, INC.

177 E. 77th St., PHC, New York NY 10075. Phone/Fax: (212)570-2340. **Contact:** Richard R. Valcourt, president. Estab. 1995. Represents 25 clients. 20% of clients are new/unpublished writers. Currently handles: 100% nonfiction books.

    ● Prior to opening his agency, Mr. Valcourt was a journalist, editor, and college political science instructor. He is also editor-in-chief of the *International Journal of Intelligence* and faculty member at American Military University in West Virginia.

Represents Scholarly books.

    O→ Not accepting new clients at this time. This agency specializes in intelligence and other national security affairs. Represents exclusively academics, journalists, and professionals in the categories listed.

How to Contact Prefers to read materials exclusively. No e-mail or fax queries. Responds in 1 week to queries; 1 month to mss. Returns materials only with SASE. Obtains most new clients through recommendations from others.

Terms Agent receives 15% commission on domestic sales; 20% commission on foreign sales. Offers written contract. Charges clients for excessive photocopying, express mail, overseas telephone expenses.

◻ VANGUARD LITERARY AGENCY

81 E. Jefryn Blvd., Suite E, Deer Park NY 11729. (718)710-3662. Fax: (718)504-4541. E-mail: sandylu@vanguardliterary.com. Website: www.vanguardliterary.com. **Contact:** Sandy Lu. Estab. 2006. Represents 15 clients. 60% of clients are new/unpublished writers. Currently handles: 20% nonfiction books; 80% novels.

    ● Prior to becoming an agent, Ms. Lu held managerial positions in commercial theater.

Represents Nonfiction books, novels, short story collections, novellas. **Considers these nonfiction areas:** Anthropology/archaeology; biography/autobiography; cooking/foods/nutrition; ethnic/cultural interests; gay/lesbian issues; history; memoirs; music/dance; popular culture; psychology; science/technology; sociology; translation; true crime/investigative; women's issues/studies. **Considers these fiction areas:** Action/adventure; confession; detective/police/crime; ethnic; historical; horror; humor/satire; literary; mainstream/contemporary; mystery/suspense; regional; thriller; women's (no chick lit).

    O→ "Very few agents in the business still edit their clients' manuscripts, especially when it comes to fiction. Vanguard Literary Agency is different. I care about the quality of my clients' works and will not send anything out to publishers without personally going through each page first to ensure that when the manuscript is sent out, it is in the best possible shape." Actively seeking literary and commercial fiction with a unique voice. Does not want to receive movie or TV scripts, stage plays or poetry; unwanted fiction genres include science fiction/fantasy, Western, YA, children's; unwanted nonfiction genres include self-help, how-to, parenting, sports, dating/relationship, military/war, religion/spirituality, New Age, gift books.

How to Contact Query with SASE, submit outline/proposal, synopsis, author bio, 10-15 sample pp. Accepts e-mail queries. No fax queries. Considers simultaneous queries. Responds in 2 weeks to queries; 6-8 weeks to mss. Returns materials only with SASE. Obtains most new clients through recommendations from others, solicitations, conferences.

Terms Agent receives 15% commission on domestic sales; 20% commission on foreign sales. Offers written contract, binding for 1 year; 30-day notice must be given to terminate contract. This agency charges for photocopying and postage, and discusses larger costs (in excess of $100) with authors prior to charging.

Tips "Do your research. Do not query an agent for a genre he or she does not represent. Personalize your query letter. Start with an interesting hook. Learn how to write a succinct yet interesting synopsis or proposal."

✪ VENTURE LITERARY

8895 Towne Centre Drive, Suite 105, #141, San Diego CA 92122. (619)807-1887. Fax: (772)365-8321. E-mail: submissions@ventureliterary.com. Website: www.ventureliterary.com. **Contact:** Frank R. Scatoni. Estab. 1999. Represents 50 clients. 40% of clients are new/unpublished writers. Currently handles: 80% nonfiction books; 20% novels.

• Prior to becoming an agent, Mr. Scatoni worked as an editor at Simon & Schuster.

Member Agents Frank R. Scatoni (general nonfiction, biography, memoir, narrative nonfiction, sports, serious nonfiction, graphic novels, narratives); Jennifer de la Fuente (literary, commercial and women's fiction, women's nonfiction, pop culture).

Represents Nonfiction books, novels, graphic novels, narratives. **Considers these nonfiction areas:** Anthropology/archaeology; biography/autobiography; business/economics; current affairs; ethnic/cultural interests; government/politics/law; history; memoirs; military/war; money/finance; multicultural; music/dance; nature/environment; popular culture; psychology; science/technology; sports; true crime/investigative. **Considers these fiction areas:** Action/adventure; detective/police/crime; literary; mainstream/contemporary; mystery/suspense; sports; thriller; women's.

⚬━ Specializes in nonfiction, sports, biography, gambling and nonfiction narratives. Actively seeking nonfiction, graphic novels and narratives.

How to Contact Considers e-mail queries only. *No unsolicited mss.* See Web site for complete submission guidelines. Obtains most new clients through recommendations from others.

Recent Sales *The 9/11 Report: A Graphic Adaptation*, by Sid Jacobson and Ernie Colon (FSG); *Untitled on Infertility*, by Cindy Margolis (Perigee/Penguin); *Phil Gordon's Little Blue Book*, by Phil Gordon (Simon & Schuster); *Super Critical*, by Todd Tucker (Free Press); *The Making of Michelle Wie*, by Eric Adelson (ESPN Books); *Online Ace*, by Scott Fischman (ESPN Books).

Terms Agent receives 15% commission on domestic sales; 20% commission on foreign sales. Offers written contract.

✪ VERITAS LITERARY AGENCY

601 Van Ness Ave., Opera Plaza, Suite E, San Francisco CA 94102. Website: www.veritasliterary.com. **Contact:** Katherine Boyle. Member of AAR, Author's Guild.

Represents Nonfiction books, novels. **Considers these nonfiction areas:** Current affairs; government/politics/law; memoirs; popular culture; women's issues/studies; narrative nonfiction, art and music biography, natural history, health and wellness, psychology, serious religion (no New Age) and popular science. **Considers these fiction areas:** Contemporary and literary fiction only.

⚬━ Does not want to receive romance, sci-fi, poetry or children's books.

How to Contact Query with SASE. This agency prefers a short query letter with no attachments. Accepts e-mail queries. No fax queries.

Recent Sales *If I am Missing or Dead*, by Janine Latus.

✪ BETH VESEL LITERARY AGENCY

80 Fifth Ave., Suite 1101, New York NY 10011. (212)924-4252. E-mail: mlindley@bvlit.com. **Contact:** Molly Lindley, assistant. Estab. 2003. Represents 65 clients. 10% of clients are new/unpublished writers. Currently handles: 75% nonfiction books; 10% novels; 5% story collections; 10% scholarly books.

• Prior to becoming an agent, Ms. Vesel was a poet and a journalist.

Represents Nonfiction books, novels. **Considers these nonfiction areas:** Biography/autobiography; business/economics; ethnic/cultural interests; health/medicine; how-to; memoirs; psychology; self-help/personal improvement; true crime/investigative; women's issues/studies; cultural criticism. **Considers these fiction areas:** Detective/police/crime; literary; Francophone novels.

⚬━ "My specialties include serious nonfiction, psychology, cultural criticism, memoir, and women's issues." Actively seeking cultural criticism, literary psychological thrillers, and sophisticated memoirs. No uninspired psychology or run-of-the-mill first novels.

How to Contact Query with SASE. Considers simultaneous queries. Responds in 2 weeks to queries; 1 month to mss. Returns materials only with SASE. Obtains most new clients through referrals, reading good magazines, contacting professionals with ideas.

Recent Sales Sold 10 titles in the last year. *James Brown's Body*, by Greg Tate (Riverhead); *Your Money or Your Life for the 21st Century*, by Vicki Robin (Penguin); *Beowulf on the Beach*, by Jack Murninghan (Three Rivers); *Shakespeare and Modern Culture*, by Marge Garber (Pantheon).

Terms Agent receives 15% commission on domestic sales; 20% commission on foreign sales. Offers written contract.

Writers' Conferences Squaw Valley Writers Workshop, Iowa Summer Writing Festival.

Tips "Try to find out if you fit on a particular agent's list by looking at his/her books and comparing yours. You can almost always find who represents a book by looking at the acknowledgements."

⊘ RALPH VICINANZA, LTD.

303 W. 18th St., New York NY 10011. (212)924-7090. Fax: (212)691-9644. Member of AAR.
Member Agents Ralph M. Vicinanza; Chris Lotts; Chris Schelling.
How to Contact This agency takes on new clients by professional recommendation only.
Recent Sales This agency prefers not to share information on specific sales.
Terms Agent receives 15% commission on domestic sales; 20% commission on foreign sales.

⊕ ⊘ WADE & DOHERTY LITERARY AGENCY

33 Cormorant Lodge, Thomas Moore St., London E1W 1AU England. (44)(207)488-4171. Fax: (44)(207)488-4172. E-mail: rw@rwla.com. Website: www.rwla.com. **Contact:** Robin Wade. Estab. 2001.
  ● Prior to opening his agency, Mr. Wade was an author; Ms. Doherty worked as a production assistant, editor and editorial director.
Member Agents Robin Wade, agent; Broo Doherty, agent.
Represents Nonfiction books, novels, juvenile books.
  ⌖ "We are young and dynamic, and actively seek new writers across the literary spectrum." Does not want to receive poetry, plays or short stories.
How to Contact Submit synopsis (1-6 pages), bio, first 10,000 words via e-mail (Word or pdf documents only). If sending by post, include SASE or IRC. Responds in 1 week to queries; 1 month to mss.
Recent Sales *The Solitude of Thomas Cave*, by Georgina Harding; *The Hunt for Atlantis*, by Andy McDermott; *The Opposite House*, by Helen Oyeyemi; *A Tangled Summer*, by Caroline Kington; *The Truth Will Out: Unmasking the Real Shakespeare*, by Brenda James.
Terms Agent receives 10% commission on domestic sales; 20% commission on foreign sales. Offers written contract; 1-month notice must be given to terminate contract.
Tips "We seek manuscripts that are well written, with strong characters and an original narrative voice. Our absolute priority is giving the best possible service to the authors we choose to represent, as well as maintaining routine friendly contact with them as we help develop their careers."

⊘ MARY JACK WALD ASSOCIATES, INC.

111 E. 14th St., New York NY 10003. (212)254-7842. **Contact:** Danis Sher. Estab. 1985. Member of AAR, Authors Guild, SCBWI. Represents 35 clients. 5% of clients are new/unpublished writers.
Member Agents Mary Jack Wald; Danis Sher; Alvin Wald.
Represents Nonfiction books, novels, short story collections, novellas, juvenile books, clients' movie/TV scripts. **Considers these nonfiction areas:** Biography/autobiography; current affairs; ethnic/cultural interests; history; juvenile nonfiction; language/literature/criticism; music/dance; nature/environment; photography; sociology; theater/film; translation; true crime/investigative. **Considers these fiction areas:** Action/adventure; contemporary issues; detective/police/crime; ethnic; experimental; family saga; feminist; gay/lesbian; glitz; historical; juvenile; literary; mainstream/contemporary; mystery/suspense; picture books; thriller; young adult; satire.
  ⌖ This agency is not accepting mss at this time. This agency specializes in literary works and juvenile works.
How to Contact Submit will request more if interested. Query by e-mail only.
Recent Sales *Ghost Walk*, by Richie Tankersley Cusick (Speak/Penguin); *Gates of Hades*, by Gregg Loomis (Leisure Books/Dorchester); *Escape From Castle Cant*, by K.P. Bath (Recorded Books).
Terms Agent receives 15% commission on domestic sales; 15-30% commission on foreign sales. Offers written contract, binding for 1 year.

⊘ WALES LITERARY AGENCY, INC.

P.O. Box 9428, Seattle WA 98109-0428. (206)284-7114. Fax: (206)322-1033. E-mail: waleslit@waleslit.com. Website: www.waleslit.com. **Contact:** Elizabeth Wales, Neal Swain. Estab. 1988. Member of AAR, Book Publishers' Northwest, Pacific Northwest Booksellers Association, PEN. Represents 65 clients. 10% of clients are new/unpublished writers. Currently handles: 60% nonfiction books; 40% novels.
  ● Prior to becoming an agent, Ms. Wales worked at Oxford University Press and Viking Penguin.
Member Agents Elizabeth Wales; Neal Swain.
  ⌖ This agency specializes in narrative nonfiction and quality mainstream and literary fiction. Does not handle screenplays, children's literature, genre fiction, or most category nonfiction.
How to Contact Query with cover letter, SASE. No phone or fax queries. Prefers regular mail queries, but

accepts 1-page e-mail queries with no attachments. Considers simultaneous queries. Responds in 3 weeks to queries; 6 weeks to mss. Returns materials only with SASE.

Recent Sales *The Floating World*, by Curtis Ebbesmeyer and Eric Scigliano (Smithsonian/HarperCollins); *Crow Planet*, by Lyanda Lynn Haupt (Little, Brown); *Shimmering Images*, by Lisa Dale Norton (St. Martin's); *A Grey Moon Over China*, by Thomas A. Day (Tor).

Terms Agent receives 15% commission on domestic sales; 20% commission on foreign sales.

Writers' Conferences Pacific Northwest Writers Conference; Willamette Writers Conference.

Tips "We are especially interested in work that espouses a progressive cultural or political view, projects a new voice, or simply shares an important, compelling story. We also encourage writers living in the Pacific Northwest, West Coast, Alaska, and Pacific Rim countries, and writers from historically underrepresented groups, such as gay and lesbian writers and writers of color, to submit work (but does not discourage writers outside these areas). Most importantly, whether in fiction or nonfiction, the agency is looking for talented storytellers."

🔲 JOHN A. WARE LITERARY AGENCY

392 Central Park W., New York NY 10025-5801. (212)866-4733. Fax: (212)866-4734. **Contact:** John Ware. Estab. 1978. Represents 60 clients. 40% of clients are new/unpublished writers. Currently handles: 75% nonfiction books; 25% novels.

• Prior to opening his agency, Mr. Ware served as a literary agent with James Brown Associates/Curtis Brown, Ltd., and as an editor for Doubleday & Co.

Represents Nonfiction books, novels. **Considers these nonfiction areas:** Anthropology/archaeology; biography/autobiography; current affairs; health/medicine (academic credentials required); history (oral history, Americana, folklore); language/literature/criticism; music/dance; nature/environment; popular culture; psychology (academic credentials required); science/technology; sports; true crime/investigative; women's issues/studies; social commentary; investigative journalism; bird's eye views of phenomena. **Considers these fiction areas:** Detective/police/crime; mystery/suspense; thriller; accessible literary noncategory fiction.

0-ᴕ Does not want personal memoirs.

How to Contact Query with SASE. Send a letter only. No e-mail or fax queries. Considers simultaneous queries. Responds in 2 weeks to queries.

Recent Sales Untitled on Afghanistan, by Jon Krakauer (Doubleday); *High School*, by Jennifer Niven (Simon Spotlight Entertainment); *Spent*, by Avid Cardella (Little, Brown); *To Kill a Page*, by Travis Hugh Culley (Villard/Random House); *Inside the Minds of School Shooters*, by Peter Langman (Palgrave Macmillan); *Spies for Hire*, by Tim Shorlock (Simon & Schuster); *The Man Who Made the Blues: A Biography of W.C. Handy*, by David Robertson (Knopf); *Abundance of Valor*, by Will Irwin (Presidio); *The Star Garden*, by Nancy E. Turner (Thomas Dunne/St. Martin's).

Terms Agent receives 15% commission on domestic sales; 20% commission on foreign sales; 15% commission on dramatic rights sales. Charges clients for messenger service and photocopying.

Tips "Writers must have appropriate credentials for authorship of proposal (nonfiction) or manuscript (fiction); no publishing track record required. I am open to good writing and interesting ideas by new or veteran writers."

🔲 WATERSIDE PRODUCTIONS, INC.

2376 Oxford Ave., Cardiff-by-the-Sea CA 92007. (760)632-9190. Fax: (760)632-9295. Website: www.waterside.com. Estab. 1982.

Member Agents Bill Gladstone; Margot Maley Hutchison; Carole McClendon; William E. Brown; Lawrence Jackel; Ming Russell; Devra Ann Jacobs.

Represents Nonfiction books. **Considers these nonfiction areas:** Art/architecture/design; biography/autobiography; business/economics; child guidance/parenting; computers/electronic; ethnic/cultural interests; health/medicine; how-to; humor/satire; money/finance; nature/environment; popular culture; psychology; sociology; sports; cookbooks.

0-ᴕ Specializes in computer books, how-to, business, and health titles.

How to Contact Query via mail or online form. Phone queries are not accepted. Obtains most new clients through referrals from established client and publisher list.

Recent Sales "We have represented bestselling authors ranging from Eckhart Tolle to Kevin Trudeau, Mellisa Rossi, Ken Milbern, Randy Fitzgerald, and David Karlins."

Tips "For new writers, a quality proposal and a strong knowledge of the market you're writing for goes a long way toward helping us turn you into a published author. We like to see a strong author platform. Two foreign rights agents on staff, Neil Gudovitz; Kimberly Valentini, help us with overseas sales."

🔲 WATKINS LOOMIS AGENCY, INC.

133 E. 35th St., Suite 1, New York NY 10016. (212)532-0080. Fax: (212)889-0506. Website: www.watkinsloomis.com/. Estab. 1908. Represents 50 clients.

Member Agents Gloria Loomis, president.

Represents Nonfiction books, novels, short story collections. **Considers these nonfiction areas:** Biography/ autobiography; current affairs; ethnic/cultural interests; history; nature/environment; popular culture; science/ technology; investigative journalism. **Considers these fiction areas:** Literary.

O– This agency specializes in literary fiction and nonfiction.

How to Contact *No unsolicited mss.* This agency does not guarantee a response to queries.

Recent Sales *Where Did I Leave My Glasses?*, by Marta Lear; *Incognegro*, by Mat Johnson and Warren Pleece; *Diablerie*, by Walter Mosley.

Terms Agent receives 15% commission on domestic sales; 20% commission on foreign sales.

◖ WAXMAN LITERARY AGENCY, INC.

80 Fifth Ave., Suite 1101, New York NY 10011. Website: www.waxmanagency.com. **Contact:** Scott Waxman. Estab. 1997. Represents 60 clients. 50% of clients are new/unpublished writers. Currently handles: 80% nonfiction books; 20% novels.

• Prior to opening his agency, Mr. Waxman was an editor at HarperCollins.

Member Agents Scott Waxman (all categories of nonfiction, commercial fiction); Byrd Leavell; Farley Chase; Holly Rooy.

Represents Nonfiction books, novels. **Considers these nonfiction areas:** Narrative nonfiction. **Considers these fiction areas:** Literary; romance (contemporary); young adult; women's; commercial.

O– "We're looking for serious journalists and novelists with published works."

How to Contact All unsolicited mss returned unopened. Query through Web site. Considers simultaneous queries. Responds in 6 weeks to queries; 8 weeks to mss. Returns materials only with SASE. Obtains most new clients through recommendations from others, solicitations, conferences.

Recent Sales *Breaking the Slump: How Great Players Survived Their Darkest Moments in Golf*, by Jimmy Roberts (Collins); *Infected*, by Scott Sigler (Crown) *The Power of Less*, by Leo Babauta (Hyperion).

Terms Agent receives 15% commission on domestic sales; 10% commission on foreign sales. Offers written contract; 2-month notice must be given to terminate contract.

◎ IRENE WEBB LITERARY

1112 Montana Ave., No. 294, Santa Monica CA 90403. E-mail: webblit@verizon.net. Website: www.irenewebb. com. **Contact:** Irene Webb. Estab. 2003.

Represents Nonfiction books, novels. **Considers these nonfiction areas:** Memoirs; popular culture; sports; true stories. **Considers these fiction areas:** Mystery/suspense; thriller; literary and commercial fiction.

O– "Irene Webb Literary is known as one of the top boutique agencies selling books to film and TV. We have close relationships with top film producers and talent in Hollywood." Does not want to receive unsolicited manuscripts or screenplays.

How to Contact Query with SASE. Accepts e-mail queries. No fax queries. Obtains most new clients through recommendations from others, solicitations.

Recent Sales Film rights to *Koko*, by Peter Straub (Phoenix Entertainment); TV series rights to *Army Wives*, by Tanya Biank to Lifetime TV.

◖ THE WENDY WEIL AGENCY, INC.

232 Madison Ave., Suite 1300, New York NY 10016. (212)685-0030. Fax: (212)685-0765. E-mail: info@wendywe il.com. Website: www.wendyweil.com. Member of AAR. Currently handles: 20% nonfiction books; 80% novels.

Member Agents Wendy Weil (commercial fiction, women's fiction, family saga, historical fiction, short stories); Emily Forland; Emma Patterson.

Represents Nonfiction books, novels.

O– "The Wendy Weil Agency, Inc. represents fiction and non-fiction for the trade market. We work with literary and commercial fiction, mystery/thriller, memoir, narrative non-fiction, journalism, history, current affairs, books on health, science, popular culture, lifestyle, and art history." Does not want to receive screenplays or textbooks.

How to Contact Query with SASE. Snail mail queries are preferred. No fax queries. Obtains most new clients through recommendations from others, solicitations.

Recent Sales *What's the Girl Worth?: A Novel*, by Christina Fitzpatrick (HarperCollins); *Miss American Pie: A Diary*, by Margaret Sartor (Bloomsbury USA); *Devil in the Details: Scenes from an Obsessive Girlhood*, by Jennifer Traig (Little, Brown).

◖ CHERRY WEINER LITERARY AGENCY

28 Kipling Way, Manalapan NJ 07726-3711. (732)446-2096. Fax: (732)792-0506. E-mail: cherry8486@aol.com. **Contact:** Cherry Weiner. Estab. 1977. Represents 40 clients. 10% of clients are new/unpublished writers. Currently handles: 10-20% nonfiction books; 80-90% novels.

Represents Nonfiction books, novels. **Considers these nonfiction areas:** Self-help/personal improvement. **Considers these fiction areas:** Action/adventure; contemporary issues; detective/police/crime; family saga; fantasy; historical; mainstream/contemporary; mystery/suspense; psychic/supernatural; romance; science fiction; thriller; westerns/frontier.

    O➔ This agency is currently not accepting new clients except by referral or by personal contact at writers' conferences. Specializes in fantasy, science fiction, Western's, mysteries (both contemporary and historical), historical novels, Native-American works, mainstream and all genre romances.

How to Contact Query with SASE. Prefers to read materials exclusively. No fax queries. Responds in 1 week to queries; 2 months to mss. Returns materials only with SASE.

Recent Sales Sold 56 titles in the last year. This agency prefers not to share information on specific sales.

Terms Agent receives 15% commission on domestic sales; 15% commission on foreign sales. Offers written contract. Charges clients for extra copies of mss, first-class postage for author's copies of books, express mail for important documents/mss.

Tips "Meet agents and publishers at conferences. Establish a relationship, then get in touch with them and remind them of the meeting and conference."

☑ THE WEINGEL-FIDEL AGENCY

310 E. 46th St., 21E, New York NY 10017. (212)599-2959. **Contact:** Loretta Weingel-Fidel. Estab. 1989. Currently handles: 75% nonfiction books; 25% novels.

    ● Prior to opening her agency, Ms. Weingel-Fidel was a psychoeducational diagnostician.

Represents Nonfiction books, novels. **Considers these nonfiction areas:** Art/architecture/design; biography/autobiography; memoirs; music/dance; psychology; science/technology; sociology; women's issues/studies; investigative journalism. **Considers these fiction areas:** Literary; mainstream/contemporary.

    O➔ This agency specializes in commercial and literary fiction and nonfiction. Actively seeking investigative journalism. Does not want to receive genre fiction, self-help, science fiction, or fantasy.

How to Contact Accepts writers by referral only. *No unsolicited mss.*

Terms Agent receives 15% commission on domestic sales; 20% commission on foreign sales. Offers written contract, binding for 1 year with automatic renewal. Bills sent back to clients are all reasonable expenses, such as UPS, express mail, photocopying, etc.

Tips "A very small, selective list enables me to work very closely with my clients to develop and nurture talent. I only take on projects and writers about which I am extremely enthusiastic."

☑ TED WEINSTEIN LITERARY MANAGEMENT

307 Seventh Ave., Suite 2407, Dept. GLA, New York NY 10001. Website: www.twliterary.com. **Contact:** Ted Weinstein. Estab. 2001. Member of AAR. Represents 75 clients. 50% of clients are new/unpublished writers. Currently handles: 100% nonfiction books.

Represents Nonfiction books by a wide range of journalists, academics, and other experts. **Considers these nonfiction areas:** Biography/autobiography; business/economics; current affairs; government/politics/law; health/medicine; history; popular culture; science/technology; self-help/personal improvement; travel; true crime/investigative; lifestyle, narrative journalism, popular science.

How to Contact Please visit website for detailed guidelines before submitting. E-mail queries **only**. No fax queries. Responds in 3 weeks to queries.

Terms Agent receives 15% commission on domestic sales; 20% commission on foreign sales; 20% commission on dramatic rights sales. Offers written contract, binding for 1 year. Charges clients for photocopying and express shipping.

Tips "Send e-queries only. See the Web site for guidelines."

ⓝ ☑ LARRY WEISSMAN LITERARY, LLC

526 8th St., #2R, Brooklyn NY. **Contact:** Larry Weissman. Represents 35 clients. Currently handles: 80% nonfiction books; 10% novels; 10% story collections.

Represents Nonfiction books, novels, short story collections. **Considers these fiction areas:** Literary.

    O➔ Actively seeking nonfiction, including food & lifestyle, politics, pop culture, narrative, cultural/social issues, journalism. Does not want to receive poetry or children's.

How to Contact Send e-queries only. Accepts e-mail queries. No fax queries.

Recent Sales *The Billionaire's Vinegar*, by Ben Wallace (Crown); *Sushi: Big Tuna, Globalization, and the Journey from Sea to Plate*, by Sasha Issenberg (Gotham); *The Shia Revival: How Conflicts Within Islam Will Shape the Future*, by Vali Nasr (W.W. Norton & Co.); *The Invisible Fist: Why the Best and the Brightest Are Selling Out and What It Means For America*, by Daniel Brook (Henry Holt).

Terms Agent receives 15% commission on domestic sales; 20% commission on foreign sales.

⚡ ⊙ WESTWOOD CREATIVE ARTISTS, LTD.

94 Harbord St., Toronto Ontario M5S 1G6, Canada. (416)964-3302. Fax: (416)975-9209. E-mail: wca_office@wc altd.com. Website: www.wcaltd.com. Represents 200+ clients.

Member Agents Deborah Wood, book-to-film agent; Aston Westwood, book-to-film agent; Linda McKnight, literary agent; Jackie Kaiser, literary agent; Hilary McMahon, literary agent; John Pearce, literary agent; Natasha Daneman, subsidiary rights director; Michael Levine, film & TV agent.

Represents Canadian literary fiction and nonfiction.

How to Contact Query with SASE. Use a referral to break into this agency. Accepts e-mail queries. No fax queries. Considers simultaneous queries.

Recent Sales A biography of Richard Nixon, by Conrad Black (Public Affairs); *The New Cold War: Revolutions, Rigged Elections and Pipeline Politics in the Former Soviet Union*, by Mark MacKinnon (Carroll & Graf).

◻ ⊘ WHIMSY LITERARY AGENCY, LLC

New York/Los Angeles. E-mail: whimsynyc@aol.com. **Contact:** Jackie Meyer. Estab. 2006. Member of Center for Independent Publishing Advisory Board. Represents 25 clients. 20% of clients are new/unpublished writers. Currently handles: 80% nonfiction books; 10% novels; 5% juvenile books; 5% other.

- Prior to becoming an agent, Ms. Meyer was with Warner Books for 19 years; Ms. Vezeris, Ms. Dempsey and Ms. Legette have 30 years experience at various book publishers.

Member Agents Jackie Meyer and P.J. Dempsey (nonfiction); Olga Vezeris (fiction and nonfiction); Nansci LeGette, senior associate in LA.

Represents Nonfiction books, novels. **Considers these nonfiction areas:** Agriculture/horticulture; art/architecture/design; biography/autobiography; business/economics; child guidance/parenting; cooking/foods/nutrition; education; health/medicine; history; how-to; humor/satire; interior design/decorating; memoirs; money/finance; New Age/metaphysics; popular culture; psychology; religious/inspirational; self-help/personal improvement; true crime/investigative; women's issues/studies. **Considers these fiction areas:** Mainstream/contemporary; religious/inspirational; thriller; women's.

- ⊶ "Whimsy looks for projects that are concept and platform driven. We seek books that educate, inspire and entertain." Actively seeking experts in their field with good platforms.

How to Contact Send a query letter via e-mail. Send a synopsis, sample chapters, bio, platform and proposal. No snail mail submissions. Accepts e-mail queries. No fax queries. Responds in 5 days to queries; 30 days to mss. Obtains most new clients through recommendations from others, solicitations.

Recent Sales *You Can Never Be Too Rich*, by Alan Haft (Wiley); *God Made Easy*, by Patrice Karst (Cider Mill Press); *Gracefully*, by Valerie Ramsey with Heather Hummel (McGraw-Hill); *Business Wargames*, by Ben Gilad (Career Press).

Terms Agent receives 15% commission on domestic sales; 20% commission on foreign sales. Offers written contract. Charges for posting and photocopying.

⊘ WINSUN LITERARY AGENCY

Website: www.winsunliterary.com/. Estab. 2004. Represents 20 clients. 50% of clients are new/unpublished writers. Currently handles: 75% nonfiction books; 20% novels; 5% juvenile books.

- Prior to becoming an agent, Mr. Littleton was a writer and a speaker.

Represents Nonfiction books, novels, juvenile books. **Considers these nonfiction areas:** Biography/autobiography; child guidance/parenting; current affairs; how-to; humor/satire; memoirs; religious/inspirational; self-help/personal improvement. **Considers these fiction areas:** Action/adventure; detective/police/crime; family saga; humor/satire; juvenile; literary; mainstream/contemporary; mystery/suspense; picture books; psychic/supernatural; religious/inspirational; romance; thriller.

- ⊶ This agency is not seeking new clients at this time. Look to the Web site for further information.

How to Contact Considers simultaneous queries. Returns materials only with SASE. Obtains most new clients through recommendations from others, conferences.

Terms Agent receives 15% commission on domestic sales; 20% commission on foreign sales. Offers written contract, binding for 1 year; 30-day notice must be given to terminate contract.

🅽 ◻ WOLFSON LITERARY AGENCY

P.O. Box 266, New York NY 10276. E-mail: query@wolfsonliterary.com. Website: www.wolfsonliterary.com/. **Contact:** Michelle Wolfson. Estab. 2007; Adheres to AAR canon of ethics. Currently handles: 40% nonfiction books; 60% novels.

- Prior to forming her own agency, Michelle spent two years with Artists & Artisans, Inc. and two years with Ralph Vicinanza, Ltd.

Represents Nonfiction books, novels. **Considers these nonfiction areas:** Business/economics; child guidance/parenting; health/medicine; how-to; humor/satire; popular culture; self-help/personal improvement; women's issues/studies. **Considers these fiction areas:** Action/adventure; detective/police/crime; erotica; family saga; mainstream/contemporary; mystery/suspense; romance; thriller; young adult; women's.

O— Actively seeking commercial fiction, mainstream, mysteries, thrillers, suspense, women's fiction, romance, YA, practical nonfiction (particularly of interest to women), advice, medical, pop culture, humor, business.

How to Contact Query with SASE. E-queries only!. Considers simultaneous queries. Responds in 2 weeks to queries; 3 months to mss. Obtains most new clients through recommendations from others, solicitations.

Terms Agent receives 15% commission on domestic sales; 25% commission on foreign sales. Offers written contract; 30-day notice must be given to terminate contract.

Writers' Conferences SDSU Writers' Conference; New Jersey Romance Writers of America Writers' Conference.

Tips "Be persistent."

☑ WOLGEMUTH & ASSOCIATES, INC

8600 Crestgate Circle, Orlando FL 32819. (407)909-9445. Fax: (407)909-9446. E-mail: ewolgemuth@cfl.rr.com. **Contact:** Erik Wolgemuth. Estab. 1992. Member of AAR. Represents 40 clients. 10% of clients are new/unpublished writers. Currently handles: 90% nonfiction books; 2% novellas; 5% juvenile books; 3% multimedia.

● "We have been in the publishing business since 1976, having been a marketing executive at a number of houses, a publisher, an author, and a founder and owner of a publishing company."

Member Agents Robert D. Wolgemuth; Andrew D. Wolgemuth; Erik S. Wolgemuth.

O— "We are not considering any new material at this time."

Recent Sales Sold 35-40 titles in the last year. Works by prominent Christian pastors and lay leaders.

Terms Agent receives 15% commission on domestic sales. Offers written contract, binding for 2-3 years; 30-day notice must be given to terminate contract.

☑ WORDSERVE LITERARY GROUP

10152 S. Knoll Circle, Highlands Ranch CO 80130. (303)471-6675. E-mail: rachelle@wordserveliterary.com. Website: www.wordserveliterary.com. **Contact:** Greg Johnson; Rachelle Gardner. Estab. 2003. Represents 70 clients. 20% of clients are new/unpublished writers. Currently handles: 30% nonfiction books; 40% novels; 10% story collections; 5% novellas; 10% juvenile books; 5% multimedia.

● Prior to becoming an agent in 1994, Mr. Johnson was a magazine editor and freelance writer of more than 20 books and 200 articles.

Member Agents Greg Johnson; Rachelle Gardner.

Represents Primarily religious books in these categories: nonfiction, fiction, short story collections, novellas.

Considers these nonfiction areas: Biography/autobiography; child guidance/parenting; memoirs; religious/inspirational.

O— Materials with a faith-based angle.

How to Contact Query with SASE, proposal package, outline, 2-3 sample chapters. Considers simultaneous queries. Responds in 4 weeks to queries; 2 months to mss. Returns materials only with SASE. Obtains most new clients through recommendations from others.

Recent Sales Sold 1,500 titles in the last 15 years. Redemption series, by Karen Kingsbury (Tyndale); *Loving God Up Close*, by Calvin Miller (Warner Faith); *Christmas in My Heart*, by Joe Wheeler (Tyndale). Other clients include Steve Arterburn, Wanda Dyson, Catherine Martin, David Murrow, Leslie Haskin, Gilbert Morris, Calvin Miller, Robert Wise, Jim Burns, Wayne Cordeiro, Denise George, Susie Shellenberger, Tim Smith, Joe Wheeler, Athol Dickson, Bob DeMoss, Patty Kirk, John Shore.

Terms Agent receives 15% commission on domestic sales; 10-15% commission on foreign sales. Offers written contract; up to 60-day notice must be given to terminate contract.

Tips "We are looking for good proposals, great writing, and authors willing to market their books, as appropriate. Also, we're only looking for projects with a faith element bent. See the Web site before submitting."

☑ WRITERS HOUSE

21 W. 26th St., New York NY 10010. (212)685-2400. Fax: (212)685-1781. Website: www.writershouse.com. Estab. 1974. Member of AAR. Represents 440 clients. 50% of clients are new/unpublished writers. Currently handles: 25% nonfiction books; 40% novels; 35% juvenile books.

Member Agents Albert Zuckerman (major novels, thrillers, women's fiction, important nonfiction); Amy Berkower (major juvenile authors, women's fiction, art/decorating, psychology); Merrilee Heifetz (quality children's fiction, science fiction/fantasy, popular culture, literary fiction); Susan Cohen (juvenile/young adult fiction and nonfiction, Judaism, women's issues); Susan Ginsburg (serious and popular fiction, true crime, narrative nonfiction, personality books, cookbooks); Michele Rubin (serious nonfiction); Robin Rue (commercial fiction and nonfiction, young adult fiction); Jodi Reamer (juvenile/young adult fiction and nonfiction, adult commercial fiction, popular culture); Simon Lipskar (literary and commercial fiction, narrative nonfiction);

Steven Malk (juvenile/young adult fiction and nonfiction); Dan Lazar (commercial and literary fiction, pop culture, narrative nonfiction, women's interest, memoirs, Judaica and humor); Rebecca Sherman (juvenile, young adult); Ken Wright (juvenile, young adult).

Represents Nonfiction books, novels, juvenile books. **Considers these nonfiction areas:** Animals; art/architecture/design; biography/autobiography; business/economics; child guidance/parenting; cooking/foods/nutrition; health/medicine; history; humor/satire; interior design/decorating; juvenile nonfiction; military/war; money/finance; music/dance; nature/environment; psychology; science/technology; self-help/personal improvement; theater/film; true crime/investigative; women's issues/studies. **Considers these fiction areas:** Action/adventure; contemporary issues; detective/police/crime; erotica; ethnic; family saga; fantasy; feminist; gay/lesbian; gothic; hi-lo; historical; horror; humor/satire; juvenile; literary; mainstream/contemporary; military/war; multicultural; mystery/suspense; New Age; occult; picture books; psychic/supernatural; regional; romance; science fiction; short story collections; spiritual; sports; thriller; translation; westerns/frontier; young adult; women's; cartoon.

> O── This agency specializes in all types of popular fiction and nonfiction. Does not want to receive scholarly, professional, poetry, plays, or screenplays.

How to Contact Query with SASE. No e-mail or fax queries. Responds in 1 month to queries. Obtains most new clients through recommendations from authors and editors.

Recent Sales Sold 200-300 titles in the last year. *Moneyball*, by Michael Lewis (Norton); *Cut and Run*, by Ridley Pearson (Hyperion); *Report from Ground Zero*, by Dennis Smith (Viking); *Northern Lights*, by Nora Roberts (Penguin/Putnam); Captain Underpants series, by Dav Pilkey (Scholastic); Junie B. Jones series, by Barbara Park (Random House). Other clients include Francine Pascal, Ken Follett, Stephen Hawking, Linda Howard, F. Paul Wilson, Neil Gaiman, Laurel Hamilton, V.C. Andrews, Lisa Jackson, Michael Gruber, Chris Paolini, Barbara Delinsky, Ann Martin, Bradley Trevor Greive, Erica Jong, Kyle Mills, Andrew Guess, Tim Willocks.

Terms Agent receives 15% commission on domestic sales; 20% commission on foreign sales. Offers written contract, binding for 1 year. Agency charges fees for copying mss/proposals and overseas airmail of books.

Tips "Do not send manuscripts. Write a compelling letter. If you do, we'll ask to see your work."

◑ WRITERS' REPRESENTATIVES, LLC

116 W. 14th St., 11th Floor, New York NY 10011-7305. (212)620-9009. Fax: (212)620-0023. E-mail: transom@writersreps.com. Website: www.writersreps.com. Estab. 1985. Represents 130 clients. 10% of clients are new/unpublished writers. Currently handles: 90% nonfiction books; 10% novels.

> • Prior to becoming an agent, Ms. Chu was a lawyer; Mr. Hartley worked at Simon & Schuster, Harper & Row, and Cornell University Press.

Member Agents Lynn Chu; Glen Hartley; Farah Peterson.

Represents Nonfiction books, novels. **Considers these fiction areas:** Literary.

> O── Serious nonfiction and quality fiction. No motion picture or television screenplays.

How to Contact Query with SASE. Prefers to read materials exclusively. Considers simultaneous queries, but must be informed at time of submission.

Recent Sales Sold 30 titles in the last year. *War Made New*, by Max Boot; *Book by Book*, by Michael Dirda; *Dangerous Nation*, by Robert Kagan; *Power, Faith and Fantasy*, by Michael B. Oren.

Terms Agent receives 15% commission on domestic sales; 20% commission on foreign sales.

Tips "Always include a SASE; it will ensure a response from the agent and the return of your submitted material."

⊘ THE WYLIE AGENCY

250 West 57th St., Suite 2114, New York NY 10107. (212)246-0069. Fax: (212)586-8953. E-mail: mail@wylieagency.com. Website: www.wylieagency.com. Ovreseas address: 17 Bedford Square, London WC1B 3JA, United Kingdom; mail@wylieagency.co.uk

Member Agents Andrew Wylie, Sarah Chalfant; Scott Moyers.

Represents Nonfiction books, novels.

> O── High-profile and prolific authors. This agency is not currently accepting unsolicited submissions, so do not query unless you are asked.

How to Contact This agency does not currently take unsolicited queries/proposals.

Recent Sales *The Way the Crow Flies: A Novel*, by Ann-Marie MacDonald (HarperCollins); *No One Belongs Here More Than You: Stories*, by Miranda July (Scribner); *The Janissary Tree: A Novel*, by Jason Goodwin (Farrar, Straus and Giroux); *This Book Will Save Your Life*, by A.M. Homes (Viking Adult). Other clients include Philip Roth, Saul Bellow, Norman Mailer, Salman Rushdie, Martin Amis and Dave Eggers.

◙ WYLIE-MERRICK LITERARY AGENCY

1138 S. Webster St., Kokomo IN 46902-6357. (765)459-8258. Website: www.wylie-merrick.com. NJ address: Gloucester Town Center, 521 Berlin-Cross Keys Road, Sicklerville, NJ 08081 **Contact:** Sharene Martin. Estab. 1999. Member of AAR, SCBWI. Currently handles: 10% nonfiction books; 85% novels; 5% juvenile books.

- • Ms. Martin holds a master's degree in language education and is a writing and technology curriculum specialist.

Member Agents Sharene Martin (juvenile, picture books, young adult); Robert Brown; Ann Boyle.

- ○━ "We prefer writers who understand the writing craft and have thoroughly researched and have a firm understanding of the publishing industry. We specialize in highly commercial literature." This agency has taken submissions for juvenile writing in the past, but is now no longer looking for new children's writers.

How to Contact Correspond via e-mail only. No phone queries, please. No fax queries. Obtains most new clients through recommendations from others, conferences.

Recent Sales *Death for Dessert*, by Dawn Richard (Harlequin Worldwide Mystery); *Mineral Spirits*, by Heather Sharfeddin (Bridge Works); *Whiskey and Tonic*, by Nina Wright (Midnight Ink); *Discreet Young Gentlemen*, by M.J. Pearson (Seventh Window); *Epoch*, by Tim Carter (Flux); *The Love of His Brother*, by Jennifer Allee (Five Star).

Terms Agent receives 15% commission on domestic sales; 20% commission on foreign sales; 20% commission on dramatic rights sales. Offers written contract.

Tips "Please see Web site for contact information. Please refer to our Web site for the most updated information about our agency. We changed the way we take queries in September 2006, and queries that don't follow our guidelines will be discarded. No phone or snail mail queries accepted."

◙ YATES & YATES, LLP

1100 Town & Country Road, Suite 1300, Orange CA 92868. Website: www.yates2.com. Estab. 1989. Represents 60 clients.

Represents Nonfiction books, novels. **Considers these nonfiction areas:** Business/economics; current affairs; government/politics/law; memoirs; religious/inspirational. **Considers these fiction areas:** Literary; regional; religious/inspirational; thriller; women's.

Recent Sales *No More Mondays*, by Dan Miller (Doubleday Currency).

◙ ZACHARY SHUSTER HARMSWORTH

1776 Broadway, Suite 1405, New York NY 10019. (212)765-6900. Fax: (212)765-6490. E-mail: kfleury@zshlitera ry.com. Website: www.zshliterary.com. Alternate address: 535 Boylston St., 11th Floor. (617)262-2400. Fax: (617)262-2468. **Contact:** Kathleen Fleury. Estab. 1996. Represents 125 clients. 20% of clients are new/unpublished writers. Currently handles: 45% nonfiction books; 45% novels; 5% story collections; 5% scholarly books.

- • "Our principals include two former publishing and entertainment lawyers, a journalist, and an editor/agent." Lane Zachary was an editor at Random House before becoming an agent.

Member Agents Esmond Harmsworth (commercial mysteries, literary fiction, history, science, adventure, business); Todd Shuster (narrative and prescriptive nonfiction, biography, memoirs); Lane Zachary (biography, memoirs, literary fiction); Jennifer Gates (literary fiction, nonfiction).

Represents Nonfiction books, novels. **Considers these nonfiction areas:** Animals; biography/autobiography; business/economics; current affairs; gay/lesbian issues; government/politics/law; health/medicine; history; how-to; language/literature/criticism; memoirs; money/finance; music/dance; psychology; science/technology; self-help/personal improvement; sports; true crime/investigative; women's issues/studies. **Considers these fiction areas:** Detective/police/crime; ethnic; feminist; gay/lesbian; historical; literary; mainstream/contemporary; mystery/suspense; thriller.

- ○━ As of early 2008, this agency was no longer accepting unsolicited work. Check the Web site for updated info.

How to Contact Query with SASE. No e-mail or fax queries. Obtains most new clients through recommendations from others.

Recent Sales *Can You Tell a Sunni from a Shiite?*, by Jeff Stein (Hyperion); *Christmas Hope*, by Donna Van Liere; *Female Chauvinist Pigs*, by Ariel Levy; *War Trash*, by Ha Jin; *Women Who Think Too Much*, by Susan Nolen-Hoeksema, PhD; *The Red Carpet*, by Lavanya Sankaran; *Grapevine*, by David Balter and John Butman.

Terms Agent receives 15% commission on domestic sales; 20% commission on foreign sales. Offers written contract, binding for 1 work only; 30-day notice must be given to terminate contract.

◙ KAREN GANTZ ZAHLER LITERARY MANAGEMENT AND ATTORNEY AT LAW

860 Fifth Ave., Suite 7J, New York NY 10065. (212)734-3619. E-mail: karen@karengantzlit.com. Website: www.karengantzlit.com. **Contact:** Karen Gantz Zahler. Currently handles: 95% nonfiction books; 5% novels.

- Prior to her current position, Ms. Zahler wrote two cookbooks, *Taste of New York* (Addison-Wesley) and *Superchefs* (John Wiley & Sons). She also participated in a Presidential Advisory Committee on Intellectual Property, U.S. Department of Commerce.

Represents Nonfiction books, novels (very selective).

○━ "We are hired for two purposes, one as lawyers to negotiate publishing agreements, option agreements and other entertainment deals and two as literary agents to help in all aspects of the publishing field. Ms. Zahler is both a literary agent and a literary property lawyer. Thus, she involves herself in all stages of a book's development, including the collaboration agreement with the writer, advice regarding the book proposal, presentations to the publisher, negotiations including the legal work for the publishing agreement and other rights to be negotiated, and work with the publisher and public relations firm so that the book gets the best possible media coverage." Actively seeking nonfiction.

How to Contact Query with SASE. Include a summary. Check the Web site for complete submission information. Accepts e-mail queries. No fax queries. Responds in 4 weeks to queries. Obtains most new clients through recommendations from others, solicitations.

Recent Sales *Life After Divorce*, by Alec Baldwin (St. Martin's Press); *Take the Lead, Lady! Kathleen Turner's Life Lessons*, by Kathleen Turner in collaboration with Gloria Feldt (Springboard Press); *Tales of a Neo-Con*, by Benjamin Wattenberg(John Wiley and Sons); more sales can be found online.

Tips "Our dream client is someone who is a professional writer and a great listener. What writers can do to increase the likelihood of our retainer is to write an excellent summary and provide a great marketing plan for their proposal in an excellent presentation. Any typos or grammatical mistakes do not resonate well. If we want to read it, we will ask you to send a copy by snail mail with an envelope and return postage enclosed. We don't call people unless we have something to report."

◪ SUSAN ZECKENDORF ASSOC., INC.

171 W. 57th St., New York NY 10019. (212)245-2928. **Contact:** Susan Zeckendorf. Estab. 1979. Member of AAR. Represents 15 clients. 25% of clients are new/unpublished writers. Currently handles: 50% nonfiction books; 50% novels.

- Prior to opening her agency, Ms. Zeckendorf was a counseling psychologist.

Represents Nonfiction books, novels. **Considers these nonfiction areas:** Biography/autobiography; child guidance/parenting; health/medicine; history; music/dance; psychology; science/technology; sociology; women's issues/studies. **Considers these fiction areas:** Detective/police/crime; ethnic; historical; literary; mainstream/contemporary; mystery/suspense; thriller.

○━ Actively seeking mysteries, literary fiction, mainstream fiction, thrillers, social history, parenting, classical music, and biography. Does not want to receive science fiction, romance, or children's books.

How to Contact Query with SASE. No e-mail or fax queries. Considers simultaneous queries. Responds in 10 days to queries; 3 weeks to mss. Returns materials only with SASE.

Recent Sales *How to Write a Damn Good Mystery*, by James N. Frey (St. Martin's Press); *The Handscrabble Chronicles* (Berkley); *Haunted Heart: A Biography of Susannah McCorkle*, by Linda Dahl (University of Michigan Press); *Garden of Aloes*, by Gayle Jandrey (Permanent Press).

Terms Agent receives 15% commission on domestic sales; 20% commission on foreign sales. Charges for photocopying and messenger services.

Writers' Conferences Frontiers in Writing Conference; Oklahoma Festival of Books.

Tips "We are a small agency giving lots of individual attention. We respond quickly to submissions."

◪ HELEN ZIMMERMANN LITERARY AGENCY

3 Emmy Lane, New Paltz NY 12561. (845)256-0977. Fax: (845)256-0979. E-mail: helen@zimmagency.com. **Contact:** Helen Zimmermann. Estab. 2004. Represents 25 clients. 50% of clients are new/unpublished writers. Currently handles: 80% nonfiction books; 20% fiction.

- Prior to opening her agency, Ms. Zimmermann was the director of advertising and promotion at Random House and the events coordinator at an independent bookstore.

Represents Nonfiction books, novels. **Considers these nonfiction areas:** Animals; child guidance/parenting; how-to; humor/satire; memoirs; nature/environment; popular culture; sports; nutrition. **Considers these fiction areas:** Family saga; historical; literary; mystery/suspense.

○━ "As an agent who has experience at both a publishing house and a bookstore, I have a keen insight for viable projects. This experience also helps me ensure every client gets published well, through the whole process." Actively seeking memoirs, pop culture, women's issues and accessible literary fiction. Does not want to receive science fiction, poetry or romance.

How to Contact Query with proposal (about 50 pages), SASE. Considers simultaneous queries. Responds in 2 weeks to queries; 1 month to mss. Returns materials only with SASE. Obtains most new clients through recommendations from others, solicitations.

Recent Sales Sold 7 titles in the last year. *Captain Freedom*, by Greg Robillard (HarperCollins)*The First Season*, by Charley Rosen (McGraw Hill); *The Cosmic Navigator*(Red Wheel Weiser); *Let the Dog Lead*, by Deborah Potter (Sunstone Press); *Chosen By a Horse*, by Susan Richards (Soho Press); *101 Things Not To Do Before You Die*, by Robert Harris (St. Martin's Press); *Truth Catcher*, by Anna Salter (Pegasus Books); *The Mini Ketchup Cookbook*, by Cameron Pearl (Running Press).

Terms Agent receives 15% commission on domestic sales. Offers written contract; 30-day notice must be given to terminate contract. Charges for photocopying and postage (reimbursed if project is sold).

Writers' Conferences BEA/Writer's Digest Books Writers' Conference

N ☐ RENEE ZUCKERBROT LITERARY AGENCY

115 West 29th St., Third Floor, New York NY 10001. (212)967-0072. Fax: (212)967-0073. E-mail: renee@rzagency.com. Website: rzagency.com. **Contact:** Renee Zuckerbrot. Estab. 2003. Represents 30 clients. Currently handles: novels; 30& nonfiction and 70% fiction.

- Prior to becoming an agent, Ms. Zuckerbrot worked as an editor at Doubleday as well as in the editorial department at Putnam.

Represents Nonfiction books, novels, short story collections.

   O→ Literary fiction, short story collections, mysteries, thrillers, women's fiction, slipstream/speculative, narrative nonfiction (focusing on science, history and pop culture). No business books, self-help, spirituality or romance.

How to Contact Query with SASE. Include a description of your manuscript or proposal. Include your publishing history, if applicable. Include a brief personal bio. Include an SASE or an e-mail address. Snail mail queries only. No e-mail or fax queries.

Recent Sales *Pretty Monster*, by Kelly Link (Penguin); *Manhattan Primeval*, by Eric Sanderson (Abrams); *Everything Asian*, by Sung Woo (Dunne/St. Martin's); *The Dart League King*, by Keith Lee Morris, *by Keith Lee Morris (Tin House)*.

Terms Agent receives 15% commission on domestic sales; 25% commission on foreign sales.

Conferences

Attending a writers' conference that includes agents gives you the opportunity to learn more about what agents do and to show an agent your work. Ideally, a conference should include a panel or two with a number of agents to give writers a sense of the variety of personalities and tastes of different agents.

Not all agents are alike: Some are more personable, and sometimes you simply click better with one agent versus another. When only one agent attends a conference, there is a tendency for every writer at that conference to think, "Ah, this is the agent I've been looking for!" When the number of agents attending is larger, you have a wider group from which to choose, and you may have less competition for the agent's time.

Besides including panels of agents discussing what representation means and how to go about securing it, many of these gatherings also include time—either scheduled or im-promptu—to meet briefly with an agent to discuss your work.

If they're impressed with what they see and hear about your work, they will invite you to submit a query, a proposal, a few sample chapters, or possibly your entire manuscript. Some conferences even arrange for agents to review manuscripts in advance and schedule one-on-one sessions during which you can receive specific feedback or advice regarding your work. Such meetings often cost a small fee, but the input you receive is usually worth the price.

Ask writers who attend conferences and they'll tell you that, at the very least, you'll walk away with new knowledge about the industry. At the very best, you'll receive an invitation to send an agent your material!

Many writers try to make it to at least one conference a year, but cost and location can count as much as subject matter when determining which one to attend. There are conferences in almost every state and province that can provide answers to your questions about writing and the publishing industry. Conferences also connect you with a community of other writers. Such connections help you learn about the pros and cons of different agents, and they can also give you a renewed sense of purpose and direction in your own writing.

SUBHEADS

Each listing is divided into subheads to make locating specific information easier. In the first section, you'll find contact information for conference contacts. You'll also learn conference dates, specific focus, and the average number of attendees. Finally, names of agents who will be speaking or have spoken in the past are listed along with details about their availability during the conference. Calling or e-mailing a conference director to verify the names of agents in attendance is always a good idea.

Costs: Looking at the price of events, plus room and board, may help writers on a tight budget narrow their choices.

Accommodations: Here conferences list overnight accommodations and travel information. Often conferences held in hotels will reserve rooms at a discount rate and may provide a shuttle bus to and from the local airport.

Additional Information: This section includes information on conference-sponsored contests, individual meetings, the availability of brochures, and more.

REGIONS

To make it easier for you to find a conference close to home—or to find one in an exotic locale to fit into your vacation plans—listings are separated into the following geographical regions:

- **Northeast** (pages 236): Connecticut, Maine, Massachusetts, New Hampshire, New York, Rhode Island, Vermont.
- **Midatlantic** (pages 239): Washington D.C., Delaware, Maryland, New Jersey, Pennsylvania.
- **Midsouth** (pages 241): North Carolina, South Carolina, Tennessee, Virginia, West Virginia.
- **Southeast** (pages 243): Alabama, Arkansas, Florida, Georgia, Louisiana, Mississippi.
- **Midwest** (pages 246): Illinois, Indiana, Kentucky, Michigan, Ohio.
- **North Central** (pages 248): Iowa, Minnesota, Nebraska, North Dakota, South Dakota, Wisconsin.
- **South Central** (pages 249): Colorado, Kansas, Missouri, New Mexico, Oklahoma, Texas.
- **West** (pages 254): Arizona, California, Hawaii, Nevada, Utah.
- **Northwest** (pages 258): Alaska, Idaho, Montana, Oregon, Washington, Wyoming.
- **Canada** (pages 260).
- **International** (pages 260).

Quick Reference Icons

At the beginning of some listings, you will find one or more of the following symbols:

- **N** Conference new to this edition
- **⁂** Canadian conference
- **🌐** International conference

Find a pull-out bookmark with a key to symbols on the inside cover of this book.

NORTHEAST (CT, MA, ME, NH, NY, RI, VT)

ASJA WRITERS CONFERENCE
American Society of Journalists and Authors, 1501 Broadway, Suite 302, New York NY 10036. (212)997-0947. Fax: (212)768-7414. E-mail: staff@asja.org; director@asja.org. Web site: www.asjaconference.org. **Contact:** Executive director. Estab. 1971. Annual conference held in April. Conference duration: 2 days. Average attendance: 600. Covers nonfiction and screenwriting. Held at the Grand Hyatt in New York. Speakers have included Dominick Dunne, James Brady, and Dana Sobel. Agents will be speaking at the event.
Costs $200+, depending on when you sign up (includes lunch).
Accommodations "The hotel holding our conference always blocks out discounted rooms for attendees."
Additional Information Brochures available in February. Registration form is on the Web site. Inquire by e-mail or fax.

BOOKEXPO AMERICA/WRITER'S DIGEST BOOKS WRITERS CONFERENCE
4700 E. Galbraith Rd., Cincinnati OH 45236. (513)531-2690. Fax: (513)891-7185. E-mail: publicity@fwpubs.com. Web site: www.writersdigest.com/bea. **Contact:** Greg Hatfield, publicity manager. Estab. 2003. Annual. Annual conference held in May the day before BookExpo America starts. The conference is at the same location as BEA. Average attendance: 500+. The conference offers instruction on the craft of writing, as well as advice for submitting work to publications, publishing houses, and agents. "We provide breakout sessions on these topics, including expert advice from industry professionals, and offer workshops on fiction and nonfiction. We also provide agents to whom attendees can pitch their work." The conference is part of the BookExpo America trade show. Registration for the conference does not allow you access to the trade show. Speakers have included Jodi Picoult, Jerry Jenkins, Steve Almond, John Warner, Donald Maass, Noah Lukeman and Jennifer Gilmore. The conference finishes with a large "Agent Pitch Slam," with up to 60 agents and editors taking pitches from writers. The slam is the largest of its kind.

BREAD LOAF WRITERS' CONFERENCE
Middlebury College, Middlebury VT 05753. (802)443-5286. Fax: (802)443-2087. E-mail: ncargill@middlebury.edu. Web site: www.middlebury.edu/blwc. **Contact:** Noreen Cargill, administrative manager. Estab. 1926. Annual conference held in late August. Conference duration: 11 days. Average attendance: 230. Offers workshops for fiction, nonfiction, and poetry. Agents, editors, publicists, and grant specialists will be in attendance.
Costs $2,345 (includes tuition, housing).
Accommodations Bread Loaf Campus in Ripton, Vermont.

GOTHAM WRITERS' WORKSHOP
WritingClasses.com, 555 Eighth Ave., Suite 1402, New York NY 10018. (212)974-8377. Fax: (212)307-6325. E-mail: dana@write.org. Web site: www.writingclasses.com. **Contact:** Dana Miller, director of student affairs. Estab. 1993. Classes are held throughout the year. There are four terms, beginning in January, April, June/July, and September/October. Offers craft-oriented creative writing courses in general creative writing, fiction writing, screenwriting, nonfiction writing, article writing, stand-up comedy writing, humor writing, memoir writing, novel writing, children's book writing, playwriting, poetry, songwriting, mystery writing, science fiction writing, romance writing, television writing, article writing, travel writing, business writing and classes on freelancing, selling your screenplay and getting published. Also, Gotham Writers' Workshop offers a teen program, private instruction ,and classes on selling your work. Classes are held at various schools in New York City as well as online at www.writingclasses.com. Agents and editors participate in some workshops.
Costs $395/10-week workshops; $125 for the four-week online selling seminars and 1-day intensive courses; $29⁵/₆-week creative writing and business writing classes.

GREEN MOUNTAIN WRITERS CONFERENCE
47 Hazel St., Rutland VT 05701. (802)236-6133. E-mail: ydaley@sbcglobal.net. Web site: www.vermontwriters.com. **Contact:** Yvonne Daley, director. Estab. 1999. Annual conference held in the summer; 2008 dates are July 28—Aug. 1. Covers fiction, creative nonfiction, poetry, journalism, nature writing, essay, memoir, personal narrative, and biography. Held at an old dance pavillion on a remote pond in Tinmouth, Vermont. Speakers have included Joan Connor, Yvonne Daley, David Huddle, David Budbill, Jeffrey Lent, Verandah Porche, Tom Smith, and Chuck Clarino.
Costs $500 before June 15; $525 after June 15. Partial scholarships are available.
Accommodations "We have made arrangements with a major hotel in nearby Rutland and 2 area bed and breakfast inns for special accommodations and rates for conference participants. You must make your own reservations."

HIGHLIGHTS FOUNDATION WRITERS WORKSHOP AT CHAUTAUQUA

814 Court St., Honesdale PA 18431. (570)253-1192. Fax: (570)253-0179. E-mail: contact@highlightsfoundation. org. Web site: www.highlightsfoundation.org. **Contact:** Kent Brown, executive director. Estab. 1985. Annual conference held July 12-18, 2008, and July 11-18, 2009. Average attendance: 100. Workshops are geared toward those who write for children at the beginner, intermediate, and advanced levels. Offers seminars, small group workshops, and one-on-one sessions with authors, editors, illustrators, critics, and publishers. Workshop site is the picturesque community of Chautauqua, New York. Speakers have included Bruce Coville, Candace Fleming, Linda Sue Park, Jane Yolen, Patricia Gauch, Jerry Spinelli, Eileen Spinelli, Joy Cowley and Pam Munoz Ryan.

Costs $2,400 (includes all meals, conference supplies, gate pass to Chautauqua Institution).

Accommodations ''We coordinate ground transportation to and from airports, trains, and bus stations in the Erie, Pennsylvania and Jamestown/Buffalo, New York area. We also coordinate accommodations for conference attendees.''

Additional Information ''We offer the opportunity for attendees to submit a manuscript for review at the conference.'' Workshop brochures/guidelines are available upon request.

THE MACDOWELL COLONY

100 High St., Peterborough NH 03458. (603)924-3886. Fax: (603)924-9142. E-mail: admissions@macdowellcolony.org. Web site: www.macdowellcolony.org. **Contact:** Admissions Director. Estab. 1907. Open to writers, playwrights, composers, visual artists, film/video artists, interdisciplinary artists and architects. Applicants send information and work samples for review by a panel of experts in each discipline. See application guidelines for details.

Costs There are no residency fees.

◼ MUSE AND THE MARKETPLACE

160 Boylston St., 4th Floor, Boston MA 02116. (617)695.0075. E-mail: info@grubstreet.org. Web site: www.grubstreet.org. Annual. The conferences are held in the late spring, such as early May. Conference duration: 2 days. Average attendance: 400. Dozens of agents are in attendance to meet writers and take pitches. Previous keynote speakers include Jonathan Franzen. The conferences has workshops on all aspects of writing.

Costs $265 for Members, $305 for Non-Members (includes 6 workshop sessions and 2 ''Hour of Power'' sessions with options for the Manuscript Mart and a ''Five-Star'' lunch with authors, editors and agents). Other passes are available for ''Saturday only'' and ''Sunday only'' guests.

◼ NECON

Northeastern Writers Conference, 330 Olney St., Seekonk MA 02771. (508)557-1218. E-mail: daniel.booth77@gmail.com. Web site: www.campnecon.com. **Contact:** Dan Booth, chairman. Estab. 1980. Annual. July 17-20, 2008. Conference duration: Four days. Average attendance: 200. The conference is dedicated to those who write fiction. Site: Held at Riger Williams University in Bristol, RI. Themes vary from year to year. Agents attend the workshop each year.

Costs $350. This includes meals and lodging.

Accommodations Attendees stay on campus in the dorm rooms. This housing cost is in the registration fee.

Additional Information Shuttle service provided to the convention site as well as the airport and train station. ''We are a very laid back, relaxed convention. However, work is accomplished each year and it's a good opportunity to network.''

◎ ODYSSEY FANTASY WRITING WORKSHOP

P.O. Box 75, Mont Vernon NH 03057. E-mail: jcavelos@sff.net. Web site: www.odysseyworkshop.org. **Contact:** Jeanne Cavelos, director. Estab. 1996. Annual workshop held in June (through July). Conference duration: 6 weeks. Average attendance: 16. A workshop for fantasy, science fiction, and horror writers that combines an intensive learning and writing experience with in-depth feedback on students' mss. Held on the campus of Saint Anselm College in Manchester, New Hampshire. Speakers have included George R. Martin, Elizabeth Hand, Jane Yolen, Harlan Ellison, Melissa Scott and Dan Simmons.

Costs $1,800/tuition; $700-1,400/on-campus apartment; approximately $550/on-campus meals. Scholarships are available.

Additional Information Prospective students must include a 15-page writing sample with their application. Accepts inquiries by SASE, e-mail, fax and phone. Application deadline April 10.

ROBERT QUACKENBUSH'S CHILDREN'S BOOK WRITING & ILLUSTRATING WORKSHOP

460 E. 79th St., New York NY 10021-1443. (212)744-3822. Fax: (212)861-2761. E-mail: rqstudios@aol.com. Web site: www.rquackenbush.com. **Contact:** Robert Quackenbush, director. Estab. 1982. Annual workshop

held during the second week in July. Conference duration: 4 days. Average attendance: Enrollment limited to 10. Workshops promote writing and illustrating books for children and are geared toward beginners and professionals. Generally focuses on picture books, easy-to-read books, and early chapter books. Held at the Manhattan studio of Robert Quackenbush, author and illustrator of more than 200 books for children. All classes led by Robert Quackenbush.

Costs $750 tuition covers all the costs of the workshop, but does not include housing and meals. A $100 nonrefundable deposit is required with the $650 balance due two weeks prior to attendance.

Accommodations A list of recommended hotels and restaurants is sent upon receipt of deposit.

STONECOAST WRITERS' CONFERENCE

University of Southern Maine, 37 College Avenue, Gorham ME 04038. (207)780-4141. Web site: www.usm.main e.edu/summer/stonecoastwc/. **Contact:** Conference Director. Estab. 1979. Annual conference held in mid-July. Conference duration: 10 days. Average attendance: 90-100. Concentrates on fiction, poetry, popular fiction, and creative nonfiction. Held at Wolfe's Neck on Casco Bay in Freeport, Maine. Speakers have included Christian Barter, Brian Turner, Chun Yu, Margo Jefferson, Mike Kimball, and Jack Neary.

Costs 2007 costs: $813/tuition; $560/housing and meals at Bowdoin College; $136/commuters. Scholarships are available for various groups.

Ⓝ THRILLERFEST

PO Box 311, Eureka CA 95502. E-mail: infocentral@thrillerwriters.org. Web site: www.thrillerwriters.org/thrille rfest/. **Contact:** Shirley Kennett. Estab. 2006. Annual. 2008 conference: July 9-12 in Manhattan. Average attendance: 700. Conference dedicated to writing the thriller. Speakers have included Sandra Brown, Eric Van Lustbader, David Baldacci, RL Stine, Steve Martini, Andrew Gross, Donald Maass, Dr. Kathy Reichs, Brad Thor and James Patterson. Two days of the conference is CraftFest, where the focus is on writing craft, and two days is ThrillerFest, where the focus is on both writers and their readers. There is also AgentFest, where authors can pitch their work to agents in attendance.

Costs Price will vary from $200 to $1,000 dollars depending on all the events attendees sign up for, including agent pitch slams, award banquets and more. Various event packages are available for attendees.

Accommodations Grand Hyatt in New York City.

VERMONT COLLEGE POSTGRADUATE WRITERS' CONFERENCE

36 College St., Montpelier VT 05651. (802)223-2133 or (802)828-8764. E-mail: roger.weingarten@tui.edu. Website: www.tui.edu/pgwc/. **Contact:** Roger Weingarten. Estab. 1996. Annual conference held in August. Conference duration: 6 days. Average attendance: 5-7/workshop. Conference will focus on novel writing, short story writing, short short story writing, creative nonfiction, poetry manuscript, and poetry. Held on the historic Vermont College campus, overlooking Montpelier. Faculty has included Rikki Ducornet, Bret Lott, Mary Ruefle, Sue William Silverman, Robin Hemley, Charles Harper Webb, Richard Jackson and Bruce Weigl.

Costs $800/tuition; $330/private room; $180/shared room; $140/meals. Limited scholarships are available.

Accommodations Single or double rooms are available in the Vermont College campus dormitories.

WESLEYAN WRITERS CONFERENCE

Wesleyan University, 294 High St., Room 207, Middletown CT 06459. (860)685-3604. Fax: (860)685-2441. E-mail: agreene@wesleyan.edu. Web site: www.wesleyan.edu/writers. **Contact:** Anne Greene, director. Estab. 1956. Annual conference held the third week of June. Average attendance: 100. Focuses on the novel, fiction techniques, short stories, poetry, screenwriting, nonfiction, literary journalism, memoir, mixed media work and publishing. The conference is held on the campus of Wesleyan University, in the hills overlooking the Connecticut River. Features a faculty of award-winning writers, seminars and readings of new fiction, poetry, nonfiction and mixed media forms—as well as guest lectures on a range of topics including publishing. Both new and experienced writers are welcome. Participants may attend seminars in all genres. Speakers have included Esmond Harmsworth (Zachary Schuster Agency), Daniel Mandel (Sanford J. Greenburger Associates), Dorian Karchmar, Amy Williams (ICM and Collins McCormick), Mary Sue Rucci (Simon & Schuster), Denise Roy (Simon & Schuster), John Kulka (Harvard University Press), Julie Barer (Barer Literary) and many others. Agents will be speaking and available for meetings with attendees. Participants are often successful in finding agents and publishers for their mss. Wesleyan participants are also frequently featured in the anthology *Best New American Voices*.

Costs 2007 Day rate is $1,050 (includes meals for 5 days). Student rate with boarding: $1,250 (includes meals and room for 5 nights); boarding student rate: $1,190 (includes meal and room for 5 nights).

Accommodations Meals are provided on campus. Lodging is available on campus or in town.

Additional Information Ms critiques are available, but not required. Scholarships and teaching fellowships are available, including the Joan Jakobson Awards for fiction writers and poets; and the Jon Davidoff Scholarships for nonfiction writers and journalists. Inquire via e-mail, fax, or phone.

WRITERS' CONFERENCE AT OCEAN PARK

P.O. Box 7146, Ocean Park ME 04063-7146. (401)598-1424. E-mail: jbrosnan@jwu.edu. Web site: www.oceanpark.org/programs/events/writers/writers.html. **Contact:** Jim Brosnan, Donna Brosnan. Estab. 1941. Annual conference held in mid-August. Conference duration: 4 days. Average attendance: 50. "We try to present a balanced and eclectic conference. In addition to time and attention given to poetry, we also have children's literature, mystery writing, travel, fiction, nonfiction, journalism, and other issues of interest to writers. Our speakers are editors, writers, and other professionals. Our concentration is, by intention, a general view of writing to publish with supportive encouragement. We are located in Ocean Park, a small seashore village 14 miles south of Portland. Ours is a summer assembly center with many buildings from the Victorian age. The conference meets in Porter Hall, one of the assembly buildings which is listed in the National Register of Historic Places." Speakers have included Michael C. White (novelist/short story writer), Betsy Shool (poet), Suzanne Strempek Shea (novelist), John Perrault (poet), Josh Williamson (newspaper editor), Dawn Potter (poet), Bruce Pratt (fiction writer), Amy McDonald (children's author), Anne Wescott Dodd (nonfiction writer), Kate Chadbourne (singer/songwriter), Wesley McNair (poet/Maine faculty member), and others. "We usually have about 8 guest presenters each year." Publishes writers/editors will be speaking, leading workshops, and available for meetings with attendees.

Costs $175+ (includes conference, reception, Tuesday evening meal). The fee does not include housing or meals, which must be arranged separately by conferees.

Accommodations An accommodations list is available. "We are in a summer resort area where motels, guest houses, and restaurants abound."

Additional Information "We have 7 contests for various genres. An announcement is available in the spring. The prizes (all modest) are awarded at the end of the conference and only to those who are registered." Send SASE in June for the conference program.

MIDATLANTIC (DC, DE, MD, NJ, PA)

ALGONKIAN WRITER WORKSHOPS

2020 Pennsylvania Ave. NW, Suite 43, Washington DC 20006. (800)250-8290. E-mail: algonkian@webdelsol.com. Web site: http://www.algonkianconferences.com/. **Contact:** Michael Neff, director. Estab. 2001. Conference duration: 5 days. Average attendance: 15/craft workshops; 60/pitch sessions. Workshops on fiction, short fiction, and poetry are held 12 times/year in various locations. Speakers have included Paige Wheeler, Elise Capron, Deborah Grosvenor and Kathleen Anderson. Agents will be speaking and available for meetings with attendees.

Costs Housing costs vary depending on the workshop's location.

Additional Information "These workshops are challenging and are not for those looking for praise. Guidelines are available online or via e-mail."

BALTIMORE WRITERS' CONFERENCE

Citylit Project, 120 S. Curley St., Baltimore MD 21224. E-mail: info@citylitproject.org. Web site: www.towson.edu/writersconference. **Contact:** Greg Wilhelm, coordinator. Estab. 1994. Annual conference held in November. Conference duration: 1 day. Average attendance: 150-200. Covers all areas of writing and getting published. Held at Towson University. Topics have included: mystery, science fiction, poetry, children's writing, legal issues, grant funding, working with an agent, and book and magazine panels. Speakers have included Dana Gioia, Alice McDermott and Nina Graybill. Agents will be speaking at the event.

Costs $80-100 (includes all-day conference, lunch and reception).

Accommodations Hotels are close by, if required.

Additional Information Writers may register through the BWA Web site. Send inquiries via e-mail.

🅽 MALICE DOMESTIC

PO Box 8007, Gaithersburg MD 20898-8007. Fax: (301)432-7391. E-mail: malicechair@malicedomestic.org. Web site: www.malicedomestic.org/. Estab. 1989. The 2008 conference was in April, in Arlington, VA. Future dates: May 1-3, 2009 and April 30—May 2, 2010. The conference is for mystery writers of all kinds and always held in the Washington, DC regional area. The conference includes authors and literary agents.

Costs $225 basic registration. This will convention activities, including Opening Reception, New Authors Breakfast and Closing Festivities. Comprehensive registration also includes your right to vote for the Agatha Awards, a souvenir Program Book, and a subscription to the Usual Suspects.

MONTROSE CHRISTIAN WRITERS' CONFERENCE

5 Locust St., Montrose PA 18801. (570)278-1001 or (800)598-5030. Fax: (570)278-3061. E-mail: mbc@montrose bible.org. Web site: www.montrosebible.org. **Contact:** MBC Secretary/Registrar. Estab. 1990. Annual conference held in July. Offers workshops, editorial appointments, and professional critiques. "We try to meet a cross-section of writing needs, for beginners and advanced, covering fiction, poetry, and writing for children. It is small enough to allow personal interaction between attendees and faculty." Speakers have included William Petersen, Mona Hodgson, Jim Fletcher, and Terri Gibbs.

Costs $150/tuition (in 2007); $35/critique.

Accommodations Housing and meals are available on site.

NEW JERSEY ROMANCE WRITERS PUT YOUR HEART IN A BOOK CONFERENCE

P.O. Box 644, South Plainfield NJ 07080-0644. E-mail: njrwconfchair@yahoo.com; njrw@njromancewriters.o rg. Web site: www.njromancewriters.org. **Contact:** Michele Richter. Estab. 1984. Annual. Annual conference held in October. 2008 dates: Oct. 24-25. Average attendance: 500. Workshops are offered on various topics for all writers of romance, from beginner to multi-published. Speakers have included Nora Roberts, Kathleen Woodiwiss, Patricia Gaffney, Jill Barnett and Kay Hooper. Appointments are offered with editors/agents.

Accommodations Special rate available for conference attendees at the Sheraton at Woodbridge Place Hotel in Iselin, New Jersey.

Additional Information Conference brochures, guidelines, and membership information are available for SASE. Massive bookfair is open to the public with authors signing copies of their books.

PHILADELPHIA WRITERS' CONFERENCE

121 Almatt Terrace, Philadelphia PA 19115-2745. E-mail: info@pwcwriters.org. Web site: www.pwcwriters.org. **Contact:** Rhonda O. Hoffman, registrar. Estab. 1949. Annual conference held in June. 2008 dates: June 6-8. Conference duration: 3 days. Average attendance: 150+. Workshops cover short stories, poetry, travel, humor, magazine writing, science fiction, playwriting, memoir, juvenile, nonfiction, and fiction. Speakers have included Ginger Clark (Curtis Brown), Sara Crowe (Harvey Klinger), Samantha Mandor (Berkley), Nancy Springer, Susan Guill, Karen Rile, Gregory Frost, and John Volkmer. Editor/agent critiques are available.

Costs Costs available online.

📷 SANDY COVE CHRISTIAN WRITERS CONFERENCE

Sandy Cove Ministries, 60 Sandy Cove Rd., North East MD 21901. (410)287-5433. Fax: (410)287-3196. E-mail: info@sandycove.org. Web site: www.sandycove.org. Estab. 1991. Annual conference held the first week in October. Conference duration: 4 days. Average attendance: 200. There are major workshops in fiction, article writing, and nonfiction books for beginner and advanced writers. The conference has plans to add tracks in screenwriting and musical lyrics. Workshops offer a wide variety of hands-on writing instruction in many genres. While Sandy Cove has a strong emphasis on available markets in Christian publishing, all writers are more than welcome. Speakers have included Francine Rivers, Lisa Bergen, Ken Petersen (Tyndale House), Linda Tomblin (*Guideposts*), and Karen Ball (Zondervan).

Costs Call for rates.

Accommodations Sandy Cove is a full-service conference center located on the Chesepeake Bay. All the facilities are first class, with suites, single rooms, and double rooms available.

Additional Information Conference brochures/guidelines are available. Visit the Web site for exact conference dates.

WASHINGTON INDEPENDENT WRITERS (WIW) SPRING WRITERS CONFERENCE

1001 Connecticut Ave. NW, Suite 701, Washington DC 20036. (202)775-5150. Fax: (202)775-5810. E-mail: info@washwriter.org. Web site: www.washwriter.org. **Contact:** Taryn Carrino. Estab. 1975. Annual conference held in June. Average attendance: 350. Focuses on fiction, nonfiction, screenwriting, poetry, children's writing, and technical writing. Gives participants the chance to hear from and talk with dozens of experts on book and magazine publishing, as well as on the craft, tools, and business of writing. Speakers have included Erica Jong, John Barth, Kitty Kelley, Vanessa Leggett, Diana McLellan, Brian Lamb, and Stephen Hunter. New York and local agents attend the conference.

Additional Information See the Web site or send a SASE in mid-February for brochures/guidelines and fees information.

WINTER POETRY & PROSE GETAWAY IN CAPE MAY

(609)823-5076. E-mail: info@wintergetaway.com. Web site: www.wintergetaway.com. **Contact:** Peter Murphy, founder/director. Estab. 1994. Annual workshop held in January. Conference duration: 4 days. Offers workshops on short stories, memoirs, creative nonfiction, children's writing, novel, drama, poetry and photography.

Classes are small, so each person receives individual attention for the new writing or work-in-progress that they are focusing on. Held at the Grand Hotel on the oceanfront in historic Cape May, New Jersey. Speakers have included Stephen Dunn (recipient of the 2001 Pulitzer Prize for poetry), Christian Bauman, Kurt Brown, Catherine Doty, Douglas Goetsch, James Richardson, Robbie Clipper Sethi and many more.

ℕ WRITERS AT THE BEACH: SEAGLASS WRITERS CONFERENCE

Writers at the Beach, PO Box 1326, Rehoboth Beach DE 19971. (302)226-8210. E-mail: contactus@rehobothbeachwritersguild.com. Web site: www.writersatthebeach.com/. **Contact:** Maribeth Fischer, mbfischer1@verizon.net. Annual. Annual conference held in the spring. Conference duration: 3 days. Annual conference on the Delaware coast featuring a variety of editors, agents and writers who present workshops on fiction writing, nonfiction writing and more. Manuscript readings are available, and a "Meet the Authors" sessions takes place. The beachcoast conference is a great opportuinity to learn and charge your batteries. Some proceeds from the conference go to charity.

Accommodations The special room rate for participants is approximately $60.

Additional Information Rehoboth Beach, a popular resort town nicknamed "The Nation's Summer Capital." is a coastal resort town in southern Delaware, 2.5 hours from both Baltimore Maryland and Washington, DC; 2 hours from Philadelphia, and just over 3 hours from New York City. During the conference, you glance outside from any number of the rooms at the Atlantic Sands to the ever-mercurial Atlantic ocean, walk the mile-long boardwalk, or sit on one of the numerous benches where you can watch the sunrise and enjoy our many migrating dolphins. This small town also offers, within a block of the hotel, an eclectic array of boutiques, cafés, souvenir shops and restaurants. And nearby Cape Henlopen State Park is home to the highest sand dune—rising over 80 feet above the shoreline—between Cape Hatteras and Cape Cod.

MIDSOUTH (NC, SC, TN, VA, WV)

◎ BLUE RIDGE MOUNTAIN CHRISTIAN WRITERS CONFERENCE

E-mail: ylehman@bellsouth.net. Web site: www.lifeway.com/christianwriters. **Contact:** Yvonne Lehman. Annual conference held in May. Conference duration: Sunday through lunch on Thursday. Average attendance: 400. A training and networking event for both seasoned and aspiring writers that allows attendees to interact with editors, agents, professional writers, and readers. Workshops and continuing classes in a vareity of creative categories are also offered.

Costs $375 (includes sessions and banquet).

Accommodations $49-84, depending on room size, at the LifeWay Ridgecrest Conference Center near Asheville, North Carolina.

Additional Information The event also features a contest for unpublished writers and ms critiques prior to the conference.

CHATTANOOGA FESTIVAL OF WRITERS

Arts & Education Council, 3069 S. Broad St., Suite 2, Chattanooga TN 37408. (423)267-1218. Fax: (423)267-1018. E-mail: info@artsedcouncil.org. Web site: www.artsedcouncil.org/page/chattanooga-festival-of-writers. **Contact:** Susan Frady Robinson, executive director. Estab. 2006. biennial. Biennial conference held in late March. Conference duration: 2 days. Average attendance: 250. This conference covers fiction, nonfiction, drama and poetry through workshops and keynote. Held in downtown Chattanooga. Speakers have included Suzette Francis, Richard Bausch, David Magee, Philip Gerard, Elizabeth Kostova and Robert Morgan.

Costs $65-175 (depending on attendees participation in workshops, luncheon and dinner).

Additional Information Visit www.chattanoogafun.com for assistance with accomodations and airfare.

ℕ CHRISTOPHER NEWPORT UNIVERSITY WRITERS CONFERENCE

1 University Place, Center for Community Learning, Newport News VA 23606-2988. (757)594-7938. Fax: (757)594-8736. E-mail: challiday@cnu.edu. Web site: writers.cnu.edu/. **Contact:** Director. Estab. 1981. Annual. Conference held in March. Conference duration: Friday evening and Saturday day. "This is a working conference." Presentations made by editors, agents, fiction writers, poets and more. Site: Christopher Newport University, Newport News, VA. Friday evening and Saturday morning consist of breakout sessions in fiction, nonfiction, poetry, juvenile fiction and publishing. Previous panels included Publishing, Proposal Writing, Internet Research and various breakout sessions. There is one keynote Saturday morning.

Accommodations Provides list of area hotels.

Additional Information Sponsors contest. Full contest info is available online.

Conferences

ⓝ CLARKSVILLE WRITERS CONFERENCE
1123 Madison St., Clarksville TN 37040. (931)645-2317. E-mail: corneliuswinn@bellsouth.net. Web site: www.a rtsandheritage.us/writers/. **Contact:** Patricia Winn. Annual. Annual conference held in the summer. Conference duration: 2 days. The conference features a variety of presentations on fiction, nonfiction and more. Previous speakers have included Robert Hicks, Jeanne Ray, David Magee, Alanna Nash, William Gay, River Jordan, Malcolm Glass, David Till.

Costs Costs available online; prices vary depending on how long attendees stay and if they attend the banquet dinner.

Accommodations Hotel specials provided every year.

ⓝ FALL WRITERS' SEMINAR
Council for the Written Word, P.O. Box 298, Franklin TN 37065. (615)790-5918. E-mail: kathyrhodes@pinkbutte rbeans.com. Web site: www.asouthernjournal.com/cww. **Contact:** Kathy Rhodes. Annual conference held in September. The Sept. 18 session addresses the five R's of creative nonfiction with Lee Gutkind. An all-day event with local and area authors, agents, editors, publishers, and/or publicists teaching the art and business of writing.

HIGHLAND SUMMER CONFERENCE
Box 7014, Radford University, Radford VA 24142-7014. (540)831-5366. Fax: (540)831-5951. E-mail: dcochran7 @radford.edu; jasbury@radford.edu. Web site: www.radford.edu/~arsc. **Contact:** JoAnn Asbury, assistant to the director. Estab. 1978. Annual conference held in June. 2008 dates: June 2-13. Conference duration: 2 weeks. Average attendance: 25. Covers fiction, nonfiction, poetry, and screenwriting. Speakers have included Bill Brown, Robert Morgan, Sharyn McCrumb, Nikki Giovanni, Wilma Dykeman, Jim Wayne Miller, David Huddle, and Diane Fisher. 2008 speakers include: Affrilachian Poet, Frank X. Walker and Poet and Novelist Darnell Arnoult.

Costs The cost is based on current Radford tuition for 3 credit hours, plus an addidtional conference fee. On-campus meals and housing are available at additional cost. In 2007, conference tuition was $717/in-state undergraduates, $1,686/for out-of-state undergraduates, $780/in-state graduates, and $1,434/out-of-state graduates.

Accommodations ''We do not have special rate arrangements with local hotels. We do offer accommodations on the Radford University campus in a recently refurbished residence hall. The 2005 cost was $26-36/night.''

Additional Information Conference leaders typically critique work done during the 2-week conference, but do not ask to have any writing sumbitted prior to the conference.'' Conference brochures/guidelines are available in March for a SASE. Inquire via e-mail or fax.

KILLER NASHVILLE
P.O. Box 680686, Franklin TN 37068-0686. (615)599-4032. E-mail: contact@killernashville.com. Web site: www .killernashville.com. **Contact:** Clay Stafford. Estab. 2006. Annual conference held in August. Next conference: Aug. 15-17, 2008. Conference duration: 4 days. Average attendance: 180+. Conference designed for writers and fans of mysteries and thrillers, including fiction and nonfiction authors, playwrights, and screenwriters. There are many opportunities for authors to sign books. Authors/panelists have included Michael Connelly, Carol Higgins Clark, Hallie Ephron, Chris Grabenstein, Rhonda Pollero, P.J. Parrish, Reed Farrel Coleman, Gwen Hunter, Kathryn Wall, Mary Saums, Don Bruns, Bill Moody, Richard Helms, Brad Strickland and Steven Womack. Literary agents and acquisitions editors attend and take pitches from writers. The conference is sponsored by Middle Tennessee State University, Mystery Writers of America, Sisters in Crime and the Nashville Scene, among others. Representatives from the FBI, ATF, police department and sheriff's department present on law enforcement procedures.

NORTH CAROLINA WRITERS' NETWORK FALL CONFERENCE
P.O. Box 954, Carrboro NC 27510-0954. (919)967-9540. Fax: (919)929-0535. E-mail: mail@ncwriters.org. Web site: www.ncwriters.org. **Contact:** Cynthia Barnett, executive director. Estab. 1985. Annual conference held in November in Research Triangle Park (Durham, North Carolina). Average attendance: 450. This organization hosts two conferences: one in the spring and one in the fall. Each conference is a weekend full of workshops, panels, book signings, and readings (including open mic). There will be a keynote speaker, along with sessions on a variety of genres, including fiction, poetry, creative nonfiction, journalism, children's book writing, screen-writing, and playwriting. ''We also offer craft, editing, and marketing classes. We hold the event at a conference center with hotel rooms available.'' Speakers have included Donald Maass, Noah Lukeman, Joe Regal, Jeff Kleinman, and Evan Marshall. Some agents will teach classes and some are available for meetings with attendees.

Costs Approximately $250 (includes 2 meals).

Accommodations Special rates are available at the Sheraton Hotel, but conferees must make their own reservations. **Additional Information** Brochures/guidelines are available online or by sending your street address to mail@ncw riters.org. You can also register online.

SEWANEE WRITERS' CONFERENCE

735 University Ave., 119 Gailor Hall, Stemlor Center, Sewanee TN 37383-1000. (931)598-1141. E-mail: cpeters@ sewanee.edu. Web site: www.sewaneewriters.org. **Contact:** Cheri B. Peters, creative writing programs manager. Estab. 1990. Annual conference held in July. Conference duration: 12 days. Average attendance: 120. "We offer genre-based workshops in fiction, poetry, and playwriting." The conference uses the facilities of Sewanee: the University of the South. The university is a collection of ivy-covered Gothic-style buildings located on the Cumberland Plateau in mid-Tennessee. Editors, publishers, and agents structure their own presentations, but there is always opportunity for questions from the audience." 2007 faculty members are fiction writers Richard Bausch, John Casey, Tony Earley, Diane Johnson, Randall Kenan, Alison Lurie, Jill, McCorkle, and Claire Messud; poets Brad Leithauser, Charles Martin, Mary Jo Salter, Alan Shapiro, Mark Strand, and Greg Williamson; and playwrights Lee Blessing and Melanie Marnich. Visiting agents include Gail Hochman and Georges Borchardt.
Costs $1,600 (includes tuition, board, basic room).
Accommodations Participants are housed in university dormitory rooms. Motel or bed & breakfast housing is available, but not abundantly so. Dormitory housing (shared occupancy) costs are included in the full conference fee. Single rooms are also available for a modest fee.
Additional Information Complimentary chartered bus service is available from the Nashville Airport to Sewanee and back on the first and last days of the conference. "We offer each participant (excepting auditors) the opportunity for a private manuscript conference with a member of the faculty. These manuscripts are due 1 month before the conference begins." Brochures/guidelines are free. The conference provides a limited number of fellowships and scholarships; these are awarded on a competitive basis.

SPRING WRITERS' WORKSHOP

Council for the Written Word, P.O. Box 298, Franklin TN 37065. (615)591-7516. E-mail: kathy@asouthernjourna l.com. Web site: www.cww-writers.org. **Contact:** Kathy Rhodes, facilitator. Annual workshop held in March. An intensive, half-day event with instruction and hands-on experience in a specific genre.

N TENNESSEE WRITERS ALLIANCE WRITERS CONFERENCE

Tennessee Writers Alliance, Inc., P.O. Box 120396, Nashville TN 37212. E-mail: inquiries@tn-writers.org. Web site: www.tn-writers.org/Workshops.asp. **Contact:** Nancy Fletcher-Blume, president. Annual. Annual conference held in June in Franklin, TN, just outside of Nashville. Conference duration: 2 days. Average attendance: 200. The conference is held at Battle Ground Academy, not far from Nashville. Previous speakers have included Robert Hicks, Tama Kieves, Richard Goodman, Ted Swindley and Carl Harris. The conference features a variety of sessions on fiction, nonfiction, playwriting, creative nonfiction, inspiring writers and more.
Costs Costs available online.
Accommodations Hotel accomodations available not far from the conference center in Franklin hotels.

SOUTHEAST (AL, AR, FL, GA, LA, MS)

FLORIDA CHRISTIAN WRITERS CONFERENCE

2344 Armour Ct., Titusville FL 32780. (321)269-5831. Fax: (321)264-0037. E-mail: billiewilson@cfl.rr.com. Web site: www.flwriters.org. **Contact:** Billie Wilson. Estab. 1988. Annual conference held in March. Conference duration: 4 days. Average attendance: 200. Covers fiction, nonfiction, magazine writing, marketing, Internet writing, greeting cards, and more. Conference is held at the Christian Retreat Center in Brandenton, Florida.
Costs $485 (includes tuition, meals).
Accommodations "We provide a shuttle from the Sarasota airport." $625/double occupancy; $865/single occupancy.
Additional Information "Each writer may submit 2 works for critique. We have specialists in every area of writing." Brochures/guidelines are available online or for a SASE.

FLORIDA FIRST COAST WRITERS' FESTIVAL

4501 Capper Road, C105, FCCJ, Jacksonville FL 32218. (904)766-6731. Fax: (904)713-4858. E-mail: dathomas@f ccj.org. Web site: www.fccj.org/wf. **Contact:** Dana Thomas. Estab. 1985. Annual conference held in the spring. Average attendance: 300. Covers fiction, nonfiction, scriptwriting, poetry, freelancing, etc. Offers seminars on narrative structure and plotting character development. Speakers have included Andrei Codrescu, Gerald

Hausman, Connie May Fowler, Leslie Schwartz, Larry Smith, Stella Suberman, Sophia Wadsworth, Amy Gash, David Hale Smith, Katharine Sands, Rita Rosenkranz, Jim McCarthy, David Poyer, Lenore Hart, Steve Berry and S.V. Date. "We offer one-on-one sessions at no additional cost for attendees to speak to selected writers, editors, and agents on a first-come, first-served basis."

Costs Visit the Web site for updated registration fees, including early bird specials.

Additional Information Sponsors a contest for short fiction, poetry, novels and plays. Novel judges are David Poyer and Lenore Hart. Entry fees: $39/novels; $15/short fiction; $7/poetry. Deadline: varies. Visit the Web site often for festival updates and details.

ⓃⓃ GULF COAST WRITERS CONFERENCE

P.O. Box 35038, Panama City FL 32412. (850)639-4848. E-mail: MichaelLister@mchsi.com. Web site: www.gulf coastwritersconference.com/. **Contact:** Michael Lister. Estab. 1999. Annual conference held in September in Panama City, Fla. 2008 dates: Sept. 18-20. Conference duration: 2 days. Average attendance: 100+. This conference is deliberately small and writer-centric with an affordable attedance price. Speakers include writers, editors and agents. Cricket Pechstein Freeman of the August Agency is often in attendance. The 2009 keynote speaker is mystery writer Michael Connelly.

HARRIETTE AUSTIN WRITERS CONFERENCE

Georgia Center for Continuing Education, The University of Georgia, Athens GA 30602-3603. E-mail: adminhawc 2008@gmail.com. Web site: harrietteaustin.org/default.aspx. **Contact:** Diane Trap. Annual conference held in July. Sessions cover fiction, poetry, freelance writing, computers, how to get an agent, working with editors, and more. Editors and agents will be speaking. Ms critiques and one-on-one meetings with an evaluator are available for $50.

Costs Cost information available online.

Accommodations Accomodations at the Georgia Center Hotel (georgiacenter.uga.edu).

NATCHEZ LITERARY AND CINEMA CELEBRATION

P.O. Box 1307, Natchez MS 39121-1307. (601)446-1208. Fax: (601)446-1214. E-mail: carolyn.smith@colin.edu. Web site: www.colin.edu/NLCC. **Contact:** Carolyn Vance Smith, co-chairman. Estab. 1990. Annual conference held in February. Conference duration: 5 days. Conference focuses on all literature, including film scripts. Each year's conference deals with some general aspect of Southern history. Speakers have included Eudora Welty, Margaret Walker Alexander, William Styron, Willie Morris, Ellen Douglas, Ernest Gaines, Elizabeth Spencer, Nikki Giovanni, Myrlie Evers-Williams, and Maya Angelou.

OZARK CREATIVE WRITERS CONFERENCE

ETSU-Box 23115, Johnson City TN 37614. (423)439-6024. E-mail: ozarkcreativewriters@earthlink.net. Web site: www.ozarkcreativewriters.org. **Contact:** Chrissy Willis, president. Estab. 1975. Annual conference held the second weekend in October, in Eureka Springs, AR. Includes programs for all types of writing. Speakers have included Dan Slater (Penguin Putnam), Stephan Harrigan (novelist/screenwriter), and Christopher Vogler.

Costs Approximately $100.

Accommodations Special rates are available at the Inn of the Ozarks in Eureka Springs, Arkansas.

Additional Information The conference has a friendly atmosphere and conference speakers are available. Many speakers return to the conference for the companionship of writers and speakers. Brochures are available for a SASE.

SANDHILLS WRITERS CONFERENCE

E-mail: akellman@aug.edu. Web site: www.sandhills.aug.edu. **Contact:** Anthony Kellman, director. Annual conference held the fourth weekend in March. Covers fiction, poetry, children's literature, nonfiction, plays, and songwriting. Located on the campus of Augusta State University in Georgia. Agents and editors will be speaking at the event.

Accommodations Several hotels are located near the university.

SLEUTHFEST

MWA Florida Chapter,. E-mail: SleuthfestRandy@yahoo.com. Web site: www.mwa-florida.org/sleuthfest.htm. Annual conference held in March. Conference duration: 4 days. Hands-on workshops, 4 tracks of writing and business panels, and 2 keynote speakers for writers of mystery and crime fiction. Also offers agent and editor appointments and paid ms critiques. Honored 2008 speakers included Lee Child and DP Lyle. A full list of attending speakers as well as agents and editors is online. This event is put on by the local chapter of the Mystery Writers of America.

Accommodations The Deerfield Beach Hilton.

⑅ SOUTH CAROLINA WRITERS WORKSHOP

P.O. Box 7104, Columbia SC 29202. (803)413-5810. E-mail: conference@myscww.org. Web site: www.myscww .org/. Estab. 1991. Annual conference in October. Next conference: Oct. 24-26, 2008 at the Hilton Myrtle Beach Resort in Myrtle Beach, SC. Conference duration: 3 days. The conference features critique sessions, open mic readings, presentations from agents and editors and more. The conference features more than 50 different workshops for writers to choose from, dealing with all subjects of writing craft, writing business, getting an agent and more. Agents will be in attendance.

Costs $289-389, depending on the package. Cheaper options available for part of the weekend. See the Web site for full registration details.

SOUTHEASTERN WRITERS WORKSHOP

P.O. Box 82115, Athens GA 30608. E-mail: info@southeasternwriters.com. Web site: www.southeasternwriters. com. **Contact:** Tim Hudson. Estab. 1975. Held annually the third week in June at Epworth-by-the-Sea, St. Simons Island, Georgia. Conference duration: 4 days. Average attendance: Limited to 100 students. Classes are offered in all areas of writing, including fiction, poetry, nonfiction, inspirational, juvenile, specialty writing, and others. The faculty is comprised of some of the most successful authors from throughout the southeast and the country. Agent-in-Residence is available to meet with participants. Up to 3 free ms evaluations and critique sessions are also available to participants if mss are submitted by the deadline.

Costs 2007 tuition was $395.

Additional Information Multiple contests with cash prizes are open to participants. Registration brochure is available in March—e-mail or send a SASE. Full information, including registration material, is on the Web site.

⑅ SPACE COAST WRITERS GUILD ANNUAL CONFERENCE

(321)956-7193. E-mail: scwg-jm@cfl.rr.com. Web site: www.scwg.org/conference.asp. **Contact:** Judy Mammay. Annual. Annual conference held in January along the east coast of central Florida. Conference duration: 2 days. Average attendance: 150+. This conference is hosted each winter in Florida and features a variety of presenters on all topics writing. Critiques are available for a price, and agents in attendance will take pitches from writers. Previous presenters have included Davis Bunn (writer), Ellen Pepus (agent), Miriam Hees (editor), Lauren Mosko (editor), Lucienne Diver (agent) and many many more.

Accommodations The conference is hosted on a beachside hotel, where rooms are available.

WORDS & MUSIC

624 Pirates Alley, New Orleans LA 70116. (504)586-1609. Fax: (504)522-9725. E-mail: faulkhouse@aol.com. Web site: www.wordsandmusic.org. **Contact:** Rosemary James DeSalvo. Estab. 1997. Annual conference held the first week in November. Conference duration: 5 days. Average attendance: 300. Presenters include authors, agents, editors and publishers. 2006 speakers included agents Deborah Grosvenor, Judith Weber, Stuart Bernstein, Nat Sobel, Jeff Kleinman, Emma Sweeney, Liza Dawson and Michael Murphy; and editors Lauren Marino, Webster Younce, Ann Patty, Will Murphy, Jofie Ferrari-Adler, Elizabeth Stein; critics Marie Arana, Jonathan Yardley, and Michael Dirda; fiction writers Oscar Hijuelos, Robert Olen Butler, Shirley Ann Grau, Mayra Montero, Ana Castillo, H.G. Carrillo. Agents and editors critique manuscripts in advance; meet with them one-on-one during the conference.

Costs $300 fee includes critiques and agent/editor meetings, all discussions. Food, wine, music events, lunches are extra. Hotel and transportation costs not included.

Accommodations Hotel Monteleone in New Orleans.

WRITING THE REGION

Gainesville Association for the Creative Arts, P.O. Box 12246, Gainesville FL 32604. (888)917-7001. Fax: (352)373-8854. E-mail: info@artsgaca.org; SarahBewley@sarahbewley.com. Web site: www.writingtheregion. com. **Contact:** Norma Homan, director. Estab. 1997. Annual conference held in July. 2008 dates: July 23-27. Conference duration: 5 days. Average attendance: 100. Conference concentrates on fiction, writing for children, poetry, nonfiction, drama, screenwriting, writing with humor, setting, character, and more. Workshop honors Pulitzer Prize-winning author Marjorie Kinnan Rawlings. Held at the Thomas Center in Gainesville, Floriday. Speakers have included Anne Hawking, Doris Booth, Sarah Bewley, Bill Maxwell, and Robert Fulton. Agent/editor appointments are available.

Costs Costs available online. Lower costs for half-day and one-day registration.

Accommodations Special rates are available at the Holiday Inn, University Center and the Residence Inn, Marriott.

 **WRITING TODAY**

Birmingham-Southern College, Box 549066, Birmingham AL 35254. (205)226-4922. Fax: (205)226-4931. E-mail: agreen@bsc.edu. Web site: www.writingtoday.org. **Contact:** Annie Green. Estab. 1978. Annual conference held during the second weekend in March. The 2009 dates are set for March 13-14. Conference duration: 2 days. Average attendance: 300-350. Conference hosts approximately 18 workshops, lectures, and readings. ''We try to offer sessions in short fiction, novels, poetry, children's literature, magazine writing, songwriting, and general information of concern to aspiring writers, such as publishing, agents, markets, and research.'' The event is held on the Birmingham-Southern College campus in classrooms and lecture halls. Speakers have included Eudora Welty, Pat Conroy, Ernest Gaines, Ray Bradbury, Erskine Caldwell, John Barth, Galway Kinnell, Edward Albee, Horton Foote, and William Styron and other renowned writers.

Costs $150 for both days (includes lunches, reception, morning coffee/rolls).

Accommodations Attendees must arrange own transportation and accommodations.

Additional Information For an additional charge, poetry and short story critiques are offered for interested writers who request and send mss by the deadline. The conference also sponsors the Hackney Literary Competition Awards for poetry, short stories, and novels.

MIDWEST (IL, IN, KY, MI, OH)

BACKSPACE WRITERS CONFERENCE

P.O. Box 454, Washington MI 48094-0454. Phone/Fax: (586)532-9652. E-mail: chrisg@bksp.org. Web site: www.backspacewritersconference.com. **Contact:** Karen Dionne, Christopher Graham. Estab. 2005. The 2008 conference will be held in New York City on Aug. 7-8. Conference duration: 2 days. Average attendance: 150. Conference focuses on all genres of fiction and nonfiction. Offers query letter workshop, writing workshop, and panels with agents, editors, marketing experts, and authors. Speakers have included Pulitzer-Prize-winning playwright Douglas Wright, Michael Cader, David Morrell, Lee Child, Gayle Lynds, Ron McLarty, C. Michael Curtis, Jeff Kleinman, Richard Curtis, Noah Lukeman, Jenny Bent, Dan Lazar and Kristin Nelson.

Costs $355 for Backspace members, $395 for non-members (includes 2-day, 2-track program and refreshments on both days, as well as a cocktail reception).

Additional Information This is a high-quality conference, with much of the program geared toward agented and published authors. Afternoon mixers each day afford plenty of networking opportunities. Go online for brochure, or request information via fax or e-mail.

COLUMBUS WRITERS CONFERENCE

P.O. Box 20548, Columbus OH 43220. (614)451-3075. Fax: (614)451-0174. E-mail: angelapl28@aol.com. Web site: www.creativevista.com. **Contact:** Angela Palazzolo, director. Estab. 1993. Annual conference held in August. Average attendance: 250+. In addition to literary agent and editor consultations, the conference offers a wide variety of fiction and nonfiction topics presented by writers, editors, and literary agents. Writing topics have included novel, short story, children's, young adult, science fiction, fantasy, humor, mystery, playwriting, finding and working with a literary agent, book proposals, query writing, screenwriting, magazine writing, travel, humor, cookbook, technical queries and freelance writing. The conference has included many writers, editors and literary agents, including Lee K. Abbott, Chuck Adams, Tracy Bernstein, Sheree Bykofsky, Oscar Collier, Lisa Cron, Jennifer DeChiara, Tracey E. Dils, Hallie Ephron, Karen Harper, Scott Hoffman, Jeff Kleinman, Simon Lipskar, Noah Lukeman, Donald Maass, Lee Martin, Erin McGraw, Kim Meisner, Doris S. Michaels, Rita Rosenkrantz, Ben Salmon and Nancy Zafris.

Additional Information For registration fees or to receive a brochure (available in the summer), visit the Web site or contact the conference by e-mail, phone, fax, or postal mail.

IMAGINATION WRITERS WORKSHOP AND CONFERENCE

Cleveland State University, English Department, 2121 Euclid Ave., Cleveland OH 44115. (216)687-4522. Fax: (216)687-6943. E-mail: imagination@csuohio.edu. Web site: www.csuohio.edu/imagination/. **Contact:** Neal Chandler, director. Estab. 1990. Annual conference is held in late June/early July. Conference duration: 6 days. Average attendance: 60. Program includes intensive workshops, panels, lectures on poetry, fiction, creative nonfiction, playwriting, and the business of writing by noted authors, editors and agents. Held at Trinity Commons, an award-winning urban renovation and ideal conference center adjacent to the CSU campus. Available both not-for-credit and for university credit.

INDIANA UNIVERSITY WRITERS' CONFERENCE

464 Ballantine Hall, Bloomington IN 47405. (812)855-1877. E-mail: writecon@indiana.edu. Web site: www.indiana.edu/~writecon. Estab. 1940. Annual conference held in June. Participants in the week-long conference

join faculty-led workshops (fiction, poetry, and creative nonfiction), take classes, engage in one-on-one consultation with authors, and attend a variety of readings and social events. Previous speakers have included Raymond Carver, Mark Doty, Robert Olen Butler, Aimee Bender, Li-Young Lee, and Brenda Hillman.

Costs Costs available online.

Additional Information "In order to be accepted in a workshop, the writer must submit the work they would like critiqued. Work is evaluated before the applicant is accepted. Go online or send a SASE for guidelines.

KARITOS CHRISTIAN ARTS CONFERENCE

24-B N. Belmont Ave., Arlington IL 60004. (847)749-1284. E-mail: bob@karitos.com. Web site: www.karitos.com. **Contact:** RuthAnne Boone, literary department head (ladyruth@ix.netcom.com. Estab. 1996. Annual conference held each summer. 2008 dates: July 31—Aug. 2. Conference duration: Thursday-Saturday night. Average attendance: 300-400. Karitos is a celebration and teaching weekend for Christian artists and writers. Writing Division will focus on teaching the craft of writing, beginning and advanced, fiction and nonfiction. Site for this year's conference is Living Waters Community Church in the Chicago suburb of Bolingbrook, Faculty has included Lori Davis, John DeJarlais, Eva Marie Everson, Lin Johnson, Patricia Hickman, Elma Photikarm, Rajendra Pillai, Jane Rubietta, Travis Thrasher and Chris Wave.

Costs Early registration: $80 (Through April 20); $120 thereafter.

KENYON REVIEW WRITERS WORKSHOP

The Kenyon Review, Kenyon College, Gambier OH 43022. (740)427-5207. Fax: (740)427-5417. E-mail: reacha@kenyon.edu. Web site: www.kenyonreview.org. **Contact:** Anna Duke Reach, Director of Summer Programs. Estab. 1990. Annual 8-day workshop held in June. Participants apply in poetry, fiction, or creative nonfiction, and then participate in intensive daily workshops which focus on the generation and revision of significant new work. Held on the campus of Kenyon College in the rural village of Gambier, Ohio. Workshop leaders have included David Baker, Ron Carlson, Rebecca McClanahan, Rosanna Warren and Nancy Zafris.

Costs $1,995 (includes tuition, housing, meals).

Accommodations Participants stay in Kenyon College student housing.

LAMB'S SPRINGFED WRITING RETREAT

Springfield Arts, P.O. Box 304, Royal Oak MI 48068-0304. (248)589-3913. Fax: (248)589-9981. E-mail: johndlamb@ameritech.net. Web site: www.springfed.org. **Contact:** John D. Lamb, director. Estab. 1999. Annual conference held in late September. Average attendance: 75. New and established writers and poets attend workshops, readings, and provocative panel discussions. Held at The Birchwood Inn, Harbor Springs, Mich. Speakers have included Thomas Lux, Michael Moore, Dorianne Laux, Billy Collins, Denise Duhamel, Jane Hamilton, Jacquelyn Mitchard, Mary Jo Salter, Brad Leithauser, Doug Stanton, Craig Holden, Chuck Pfarrer, Ivan Raimi, Jonathan Rand and M.L. Liebler.

Costs $535-600/single occupancy; $460-500/double occupancy; $360/no lodging (includes workshops, meals).

Accommodations Attendees stay in comfortable rooms with 1 king bed or two queens. Arranges shuttle ride from Pellston Airport in Pellston, Mich.

Additional Information Attendees may submit their work for craft discussion and/or conference tutorials; send 3 copies of 3 poems or 5 pages of prose.

⊚ MAGNA CUM MURDER

The Mid America Crime Writing Festival, The E.B. and Bertha C. Ball Center, Ball State University, Muncie IN 47306. (765)285-8975. Fax: (765)747-9566. E-mail: magnacummurder@yahoo.com; kennisonk@aol.com. Web site: www.magnacummurder.com. **Contact:** Kathryn Kennison. Estab. 1994. Annual conference held in October. 2008 dates: Oct. 24-26 in Muncie, IN. Average attendance: 350. Festival for readers and writers of crime writing. Held in the Horizon Convention Center and Historic Hotel Roberts. Dozens of mystery writers are in attendance and there are presentations from agents, editors and professional writers. The Web site has the full list of attending speakers.

Costs $195+ (includes breakfast, boxed lunches, opening reception, Saturday evening banquet).

⬚ MIDWEST LITERARY FESTIVAL

Mayors Office of Special Events, 44 East Downer Place, Aurora IL 60507. (630)844-4731. E-mail: info@midwestliteraryfestival.com; mayorsoffice@aurora-il.org. Web site: www.midwestliteraryfestival.com/press001.htm. Estab. 2002. Annual. Annual conference held in the fall. Conference duration: 3 days. Average attendance: 250+. Annual conference in downtown Aurora, IL, featuring dozens of screenwriters, fiction writers and nonfiction writers—both local and national—who present workshops, meet with writers, and more. Agents in attendance will take pitches from writers and workshop critiques are available. Previous keynote speakers have included

Helen Thomas, Joyce Carol Oates, Harry Shearer. Other speakers have included David Morrell, Les Edgerton, Elizabeth Kostova. The conference is paired witha large book festival and book sale.
Costs Costs available online.
Accommodations Hotels are available near the hotel.

MIDWEST WRITERS WORKSHOP
Department of Journalism, Ball State University, 2800 Bethel Ave., Muncie IN 47306. (765)282-1055. Fax: (765)285-5997. E-mail: info@midwestwriters.org. Web site: www.midwestwriters.org. **Contact:** Jama Bigger, registrar. Estab. 1974. Annual workshop held in July. 2008 dates: July 24-26. Conference duration: 3 days. Covers fiction, nonfiction, poetry, writing for children, how to find an agent, memoirs, Internet marketing and more. Speakers have included Steve Brewer, Crescent Dragonwagon, Dennis Hensley, Nickole Brown, Nelson Price, Hanoch McCarty, Jane Friedman (Writer's Digest Books) and more.
Costs $90-275; $25/ms evaluation.

WRITE-TO-PUBLISH CONFERENCE
WordPro Communications Services, 9118 W Elmwood Dr., #1G, Niles IL 60714-5820. (847)296-3964. Fax: (847)296-0754. E-mail: lin@writetopublish.com. Web site: www.writetopublish.com. **Contact:** Lin Johnson, director. Estab. 1971. Annual conference held June 3-6, 2009. Conference duration: 4 days. Average attendance: 250. Conference on writing fiction, nonfiction, devotions, and magazine articles for the Christian market. Held at Wheaton College in Wheaton, Illinois. Speakers have included Dr. Dennis E. Hensley, agent Chip MacGregor, Ken Peterson (Tyndale House), Craig Bubeck (Cook), Joan Alexander, Allan Fisher (Crossway Books & Bibles), Joyce Hart (Hartline Literary Agency), Betsy Newenhuyse (Moody Publishers), and Ginger Kolbaba (Marriage Partnership).
Costs $450 (includes all sessions, Saturday night banquet, 1 ms evaluation); $95/meals.
Accommodations Campus residence halls: $220/double; $300/single. A list of area hotels is also on the Web site.

NORTH CENTRAL (IA, MN, NE, ND, SD, WI)

GREEN LAKE WRITERS CONFERENCE
W2511 State Road 23, Green Lake Conference Center, Green Lake WI 54941-9599. (920)294-3323. E-mail: janwhite@glcc.org. Web site: www.glcc.org. **Contact:** Program coordinator. Estab. 1948. The 60th annual conference will be Aug. 17-22, 2008. Conference duration: 1 week. Attendees may be well-published or beginners, may write for secular and/or Christian markets. Leaders are experienced writing teachers. Attendees can spend 11.5 contact hours in the workshop of their choice: fiction, nonfiction, poetry, inspirational/devotional. Seminars include specific skills: marketing, humor, songwriting, writing for children, self-publishing, writing for churches, interviewing, memoir writing, the magazine market. Evening: panels of experts will answer questions. Social and leisure activities included. GLCC is in south central WI, has 1,000 acres, 2.5 miles of shoreline on WI's deepest lake, and offers a resort setting.
Additional Information Brochure and scholarship info from Web site or contact Jan White (920-294-7327). To register, call 920-294-3323.

IOWA SUMMER WRITING FESTIVAL
C215 Seashore Hall, University of Iowa, Iowa City IA 52242. (319)335-4160. Fax: (319)335-4039. E-mail: iswfestival@uiowa.edu. Web site: www.uiowa.edu/~iswfest. **Contact:** Amy Margolis, director. Estab. 1987. Annual festival held in June and July. Conference duration: Workshops are 1 week or a weekend. Average attendance: Limited to 12 people/class, with over 1,500 participants throughout the summer. ''We offer courses across the genres: novel, short story, poetry, essay, memoir, humor, travel, playwriting, screenwriting, writing for children, and women's writing.'' Held at the University of Iown campus. Speakers have included Marvin Bell, Lan Samantha Chang, John Dalton, Hope Edelman, Katie Ford, Patricia Foster, Bret Anthony Johnston, Barbara Robinette Moss, among others.
Costs $500-525/week; $250/weekend workshop. Housing and meals are separate.
Accommodations Iowa House: $75/night; Sheraton: $88/night (rates subject to change).
Additional Information Brochures are available in February. Inquire via e-mail or fax.

NEBRASKA SUMMER WRITERS' CONFERENCE
Department of English, University of Nebraska, Lincoln NE 68588-0333. (402)472-1834. E-mail: nswc@unl.edu. Web site: www.nswc.org. **Contact:** Jonis Agee, director. Annual conference held in June. Conference duration: 1 week. Faculty include Sara Gruen, Ron Hansen, Li-Young Lee, Sean Doolittle, Lee Martin, Dorianne Laux,

Jim Shepard, Judith Kitchen, Joe Mackall, Hilda Raz, William Kloefkorn, agent Sonia Pabley, Timothy Schaffert, Brent Spencer, Stan Sanvel Rubin, agent Emma Sweeney, Jane Von Mehren (vice president, Random House). **Costs** Costs available online.

UNIVERSITY OF NORTH DAKOTA WRITERS CONFERENCE

Department of English, 110 Merrifield Hall, 276 Centennial Drive, Stop 7209, Grand Forks ND 58202. (701)777-3321. E-mail: english@und.edu. Web site: www.undwritersconference.org. **Contact:** Liz Harris-Behling or Heidi Czerwiec, co-directors. Estab. 1970. Annual conference held in March. Offers panels, readings, and films focused around a specific theme. Almost all events take place in the UND Memorial Union, which has a variety of small rooms and a 1,000-seat main hall. Future speakers include Stuart Dybek, Mary Gaitskill, Li-Young Lee, Timothy Liu, Leslie Adrienne Miller, Michelle Richmond, Miller Williams and Anne Harris.
Costs All events are free and open to the public. Donations accepted.

WISCONSIN BOOK FESTIVAL

222 S. Bedford St., Suite F, Madison WI 53703. (608)262-0706. Fax: (608)263-7970. E-mail: alison@wisconsinbookfestival.org. Web site: www.wisconsinbookfestival.org. **Contact:** Alison Jones Chaim, director. Estab. 2002. Annual festival held in October. Conference duration: 5 days. The festival feature readings, lectures, book discussions, writing workshops, live interviews, children's events, and more. Speakers have included Michael Cunningham, Grace Paley, TC Boyle, Marjane Satrapi, Phillip Gourevitch, Myla Goldberg, Audrey Niffenegger, Harvey Pekar, Billy Collins, Tim O'Brien and Isabel Allende.
Costs All festival events are free.

WISCONSIN REGIONAL WRITERS' ASSOCIATION CONFERENCES

E-mail: vpresident@wrwa.net. Web site: www.wrwa.net. **Contact:** Nate Scholze, fall conference chair; Roxanne Aehl, spring conference chair. Estab. 1948. Annual conferences are held in May and September. Conference duration: 1-2 days. Provides presentations for all genres, including fiction, nonfiction, scriptwriting, and poetry. Presenters include authors, agents, editors, and publishers. Speakers have included Jack Byrne, Michelle Grajkowski, Benjamin Leroy, Richard Lederer, and Philip Martin.
Additional Information Go online for brochure or make inquiries via e-mail or with SASE.

SOUTH CENTRAL (CO, KS, MO, NM, OK, TX)

AGENTS AND EDITORS CONFERENCE

Writers' League of Texas, 1501 W. Fifth St., Suite E-2, Austin TX 78703. (512)499-8914. Fax: (512)499-0441. E-mail: wlt@writersleague.org. Web site: www.writersleague.org. **Contact:** Kristy Bordine, membership director. Estab. 1982. Annual conference held in the summer. Conference duration: 3 days. Average attendance: 300. Provides writers with the opportunity to meet top literary agents and editors from New York and the West Coast. Topic include: finding and working with agents and publishers, writing and marketing fiction and nonfiction, dialogue, characterization, voice, research, basic and advanced fiction writing, the business of writing, and workshops for genres. Speakers have included Malaika Adero, Stacey Barney, Sha-Shana Crichton, Jessica Faust, Dena Fischer, Mickey Freiberg, Jill Grosjean, Anne Hawkins, Jim Hornfischer, Jennifer Joel, David Hale Smith and Elisabeth Weed.
Costs $295-$345.
Additional Information Contests and awards programs are offered separately. Brochures are available upon request.

ASPEN SUMMER WORDS LITERARY FESTIVAL & WRITING RETREAT

Aspen Writers' Foundation, 110 E. Hallam St., #116, Aspen CO 81611. (970)925-3122. Fax: (970)925-5700. E-mail: info@aspenwriters.org. Web site: www.aspenwriters.org. **Contact:** Natalie Lacy, programs manager. Estab. 1976. Annual conference held the fourth week of June. Conference duration: 5 days. Average attendance: 150 at writing retreat; 300 + at literary festival. Retreat for fiction, creative nonfiction, poetry, magazine writing, food writing, and literature. Festival includes author readings, craft talks, panel discussions with publishing industry insiders, professional consultations with editors and agents, and social gatherings. Retreat faculty members include (in 2007: Andrea Barzi, Katherine Fausset, Anjali Singh, Lisa Grubka, Amber Qureshi, Joshua Kendall, Keith Flynn, Robert Bausch, Amy Bloom, Percival Everett, Danzy Senna, Bharti Kirchner, Gary Ferguson, Dorianne Laux. Festival presenters include (in 2007): Wole Soyinka, Chimamanda Ngozi Adichie, Alaa Al Aswany, Henry Louis Gates, Jr., Leila Aboulela, and many more!
Costs (In 2007:) $475/retreat; $175-250/seminar; Tuition includes daily continental breakfast and lunch, plus

one evening reception; a limited number of half-tuition scholarships are available; $200/festival; $35/professional consultation.

Accommodations Discount lodging at the conference site will be available. $170/one-bedroom condo; $255/two-bedroom condo; $127.50/shared two-bedroom condo.

Additional Information Workshops admission deadline is April 1 for the 2008 conference, or until all workshops are filled. Juried admissions for some workshops; writing sampl required with application to juried workshops. Mss will be discussed during workshop. Literary festival and some retreat programs are open to the public on first-come, first-served basis; no mss required. Brochure, application and complete admissions information available on Web site, or request by phone, fax or e-mail. Include mailing address with all e-mail requests.

AUSTIN FILM FESTIVAL & CONFERENCE

1145 W 5th St., Suite 210, Austin TX 78703. (512)478-4795. Fax: (512)478-6205. Web site: www.austinfilmfestival.com. **Contact:** Linnea Toney, conference director. Estab. 1994. Annual conference held in October. Conference duration: 4 days. Average attendance: 2,200. This festival is the first organization of its kind to focus on writers' unique creative contribution to the film and television industries. The conference takes place during the first four days of the festival. The event presents more than 75 panels, round tables and workshops that address various aspects of screenwriting and filmmaking. The Austin Film Festival is held in downtown Austin at the Driskill and Stephen F. Austin hotels. The AFF boasts a number of events and services for emerging and professional writers and filmmakers. Past participants include Robert Altman, Wes Anderson, James L. Brooks, Joel & Ethan Coen, Russell Crowe, Barry Levinson, Darren Star, Robert Duvall, Buck Henry, Dennis Hopper, Lawrence Kasdan, John Landis, Garry Shandling, Bryan Singer, Oliver Stone, Sandra Bullock, Harold Ramis and Owen Wilson.

Costs Approximately $300 for early bird entries (includes entrance to all panels, workshops, and roundtables during the 4-day conference, as well as all films during the 8-night film exhibitions and the opening and closing night parties). Go online for other offers.

Accommodations Discounted rates on hotel accommodations are available to attendees if the reservations are made through the Austin Film Festival office.

Additional Information The Austin Film Festival is considered one of the most accessible festivals, and Austin is the premier town for networking because when industry people are here, they are relaxed and friendly. The Austin Film Festival holds annual screenplay/teleplay and film competitions, as well as a Young Filmmakers Program. Check online for competition details and festival information. Inquire via e-mail or fax.

THE GLEN WORKSHOP

Image, 3307 Third Avenue W., Seattle WA 98119. (206)281-2988. Fax: (206)281-2335. E-mail: glenworkshop@imagejournal.org; jmullins@imagejournal.org. Web site: www.imagejournal.org/glen. Estab. 1991. Annual workshop held in August. Conference duration: 1 week. Workshop focuses on fiction, poetry, spiritual writing, playwriting, screenwriting, songwriting, and mixed media. Writing classes combine general instruction and discussion with the workshop experience, in which each individual's works are read and discussed critically. Held at St. John's College in Santa Fe, New Mexico. Faculty has included Scott Cairns, Jeanine Hathaway, Bret Lott, Paula Huston, Arlene Hutton, David Denny, Barry Moser, Barry Krammes, Ginger Geyer, and Pierce Pettis.

Costs 2007 costs: $500-960 (includes tuition, lodging, meals); $395-475/commuters (includes tuition, lunch). A limited number of partial scholarships are available.

Accommodations Offers dorm rooms, dorm suites, and apartments.

Additional Information "Like *Image*, the Glen is grounded in a Christian perspective, but its tone is informal and hospitable to all spiritual wayfarers." Depending on the teacher, participants may need to submit workshop material prior to arrival (usually 10-25 pages).

◎ GLORIETA CHRISTIAN WRITERS CONFERENCE

CLASServices, Inc., 3311 Candelaria NE, Suite 1, Albuquerque NM 87107-1952. (800)433-6633. Fax: (505)899-9282. E-mail: info@classervices.com. Web site: www.glorietacwc.com. **Contact:** Linda Jewell, seminar manager. Estab. 1997. Annual. Annual conference held in October. Conference duration: Wednesday afternoon through Sunday lunch. Average attendance: 350. Includes programs for all types of writing. Agents, editors, and professional writers will be speaking and available for meetings with attendees.

Costs 2007 costs: $450/early registration (1 month in advance); $495/program only. Critiques are available for an addition charge.

Accommodations Hotel rooms are available at the LifeWay Glorieta Conference Center. Santa Fe Shuttle offers service from the Albuquerque or Santa Fe airports to the conference center. Hotel rates vary. "We suggest you make airline and rental car reservations early due to other events in the area."

Additional Information Brochures are available April 1. Inquire via e-mail, phone, or fax, or visit the Web site.

HEARTLAND WRITERS CONFERENCE

P.O. Box 652, Kennett MO 63857. (573)297-3325. Fax: (573)297-3352. E-mail: hwg@heartlandwriters.org. Web site: www.heartlandwriters.org/conference.html. **Contact:** Harry Spiller, conference coordinator. Estab. 1990. Biennial (even years) conference held in June. 2008 date: June 7. Conference duration: 3 days. Average attendance: 160. Covers popular fiction (all genres), nonfiction, children's writing, screenwritin, and poetry. Held at the Best Western Coach House Inn in Sikeston, Missouri. Speakers have included Alice Orr, Jennifer Jackson, Ricia Mainhardt, Christy Fletcher, Sue Yuen, and Evan Marshall. Agents will be speaking and available for meetings with attendees.

Costs $215 for advance registrants; $250 for general registration (includes lunch on Friday and Saturday, awards banquet on Sunday, hospitality room, and get-acquainted mixer Thursday night).

Accommodations Blocks of rooms are available at a special rate ($55-85/night) at the conference venue and 2 nearby motels.

Additional Information Brochures are available in late January. Inquire via e-mail or fax.

TONY HILLERMAN WRITERS CONFERENCE

304 Calle Oso, Santa Fe NM 87501. (505)471-1565. E-mail: wordharvest@wordharvest.com. Web site: www.wordharvest.com/index.php/hillermanconference. Estab. 2001. Annual conference held in November. 2008 dates: Oct. 30—Nov. 2. Conference duration: 4 days. Average attendance: 150-200. Workshops on writing good dialogue, building your platform, writing series that sell, and adding humor to your writing are geared toward mystery writers. Held at the Hyatt Regency in Albuquerque, New Mexico. Speakers have included Tony Hillerman, Michael McGarrity, J.A. Jance, Margaret Coel, Sean Murphy, Virginia Swift, James D. Doss, Gail Larsen, Luther Wilson, and Craig Johnson. 2008 guests include: James Rollins, Michael McGarrity, Craig Johnson, Pari Noskin Taichert and Sandi Ault. The conference has both a short story writing contest and a mystery writing contest.

Costs $250-450, depending on if attendees want an entire weekend pass or just one day. Full cost information available online.

Accommodations Approximately $99/night at the Hyatt Regency.

NETWO WRITERS ROUNDUP

Northeast Texas Writers Organization, P.O. Box 411, Winfield TX 75493. (903)856-6724. E-mail: netwomail@netwo.org. Web site: www.netwo.org. **Contact:** Galand Nuchols, president. Estab. 1987. Annual conference held in April. Conference duration: 2 days. Presenters include agents, writers, editors, and publishers. Agents in attendance will take pitches from writers. The conference features a writing contest, pitch sessions, critiques from professionals, as well as dozens of workshops and presentations.

Costs $60+ (discount offered for early registration).

Additional Information Conference is co-sponsored by the Texas Commission on the Arts. See Web site for current updates.

THE NEW LETTERS WEEKEND WRITERS CONFERENCE

University of Missouri-Kansas City, 5101 Rockhill Rd., Kansas City MO 64110-2499. (816)235-1168. Fax: (816)235-2611. E-mail: newletters@umkc.edu. Web site: www.newletters.org. **Contact:** Betsy Beasley or Sharon Seaton. Estab. 1970s (as The Longboat Key Writers Conference). Annual conference held in late June. Conference duration: 3 days. Average attendance: 60. The conference brings together talented writers in many genres for seminars, readings, workshops, and individual conferences. The emphasis is on craft and the creative process in poetry, fiction, screenwriting, playwriting, and journalism, but the program also deals with matters of psychology, publications, and marketing. The conference is appropriate for both advanced and beginning writers. The conference meets at the university's beautiful Diastole Conference Center. Two- and 3-credit hour options are available by special permission from the Director Robert Stewart.

Costs Participants may choose to attend as a noncredit student or they may attend for 1 hour of college credit from the University of Missouri-Kansas City. Conference registration includes Friday evening reception and keynote speaker, Saturday and Sunday continental breakfast and lunch.

Accommodations Registrants are responsible for their own transportation, but information on area accomodations is available.

Additional Information Those registering for college credit are required to submit a ms in advance. Ms reading and critique are included in the credit fee. Those attending the conference for noncredit also have the option of having their ms critiqued for an additional fee. Brochures are available for a SASE after March. Accepts inquiries by e-mail and fax.

NIMROD/HARDMAN AWARDS CELEBRATION & WRITING WORKSHOP

Nimrod, University of Tulsa, 800 S. Tucker Drive., Tulsa OK 74104-3189. (918)631-3080. Fax: (918)631-3033. E-mail: nimrod@utulsa.edu. Web site: www.utulsa.edu/nimrod. **Contact:** Francine Ringold, editor-in-chief.

Managing Editor: Eilis O'Neal. Estab. 1978. Annual conference held in October. Conference duration: 1 day. Offers one-on-one editing sessions, readings, panel discussions, and master classes in fiction, poetry, nonfiction, memoir, and fantasy writing. Speakers have included Myla Goldberg, B.H. Fairchild, Colleen McElroy, Gina Ochsner, Kelly Link, Rilla Askew, Matthew Galkin, and A.D. Coleman.
Additional Information Full conference details are online in August.

PIKES PEAK WRITERS CONFERENCE

4164 Austin Bluffs Pkwy., #246, Colorado Springs CO 80918. (719)531-5723. E-mail: info@pikespeakwriters.com. Web site: www.pikespeakwriters.com. Estab. 1993. Annual conference held in April. Conference duration: 3 days. Average attendance: 400. Workshops, presentations, and panels focus on writing and publishing mainstream and genre fiction (romance, science fiction/fantasy, suspense/thrillers, action/adventure, mysteries, children's, young adult). Agents and editors are available for meetings with attendees on Saturday.
Costs 2007 costs: $295/PPW members; $350/nonmembers (includes all meals).
Accommodations Marriott Colorado Springs holds a block of rooms at a special rate for attendees until late March.
Additional Information Readings with critiques are available on Friday afternoon. Also offers a contest for unpublished writers; entrants need not attend the conference. Deadline: November 1. Registration and contest entry forms are online; brochures are available in January. Send inquiries via e-mail.

ROCKY MOUNTAIN FICTION WRITERS COLORADO GOLD

Rocky Mountain Fiction Writers, P.O. Box 545, Englewood CO 80151. E-mail: conference@rmfw.org. Web site: www.rmfw.org/default.aspx. **Contact:** Conference Director. Estab. 1983. Annual conference held in September/October. Conference duration: 3 days. Average attendance: 250. Themes include general novel-length fiction, genre fiction, contemporary romance, mystery, science fiction/fantasy, mainstream, and history. Speakers have included Terry Brooks, Dorothy Cannell, Patricia Gardner Evans, Diane Mott Davidson, Constance O'Day, Connie Willis, Clarissa Pinkola Estes, Michael Palmer, Jennifer Unter, Margaret Marr, Ashley Krass, and Andren Barzvi. Approximately 4 editors and 5 agents attend annually.
Costs Costs available online.
Accommodations Special rates will be available at a nearby hotel.
Additional Information Editor-conducted workshops are limited to 10 participants for critique, with auditing available.

SANTA FE WRITERS CONFERENCE

Southwest Literary Center, 826 Camino de Monte Rey, A3, Santa Fe NM 87505. (505)577-1125. Fax: (505)982-7125. E-mail: litcenter@recursos.org. Web site: www.santafewritersconference.com. **Contact:** Jenice Gharib, director. Estab. 1985. Annual conference held in June. Conference duration: 5 days. Average attendance: 50. Conference offering intimate workshops in fiction, poetry, and creative nonfiction. Speakers have included Lee K. Abbott, Alice Adams, Lucille Adler, Francisco Alarcon, Agha Shahid Ali, Rudolfo Anaya, Max Apple, Jimmy Santiago Baca, Madison Smartt Bell, Marvin Bell, Molly Bendall, Elizabeth Benedict, Roo Borson, Robert Boswell, Kate Braverman, Mei-Mei Berssenbrugge, Ron Carlson, Denise Chavez, Lisa D. Chavez, Alan Cheuse, Ted Conover, Robert Creeley, C. Michael Curtis, Jon Davis, Percival Everett, Jennifer Foerster, Richard Ford, Judith Freeman, Samantha Gillison, Natalie Goldberg, Jorie Graham, Lee Gutkind, Elizabeth Hardwick, Robert Hass, Ehud Havazelet, Elizabeth Hightower, Tony Hillerman, Brenda Hillman, Tony Hoagland, Garrett Hongo, Lewis Hyde, Mark Irwin, Charles Johnson, Diane Johnson, Teresa Jordan, Donald Justice, Laura Kasischke, Pagan Kennedy, Brian Kiteley, William Kittredge, Carolyn Kizer, Verlyn Klinkenborg, Karla Kuban, Mark Levine, Alison Lurie, Tony Mares, Kevin McIlvoy, Christopher Merrill, Jane Miller, Mary Jane Moffat, Carol Moldow, N. Scott Momaday, David Morrell, Antonya Nelson, Susan Neville, John Nichols, Sharon Niederman, Naomi Shahib Nye, Grace Paley, Ann Patchett, Margaret Sayers Peden, Michael Pettit, Robert Pinsky, Melissa Pritchard, Annie Proulx, Ron Querry, Judy Reeves, Katrina Roberts, Janet Rodney, Pattiann Rogers, Suzanna Ruta, David St. John, Scott Sanders, Bob Shacochis, Julie Shigekuni, John Skoyles, Carol Houck Smith, Gibbs M. Smith, Roberta Smoodin, Marcia Southwick, Kathleen Spivack, Gerald Stern, Robert Stone, Arthur Sze, Elizabeth Tallent, Nathaniel Tarn, James Thomas, Frederick Turner, Leslie Ullman, David Wagoner, Larry Watson, Rob Wilder, Eleanor Wilner, Diane Williams, Kimberly Witherspoon, Charles Wright, Dean Young, Norman Zollinger.
Costs $575+.
Accommodations A special rate is offered at a nearby hotel.
Additional Information Brochure are available online or by e-mail, fax, or phone.

SCENE OF THE CRIME CONFERENCE

Kansas Writers Association, P.O. Box 2236, Wichita KS 67201. (316) 618-0449; (316)208-6961. E-mail: info@kwawriters.org. Web site: www.kwawriters.org/sceneofthecrime.htm. **Contact:** Gordon Kessler. Annual. Annual

conference held in April. Features agent/editor consultations, mixer, banquet and two days of speaker sessions with detectives, government agents, CSI professionals, editors, agents and authors. A full list of each year's speakers is available to see in full on the Web site.
Accommodations Wichita Airport Hilton.

THE SCREENWRITING CONFERENCE IN SANTA FE

P.O. Box 29762, Santa Fe NM 87592. (866)424-1501. Fax: (505)424-8207. E-mail: writeon@scsfe.com. Web site: www.scsfe.com. **Contact:** Larry N. Stouffer, founder. Estab. 1999. Annual conference held the week following Memorial Day. Average attendance: 175. The conference is divided into 2 componants: The Screenwriting Symposium, designed to teach the art and craft of screenwriting, and The Hollywood Connection, which speaks to the business aspects of screenwriting. Held at The Lodge in Santa Fe.
Costs $695 for The Screenwriting Symposium; $200 for The Hollywood Connection. Early discounts are available. Includes 9 hours of in-depth classroom instruction, over 2 dozen workshops, panel discussions, a screenplay competition, academy labs for advanced screenwriters, live scene readings, and social events.

SOUTHWEST WRITERS CONFERENCE MINI-CONFERENCE SERIES

3721 Morris St. NE, Suite A, Albuquerque NM 87111. (505)265-9485. E-mail: swwriters@juno.com. Web site: www.southwestwriters.org. Estab. 1983. Annual mini-conferences held throughout the year. Average attendance: 50. Speakers include writers, editors, agents, publicists, and producers. All areas of writing, including screenwriting and poetry, are represented.
Costs Fee includes conference sessions and lunch.
Accommodations Usually have official airline and hotel discount rates.
Additional Information Sponsors a contest judged by authors, editors from major publishers, and agents from New York, Los Angeles, etc. There are 19 categories. Deadline: May 1. Entry fee is $29/members; $44/nonmembers. There are monthly contests with various themes—$5/member, $10/non-member. See Web site for details. Brochures/guidelines are available online or for a SASE. Inquire via e-mail or phone. A one-on-one appointment may be set up at the conference with the editor or agent of your choice on a first-registered, first-served basis.

STEAMBOAT SPRINGS WRITERS CONFERENCE

Steamboat Springs Arts Council, P.O. Box 774284, Steamboat Springs CO 80477. (970)879-8079. E-mail: sswriters@cs.com. Web site: www.steamboatwriters.com. **Contact:** Harriet Freiberger, director. Estab. 1982. Annual conference held in mid-July. Conference duration: 1 day. Average attendance: approximately 35. Attendance is limited. Featured areas of instruction change each year. Held at the restored train depot. Speakers have included Carl Brandt, Jim Fergus, Avi, Robert Greer, Renate Wood, Connie Willis, Margaret Coel and Kent Nelson.
Costs $45 prior to June 1; $55 after June 1 (includes seminars, catered lunch). A post-conference dinner is also available.
Additional Information Brochures are available in April for a SASE. Send inquiries via e-mail.

TAOS SUMMER WRITERS' CONFERENCE

Department of English Language and Literature, MSC 03 2170, University of New Mexico, Albuquerque NM 87131-0001. (505)277-5572. Fax: (505)277-2950. E-mail: taosconf@unm.edu. Web site: www.unm.edu/~taosconf. **Contact:** Sharon Oard Warner, Barbara van Buskirk. Estab. 1999. Annual conference held in July. Conference duration: 9 days. Offers workshops in novel writing, short story writing, screenwriting, poetry, creative nonfiction, travel writing, historical fiction, memoir, and revision. Participants may also schedule a consultation with a visiting agent/editor.
Costs $300/weekend; $600/week; discounted tuition rate of $250/weekend workshop with weeklong workshop or master class registration.
Accommodations $60-100/night at the Sagebrush Inn; $89/night at Comfort Suites.

WRITING FOR THE SOUL

At the Broadmoor Hotel in Colorado Springs, Jerry B. Jenkins Christian Writers Guild, 5525 N. Union Blvd., Suite 200, Colorado Springs CO 80918. (866)495-5177. Fax: (719)495-5181. E-mail: paul@christianwritersguild.com. Web site: www.christianwritersguild.com/conferences. **Contact:** Paul Finch, admissions manager. Annual conference held in late January and/or early February. Workshops and continuing classes cover fiction, nonfiction, magazine writing, children's books, and teen writing. Appointments with more than 30 agents, publishers, and editors are also available. The keynote speakers are Lee Strobel, Dallas Jenkins, and Richard Lederer. The conference is hosted and emcee'd by Jerry B. Jenkins.
Costs $635/guild members; $795/nonmembers.
Accommodations $150/night at the Broadmoor Hotel in Colorado Springs.

WEST (AZ, CA, HI, NV, UT)

BIG SUR WRITING WORKSHOPS
Henry Miller Library, Highway One, Big Sur CA 93920. Phone/Fax: (831)667-2574. E-mail: magnus@henrymille r.org. Web site: www.henrymiller.org/CWW. **Contact:** Magnus Toren, executive director. Annual workshops held in December for children's/young adult writing and in March for adult fiction and nonfiction.
Accommodations Big Sur Lodge in Pfeiffer State Park.

◎ BYU WRITING AND ILLUSTRATING FOR YOUNG READERS WORKSHOP
348 HCEB, Brigham Young University, Provo UT 84602. (801)422-2568. E-mail: cw348@byu.edu. Web site: wfyr.byu.edu. Estab. 2000. Annual workshop held in June. 2008 dates: June 16-20. Conference duration: 5 days. Average attendance: 100. Learn how to write/illustrate and publish in the children's and young adult fiction and nonfiction markets. Beginning and advanced writers/illustrators are tutored in a small-group setting by published authors/artists and receive instruction from editors, a major publishing house representative and a literary agent. Held at Brigham Young University's Harmon Conference Center. Speakers have included Edward Necarsulmer, Tracy Gates, and Jill Davis.
Costs Costs available online.
Accommodations A block of rooms is reserved at the Super 8 Motel for around $49/night. Airport shuttles are available.
Additional Information Guidelines and registration are on the Web site.

◎ DESERT DREAMS
Phoenix Desert Rose Chapter No. 60, PO Box 27407, Tempe AZ 85285. (866)267-2249. E-mail: info@desertroser wa.org; desertdreams@desertroserwa.org. Web site: desertroserwa.org. **Contact:** Susan Lanier-Graham, conference coordinator. Estab. 1986. Conference held every other April. Conference duration: 3 days. Average attendance: 250. Covers marketing, fiction, screenwriting, and research. Upcoming speakers and agents will include Jessica Faust (BookEnds), Deirdre Knight (The Knight Agency), other agents, editors, Vicki Lewis Thompson, Lori Wilde, Mary Jo Putney, Sherrilyn Kenyon and more. Agents and editors will be speaking and available for meetings with attendees.
Costs $218+ (includes meals, seminars, appointments with agents/editors).
Accommodations Discounted rates for attendees is negotiated at the Crowne Plaza San Marcos Resort in Chandler, Ariz.
Additional Information Send inquiries via e-mail. Visit Web site for updates and complete details.

EAST OF EDEN WRITERS CONFERENCE
P.O. Box 3254, Santa Clara CA 95055. E-mail: vp@southbaywriters.com; pres@southbaywriters.com. Web site: www.southbaywriters.com. **Contact:** Vice President/Programs Chair of South Bay Writers. Estab. 2000. Biannual confereence held in September. 2008 dates: Sepy. 5-7. Average attendance: 300. Writers of all levels are welcome. Pitch sessions to agents and publishers are available, as are meetings with authors and editors. Workshops address the craft and the business of writing. Location: Salinas, Calif.—Steinbeck Country.
Costs Costs vary. The full conference (Friday and Saturday) is approximately $250; Saturday only is approximately $175. The fee includes meals, workshops and pitch/meeting sessions. Optional events extra.
Accommodations Negotiated rates at local hotels—$85 per night, give or take.
Additional Information The East of Eden conference is run by writers/volunteers from the California Writers Club, South Bay Branch. For details about our next conference(s), please visit our Web site or send an SASE.

LA JOLLA WRITERS CONFERENCE
P.O. Box 178122, San Diego CA 92177. (858)467-1978. Fax: (858)467-1971. E-mail: jkuritz@san.rr.com. Web site: www.lajollawritersconference.com. **Contact:** Jared Kuritz, co-director. Estab. 2001. Annual conference held in October. Conference duration: 3 days. Average attendance: 200. "In addition to covering nearly every genre, we also take particular pride in educating our attendees on the business aspect of the book industry by having agents, editors, publishers, publicists, and distributors teach classes. Our conference offers 2 types of classes: lecture sessions that run for 50 minutes, and workshops that run for 110 minutes. Each block period is dedicated to either workshop or lecture-style classes. During each block period, there will be 6-8 classes on various topics from which you can choose to attend. For most workshop classes, you are encouraged to bring written work for review." Literary agents from The Andrea Brown Literary Agency, The Dijkstra Agency, The McBride Agency and Full Circle Literary Group have participated in the past.
Costs Costs are available online.
Accommodations "We arrange a discounted rate with the hotel that hosts the conference. Please refer to the Web site."

Additional Information "Our conference is completely non-commercial. Our goal is to foster a true learning environment. As such, our faculty is chosen based on their expertise and willingness to make themselves completely available to the attendees." Brochures are online; send inquiries via e-mail or fax.

LAS VEGAS WRITERS CONFERENCE

Henderson Writers Group, 614 Mosswood Drive, Henderson NV 89015. (702)564-2488. E-mail: info@lasvegaswritersconference.com. Web site: www.lasvegaswritersconference.com/. **Contact:** Jo Wilkens, president. Annual. Annual conference just outside of Las Vegas. 2008 dates: April 17-19. Conference duration: 3 days. Average attendance: 140. "Join writing professionals, agents, industry experts and your colleagues for four days in Las Vegas, NV, as they share their knowledge on all aspects of the writer's craft. One of the great charms of the Las Vegas Writer's Conference is its intimacy. Registration is limited to 140 attendees so there's always plenty of one-on-one time with the faculty. While there are formal pitch sessions, panels, workshops, and seminars, the faculty is also available throughout the conference for informal discussions and advice. Plus, you're bound to meet a few new friends, too. Workshops, seminars and expert panels will take you through writing in many genres including fiction, creative nonfiction, screenwriting, poetry, journalism and business and technical writing. There will be many Q&A panels for you to ask the experts all your questions."
Accommodations Sam's Town Hotel and Gambling Hall.

MAUI WRITERS CONFERENCE

P.O. Box 1118, Kihei HI 96753. (808)879-0061. Fax: (808)879-6233. E-mail: writers@mauiwriters.com. Web site: www.mauiwriters.com. **Contact:** Shannon Tullius. Estab. 1993. Annual. Annual conference held at the end of August (Labor Day weekend). 2008 dates: Aug. 29—Sept. 1. Conference duration: 4 days. Average attendance: 600. Covers fiction, nonfiction, poetry, screenwriting, children's/young adult writing, horror, mystery, romance, science fiction, and journalism. Though previously held in Maui, the conference moved to Honolulu in 2008. Speakers have included Kimberley Cameron (Reece Halsey North), Susan Crawford (Crawford Literary Agency), Jillian Manus (Manus & Associates), Jenny Bent (Trident Media Group), Catherine Fowler (Redwood Agency), James D. Hornfischer (Hornfischer Literary Management), and Debra Goldstein (The Creative Culture). Many of these agents will be at the 2007 conference, where they will be on panels discussing the business of publishing and will be available for one-on-one consultations with aspiring authors.
Costs $600-1,000. See the Web site for full information.
Additional Information "We offer a comprehensive view of the business of publishing, with more than 1,500 consultation slots with industry agents, editors, and screenwriting professionals, as well as workshops and sessions covering writing instruction. Consider attending the MWC Writers Retreat immediately preceding the conference. Write, call, or visit our Web site for current updates and full details on all of our upcoming programs."

MENDOCINO COAST WRITERS CONFERENCE

1211 Del Mar Dr., Fort Bragg CA 95437. (707)962-2600, ext. 2167. E-mail: info@mcwc.org. Web site: www.mcwc.org. **Contact:** Barbara Lee, registrar. Estab. 1988. Annual conference held in August. 2008 dates: July 31—Aug. 3. Conference duration: 3 days. Average attendance: 90. Provides workshops for fiction, nonfiction, scriptwriting, children's, mystery, and writing for social change. Held at a small community college campus on the northern Pacific Coast. Speakers have included Jandy Nelson, Paul Levine, Sally Werner, John Lescroart, and Maxine Schur. Agents will be speaking and available for meetings with attendees.
Costs $400 + (includes panels, meals, 2 socials with guest readers, 1 public event, 1 day intensive in 1 subject and 2 days of seveal short sessions).
Accommodations Information on overnight accommodations and shared rides fromt he San Francisco Airport is made available.
Additional Information Emphasis is on writers who are also good teachers. Brochures are online or available with a SASE after January. Send inquiries via e-mail.

MOUNT HERMON CHRISTIAN WRITERS CONFERENCE

37 Conference Drive, Mount Hermon CA 95041. E-mail: info@mounthermon.org. Web site: www.mounthermon.org/writers. **Contact:** Conference director. Estab. 1970. Annual conference held in the spring. 2008 dates were March 14-16, 2008. Average attendance: 450. "We are a broad-ranging conference for all areas of Christian writing, including fiction, children's, poetry, nonfiction, magazines, books, inspirational and devotional writing, educational curriculum and radio and TV scriptwriting. This is a working, how-to conference, with many workshops within the conference involving on-site writing assignments. The conference is sponsored by and held at the 440-acre Mount Hermon Christian Conference Center near San Jose, California, in the heart of the coastal redwoods. The faculty-to-student ratio is about 1 to 6. The bulk of our more than 60 faculty members are editors and publisher representatives from major Christian publishing houses nationwide." Speakers have

included Janet Kobobel Grant, Chip MacGregor, Karen Solem, T. Davis Bunn, Sally Suart, Debbie Macomber, Jerry Jenkins and others.

Accommodations Registrants stay in hotel-style accommodations. Meals are taken family style, with faculty joining registrants.

Additional Information "The residential nature of our conference makes this a unique setting for one-on-one interaction with faculty/staff. There is also a decided inspirational flavor to the conference, and general sessions with well-known speakers are a highlight." Registrants may submit 2 works for critique in advance of the conference, then have personal interviews with critiquers during the conference. Brochures/guidelines are available December 1. All conference information is now online only. Send inquireies via e-mail or fax. Tapes of past conferences are also available.

NATJA ANNUAL CONFERENCE & MARKETPLACE

North American Travel Journalists Association, 531 Main St., #902, El Segundo CA 90245. (310)836-8712. Fax: (310)836-8769. E-mail: chelsea@natja.org; elizabeth@natja.org. Web site: www.natja.org/conference. **Contact:** Elizabeth H. Beshear, executive director. Estab. 2003. Annual. Annual conference held in May or June. 2008 dates: June 24-27 in Oklahoma City. Conference duration: 3 days. Average attendance: 250. Provides professional development for travel journalists and gives them the chance to market themselves to destinations and cultivate relationships to further their careers. Previous speakers have included Lisa Lenoir (*Chicago Sun-Times*), Steve Millburg (*Coastal Living*) and Peter Yesawich. The dates and location of this event changes each year, so checking the Web site is the best way to go.

Costs $350+ for media attendees (includes hotel accommodations, meals, in-conference transportation); $100 extra for round-trip airline tickets.

Accommodations Different destinations host the conference each year, all at hotels with conference centers.

Additional Information E-mail, call, or go online for more information.

NO CRIME UNPUBLISHED™ MYSTERY WRITERS' CONFERENCE

E-mail: sistersincrimela@yahoo.com. Web site: www.sistersincrimela.com. Estab. 1995. Annual conference held in June. Next conference June 2009. Conference duration: 1 day. Average attendance: 150. Conference on mystery and crime writing. Offers craft and forensic sessions, a keynote speaker, a luncheon speaker, author and agent panels, and book signings.

Additional Information Conference information is available on the Web site.

🄽 NORTHERN COLORADO WRITERS CONFERENCE

2107 Thunderstone Court, Fort Collins CO 80525. (970)282-7754. E-mail: kerrie@ncwc.biz. Web site: www.ncwc.biz/. **Contact:** Kerrie Flanagan. Estab. 2006. Annual. Annual conference held in the spring in Colorado. Conference duration: 3 days. The conference features a variety of speakers, agents and editors. There are workshops and presentations on fiction, nonfiction, screenwriting, staying inspired, and more. Previous agents who have attended and taken pitches from writers include Jessica Regel, Kristen Nelson and Rachelle Gardner. Each conference features more than 30 workshops from which to choose from.

Costs $200-300, depending on what package the attendee selects.

Accommodations The conference is hosted at the Fort Collins Hilton, where rooms are available at a special rate.

SAN DIEGO STATE UNIVERSITY WRITERS' CONFERENCE

SDSU College of Extended Studies, 5250 Campanile Dr., San Diego State University, San Diego CA 92182-1920. (619)594-2517. Fax: (619)594-8566. E-mail: jgreene@mail.sdsu.edu; rbrown2@mail.sdsu.edu. Web site: www.ces.sdsu.edu/writers. **Contact:** Jim Greene, program coordinator. Estab. 1984. Annual conference held in January/February. 2009 dates: Feb. 6-8. Conference duration: 2 days. Average attendance: 375. Covers fiction, nonfiction, scriptwriting and e-books. Held at the Doubletree Hotel in Mission Valley. Each year the conference offers a variety of workshops for the beginner and advanced writers. This conference allows the individual writer to choose which workshop best suits his/her needs. In addition to the workshops, editor reading appointments and agent/editor consultation appointments are provided so attendees may meet with editors and agents one-on-one to discuss specific questions. A reception is offered Saturday immediately following the workshops, offering attendees the opportunity to socialize with the faculty in a relaxed atmosphere. Last year, approximately 60 faculty members attended.

Costs Approximately $365-485 (2009 costs will be published with a fall update of the Web site).

Accommodations Doubletree Hotel (800)222-TREE. Attendees must make their own travel arrangements.

SAN FRANCISCO WRITERS CONFERENCE

1029 Jones St., San Francisco CA 94109. (415)673-0939. Fax: (415)673-0367. E-mail: sfwriterscon@aol.com. Web site: www.sfwriters.org. **Contact:** Michael Larsen, director. Estab. 2003. Annual conference held President's Day weekend in February. Average attendance: 400+. Top authors, respected literary agents, and major publishing houses are at the event so attendees can make face-to-face contact with all the right people. Writers of nonfiction, fiction, poetry, and specialty writing (children's books, cookbooks, travel, etc.) will all benefit from the event. There are important sessions on marketing, self-publishing, and trends in the publishing industry. Plus, there's an optional 3-hour session called Speed Dating for Agents where attendees can meet with 20+ agents. Speakers have included Gayle Lynds, Jennifer Crusie, Alan Jones, Lalita Tademy, Jamie Raab, Mary Roach, Bob Mayer, Firoozeh Dumas, Zilpha Keatley Snyder. More than 20 agents and editors participate each year, many of whom will be available for meetings with attendees.

Costs $600+ with price breaks for early registration (includes all sessions/workshops/keynotes, Speed Dating with Editors, opening gala at the Top of the Mark, 2 continental breakfasts, 2 lunches). Optional Speed Dating for Agents is $45.

Accommodations The Intercontinental Mark Hopkins Hotel is a historic landmark at the top of Nob Hill in San Francisco. Elegant rooms and first-class service are offered to attendees at the rate of $152/night. The hotel is located so that everyone arriving at the Oakland or San Francisco airport can take BART to either the Embarcadero or Powell Street exits, then walk or take a cable car or taxi directly to the hotel.

Additional Information Present yourself in a professional manner and the contact you will make will be invaluable to your writing career. Brochures and registration are online.

SANTA BARBARA WRITERS CONFERENCE

P.O. Box 6627, Santa Barbara CA 93160. (805)964-0367. E-mail: info@sbwritersconference.com. Web site: www.sbwritersconference.com. **Contact:** Marcia Meier, conference diretor. Estab. 1973. Annual conference held in June. Average attendance: 450. Covers poetry, fiction, nonfiction, journalism, playwriting, screenwriting, travel writing, young adult, children's literature, chick lit, humor, and marketing. Speakers have included Kenneth Atchity, Michael Larsen, Elizabeth Pomada, Bonnie Nadell, Stuart Miller, Angela Rinaldi, Katherine Sands, Don Congdon, Mike Hamilburg, Sandra Dijkstra, Paul Fedorko, Andrea Brown and Deborah Grosvenor. Agents appear on a panel, plus there will be an agents and editors day when writers can pitch their projects in one-on-one meetings.

Accommodations Fess Parker's Doubletree Resort.

Additional Information Individual critiques are also available. Submit 1 ms of no more than 3,000 words in advance (include SASE). Competitions with awards are sponsored as part of the conference. E-mail or call for brochure and registration forms.

⊚ SOCIETY OF CHILDREN'S BOOK WRITERS & ILLUSTRATORS ANNUAL SUMMER CONFERENCE ON WRITING AND ILLUSTRATING FOR CHILDREN

8271 Beverly Blvd., Los Angeles CA 90048-4515. (323)782-1010. Fax: (323)782-1892. E-mail: scbwi@scbwi.org. Web site: www.scbwi.org. **Contact:** Stephen Mooser, president. Estab. 1972. Annual conference held in early August. Conference duration: 4 days. Average attendance: 1,000. Held at the Century Plaza Hotel in Los Angeles. Speakers have included Andrea Brown, Steven Malk, Scott Treimel, Ashley Bryan, Bruce Coville, Karen Hesse, Harry Mazer, Lucia Monfried, and Russell Freedman. Agents will be speaking and sometimes participate in ms critiques.

Costs Approximately $400 (does not include hotel room).

Accommodations Information on overnight accommodations is made available.

Additional Information Ms and illustration critiques are available. Brochure/guidelines are available in June online or for SASE.

SQUAW VALLEY COMMUNITY OF WRITERS WORKSHOP

P.O. Box 1416, Nevada City CA 95959-1416. (530)470-8440. E-mail: info@squawvalleywriters.org. Web site: www.squawvalleywriters.org/writers_ws.htm. **Contact:** Ms. Brett Hall Jones, executive director. Estab. 1969. Annual conference held the first full week in August. Conference duration: 1 week. Average attendance: 124. Covers fiction, nonfiction, and memoir. Held in Squaw Valley, California—the site of the 1960 Winter Olympics. The workshops are held in a ski lodge at the foot of this spectacular ski area. Literary agent speakers have recently included Betsy Amster, Julie Barer, Michael Carlisle, Elyse Cheney, Mary Evans, Christy Fletcher, Theresa Park, B.J. Robbins and Peter Steinberg. Agents will be speaking and available for meetings with attendees.

Costs $750 (includes tuition, dinners). Housing is extra.

Accommodations Single room: $550/week; double room: $350/week per person; multiple room: $210/week per person. The airport shuttle is available for an additional cost.

Additional Information Brochures are available online or for a SASE in March. Send inquiries via e-mail.

WRANGLING WITH WRITING

Society of Southwestern Authors, P.O. Box 30355, Tucson AZ 85751-0355. (520)546-9382. Fax: (520)751-7877. E-mail: Penny Porter (wporter202@aol.com); Carol Costa (Ccstarlit@aol.com). Web site: www.ssa-az.org/conference.htm. **Contact:** Penny Porter, Carol Costa. Estab. 1972. Annual. Sept. 27-28, 2008. Conference duration: 2 days. Average attendance: 350. Conference offers 36 workshops covering all genres of writing, plus pre-scheduled one-on-one interviews with 30 agents, editors, and publishers representing major book houses and magazines. Speakers have included Ray Bradbury, Clive Cussler, Elmore Leonard, Ben Bova, Sam Swope, Richard Paul Evans, Bruce Holland Rogers and Billy Collins.

Costs 2007 costs were $275/members; $350/nonmembers. Five meals included.

Additional Information Brochures/guidelines are available as of July 15 by e-mail address above.

NORTHWEST (AK, ID, MT, OR, WA, WY)

N ALASKA WRITERS GUILD SPECULATIVE FICTION CONFERENCE

Alaska Writers Guild, 9138 Arlon St., Ste. A-3 Box 910, Anchorage AK 99507. (907)783-0430. E-mail: info@alaskawritersworkshop.com. Web site: www.akwworkshop.alaskawriters.com/. **Contact:** Director. Annual. Oct. 1-5, 2008. Conference duration: 4 days. Agents, editors and professional writers will present on the business and craft of writing for four days. The complete list of each year's faculty is available online. A manuscript critique program is also available.

Costs $375-475.

Accommodations "Coast International Inn, has contracted with us for a great room rate, $59 per night, for the duration of the conference, as well as for four nights previous to, and four nights after, the actual conference. Space is limited, so do not procrastinate! Contact Coast International Inn at (907)243-2233. Ask for the Alaska Writers Guild or utilize our booking number (1435), to receive the discounted rate."

Additional Information Activities include a reception with appetizers will be held the night of arrival. Morning and afternoon sessions will be held the following three days, breakfast and lunch provided. Thursday or Friday evening will be spent in panel discussion with the entire faculty. Saturday night there will be a banquet dinner and awards ceremony for the associated Ralph Williams Memorial Speculative Fiction Short Story Contest winner(s). Sunday morning will include farewell brunch before check-out. During morning and afternoon sessions, one-on-one consultations with faculty will be held by appointment only.

CLARION WEST WRITERS' WORKSHOP

340 15th Ave. E, Suite 350, Seattle WA 98112-5156. (206)322-9083. E-mail: info@clarionwest.org. Web site: www.clarionwest.org. **Contact:** Leslie Howle, executive director. Annual workshop that usually goes from late June through early July. Conference duration: 6 weeks. Average attendance: 18. Conference prepares students for professional careers in science fiction and fantasy writing. Held near the University of Washington. Deadline for applications is March 1. Agents are invited to speak to attendees.

Costs $3,200 (for tuition, housing, most meals). $100 disocunt if application received prior to March 1. Limited scholarships are available based on financial need.

Additional Information This is a critique-based workshop. Students are encouraged to write a story every week; the critique of student material produced at the workshop forms the principal activity of the workshop. Students and instructors critique mss as a group. Students must submit 20-30 pages of ms to qualify for admission. Conference guidelines are available for a SASE. Visit the Web site for updates and complete details.

FLATHEAD RIVER WRITERS CONFERENCE

P.O. Box 7711, Kalispeil MT 59904-7711. E-mail: answers@authorsoftheflathead.org. Web site: www.authorsoftheflathead.org. **Contact:** Val Smith. Estab. 1990. Annual conference held in early mid-October. Conference duration: 3 days. Average attendance: 100. "We provide several small, intense 3-day workshops before the general weekend conference." Workshops, panel discussions, and speakers focus on novels, nonfiction, screenwriting, short stories, magazine articles, and the writing industry. Held at the Grouse Mountain Lodge in Whitefish, Montana. Past speakers have included Sam Pinkus, Randy Wayne White, Donald Maass, Ann Rule, Cricket Pechstein, Marcela Landres, Amy Rennert, Ben Mikaelsen, Esmond Harmsworth, Linda McFall, and Ron Carlson. Agents will be speaking and available for meetings with attendees.

Costs $150 (includes breakfast and lunch, but not lodging).

Accommodations Rooms are available at a discounted rate of $100/night. Whitefish is a resort town, so less expensive lodging can be arranged.

Additional Information "By limiting attendance to 100 people, we assure a quality experience and informal, easy access to the presenters and other attendees." Brochures are available in June; send inquiries via e-mail.

IDAHO WRITERS LEAGUE WRITERS' CONFERENCE

P.O. Box 492, Kootenai, ID 83840. (208)290-8749. E-mail: president@idahowritersleague.com. Web site: www.i dahowritersleague.com/Conference.html. **Contact:** Sherry Ramsey. Estab. 1940. Annual floating conference. Next conference: Sept. 25-27, 2008. Average attendance: 80+. We have such writers as magazine freelance and children's book author, Kelly Milner Halls; and author of the 2006 Christian Women's Fiction Book of the Year, Nikki Arana.

Costs Cost: $125.

Additional Information Check out our Web site at www.idahowritersleague.com. Conference will be held at the Coeur d'Alene Inn in Coeur d'Alene, Idaho.

JACKSON HOLE WRITERS CONFERENCE

PO Box 1974, Jackson WY 83001. (307)413-3332. E-mail: tim@jacksonholewritersconference.com. Web site: jacksonholewritersconference.com/. Estab. 1991. Annual conference held in June. 2008 dates: June 26-29. Conference duration: 4 days. Average attendance: 70. Covers fiction and creative nonfiction and offers ms critiques from authors, agents, and editors. Agents in attendance will take pitches from writers. Paid manuscript critique programs are available.

Costs $360-390.

PNWA SUMMER WRITERS CONFERENCE

PMB 2717, 1420 NW Gilman Blvd., Issaquah WA 98027. (425)673-2665. E-mail: pnwa@pnwa.org. Web site: www.pnwa.org. Estab. 1955. Annual. All conferences are held in July. Conference duration: 4 days. Average attendance: 400. Attendees have the chance to meet agents and editors, learn craft from authors and uncover marketing secrets. Speakers have included J.A. Jance, Sheree Bykofsky, Kimberley Cameron, Jennie Dunham, Donald Maass, and Jandy Nelson.

Costs For cost and additional information, please see the Web site.

Accommodations The conference is held at the Hilton Seattle Airport & Conference Center.

Additional Information PNWA also holds an annual literary contest every February with more than $12,000 in prize money. Finalists' manuscripts are then available to agents and editors at our summer conference. Visit the Web site for further details.

PORT TOWNSEND WRITERS' CONFERENCE

Box 1158, Port Townsend WA 98368. (360)385-3102. Fax: (360)385-2470. E-mail: info@centrum.org. Web site: http://www.centrum.org/writing/. **Contact:** Carla Vander Ven. Estab. 1974. Annual conference held in mid-July. Average attendance: 180. Conference promotes poetry, fiction, and creative nonfiction and features many of the nation's leading writers. All conference housing and activities are located at beautiful Fort Worden State Park, a historic fort overlooking the Strait of Juan de Fuca, with expansive views of the Olympic and Cascade mountain ranges.

Costs $575/critiqued workshops; $495/open enrollment workshops.

Accommodations $190-380. Participants stay in dorms; meals are taken together in the For Worden Commons. Visitors may also choose to stay in one of Port Townsend's rentals, bed and breakfasts, or hotels.

Additional Information The conference focus is on the craft of writing and the writing life, not on marketing. Guidelines/registration are available online or for SASE.

WHIDBEY ISLAND WRITERS' CONFERENCE

Whidbey Island Writers' Association, P.O. Box 1289, Langley WA 98260. (360)331-6714. E-mail: wiwa@whidbe y.com. Web site: www.writeonwhidbey.org. **Contact:** Pam Owen, Director. Annual conference held in March. 2008 dates were Feb. 28 through March 2. Conference duration: 3 days. Average attendance: 250. The 11th annual conference, located near Seattle, combines preconference workshops, signature fireside chats, professional instruction and island hospitality to encourage and inspire writers. Check out this year's upcoming talent on our Web site. Covers fiction, nonfiction, screenwriting, writing for children, poetry, travel, and nature writing. Class sessions include "Dialogue That Delivers" and "Putting the Character Back in Character." Held at a conference hall, with break-out fireside chats held in local homes near the sea. 2008 speakers include Elizabeth George, Maureen Murdock, Steve Berry, M.J. Rose, Katharine Sands, Doris Booth, Eva Shaw, Stephanie Elizondo Griest.

Costs $350+. Volunteer discounts are available; early registration is encouraged.

Additional Information Brochures are available online or for a SASE. Send inquiries via e-mail.

WILLAMETTE WRITERS CONFERENCE

9045 SW Barbur, Suite 5-A, Portland OR 97219. (503)452-1592. Fax: (503)452-0372. E-mail: wilwrite@willamett ewriters.com. Web site: www.willamettewriters.com. **Contact:** Conference director. Estab. 1968. Annual confer-

ence held in August. 2008 dates: Aug. 1-3. Average attendance: 600. "Williamette Writers is open to all writers, and we plan our conference accordingly. We offer workshops on all aspects of fiction, nonfiction, marketing, the creative process, etc. Also, we invite top-notch inspirational speakers for keynote addresses. We always include at least 1 agent or editor panel and offer a variety of topics of interest to screenwriters and fiction and nonfiction writers. Speakers have included Laura Rennert, Kim Cameron, Paul Levine, Angela Rinaldi, Robert Tabian, Joshua Bilmes and Elise Capron. Agents will be speaking and available for meetings with attendees.
Costs Costs available online.
Accommodations If necessary, arrangements can be made on an individual basis. Special rates may be available.
Additional Information Brochure/guidelines are available for a catalog-sized SASE.

WRITE ON THE SOUND WRITERS' CONFERENCE

Edmonds Arts Commission, 700 Main St., Edmonds WA 98020. (425)771-0228. Fax: (425)771-0253. E-mail: wots@ci.edmonds.wa.us. Web site: www.ci.edmonds.wa.us/ArtsCommission/wots.stm. **Contact:** Conference Coordinator. Estab. 1985. Annual conference held in October. Conference duration: 2.5 days. Average attendance: 200. Features over 30 presenters, a literary contest, ms critiques, a reception and book signing, onsite bookstore, and a variety of evening activities. Held at the Frances Anderson Center in Edmonds, just north of Seattle on the Puget Sound. Speakers have included Elizabeth George, Dan Hurley, Marcia Woodard, Holly Hughes, Greg Bear, Timothy Egan, Joe McHugh, Frances Wood, Garth Stein and Max Grover.
Costs $108 before September 19; $130 after September 19; $68/day; $25/ms critiques.
Additional Information Brochures are available Aug. 1. Accepts inquiries via phone, e-mail and fax.

CANADA

📇 BLOODY WORDS

64 Shaver Ave., Toronto ON M9B 3T5, Canada. E-mail: chair2008@bloodywords.com; info@bloodywords.com; registrar@bloodywords.com. Web site: www.bloodywords.com. **Contact:** Caro Soles. Estab. 1999. Annual conference held in June. 2008 dates: June 6-8. Conference duration: 3 days. Average attendance: 250. Focuses on mystery fiction and aims to provide a showcase for Canadian mystery writers and readers, as well as provide writing information to aspiring writers. "We will present 3 tracks of programming: Just the Facts, where everyone from coroners to toxicologists to tactical police units present how things are done in the real works; and What's the Story—where panelists discuss subjects of interest to readers; and the Mystery Cafe, where 12 authors read and discuss their work."
Costs $175 + (Canadian).
Accommodations A special rate will be available at The Downtown Marriott Hotel in Toronto, Ontario.
Additional Information Registration is available online. Send inquiries via e-mail.

📇 FESTIVAL OF WORDS

217 Main St. N., Moose Jaw SK S6J 0W1, Canada. (306)691-0557. Fax: (306)693-2994. E-mail: word.festival@sasktel.net. Web site: www.festivalofwords.com. **Contact:** Donna Lee Howes. Estab. 1997. Annual festival held in July. 2008 dates: July 17-20. Conference duration: 4 days. Average attendance: 1,500.
Accommodations A list of motels, hotels, campgrounds, and bed and breakfasts is provided upon request.
Additional Information "Our festival is an ideal place for people who love words to mingle, promote their books, and meet their fans." Brochures are available; send inquiries via e-mail or fax.

📇 SURREY INERNATIONAL WRITERS' CONFERENCE

10707 146th St., Surrey BC V3R 1T5, Canada. (640)589-2221. Fax: (604)589-9286. Web site: www.siwc.ca. **Contact:** Lisa Mason. Estab. 1992. Annual conference held in October. 2008 dates: Oct. 24-26. Conference duration: 3 days. Average attendance: 600. Conference for fiction, nonfiction, scriptwriting, and poetry. Held at the Sheraton Guildford Hotel. Speakers have included Donald Maass, Meredith Bernstein, Charlotte Gusay, Denise Marcil, Anne Sheldon, and Michael Vidor. Agents will be speaking and available for one-on-one meetings with attendees.
Costs Approximately $450. See Web site for full cost information and list of upcoming speakers for the next year.
Accommodations Attendees must make their own hotel and transportation arrangements.

INTERNATIONAL

🌐 AUSTRALIAN PUBLISHERS AND AUTHORS BOOKSHOW

NSW Writers' Centre, P.O. Box 1056, Rozelle Hospital Grounds, Balmain Road, Rozelle NSW 2039, Australia. (61)(2)9555-9757. Fax: (61)(2)9818-1327. E-mail: nswwc@nswwriterscentre.org.au. Web site: www.nswwriter

scentre.org.au. **Contact:** Irina Dunn, executive director. Annual event held the third week in November. Books and magazines from independent, Australian-owned publishing companies, distributors, small presses, niche publishers, self-publishers, and print-on-demand publishers will be showcased. Writers, librarians, booksellers, and members of the public and literary organizations are invited to attend to see what local publishers are doing. Books will also be available for purchase.

Additional Information See the Web site for a complete list concerning program of festivals. There are multiple events with this organization each year. Topics covered during the year include writing novels, short stories, poetry, plays.

BYRON BAY WRITERS FESTIVAL

Northern Rivers Writers' Centre, P.O. Box 1846, 69 Johnson St., Byron Bay NSW 2481, Australia. 040755-2441. E-mail: jeni@nrwc.org.au. Web site: www.byronbaywritersfestival.com. **Contact:** Director. Estab. 1996. Annual festival held the first weekend in August at Becton's Byron Bay Beach Resort. Conference duration: 3 days. Celebrate and reflect with over 100 of the finest writers from Australia and overseas. Workshops, panel discussions, and poetry readings will also be offered.

Costs Early bird: $145/nonmembers; $125/NRWC members and students.

GENEVA WRITERS CONFERENCE

Geneva Writers Group, Switzerland. E-mail: info@GenevaWritersGroup.org. Web site: www.genevawritersgroup.org/conference.html. Estab. 2002. Annual. Conference held in Geneva, Switzerland. The 2008 conference was held at Webster University. Conference duration: 2 days. Past speakers and presenters have included Thomas E. Kennedy, Nahid Rachlin, Jeremy Sheldon, Kwame Kwei Armah, Philip Graham, Mimi Schwartz, Susan Tiberghien, Jo Shapcott, Wallis Wilde Menozzi, David Applefield, Laura Longrigg, Bill Newlin, Zeki Ergas, D-L Nelson, Sylvia Petter, Alistair Scott.

Conferences

Glossary

#10 Envelope. A standard, business-size envelope.

Acquisitions Editor. The person responsible for originating and/or acquiring new publishing projects.

Adaptation. The process of rewriting a composition (novel, story, film, article, play) into a form suitable for some other medium, such as TV or the stage.

Advance. Money a publisher pays a writer prior to book publication, usually paid in installments, such as one-half upon signing the contract and one-half upon delivery of the complete, satisfactory manuscript. An advance is paid against the royalty money to be earned by the book. Agents take their percentage off the top of the advance as well as from the royalties earned.

Adventure. A genre of fiction in which action is the key element, overshadowing characters, theme and setting.

Auction. Publishers sometimes bid for the acquisition of a book manuscript with excellent sales prospects. The bids are for the amount of the author's advance, guaranteed dollar amounts, advertising and promotional expenses, royalty percentage, etc. Auctions are conducted by agents.

Author's Copies. An author usually receives about 10 free copies of his hardcover book from the publisher; more from a paperback firm. He can obtain additional copies at a price that has been reduced by an author's discount (usually 40 percent of the retail price).

Autobiography. A book-length account of a person's entire life written by the subject himself.

Backlist. A publisher's list of books that were not published during the current season, but that are still in print.

Backstory. The history of what has happened before the action in your script takes place, affecting a character's current behavior.

Bible. The collected background information on all characters and story lines of all existing episodes, as well as projections of future plots.

Bio. A sentence or brief paragraph about the writer; includes work and educational experience.

Blurb. The copy on paperback book covers or hardcover book dust jackets, either promoting the book and the author or featuring testimonials from book reviewers or well-known people in the book's field. Also called flap copy or jacket copy.

Boilerplate. A standardized publishing contract. Most authors and agents make many changes on the boilerplate before accepting the contract.

Book Doctor. A freelance editor hired by a writer, agent or book editor who analyzes problems that exist in a book manuscript or proposal and offers solutions to those problems.

Book Packager. Someone who draws elements of a book together—from the initial concept to writing and marketing strategies—and then sells the book package to a book publisher and/or movie producer. Also known as book producer or book developer.

Bound Galleys. A prepublication—often paperbound—edition of a book, usually prepared from photocopies of the final galley proofs. Designed for promotional purposes, bound galleys serve as the first set of review copies to be mailed out. Also called bound proofs.

Category Fiction. A term used to include all types of fiction. See *genre*.

Clips. Samples, usually from newspapers or magazines, of your published work. Also called tearsheets.

Commercial Fiction. Novels designed to appeal to a broad audience. These are often broken down into categories such as western, mystery and romance. See *genre*.

Concept. A statement that summarizes a screenplay or teleplay—before the outline or treatment is written.

Confession. A first-person story in which the narrator is involved in an emotional situation that encourages sympathetic reader identification, concluding with the affirmation of a morally acceptable theme.

Contributor's Copies. Copies of the book sent to the author. The number of contributor's copies is often negotiated in the publishing contract.

Co-Publishing. Arrangement where author and publisher share publication costs and profits of a book. Also called co-operative publishing.

Copyediting. Editing of a manuscript for writing style, grammar, punctuation and factual accuracy.

Copyright. A means to protect an author's work.

Cover Letter. A brief letter that accompanies the manuscript being sent to an agent or publisher.

Coverage. A brief synopsis and analysis of a script provided by a reader to a buyer considering purchasing the work.

Creative Nonfiction. Type of writing where true stories are told by employing the techniques usually reserved for novelists and poets, such as scenes, dialogue and detailed descriptions. Also called literary journalism.

Critiquing Service. An editing service offered by some agents in which writers pay a fee for comments on the salability or other qualities of their manuscript. Sometimes the critique includes suggestions on how to improve the work. Fees vary, as does the quality of the critique.

Curriculum Vitae (CV). Short account of one's career or qualifications.

D Person. Development person; includes readers, story editors and creative executives who work in development and acquisition of properties for TV and film.

Deal Memo. The memorandum of agreement between a publisher and author that precedes the actual contract and includes important issues such as royalty, advance, rights, distribution and option clauses.

Development. The process in which writers present ideas to producers who oversee the developing script through various stages to finished product.

Division. An unincorporated branch of a company.

Docudrama. A fictional film rendition of recent news-making events or people.

Electronic Rights. Secondary or subsidiary rights dealing with electronic/multimedia formats (the Internet, CD-ROMs, electronic magazines).

Elements. Actors, directors and producers attached to a project to make an attractive package.

El-Hi. Elementary to high school. A term used to indicate reading or interest level.

Episodic Drama. An hour-long, continuing TV show, often shown at 10 p.m.

Erotica. A form of literature or film dealing with the sexual aspects of love. Erotic content ranges from subtle sexual innuendo to explicit descriptions of sexual acts

Ethnic. Stories and novels whose central characters are African American, Native American, Italian American, Jewish, Appalachian or members of some other specific cultural group. Ethnic fiction usually deals with a protagonist caught between two conflicting ways of life: mainstream American culture and his ethnic heritage.

Evaluation Fees. Fees an agent may charge to evaluate material. The extent and quality of this evaluation varies, but comments usually concern the salability of the manuscript.

Exclusive. Offering a manuscript, usually for a set period of time, to just one agent and guaranteeing that agent is the only one looking at the manuscript.

Experimental. Type of fiction that focuses on style, structure, narrative technique, setting and strong characterization rather than plot. This form depends largely on the revelation of a character's inner being, which elicits an emotional response from the reader.

Family Saga. A story that chronicles the lives of a family or a number of related or interconnected families over a period of time.

Fantasy. Stories set in fanciful, invented worlds or in a legendary, mythic past that rely on outright invention or magic for conflict and setting.

Film Rights. May be sold or optioned by the agent/author to a person in the film industry, enabling the book to be made into a movie.

Floor Bid. If a publisher is very interested in a manuscript, he may offer to enter a floor bid when the book goes to auction. The publisher sits out of the auction, but agrees to take the book by topping the highest bid by an agreed-upon percentage (usually 10 percent).

Foreign Rights. Translation or reprint rights to be sold abroad.

Foreign Rights Agent. An agent who handles selling the rights to a country other than that of the first book agent. Usually an additional percentage (about 5 percent) will be added on to the first book agent's commission to cover the foreign rights agent.

Genre. Refers to either a general classification of writing, such as a novel, poem or short story, or to the categories within those classifications, such as problem novels or sonnets. Genre fiction is a term that covers various types of commercial novels, such as mystery, romance, Western, science fiction and horror.

Ghostwriting. A writer puts into literary form the words, ideas, or knowledge of another person under that person's name. Some agents offer this service; others pair ghostwriters with celebrities or experts.

Gothic. Novels characterized by historical settings and featuring young, beautiful women who win the favor of handsome, brooding heroes while simultaneously dealing with some life-threatening menace—either natural or supernatural.

Graphic Novel. Contains comic-like drawings and captions, but deals more with everyday events and issues than with superheroes.

High Concept. A story idea easily expressed in a quick, one-line description.

Hi-Lo. A type of fiction that offers a high level of interest for readers at a low reading level.

Historical. A story set in a recognizable period of history. In addition to telling the stories of ordinary people's lives, historical fiction may involve political or social events of the time.

Hook. Aspect of the work that sets it apart from others and draws in the reader/viewer.

Horror. A story that aims to evoke some combination of fear, fascination and revulsion in its readers—either through supernatural or psychological circumstances.

How-To. A book that offers the reader a description of how something can be accomplished. It includes both information and advice.

Imprint. The name applied to a publisher's specific line of books.

Independent Producers. Self-employed entrepreneurs who assemble scripts, actors, directors and financing for their film concepts.

IRC. International Reply Coupon. Buy at a post office to enclose with material sent outside the country to cover the cost of return postage. The recipient turns them in for stamps in their own country.

Joint Contract. A legal agreement between a publisher and two or more authors that establishes provisions for the division of royalties the book generates.

Juvenile. Category of children's writing that can be broken down into easy-to-read books (ages 7-9), which run 2,000-10,000 words, and middle-grade books (ages 8-12), which run 20,000-40,000 words.

Literary. A book where style and technique are often as important as subject matter. Also called serious fiction.

Logline. A one-line description of a plot as it might appear in *TV Guide*.

Mainstream Fiction. Fiction on subjects or trends that transcend popular novel categories like mystery or romance. Using conventional methods, this kind of fiction tells stories about people and their conflicts.

Marketing Fee. Fee charged by some agents to cover marketing expenses. It may be used to cover postage, telephone calls, faxes, photocopying or any other expense incurred in marketing a manuscript.

Mass Market Paperbacks. Softcover books, usually 4×7, on a popular subject directed at a general audience and sold in groceries, drugstores and bookstores.

Memoir. An author's commentary on the personalities and events that have significantly influenced one phase of his life.

MFTS. Made for TV series.

Midlist. Those titles on a publisher's list expected to have limited sales. Midlist books are mainstream, not literary, scholarly or genre, and are usually written by new or relatively unknown writers.

Miniseries. A limited dramatic series written for television, often based on a popular novel.

MOW. Movie of the week. A movie script written especially for television, usually seven acts with time for commercial breaks. Topics are often contemporary, sometimes controversial, fictional accounts. Also called a made-for-TV movie.

Multiple Contract. Book contract with an agreement for a future book(s).

Mystery. A form of narration in which one or more elements remain unknown or unexplained until the end of the story. Subgenres include: amateur sleuth, caper, cozy, heist, malice domestic, police procedural, etc.

Net Receipts. One method of royalty payment based on the amount of money a book publisher receives on the sale of the book after the booksellers' discounts, special sales discounts and returned copies.

Novelization. A novel created from the script of a popular movie and published in paperback. Also called a movie tie-in.

Novella. A short novel or long short story, usually 25,000-50,000 words. Also called a novelette.

Occult. Supernatural phenomena, including ghosts, ESP, astrology, demoniact possession and witchcraft.

One-Time Rights. This right allows a short story or portions of a fiction or nonfiction book to be published again without violating the contract.

Option. Instead of buying a movie script outright, a producer buys the right to a script for a short period of time (usually six months to one year) for a small down payment. If the movie has not begun production and the producer does not wish to purchase the script at the end of the agreed time period, the rights revert back to the scriptwriter. Also called a script option.

Option Clause. A contract clause giving a publisher the right to publish an author's next book.

Outline. A summary of a book's content (up to 15 double-spaced pages); often in the form

Resources

of chapter headings with a descriptive sentence or two under each one to show the scope of the book. A script's outline is a scene-by-scene narrative description of the story (10-15 pages for a ½-hour teleplay; 15-25 pages for 1-hour; 25-40 pages for 90 minutes; 40-60 pages for a 2-hour feature film or teleplay).

Picture Book. A type of book aimed at ages 2-9 that tells the story partially or entierly with artwork, with up to 1,000 words. Agents interested in selling to publishers of these books often handle both artists and writers.

Pitch. The process where a writer meets with a producer and briefly outlines ideas that could be developed if the writer is hired to write a script for the project.

Platform. A writer's speaking experience, interview skills, Web site and other abilities which help form a following of potential buyers for his book.

Proofreading. Close reading and correction of a manuscript's typographical errors.

Property. Books or scripts forming the basis for a movie or TV project.

Proposal. An offer to an editor or publisher to write a specific work, usually a package consisting of an outline and sample chapters.

Prospectus. A preliminary written description of a book, usually one page in length.

Psychic/Supernatural. Fiction exploiting—or requiring as plot devices or themes—some contradictions of the commonplace natural world and materialist assumptions about it (including the traditional ghost story).

Query. A letter written to an agent or a potential market to elicit interest in a writer's work.

Reader. A person employed by an agent or buyer to go through the slush pile of manuscripts and scripts and select those worth considering.

Regional. A book faithful to a particular geographic region and its people, including behavior, customs, speech and history.

Release. A statement that your idea is original, has never been sold to anyone else, and that you are selling negotiated rights to the idea upon payment.

Remainders. Leftover copies of an out-of-print or slow-selling book purchased from the publisher at a reduced rate. Depending on the contract, a reduced royalty or no royalty is paid on remaindered books.

Reprint Rights. The right to republish a book after its initial printing.

Romance. A type of category fiction in which the love relationship between a man and a woman pervades the plot. The story is told from the viewpoint of the heroine, who meets a man (the hero), falls in love with him, encounters a conflict that hinders their relationship, and then resolves the conflict with a happy ending.

Royalties. A percentage of the retail price paid to the author for each copy of the book that is sold. Agents take their percentage from the royalties earned and from the advance.

SASE. Self-addressed, stamped envelope. It should be included with all correspondence.

Scholarly Books. Books written for an academic or research audience. These are usually heavily researched, technical, and often contain terms used only within a specific field.

Science Fiction. Literature involving elements of science and technology as a basis for conflict, or as the setting for a story.

Screenplay. Script for a film intended to be shown in theaters.

Script. Broad term covering teleplay, screenplay or stage play. Sometimes used as a shortened version of the word manuscript when referring to books.

Serial Rights. The right for a newspaper or magazine to publish sections of a manuscript.

Simultaneous Submission. Sending the same manuscript to several agents or publishers at the same time.

Sitcom. Situation comedy. Episodic comedy script for a television series. The term comes from the characters dealing with various situations with humorous results.

Slice of Life. A type of short story, novel, play or film that takes a strong thematic approach, depending less on plot than on vivid detail in describing the setting and/or environment, and the environment's effect on characters involved in it.

Slush Pile. A stack of unsolicited submissions in the office of an editor, agent or publisher.

Spec Script. A script written on speculation without confirmation of a sale.

Standard Commission. The commission an agent earns on the sales of a manuscript or script. For literary agents, the commission percentage (usually 10-20 percent) is taken from the advance and royalties paid to the writer. For script agents, the commission (usually 15-20 percent) is taken from script sales. If handling plays, agents take a percentage from the box office proceeds.

Subagent. An agent handling certain subsidiary rights, usually working in conjunction with the agent who handled the book rights. The percentage paid the book agent is increased to pay the subagent.

Subsidiary. An incorporated branch of a company or conglomerate (e.g., Knopf Publishing Group is a subsidiary of Random House, Inc.).

Subsidiary Rights. All rights other than book publishing rights included in a book publishing contract, such as paperback rights, book club rights and movie rights. Part of an agent's job is to negotiate those rights and advise you on which to sell and which to keep.

Syndication Rights. The right for a station to rerun a sitcom or drama, even if the show originally appeared on a different network.

Synopsis. A brief summary of a story, novel or play. As a part of a book proposal, it is a comprehensive summary condensed in a page or page and a half, single-spaced. See *outline*.

Teleplay. Script for television.

Terms. Financial provisions agreed upon in a contract.

Textbook. Book used in a classroom at the elementary, high school or college level.

Thriller. A story intended to arouse feelings of excitement or suspense. Works in this genre are highly sensational, usually focusing on illegal activites, international espionage, sex and violence.

TOC. Table of Contents. A listing at the beginning of a book indicating chapter titles and their corresponding page numbers. It can also include brief chapter descriptions.

Trade Book. Either a hardcover or softcover book sold mainly in bookstores. The subject matter frequently concerns a special interest for a general audience.

Trade Paperback. A soft-bound volume, usually 5×8, published and designed for the general public; available mainly in bookstores.

Translation Rights. Sold to a foreign agent or foreign publisher.

Treatment. Synopsis of a television or film script (40-60 pages for a two-hour feature film or teleplay).

Unsolicited Manuscript. An unrequested manuscript sent to an editor, agent or publisher.

Westerns/Frontier. Stories set in the American West, almost always in the 19th century, generally between the antebellum period and the turn of the century.

Young Adult (YA). The general classification of books written for ages 12-17. They run 50,000-60,000 words and include category novels—adventure, sports, career, mysteries, romance, etc.

Resources

Literary Agents Specialties Index

This index is divided into fiction and nonfiction subject categories. To find an agent interested in the type of manuscript you've written, see the appropriate sections under the subject headings that best describe your work.

FICTION

Action/Adventure

Experimental

Family Saga

Writers House 229
Zachary Shuster Harmsworth 231

Glitz

Anderson Literary Management, LLC 89
August Agency, LLC, The 91
Baker's Mark Literary Agency 93
Balzer Agency, The Paula 94
Browne, Ltd., Pema 104
DeChiara Literary Agency, The Jennifer 114
Dystel & Goderich Literary Management 119
Fairbank Literary Representation 125
Fielding Agency, LLC, The 126
Greenburger Associates, Inc., Sanford J. 137
Harris Literary Agency, Inc., The Joy 141
Harwood Limited, Antony 142
Hawkins & Associates, Inc., John 142
International Transactions, Inc. 147
Jabberwocky Literary Agency 148
Jellinek & Murray Literary Agency 149
JET Literary Associates 149
Larsen/Elizabeth Pomada, Literary Agents, Michael 158
Lazear Agency Group, Inc. 159
Levine Literary Agency, Paul S. 161
Lippincott Massie McQuilkin 163
Lyons Literary, LLC 168
Mainhardt Agency, Ricia 170
Mendel Media Group, LLC 176
Mura Literary, Dee 179
Pepus Literary Agency, Ellen 187
Pevner, Inc., Stephen 188
Picard, Literary Agent, Alison J. 189
PMA Literary and Film Management, Inc. 190
Redhammer Management, Ltd. 194
RLR Associates, Ltd. 199
Sanders & Associates, Victoria 205
Scribe Agency, LLC 208
Spieler Agency, The 213
Wald Associates, Inc., Mary Jack 224
Writers House 229
Zachary Shuster Harmsworth 231

Hi-Lo

Harris Literary Agency, Inc., The Joy 141
Harwood Limited, Antony 142
Hawkins & Associates, Inc., John 142
Lazear Agency Group, Inc. 159
Writers House 229

Historical

Ahearn Agency, Inc., The 86
Aitken Alexander Associates 86
Alive Communications, Inc. 87
Anderson Literary Management, LLC 89
August Agency, LLC, The 91
Avenue A Literary 92
Baker's Mark Literary Agency 93
Balzer Agency, The Paula 94
Barer Literary, LLC 94
Barrett Books, Inc., Loretta 94
Belli Literary Agency, Lorella 95
Bennett & West Literary Agency 96
Blumer Literary Agency, Inc., The 98
Books & Such Literary Agency 99
Bradford Literary Agency 100
Brandt Agency, The Joan 101
Brandt & Hochman Literary Agents, Inc. 101
Browne & Miller Literary Associates 104
Browne, Ltd., Pema 104
Carvainis Agency, Inc., Maria 106
Cheney Literary Associates, LLC, Elyse 108
Chudney Agency, The 108
Clark Associates, WM 108
Cornerstone Literary, Inc. 110
Daniel Literary Group 112
Dawson Associates, Liza 113
DeChiara Literary Agency, The Jennifer 114
Delbourgo Associates, Inc., Joelle 115
Doyen Literary Services, Inc. 117
Dupree/Miller and Associates Inc. Literary 119
Eady Associates, Toby 120
English Literary Agency, The Elaine P. 124
Farris Literary Agency, Inc. 126
Fielding Agency, LLC, The 126
Finch Literary Agency, Diana 127
Firebrand Literary 128
Golomb Literary Agency, The Susan 135
Goodman Literary Agency, Irene 136

Horror

Literary

Specialties Index

Occult

Picture Books

Plays

Poetry

Poetry in Translation

Psychic/Supernatural

Specialties Index

Translation

Westerns/Frontier

Women's

Young Adult

NONFICTION

Agriculture/Horticulture

Americana

Art/Architecture/Design

Biography/Autobiography

Specialties Index

Business/Economics

Child Guidance/Parenting

Computers/Electronics

Cooking/Foods/Nutrition

Crafts/Hobbies

Education

Ethnic/Cultural Interests

Health/Medicine

History

Specialties Index

Humor/Satire

Interior Design/Decorating

Memoirs

Specialties Index

Specialties Index

Psychology

Science/Technology

Self-Help/Personal Improvement

Sex

Sociology

Theater/Film

True Crime/Investigative

Women's Issues/Studies

Agents Index

General Index

General Index

General Index